Approaches to Planned Change

PUBLIC ADMINISTRATION AND PUBLIC POLICY

A Comprehensive Publication Program

Executive Editor

NICHOLAS HENRY

Center for Public Affairs
Arizona State University
Tempe, Arizona

Publications in Public Administration and Public Policy

1. Public Administration as a Developing Discipline (in two parts)
   by Robert T. Golembiewski
2. Comparative National Policies on Health Care
   by Milton I. Roemer, M.D.
3. Exclusionary Injustice: The Problem of Illegally Obtained Evidence
   by Steven R. Schlesinger
4. Personnel Management in Government: Politics and Process
   by Jay M. Shafritz, Walter L. Balk, Albert C. Hyde, and David H. Rosenbloom
5. Organization Development in Public Administration (in two parts)
   edited by Robert T. Golembiewski and William B. Eddy
6. Public Administration: A Comparative Perspective
   Second Edition, Revised and Expanded
   by Ferrel Heady
7. Approaches to Planned Change (in two parts)
   by Robert T. Golembiewski

Other volumes in preparation

Developmental Editors

Approaches to Planned Change

(in two parts)

Part 2

Macro-Level Interventions and Change-Agent Strategies

ROBERT T. GOLEMBIEWSKI

The University of Georgia
Athens, Georgia

MARCEL DEKKER, INC. New York and Basel

Library of Congress Cataloging in Publication Data

Golembiewski, Robert T
Macro-level interventions and change-agent strategies.

(His Approaches to planned change ; pt. 2)
Includes bibliographical references and indexes.
1. Organizational change. I. Title.
HD58.8.G64 pt. 2 658.4'06s [658.4'06] 79-17211
ISBN 0-8247-6804-3

Parts of this book were previously published under the title *Renewing Organizations: The Laboratory Approach to Planned Change*, Copyright 1972, F. E. Peacock Publishers, Inc., Itasca, Illinois.

MARCEL DEKKER, INC.
270 Madison Avenue, New York, New York 10016

Current printing (last digit):
10 9 8 7 6 5 4 3 2 1

PRINTED IN THE UNITED STATES OF AMERICA

To that tiny stranger
who first came and stayed to fill our home and hearts
and minds

To that kaleidoscopic self
which wondrously reveals an expanding crowd within:
Dump and 'bott,' Bumbumniecki and Mad Gerbel,
Mrs. Dettelson and Allison, Stephanie Dickinson,
Rebecca Nurse, and the roaring mouse's Queen

To that mega-package of will and want
that seeks to mark increasingly more of the world
as her own

To that phenom and those phenomena of the past four years:
Lordie, save us from four years more.

To that Tiger of the next years four.

In short, to Alice herself, who has evolved in as
protean ways as this book, between then and now.

Preface

Approaches to Planned Change may be pardoned if it experiences a written work's equivalent of an identity crisis. Is it a second edition of *Renewing Organizations*, or no?

Let readers judge for themselves. Consider the two basic similarities between this work and its predecessor. Despite the 7 years that have passed since the publication of *Renewing Organizations*, the broad introductory framework of the original still seems serviceable and hence is substantially retained in the first three chapters below. These chapters provide an orienting structure for a literature that has sprawled and burgeoned wondrously over the last few years. Moreover, both writing programs propose that Organization Development clearly is here to stay. That conclusion was argued for in *Renewing Organizations*, and it seems certain now.

Now consider the points of difference between *Renewing Organizations* and this 1979 effort. Overall, to begin, perhaps 70 percent of the material below did not appear in any form in the earlier book. In addition to seeking to accommodate the great burst of research and experience that has accumulated since the appearance of the first edition, moreover, basic structural changes also characterize this effort. Not only have large portions of manuscript prominent in the first edition disappeared, but many of the retained portions have been variously shuffled about. This will emphasize relationships and insights that were not obvious earlier, as well as correct poor judgment and artless placement.

The most obvious difference from *Renewing Organizations* is that one book has now become two. The level of interaction constitutes the dominant criterion for the separation: Part 1 basically deals with micro-interventions, those aimed at individuals and small groups, while Part 2 focuses on macro-level interventions relevant to large organizations. Although dominant, the focus on levels of intervention is conveniently supplemented by other kinds of materials. In addition, that is, Part 1 begins with a number of introductory concerns and orienting perspectives, and Part 2 ends with a major block of materials relating to intervenors and the complex act of intervening.

Great pleasure fills me as I write this Preface, but I also recognize pain—basically that pain involved in letting-go. Each month brings fresh and exciting experience and research that begs to be recognized and assimilated, and mulling over the materials constantly suggests ways to highlight insights previously slighted or unrecognized, constantly pinpoints places where the felicitous phrase could better capture an idea and better attract the reader's eye and mind. Hence, active waiting to let go has been a very rewarding posture on this project, which is long past term. The fact is that I have put off completing this revision several times—finding one excuse or another to set this work aside, to begin and publish perhaps six other books while this revision waited. Waiting presents a strong temptation even now, with two substantial piles of manuscript before me.

As in all human affairs, however, letting-go can only be postponed so long. For this revision—warts and blemishes and all—that time is now. The timing could not be more appropriate, it just occurs to me. The two of us—wife and husband, mother and father—have experienced a recent and major letting-go with two of our children who, born close together, boogied-off to college close together. And our son will soon follow his sisters, his senior year in high school now closing with a rush. The two-part volume thus constitutes just another letting-go, if long delayed, and a far less impactful one at that.

Robert T. Golembiewski

Contents

Contents of Part 1

Approaches to Planned Change

Section 1

SOME INTERVENTIONS IN LARGE ORGANIZATIONS

Chapter 1

CHANGING PATTERNS OF INTERPERSONAL AND INTERGROUP RELATIONS

Building Organizations to Order

Early applications of the laboratory approach in complex organizations were preoccupied with reinventing the wheel. This is no criticism of anyone or anything, because incremental advance is reasonable and perhaps even unavoidable in the early development of any technology. Simple facts remain: the early developmental history of organization development (OD) efforts based on the laboratory approach has come out very much like the experience of similar behavioral science applications, and it took valuable time to relearn those old lessons.

No need to feign suspense. Three general points describe well enough the early developmental history of OD. *First,* OD applications dominantly were interaction-centered, due no doubt in very substantial and understandable degree to the vogue of the T-group and its undoubted power for encouraging choice and change in small groups. It seemed reasonable to apply the same leverage in large organizations, which to some appeared to be only a collection of small groups.

Second, attention in early OD tended to fixate on techniques rather than a set of values, again in large part due to the burgeoning reliance on one technique, the T-group. This is a momentous if understandable fixation, and stands in marked contrast to the value or ethical preoccupation—both early[1] and late[2]—of the very laboratory approach that generated the development of the T-group. Two prime consequences stand out. The focus on techniques stood work in the tradition of the laboratory approach on its head, as it were, and it also discouraged for a time the invention or application of the fuller panoply of techniques consistent with the values of the laboratory approach.

Third, the possibility of technostructural redesign largely was neglected in early OD work.[3] The neglect has complex roots, and some observers even see the two organizational approaches as basically antagonistic. Bartunek, Gujral, and Pondy do not go quite that far, but almost, even as they seek to increase OD's emphasis on technostructural design. They observe that:[4]

> Each approach represents more than a technology for organizational improvement: OD and design come from different traditions, make different assumptions, and have differing philosophical and theoretical foundations.
>
> We do not believe that, on a philosophical level, the two approaches are totally capable of being integrated. Nor do we believe that an attempt to integrate them on this level is advisable. Rather, we believe that interfacing the two approaches on a philosophical level requires an approach that preserves and encourages the unique development of each.

Perhaps the dominant consequence of the neglect of technostructural design threatened restricting OD to the Band-Aid business, providing only topical relief for problems that inhere in the design of work which—because it remains unchanged—keeps generating the same symptoms which interaction-centered OD can alleviate but not cure.

This initial block of seven chapters will provide detailed counterpoint about the developmental history of OD, as it encompasses interaction-centered and technostructural orientations, as well as the complex linking processes generated by each of them that impact on the other.

This first chapter provides a kind of introductory before and after perspective on the developmental history of OD in large organizations. The early emphasis is on the premises from which early applications tended to start, as well as on those premises that underlay more recent OD efforts. The latter part of this chapter summarizes two major OD efforts that consciously seek to build on this developmental history. The goal of both efforts is comprehensive change in an organization's climate or style, to induce or reinforce behavioral and attitudinal changes by individuals that are consistent with the values of the laboratory approach.

Organization Change via the Laboratory Approach
Some Overall Tendencies

In the broadest possible summary, the history of organization change via the laboratory approach implies more repeating of history than learning from it. Two themes support this characterization.

Emphases Early and Later

Initial efforts at organization reform tended to emphasize training experiences for individuals who, after their numbers reached some critical mass, could later begin inducing changes in their organization. The general model was:

(1)		(2)		(3)
Model A: Individuals have stranger training experiences, as via T-groups, to develop skills and values of process orientation	→	Team development at work, which blends concern with process and task	→	Organizational change

The more contemporary emphasis directly seeks changes in the organization, to build upon as well as to facilitate individual change. In short, it not only gets to organization applications, it begins with them. This contemporary emphasis may be generalized as:

(1)		(2)
Model B: Work units have family experiences with laboratory approach, either in T-groups or in various development activities derived from the laboratory approach	↗	Change in individual's behavior, attitudes, and values
		↕
	↘	Organizational change in climate, style, or values, which reinforces and induces changes by individuals

This section variously looks at this shift in emphasis about what is cart and what is horse. The choice of one basic intervention strategy or the other is a critical one, not that one is necessarily better but in the sense that each basic strategy implies its own internal logic.

Delayed Learning from Experience

As it turns out, organizational applications of the laboratory approach could well have taken to heart the experience of other behavioral science applications. Consider the striking case of a 2-week training program to increase certain specific attributes and skills of foremen at International Harvester Company. The case goes back to the mid-1940s. Initially, changes in attitudes of individual foremen occurred in the expected direction, but soon back-home relations showed their awesome strength. No sooner had the foremen returned to work than changes due to training not only began to decay, but they actually reversed. So great was the reversal, in fact, that after a short period back at work the trained foremen actually scored lower on the target variables than a control group of foremen who had experienced no training. The only trained foremen who retained their increases, significantly, worked for superiors who themselves scored high on the target attitudes. As Gene W. Dalton concludes:

> Daily interaction completely negated the effect of the training program. The foremen's ties had been interrupted only during the two week training period. They then returned to a situation where the most significant relationship was with their own supervisors. No continuing new relationships had been established which would act to confirm and reinforce any attitude changes begun in the training program.[5]

Experience with other behavioral science applications in other organizations more or less ran to a similar pattern.[6] They never scored because they seldom got past first base, as it were.

Such early experience with other behavioral science applications did not inspire initial organizational applications based on the laboratory approach, however. For a variety of reasons, Model A became the usual guiding concept. In part, unrealistic expectations or even naïveté about the ease of transfer into organizations of the commonly potent learning gained in stranger T-groups explains this inhibited follow-though. Moreover, the general popularity of stranger T-group experiences, plus a shortage of skilled organization analysts, no doubt contributed to a lack of concentrated attention on the problems of the transfer into organizations of any learning gained in stranger experiences.

Accumulating Evidence of Inadequacies

It was not long before applications of the laboratory approach to large organizations began to point up some central problems with its leading concept, however. Six themes reflect these inadequacies.

First, Model A above rests heavily on the sanguine effects of personal insight on organization systems. Experience clearly demonstrates that personal insight and organization change are not necessarily linked, however. Specifically, personal insight does imply some control over intellectual and emotional aspects of some issues. But, one can have insight by the yard, with little or no control over the strategies necessary for organization change.[7]

Second, the relevance to the work site of material discussed in stranger experiences was not always clear and direct. For example, Sheldon Davis pungently reacts to the lack of follow-up at work after stranger training experiences. "Say a man has a good experience. He comes back to the job full of new values—and sits down in the same crummy atmosphere he left a week before. He may be changed, but his environment isn't. How can he practice confrontation with a boss and a secretary and colleagues who don't even know what it's all about? In a few weeks he's either completely dazed or has reverted, in self-defense, to the old ways."[8]

Third, indeed, a stranger experience might even complicate the subsequent raising of an issue at the work site, which is the only place it can be resolved. This point applies in several senses. The stranger experience might only dissipate feelings or reactions that could have motivated action at the work site. Hence, these potential motivators might be ventilated in a context where the underlying problem may be explorable, but where it is definitely not resolvable.

Fourth, a stranger experience lacks a critical reality of all back-home organizations—the authority structure. At the very least, this deprives participants of a learning experience that is highly relevant in all organizations[9] and, indeed, in all of life. Worse effects also are possible. Consider "unfreezing" in the typical T-group, which is facilitated (as Bernard Bass describes it) "by removing the familiar props and customary social mechanisms, by violating the expectations of trainees, and by creating an ambiguous, unstructured situation for them of unclear goals and minimum cues."[10] Bass is concerned that this aspect of the T-group technology might generate serious consequences in some cases while it facilitates learning in others. For example, this aspect of the technology might foster feelings among some trainees which reflect Bakunin's broadside that: "All exercise of authority perverts and all submissiveness to authority humiliates." Bass worries that:

> it may be that some laboratory participants lose their confidence to use authority which may be needed in the future for organizational reasons. This may be neither the intent of the program nor a logical outcome, but it may occur just the same. At the same time, there may be a correspondingly reduced acceptance of submissive behavior that may be necessary at times for the interests of good organization. In short, the "destruction" of the customary authority structure in the T-Group in order to promote exploration and change in the individual participants, coupled with an emphasis on the values of democracy and consensus, may produce, in some participants at least, sufficient antiauthoritarian leadership attitudes to reduce their contributions to the organization at times when such directive leadership is required.[11]

Fifth, greater appreciation evolved concerning the complexity of the linkages between a stranger experience and increased effectiveness of individuals as they readopt specific organization roles. In part, this complexity derives from the fact that various tasks tend to imply their own specific demands.[12] Accumulating experience showed there could be no guarantee that enhanced individual mental health and maturity will meet all such demands.[13] Consequently, as Bass concludes, training people "to be better diagnosticians with greater tolerance and social awareness" is perhaps necessary but not sufficient for organization development.[14]

Sixth, stranger experiences by definition do not provide the continuous reinforcement that is useful and perhaps necessary to transfer individual learning into organization contexts. Indeed, some frustration may set in as individuals fail to gain reinforcement at work. Consequently, they might have "to relearn negatively" in order to get back in phase with organization norms. This is psychically herniating.

Important Shifts in OD Designs

Such factors encouraged important shifts in opinion about OD designs in complex organizations.[15] Four effects will illustrate the broader range. *First,* in the most simple sense, more realistic expectations developed about the impact of stranger experiences on managerial behavior. Thus, Ernest G. Miller concludes that organization climate is critical to general changes in member behavior. "Few if any evaluative studies of T-Group training," he explains, "can be expected to show notable and continuing impact upon managerial behavior unless that training is linked to a continuing program of team building or organizational development."[16]

Multiple morals are implied in this new realism. To illustrate, one can begin an OD program following Model A, if that seems appropriate in a specific case. But one must always be aware of the fact that any persisting changes from a stranger experience will require reinforcement at work. Moreover, some of these changes may directly conflict with back-home organizational norms or structure. This can create some nasty conflict situations. Indeed, if no possibility exists for changes in the host organization, training in stranger groups is at least questionable and probably undesirable.

Second, early OD efforts encouraged a shift in attention from individual skills to changes in organizational values or attitudes. This may seem a minor shift, but it is actually critical. That is, if the focus is on changes in individual skills, the intense stranger experience is the preferred vehicle, and the more intensive, the better. If the focus is on changes in organizational values and attitudes, the learning thrust is toward:[17]

- A new "view of the possible" for guiding interpersonal and intergroup relations at work, with the values of the laboratory approach generating an ideal which can be compared by organization members as to its need-gratification potential with the actual relations in their organization
- An enhanced sense of collaboration among organization members that derives from sharing the values and norms of the laboratory approach, of membership in a common social order
- Improving trust, respect, and communication among members of the organization
- A reduced sense of individual needs as inevitably opposed to "the organization"

The more appropriate vehicle for such learning is a family experience, whether in a T-group or in some learning design. Some sparse empirical research consistently supports the greater effectiveness and appropriateness of such family experiences when the goal is organizational change.[18] Moreover, even when family groups are employed, effectiveness seems to vary with the extensiveness of pretraining and posttraining activities.[19] This implies a reasonable need by participants to feel a part of a long-run program as a condition of their fuller commitment to working toward a change in organizational values and climate.

Notice also that emphasis on values represents an effort in education, or re-education, which helps distinguish the laboratory approach from therapy, as it is conventionally understood. Moreover, values are seen as strategic in inducing appropriate skills, but the reverse probably is not the case. "The development of valid values will tend to lead automatically to the development of proper skills," Chris Argyris observes. "Skills follow values; values rarely follow skills."[20] Finally, the emphasis on values provides a systematic and common frame of reference for individuals and groups which can have self-reinforcing consequences. The goal, as James Clark notes, is the creation of social orders at work, of "effective sociotechnical systems which support the kind of human encounters in which there is greater likelihood that people's authentic beings will be expressed in relation to one another and their work."[21] Once established, the dynamics of enhanced authenticity have self-heightening effects.[22]

Third, OD designs based on Model B became more common. Witness the position of Jack and Lorraine Gibb. "The group experience is more powerful and permanent if it is imbedded in significant organizational life," they conclude. "Training in a natural team is far more powerful than training in the heterogeneous groups that are common in group therapy and sensitivity training."[23]

Fourth, OD designs have begun diversely to cope with the inadequacies summarized above. Some of these designs utilize T-groups directly; others concentrate on intergroup processes via a variety of other designs and initially seek to change patterns of interaction, while others first seek structural change and then try to induce or reinforce behaviors, attitudes, or values consistent with that structure. Several examples suggest the range of such designs:[24]

- Designs of stranger experiences following Model A involve T-groups in quasi-organizational activities—as in planning aspects of their own experience or in developing a special purpose organization[25] where process and content issues must be dealt with simultaneously—to highlight issues re the transfer of learning.
- Designs of stranger experiences following Model A facilitate later organizational transfer of learning, as by an initial focus on managerial styles in Blake's Phase I, which provides a relatively direct base for subsequent work in family groups.[26]

- Designs of learning experiences blend Models A and B by combining aspects of stranger and family experiences: for example, time is divided during a training period between work in T-groups composed of individuals from different organizations which deal with here-and-now interpersonal and intergroup processes, and in homogeneous family units which deal with common back-home issues.[27]
- Designs of family experiences following Model B concentrate on team-development activities re work issues, rather than on T-groups, the consultant's role being to introduce gradually concerns relating to interpersonal and intergroup processes.[28]
- Designs of either family or stranger experiences use simulations of a business game, each play of which is followed by a detailed review led by professional trainers who deal with content issues as well as with process analysis,[29] but not in a T-group context.
- Designs for family groups attempt to induce processes associated with the laboratory approach, as by increasing feedback in a family group, but without resort to a T-group.[30]
- Designs for family groups emphasize structural change consistent with the laboratory approach, and behavior, attitudes, and values consistent with that structure can then be induced and/or reinforced by various OD designs.

Why the Delayed Learning re OD Applications?

Perversity did not of course lead advocates of the laboratory approach to rediscover painfully and late what had been learned in other applications of the behavioral sciences in organizations. Major conceptual and practical concerns influenced, perhaps even dictated, the direction that the laboratory approach would initially take in complex organizations. Consider voluntarism, which ranks high in the pantheon of values of the laboratory approach. Stranger experiences maximize voluntarism, which was seen as crucial in inducing several desired learning outcomes. Thus, it was seen as reducing resistance to change as well as defensiveness, while it facilitated unfreezing and the learner's psychological owning of the consequences of the learning experience. These are important considerations in any learning, and they cannot be casually jeopardized. In contrast, family experiences patently had to contend with the question of how much (if any) voluntarism could be sacrificed without perverting the essence of the laboratory approach. Consequently, as proponents of the laboratory approach were feeling their early way, stranger experiences it tended to be.

The conceptual bind over voluntarism had its practical sides also. Opponents of the laboratory approach, whatever their motives, patently had a powerful weapon in a strict interpretation of voluntarism. Winn clearly reflects the point in this summary of his own early experience in Alcan: Canada:

> There is no problem with regard to securing as many as 200 or more participants from its managerial and professional ranks for the many [stranger] two-week laboratories organized every year. The participants come voluntarily, and most of the personnel look forward with a great deal of anticipation to this experience. The situation changes drastically, however, when it comes to filling the places for a family or intergroup laboratory. Voluntarism decreases markedly, and resistances reappear in strength. It is all right to play "the behavior-change game" away from subordinates or peers or work companions, but it is not quite the same to play this "forbidden game" at one's work. It is too threatening.[31]

As is common, then, convenience reinforced an apparent principle. The early bind should be apparent. For example, Winn advises that major efforts to allay anxieties, to publicize the value of family experiences, and so on, were necessary to encourage work-site applications. Patently, however, such efforts in large part rest on prior resolution of the issues they are intended to solve. Hence, it is understandable that emphasis on family experiences did not emerge early, full blown.

Support for OD Applications in Complex Organizations

Six positive developmental forces illustrate the existing base of success experiences that support future applications of the laboratory approach in organizations.

First, and especially in the past decade, major organizational showcases have highlighted the potential of the laboratory approach, in business and in government. Some of these showcase applications were basically *wunderkinder* whose virtues spread by personal contact among cognoscenti, and later even engaged the interest of the mass media.[32] Other examples had a more definite research thrust[33] and added significant counterpoint to more pragmatic claims about the possibility of a more humane and effective organizational life based on the laboratory approach. Moreover, some of these applications followed Model A and developed designs to encourage the transfer of initial learning into organization contexts,[34] while other applications were seminal efforts to innovate Model B approaches.[35]

Second, the applications tended to establish that powerful group forces could be induced in settings other than "cultural islands" such as a stranger T-group. The appreciation of which designs were more appropriate for which broad types of situations also increased correspondingly. For example, some of these innovative designs utilized family T-groups in novel ways with positive results. An experience at Non-Linear Systems is illustrative. An entire work unit was exposed to sensitivity training as an initial experience, with no apparent loss in potency and with important advantages. These advantages included:[36]

- Presence of superiors reduces participants' fantasies about tales being carried to the boss by the trainer or fellow participants.
- Reinforcement of any new behaviors resulting from the training is easier, and any learning can be more-or-less immediately applied to the job.
- Interpersonal relationships and communication among participants are improved on the job because of reductions in the mass of, and multiple ignorance about, true feelings and reactions that are characteristic even among work colleagues of long standing.
- A conscious discipline operates in family groups. They focus on improved interpersonal relationships and communications relevant at work, rather than on the generalized personal development of individual participants. This eases the task of translating any learning in job-oriented terms and provides more-or-less common criteria for data introducible into the training session.

Third, such applications reinforce the critical role of transfer. Thus, the need to reinforce any individual learning by corresponding changes in organizational climate and/or structure—as by team-development activities, or some such—was more appreciated. In addition, several showcase applications provided greater motivation for organization activities that followed after the initial stranger training experience. Finally, the issue of voluntarism eased somewhat. In part, this resulted from a better job of meeting participant anxieties, as well as from positive reports about personal and organizational consequences of the newly available showcase applications. In part, also, voluntarism was less salient because of the availability of various non-T-group designs for OD starters that implied less potential for personal trauma.

Fourth, a number of the showcase applications implied that changes induced by successful OD efforts based on the laboratory approach persisted over extended periods. This eliminated many cheap victories possible before the results of such longitudinal studies were available. The granddaddy of all longitudinal studies covers a period of some 8 years, in fact. Major changes were reported in before and after comparisons covering the first few years of the OD effort.[37] Approximately 6 years later, although the results were "somewhat mixed and with a few contrary elements," a research team reported that the "organization, far from reverting to its prior condition, has during recent years made additional progress toward the organizational goals envisioned by the owners and managers . . . , and envisioned as well by superiors and production employees at a somewhat later time." The two principal investigators concluded, somewhat facetiously, that:

> We confess a brief regret that there was not an opposite outcome for we are rather better equipped with ideas about organizational stability and regression than we are with ideas about organizational change and continuing development. For example, before the data became available, we were prepared to make some remarks about the "Hawthorne effect"–about the superficiality and transient quality of organizational and behavioral changes induced under conditions of external attention and pressure; but it boggles the mind to think of a "Hawthorne effect" persisting for over eight years among people half of whom were not on the scene at the time of the original change.[38]

Fifth, the showcase applications stressed the value of a "system orientation."[39] That is, it might be appropriate to begin working to change patterns of interaction by T-group methods as a starter in a specific case, but any OD program sooner rather than later should seek "mutually reinforcing change actions across the psychological, organizational, and technological domains." As two researchers summarize a basic thrust of their own breakthrough OD effort:

> A central idea was to make structural changes in the organization that matched the work system and did not violate reasonable assumptions about the values and motives of individual members. . . . The idea of systematic consistency is surely an elementary one, no more than common sense–a habit of thought for those who have learned to view the factory as a total system in which all elements are interdependent. The interdependence of elements tends to preserve, to enhance, and to "lock in" the central characteristics of the system and thus to prevent retrogression.[40]

Sixth, showcase OD applications began to reflect a major interest in economic and performance variables. Perhaps the prime example is the parallel research study of an OD application of Blake's Managerial Grid.®*[41] Basically, the Grid seeks to induce a specific style of management, building from a concern with individuals and working on successively larger groupings as the training proceeds. The results of that training-research effort had been reviewed very positively in the popular literature, and for good reason. The research effort was comprehensive and touched on many variables of central concern to both students and managers of complex organizations. For example, one summary article stresses these results of that seminal OD application.

> The firm experienced a considerable increase in profits and a decrease in costs. The researchers attributed 56% of the profit to increase in non-controllable factors, 31% to a reduction in manpower, and 13% (amounting to several million dollars) to improved operating procedures and higher productivity per man-hour. The increase in productivity per employee was

*The word Grid is a registered service mark of Scientific Methods, Inc.

> achieved without increased investment in plant and equipment. Other criterion changes cited were an increased frequency of meetings, increased transfers within the plant and to other parts of the organization, a higher frequency of promotion for young line managers as opposed to staff men with more tenure, and a greater degree of success in solving organizational problems.[42]

Similarly, Beckhard summarized the results of another OD program. He stressed a dramatic improvement in profits in the year following the OD program, for example, which came in the face of stabilized profits in the industry. Beckhard also stressed evidence of improved interpersonal and intergroup relations, such as very low turnover in an industry characterized by high mobility. In addition, he noted various increases in the effectiveness of performance in most units, such as reduced costs as a function of sales. To be sure, Beckhard did not attribute all these changes entirely to the OD educational effort. But, he also urged that the OD program "has made a significant contribution through developing attitudes of commitment to company objectives a shared value of concern for costs, and a measurable increase in operating efficiency of almost all units."[43]

In summary, the combined effect of such positive forces was to encourage numerous training-research programs that seek to establish in comprehensive practical and theoretical detail the conditions and consequences of specific OD designs. The early developmental history of the laboratory approach to OD, in short, was that promising.

Two Complex Applications of the Laboratory Approach

Changing Organization Climate*

The designs and results of two OD efforts to change the organization "climate" or "style" of several sales units in a business organization illustrate an attempt to apply, in an ongoing organization, the developmental lessons just sketched. The illustration has two thrusts: it should establish that quite a bit is known about which OD training designs tend to lead to which consequences; and it demonstrates that we often know better than we can do, because of lack of resources or because of the intransigence of specific practical situations.

Building Organizations to Order

The common OD learning design sought to create a specific kind of social order, as well as to provide experience with appropriate skills and attitudes. The first OD effort—a pilot study—dealt with fifteen managers who supervised the national

*This section essentially follows Robert T. Golembiewski and Stokes B. Carrigan, "Planned Change Through Laboratory Methods," *Training and Development Journal,* Vol. 27 (March 1973), pp. 18-27.

sales of a well-known personal consumption product. The men represented three hierarchical levels and had eighty salesmen in the field reporting to them. Sales were in excess of $40 million during 1968. In the second OD effort, a replication of the training design, more managers at more hierarchical levels were involved. The common goal in both studies was change in "climate" which, following Tagiuri, is defined here as "the relatively enduring quality of the total environment that (1) is experienced by the occupants, (2) influences their behavior, and (3) can be described in terms of the values of a particular set of characteristics (or attributes) of the environment."[44]

Some Initial Limitations

This description is limited in a number of senses. Thus, only a sketch of the learning design is provided. Further detail can be found elsewhere.[45] Moreover, this section summarizes the thrust of two published pieces, as well as two long, unpublished papers.[46] Nuances in the data consequently cannot receive due attention. Finally, the major limit inheres in the lack of control groups in the research design. The design in this case is a modified time-series design, which does not eliminate as many alternative explanations of results as does the control group design.[47]

These limits are not deemed invalidating, but they do imply the usual state of the art reservations appropriate to developing areas of concern. Despite the unavoidable lack of control groups, for example, the results seem due to the training design rather than to the passage of time or some other cause. Despite these limits, the data imply real progress toward the goal of building organizations that are built to order in the sense of having climates that their members consider desirable.

Laboratory Approach as Value Filled

In overview, the laboratory approach to planned change rests on a relatively specific set of values, attitudes, and behavioral skills that are ideals to be approached in interpersonal and intergroup relations. That is, the laboratory model is overtly value filled, not value neutral. The values, attitudes, and behavioral skills appropriate to the laboratory model cannot be spelled out here. However, these few prescriptions illustrate how the laboratory model is value filled:

- Full and free communication
- Reliance on open consensus in managing conflict, as opposed to using coercion or compromise
- Influence based on competence rather than on personal whim or formal power
- Expression of emotional as well as task-oriented behavior

- Acceptance of conflict between the individual and the organization, to be coped with willingly, openly, and rationally

Rationale for Planned Change

The rationale for the laboratory approach to planned change in organizations rests on a basic premise. Directly, it is both useful and possible to develop conditions at work such that individual needs and organization demands can become increasingly congruent. This premise does not imply a Pollyanna-like neglect of those many factors in organizations that can frustrate individual needs. These factors do exist, and will continue to exist. However, we can do more than is normally done to increase the congruence between what individuals want and what their organizations demand of them. It is this goal of doing more than is normally done that inspires the present designs.

There are many ways of illustrating the usefulness of intentionally increasing the congruence of individual needs and organization demands, no one of them entirely satisfactory. For present purposes, both individuals and organizations can be shown to have a common stake in developing what have been called "regenerative communication sequences." Or, to say much the same thing, both individuals and organizations have a significant stake in avoiding degenerative communication sequences or, once they have developed, in reversing them.

The significance to individuals of degenerative communication sequences may be illustrated briefly. Figure 1 depicts such a sequence as a circular model with four elements that are mutually heightening. Only the distinction between being "open" and "owning" needs to be made explicitly. Assume A says to B: "Some people feel you are unscrupulous." If some people do in fact feel that way, A is being open. But, if A is one of these people, A is not owning up to his reaction about B.

Degenerative Interaction Effects. What is there to choose between these two idealized communication sequences? For details, consult Chapters 1 and 2 of Part 1. Here note only that individuals need relationships that are honest, caring, and nonmanipulative, to make the point one way. Hence, their needs tend to be deprived by degenerative communication sequences, which are nonhonest, noncaring, and usually manipulative in effect if not always in intention. To approach the point in another way, individuals have their needs frustrated by degenerative sequences, because once caught in such a sequence you often cannot win for losing.

A degenerative communication sequence is circular and self-heightening so that, for example, when trust is low even authentic openness tends to be misperceived as dishonest or manipulative. Of course, such misperception tends to lower the trust still further. The circularity is even more diabolical because it encourages self-fulfilling prophecies. For example, if I perceive others as initially

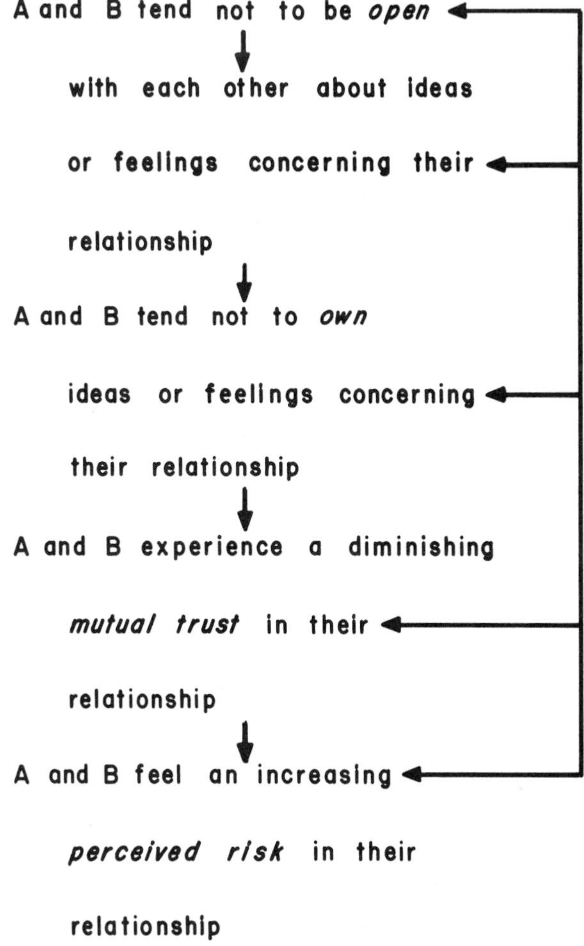

Figure 1 A typical degenerative communication sequence between individuals.

hostile in intention, I am likely to act toward them in ways that encourage their hostility in fact toward me. The effect is likely even in those cases where I see initial hostility where none existed. This sketches a sad game that people often play.

The circularity of degenerative communication sequences tends toward a common outcome. Individuals feel diminished and demeaned as persons, enmeshed in an increasingly inauthentic relationship in which it is difficult or impossible to make desired outcomes happen. A person in a degenerative communication sequence is like the unlucky soul in quicksand. The more she struggles, the worse things are likely to become.

Regenerative Interaction Effects. These few comments suggest the significant stake that individuals should feel in the quality of their communication sequences. The ideal is a life space characterized by regenerative sequences in which, almost literally, the individual cannot lose for winning. Illustratively, even when things go badly wrong, the individual in a regenerative sequence is in a better situation to cope successfully and hence to enhance his self-esteem and that of others with whom he interacts. He has better information about problems and about his efforts to cope with them, and he has the trust of others to help him over the rough spots.

The significant stake that organizations have in carefully managing such degenerative communication sequences should have been established by the discussion in Chapter 3 of Part 1, which details their troubling negative outcomes. Those outcomes are serious enough, and common enough, to imply the clear organizational stake in avoiding or reversing degenerative communication sequences between individuals.

The Learning Design

The rationale above inspired a learning design which seeks to reverse degenerative communication sequences, as well as to reinforce regenerative communication sequences. This design has three basic elements. *First,* members of small organization units are provided with an off-site learning experience that centers around values, attitudes, and behavioral skills appropriate for avoiding or reversing degenerative communication sequences. The off-site learning experience utilizes sensitivity training or T-grouping in small groups composed of peers who work together.

Second, immediately after the initial experience, the design begins to extend the learning gained in small groups into the larger workaday organization. Such extensions are variously encouraged, as by permitting organizational peers to confront their hierarchical superiors as a test of the values, attitudes, and behavioral skills reinforced or developed in the initial training. "Confronting," in the present sense, involves four elements that are the focal points in the initial training:

- To be in touch with one's feelings, reactions, or ideas
- To be able to identify the stimuli which induce specific feelings, reactions, or ideas
- To develop relations of trust that permit individuals to express their feelings, reactions, or ideas

- To express one's feelings, reactions, or ideas while encouraging others to do likewise

In summary, the initial two phases of the learning design provide experience with relevance and skills, whose transfer to relations at work is tested in work-related confrontations between organizational superiors and subordinates.

Third, the learning design calls for a "reinforcement experience" some 9 to 12 months after the initiation of the program of change. This provides a kind of "booster shot" for the values, attitudes, and behavioral skills that were developed or reinforced in the two earlier training phases. The reinforcement experience typically lasts a day or more. It focuses on the progress that has been made toward the ideals of the laboratory model to that point, as well as on what can be done in the future to sustain or extend that progress.

Targets for Change

The ability of the learning design sketched above to induce changes in interpersonal and intergroup relations appropriate for more effectively meeting individual needs and organization demands was tested in two kinds of small organization units. Exhibit 1 broadly distinguishes their two sets of properties. The learning design was expected to induce similar patterns of change in interpersonal and intergroup relations in the two types of organization units, but greater magnitudes of change were expected in the growth-oriented units. In fact, any result other than a major deterioration in relationships was considered attractive in the stability-oriented units.

The rationale for the expected difference in change can be illustrated briefly. In essence, the stability-oriented units were seen as facing more intense degenerative communication sequences and, in effect, the training design in these units consequently had to swim against their tide. For example, the learning design could successfully highlight the usefulness of high trust and low risk. But the environment would keep generating unavoidable concerns in stability-oriented units that served to lower trust and increase risk, as in the threat that reductions in manpower above and beyond normal attrition would be made. Being "safe" and not "rocking the boat" would be more likely in stability-oriented units, then, with the prime consequence of making even more difficult what at best would be a major adjustment to changing market conditions. Growth-oriented units would not be without their own problems, of course, but they would not face such dismal inevitabilities or probabilities.

There were eight experimental units altogether, all engaged in marketing activities in two separate areas of the same large firm. Each unit was compsoed of six to ten managers, with two units being growth oriented and six being stability oriented. See Figure 2. The training design was extended level by level.

Exhibit 1 Two Contrasting Types of Organization Units

Growth-Oriented Units	Stability-Oriented Units
1. Short organizational histories.	1. Several decades of organizational history.
2. Marked flexibility in policies and procedures.	2. Traditional policies and procedures.
3. Product lines that are new in markets that are sharply expanding.	3. Product lines that are aging in markets that are "mature" and perhaps declining.
4. Profit opportunities are attractive.	4. Profit opportunities still good, but declining, and perhaps precipitously so.
5. Substantial growth in personnel and expanding opportunities for promotion.	5. Substantial reductions in personnel will occur, hopefully by attrition only, and opportunities for promotion are few.
6. Of apparently growing present and future importance to parent corporation.	6. Traditionally the source of corporate leadership, but units may play lesser role in corporation of the future.
7. Look forward to continued growth.	7. Seek stability or even a gentle decline.

The details of the training design resemble a complex Chinese laundry ticket, but their thrust can be outlined economically. Globally, the acceptability of the laboratory approach to planned change was tested at a variety of organization levels above the two "systems" whose climates were to be changed, national field sales managers X and Z. The initial learning of relevance here took place in subsystemic groups of peers, for example, the group of six regional managers in the Eastern division. The T-group was the basic training vehicle in this first stage, and the primary goal was to provide the managers with a learning experience that emphasized the values, attitudes, and behavioral skills appropriate for inducing:

- High levels of openness
- High levels of owning
- High levels of mutual trust
- Low levels of perceived risk

Extensions of this learning were then tested as subordinates confronted their immediate superiors. For example, each group of regional managers in the

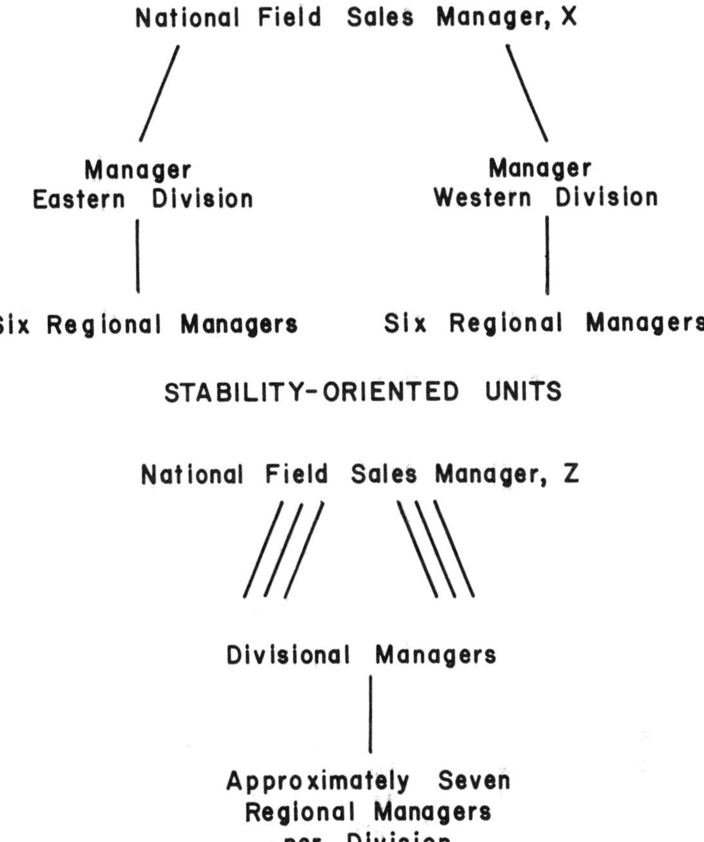

Figure 2 Skeletal organizations of two field sales units.

stability-oriented units confronted its divisional manager as well as the national sales manager, Z, with the focus on work-related concerns. The common goal of the initial learning, whose testing was begun by the confrontations, was to change the system-wide climate of interpersonal and intergroup relations of each of the broad organization units presided over by the two national sales managers. The intended approach was to transfer into the broad organization contexts the values, attitudes, and behavioral skills that were developed in the small units during the initial training phase. In effect, the design involved nothing less than the building of a new social order, complete with supporting norms and behavioral skills.

Measuring Planned Change

The degree of systemic change induced by the learning design was measured with managerial self-reports on the Likert Profile of Organization Characteristics.[48] Managers in the growth-oriented units rated one form of the profile four times over an 18-month period, and managers from stability-oriented units responded to a shorter form of the profile six times over a 245-day interval. In all cases, respondents were instructed to keep their total marketing system in mind when responding to the Likert Profile. The reference organization in each case is the system "national field sales." The form of the Likert Profile used here taps six basic organizational processes, and attempts to characterize an organization in terms of four systems of management on each profile item. The six processes deal with: leadership; motivation; communication; decisions; control; and goals. Several profile items relate to each process, with each item being anchored by four descriptive statements that provide a working description of each of the four systems of management. Individual items are scored on a 1- to 20-point scale, which is subdivided into these four management systems:

System 1: Exploitative-authoritative

System 2: Benevolent-authoritative

System 3: Consultative

System 4: Participative group

The profile was introduced in Chapter 6 of Part 1.

Two additional points about the profile deserve note. A System 4 organization is assumed to be most consistent with the values of the laboratory approach sketched above. Hence, a System 4 organization should both induce and require regenerative communication sequences more than the other systems.[49]

Now and Ideal Scores

The summary below of the results of the program of planned change will take advantage of an interesting property of the Likert Profile. That is, each profile item can be rated as Now and as Ideal. This permits useful contrasts of preferred and existing organization relations. Requests for Now scores direct the rater to respond as to where she now sees her organization; Ideal scores reflect where the rater would prefer the reference organization to be on each item.

The assumptions underlying the use of the Likert Profile are direct and can be spelled out briefly. System 4 organizations imply values, attitudes, and behavioral skills that are most consistent with OD. Hence, the success of the present program of planned organizational change can be defined in terms of movement toward System 4 ratings. System 4 ratings on the Likert Profile are most likely to induce regenerative, and to reverse or limit degenerative, communication sequences. Similarly, System 4 ratings imply a greater congruence of individual needs and organization demands than do the other three systems of organization in the Likert schema.

Results Imply Success

Managerial responses to the Likert Profile indicate that the learning design had the anticipated effects on interpersonal and intergroup relations in both kinds of organization units. These results come from two separate sets of studies, with somewhat different research designs and measuring instruments. The differences are mostly minor and technical in nature, and can be neglected here.

The results from the two studies can be highlighted in terms of five emphases. For convenience, the results will be reported in terms of the following conventions. Changes in managerial self-reports toward System 4 will be referred to as "increases," "positive" changes, or "changes toward the laboratory model." Changes trending toward System 1 will be referred to as "decreases," or "negative" changes or "changes away from the laboratory model."

First, managers in both kinds of units preferred a System 4 organization but acknowledged working under other systems. The conclusion can be illustrated by the growth-oriented units. In comparisons of forty-eight items, Ideal scores on the first administration of the profile were in all cases greater than Now scores. In fact, forty-three of the forty-eight cases showed statistically significant differences. To a similar point, the mean Ideal scores were in System 4 and the mean Now scores in low System 3. The profile scores can be summarized as shown:

System	Ideal	Now
1. Exploitative-authoritative	0	0
2. Benevolent-authoritative	0	1
3. Consultative	3	41
4. Participative group	45	6

These data establish that managers desired more System 4 properties at work than their organizations provided. The pattern is similar for the stability-oriented units, although for a variety of technical reasons, flat comparisons are more difficult to make.

Second, the learning in T-groups apparently was both impactful and was extended to relations at work, judging from changes in responses to the Likert Profile in the administration following each initial training experience. As expected, the change is more dramatic for the growth-oriented units. This difference may be due to factors in addition to the expected greater difficulty of inducing change in the stability-oriented units, however. Thus, first posttraining measures were some 4 months after the initial training in the case of the former units, while the interval was only 20 to 30 days for the latter units.

Common Pattern Reflected

The data clearly reflect a common pattern of changes in existing interpersonal and intergroup relations for both kinds of units, while the magnitudes of change apparently differ. Changes in Now scores, of course, measure changes in the existing relations.

Changes Toward System 4. In the growth-oriented units, managerial self-reports reveal a very sharp change toward System 4, that is, toward an organization style consistent with the laboratory approach. Specifically, in forty-eight comparisons of pretreatment with posttreatment scores, expected increases occur in forty-seven, and twenty-eight of these cases reach the 0.05 level of statistical significance, or better. This is most impressive evidence of systemic change.

For the stability-oriented units, the pattern of change trends dominantly in the same direction but is of smaller magnitude. Specifically, 82 percent of the self-ratings on Now scores increase between the pretest and the administration of the Likert Profile immediately following the training intervention. Although only 4 percent of these increases attain statistical significance, and some of the increases are small, most observers see even holding steady as a major triumph.[50]

In the first self-rating on the profile following the initial training experience the Ideal scores in both kinds of units change pretty much as do the Now scores. Consequently, a pattern of rising expectations had been set in motion by the training design. Managers were demanding even more gratification of their needs at work while they reported that the style of their relations at work was in fact becoming more need-gratifying.

In summary, the pattern is one of overwhelming change in existing relations toward System 4. The initial training experience had the intended effects, although their magnitudes clearly differ.

Third, some decay of the change in both kinds of organization units did occur following the initial spurt of changes, but most of the gain was retained. This implies a mostly successful testing of the initial learning, a two steps forward and one step back that suggests an incremental pattern of change. A variety of considerations, practical and theoretical, led to a prediction that this learning fade-out would occur.

A pattern of modest regression affects both Now and Ideal scores, but the former apparently more than the latter. Consider the stability-oriented units. About 2 months after the initial training experience, a modest regression in the self-ratings was observed. On the Now scores, self-ratings trend negatively in about 50 percent of the cases. Some 35 percent of the Ideal scores also trend negatively. None of these regressive changes attain statistical significance. These changes away from System 4 erode only part of the positive changes apparently induced by the learning design.

About 8 months into the program of change, despite the regression and before any additional planned training inputs were made, about 70 percent of the changes in scores from managers in the stability-oriented units still show increases over the set of self-ratings immediately preceding the initial training experience. Only 6 percent of these cases achieve statistical significance, but they are all changes toward System 4.

The growth-oriented units show an even more marked tendency to retain the initial movement toward System 4 on Now and Ideal scores. Approximately 12 months after the initial training, more than 96 percent of the self-ratings approach System 4 more closely than did the scores immediately before the initial training. Some 30 percent of these changes still retain statistical significance. Impressively, only 1.1 percent of the changes are toward System 1, despite some rocky intervening organizational history. None of these negative changes attains statistical significance.

Reinforcement Experience Useful. *Fourth,* a "reinforcement experience" proved useful for reversing or at least arresting the fade-out of changes in interpersonal and intergroup relations. Such reinforcement was programmed about a year after the initial training and had three objectives: to permit trainees to review their relative success in behaving consistently with the values of the laboratory approach, to reassess their commitment to those values, and to plan for the future.

Some Partial Erosion. The changes in managerial self-ratings that follow a reinforcement experience strongly imply its ability to arrest learning fade-out, again more so in the growth-oriented units. To sample the data in the stability-oriented units, an overwhelmingly positive pattern of change was observed between the self-ratings immediately before the reinforcement experience and those approximately 30 days later. Specifically, almost 80 percent of the changes in Now scores following the reinforcement experience are positive. Only a handful of these changes attain usually accepted levels of statistical significance.

The reinforcement experience also clearly had a major impact on the growth-oriented units. As the summary data in Table 1 reflect, the full observational period can be characterized in terms of three phases. In the first column, a massive change in self-ratings follows the initial training experience. The second column reflects a significant regression in which almost three-quarters of the scores decrease. This regression is substantial, but it erodes only part of the change induced by the initial training experience. Note the most prominent evidence of this partial erosion. In the first column, more than 56 percent of the

Table 1 Summary of Now Scores Only, Three Comparisons

	Rating After Initial Training vs. First Rating (Percent)	Third Rating vs. Rating After Initial Training (Percent)	Rating After Reinforcement vs. First Rating (Percent)
Statistically significant changes toward lab approach	56.3	0.0	35.4
Changes toward lab approach	39.5	23.0	43.8
No changes	0.0	2.1	6.3
Changes away from lab approach	4.2	66.5	14.6
Statistically significant changes away from lab approach	0.0	8.4	0.0
	100.0	100.0	100.1

changes toward the laboratory appraoch are statistically significant. In contrast, less than 10 percent of the changes away from the lab approach in the second column are statistically significant. Finally, following the reinforcement experience, the regression is reversed and scores return to the very high level immediately following the initial learning experiences, as the third column in Table 1 shows.

Fifth, the reinforced changes in the styles of interpersonal and intergroup relations tend to persist over extended periods. The record of the growth-oriented units is illustrative. Comparisons of the self-ratings on the Likert Profile before the training experience with the self-ratings 18 months later establish both the definite pattern and the substantial magnitude of the changes that persisted over the full period of observation. Table 2 presents summary data for the full 18-month period of observation in the growth-oriented units.

The pattern is similar in the stability-oriented units, but the magnitudes of change are smaller. The observational period is approximately 10 months. Again comparing the last self-rating with the one immediately before the initial training experience, 88 percent of the changes in Now and Ideal scores show increases. For growth-oriented units the corresponding figure is 84.4 percent, which is not very different. However, only 6 percent of the changes in stability-oriented units attain usually accepted levels of statistical significance. In contrast, for the growth-oriented units, between 35 and 50 percent of the changes in scores retain statistical significance after 18 months.

Table 2 Summary of Change over Full 18-Month Observation Period

	Now Scores (Percent)	Ideal Scores (Percent)
Statistically significant changes toward lab approach	35.4	50.0
Changes toward lab approach	43.8	39.6
No changes	6.3	6.3
Changes away from lab model	14.6	4.1
Statistically significant changes away from lab model	0.0	0.0
	100.1	100.0

Cautious but Real Optimism

In conclusion, the heavy preponderance of evidence implies the efficacy of the training design in inducing marked and persisting changes in the style of interpersonal and intergroup relations.

This conclusion is tentative, of course, and awaits further needed testing. In the case of the growth-oriented units, however, the pattern of change is so consistent and the magnitudes are so great that the effects can hardly be considered random. For the stability-oriented units, the dominant pattern of change is similar. However, the small magnitudes admit the possibility that the effects may be due to random causes rather than to the training design interacting with the specific type of organization unit. The consultants feel more comfortable in attributing the reduced magnitudes of change to the character of the stability-oriented units, as opposed to random forces that somehow trend to such a definite pattern.

Whatever future research shows, the possibilities are exciting. It is still too early to build organizations to order. But, results like those above, and similar findings,[51] imply that the science/art of planned change in organizations has developed sufficiently to provide major hope that individual needs can be made more congruent with organization demands. At the risk of being melodramatic, in any case, the view here is that the success in increasing this congruence in organizations will significantly determine the degree of freedom that humans will experience in contemporary life.

Notes

1. Leland P. Bradford, Jack R. Gibb, and Kenneth D. Benne (eds.), *T-Group Theory and Laboratory Method* (New York: Wiley, 1964), esp. pp. 216-247. The role of values also was prominent in the "group dynamics" literature which contributed to the evolution of the laboratory approach, most prominently in the work on leadership and group "climates" or "atmospheres."
2. Kenneth D. Benne, Leland P. Bradford, Jack R. Gibb, and Ronald O. Lippitt (eds.), *The Laboratory Method of Changing and Learning* (Palo Alto, Calif.: Science and Behavior Books, 1975), esp. pp. 72-106.
3. Ralph H. Kilmann, "Structural Designs for OD Programs," *Working Paper Series 231,* Graduate School of Business, University of Pittsburgh, esp. p. 27.
4. Jean M. Bartunek, Vishal Gujral, and Louis R. Pondy, "On the Complementarity of Organization Development and Design," pp. 1-2. Paper presented at 1977 Annual Meeting, Academy of Management, Kissimmee, Fla., August 14-17.
5. Gene W. Dalton, "Influence and Organizational Change," in Anant R. Negandhi and Joseph P. Schwitter (eds.), *Organizational Behavior Models* (Kent, Ohio: Comparative Administration Research Institute, 1970), p. 90.
6. Arnold Tannenbaum and Stanley Seashore, "Some Changing Conceptions and Approaches to the Study of Persons in Organizations" (Ann Arbor, Mich.: University of Michigan, Institute for Social Research, not dated), mimeographed.
7. Warren G. Bennis, "A New Role for the Behavioral Sciences: Effecting Organizational Change," *Administrative Science Quarterly,* Vol. 8 (September 1963), p. 138.
8. Davis is quoted in John Poppy, "New Era in Industry: It's OK to Cry in the Office," *Look,* July 9, 1968, p. 65.

   K. Bamforth, "T-Group Methods Within a Company," in G. Whitaker (ed.), *ATM Occasional Papers,* Vol. 2 (Oxford, England: Basil Blackwell, 1965), reports a similar effect in T-groups composed of "diagonal slices" of an organization. That is, their members represent different hierarchical levels but include no immediate superiors or subordinates. The effect encouraged Bamforth to discontinue direct use of T-groups.
9. Sharon Lieder and Newton Margulies, "A Sensitivity Training Design for Organizational Development," *Social Change,* Vol. 1, no. 1 (1971), p. 6; and Robert T. Golembiewski and Arthur Blumberg, "Training and Relational Learning," *Training and Development Journal,* Vol. 21 (November 1967), pp. 35-43.
10. Bernard M. Bass, "The Anarchist Movement and the T-Group," *Journal of Applied Behavioral Science,* Vol. 3 (April 1967), p. 215.

11. Ibid., pp. 215-216.
12. At a trivial level, see Robert T. Golembiewski, *The Small Group* (Chicago: University of Chicago, 1962), esp. pp. 201-204, for a discussion of task effects.
13. To choose an extreme example, see William J. Goode and Irving Fowler, "Incentive Factors in a Low Morale Plant," *American Sociological Review*, Vol. 14 (October 1949), pp. 618-624. In the organization described there, it is reasonable to conclude, poor mental health was more appropriate for organizational success.
14. For one case where T-group training was not sufficient for organizational success, see Samuel D. Deep, Bernard M. Bass, and James A. Vaughn, "Some Effects on Business Gaming of Previous Quasi-T-Group Affiliations," *Journal of Applied Psychology*, Vol. 51, no. 5 (1967), pp. 426-431.
15. Generally, see Wendell L. French and Cecil H. Bell, Jr., *Organization Development* (Englewood Cliffs, N.J., Prentice-Hall, 1973), esp. pp. 21-29; and Edgar F. Huse, *Organization Development and Change* (St. Paul, Minn.: West Publishing, 1975), esp. pp. 25-29, 235-238.
16. Ernest G. Miller, "The Impact of T-Groups on Managerial Behavior," *Public Administration Review*, Vol. 30 (May 1970), p. 297.
17. Adapted from Paul C. Buchanan, "Laboratory Training and Organization Development," *Administrative Science Quarterly*, Vol. 14 (September 1969), p. 221.
18. Robert B. Morton and A. Wight, "A Critical Incidents Evaluation of an Organizational Training Laboratory" (Sacramento, Calif.: Aerojet General Corporation, Personnel Department, 1964), mimeographed; and Reed M. Powell and John F. Stinson, "The Worth of Laboratory Training," *Business Horizons*, Vol. 14 (August 1971), pp. 87-95.
19. Frank Friedlander, "A Comparative Study of Consulting Processes and Group Development," *Journal of Applied Behavioral Science*, Vol. 4 (October 1968), pp. 377-399.
20. Chris Argyris, *Interpersonal Competence and Organizational Effectiveness* (Homewood, Ill.: Dorsey, 1962), p. 135.
21. James J. Clark, "Task Group Therapy," mimeographed, p. 11.
22. Robert Tannenbaum and Sheldon A. Davis, "Values, Men, and Organizations," *Industrial Management Review*, Vol. 10 (Winter 1969), pp. 67-83.
23. Jack R. Gibb and Lorraine M. Gibb, "Role Freedom in a TORI Group," in Arthur Burton (ed.), *Encounter* (San Francisco: Jossey-Bass, 1969), p. 47.
24. Bass, "The Anarchist Movement and the T-Group," pp. 222-225, provides the model for the catalog that follows.
25. Richard E. Byrd, "Training in a Non-Group," *Journal of Humanistic Psychology*, Vol. 7 (1967), pp. 18-27.
26. Robert R. Blake and Jane S. Mouton, *The Managerial Grid* (Houston, Tex.: Gulf Publishing, 1964).

27. Robert B. Morton and Bernard M. Bass, "The Organizational Training Laboratory," *Training Directors Journal,* Vol. 18 (October 1964), pp. 2-18.
28. Bamforth, "T-Group Methods Within a Company."
29. Alan B. Wagner, "The Use of Process Analysis in Business Decision Games," *Journal of Applied Behavioral Science,* Vol. 1 (October 1965), pp. 387-408.
30. Robert T. Golembiewski and Arthur Blumberg, "Confrontation as a Training Design in Complex Organizations," *Journal of Applied Behavioral Science,* Vol. 3 (December 1967), pp. 525-547; and Matthew B. Miles, Paula Holzman Calder, Harvey A. Hornstein, Daniel M. Callahan, and R. Steven Schiavro, "Data Feedback and Organizational Change in a School System." Paper presented at Annual Meeting, American Sociological Association, Miami Beach, Fla., August 29, 1966.
31. Alexander Winn, "Social Change in Industry: From Insight to Implementation," *Journal of Applied Behavioral Science,* Vol. 2 (April 1966), p. 81.
32. TRW Systems is perhaps the best example. See Sheldon A. Davis, "Organic Problem-Solving Method of Organizational Change," *Journal of Applied Behavioral Science,* Vol. 3 (January 1967), pp. 3-21. See also a set of brief Harvard case studies describing the OD program at TRW and its roots in the laboratory approach, in Gene W. Dalton, Paul R. Lawrence, and Larry E. Greiner (eds.), *Organizational Change and Development* (Homewood, Ill.: Irwin-Dorsey, 1970), pp. 114-153. Popular attention to TRW's efforts came through such vehicles as John Poppy's "New Era in Industry: It's OK to Cry in the Office," pp. 64-76.
33. For a convenient summary review of thirty-seven pieces of such research, see Larry E. Pate, Warren R. Nielsen, and Paula C. Bacon, "Advances in Research on Organization Development: Toward A Beginning," pp. 389-394, in Robert L. Taylor, Michael J. O'Connell, Robert A. Zawacki, and D. D. Warrick (eds.), *1976 Proceedings,* Academy of Management. For convenient, annotated bibliographies to the OD literature, see Jerome L. Franklin, *Organization Development: An Annotated Bibliography* (Ann Arbor, Mich.: Institute for Social Research, 1975), and Kenneth J. Murrell and Peter B. Vaill, *Organization Development: Sources and Applications* (Washington, D.C.: Organization Development Division, American Society for Training and Development, 1975).
34. Project ACORD in the U.S. Department of State used an initial "cousin" experience following Model A, for example, and helped develop such approaches to organizational transfer of learning as third-party consultation, which is described in Chapter 6. Alfred J. Marrow, *Making Waves on Foggy Bottom* (Washington, D.C.: NTL Institute, 1974).
35. Arthur H. Kuriloff and Stuart Atkins, "T-Group for a Work Team," *Journal of Applied Behavioral Science,* Vol. 2 (January 1966), p. 63. They note that: "Superiors and subordinates together attended the [T-Group] sessions. This has not been usual. . . ."

36. Ibid., p. 64.
37. Alfred J. Marrow, David G. Bowers, and Stanley E. Seashore, *Management by Participation* (New York: Harper and Row, 1967).
38. Stanley E. Seashore and David G. Bowers, "Durability of Organizational Change," *American Psychologist,* Vol. 25 (January 1970), p. 232.
39. Michael Beer and Edgar F. Huse, "A Systems Approach to Organizational Development," *Journal of Applied Behavioral Science,* Vol. 8 (January 1972), pp. 79-101.
40. Seashore and Bowers, "Durability of Organizational Change," p. 233.
41. Robert R. Blake, Jane S. Mouton, Louis B. Barnes, and Larry E. Greiner, "Breakthrough in Organization Development," *Harvard Business Review,* Vol. 42 (November 1964), pp. 133-135; and Robert R. Blake, Jane S. Mouton, Richard L. Sloma, and Barbara Peek Loftin, "A Second Breakthrough In Organization Development," *California Management Review,* Vol. 11, no. 2 (1968), pp. 73-78.

    General support for the expected effects of Phase I is provided, for example, by Michael Beer and S. W. Kleinsath, "The Effects of the Managerial Grid Lab on Organizational and Leadership Dimensions." Paper presented at the Annual Meeting, American Psychological Association, Washington, D.C., September 1967.
42. Julius E. Eitington, "Assessing Laboratory Training Using Psychology of Learning Concepts," *Training and Development Journal,* Vol. 25 (February 1971), p. 15.

    Note that other studies do not replicate some of these effects, both at earlier or later phases of Grid training. See Peter B. Smith and Trudie F. Honour, "The Impact of Phase I Managerial Grid Training," *Journal of Management Studies,* Vol. 6 (October 1969), esp. pp. 319-322; S. R. Maxwell and Martin G. Evans, "An Evaluation of Organizational Development: Three Phases of the Managerial Grid." Mimeographed working paper, School of Business, University of Toronto, July 1971; and Robert T. Keller, "A Longitudinal Assessment of an Organizational Development Intervention." Paper presented at 1977 Annual Meeting, Academy of Management, Kissimmee, Fla., August 14-17.
43. Richard Beckhard, *Strategies of Organization Development* (Reading, Mass.: Addison-Wesley, 1969), pp. 23-24.
44. Renato Tagiuri, "The Concept of Organization Climate," p. 24, in Tagiuri and George H. Litwin (eds.), *Organizational Climate* (Boston: Division of Research, Harvard University, 1968).
45. For details, see Robert T. Golembiewski and Arthur Blumberg, "Sensitivity Training in Cousin Groups: A Confrontation Design," *Training and Development Journal,* Vol. 23 (August 1969), pp. 18-23.
46. The design and results of the study with growth-oriented units has appeared as Robert T. Golembiewski and Stokes B. Carrigan, "Planned Change in

Organization Style Based on Laboratory Approach," *Administrative Science Quarterly,* Vol. 15 (March 1970), pp. 79-93; and "The Persistence of Laboratory-Induced Changes in Organization Styles," *Administrative Science Quarterly,* Vol. 15 (September 1970), pp. 330-340. The research on Stability-oriented units is summarized in two long unpublished papers, "Changing Climate in a Complex Organization: I and II." The research team includes Robert T. Golembiewski, Robert Munzenrider, Arthur Blumberg, Stokes B. Carrigan, and Walter R. Mead.

For similar effects of OD efforts on classroom climate, see Christopher B. Keys and Rhoda K. Kreisman, "Organization Development, Classroom Climate, and Grade Level," *Group and Organization Studies,* Vol. 3 (June 1978), esp. pp. 233-234. They stress that OD can "create, in schools, the sense of community [and] a new feeling of autonomy."

47. Donald T. Campbell, "From Description to Experimentation," pp. 212-242, in Chester W. Harris (ed.), *Problems In Measuring Change* (Madison, Wisc.: University of Wisconsin, 1963).

48. Rensis Likert, *The Human Organization* (New York: McGraw-Hill, 1967).

49. For data supporting this point of view, consult Rensis Likert and Jane Gibson Likert, *New Ways of Managing Conflict* (New York: McGraw-Hill, 1976), esp. pp. 86-106.

50. If only "major changes" are considered for the stability-oriented units, the picture does not change essentially. Let us arbitrarily define "major changes" as those on which mean scores change by ±1.0 or greater. In this case, for the Now scores, 70 percent of the changes are positive, only 13 percent are negative, while 17 percent show differences less than ±1.0.

51. See especially Jerome L. Franklin, "Characteristics of Successful and Unsuccessful Organization Development," *Journal of Applied Behavioral Science,* Vol. 12 (October 1976), esp. p. 483.

Chapter 2

SHAPING JOBS AND AUTHORITY RELATIONSHIPS
Permanently Building Organization Development Values into the Structure of Work

The *summum bonum* of OD involves building organization structures and jobs consistent with laboratory values. This constitutes the permanent solution for moving beyond the bureaucratic organization. Put another way, technostructural and human-processual approaches then would work together toward a common set of values, inducing the same or similar mutually reinforcing dynamics.

This chapter must have an incomplete character, for much remains unknown or doubtful about its target. However, three points seem relatively clear about the importance of the structural emphasis below:

- Changes in organization structures or roles often can usefully precede efforts toward educational or cultural change, such as those implied by interaction-centered OD approaches.[1]
- Changes in organization structures or roles are likely to be more convenient and perhaps more effective at lower levels of organization than are educational or cultural interventions.[2]
- Changes in organization structures or roles have to be carefully monitored so that the end does not come to justify the means, as in an autocratic imposition of a participative intervention.

This chapter reviews three ways of approaching the *summum bonum* of OD. Thus, the first section provides a brief primer on two alternative ways of organizing work—the familiar approach called "bureaucracy"; and the alternative approach more consistent with OD values. The analysis focuses upon the comparison of alternative skeletal organization structures—their underlying theoretical propositions and their probable impacts on attitudes and behaviors.

The choice of this introductory emphasis is deliberate and seeks to provide a common conceptual basis for two other efforts at permanent structural change reviewed in the last three sections of this chapter. One of those efforts deals with micro-structures and the other two with macro-structures. If the first section of this chapter is considered a general treatise on humans, then two other sections busy themselves with a specific discussion of Mutt, while a fourth deals in detail with Jeff.

Those who have neglected to read their funny papers no doubt will prefer a less fanciful introduction to what follows. The pure vanilla of it? The first section of this chapter seeks to show how two sets of simple ideas can generate different jobs or tasks that have contrasting effects on the persons performing them, in general. The following three sections deal with specifics, the first involving top levels of organization. Attention then shifts to the lowest levels via "job enrichment" or "job enlargement," based on Herzberg's familiar distinction between motivators and satisfiers. Some rules of thumb for workaday-level applications more likely to succeed than fail also get attention. Finally, middle management levels will be shown to be amenable to ways of organizing that also approach OD values.

The concluding section deals with two contrasting structurings of large organizations. Most attention will go to a retail food chain seeking to move from a basically centralized mode of operation to one with dominant features of decentralization, but a cursory look also will be given to a state agency taking a similar structural approach. Again, the two basic models introduced in the first section below constitute the conceptual framework in terms of which this successful effort at macro-structural change can be understood.

Alternative General Models for Structuring Work

Expressing and Reinforcing OD Values in Formal Organizations

We live in a transitional period, and the following analysis extends what is already happening into a reasonably coherent view of what the future implies. The effort remains somewhat speculative, but is grounded in the major forces generalized in Exhibit 1. The reader can easily generate the awesome implications of that exhibit. To illustrate, you can more easily order someone to obey when work and decisions are programmed. Ordering someone to be creative is another matter.

Exhibit 1 Two Contrasting Emphases in Organizing

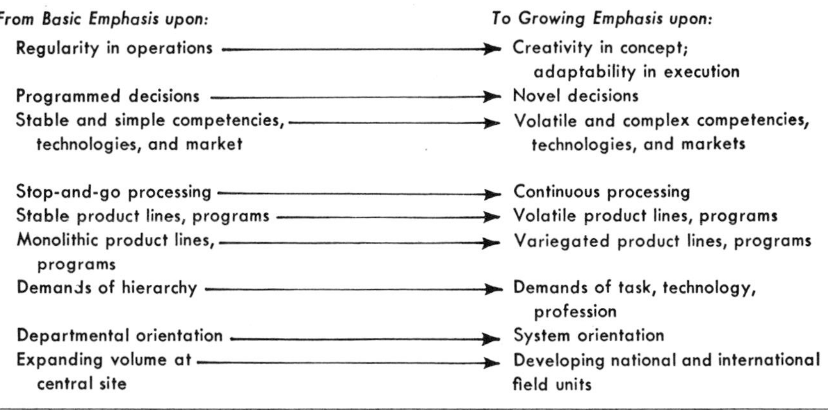

From Basic Emphasis upon:	*To Growing Emphasis upon:*
Regularity in operations	Creativity in concept; adaptability in execution
Programmed decisions	Novel decisions
Stable and simple competencies, technologies, and market	Volatile and complex competencies, technologies, and markets
Stop-and-go processing	Continuous processing
Stable product lines, programs	Volatile product lines, programs
Monolithic product lines, programs	Variegated product lines, programs
Demands of hierarchy	Demands of task, technology, profession
Departmental orientation	System orientation
Expanding volume at central site	Developing national and international field units

Source: See Note 111.

Structuring Work as an Exercise in Four Variables

Probable changes in organizational patterns consistent with such diverse technological trends can be described in terms of four polarities. Different times and technologies give different emphases to these four polarities:

- Differentiation and integration
- Repression and wriggle room, or freedom to act
- Stability and newness
- Function and flow of work

These four polarities imply variegated structures for work, as four points establish. *First,* any organizing pattern reflects relative emphases on differentiation and integration. Following Paul R. Lawrence and Jay W. Lorsch, "differentiation" can be defined in terms of the development among the several units of an organization of "different formal reporting relationships, different criteria for rewards, and different control procedures." In summary, differentiation is defined in terms of "the difference in cognitive and emotional orientation among managers in different functional departments." Integration refers to "the quality of the state of collaboration that exists among departments that are required to achieve unity of effort by the demands of the environment."[3]

Although organizations of the future will increasingly emphasize integration, bureaucracy dominated over the first half of this century. The concept "bureaucracy" is rooted in differentiation, as these properties imply:

- A well-defined chain of command that vertically channels formal interaction
- A system of procedures and rules for dealing with all contingencies at work, which reinforces the reporting insularity of each bureau
- A division of labor based upon specialization by major function or process that vertically fragments a flow of work
- Promotion and selection based on technical competence defined consistently with the first three points above
- Impersonality in relations between organization members and between them and their clients

More recently, integration has received increasing emphasis.[4] The "system approach" and the computer underlay the major contemporary technical expressions of this integrative thrust. Behaviorally, integration implies meeting both human needs and technical demands at work.

Second, any pattern for organizing impacts on repression and "wriggle room." That is, every structure intentionally limits behavior, but some do so significantly more than others. Increasingly, an emerging integrative emphasis seeks an organizational climate having the minimal constraints consistent with quality performance. This is the essence of the contemporary stress on management by objectives, as well as of AT&T's vertical loading of jobs to be described later in this chapter.

There is no mistaking the root cause of today's deemphasis on repression. Contemporary organizations reflect a growing need for an organic and evolving integration, as opposed to a mechanical structuring. The consequences are profound. In short, adherence to a mechanical system can be enforced, but commitment to an organic integration can only be elicited and encouraged. Put another way, the integrity of a stable and simple technology may be safeguarded by culling deviants. But changing and complex technologies require the careful husbanding of selected kinds of innovation or adaptability in a widening range of employees. Hence the growing importance of wriggle room, or freedom to act.

The change in emphasis on repression and wriggle room may be characterized broadly, and with essential accuracy. The bureaucratic spirit is oriented toward developing a system to guard against humans at their worst, to preclude error or venality. Flows of work are differentiated as functions or positions or motions, and surplus repression is the glue used to pull them together. The integrative spirit, on the other hand, is oriented toward creating an environment in which humans can approach their productive best.

Costs must be paid whether the thrust is integrative or fragmenting, of course. The costs of the bureaucratic logic are repression and narrowed developmental opportunities; and the costs of freedom to act may be calculated in terms of lessened control over behavior, or of more complex decision-making processes which hopefully facilitate the implementing of decisions. Thus, integration constitutes no facile panacea. Rather, technological developments require that we cope with the costs of the integrative model because we can no longer, in general, bear the costs of the differentiating model.

Third, the relative emphasis on stability and newness also has profound implications for organization structures. The acceleration of newness has been described in many places. Hence, the bare notice here that the all-but-overwhelming newness that is a trademark of our times is poorly served by bureaucratic properties. In summary, the bureaucratic model better serves the trends listed in the left column of Exhibit 1 than it meets those listed on the right.

Fourth, different emphases on the three polarities above imply different organization structures built around functions and flows of work, respectively. Illustrating this conclusion requires a major input.

Two Alternative Models for Organizing

Demonstrating that different emphases on the polarities above will generate different organization structures is straightforward,[5] if involved. To begin, take an easy case: the organization of three activities, A, B, and C, which when combined yield some product or service. Figure 1 presents the skeletal structure consistent with these four emphases: differentiation, repression, stability, and flow of work.

The ways in which the two structures reflect extreme emphases on the four polarities can be suggested briefly. For example, Figure 1 essentially puts the same or similar activities together in its basic units of organization. That is, the model builds on departments differentiated by kinds of activities, usually called "functions" at high levels of organization and "processes" at lower levels. Relatedly, the narrow span of control is well designed to facilitate surplus repression in the details in operation. That is, the structure encourages centralization of decision-making at the level of M_{ABC}, who alone can make reasonable decisions about the flow of work, A + B + C. Hence, he alone controls a "managerial unit," the size of which is indicated by the broken-line circle. Finally, the model presumes a *stable* state. The underlying model implies a mechanical meshing of parts rather than of a dynamic flow of work.

Figure 2 presents an alternative structure consistent with the principal adaptations that have been made to the ongoing organizational revolution. These adaptive arrangements include: decentralization, project management, matrix overlays, independent profit centers, management by objectives, autonomous teams, and numerous other variations on the same central theme.

As the Figure 2 model suggests, these adaptations stress integration, wriggle room, change, and flow of work. The compound conclusion will only be illustrated here. To begin, the unorthodox model organizes around integrative departments, that is, it groups together activities related in a total flow of work.

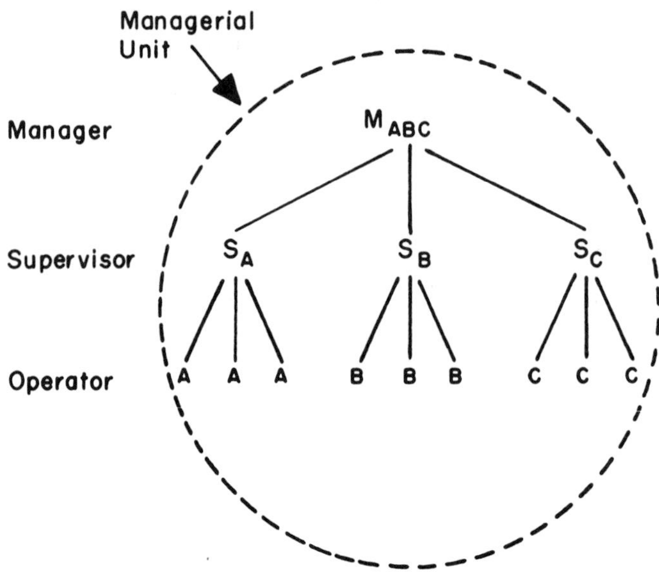

Figure 1 A structure consistent with values of bureaucracy: emphasis on differentiation, repression, stability, and function. Underlying properties: Authority is a vertical, or hierarchical, relation. Departments are organized around the same or similar activities, called "functions" at high levels of organization and "processes" at low levels, that is, "like" activities are put together. Only a relatively small number of people should report directly to any superior.

This integrative thrust at the departmental level can also be extended to the operators, as through job rotation and job enlargement. In addition, the model seeks the *minimum control* consistent with end-item quality and quantity. The multiple opportunities for self-discipline and self-control built into the model, for example, reduce the need for external repression in tying individual needs to organizational goals. The key factors are teams which control a flow of work whose performance is easily and meaningfully comparable.

Implicitly, the role of higher management changes profoundly in a Figure 2 structure. The emphasis is on developing and monitoring measures of performance, and on responding to exceptions as that is necessary by training, by redefining policies, or by disciplinary action. Higher management in Figure 1 is far more in the fire-fighting business and stands more oriented toward enforcing than eliciting.

Moreover, Figure 2 variously facilitates adapting to *change* and to *growth.* For example, Figure 1 structures tend to grow tall very quickly, with consequent increases in reaction time, in communication costs, and so on. The limited span of control is the major culprit. Figure 2 structures are much less growth-sensitive and can remain relatively flat even with manifold increases in size.

Finally, Figure 2 structures departmentalize around *flows of work* as opposed to functions. Each S now controls a managerial unit.

The two structures represent ideal types or analytical extremes. In practice, they can be approached only in degree, often in complex mixtures. But approaches to one ideal model or the other will tend to generate significantly different consequences. The vertical loading of work described below, for example, illustrates the movement from a Figure 1 to a Figure 2 job at the operator's level. This movement implies major changes in the role of the manager, as well as a freer work environment which emphasizes self-control.[6]

In a more complex organization, similarly, the two structures can motivate radically different hierarchies. Consider the U.S. Department of State's effort to create autonomous "program managers" who reported directly to the Deputy Undersecretary of State for Administration. Following a Figure 2 structure made the organization much "flatter."[7] For example, one manager in it reports to the Deputy Undersecretary. Prior to the reorganization, this towering chain of command loomed above that manager: Division Head, Office Director, Deputy Director of Personnel, Director of Personnel, Deputy Assistant Secretary for Administration, Assistant Secretary for Administration, and Deputy Undersecretary.[8]

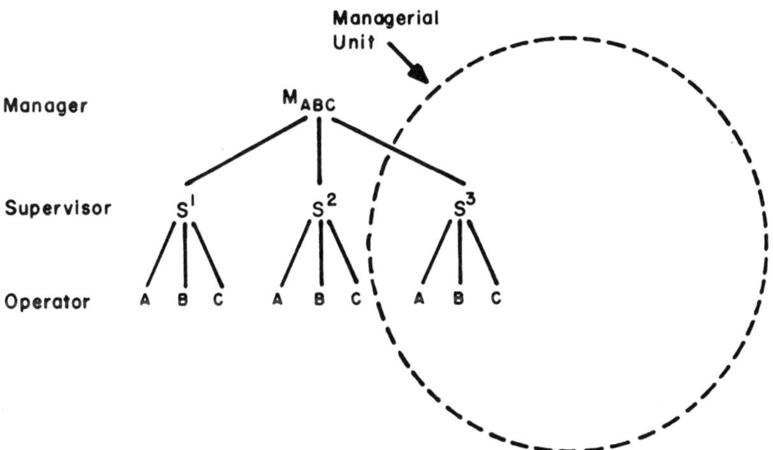

Figure 2 An alternative structure: emphasis on integration, wriggle room, change, and flow of work. Underlying properties: Authoritative relations occur up, down, and across the organization, and all these vectors should be directed to similar goals by an effective structure. Departmentation reflects the flow of work; that is, related activities are put together whether they are "like" or "unlike." A relatively large number of people may report to any superior, given a structure that facilitates measuring performance.

Alternative Structures and Quality of Interaction Systems

If the examples above seem to suggest that the laboratory approach to OD better suits the structure in Figure 2 than in Figure 1, that suggestion is intended. This section and the ones to follow seek to establish the point. Note that OD applications also are useful in a Figure 1 structure, especially in providing a palliative for the interpersonal and intergroup difficulties that tend to be induced by that structure.

There is a gentle way of reflecting the greater complementarity of the laboratory approach to OD and a Figure 2 structure. Usefully, it also highlights the value of the laboratory approach even where a Figure 2 structure does not, and perhaps cannot, exist. Recall the notion of a degenerative interaction system, which involves a self-heightening model of four variables:

→ Low openness
→ Low owning
→ Low trust
→ High risk

Such degenerative sequences are at once one of the prime targets for change in applications of the laboratory approach, one of the common products of a Figure 1 structure, and a major impediment to change. Evidence also suggests that Figure 2 structures tend to induce forces that reverse degenerative sequences, as well as to reinforce regenerative sequences.[9]

Conveniently, a miniature-argument sketches the fuller sense in which Figure 1 structures can encourage degenerative sequences. Consider only that A + B + C generate some product or discrete subassembly and consequently must collaborate. But, individual supervisors are responsible only for A or B or C, and thus tend to be drawn into zero-sum competitive games which fragment that which requires integration. For example, the very act of departmentalizing in a Figure 1 structure around like or similar activities encourages we vs. they dynamics. Illustratively, powerful reasons encourage As to identify in vertical cliques—reasons such as promotions, pay increases, and so on. And organization dilemmas often make the worst of these reasonable identifications.[10] Thus, an S_A and an S_B could get involved in a question over the allocation of some costs in dispute, and any resulting socioemotional disturbance would at once be reinforced by the fragmentation inherent in a Figure 1 approach to departmentation, while it also contributes to that fragmentation.

Such fragmenting tendencies in a Figure 1 structure imply reduced openness and owning between (for example) the units headed by S_A and S_B, which could lead to chronically low trust and paralyzing risk. The probabilities of such an outcome are increased by the problems of assessing validly and reliably the relative contributions to performance of A, B, and C, which issue plagues Figure 1 structures. The classic question is: How many As are equal to how many Bs? Appropriate standards are difficult to set and perhaps even harder to change, while they also involve major elements of arbitrariness. This combination encourages disputes, because all parties can rightly claim much virtue for their positions.

Moreover, M_{ABC} in a Figure 1 structure may have a vested if paradoxical interest in reinforcing such degenerative sequences. Assume her interest is avoiding low output. Note also that low output can be preserved tactfully only by the close cooperation of the three supervisors and their units. A certain measure of degenerative interaction between the Figure 1 units might seem a reasonable price to pay to avoid such an unwanted collaboration.

From many perspectives, then, Figure 1 structures often imply a high risk of trusting, of being open, and of owning one's ideas and feelings with those who are involved in the same flow of work.

Figure 2 structures trend oppositely. In a pure Figure 2 structure, performance of the units headed by S_1, S_2, and S_3 may be meaningfully compared, and at least some important elements such as productivity levels can be changed by the independent efforts of any individual work unit. This massive datum induces attractive relationships between A + B + C in each of the three supervisory units. The structure encourages integration of what needs to be integrated—the several activities and persons necessary to produce some product or service. If A and B in S_1 are not open with one another, to bowdlerize the point, it could effect their mutual performance and consequently might come out of their combined hides.

Consider an approximate but powerful contrast. Tersely, it is risky in a Figure 2 structure not to be open, not to own, and not to trust those in the same flow of work. Tersely, also, it is risky in a Figure 1 structure for an individual to be open, owning, and trusting with all those in the same flow of work. The difference is awesome.

The same point can be made in many other ways. We vs. they relationships no doubt will exist in a Figure 2 structure between the units headed by S_1, S_2, and S_3, but relationships between those units are not critical to performance, except where massive antagonism between the units exists. In Figure 2 structures, in contrast, the probable we vs. they relationships also should be integrative. It is by just such central tendencies that the Figure 2 structures induce more attractive consequences than the Figure 1 structures.

Some Major Consequences of Alternative Structures

Exhibit 2 at once consolidates, builds upon, and extends these illustrative differences between the two structural types. The exhibit has been adapted somewhat for present purposes, but it is faithful to the existing research literature or to reasonable inferences where that literature is lacking.

Exhibit 2 Comparisons of the Consequences of Two Structural Types, Using Selected Properties of Performance

Selected Properties	Figure 1 Structure Functional Model	Figure 2 Structure Flow-of-Work Model
1. Information Overload	1a. Tends toward information overload at level of integrative managers like M_{ABC}	1a. Reduces information overload at level of managers like M_{ABC}
	1b. Lengthens the social and psychological distances between the points at which messages originate, at which decisions are made, and at which actions will be taken	1b. Shortens the distance between points at which messages originate, at which decisions are made, and at which actions will be taken
	1c. Decreases the probability that messages will get through, at least without distortion	1c. Increases the probability that messages will get through, and with minimal distortion
	1d. Decreases likelihood that messages will be acted on	1d. Increases likelihood that messages will be acted on
2. Response Time	2a. Increases response time, due to longer communication chains	2a. Reduces response time, due to shorter chains
	2b. Prone to responses that are too little, too late, and to a paralysis of analysis.	2b. Increases the probability of timely awareness/response to rapidly changing conditions
	2c. Prone to errors of omission, to failure to communicate and/or to act	
3. Management Review	3a. Tends to refer decisions to higher management for prior review	3a. Tends to make decisions at lower levels, with later review at higher levels
	3b. Decreases likelihood of errors of commission at lower levels	3b. Increases likelihood of errors of commission at lower levels
	3c. Subjects decisions to considered judgment at various levels	3c. Decreases likelihood that decisions will benefit from top-level perspective
4. Decision Locus	4a. Centralizes decision-making	4a. Decentralizes decision-making
	4b. Decisions may suffer from lack of detailed and up-to-date information about operating situation	4b. Decisions may suffer in that they are so responsive to specific operating situation
5. Mutual Influence	5a. Reduces mutual influence across functional lines	5a. Increases and legitimates mutual influence across functional lines
	5b. Requires either informal bargaining or cumbersome up-over-and-down linkages of separate hierarchical chains of command that are integrated only far above the operating level	5b. Functions are integrated near the operating level via identification with a common flow of work
6. Competition/ Collaboration	6a. Encourages intergroup competition between functions	6a. Encourages collaboration between functions in same flow of work
	6b. Encourages we/they attitudes that fragment flow of work or, alternatively, a "mind your own business and we'll mind ours" attitude that isolates functions	6b. Encourages "we" attitudes that integrate contributors to a flow of work and that induce helping relationships between the several functions

Exhibit 2 (Continued)

Selected Properties	Figure 1 Structure Functional Model	Figure 2 Structure Flow-of-Work Model
	6c. Encourages blaming of other functions for problems	6c. May induce some competition between units monitoring different flows of work
		6d. Reduces blaming of other functions for problems
7. Dependence/ Independence	7a. Encourages dependence on higher authority and unwillingness to act without specific authorization	7a. Encourages aggressiveness and independence of higher authority, plus an eagerness to act without specific authorization
	7b. Gives higher management a sense of significance and of being in control	7b. May isolate higher management from the action
	7c. Equilibrates higher management's authority and responsi-	7c. May lessen the sense of control by higher management

Source: Adopted from Roger Harrison, "Effective Organization for Startup," mimeographed (Cambridge, Mass.: Development Research Associates, Inc., July 8, 1970), p. 14.

Note that each structural form has advantages and disadvantages. The critical issue then becomes one of choosing the structure which best meets the set of actual operating conditions, and the relevant challenge involves coping with the more-or-less inevitable problems generated by the structure that is chosen. Beyond this, start-up seems to require structural properties like those in the right column of Exhibit 2. After the shakedown period, however, the need may shift to regularity in operations, programmed decisions, and other properties of a Figure 1 structure.[11] Roger Harrison contrasts the differences between start-up and steady-state operations in these revealing terms:

> A startup organization has a radically different climate from those operating under normal conditions. The best way of capturing the flavor of these differences is to consider the startup operation as a "wartime" battle situation, compared with normal "peacetime" conditions. . . .
>
> The time pressure, the crisis decision-making amid grave responsibilities, the difficulties of communication, the stress on individuals, the fluidity and lack of structure of the organization are all typical of combat situations.
>
> During normal operations . . . most organizations value *efficiency* and *economy*. This leads, for example, to rules for the use and procurement of materials and manpower which are oriented towards *conservation* and *control*. During startup . . . the appropriate priorities are *delivery* and *performance* because of the greatly increased cost of having materials and services too little and too late. A degree of inefficiency and waste must be tolerated in favor of effectiveness. The costs of the wastage are frequently small compared to the costs of delay in startup.[12]

Four Major Structural Challenges

Various emphases on each of the organizational polarities imply major challenges for management thought and practice. The interaction will be illustrated, if only briefly, to sketch the implications of the laboratory approach to OD for the development of leading ideas and practices.

Differentiation and Integration

At least three major challenges are involved in shifting emphasis from differentiation toward integration. Basically, the interest here is in "what" needs to be done, rather than in "who" will do it. "Who" questions do get some attention, however.

Developing Strategies for Motivation and Collaboration. *First,* new strategies must be developed for motivating individuals and groups while facilitating interpersonal and intergroup collaboration. Inducing win or lose competition between individuals and groups has been *the* standby strategy, and it does have its attractions. Much experience has been accumulated about "cattle prod" activities useful for inducing rivalry or win or lose competition. Triggering rivalry or conflict is easy; keeping it within bounds often is difficult. Moreover, the competitive strategy can generate substantial energies, as every football coach and military officer knows.

The disadvantages of win or lose competition loom increasingly significant,[13] however, particularly in organizations with structures like that in Figure 1. Overall, technological demands increasingly require fluid collaboration between functions or processes. However, great potential for conflict and rivalry is built into Figure 1 structures.

The awkward effects of Figure 1 structures in this regard become particularly marked in industries like aerospace, but these effects are clear enough even in organizations with more routine missions. For example, the work of departments in an orthodox structure is not directly comparable, which often precludes reliable and nonarbitrary measures of performance. Each department provides only a partial contribution to a variety of flows of work, which implies major problems in factoring out departmental success and failure. Because of this complexity, one department may win only as another department loses, for example, in a cost-accounting allocation.

In contrast, structures like that in Figure 2 require that S perform a managerially integrative role. S can take a generalist role in fact as well as intent, in that in supervising the managerial unit defined by the broken-line circle, he can and indeed must make reasonable decisions about a total flow of work. These integrative features of Figure 2 structures have numerous advantages. Because the basic units of organization below M_{ABC} are autonomous and control an entire flow of work, for example, reliable and nonarbitrary measurement of performance is relatively simple. In addition, the basic unit of organization includes the full sequence of operations. As a consequence, effort and performance are more likely to be congruent. Moreover, the wins of one department do not preclude wins by others. In summary, even the competition in Figure 2 structures has integrative tendencies.

In addition, the issue of the broader usefulness of the laboratory approach has a "heads I win, tails you lose" quality about it. Behaviors and values consistent with the laboratory approach are critical in managing a Figure 2 structure, and especially in changing over to such a structure. Specifically, those structures basically permit decentralized patterns of delegation. And, as Argyris observes,

> For decentralization to work, open superior-subordinate relationships are required, where trust is high, where conformity, fear, dependence are low, where experimentation and risk-taking are prominent. These qualities cannot be issued, ordered, or even delegated. . . .
>
> The need is to find ways to uncover, to unfreeze these values wherever they exist. There is also a need to find ways to help man increase and strengthen these values because, lying dormant for years, they have tended to become weak, soft, and seemingly not very effective—especially in the tense, action-packed world of industrial life.[14]

The development of the integrative teams called for by Figure 2 structures at once requires similar appropriate values, and also contributes to them. That is, those teams have a very special character, which Leonard Sayles and Margaret Chandler incisively capture. Their managers, we are told, ". . . must create a system that will make . . . the organizations it embraces and the people in them . . . do what is needed in a system that is *self-forcing* (for excellence) and *self-enforcing.*"[15]

There may be cases in which a Figure 2 structure cannot be approached. But even there—perhaps especially there—high priority may be appropriate for the development of OD strategies that facilitate interpersonal and intergroup collaboration. For example, the interdepartmental conflicts and rivalries encouraged by traditional structures may be ameliorated by improving the processes of interpersonal and group interaction. Consider the chief executive of a Figure 1 organization who spotlighted the diverse forces induced by the traditional structure in these words:

> The trouble with ABC is that nobody aside from me ever gives one damn about the overall goals of this place. They're all seeing the world through the lenses of their departmental biases. What we need around here are people who wear the ABC hat, not the engineering hat or the sales hat or the production hat.[16]

This complaint inspired the development of the ABC Hats, a group representing several functions and hierarchical levels that filled the integrative gaps. Organizational applications of sensitivity training seek similar integration via improved interpersonal and group relations.

Improving interpersonal and intergroup relations in a Figure 1 structure implies an uphill struggle, all the way. Whatever improvement in communication results from sensitivity training or from a team-building experience, the structure will tend to keep on generating conflict and rivalry. Consequently, booster shots are necessary.

Developing an Integrative Role. Massive attention also must be given to developing a viable integrative role. Consider two possible approaches: some integrative role may be grafted to the basic functional structure in Figure 1, or integrative teams may become the basic units of departmentation, as in Figure 2. Both cases present problems. The second case is more attractive in concept, but for most organizations it would mean a major and perhaps difficult OD effort.

Consequently, integrative roles in organizations tend to be superimposed on a Figure 1 structure, as by establishing an interdepartmental coordinating committee or a project manager. Both are integrative overlays designed to counteract the fragmenting tendencies of the traditional structure of departments organized by functions or processes. To illustrate, the project manager develops a temporary integrative team to do some specific job, making requests for personnel as necessary from the functional departments. Team members then respond to two authoritative sources: to their more-or-less temporary project manager, and to the head of the functional department to which they will return when the project is complete. The resulting multiple lines of authority are sometimes called a "matrix overlay."

Integrative arrangements superimposed on a traditional structure can help reduce the conflict and rivalry characteristic of a Figure 1 structure, but they are tricky.[17] Thus, questions of multiple authority may vex personnel administration, or power may remain in the permanent functional departments, and this can make life difficult for integrative agents such as project managers or interdepartmental coordinating committees. In both cases, in addition, what is to be done with a project manager when his project is terminated? The experience in the aerospace industry does not suggest any easy ways out. Making conscious arrangements for an integrative role, then, implies serious problems.[18]

Developing Values Supporting Unity. Shared values that encourage organizational unity must be developed and broadly accepted. Otherwise, a significant shift of emphasis toward integration is unlikely. Prevailing organizational values—the "values of bureaucracy"—are hierarchy-serving in that they reinforce vertical superior-subordinate relations. But they do so only at the expense of inhibiting the development of horizontal and vertical socioemotional ties that can integrate individuals or groups performing different functions in different departments in a Figure 1 structure. Since today's organizations increasingly must be integrative, and since they increasingly must stress dynamic knowledge-gathering because they are truth-requiring, the values of bureaucracy will increasingly generate troublesome consequences.

The specific alternative to the values of bureaucracy is not yet clear. However, the following climate of beliefs suggests at least a first-generation response to the knowledge-gathering and truth-requiring demands of today's technology:[19]

- Full and free communication, regardless of rank or power
- Reliance on confronting processes in dealing with conflict, as opposed to coercion or compromise
- Basing influence on technical competence and knowledge, as opposed to personal whim or hierarchical status
- An atmosphere that easily admits emotional expression as well as task-oriented behavior
- Acceptance of conflict between the individual and the organization which is to be coped with openly

Getting acceptance of such values in principle, and working toward them in practice, should constitute a major near-future challenge.

Repression and Wriggle Room

Two approaches toward achieving wriggle room deserve special attention. One approach involves shaping organizations to fit people in the design of tasks and structure. Historically, people were fitted to the organization. Many observers have argued the merits of tailoring tasks to individuals,[20] as through job enlargement, and the following section will provide appropriate chapter-and-verse. So here note only that job enlargement is easier in a Figure 2 structure.

Relatedly, interaction processes can also usefully be tailored to individuals. Argyris has posited human needs that typically are frustrated in large organizations, especially in organizations patterned after Figure 1.[21] Building satisfying interaction processes into organizations is a gargantuan task, and only scarcely begun. Thus, some change agents attempt to use sensitivity training in family groups to try to improve relationships in an organization, which may raise major issues with traditional ways of organizing and managing. Others argue that building need-satisfying interaction into organizations is hopelessly utopian. Many variations exist between those anchor positions.

A second approach to achieving wriggle room involves the development of new forms of organizational representation. As an example, greater managerial concern for due process and sharing of influence seems necessary. The choice is a matter of real consequence. That is, influence-sharing or due process can be granted with top management support in sensitive dialogue with employees whose needs and capabilities are diversely evolving; or at a polar extreme, they can be wrested away by employees after heated battle with a boulwareian management.

No doubt much of the near-future resolution of issues involving due process and influence sharing will be in familiar terms: employee unionization, more-or-less grudging management assent, and more-or-less successful efforts at rapprochement. Increasingly, however, the resolution will involve the breaking of new and uncertain ground. At least at managerial levels in many organizations, for example, determined efforts are underway to develop new and enhanced representational vehicles, encompassing "tell all" dinners, management councils, and God knows what. Only the brave fool would try to guess the product of this maelstrom, or even whether we can avoid a kind of organizational totalitarianism born of ineptness or unwillingness in developing appropriate values and vehicles.[22]

Stability and Newness

Any shift in today's organizations toward newness implies at least two major challenges. *First,* the "change function" must be given greater priority, with such attendant challenges as to better equip people to tolerate ambiguity. We have only clues as to how to cope successfully with such an increased priority, both as to mechanics and organization. But the trends are there for everyone to see in the rapid evolution of project or task-force structures which are intentionally temporary, unlike the bureaucratic structure of Figure 1. For example, the project organization for the C-5A transport had a planned 5-year life, involved tens of thousands of employees, 6000 separate companies, and astronomical volumes of all manner of resources. "What we see here is nothing less than the creation of a disposable division," Toffler observes, "the organizational equivalent of paper dresses or throw-away tissues."[23]

In order to facilitate change, at the very least, an appropriate reward system becomes necessary. However, existing reward systems usually are keyed to how much one produces or how long one has been a producer. Neither bias facilitates change; both biases are at best irrelevant to change, and may be inimical to it. Likely reinforcers of change imply a host of problems. I have in mind one labor agreement that rewards employees for their willingness to be retrained continually, as opposed to rewarding them for their productivity or for seniority. Such arrangements imply very significant labor/management issues, with which we have precious little experience.

Organizationally, increased emphasis on change also poses real problems. The issues are sharply joined in the evolving role of the intervenor devoted to facilitating change and inducing appropriate interpersonal and intergroup climates for change. Where is the change agent to be located? Who is to be the change-agent?

Working answers to such questions have tended to be unsatisfactory. Relying on external change-agents has some real advantages, but this places the change agent outside the organization's authority and reward structure and may compromise his or her effectiveness. Relying on internal change agents ties them into the system, but this cuts both ways. If things got rough for them, staff members who became change agents might be motivated to become a kind of gestapo in the pursuit of their own interests.[24] Embody the change-agent role in a "staff" member or unit, and that implies all of the problems that have plagued line-staff relations. Relying on change agents in the "line" provides no surefire alternative. If the line manager becomes the change agent, you avoid many ticklish authority problems but you run the risk of placing reliance for change in an individual who may be overbusy with day-to-day problems. Moreover, no guarantee exists that line officials will have the appropriate skills or training, or even the interest.

In summary, managing the change-agent role implies one grand job conceived in its broad sense as an amalgam of line and staff responsibilities.

Second, a commitment to newness versus stability implies a growing need to develop and disband both large and small work units quickly. Moreover, the need to revitalize today's organizations to prepare them for adapting to tomorrow's markets or programs also encourages seeing them as temporary social systems.

Managing temporary social systems presents a formidable task in at least two major ways. Such management requires that people develop a kind of instant but still intense commitment. This is difficult, but seemingly unavoidable. Complex systems often permit no alternative to the technical and social compatibility of team members. In addition, organization members will need to learn how to experience the loss of one temporary social system in ways that do not inhibit their commitment to future systems.

We are gaining some experience with effective management of new social systems, as via team development, or team-building. Chapter 6, especially, speaks to this point.

Less is known about disbanding a temporary social system in ways that do not inhibit the commitment of its members to future systems. Work with sensitivity training suggests that such separation anxiety can be effectively managed. However, socioemotional debriefing is still uncommon. Chapter 5 provides a summary of available research and experience. Here note only one prominent feature in the aerospace industry–socioemotional turmoil associated with developing, and more particularly with terminating, project teams. Members of teams gear themselves up to unflinching commitment, work long and hard. When the project is concluded, emotional depression often sets in, marital difficulties seem unusually common and severe, and so on. Both research and popular news magazines have painted an alarming picture of this new problem, which we can expect to become increasingly common.[25]

Managing temporary social systems also implies two major technical issues. One issue involves structural arrangements that encourage quick group identification and that also permit reinforcement by reward systems keyed to meaningful measures of performance. These dual goals are within reach. That is, both identification and the measurement of performance will be facilitated as organizations move toward Figure 2 structures. The point is of crucial significance.

Figure 2 structures also permit convenient changes in incentive systems and philosophy. In one traditional structure, to illustrate the point by contrast, a very complex system of different wage rates for specific jobs required an elaborate supervisory and clerical apparatus for wage administration. Under a Figure 2 structure, a simpler system was possible. Management negotiated a base price tied to output with a producing team that controlled the entire flow of work, and the unit handled the internal distribution of its income.[26] That is, group incentives in a Figure 2 structure can help integrate a flow of work and reinforce the allegiances encouraged by that structure. Supervision is consequently simplified. Compensation systems in traditional structures, in contrast, tend to fragment flows of work and to complicate supervision.

A second major technical issue in managing temporary social systems concerns position classification. Figure 2 structures, and the temporary teams within them, encourage classification plans that place rank in the individual rather than in the job. On this source, the federal public service can expect special problems in managing temporary social systems. Although recent policies permit some recognition of the impact of the individual on the job, the federal approach to classification emphasizes rank in position.

Function and Flow of Work

Basic structural change that shifts emphasis from particularistic to integrative departmentation, from function to the flow of work, will make it easier to respond effectively to contemporary challenges. But the change will be difficult, requiring the development of a solid core of OD specialists who can maintain real momentum in long-run programs of change. Ideally, perhaps, every manager should be his or her own OD specialist. Practically, the OD function often will become a personnel speciality.

Structural arrangements for a suitable redefinition of line-staff relations also seem clear, in general. A Figure 2 structure, for example, could provide a common organizational home for both a line manager and a staff personnel member. Their shared responsibility for the success of a total managerial unit would encourage a team effort, rather than line versus staff tension. The approach gets much support from theoretical analysis[27] as well as from empirical research.[28] In contrast, Figure 1 structures are organized around separate functions or processes. This encourages fragmentation of line from staff and differentiation between line and staff.

Realistically, OD specialists can anticipate a formidable and multidimensional task.[29] Even assuming the development of a core of OD specialists, three specific reorientations in outlook seem necessary. They will only be sketched. *First,* an emphasis on flow of work as opposed to functions will require a bottom-up approach to organizing work and to locating services. Given a top-down approach, services tend to drift upward in the typical hierarchy. For example, staff probably would report to M_{ABC} in Figure 1, even though many of their inputs might be made at the level of S_A or below.

A bottom-up approach would generate a different pattern. The point may be illustrated briefly. Typically, an overhead staff unit would both design and monitor patterns of work motions. In one large electronics firm, however, "time and methods" have been handled differently. Employees are themselves instructed in the basics of motion analysis by a very small overhead staff. These employees then design and monitor their own work-motion patterns.

Such bottom-up approaches as the example above imply multiple problems. Thus, they may raise troublesome status questions for both M_{ABC} and the individuals who report to him. Moreover, suitable work environments for such approaches must have one or both of two characteristics: employee efforts must be measurable, easily and validly; or the employees must be motivated to apply the principles of motion analysis. These are major problems, but less troublesome than the enforcement and evasion likely under a top-down approach to motion analysis. For example, Figure 2 structures can help significantly to reduce problems of both measuring and motivating performance.[30]

Second, shifting emphasis to the flow of work requires a new line-staff concept. Analytic work strongly implies this reorientation, and accumulating research and practice confirms the thrust of such theorizing—at least in general terms, and often in specific details.[31] Consider only one aspect of the theoretical work—that focusing on the multiple mischief of conceiving staff as a glorified prosthetic device, as a kind of enlargement of the senses of M_{ABC} in Figure 1. Such a notion does encourage centralized identification, which often will appeal to top management. Moreover, a centralized location always will be necessary for some staff, at least some of the time. Often too much is made of a good thing, however, with obvious costs in increased managerial complexity, heightened line-staff conflict, long communication chains, and a general rigidifying of relations at work. Hence evolving research and experience suggests the strong need to move away from the traditional line-staff notion to cope with today's complex and fast-paced organizations. The experience of General Foods Corporation with its "Total Quality System" is illustrative. TQS is defined as ". . . a documented system which identifies authority and responsibility for *all* activities related to manufacturing products, within specifications," with feedback loops throughout the Marketing → Manufacturing → Delivery cycle. TQS involves the traditional line units, and melds with them the "old" Quality Control function which focuses on "doing things right" and the "new" Quality Assurance which emphasizes "doing the right things." The goals–to improve communication with technical people, to facilitate change, to involve people from many levels in problem-solving and decision-making, and to satisfy government requirements–cannot be met within traditional line/staff constraints, at least not within acceptable time-frames. What is needed? In the case of Quality Assurance, for example, major movement away from the model of Figure 1 structures was necessary: ". . . from a single function activity to a complex network of activities at all organization levels which require new understanding and new relationships" so that structure can follow the flow of work, rather than the other way around.

Third, greater emphasis on the flow of work will require basic value reorientations in wide segments of the population. This resocialization of adults will require both defusing and infusing of values, as it were. As some intriguing research demonstrates, at least middle-class children seem to be acquainted with the essentials of a Figure 1 structure as early in life as the third or fourth grade.[32] This suggests the extent of the value defusing that will be required, and it implies a major training burden that extends far beyond the work place into the value-generating processes of the socialization of children.

There seems a solid base on which to infuse values more appropriate for Figure 2 structures, however. Thus, many observers explain the fascination with McGregor's Theory X, Theory Y formulation in terms of a broad managerial desire to increase the congruence between their personal values and presently legitimate organization values. The former values tend toward Theory Y; the latter are Theory X-ish, decidedly. In addition, some evidence shows that managers in larger and technologically sophisticated firms tend toward more frequent espousal of Theory Y attitudes.[33]

Alternative Ways to Meet Structural Challenges

The contrasts above may be overly abstract, and moot about the range of possible structural applications that approach OD values and which, in general, are more consistent with a Figure 2 structure than that sketched in Figure 1.[34] The goal here is modest, for an adequate treatment of structural design would require a lengthy treatise.[35] But the sketches below do provide a useful sense of the broad range of structural alternatives to the traditional model. Five structural alternatives get brief attention.

Job Enrichment

Thinking of what follows as a continuum of increasingly comprehensive structural approaches should be helpful and, consistent with that notion, job enrichment can be conceived as anchoring the skinny end of the continuum. The second section below will provide substantial detail on this structural intervention, so we can be content here with three limited but significant points. *First,* this attempt to build Figure 2 properties into work at the operating level has received fulsome attention—in scholarly and workaday circles,[36] in this country as well as abroad.[37]

Second, the point does not always get appropriate emphasis, but job enrichment clearly provides a vehicle for approaching basic OD values at work. No Pollyanna vision is intended or appropriate but, clearly, job enrichment can relate to the central normative OD challenge of shifting the balance in organizations from repression toward freedom. Without any doubt, the intervention has been applied by those with only narrower economic or tactical considerations in mind, just as a clever knife-sharpening technique might be used to save lives medically, or to take them criminally, or both.[38] Evidence assembled in the second section below implies that failure to be sensitive to the value implications of job enlargement helps account for failures in applications, as when managements do not understand the difference between a job with more components, as distinguished from a job whose components create greater employee control over work.

Third, on definite balance, job enlargement seems to be one of those interventions where a mutuality between individual needs and organization demands can exist. Consider Alber's conclusion that job enlargement can generate "very important economic returns," while "employees usually benefit also." He notes:[39] "In short, we have a win-win outcome in which both parties stand to gain a great deal from the changes in the way work is performed." But Alber carefully also adds:

> These benefits, while real, are not free. A sizeable sum of money may have to be spent in the form of increased wages, additional learning, training, and project implementation before the benefits can be realized. And even then it is not uncommon for an organization to suffer from a deterioration in such areas as quality, production output, absenteeism, or turnover.

Table 1 summarizes the range of organizational and individual pay-offs to which Alber refers; quite an impressive catalog, that, even though the literature contains many exceptions and some theoretical and practical puzzles.[40]

Unit Integrators

Providing for work-unit "integrators" seems a step up the ladder of comprehensiveness in moving toward the properties of a Figure 2 structure, compared to job enlargement. Briefly, Figure 1 structures tend to fragment subunits and create conflict both within these subunits and between them. Often, the supervisor gets pulled into these divisive games, since she will tend to represent her subunit's specialty.

Table 1 Summary of Benefits of Job Enrichment

Benefits	N[a]	Percentage Improvement
Quality		
Rejected items not meeting quality standards	34	20
Customer complaints	25	23
Resource utilization		
Machine breakdowns (average)	9	11
Change in labor force idle time (approximate)	29	8
Production output	50	21
Operating benefits		
Accident rate per 100 workers or man hours lost due to accidents	15	6
Late deliveries	19	29
Grievances filed per unit of time	24	16
Change in job satisfaction determined by formal studies, surveys	39	32
Absenteeism	38	32
Turnover	47	18

[a]Represents the number of companies out of a total sample of fifty-eight where benefit was applicable. Only firms that had gains are included in the table.
Source: From Antone F. Alber, "Job Enrichment Programs Seen Improving Employee Performance, But Benefits Not Without Cost," *World of Work Report,* Vol. 3 (January 1978), p. 9.

Without any basic structural change, one government agency used nonsupervisory professionals specifically responsible for integration or conflict management between subunits. Even that modest innovation seems responsive to a real need. Stumpf reports on four small work units in which one person in each unit performed an integrative role for that unit. He concludes: "Each unit's performance before and after introduction of the integrator was analyzed. The productivity of the integrated units improved during the 2-year observation period and was significantly higher than that of comparison groups."[41]

Autonomous Groups and Sociotechnical Approaches

The discovery of "autonomous groups" in Great Britain after World War II has an important place in organizational history. These were surviving forms of organization from less mechanized eras, but which had some distinct economic advantages in more complex technologies,[42] and the analysis of their dynamics spotlighted what Trist calls a "second design principle—the redundancy of functions" which is alternative to organizing around separate specialties as in Figure 1 structures. Conceptually, in a basic sense, the discovery emphasized how social or human factors not only interact with technological factors, but also how they can be primary. The prevailing tradition had seen the arrows of effect going in the other direction, in substantial or total measure. The initial insight evolved into the notion of a "socio-technical system," which has been elaborated in great detail[43] but basically rests on two fundamental concepts:[44]

- The joint operation at work of a social system and a technological system, with desired outcomes requiring the melding of both systems
- The continuous interaction of the sociotechnical system with an external environment which influences, and is influenced by, that system

Trist correctly notes that autonomous teams are generally found at low levels of organization—where "they remain in themselves no more than component organizational processes, and thus represent micro changes"[45]—but they have had a recent highly publicized renaissance. General Food's Topeka dog-food plant constitutes a typical example. Its basic organization clearly reflects properties of the Figure 2 structure. Walton notes:[46]

> The new plant had the following features: self-managing teams assumed responsibility for large segments of the production process. The teams were composed of from 7 to 14 members, large enough to embrace a set of interrelated tasks and small enough to permit face-to-face meetings for decision making and coordination. Activities typically performed by separate units—maintenance, quality control, custodianship, industrial engineering, and personnel—were built into the operating team's responsibilities. For example, team members screened job applicants for replacements on their own team.

Numerous studies support the general superiority of the results of this structural innovation,[47] but these effects seem to vary as do three conditions of work:[48]

- The degree of group control over the task boundary, as in being able to influence the broader environment
- The degree of group control over its internal activities
- The degree to which the task constitutes an autonomous whole

More specifically, astute observers recommend that "real autonomy" implies at least four criteria. The work group should decide the work methods to be used, who shall be members, who will exercise internal leadership and direction, if anyone, and how tasks will be allocated.[49]

Such criteria of autonomy might not hold in specific cases and, even if they do, various external forces might erode or even overwhelm them. At Topeka, for example, some disenchantment set in after several years, triggered by a slowly dawning but major reaction from the parent firm: pioneering managers found their careers hurt rather than helped, to put it directly, apparently in substantial measure because of the dissatisfaction about the restructuring expressed by supervisors and middle managers whose traditional functions were substantially reduced or eliminated by the Topeka changes.[50] If the "broader environment" does not change in this crucial regard, obviously, one can reasonably predict disenchantment will spread at Topeka.

Multihierarchical Modes

Still more comprehensive responses to the structural challenges above get expressed in multihierarchical modes such as the various forms of "matrix." Basically, the variants above all still retain the sense of *a* hierarchy, even as they modify it or organize it in different ways. In the matrix, specific managers may have two or more formal bosses, to whom they are expected to respond. Multihierarchies not only exist, but intentionally so. The details are far too complex for this treatment but, in general, matrix structures may be appropriate when:[51]

- Two or more critical sectors exist in an organization, be they functions, products, territories, or whatever.
- Uncertain, complex, and interdependent tasks are involved.
- Economies of scale are possible, as contrasted with necessary redundancy of resources or slow response to requests for service.

Nonhierarchical Modes

Various nonhierarchical modes constitute the most radical forms of restructuring, in networks, bargaining or exchange systems, and so on. Note here only that a substantial tradition of thought sees an end to many social problems in an "end to hierarchy."[52] This second part of the volume gives some attention to nonhierarchical models, but not in great depth. For example, the reader is directed to the reliance on ad hoc groups for feedback in Chapter 3, the use of temporary learning environments sketched in several chapters, and the development of "collateral organizations" dealt with in Chapter 5.

Nonhierarchical Assumptions in the Women's Information Center. * A brief case study illustrates one way in which nonhierarchical modes can develop. Attention here focuses on the assumptions underlying a third-sector organization, the

*This section was written expressly for this volume by Kathleen Porter, while a graduate student at Syracuse University.

Women's Information Center. Info, or the Center, is an "alternative" organization, and the idea of collectivity permeates its structures and processes. The salient characteristics of the Center collectivity are: leadership is shared; women take turns with tasks; and there is equal ownership of the outcomes of any project.

Several major assumptions underlay the workings of the Center, and they relate to Info's dominant nonhierarchical thrusts. These major assumptions, in effect, serve to inhibit any incipient hierarchical tendencies, some of which exist in Info, as later discussion will show.

The personal is the political. This suggests that what happens to us as individuals, what we do, and how we feel determine the quality of our shared public activities. Sharing our personal selves and building our sense of personal power will result in positive structures and interactions.

Knowledge is power. If we know all that we need to know, we can make the best choices. To keep information away from us diminishes our freedom of action and, as a result, our personal power. Hence, at all meetings the agenda is written on a large sheet of newsprint, with estimated time of completion next to each item. At the beginning of each meeting, the agenda gets reviewed and the group can opt to change it.

Consensus is the only appropriate decision-making mode. At Info, consensus is the only mode allowed. Staff members are particularly adamant about the inferiority of democratic decision-making, as well as strictly hierarchical modes. They believe that every woman must feel comfortable with the decision in order that the decision be adequately implemented. Voting implies that the minority will feel disenfranchised, unrepresented, and, therefore, resentful. This probable disaffection implies that the task will not be carried out well, and conflict will occur during implementation. The Center staff encourages conflict during the decision-making process and will allow meetings to continue until the conflict is resolved.

Feelings are real and valid and must be acted on. Info exudes a strong anti-rationalist strain, and a concomitant faith in emotion and in intuition. This is in reaction to the dominant mode in other organizations which emphasize what the individual knows or thinks, often along with the psychological contract that the individual must ignore what he or she is feeling. As a result, action in Info typically rests on intuitions concerning a particular project or person. The dominant language forms at Info reflect that mode: "I am feeling," "I sense," and "I am responding to." This contrasts with "I think," "I believe," and "I know." The belief in the validity of feelings gets its basic expression in the encouragement of confrontation as well as in the open expression of affection.

We can control our own lives. A fierce sense of independence is the natural outgrowth of the rejection of a middle-class life style. Info members see themselves as forging a new social structure in the midst of the old one, and hence feel obliged not to depend on existing social institutions. Too many possessions imply dependence, as does owning insurance of any kind, sending children to city schools, and getting medical check-ups. Another major expression of independence involves learning skills not normally associated with women. The Feminist School, a branch of Info, offers courses in auto mechanics, home repair, self-defense, assertiveness training, and the like.

To demonstrate the way in which nonhierarchical thrusts work, consider a typical Info staff meeting. These meetings take place every Thursday morning at 9:30. The facilitator and cofacilitator, chosen at the previous meeting, arrive around 9:00 to put up the agenda, start the coffee, and lay out the doughnuts. The agenda is formed from a list of items which has been developed over the week, each item, project, concern, or request having been contributed by a woman who places her name next to it. The two facilitators prioritize the list, with estimated times. The first two items always are: "Personal Sharing" and "Agenda Review." Personal sharing begins every meeting. Each woman tells how she is feeling that morning, and often explains why. The theory is that the group will be in a better position to deal with any given individual if her state of mind, her energy level, and her emotional state are known. The group offers support to each individual, as seems appropriate. Typical sharing will reveal: "I feel energized today: I'm ready to go"; "I have a terrible hangover"; or "I had a fight with my lover and I'm feeling drained and ready to cry."

Two other agenda features also deserve note. In the middle of the agenda, the facilitators place an "energizer," "group stretch," or "song." These refer to activities, games, or exercises to work off tensions and refocus energies. There is also a coffee break. In addition, each agenda concludes with an "Evaluation," presided over by the cofacilitator. She writes three columns on a large sheet of newsprint. The columns are headed, "plus," "minus," and "change." She is not allowed to respond to what others say, but she can add her own items. Members of the group then call out to her things they liked about the meeting, things they disliked, and things they would like to see changed. The cofacilitator writes them down without evaluating them. Typical remarks might include: "I loved the way we all listened to each other"; "I'm glad Mary shared her feelings about that with us"; "The doughnuts were good"; or "We spent too much time talking about pledges."

In terms of the vocabulary introduced in Chapter 1 of Part 1, Info seeks a regenerative system which engenders great trust in its members. Since the welfare of each individual is of prime importance to the group, openness is considered essential to the functioning of the group. Owning is also an important characteristic of the process since each woman takes responsibility for leadership, for generating agenda items, and for decision-making. Obviously, the risk associated with openness is quite low in this organization.

In this observer's view, Info gives almost unique attention to process, and yet task performance does not suffer. In fact, things get done quite easily because the group is so harmonious. This is particularly striking because Info attracts many troubled women. These troubled women can and do become burdensome to the group now and then: they might insist on bringing the group back to their problems again and again, or they might become aggressive and hostile. However, because confrontation is part of the process, someone always tells the woman the effect she is having on the speaker, for example, "I'm feeling frustrated, Anne, because we need to talk about fund raising. I'll be glad to talk to you later in private." In nine cases out of ten, the new woman, who has come to Info for help with personal problems, will learn appropriate modes of behavior in the group setting. Occasionally, a woman will leave the Center because she cannot or will not change her behavior and has not received support for it.

The Info picture above must be qualified in two major regards. First, Info has two paid staff members. They believe in consensus, but they also have very strong notions of what activities the Center ought to engage in. They are both articulate and persuasive women. I often strongly suspect that the consensus arrived at reflects the group's belief that the staffers really *do* know what is best for Info and that they, less experienced and newer, should bow to greater wisdom.

Second, Info has always been besieged by financial difficulties. The two "paid staff" frequently do not get paid. The staff, over a period of time, has made a decision not to write grant proposals in the belief that Info would then become obliged to fulfill demands made on them by an immoral government agency or an immoral corporation. The Rape Crisis Center, then housed in the same building as Info, received a large federal grant 2 years ago. Info insisted that Rape Crisis share the money with them in the spirit of collectivity. They argued that Rape Crisis had no obligation to fulfill its government contract because the government is immoral. When Rape Crisis refused, the resentment and bitterness reached an intolerable level. Rape Crisis women were characterized as middle-class and as having bought into the male-dominated power structure. Rape Crisis was pressured out of the building.

The same ambivalence, lack of clarity, and conflicting feelings about money were also manifested in the departure of two other previous "paid staff" members. They left at separate times, but the circumstances were strikingly similar. Neither had been paid for some time. Both lived in nuclear family situations, and as a consequence needed money more immediately than if they had lived in a collective. Both asked, at staff meetings, that their back pay be given them when Info could get the money. The group agreed that special efforts would be made to raise the money to pay the back salaries. After the women left, the issue was raised again at separate staff meetings for each woman, and a new decision was reached not to pay the back salaries. One of the women has become so embittered that she refuses to see women she was once close to, or even to speak of Info without contempt.

My personal interpretation of this kind of behavior is that it reflects a fear of the larger society, a sense that what has been so carefully built can be destroyed by contamination from the values and standards of a corrupt system. It also, I think, suggests a submerged desire for the goodies this society can give. After all, these women were socialized by the striving middle class and may not be completely able to dissociate money and power; hence, perhaps, the strong resentment felt toward Rape Crisis.

I believe it will become increasingly important for the staff at Info to clarify their feelings about money. If they are to cope effectively with their own insolvency and the financial needs of potential staff members, they must come to closure on this issue. Even more importantly, the issue of money has already caused a divisiveness and bitterness alien to Info's aims and values. "Women," they seem to be saying, "ought to feel good about themselves and in control of their lives—unless their sense of self is expressed through wanting or receiving money. In that case, they have betrayed us and are no longer to experience the growth and support we can offer."

As serious as this issue can potentially become, I believe that the Women's Information Center is a unique organization, even among feminist organizations. It insists upon putting into practice beliefs about human potential that many voice but few have the courage to practice. It will be an interesting organization to watch.

Introducing Three Structural Variants

Positions illustrated above can be still better defined by three illustrations of how structural challenges can be met. In order, the three succeeding sections deal with:

- Concerns appropriate toward the top of large organizations, with specific focus on the pathology common there and on how "self-forcing, self-enforcing" (SF,SE) approaches can moderate that pathology
- Concerns appropriate toward the lower organizational reaches, with specific focus on job enrichment strategies and on guidelines for their successful implementation based on the OD tradition
- Concerns appropriate at the lower-middle levels of organization, with specific attention to reorganization of food stores and a public agency to approach properties of Figure 2 structures

Directly, these three illustrations reflect in detail the several advantages of moving from the Figure 1 structure toward the Figure 2, and they also sketch some of the lessons implicit in experience with efforts to embody in practice the various theoretical advantages inherent in Figure 2 structures.

Usual Organizational Ways to Pursue Excellence at Top Levels
Some Dire Probabilities and OD
Defenses Against Them

The pursuit of excellence constitutes the avowed goal of most models for organizing work, but intent does not necessarily translate into action. That puts it mildly. Directly, this discussion shows how the traditional model for organizing work is likely to have many unanticipated and unfavorable consequences. And this section also sketches some OD defenses against those consequences, defenses short of basic structural reorganization.

Numerous approaches could be taken to elaborate the brief probabilistic profile above of the ways Figure 1 structures at top levels encourage getting in trouble and, in effect, to detail how Figure 2 structures provide some safeguards against worse coming to worst. The approach here is a distillation of masses of descriptive literature,[53] the narrower research literature,[54] as well as my own personal experience in Anglo-American cultures and in socialist countries.[55] And the focus is on executive and senior levels of management.

Let the essential point be put boldly. Figure 1 structures seem to have a range of effects that are substantially independent of both individuals and the broad socioeconomic and political contexts in which individuals operate. The present approach details a number of the more troublesome of these central tendencies of the traditional structure, and then it details a number of the things that OD efforts seek to do, short of a fundamental restructuring of work on the pattern of Figure 2. Two purposes motivate this effort, then: to sketch some of the darker probabilities inherent in the common approach to organizing work, and also to suggest how to ameliorate these all-but-universal consequences of the traditional model for organizing work at high levels.

How Things Can Go Sour

No list of awkward central tendencies inherent in the traditional model, even a *very* long list, would be exhaustive. So, the seven emphases below are only bare illustrations of a far longer litany. This introduction to what follows does not constitute an apology, however, for those illustrations are both characteristic and significant. The several emphases will vary in impact from organization to organization, to be sure, as well as from time to time and between different situations even in the same organization. In the same breath, however, one can legitimately maintain that these emphases represent many significant ways that things can go sour under the traditional structure.

One-to-One Bias

Perhaps the quintessential tendency of the traditional structure encourages the development of sets of one-to-one relationships between the chief executive and his or her immediate subordinates–in the terminology of Figure 1, for example, between $M_{A\,BC}$ and S_A, $M_{A\,BC}$ and S_B, and so on. Basically, this bias seems intentional, the apparent consequence being to facilitate $M_{A\,BC}$'s close control over his subordinates or, perhaps better still, to permit him to reinforce his dominance by segmenting the downward flow of communication and thereby lowering the likelihood of collusive action by them against him. This bias also contributes to the real insularity and isolation of the chief executive, which may be expressed in terms such as:

- "I carry all the responsibility, and the burdens are onerous and the life lonely."
- "Nobody around here but me takes the interests of the entire organization into account. They see mostly their own part of the total operation, and their particularism only makes my job all that much harder."

Such complaints have the ring of reality to them, but they are not just "human nature" but constitute (in large part, at least) an artefact of the traditional approach to organizing work.

Only Squealers Evaluate Peers, Except in Extremis

In part, in spite of the one-to-one bias, and perhaps in even more basic senses *due* to it, individual subordinates will be cautious about sharing with $M_{A\,BC}$ their evaluations of the performance of their peers, especially when those reactions are negative.

The common consequence has complex motivations, often exacerbated by the fact that measuring performance and assigning responsibility can be very difficult at all levels in the traditional structure. Many other considerations encourage peers to withhold judgments about one another from their common superior. Perhaps the basic issue is one of fairness, or the perception of fairness even when conditions encourage harsh evaluations. Then again, self-protection may be critical as in the belief (or hope) that, "If I don't rat, maybe they won't either." Further, $M_{A\,BC}$ understands that her subordinates may be variously competitive, so she may be very leery of evaluative feedback from them which could merely be vicious maneuvering for competitive position by the more unscrupulous of her subordinates. In short, encouragement by $M_{A\,BC}$ to "take off the kid gloves" might have wide-ranging and troublesome effects. That is a disciplining fact. And ultimately, perhaps, $M_{A\,BC}$'s concern may be that if one subordinate undercuts one of her peers, for good reason or ill, such a subordinate might not hesitate at some point in doing M_{ABC}'s career the same kind of service.

When things get bad enough, of course, such restraints against evaluating peers can diminish or disappear. But my experience is that things have to get very bad indeed before the "stop" signal changes to "go." Except in extreme cases, then, only squealers negatively evaluate peers. Perhaps the major consequence is that even desperately needed personnel actions occur very slowly, and often long after the point at which action was appropriate.

"Chest Your Mitt"

Peer evaluation also will be untimely and unlikely to the degree that subordinates follow the advice of the serious card player: "Keep those pasteboards close to your vest and the other players will know less about your likely moves." Peer evaluation thus might be difficult because of sheer lack of relevant information.

Such behavior by subordinates typically has mixed consequences. Peers may gain some security in that they lack relevant information to undercut each other, but the basic approach can be seriously damaging to performance. Consider the mixed consequences if subordinates "chest their mitt" with respect to M_{ABC}, as well as with respect to each other. There the stakes differ, clearly, and so also might the tactics and the strategy. Many organizational superiors do not like "being surprised," for example, so what to reveal and when may be the organizational difference between the quick and the dead.

Focus on Jurisdictions and Roles

No doubt the most common approach to not being found wanting is expressed in an insistent emphasis on jurisdictions and roles, but an emphasis often coupled with a willingness to accept unclarity or even conflict about who does what, when, where, and how. This may seem a paradoxical combination, but it constitutes the ideal defense. For every task in this view should have a home, which seems comforting, while unclarity and conflict may simply signal an activity of such quality that no one will accept it, and this provides multiple safeguards. The manager can argue simultaneously that someone should do the thing, but that it is not his thing.

Where all roles are tightly defined—which conditions may be approached in some venerable and stable-state organizations—this room for maneuvering disappears, of course. But the maneuvering area often is kept large by powerful forces: new processes, new products, and generally by change. Moreover, some roles are variously "losers," in that they can never be done without inducing conflict, acrimony, and so on. No one wants them, and that fact also contributes to a substantial area of unclarity or conflict about jurisdictions and roles. What is true in Poland seems true universally. "Success usually has a thousand parents," goes an old saying. "But failure is always an orphan."

We Versus Him, but Only on Particulars

If an M_{ABC} is insistent and consistent enough, subordinates may get into gentle we or him games. For example, they may complain about the lack of delegation or the associated slowness of getting information shoved up the hierarchy, of getting some decision made, and then having that decision trickle down throughout the hierarchy. At a sophisticated level, subordinates might complain about the lack of trust that M_{ABC} has in them, with guilt-inducing undertones that M_{ABC} has forgotten how things were when he was an underling. Or—more powerful still, although a double-edged sword—subordinates might note (carefully) that M_{ABC} is simply not a very trusting person, which breeds distrust throughout the organization and may lead to collective pathologies which M_{ABC} should wisely prefer to avoid.

Such we or him alliances probably will be quite specific as well as gentle, except in very deep extremes. Take gentleness first. Basically, such complaints remain safe because they imply a subordinate's desire to do an effective job, despite differences about how that might be done is a specific case. No iconoclasm there. Even the maladroit subordinate has easy ways of getting out from under a suddenly irate superior, as in variations on the theme of: "Please don't punish me for really wanting to do a first-class job." Moreover, full-fledged and aggressive rejections of a formal leader seem to be quite rare, as the classic experiments with children's groups demonstrate.[56] Indeed, organization members often support the hierarchy, even when its actions are clearly pathologic. Why authorities are usually obeyed is a very heavy issue, with deep roots in our socialization.[57] Moreover, the practical reality is that organizations have a way of supporting the hierarchy, right or wrong, and there seems apparent safety in the explanation that "I was just following orders."[58] This constitutes the essential tragedy of Captain Queeg of *The Caine Mutiny,* whom the U.S. Navy supported as a hierarchical figure even as it helped destroy him as a person. Basically, except for the prison sentence against Lieutenant Calley, that also seems the basic lesson for careful observers of the My Lai (and perhaps other) massacres in Viet Nam.

Of End-Runs and By-Passes

The common cumulative consequence of such tendencies as the five above has two faces, from a critical perspective: information gets shared less and less quickly, while its validity becomes more and more suspect; and M_{ABC} needs timely and valid information, more and more and more. This dualism induces behavior that exacerbates the very behaviors that underlay the dualism:

- M_{ABC} often will seek to develop unofficial sources of information, as by "going over the heads" of his immediate subordinates.
- M_{ABC} may delegate less.

- M_{ABC} may take longer to make decisions, given her basic questions about the quality of the intelligence available to her.
- Subordinates reasonably will read lower trust into these actions by M_{ABC}.
- Subordinates may grow more fearful, look assiduously for "booby traps," and hence organizational dynamics may slow down, or issues may "orbit" for long periods.

Signs of Neurosis → Psychosis

The sum of it is that, at some point that cannot now be specified, things get bad enough that we can meaningfully speak of an organization moving into a neurotic phase, and perhaps then into a full-blown psychosis.[59] Somewhere along this critical line of development, for example, an organization moves: from endemic and pervasive rumors which most everyone fears but which most question; to a belief by many that even extravagant rumors probably are true although means of testing them are less and less available; and finally to that condition where even those who fabricated and propagated palpably impossible rumors soon *know* them to be true!

Before the critical point of moving into the equivalent of an organizational neurosis, wherever it is, we may meaningfully speak of more or less healthy states of an organization. That is, every organization has some symptoms like those sketched above. Most pass with the organizational equivalent of a bit of a sour stomach. If things worsen, we may speak colorfully of various degrees of organizational constipation, which can be uncomfortable but not dangerous if matters are dealt with in good enough time.

Ways of Swimming Against the Tide

Given that fundamental reorganization is often either inconvenient or inappropriate, what can be done in the face of such dismal tendencies? Or is it simply better to give up the sense and the search for excellence in performance? Given my reading and experience, many organizations—like NASA and the Metropolitan Atlanta Rapid Transit Authority, to choose two public agencies with celestial and earthly missions, respectively—are evolving programs of controls supplementary to the ones normally encountered in organizations.[60] Basically, these new controls concentrate on the quality of relationships between people, relationships into which are intentionally infused growing senses of interdependence and of collaboration. Referring to these new controls as "supplementary" in no sense implies "secondary," and even less is the reference to "ancillary." These controls are as vital as more formal managerial controls and, depending upon one's taste in such matters, perhaps more so. So pervasive were these new controls in NASA, for example, that two skilled observers refer to that agency's management system as "self-forcing, self-enforcing."[61]

What constitutes a "self-forcing, self-enforcing" (SF,SE) system? Each case remains *sui generis* in central particulars. But much can be suggested about such systems by describing a few of the things which they intentionally increase, as well as by describing a few of the elements they seek to decrease.

Things Increased by SF,SE Systems

Six reinforcing features suggest the fuller range of forces which SF,SE systems deliberately try to increase. *First* and paramountly, such systems aggressively use multiple ways of generating valid and mutual knowledge of the several worlds of the collaborators. The regimen may call for various OD designs such as team-building, confrontation designs, or whatever. In addition, formal work assignments often are made with gains in such mutual knowledge in mind. Finally, formal and informal contacts of the broadest range are utilized. Enthusiasm can even get out of hand, even given its lofty intentions. One ambitious mission chief, for example, required that his immediate team play poker, all night, once a week, in the early stages of getting down to business. One can learn a lot about his colleagues under such circumstances, and perhaps also about their wives! Transfers of any learning in this case to the work site, or the relevance of that learning to work, will not detain us here.

Second, great efforts are devoted to cultivating a growing sense of an organization that is "problem solving," as contrasted with "hierarchy serving" or "rôle bound." NASA's Wehrner von Braun used the term "automatic responsibility" to capture the sense of the intent. That is, if one saw that some new "it" needed doing, the point was how much he or she got done before a review session with his immediate superior. The key issue was most definitely not how assiduously he worked at establishing into whose role or jurisdiction that "it" might most reasonably fall.

Patently, this desired orientation constitutes no easy piece, for it risks jurisdictional conflicts, and executives must stand firm about accepting some potential conflict or redundacy to get a good start on problem-solving.

Third, and relatedly, SF,SE systems tend to include a sense of "creative redundancy"–that is, such systems imply alternative centers of responsibility, resources, and the like. Thus, NASA often let several developmental contracts on a project, with multiple goals. The choice between contractor options could reinforce NASA's control; the arrangement might generate novel options; contractors might feel some competitive pressures to reduce costs or to exercise initiative; more contractors might develop experience and expertise; and so on.

Redundancy can get out of hand, of course, becoming only an excuse for indecision, profligate use of resources, and so on. So, willingness to use redundancy openly and consciously requires "tough management" of risky but yet potentially rewarding situations.

Fourth, ways to make problems visible to multiple publics get priority attention in SF,SE systems. Numerous and diverse opportunities are created to share plans and progress, with aggressive feedback invited and often required.

Participants may contract "meeting-itis," but the dead-serious goals concern generating an "early warning" system which can be read by sensitive observers, as well as inducing feedback from all and sundry. The possible pathology is an organizational analogue of a crucifixion. The quality and depth and variety of personal relationships are central here in fine-tuning this multichannel feedback, in order to keep it constructive and challenging. This does not preclude tough criticism, which perhaps gets vicious in cases. In these cases, "constructive" may mean only that participants are sure that the target of heavy criticism had plenty of earlier and gentler indications and that, on the bottom line, participants have the summary feeling that the target "got what he or she deserved and needed, and not any too soon, either."

Fifth, SF,SE systems all seem to develop variations of *the* one mortal sin, or unforgivable error. Typically, *the* unforgivable involves hiding an error, which may prove costly and always inhibits learning from the error, perhaps by self and especially by others.

Executives must exert delicate control here, obviously. Errors can be opportunities for learning, on the one hand, but each individual has some kind of a quota of providing opportunities for such learning. On the other hand, much patience here is a good quality, especially early in a work history, for executives do not want to encourage hiding errors as a consequence of too precipitous action against someone who seemed to provide too many unexpected opportunities for learning.

Sixth, executives must work hard to develop norms and rewards that promote interdependence, as well as provide major penalties for failure or inability to collaborate. The worst case is that in which an executive preaches collaboration, yet directs juicy rewards (as by grants of delegation, salary, or whatever) to that individual who makes progress by single-mindedly arranging his or her affairs to complicate the work of others. Such a person gets a job done, goes a common organizational metaphor, but only by leaving the field of battle crowded with the dead and walking wounded, with the tidying up to be done for long periods thereafter by those who never even got a battle star!

Things Decreased by SF,SE Systems

Several complementary reductions of forces or attitudes also constitute a critical part of SF,SE systems. Four points illustrate the broader family of reductions, with many of the latter having meaning only for specific organizations. *First,* reductions are sought in the tendency to overrely on formal authority. Perhaps even better said, the bias might be that overreliance on informal means can exist only in rare cases.

This may read like it makes life easy for executives. The opposite is the case, however, if the SF,SE logic really takes hold. As I read the Polaris effort,[62] for example, it appears to say that the need for a manager to fire anyone should be seen as a systemic failure, especially if the target were surprised. Not that firings or reshufflings never occurred. They did, often with only 24-hours' notice. Rather, the view was that if the Polaris management system were really working, appropriate improvements would have been made *before* any formal action became necessary, hopefully *long before.* Or, failing that, the target of the firing should have had ample notice that his efforts at improvement were seen as ineffective, so that resignation would have occurred or at least that formal action would not have come as a surprise.

In sum, vigilant executive monitoring of the management system rather than high-level indolence and lack of resolve are required to make SF,SE systems work well.

Second, sharp decreases are sought in the common tendency to avoid responsibility for error, or to "relocate" that responsibility. The reference here is to situations in which real doubt or dispute exists about responsibility. Whether in open-and-shut or doubtful cases, avoiding or relocating responsibility is accurately (if quite indelicately) described as "throwing dead cats into the backyards of others."

Various mechanisms can serve this end of seeking to have managers and employees "own up." In one case, for example, an executive used a central budget category against which to charge costs which were in dispute, rather than force some all-or-none resolution. Note, however, that this executive was most sensitive to the total level of charges against this budget category. In turn, his subordinates were eager to save the fund for "the really tough cases," an attitude which apparently encouraged them to reach satisfying decisions for those potentially troublesome allocations of costs about which bitter-end disagreement did not exist, but about which legitimate questions did exist. The budget category was most useful, all basically recognized, when used least. And it probably would vanish unless used sparingly.

Third, major reductions in the balkanization of organization units comprise a central preoccupation of SF,SE systems. The antigoal is the sense of "what we do here is our business, so stay out unless we invite you." This sense might be manifest in diverse forms, some more subtle and others far more gross than the illustration given.

How to curb such balkanization? Personnel assignments clearly are crucial, as are specific guidelines as to the openness required by dynamic systems. Some executives, try as they might, cannot get over old habits in this regard. This seems particularly true in my experience of managers who earlier learned to use subunit isolation, laced with paranoid suspicion, as their way of enhancing cohesiveness in their immediate subunit. This is a primordial strategy and often works, but it does require an "enemy." In fact, a person in a highly specialized function might be able to use this strategy throughout a career, but it is usually bad news for a person with integrative responsibilities such as $M_{A\,BC}$ in Figure 2, that is, a manager or executive with integrative responsibilities for blending several specialties. Such a manager might succeed in pairing-off the "us" versus a top management "them," but this requires very subtle balancing to avoid Armaggedon. And what if the manager became one of "them"? A manager who walks on water, as it were, might forever be able to use the strategy and continue to rise in the hierarchy. But such a rare bird would probably "make it" to substantial levels, no matter what the strategy.

Fourth, SF,SE systems make related efforts to reduce the many varieties of "tunnel vision," both individual and professional. The point does not require much elaboration. Where we sit significantly influences, if it does not determine, what we see. The remedy here lies in developing knowledge and skills that permit some enlargement of where one can sit, to risk a bad pun. Such learning is relevant to "taking the role of the other," a goal variously served by several of the designs and approaches mentioned above, among them being team development and the confrontation design. In effect, they provide data about how others see us and also permit practice in getting us to appreciate the reality seen by the other.

Organizing Jobs in Human Terms at Lower Levels
Motivation Through Work Itself

The argument now takes two definite turns. The focus shifts to the worm's-eye view of the bird, as it were—it looks at lower organization levels rather than focuses on executive levels. Moreover, the argument more definitely shifts to structural changes and away from interaction patterns. The typical OD emphasis, as in the section above, is on interaction. In large part, this reflects the early and strong bias of major OD practitioners who worked at the highest organization levels, where the quality of interaction is extremely important and structural constraints are minimized.[63] Relatedly, many OD applications have been in host organizations whose technology is interaction-centered, for example, marketing organizations, welfare or service agencies, and so on.

This primary emphasis on interaction versus structure is an awkward one, however. That is, OD is conceptually centered on the simultaneous satisfaction of human needs and organization demands, and it is system-oriented. Consequently, if the satisfaction of human needs in any particular case can be attained by affecting only patterns of interaction, so be it. But, if the system for analysis is technology-rich, or if the satisfaction of human needs is mediated in significant ways by organization structure or task configurations—both of which are often the case[64]—applications of the laboratory approach must emphasize structure. Otherwise, those applications will be false to the logic of the approach. Hence, OD applications based on the laboratory approach should be interaction-centered or structure-oriented, or both, as the specific situation requires.

A Concept for Need-Satisfying Work

Relatively few OD applications are structure-oriented,[65] but the nature of the tie-in seems clear enough. For example, early work with Frederick Herzberg's concept of motivation[66] has been promising, despite the fact that important methodological questions have been raised about its underlying two-factor model.[67] Basically, Herzberg's approach stresses that the individual's needs at work are met essentially by the nature of the work. The major *motivators* that can be built into work are:[68]

- The actual achievement of the employee
- The objective recognition that the employee attains for the achievement, which must be distinguished from the "recognition" accorded as a public relations gesture
- Increased responsibility assigned to the employee because of performance
- Increased opportunities to grow in knowledge about a task and in ability to perform it
- Increased chance for advancement to a higher order of task

Another class of factors, *maintenance* or *hygiene factors,* is also distinguished by Herzberg. These factors can prevent trouble, as it were, but they do not eliminate its causes. Some hygiene factors are:

- Company policies and administration
- The technical or interpersonal quality of supervision
- Working conditions
- Salaries, wages, and benefits, which can sometimes but not usually be classified as motivators because they are indicators of success

Roughly, the presence of motivators in work can raise the ceiling for effort; the presence of hygiene factors provides a floor that will prevent motivation from falling to dangerously low levels. Looked at from another perspective, attractive hygiene factors can encourage an employee to do enough to stay in the system. The presence of motivators, in sharp contrast, can motivate an individual to approach his or her best effort at work.

"Green-Lighting"

One well-known approach to implementing Herzberg's concept uses the group as the agent of change. Robert N. Ford at AT&T uses "natural families" of supervisors in a creative way. A concept for structuring jobs is explained to the supervisors, who then develop the specific plan for implementing the concept in "green-lighting" (or brainstorming) sessions that are facilitated but not directed by an outside resource person. Ford does not give great detail about these sessions.[69] But, they clearly have two goals: to make use of the information possessed by the supervisors; and to encourage their ownership of the job-enrichment program, as it applies to their specific organization units.

Experimenting with a Specific Job

Robert Ford spearheaded several efforts to build motivation into work in low-level tasks or jobs, and these tended to be successful. About the concept of providing satisfaction of human needs at work, Ford explained: "The theory is quite clear on one point. You can't motivate people from outside [themselves] for long. But you can give them a chance to succeed and to improve at tasks that challenge them. Then they will develop their own drives toward tasks."[70] To engage such energies one should

- Load the task with true work motivators
- Remove the dissatisfiers, the inadequate hygiene factors
- Remember that good hygiene factors will not compensate for a boring job

AT&T experimented with a substantial number of jobs. Overall, these had been work-simplified to the point that they were need-depriving. In summary, work simplification might have reduced the training burden, but it often created problems of morale and motivation. AT&T was particularly concerned with one reflection of these problems—turnover that often reached epidemic proportions.[71] This turnover increasingly came to be seen as a consequence of the need-depriving ways in which work was structured.

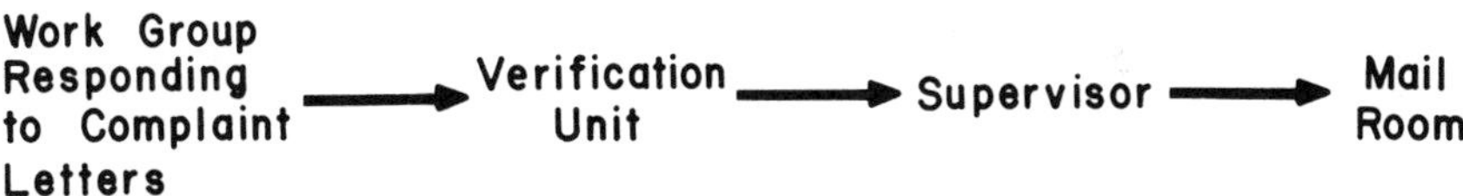

Figure 3 Initial motivator-poor organization of work of correspondents.

Consider the flow of work illustrated in Figure 3.[72] Members of the work group were college trained and responded to a wide variety of letters, some of which raised complicated issues. Their work flow was motivator-poor, in numerous senses.

- Verifiers checked every proposed response, which set narrow limits on the responsibility of the members of the work group.
- Employees responding to complaint letters felt little sense of achievement, because both verifiers and the supervisor often changed a response without informing the employee.
- The employee had no regular way of learning how well he had done, although he might get some "negative recognition" in responses changed by verifiers or supervisor.
- At least for many months, responses by new employees were signed by verifiers or the supervisor, which diluted the responsibility an employee could feel for performance.
- Few opportunities to grow in task knowledge or for promotion based on performance were available.

Various levels of supervision became involved in making this job richer in motivators. Their guide was to increase the "vertical loading" of work, enlarging or rearranging a job to make it more challenging. "Horizontal loading," in contrast, adds task elements to a job without making it more challenging, as by enlarging the brain surgeon's job by assigning the clean-up duties as well. Vertical loading of a job attempts to follow guidelines such as those in Exhibit 3.

Exhibit 3 Enriching the Work of Correspondents by Adding Motivators

Method of Loading	*Motivators Involved*
1. Removing some controls without removing responsibility	1. Responsibility; personal achievement
2. Increasing the accountability of individuals for their own work	2. Responsibility; recognition
3. Giving a person a whole natural unit of work	3. Responsibility; achievement; recognition
4. Giving a person greater job freedom, or additional authority	4. Responsibility; achievement; recognition
5. Making periodic reports available directly to the employee rather than to the supervisor	5. Internal recognition
6. Introducing new and more difficult tasks into the job	6. Growth and learning
7. Assigning specialized tasks to employees to help them become expert	7. Responsibility; growth; advancement

Source: Based on Robert N. Ford, *Motivation Through the Work Itself* (New York: American Management Association, 1969), p. 24.

The reorganized work flow for responding to complaint letters variously reflects these guidelines. Basically, respondents were given greater opportunities to gain recognition for their efforts, as well as to be responsible for them. Figure 4 suggests how these goals were approached. The simple changes in the job were designed to add variously motivators to permit greater satisfaction of individual needs and, hence, to induce lower turnover and higher quality. Existing levels of output were to be maintained.

The efficacy of restructuring work as in Figure 4 involves broad philosophic issues as well as detailed steps. The opposed philosophic persuasion argues that work is not, cannot, and (apparently) should not be a central concern for the overwhelming bulk of people, and often proposes that attention consequently ought to be given to such factors as job security rather than to job design.[73] The approach in Figure 4 maintains that work can be made less need-depriving and, consequently, more central in the scheme of things for more people.

Ford's approach to reducing those costs is to enrich the flow of work. In the specific case of the respondents to complaint letters, such methods were as follows.

- Individual respondents were given full responsibility for responses.
- Subject-matter specialists were chosen within the work group to provide immediate advice.
- The rate of verification was related to experience of respondent.
- The freedom of respondents was increased, as by reducing the degree of overhead supervision.
- The supervisor became less another review level and more a facilitator, as responses were routed directly from verifiers to the mail room, with the supervisor now conducting sample reviews at individual work locations and counseling individual respondents.
- Respondents were variously encouraged to own their responses, as by signing their own letters, personalizing the responses, and having responsibility for them.
- Responsibility for pace of work was left to respondents, with only general admonitions about a "full day's work."
- Respondents could take personally initiated opportunities for growth by seeking advice of subject-matter experts and, indeed, could aspire to that position.

The cumulative impact of such factors in the case of the correspondents was to induce major changes in the climate of interpersonal and intergroup relations, to judge from the verbal reports. Cooperation increased; relationships seemed to be less "phony" and more leavened by the realities of performance; and an atmosphere of freedom *cum* accountability prevailed, with greater self-control and

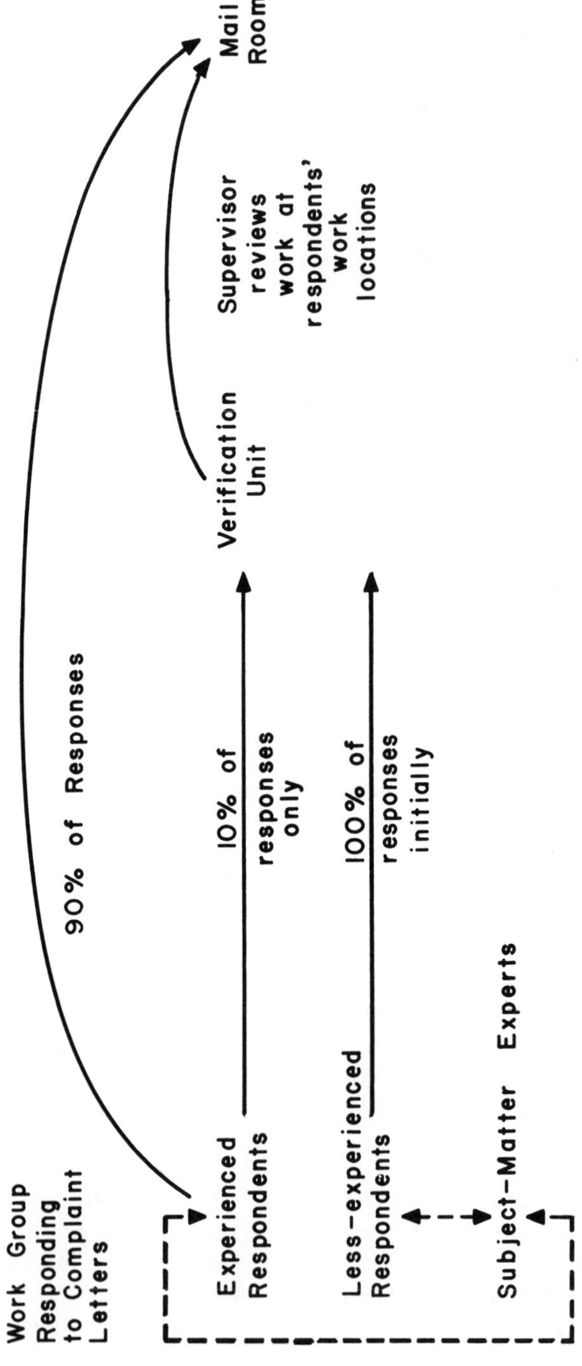

Figure 4 Restructured motivator-rich organization of work of correspondents. [*Source:* Based on Robert N. Ford, *Motivation Through the Work Itself* (New York: American Management Association, 1969), pp. 24-26.]

self-initiative by employees and less pressure from supervisors. Overall, the spirit was one of greater responsibility for a task, greater freedom in performing it, and greater initiative in seeking help when wanted.[74]

Some Quantitative Results

The descriptions above suggest that the new vertically loaded job was more need-satisfying for individuals. Specifically, only one respondent resigned because of her dislike of the responsibilities. Moreover, the verifiers—who lost some of their previous power—apparently did not prove troublesome in the transition.

But what of organization demands? AT&T was primarily interested in reduced turnover and increased quality of service to the customer. Data from the case sketched above, as well as from others, suggest that simultaneous satisfaction of individual needs and organization demands did occur. The richness of data can only be sampled here. Although no specific figures are given, Ford notes that turnover for the experimental group "was greatly reduced during the period of the study," while turnover in a control group remained at previous levels.

Quality of service in the experimental group also increased sharply, as Figure 5 shows. Three points amplify this conclusion. *First,* the index of the experimental group is initially lower than that of a control group, both in February and in April, when the study began. But the index for the experimental group reaches a substantially higher level 6 months later, after an initial dip. This initial dip in the index of the experimental group is attributed to the learning required by the vertical loading of jobs.

Second, a sharp decay is evident in the customer service index, for both experimental and control groups, in the months preceding the study. Hence, management's major concern.

Third, an upward trend also occurs in the index for the control group during the period of the study. Managers of the controls variously attempted to raise quality. They succeeded, at least in the short run, for Figure 5 reflects an ongoing improvement in quality independent of the job-loading program. That is, there are two ways to skin this particular cat, at least in the short run, even though one way seems to be more rewarding. Moreover, it is not known whether the techniques used in the control group to raise quality had any adverse long-run consequences.

Some Conditions for Successful Applications

The illustration above represents a classic case of success, and it and other similar successes in some circles have encouraged a kind of "can't miss" status for job enlargement interventions. As Frank and Hackman boldly put the point: "Now,

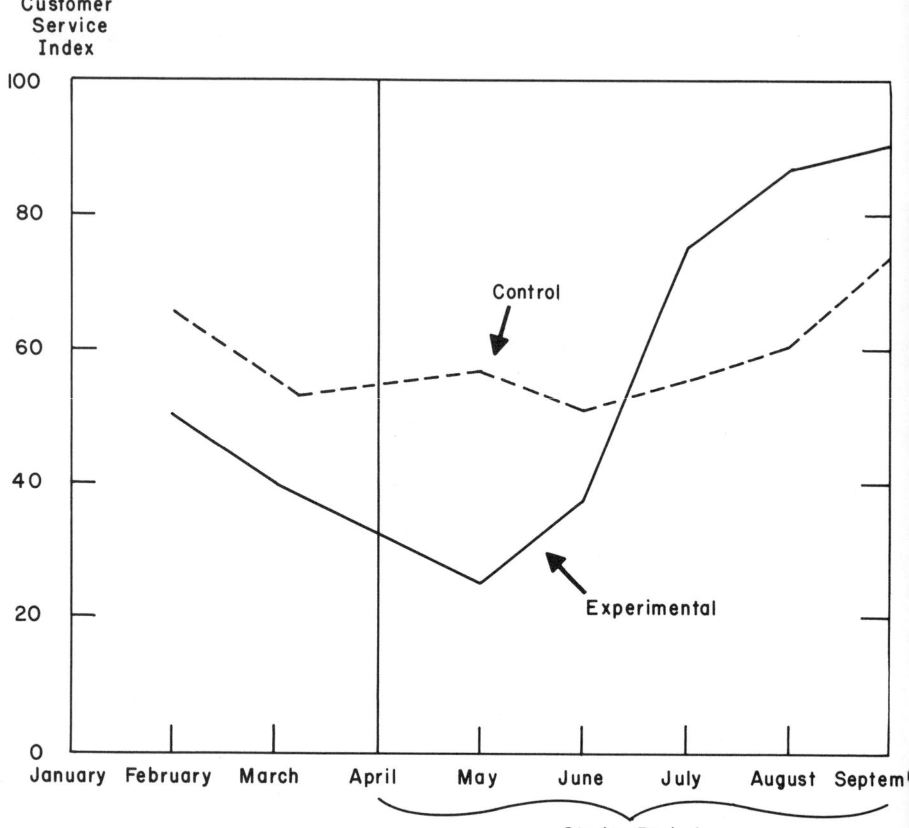

Figure 5 Trends in customer service index. [*Source:* Robert N. Ford, *Motivation Through the Work Itself* (New York: American Management Association, 1969), p. 33.]

as reports of its success are multiplying, job enrichment is being acclaimed by some as the cure for problems ranging from inflation to drug abuse."[75]

At the same time, job enlargement has always had its critics.[76] Moreover, despite the fact that "job enrichment failures" seldom have been written up in professional journals,[77] knowledge about such applications is spreading among scholars and practitioners.

These two opposed clusters of opinion may imply a dilemma for some observers, but the view here is that it is not necessary either to support or to reject job enlargement. Rather, the present view proposes that any intervention is likely to work only under a range of facilitating conditions. Hence, the prejudice here is to scan reports of both successful and unsuccessful applications to determine how to isolate sets of relatively propitious and hostile conditions for job enlargement as an OD intervention. The sense of the point inheres in this summary of the results of four major job-enlargement experiments in Norway.[78]

- Job enlargement efforts often seem to work, at least for a while: that is, on balance, production and satisfaction tend to rise, and absenteeism goes down.
- At times, vested interests get violated by job enlargement, and they resist. Thus, existing norms may inhibit or complicate redesign, or the workers may fear the job enlargement constitutes only a clever disguise for a speed-up effort.
- Higher-level management sometimes will suspend experiments, or fail to reinforce and reward appropriate learning or change.
- Diffusion to other sites will be limited, for diverse reasons.

This brief survey implies both a central tendency for job enlargement to succeed in some senses, even as diverse conditions can vitally affect the degree and character of that success.

Provisionally, in fact, some such set of facilitative conditions does seem to be emerging. Those emphasized here are an amalgam from several sources,[79] but with overall guidance from Frank and Hackman.[80]

Higher-Order Perspectives Are Needed

Perhaps basically, job enlargement needs to be disciplined by "higher-order perspectives," both normative and empirical. These perspectives provide context for the job-enrichment effort, as it were, as well as permit consistent and congruent decisions concerning the many matters of choice that will be raised in any application. Frank and Hackman phrase the need for such guiding theory in an especially compelling way:[81]

> Although some theories may be objectively "better" than others, our observations suggest that the specific details of various theories may not be as important as the fact that *some* theory is used to guide the implementation of change—and to keep change activities focused on the intended objectives. Moreover, a good theory can help identify and specify the kinds of data needed in planning and evaluating the changes; and it can also alert change agents to special problems and opportunities that may develop as the project unfolds.

Normatively, the value of such higher-order perspectives can be suggested easily. Assume a kind of General Bullmoose attitude underlies the intervention—an autocratic managerial initiative to install job enlargement, whose putative and opposed spirit is that employees will derive greater satisfaction from work when they are able to exercise greater control over their work site. Employees might respond to such incongruities by suspicious and rejecting reactions to the intervention, the general fear being that "there must be a hook somewhere in the bait."

The nasty dilemma merely requires stating. Job enlargement is attractive to many employees because it permits a greater sense of responsibility and participation in decision-making, after the job is changed. But, most employees apparently prefer to feel that sense of responsibility and participation *before the job is changed,* so much so in fact that they might resist an autocratic initiative to force on them "what is really good for them." In this case, as in practically all others, one cannot have his cake and also eat it. Illustratively, participation throughout the process by all concerned–employees, management, and unions–seems a precondition for successful applications.[82] The reasons for this precondition seem sound. In one case, degree and method of participation related directly not only to satisfaction. Moreover, participating employees reported their job changes were "better" than those who had identical changes imposed on them.[83]

Empirically, job enrichment also needs to be imbedded in higher-order theoretical formulations detailing the major covariants involved in successful applications. This need is often neglected in critical particulars. Consider only three examples. Thus, job enlargement expectations often have neglected the obvious fact that traditional organization structures are poor hosts for enlarged jobs, as the opening section of this chapter establishes. Many applications have sought to graft enlarged jobs at the lowest levels into a management structure that retains essential Figure 1 features. This asks for trouble, in a simple yet profound way. That is Davis's basic message when he argues that the *individual job* is not the most strategic place from which to start improvements in the quality of work. Davis proposes beginning with the design of the *work system.*[84] As the preceding section implies, basic decisions about the general system for organizing should be made first, and then the design of individual jobs becomes a derivative rather than a primary task. Moreover, empirical analysis must establish the proper psychological characteristics of enlarged jobs. Research and experience, to be specific, indicate that usefully enlarged jobs[85]

- Have a content that is reasonably demanding or challenging in terms other than sheer endurance, and provide some variety
- Permit learning on the job
- Provide some area of individual decision-making
- Permit some social support and recognition
- Permit the individual to relate his life to what he does at work
- Give a sense of leading to a desirable future

Similarly, job enlargement applications often suffer from a lack of guidance by a theory of groups. That is, job enlargement is most likely to be conceptually associated with such theory fragments as that of Herzberg,[86] whose bias is essentially individualistic. That is, briefly, Herzberg argues that job enlargement gratifies individual needs, and thus motivates individual employees to approach their tasks with greater zest. This leaves the typical intervenor poorly equipped to anticipate and deal with transindividual reactions of employees, as when interpersonal relations or group norms are violated by job enlargement efforts. This effect has been reported in the literature[87] and is probably ubiquitous. For job enlargement often involves changes in a *system* of jobs and relationships, and thus perforce the intervenor must operate at a transindividualistic level of abstraction, short of settling for a low batting average. Relatedly, the lack of supporting theory of groups in job-enlargement applications can forfeit the substantial power of the group as an agent of change.

Finally, only folly permits the assumption that job enrichment will apply always and everywhere, but most applications make the assumption to which even brief reflection gives the lie. For example, some employees, at least at certain stages of their lives, might prefer a monotonous and boring yet secure job.[88] The sometimes profound individual differences that exist between employees—in knowledge and skills as well as in needs and goals[89]—also urge that job enrichment does not attract everyone all of the time. Consistently, some successful job-enlargement applications, as Chapter 8 suggests, seem to owe part of their success to the lack of insistence that everyone must always play the game. Or, take a somewhat trickier example. Job enrichment in a recessionary or stabilizing economy may only mean to many that there will be fewer jobs to go around, and most people will prefer a boring job if the alternative threatens their employment or that of their co-workers. The success or failure of a job-enlargement intervention, then, may hinge on whether employees do (or do not) feel a relative security of employment. Some organizations consequently guarantee that every effort will be made to avoid lay-offs or firings following job enlargement.

To make a long story short, then, we need an empirical theory that tells us where and when and how job enlargement is more likely to succeed. And "success" and "failure" also need careful delimiting, for job enlargement is no universal remedy for what ails organizations. As Barret and Reilly wisely caution:[90]

> Can restructuring the workplace solve the problem of alienation in our time? There are diseases of the soul that do not originate in the factory: healthy people do not become heartless bosses or cruel foremen; healthy people do not feel debased or dehumanized by menial work or intimidated by blustering superiors. Sick people—alienated people—are not made whole by an interesting job.

Detailed Prior Diagnosis is Critical

Since job enrichment seems so straightforward to so many, this discussion stresses the need for comprehensive diagnosis before recommending the intervention. The diagnosis would involve not only the tasks in question, but also the technical and social contexts in which the tasks are imbedded. Seldom can you jiggle one part of a system without causing effects throughout it.

Any brief catalog of the foci for diagnosis will inevitably be false to the more complex reality of any work site, but a few factors will suggest the broader range of issues. Frank and Hackman provide guidance here, beginning with the basic premise that the specific work site will be influential in determining the success or failure of any application of job enlargement. And, detailed diagnosis alone will highlight those characteristics of the work site.[91] Important foci for diagnosis include the following questions.

- How committed is management to job enrichment, especially to its implied but basic exchange? That is, greater employee control over work often seems the quid pro quo for improvements in productivity.
- Can the jobs in question be meaningfully enlarged, and especially without creating broader technical or interpersonal problems in the process?
- Does the job enlargement involve individual tasks, or an interrelated system of individual tasks?
- Do the envisioned changes in jobs merely demand more activities of the employee, or do they permit greater variety, more employee control over work, and so on? "Horizontal" job enlargement implies the same old stuff, only more so, but it is attractive to management and raises no issues of basic redefinition of authority relations, of "who is in control."
- Are employees ready to accept an enlarged job, new skills, and greater responsibility? Or are they so fixated on bread-and-butter issues or so mistrustful of management as to have little energy for the transitions and learning required by job enlargement?
- What consequences of the job enlargement for the broader social and technical systems are not explicitly a part of the enlargement effort?

Organic, Implementation-Oriented Approach Seems Preferable

Most discussion of job enlargement is concept-centered, and applications are much the worse for it. That is, perhaps 90 percent of the success of job enlargements interventions is determined by how the concept is implemented, but the concept gets 90 percent of the attention. To put this critical point another way, the sociotechnical analysis in the job enlargement literature can be very good, but the attention to implementation often limps. For example, Emery and Thorsrud reflect this central poverty in a case in which employees feared a successful job enlargement experiment would merely "axe" some of them. "Explanations," they note, "did little to dispel these fears." The authors conclude: "We had, however, *no choice other than to . . . hope* that the backing we had outside the department and our face-to-face contacts on the shop floor would gradually change the situation."[92]

This puts it the wrong way around. The typical job enlargement concept itself is quite simple, but implementation can be tangled and torturous, especially so because basic job-enlargement ideas provide little guidance about how to anticipate and resolve the issues involved in going from concept to real-time. As two chagrined experimenters with job enlargement observe: ". . . as yet there is no neat 'package' available for installing job enrichment (and indeed, there never may be)." As a consequence, it seems essential that change agents will have to learn as they go how most effectively to design, implement, and manage enriched jobs in their own organizations.[93]

Here such higher order perspectives as OD theory and values can be critical in job-enlargement interventions, for OD provides one approach to implementing concepts such as job enlargement: It emphasizes issues related to change; and suggests approaches and designs that can help induce required processes and dynamics, especially when groups are involved.

The emphasis here on implementation is not motivated simply by respect of Murphy's Law–that if something can go wrong in a job-enrichment application, it will. Much more, this emphasis is motivated by the organic, more open-ended, and multilateral model of change encouraged when one emphasizes OD implementation–looking from the "bottom, up" as well as from the "top, down." The worm's-eye view of the bird can profoundly modify the bird's-eye view, as it were. And the multilateral view implies the need to share ownership of the intervention, as well as responsibility for it. In contrast, being basically concept-oriented encourages a more elitist model of change: of a professedly enlightened "us" unilaterally planning something that will be good for "them," while "we" variously fail to involve "them," to take into account their goals and views of the work site, and so on. As Frank and Hackman express one lesson learned from their own abortive effort at job enlargement, which was basically unilateral, downward directed, and concept oriented:[94]

> Contingency plans should be prepared ahead of time to deal with the inevitable "spin-off" problems and opportunities that emerge from work redesign activities. By making explicit contingency plans for dealing with possible problems, at least two advantages accrue. First, employees, managers, and consultants all will be well aware (and share the awareness) that certain types of problems (e.g., tension in superior-subordinate relationships; technical problems; coordination difficulties at the interfaces of work systems, and so on) are likely to emerge as the change project develops. This simple understanding may help keep surprise and dismay at manageable

levels when the problems do in fact appear, and thereby decrease the opportunity for people to conclude prematurely that "it failed."

Second, preplanning for possible problems can lead to an objective increase in the readiness of all parties to deal with those problems that do emerge.

Timely Feedback Is Central to Success

Relatedly, the value of organic, multilateral approaches to implementing job-enrichment programs is nowhere clearer than in helping to induce the real-time feedback that is required for fine-tuning any application. Directly, the success of job enlargement will in large part be determined by how it is perceived by employees, by what their expectations about it are. If an application is perceived as "more of the same," it will also no doubt be more of the same in terms of productivity and satisfaction. Moreover, if the work in point of fact remains the same—despite efforts to change it—one can hardly expect the intervention to generate salubrious effects. Viable feedback linkages between employees, intervenors, and managers are necessary to provide such information.

The point here is not that only perceptions matter. Nor is it that job enrichment concepts can contribute nothing to meeting employee needs. Rather, employee perceptions or expectations are seen as potent intervening variables which can, over a broad range, serve to mask or abort the need-gratifying potential in interventions such as job enrichment.[95]

A Retail Food Chain Decentralizes
Profoundly Changing an Organization's Structure

Let us shift attention from the numerous if variably successful efforts at structural change through job enlargement, and go hunting for bigger and rarer game. Relatively few OD efforts initially emphasize basic changes in an organization's structure, as in moving from the traditional toward the alternative structure described in the opening section of this chapter.[96] Briefly, the implied learning progression in most OD efforts has some such form:

Attitudinal change → behavioral change → structural change

In practice, structural change not only gets late attention, but it usually gets no attention, so pervasive has been the emphasis on interaction.

This pervasive bias definitely seems OD's loss. Not only is structure a powerful determinant and reinforcer of behavior, but work is often structured at major cross-purposes with OD values.[97] Illustratively, the alternative structure for organizing work sketched in Figure 2 seems to induce and/or reinforce behaviors and attitudes consistent with the values underlying OD efforts. That is, accumulating evidence implies the value of this basic but neglected sequence of learning:

$$\text{Structural change} \begin{array}{l} \nearrow \text{attitudinal change} \\ \qquad\qquad \updownarrow \\ \searrow \text{behavioral change} \end{array}$$

Or, perhaps, the sequence might be:

Structural change → behavioral change → attitudinal change

The substantial loss deriving from the general neglect of structural change can be suggested here conveniently. The description below will detail the design and the consequences of a change in a retail food chain's structure from a centralized toward a decentralized pattern, and it will also sketch the generally attractive consequences of that transition.

Initial Centralized Structure*

A large retail food chain was organized in the traditional way and relied heavily on "close supervision" as the basic way of life, which managers generally described "as getting my ass kicked" and resented for "being treated like a child." The structure in Figure 6, very much like the traditional model introduced in the opening section of this chapter, implied a number of common problems. Basically, the store manager was limited in his ability to supervise the entire store. The reasons are many, but prominent among them are the several separate chains of command that influence what went on in the store. To explain, "store operations" are distinguished quite sharply from "merchandising." Store operations involve the mechanics of getting the work done—stocking shelves, checking out customers, and so on. Merchandising involves the development of creative sales programs that provide a variety of products sufficiently attractive to bring in enough customers to generate acceptable profits.

The structural embodiment of this basic distinction is the structure in Figure 6. That structure contains a "store operations" hierarchy, with individual store managers being held on a short leash by the district manager. That structure also contains three other specialist merchandising chains of command—for grocery, meat, and produce. Merchandising policies filter down from these three centers of influence to the several department heads in each store, with meat and produce being tied especially closely to their respective merchandisers and coordinators.

*Based on Robert A. Luke, Jr., Peter Block, Jack M. Davey, and Vernon R. Averch, "A Structural Approach to Organizational Change," *Journal of Applied Behavioral Science,* Vol. 9 (September 1973), pp. 611-635.

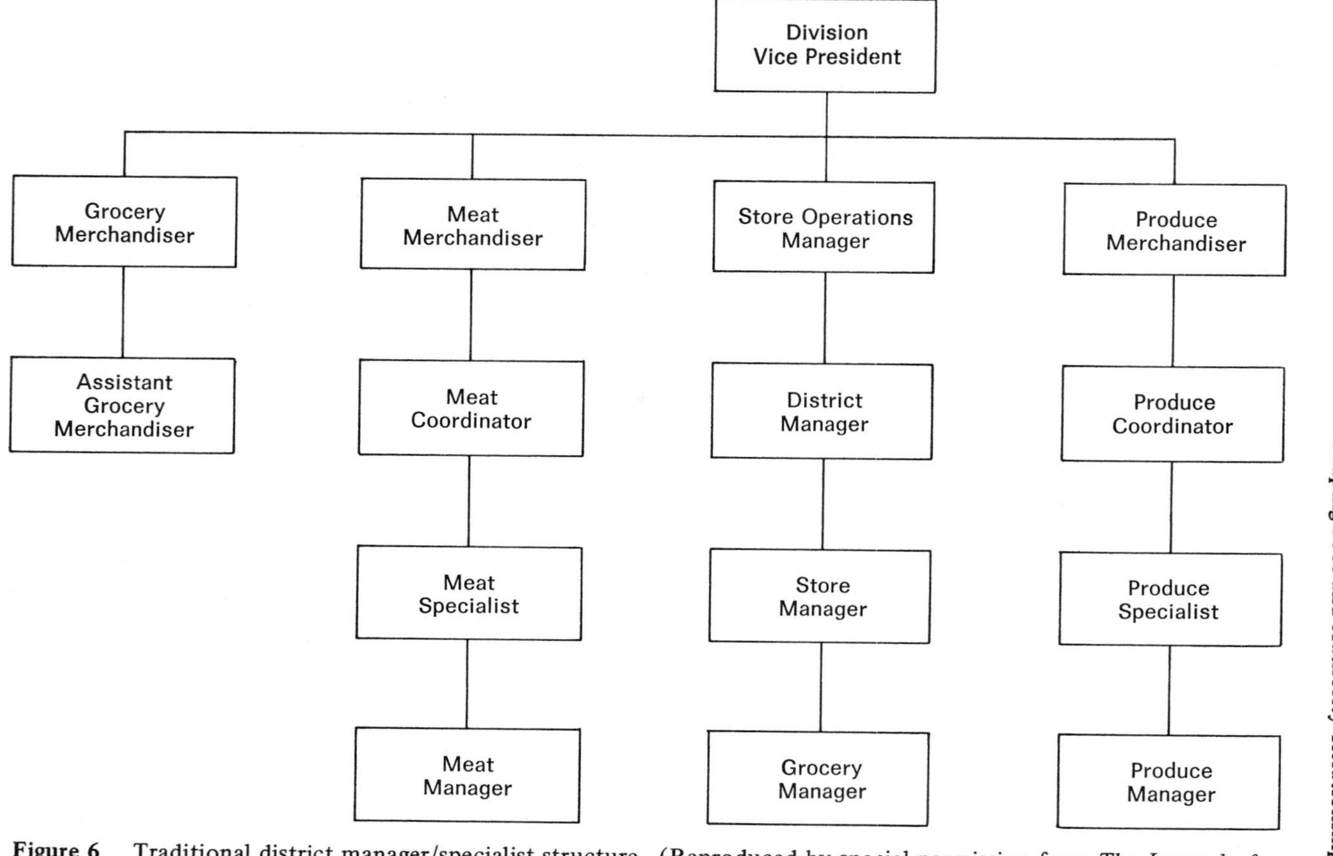

Figure 6 Traditional district manager/specialist structure. (Reproduced by special permission from *The Journal of Applied Behavioral Science.* "A Structural Approach to Organizational Change," by Robert A. Luke, Jr., Peter Block, Jack M. Davey, and Vernon Averch. Vol. 9, no. 5, p. 615. Copyrighted by NTL Institute, 1973.)

The typical store manager made a reasonable adaptation. He basically left the meat and produce to his managers and their merchandising specialists. And the store manager focused his attention on pleasing his district manager, supervising the grocery quite directly, and also overseeing the up-front activities in his store (for example, check-out counters, and so on). As several observers conclude: "This limited his ability to manage the entire store."

The district manager's (DM) adaptation was somewhat similar, albeit complicated by the fact that a DM supervised ten to fifteen stores. The DM tended to be tough with individual store managers, to emphasize day-to-day operations, and to fight whatever fires attracted or demanded his attention. Obviously, the DM's pace was hectic.

These arrangements sufficed for a substantial period, but then began to generate more and more unwanted consequences. The generic problem? No one had substantial responsibility for an individual store, even though its several major activities were closely scrutinized by several separate chains of command. As one major result, the development of managers was stunted. A more specific frustration of the firm's executives with the traditional structure was the tardy installation of a new grocery management system, which required that DMs train store managers. Such training did not have a high priority in the minds of most DMs, however, apparently because of the press of day-to-day activities, and perhaps because "training" and the normal "pushing" roles of the DM were not compatible.

Both the generic and the specific inadequacies of the traditional structure grew more grating on the firm's executives; for a growing pool of tested managers capable of rapid and successful innovation were seen as not only already central in the firm's success, but also as rapidly escalating in future significance.

Toward a Decentralized Structure

The tardy installation of the new system could have been handled in several ways, but the firm in this case opted to experiment with a major structural reshuffling of responsibilities. The overall sense of the structural change is implied by Figure 7, which details a radical lowering of the locus of effective decision-making to the level of the store manager. Basically, some employees gained responsibilities, and others lost them. New and substantial responsibilities are delegated to the store managers. This new integrative role brought together authority that was previously scattered in several positions. To explain: the old DM loses his line authority and becomes a consultant, or management development coordinator; and the MDC becomes a member of a consulting team with no line authority, along with the old meat and produce specialists who also become consultants. Moreover, the store operations manager now supervises all store operations.

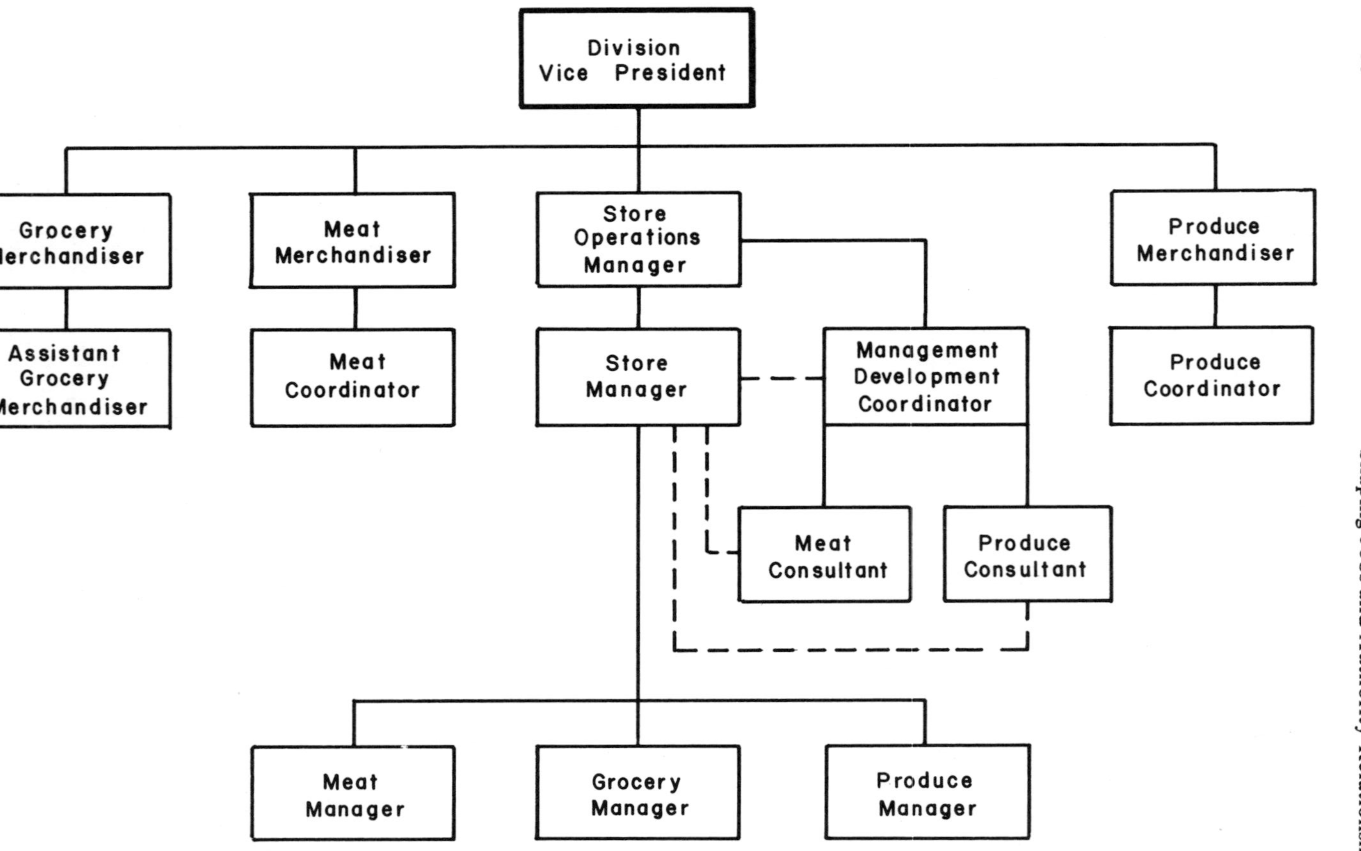

Figure 7 Proposed consultant-decentralized structure. (Reproduced by special permission from *The Journal of Applied Behavioral Science.* "A Structural Approach to Organizational Change," by Robert A. Luke, Jr., Peter Block, Jack M. Davey, and Vernon Averch, Vol. 9, no. 5, p. 616. Copyrighted by NTL Institute, 1973.)

The total sense of the experiment involves movement from the traditional structure in Figure 1 toward the unorthodox structure in Figure 2. In short, the store manager becomes more a supervisor of a managerial unit, with much fuller control over the total flow of work. An anticipated result is a major developmental opportunity for the store managers—to interpret the structural transition from the bottom, up—as well as more focused responsibility for the management of the total store. Looked at downward from the executive's perspective, each store now could be managed more by looking at the "bottom-line" of overall performance, rather than by close supervision of details.

Design for Implementing Structural Change

The structural changeover required new attitudes and behaviors from many, that was always clear. A five-step transition developed, in part through anticipation and advanced planning, and in part because of evolving and unprogrammed necessity.

First, the firm's president authorized an experiment with the new structure in one district. One consultant was chosen, and care was taken not to stack the deck one way or the other in choosing the districts, so that comparisons would validly reflect any differences in performance between the two structural forms. All districts had ten to fifteen stores. Except for the one experimental district, all others retained the traditional structure.

Second, great care was taken in the selection of the MDC, or management development coordinator, from among existing district managers. Previous experience clearly established the central role of the MDC, and the consequent significance of the selected individual's ability to convert from an ordering to a consulting mode.[98] To reinforce his role—as well as to express confidence in him—MDC was allowed to select the other two members of the consulting team, who came from corporate and divisional merchandisers. The consulting team would work with (and for) each of the fifteen store managers in the experimental district.

Third, the need for training to ease the transition got priority. As a result, both off-line and real-time opportunities were provided. There were two off-line training experiences.

- The new consulting team—MDC, meat consultant, and produce consultant—were all highly competent in store methods, but they were seen as needing "training in human relations and consultation skills to perform their new roles effectively" (p. 618), since these new roles lacked line authority and emphasized interpersonal competencies. A week-long sensitivity-training experience was the method for working toward greater human relations skills.

- The week before actual structural change, a 2-day workshop was held for the consulting team, the relevant managers, and division management. The focus was on how the consulting team and division management would respond to anticipated problems in the experimental district.

Real-time training on the job also was provided, with consultants observing the style and methods of the three members of the consulting team as they visited stores. Counseling and coaching sessions were used to demonstrate how the consultants-to-be had to adjust from their previous controlling mode, as well as to help develop appropriate consulting skills.

Fourth, a set of ground rules for consultant behavior guided both the transition and training for it. Exhibit 4 contrasts the new ground rules with those commonly used by district managers and merchandisers in their traditional roles. The contrasts between the appropriate behaviors are marked, patently.

Exhibit 4 Differences in Ground Rules for Consultant Versus Traditional District Manager

Ground Rules for Consultant District	Ground Rules for DM District
1. Consultants will make appointments for store visits and develop a quarterly contract with each manager.	DM visits stores unannounced to inspect for adherence to company standards.
2. Store managers' performance will be evaluated by the store operations manager. MDC team will have no evaluation responsibilities for managers.	DM evaluates a manager's performance and conveys his evaluation to the store operations manager.
3. Store managers are responsible for total store results.	Store manager responsible for results in grocery and front-end departments only. Perishable specialists responsible for results in meat and produce departments.
4. Consultants' performance would be evaluated by store operations manager on the basis of their ability to perform as consultants and on the basis of managers' opinion of their helpfulness.	District manager and specialists' performance evaluated by store operations on the basis of results in the stores.

Fifth, a midcourse correction was provided about 3 months after installation of the new structure. Participants had changed too much, as it were. That is, some store managers reveled in their new authority and freedom, and did not even ask for the help of the consultant team. Relatedly, some consultants had become overtimid in their new role, so concerned were they about slipping back into a controlling mode. Associated problems were discussed, and the following modifications were made.[99]

- The MDC members, still acting as consultants and not supervisors, could take more initiative in pointing out problems and suggesting solutions, but it was still the manager's decision to act on the consultant's recommendations. A consultant was given the option of not working with a manager if he felt a particular manager was avoiding him.
- The corporate meat merchandiser agreed to design a management training program for the managers. This represented the first such training program for store managers by a merchandising office.
- The ground rule was established that when a representative of divisional and/or corporate management visits a store, he will inform the manager of his observations and can suggest that the manager call his consultant. Previously, top-echelon visitors would order the manager to make changes on the spot or inform store operations but not the manager.

Some Consequences of Structural Change

The transition was hardly smooth, for detailed reasons that cannot be dwelt on here,[100] but it had major and generally attractive consequences over the first year of its life. Three clusters of these consequences are distinguished here, but greater detail is conveniently available.[101]

Attitude Change Among Executives

Perhaps the most significant change occurred in executive perceptions of their managers. After 1 year down the track, most executives of the firm believed that, with appropriate support and training, 75 to 80 percent of the firm's managers can come to contribute more significantly to the firm and to themselves. The close supervision common in the firm, in contrast, implies a less optimistic view: that managers have to be jostled, even coerced, to perform even at an elemental level of supervision.

Behavioral Change Among Managers and Consultants

Most required behavioral changes seem to have occurred. Store managers relished their new role, although two had to be transferred to other districts because they were less adept at assuming responsibility for a total store than they were at doing what had been sufficient in the old structure—pleasing their district manager. In addition, the consultants changed their behaviors appropriately, although they still fondly remembered the sweet taste of having line authority. Moreover, only middling resistance developed, and that came from the most likely source—corporate and divisional merchandisers, who lost some staff in the experiment and could see more lost staff and influence in the cards if the experiment were successful. Indeed, most of this resistance seemed to come early in the game, and implies how hard old habits die. Notice the early failure of corporate and divisional merchandisers to change their perspective:[102]

> the Merchandisers continued to see the produce and meat consultants as [still] their staff and would ask them to go to stores to resolve particular problems. This put pressure on the consultants: to be consultants rather than bosses, they could not carry out the orders of the Merchandisers. Merchandisers and Coordinators were supposed to communicate directly with the Store Managers within the new structure. . . .

It appears that the midcourse correction described above helped to bring about the needed change in perspective.

Changes in Performance

Various measures of performance indicate that, on very substantial balance, the stores in the consulting district improved. Table 2 suggests the point economically. That is, if the firm's six districts are rank-ordered, the overall rankings put the experimental district in next-to-last place in the year before the structural change. In the year after, in contrast, the district with the consulting team placed first in overall performance.

All in all, then, the changes in performance suggest that the new structure had the expected effects. The broad theoretical effects that derive from movement toward the unorthodox structure are sketched more fully in the opening section of this chapter. Those expected results are at once consistent with the changes observed in this case, while they extend far beyond what was measured in it. Moreover, the two managerial replacements do not credibly explain the positive changes. Indeed, the serious difficulties experienced by the two managers after the structural change probably serve to understate the positive changes summarized above.

Some Ethical Concerns

The blush of enthusiasm about attractive consequences should not obscure some ethical issues raised by this approach to OD through basic structural change. Three such concerns are briefly introduced here.

Table 2 Comparisons of the Rankings of Firm's Six Divisions, Before and After Structural Change

District	Sales		Sales per Man Hour		Labor (percent)		District Rankings[a]		Difference
	1971	1972	1971	1972	1971	1972	1971	1972	
1.	2	6	4	6	5.5	6	4	6	-2
2.	6	1	1	4	2.5	2.5	3	2	+1
3.	4	5	2	2	1	5	2	4.5	-2.5
4.	1	3	3	5	2.5	4	1	4.5	-3.5
5. (Consulted)	3	2	5	1	5.5	1	5	1	+4.0
6.	5	4	6	3	4	2.5	6	3	+3.0

[a]Determined by ranking of sum of ranks for each year.

First, the implied role of the OD intervenor as architect has both expanding and limiting features. That role is obviously an additional way of approaching OD values, but care needs to be exercised that this expansion is not bought at the cost of reduced ownership by the client system. This problem is mitigated in the present case by the fact that a group of executives had been worrying over the present problems for a substantial time. The intervenors described one approach to meeting their concerns which was finally chosen from among three options considered.

In many other cases, however, the approach via structural change runs the risk of jeopardizing ownership and commitment of those who will make the change work. And, the approach via structural change may be open to charges of "elitism" or even "manipulation." No elaborate general guidelines seem appropriate, except that the structural change should be approached in ways consistent with OD values and that, wherever one begins, both structural and interactional changes typically will be necessary. The rub, of course, is that the technically appropriate structural change may not be acceptable. Hence, the appropriateness of the approach by Beer and Driscoll to the ethical and practical issues involved in determining when the strategy of changing structure should be the strategy of choice, as contrasted with people changing or educational strategies. When those in control make a good diagnosis, Beer and Driscoll advise, "structural changes can be made first." Where diagnosis is less certain—as in organizations with complex and shifting tasks—"educational interventions aimed at knowledge and attitude change must come first, so that the people who will be most affected by the structural changes can be involved in determining what form those changes will take."[103]

Second, some parts of the client system may look at structural interventions with suspicion or even hatred. In this case, as in most similar cases, someone won and someone lost. Thus, almost all store managers are in the former category; and the merchandisers are in the latter category, viewed from the perspective of immediate self-interest.

The situation is not like the typical sensitivity training group, where most everyone sees self as coming off a winner and the intervenor is usually much admired and even loved. Sharp cross-currents may be expected by the change agent intervening as architect, and those cross-currents must be dealt with openly and as fully as possible. At the very least, they should come as no surprise.

Third, especially serious issues inhere in the fact that a restructured job may be beyond the capabilities of people—even with ample support and training—who performed at least adequately before the change. That was the case with two of the fifteen managers in the present case, those transferred to a district where they would receive more direct and close supervision. Two transfers of managers inside the district also were made.

The consequences of the inability to adapt were benign in this case, but the general point is still significant. Fall-out is to be expected: Some managers can become so accustomed to pleasing a district manager, and so dependent on him, that change of the kind required is very difficult or even impossible. Hence, fall-out is encouraged if not predetermined by past organization practices. Consequently, organizational support and training should be made available so that fall-out is minimized, and should it occur, reasonable and humane alternatives should be made available, and not only because this is likely to reduce resistance to change. That is also the proper thing to do.

A Public-Sector Analogue

Approaches to Figure 2 in the public sector have been rare, but they share much in common with the detailed illustration above. So, brief reference to the structural change in New York's Rehabilitation Services of the Division of Youth will suffice here to suggest what has already been established in detail, albeit in general and business contexts.

Rehabilitation Services initially were organized in terms of Figure 1, and this structure generated a familiar family of effects. That structure can be simplified in this way:[104]

Rehabilitation Services

in-take assessment placement after-care facility personnel

In brief, Services departmentalized in terms of major function, and its "managerial unit" encompassed the total organization. The prime consequences should surprise no reader of the pages introducing this chapter. To summarize very briefly, these effects of the basic structure were most prominent:

- "This assembly-line approach meant that no one person was responsible for a particular youth; hence the service flow was often inconsistent and haphazard."[105]
- "Communications . . . were sometimes nonexistent and often strained and hostile."[106]
- "Relationships between functions were often based on personality of staff members rather than service to youth. . . ."[107]

Moreover, the easy explanation of these effects can be ruled out. The Services had "numerous committed, creative, and talented staff members," a diagnostic report notes.

That the effects above had structural causes, in the main, can be inferred from the results of a reorganization. The Services switched to a Figure 2 model, and profound changes in behavior and attitude occurred. Basically, the Services departmentalized around relatively autonomous units, Youth Service Teams, and each team comprised a managerial unit, for most purposes. The basic structure thus became:

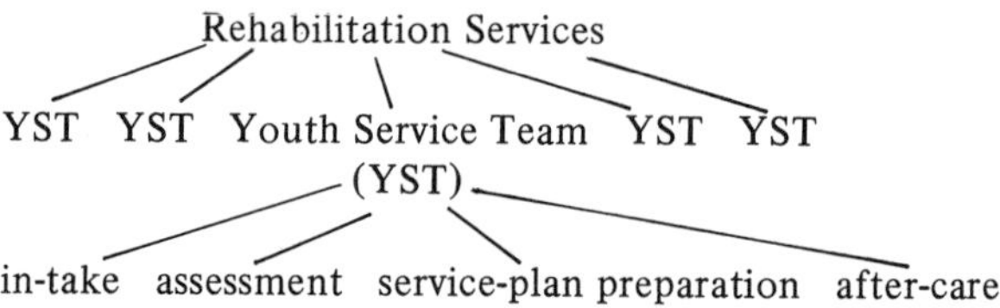

The new structure was designed and implemented in an OD mode, and its effects include:

- A "shift from compartmentalizations of service to continuity of services."[108]
- Decisions about placement are made "closer to the information upon which the placement decision is based. . . ."[109]
- ". . . management by authority and circumvention of structure has given way to collaborative problem solving."[110]

Notes

1. Michael Beer, "The Technology of Organization Development," p. 983, in Marvin D. Dunnette (ed.), *Handbook of Industrial and Organizational Psychology* (Chicago: Rand McNally, 1976).
2. Michael Beer and Edgar F. Huse, "A Systems Approach to Organizational Development," *Journal of Applied Behavioral Science,* Vol. 8 (January 1972), pp. 79-101.
3. Paul R. Lawrence and Jay W. Lorsch, *Organization and Environment* (Boston: Harvard Graduate School of Business Administration, 1967), pp. 10-11.
4. For example, see Jay Galbraith, *Designing Complex Organizations* (Reading, Mass.: Addison-Wesley, 1973).
5. A detailed comparison of these models is provided in Robert T. Golembiewski, *Men, Management, and Morality* (New York: McGraw-Hill, 1965). For corroborative evidence, see Elliott Chapple and Leonard R. Sayles, *The Measure of Management* (New York: Macmillan, 1971); and Eric Trist, Gurth W. Higgin, H. Murray, and A. B. Pollack, *Organizational Choice* (London: Tavistock Institute, 1963). The presentation here is simplified, as a comparison with other sources can establish. See Jay Galbraith, *Designing Complex Organizations* (Reading, Mass.: Addison-Wesley, 1973),

pp. 14-15, who distinguishes two basic approaches to organizational design: (1) reduce the need for information processing, which can be approached by creating slack resources or by developing self-contained units: (2) increase the capacity to process information, as by investing in vertical information systems or by improving lateral relations. Basically, the analysis here emphasizes organizing around self-contained units and improving lateral relations.

6. Robert N. Ford, *Motivation through the Work Itself* (New York: American Management Association, 1969).
7. Alfred J. Marrow, "Managerial Revolution in the State Department," *Personnel,* Vol. 43 (November-December 1966), pp. 6-7. See also Marrow's *Making Waves on Foggy Bottom* (Washington, D.C.: NTL Institute, 1974); and Donald P. Warwick, *A Theory of Public Bureaucracy: Politics, Personality, and Organization in the State Department* (Cambridge, Mass.: Harvard University, 1975).
8. Robert T. Golembiewski, *Organizing Men and Power: Patterns of Behavior and Line-Staff Models* (Chicago: Rand McNally, 1967), p. 153.
9. Golembiewski, *Organizing Men and Power,* pp. 60-267.
10. Leonard R. Sayles, *Managerial Behavior* (New York: McGraw-Hill, 1964), esp. pp. 58-82. Specifically, the relevance of regenerative systems increases, as does the scope and complexity of the task. Leonard R. Sayles and Margaret Chandler, *Managing Large Systems* (New York: Harper and Row, 1971), p. 26, provide incisive illustration: ". . . in very large programs with long lead times incremental decisions must be made before the results of prior decisions are known. Step 4 depends on what happens in Step 3, but it may be necessary to begin 4 without knowing the results of 3." Patently, low openness and trust in such a case could be catastrophic.
11. Floyd C. Mann and Richard Hoffman, *Automation and the Worker: A Study of Social Change in Power Plants* (New York: Holt, Rinehart, Winston, 1960).
12. Roger Harrison, "Effective Organization for Startup," mimeographed (Cambridge, Mass.: Development Research Associates, July 8, 1970), pp. 3 and 5.
13. To extend the argument, win/lose competition also is less useful at an interfirm or internation level. The magnitude of many projects requires exquisite coordination between "competing" firms, for example. And I have heard a major aerospace official say that, whatever the political issues between us, acute practical considerations require advanced cooperation between American and foreign firms as well as governments to cope with various projects in space, transportation, and so on.
14. Chris Argyris, *Interpersonal Competence and Organizational Effectiveness* (Homewood, Ill.: Dorsey, 1962), p. 4.
15. Sayles and Chandler, *Managing Large Systems,* p. 104.

16. Warren G. Bennis, "Organizations of the Future," *Personnel Administration,* Vol. 30 (September 1967), p. 16.
17. Richard M. Hodgetts, "Leadership Techniques in the Project Organization," *Journal of the Academy of Management,* Vol. 11 (June 1968), pp. 211-220; and Gordon L. Lippitt, "Team Building for Matrix Organizations," in Gordon L. Lippitt, Leslie E. This, and Robert G. Bidwell, Jr., *Optimizing Human Resources* (Reading, Mass.: Addison-Wesley, 1971), pp. 158-170.
18. Hans J. Thamhain and David L. Wilemon, "Conflict Management in Project Life Cycles," *Sloan Management Review,* Vol. 16 (Spring 1975), pp. 31-50.
19. Warren G. Bennis, *Changing Organizations* (New York: McGraw-Hill, 1966), pp. 15-16.
20. David S. Brown, "Shaping the Organization to Fit People," *Management of Personnel Quarterly,* Vol. 5 (Summer 1966), pp. 12-16.
21. Chris Argyris, *Personality and Organization* (New York: Harper and Row, 1957), especially pp. 49-53.
22. For a useful review of some of these issues, see William G. Scott, *The Management of Conflict: Appeals Systems in Organizations* (Homewood, Ill.: Irwin, 1965).
23. Alvin Toffler, *Future Shock* (New York: Random House, 1970), pp. 119-120.
24. The temptation is great where such change agents use sensitivity training sessions, for example, during which much data about individuals and groups may be divulged. A similar problem faces such professionals as psychiatrists or lawyers employed by organizations.
25. Warren G. Bennis and Philip E. Slater, *The Temporary Society* (New York: Harper and Row, 1968).
26. P. G. Herbst, *Autonomous Group Functioning* (London: Tavistock, 1962).
27. Golembiewski, *Organizing Men and Power.*
28. Robert R. Blake and Jane Srygley Mouton, *Corporate Excellence through Grid Organizational Development* (Houston: Gulf Publishing, 1968), Appendix II; Philip J. Browne, "Organizational Images: An Exploratory-Descriptive Study" (Ph.D. dissertation, University of Oregon, 1971); and Brown and Robert T. Golembiewski "Line-Staff Concept Revisited: An Empirical Study of Organizational Images," *Academy of Management Journal,* Vol. 17 (September 1974), pp. 406-417.
29. For one detailed analysis of the ebb-and-flow of a major OD program, see Warwick, *A Theory of Public Bureaucracy.*
30. Golembiewski, *Organizing Men and Power,* pp. 99-110 and 154-173. For a classic description of the multiple problems that can hamstring such changeovers, consult Herbert Kaufman, *The New York City Health Centers* (New York: Inter-University Case Program, Case No. 9).

31. For the analytic argument, consult Golembiewski, *Organizing Men and Power.* For some relevant research, see Robert T. Golembiewski, "Personality and Organization Structure: Staff Models and Behavioral Problems," *Academy of Management Journal,* Vol. 9 (September 1967), pp. 211-230; and Brown and Golembiewski, "Line-Staff Concept Revisited." The lessons from operating experience are reflected in such sources as Tony Olkiewicz and Bill Bevans, "Total Quality System," Personnel Department, General Foods Corporation, White Plains, N.Y., April 1978, esp. pp. 3, 6, and 8.

32. Herbert G. Wilcox has accumulated evidence of this socialization effect with an interesting research design. "The Culture Trait of Hierarchy in Middle Class Children," *Public Administration Review,* Vol. 28 (May 1968), pp. 222-235.

33. Mason Haire, E. E. Ghiselli, and Lyman W. Porter, "Cultural Patterns in the Role of the Manager," *Industrial Relations,* Vol. 2 (February 1963), pp. 95-118.

34. A useful normative comparison to this volume is provided by Golembiewski, *Men, Management, and Morality.*

35. For major emphases in such a treatment, consult such sources as Noel M. Tichy, "When Does Work Restructuring Work?" *Organizational Dynamics,* Vol. 5 (Summer 1976), esp. pp. 66-69; and Louis E. Davis, "Evolving Alternative Organization Designs: Their Sociotechnical Bases," *Human Relations,* Vol. 30, no. 3 (1977), pp. 261-273.

36. Conveniently, consult the full-issue symposium of Richard B. Petersen (ed.), "Current Perspectives in Job Design," *Journal of Contemporary Business,* Vol. 6, no. 2 (1977).

37. "French Government Funds Spur Innovative Job-Enrichment Plans," *World of Work Report,* Vol. 2 (November 1977), p. 123; and Newton Margulies, Penny L. Wright, and Richard W. Scholl, "Organization Development Techniques: Their Impact on Change," *Group and Organization Studies,* Vol. 2 (December 1977), esp. pp. 439-441.

38. This crucial point constitutes the central thrust of warnings against technocratic myopia, warnings typified by: Loren Baritz, *The Servants of Power* (Middletown, Conn.: Wesleyan University, 1960); and Ethan A. Singer and Leland M. Wooton, "The Triumph and Failure of Albert Speer's Administrative Genius: Implications for Current Management Theory and Practice," *Journal of Applied Behavioral Science,* Vol. 12 (January 1976), pp. 79-103.

39. Antone F. Alber, "Job Enrichment Programs Seen Improving Employee Performance, But Benefits Not Without Cost," *World of Work Report,* Vol. 3 (January 1978), p. 8.

40. Edwin A. Locke, David Sirota, and Alan D. Wolfson, "An Experimental Case Study of Successes and Failures of Job Enrichment in a Government Agency," *Journal of Applied Psychology,* Vol. 61, no. 6 (1976), pp. 701-711, for example, puzzle over the failure of an application to impact on

employee attitudes even as it was associated with higher productivity and reduced absenteeism.

41. Stephen A. Stumpf, "Using Integrators to Manage Conflict in a Research Organization," *Journal of Applied Behavioral Science,* Vol. 13 (October 1977), p. 507.

42. Eric Trist, "Retrospect and Prospect," *Journal of Applied Behavioral Science,* Vol. 13 (July 1977), p. 275; and Margulies, Wright, and Scholl, "Organization Development Techniques," pp. 441-443.

43. For example, by Thomas G. Cummings, "Sociotechnical Systems: An Intervention Strategy," pp. 187-215, in W. Warner Burke (ed.), *Current Issues and Strategies in Organization Development* (New York: Human Science, 1977); and Richard N. Ottaway, "A Change Strategy to Implement New Norms, New Styles and New Environment in the Work Organization," *Personnel Review,* Vol. 5 (Winter 1976), pp. 13-18.

44. Cummings, "Sociotechnical Systems," p. 188.

45. Trist, "Retrospect and Prospect," p. 275.

46. Richard E. Walton, "Work Innovations at Topeka: After Six Years," *Journal of Applied Behavioral Science,* Vol. 13 (July 1977), p. 422.

47. Ibid., pp. 422-423; and "Self-Work Teams at Butler Plant Cut Costs, Raise Profitability," *World of Work Report,* Vol. 2 (November 1977), p. 124.

48. Thomas G. Cummings and Walter H. Griggs, "Worker Reactions to Autonomous Work Groups," *Organization and Administrative Sciences,* Vol. 4 (1976-1977), pp. 87-100.

49. Josep F. Bolweg, *Job Design and Industrial Democracy: The Case of Norway,* Vol. 3, International Series on the Quality of Working Life, p. 36.

50. "Stonewalling Plant Democracy," *Business Week,* March 28, 1977, pp. 78-82.

51. Stanley M. Davis and Paul R. Lawrence, *Matrix* (Reading, Mass.: Addison-Wesley, 1977), esp. p. 20.

52. As in Frederick Thayer, *An End to Hierarchy! An End to Competition!* (New York: New Viewpoints, 1973). See also P. G. Herbst, "Non-Hierarchical Forms of Organization," *Acta Sociologica,* Vol. 19, no. 1 (1976), pp. 65-75; and his *Alternative to Hierarchies* (Leiden, The Netherlands: Martinus Nijhoff, 1976).

53. A broad range of literature is relevant here. Illustratively, see: Sayles and Chandler, *Managing Large Systems;* Alfred D. Chandler, *Strategy and Structure* (Boston: Massachusetts Institute of Technology, 1962); Golembiewski, *Men, Management, and Morality;* Golembiewski and Allan Kiepper, "MARTA: Toward An Effective, Open Giant," *Public Administration Review,* Vol. 36 (January 1976), pp. 46-60; and Harvey M. Sapolsky, *POLARIS* (Cambridge, Mass.: Harvard University, 1972).

54. To get a flavor of the supporting detailed empirical research, consult Johannes M. Pennings, "Dimensions of Organizational Influence and Their Effectiveness Correlates," *Administrative Science Quarterly,* Vol. 21 (December 1976), pp. 688-699.
55. Only a sparse literature deals with organizations in socialist countries, and OD effort there has only begun, most notably in Poland.
56. Readers may remember that the "aggressive reactions" to adult leaders with autocratic styles were quite rare in the Lewin, Lippitt, and White classic experiments with group atmospheres or climates. For an intriguing overview, consult Robert Munzenrider, *Organization Climates.* Ph.D. dissertation, University of Georgia, 1976, Chapters I and II.
57. The controversial Milgram experiments graphically reflect the degree of acceptance of authority, even when another individual is apparently being hurt. See Stanley Milgram, *Obedience to Authority* (New York: Harper and Row, 1974).
58. This was the basic Nazi defense about war atrocities during World War II, of course, although Allied courts did not accept it.
59. The analogy is nicely developed by Jerry B. Harvey and D. Richard Albertson, "Neurotic Organizations: Symptoms, Causes and Treatments," Parts I and II, *Personnel Journal,* Vol. 50 (September 1971), pp. 694-699 and (October 1971), pp. 770-777.
60. Sapolsky, *POLARIS;* Sayles and Chandler, *Managing Large Systems;* and Golembiewski and Kiepper, "MARTA."
61. Sayles and Chandler, *Managing Large Systems.*
62. Sapolsky, *POLARIS.*
63. W. Warner Burke, "Organization Development in Transition," *Journal of Applied Behavioral Science,* Vol. 12 (January 1976), esp. pp. 27-28, notes the recent change in this regard.
64. This has been a dominant theme of much research over the past two or three decades, of course. For one approach, see Newton Margulies, "Organizational Culture and Psychological Growth," *Journal of Applied Behavioral Science,* Vol. 5 (October 1969), pp. 491-508.
65. The most prominent application of the laboratory approach to a structured work environment is provided by Alfred D. Marrow, David G. Bowers, and Stanley Seashore, *Management by Participation* (New York: Harper and Row, 1967). But little attention is given to the specific linkages of the socioemotional and technical systems. It appears the laboratory approach was more or less used to reduce resistance to the technical changes.
66. Frederick Herzberg, et al., *The Motivation to Work* (New York: Wiley, 1959); and Herzberg, *Work and the Nature of Man* (Cleveland, Ohio: World Publishing, 1966).

67. For example, factor-analytic studies show that much covariation in data batches can be accounted for by motivator and hygiene clusters of variables. But the same research indicates that the two-factor model requires modification. Robert B. Ewen, Charles L. Hulin, Patricia Cain Smith, and Edwin A. Locke, "An Empirical Test of the Herzberg Two-Factor Theory," *Journal of Applied Psychology*, Vol. 50 (November 6, 1966), pp. 544-550; and Charles L. Hulin and Patricia A. Smith, "An Empirical Investigation of Two Implications of the Two-Factor Theory of Job Satisfaction," *Journal of Applied Psychology*, Vol. 51, no. 5 (1967), pp. 396-402.
68. See Robert N. Ford, *Motivation Through the Work Itself* (New York: American Management Association, 1969), pp. 23-26.
69. Ibid., pp. 153-158.
70. Ibid., p. 25.
71. Ibid., pp. 13-15.
72. This account is synthesized from ibid., pp. 26-41. Also, see William W. Dettelback and Philip Kraft, "Organization Change through Job Enrichment," *Training and Development Journal*, Vol. 25 (August 1971), pp. 2-7. Similar and earlier efforts toward greater need satisfaction through job design had developed independent of Herzberg's major distinction between motivators and hygiene factors. See especially Louis E. Davis, "Job Design and Productivity," *Personnel*, Vol. 33 (March 1957), esp. pp. 419-427, and his "The Design of Jobs," *Industrial Relations*, Vol. 6, no. 1 (1966), pp. 21-45.
73. One argument of this genre is provided by Mitchell Fein, *Motivation for Work*, Monograph No. 4 (New York: American Institute of Industrial Engineers, 1971).
74. Ford, *Motivation Through Work Itself*, pp. 31-41.
75. Reproduced by special permission from *The Journal of Applied Behavioral Science*. "A Failure of Job Enrichment: The Case of the Change That Wasn't," by Linda L. Frank and J. Richard Hackman, Vol. 11, no. 4 (October 1976), p. 414. Copyright by NTL Institute, 1976.
76. William Gomberg, "Job Satisfaction: Sorting Out the Nonsense," *AFL-CIO American Federationist* (June 1973). For a balanced view, see Frank Friedlander and L. Dave Brown, "Organization Development," *Annual Review of Psychology*, Vol. 25 (1974), pp. 322-325.
77. Frank and Hackman, "A Failure of Job Enrichment"; J. Richard Hackman, "On the Coming Demise of Job Enrichment," in Eugene L. Cass (ed.), *Man and Work in Society* (New York: Van Nostrand-Reinhold, 1975); and Samuel C. Florman, "The Job-Enrichment Mistake: Limitations of the Work Ethic," *Harper's Magazine*, Vol. 252 (May 1976), pp. 18-22.
78. Fred Emery and Einar Thorsrud, *Democracy at Work* (Leiden: The Netherlands: Martinus Nijhoff, 1976).

79. Beer, "The Technology of Organization Development," pp. 971-976; E. M. Glaser, *Improving the Quality of Worklife . . . And in the Process, Improving Productivity* (Los Angeles: Human Interaction Research Institute, 1974); and David Sirota and A. D. Wolfson, "Job Enrichment: What are the Obstacles?" *Personnel,* Vol. 49 (May 1972), pp. 8-17.

80. Frank and Hackman, "A Failure of Job Enrichment," esp. pp. 429-435.

81. Ibid., p. 430.

82. Bolweg, *Job Design and Industrial Democracy,* pp. 37-38.

83. Irmtraud Streeker Seeborg, "The Influence of Employee Participation in Job Design," *Journal of Applied Behavioral Science,* Vol. 14 (January 1978), p. 87.

84. Louis E. Davis, "Developments in Job Design," pp. 67-73, in Peter B. Warr (ed.), *Personal Goals and Work Design* (London: Wiley, 1975).

85. Bolweg, *Job Design and Industrial Democracy,* p. 34.

86. Herzberg, et al., *The Motivation to Work.*

87. Frank and Hackman, "A Failure of Job Enrichment," esp. p. 430.

88. Kae H. Chung and Monica F. Ross, "Differences in Motivational Properties Between Job Enlargement and Job Enrichment," *Academy of Management Review,* Vol. 2 (January 1977), pp. 113-122.

89. J. Richard Hackman, "Work Design," pp. 115-128, in J. Richard Hackman and J. Lloyd Suttle, *Improving Life at Work* (Santa Monica, Calif.: Goodyear Publishing, 1977).

90. Anthony G. Barret, Jr., and Anthony J. Reilly, "Abstracts," *Group and Organization Studies,* Vol. 1 (September 1976), p. 374.

91. Frank and Hackman, "A Failure of Job Enrichment," pp. 429-435. For an empirical method for isolating areas in organizations especially amenable to job enlargement, see Randall B. Dunham, "Reactions to Job Characteristics: Moderating Effects of the Organization," *Academy of Management Journal,* Vol. 20 (March 1977), esp. p. 62. Also relevant would be employee responses to such scales as the Likert Profile, the nature of the macro-organization structure as sketched by contrast in the second section of this chapter, and an organization's basic values or character or stage of development (see Chapter 8).

92. Emery and Thorsrud, *Democracy at Work,* p. 37.

93. Frank and Hackman, "A Failure of Job Enrichment," p. 434.

94. Ibid., p. 433.

95. For impressive evidence of the significance of such efforts, see Albert S. King, "Expectation Effects in Organizational Change," *Administrative Science Quarterly,* Vol. 19 (June 1974), pp. 221-230.

96. For an early exception in business see Richard Beckhard, "An Organization Improvement Program in a Decentralized Organization," *Journal of Applied*

Behavioral Science, Vol. 2 (January 1960), pp. 3-26. For one of the few public sector applications, consult notes 104 to 110 below and their accompanying text.

97. John M. Ivancevich and James H. Donnelly, Jr., "Relation of Organizational Structure to Job Satisfaction, Anxiety-Stress, and Performance," *Administrative Science Quarterly,* Vol. 20 (June 1975), pp. 272-280.
98. Paul Lawrence, *The Changing of Organizational Behavior Patterns* (Boston: Division of Research, Harvard Business School, 1958).
99. Reproduced by special permission from *The Journal of Applied Behavioral Science,* "A Structural Approach to Organizational Change," by Robert A. Luke, Jr., Peter Block, Jack M. Davey, and Vernon Averch, Vol. 9, no. 5 (1973), pp. 622-623.
100. Ibid., esp. pp. 623-628.
101. Ibid., esp. pp. 626-631.
102. Ibid., p. 622.
103. Michael Beer and James W. Driscoll, "Strategies for Change," p. 373, in Hackman and Suttle, *Improving Life at Work.*
104. Donald K. Carew, Sylvia I. Carter, Janice M. Gamache, Rita Hardiman, Bailey Jackson III, and Eunice M. Parisi, "New York State Division for Youth: A Collaborative Approach to the Implementation of Social Change in a Public Bureaucracy," *Journal of Applied Behavioral Science,* Vol. 13 (July 1977), pp. 327-329.
105. Ibid., p. 328.
106. Ibid., p. 327.
107. Ibid., p. 329.
108. Ibid., p. 335.
109. Ibid., p. 336.
110. Ibid., p. 337.
111. Robert T. Golembiewski, *Renewing Organizations: The Laboratory Approach to Planned Change* (Itasca, Ill.: F. E. Peacock, 1972).

Chapter 3

FILLING THE GAPS IN NETWORKS OF AUTHORITY
Ad Hoc Interventions Supplement Formal Structures

Life often presents problems, both aggravating and beyond our ability to change. Indeed, life itself is fundamentally tragic in that the game is played with that penultimate trump card—death—in somebody else's hand. So it is well enough to spot evil or ineffectiveness, and root it out. But life also means continuous coping with some situations and conditions that are variously beyond our capacity to change. We can only do better or worse at coping with them.

In this fundamental sense, Chapter 2 deals with the glamorous issues of root-and-branch change in organizations. This chapter deals with amelioration rather than with basic reconstruction. Indeed, this chapter's title might well be: Making Constructive Response to What Exists. Sometimes, what exists is in a fundamental sense truly unalterable. Most times, what exists is alterable but unaltered for various reasons: people in authority may be unwilling to seek permanent change, despite seeing some real problems with what exists; others may lack wit or courage; still others might be unwilling to exchange what has worked pretty well, on balance, for something more or less unknown.

The chapter deals with three ad hoc OD interventions, each of which basically accepts what exists, and yet seeks to do somewhat better than what exists. In this sense, this chapter reflects on efforts to fine-tune existing institutions or processes, to improve some outcomes while essentially maintaining those institutions or processes.

The first ad hoc intervention illustrated here reports on an effort toward collaborative authority in a restricted area, the design of a job description.

Basically, a manager was willing to depart somewhat from his usual style to solve a particular problem, which was a source of some concern to him. But that manager also was generally content with his usual style and its effects, and did not fundamentally wish to change that style. The illustration, in short, deals with bending rather than breaking.

A second intervention is somewhat more complicated and involves the efforts of a new manager to establish a basic difference from his predecessor in the matter of wanting "straight feedback," and in being willing to respond to it. But, the new manager also wanted to preserve the old formal channels of communication, after blowing the old obstructions out of communication tubes, as it were. The intervention of choice, then, used ad hoc groups to demonstrate the new manager's desire for upward feedback. A successful experience with these temporary groups, it was hoped, would later encourage organization members to use regular channels of communication in different ways than had developed under the past manager.

A third ad hoc intervention is more complex still, dealing as it does with a central dilemma in organizations: how to organize so as to perform well in day-to-day matters while also anticipating the future to better prepare for and adjust to it. Many resolutions to this dilemma have been proposed, perhaps the most common of which is the distinction between "line" and "staff." That is, "line" officials specialize in day-to-day operations, while "staff" concentrates on change and adaption. So problemmatic is this approach,[1] however, that two observers conclude: "Perhaps no area in organization theory stands more in need of clarification than the line-staff concept."[2]

In a nutshell, we will have to try harder to do better. One such effort is the use of "collateral organizations," an intervention which essentially uses temporary groupings for limited problem-solving purposes. The collateral organization phases in and then fades out when its purpose is accomplished, with a relatively specific set of values prescribing appropriate behaviors for members. The formal organization persists as collaterals wax and wane. The goal, patently, is to respond to specific problems without compromising or undercutting the existing formal structure.

Usual notions admit of only one kind of structure at work, which raises the dilemma of whether that one structure should be biased toward steady-state or novel activities. However that choice is made, something is usually lost because most organizations must balance both the novel and the steady-state. The notion of collateral organizations seeks to avoid this loss by rejecting the guiding notion that there can be only one authoritative structure.

A Narrow Intervention Implying Collaborative Authority
Writing a Job Description for Self or a Superior

One OD design based on a collaborative concept of authority in the writing of a job description was inspired by a specific problem. The position in question had caused trouble for over a decade. As one sign, the average tenure in the position over the previous 12 years had been 11 months, followed in all cases by the incumbent being demoted or leaving the company. Consequently, the position had developed quite a reputation, but there was no dearth of fresh candidates for it. Substantial financial rewards encouraged people to try their hand at riding this particular tiger, and the position provided enough visibility in the industry that other outside major opportunities could reasonably be expected. By this time, the position had become an inside joke in the industry, and anything more than a year's tenure was considered a successful performance.

Sketch of an Organizational Problem

The basic difficulty faced by incumbents lay in their being in the middle between headquarters and field units. Over time, the field units more and more became "baronies that go their own way as if there were no corporate interests distinct from their own." Headquarters responded by creating an integrative executive position between the field units and the responsible corporate official. Heads of the field units felt demoted by the insertion of the integrative executive between them and their previous superior. Moreover, that integrative executive was seen as a "headquarter's man," even though he invariably was selected from field personnel.

The field units struggled to preserve their prerogatives, and jurisdictional disputes became the order of the day. Sooner rather than later, the test of power would come, and the integrative executive at that moment was the consistent loser. Headquarters wanted more influence over the field, but not at the expense of creating morale problems among the field personnel in what clearly was a seller's labor market.

One of the first official duties of a newly promoted corporate official was to remove another occupant of the integrative executive position—he had lasted only 9 months—an act apparently followed by a major resolution to slow down the revolving door. The new corporate official had in mind three willing candidates for the position, all from among the six field officials who would be directly supervised by the new integrative executive. And the corporate official had a goal: to keep the incumbent in office at least 18 months.

Design Based on Collaborative Authority

This writer was asked to develop a design to meet the corporate official's goal, and he took a direct approach. The job description for the integrative executive's position was to be rewritten by the six field managers, three of whom were candidates for the position and all of whom would be affected in direct ways by the outcome. In addition, as one factor in his choice of the integrative executive, the corporate official would periodically observe the six field men as they developed the job description.[3] Two consultants would be available throughout the design, both of whom were known to all the field men and to the corporate official. The process observers' goal was to help each of the men show to best advantage.

The corporate official accepted the design, after brief consideration. Three days were quickly set aside for it, with the corporate official specifying only a few features of the job description he considered desirable, although he was not adamant about any of them. The corporate official could envision circumstances under which he would veto some job descriptions. Basically, however, he made a major commitment to a collaborative exercise of authority.

Five features of this design are most prominent. *First,* the design emphasized the induction of empathy for the holder of the position for which the new job description was to be written, and such consideration was an expected result of "taking the role of the other."[4] At least three of the field men were avowed candidates for the job of that Other for whom they were writing a job description. For them, the exercise was very real. Commonly, the field men would evaluate a portion of a job description in such terms: "Now if you were in that slot, and situation X arose, how would you react to it, given element Y in the job description?"

Second, the design hoped to simulate some of the cross-pressure situations that the integrative executive would later face. "So this is how it feels to be in-between," was a typical reflection that the design at times had such an effect. Problem situations were talked through in terms of the provisions of alternative job descriptions, with the goals of anticipating difficulties and of developing some sense of how they might be managed.

Third, the design hoped to increase the sense of owning the job description by all field personnel, as well as by the eventual choice for the integrative executive. The associated theme is, more or less: You made your bed, now . . . and so on.

Fourth, the design intended reducing the potential for jurisdictional conflcits, which had been so divisive over the previous decade. Such reduction could come in two ways: by clarifying what the likely jurisdictional issues would be, given various job descriptions; and by working toward the creation of norms and attitudes that could be applied to the resolution of jurisdictional issues that might develop later.

Fifth, the design sought to introduce another reality element into the choice of the new integrative executive. The promotion choice would be based in some part on public performance on a common task. That is, if X could not work effectively with the others in the learning situation, this would be an important datum that should be considered in making the eventual choice. As it developed, indeed, the 3-day design showed one field official in such a good light that the corporate official felt it necessary to reshuffle his rankings in a major way. His initial first choice still got the promotion, however.

Did the Design Work?

There is no simple evaluation of this design. The corporate official found it easy to live with the job description, even though he would have written it much differently. Moreover, the corporate official's goal was met, and that eminently satisfied him. At last reckoning, the new integrative executive had been in office for 28 months. How much of that tenure can be attributed to the design is moot, of course. Only one point is not debatable. The design was a grueling one for all concerned. The participants drifted away quickly when the job description was completed and after the choice for the new integrative executive was announced. "I slunk home to stick my head in the sand," one participant announced. "I bled through every pore for the guy who was to fill that job description. And I wasn't even a candidate!"

Engaging Vertical Feedback Processes in Large Organizations
Using Ad Hoc Groups to Communicate up the Hierarchy

The primal linkage in organizations is vertical, between one hierarchical level and another level with broader responsibilities. Indeed, without viable vertical linkages, not even modest-sized organizations could exist for very long. Moreover, despite devices for reducing the social distance between hierarchical levels, such as decentralized patterns of delegation, power sharing, and the like, hierarchical levels there will be. Hence, the quality of upward communication will remain a critical factor in an organization's effectiveness.

The illustration below deals with one OD design for engaging feedback processes in large organizations,[5] under inhospitable circumstances. The intent was to provide a quick stimulant to unclog vertical feedback channels, as it were, after which temporary booster it was hoped that the formal chain of command could do the required job. The following analysis will move from a description of the organizational context in which the OD design was introduced, to a discussion of the nature of the design and its consequences. The illustration will conclude with a rationale that helps explain the effectiveness of the simple design.

An Existing Degenerative System Between Hierarchical Levels

The organizational context into which the OD design was introduced was a classic degenerative system, and for credible reasons. *First,* the parent organization was beset by a variety of massive problems that called into serious question what and how it had traditionally done.

Second, the prime consequence was a massive holding-action. From lower levels, it appeared to be inaction born of indecisiveness and unwillingness to "bite the bullet." To those at the executive levels, the holding action was unavoidable as necessary data were being gathered, as options were being analyzed, and so on.

Third, the overall organizational climate was characterized by rumors and secrecy. That is, rumors flourished in the absence of clear statements of where the organization was going. And secrecy characterized executive deliberations, because news of even the most tentative possible option would sweep through the organization as that day's infallible pronouncement.

Fourth, a mutual despair clearly set in. Those at lower levels of organization often concluded that management decision-making did not inspire confidence. Those at upper levels emphasized the lack of impulse control of those subordinate to them, as well as their lack of comprehension of the complex issues that needed deliberate thrashing out.

Fifth, major personnel reductions-in-force traumatized the organization. A major reduction in 1969 was widely regarded as the purge to end all purges. The usual explanations about "trimming the fat" and "tightening the belt" were common, and they may have induced some overconfidence among the survivors. The unexpected other shoe fell about a year after the first reduction-in-force and cut very deeply. The organization was shaken, especially because it appeared that: "The organization is asking for more loyalty from its employees, but it seems to feel little loyalty to its employees."

Middle managers felt particularly whipsawed. They had to absorb the reasonable concerns of their employees, but they received little of substance from the executive levels. The managers were truly in the middle, above the lower levels and outside the confidences of the executive suite.

New Division Manager Seeks to Establish Viable Vertical Linkages

In the aftermath of the second reduction-in-force, a new division manager appointed from outside the organization set as one of his major priorities the reestablishment of solid communication links with his middle managers. At the initiative of an OD specialist, the division manager authorized a simple feedback design, to dramatize his intentions as well as to begin massive upward communication. The design involved all middle managers—approximately sixty of them—meeting in five-man groups composed of the widest possible range of functions or activities. Their charge was simple. They were to prepare reports for the division manager, of no specified form, but touching at least on: what they liked about their division and company and what they disliked, or what they were concerned about. The groups attended two scheduled meetings and continued to meet on their own initiative afterwards. The division manager then would meet with each of the ad hoc groups to discuss their reports, share information, clarify ambiguities, and so on.

An Illustrative Report

The basic intent was to reverse a degenerative sequence, and the ad hoc groups had decided on the specific levels of openness which they felt were risky enough. The reports covered a broad range, some with dazzle and some cautiously. One group, for example, described its feelings of being a mushroom: "Kept in the dark, up to their necks in fertilizer, and waiting to be canned." Quite revealing, that metaphor. Exhibit 1 represents one of the most extensive and open of these reports. Brief or descriptive labels have been substituted for names of products, projects, or references that have no meaning to the outside reader. Otherwise, the report appears as it was submitted.

Designs like that above have proved widely useful in large organizations. For example, "sensing groups" constitute one variety of the genre.[6] As used in TRW, employees in unstructured, small groups generate wide ranges of thoughts and feelings about their jobs and the organizations in which they work, with the goal of providing the raw data to which managerial response might be tailored. Over the years, more than 20,000 TRW employees have participated in ad hoc sensing groups with one focus or another. Similarly, temporary sensing groups also were used in SmithKline Corp. to help design a major opinion survey. More or less, such usages all employ various modifications of the approach used at Detroit Edison for "concern groups" that focus on issues at work that bother members. The focus may be broadly on the job, or narrowly on a specific area. In all cases, the central question form remains: What bugs you about . . .? Cash and Minter provide these guidelines for convenors of concern groups, whose membership will vary from situation to situation but whose anonymity always will be preserved:

- The sessions present employees with an opportunity to share ideas, frustrations, and feelings about aspects of their work which concern them.
- The convenor records the concerns expressed, being careful to check continuously with participants concerning the appropriateness of his interpretations.

Exhibit 1 Feedback Report Induced by OD Design

CONFIDENTIAL

January 22, 1971

Memo To: Division Manager

From: Messrs. A, B, C, D, and E

Subject: Division Feedback Exercise

Attached is an outline of our discussions during last week's feedback session and subsequent meetings. We appreciate the opportunity to bring these matters to your attention.

DIVISION FEEDBACK EXERCISE

Positive Signs

We sense stronger leadership at the top, and have guarded optimism that the Division Manager will develop a strong team.

We have seen examples of greater decisiveness; greater willingness to take positive action after reasonable evaluation of pertinent facts and opinions (programs L and Z).

Division must have a more articulate voice to express its viewpoint to top management. Recent events (A, B, C, and D are samples) are promising examples of what we'd like to see more of.

The strong commitment to management by objectives (MBO), while the implementation will be painful at times, should get us results in the long run.

Concerns

Planning and Priorities

1. Top management should have better appreciation/feeling for what is reasonable and/or realistic when making requests for action or initiating work projects. Since top management tends to deal in more abstract, philosophical problems, we feel they lose sight, from time to time, of nuts and bolts of how things are done on the firing line.
2. Great deal of concern expressed for where we're going and how we're going to get there. Considerable reservations (or lack of faith) in some recent and/or planned ventures implemented as stop-gap measures; for example:
   a. Product A—question $ payoff in view of eroding market potential.
   b. Product B—extremely time-consuming effort that will probably lose money.
   c. Product C—turned out to be a real detraction from earnings.
3. We are concerned about the arbitrary and uncoordinated manner in which cost-reduction programs are being implemented. Some of the steps taken indicate top management has no confidence in the ability of middle management to operate efficiently within budget guidelines.

   Management should explain what each policy change means in terms of savings and report this information honestly.

Recommendations

1. Top management should develop greater knowledge/appreciation of complexities of their areas of responsibility. Also they should not always assume attitude their people can do anything and/or surmount all odds. But, middle management should say no or be more forceful in advising superiors of unrealistic requests.
2. Feel major problem with this area of concern involves a lack of communications from top management on what's behind these projects in terms of decision-making process, alternatives, and financial risks. Perhaps if people knew more about these matters, they'd have more confidence in getting various ventures underway.
3. Undoubtedly, many of the changes will result in significant reductions in our operating cost and therefore are needed. However, when the changes are strung out consecutively, each one seems only to put another nail in the coffin. It would be much better to plan the necessary changes and make them simultaneously, so the employees could concentrate on what needs to be done to improve our future rather than worry about what further jobs, benefits, and privileges will be lost.

   In the case of cost-reduction programs or travel policy changes, we would appreciate the opportunity to participate in finding solutions to the problems rather than merely accepting a dictated alternative. This would give us a sense of "ownership" in the decision and more commitment to its successful implementation.

Exhibit 1 (Continued)

4. We are concerned that the current profit center approach of charging for services can work against positive benefits. We suspect that Subsidiaries M and O probably are not taking advantage of services in other areas of the company because they cannot afford the cost. For the budget people, this probably seems proper, but if the spin-off operations become less efficient because of this, it can only work to the disadvantage of the corporation.	4. Don't let "budgets" (particularly where fixed overhead costs are involved) influence what is and should be done. Something between a no-charge system and total charging where even a discussion is entered on the charge sheet could surely be worked out.
Human Resources	
5. Workloads have increased to the point where there is some concern with our ability to get the job done in the best possible manner. Time and priority pressures are causing managers to sacrifice attention to the kind of supervisory (and development of subordinate) duties they feel are necessary. This situation can have detrimental effects on: a. morale b. efficiency c. development of adequate back-up talent	5. While we recognize that all workloads will and should be heavier than in the past, we must: a. minimize unnecessary or unrealistic projects b. have earlier dropping of projects that have little chance for real success c. be satisfied with less information for decision-making. Must give recognition to the need for supervisory/managerial requirements in priority setting. Should also give managers more input in judging value of assignments and allow more questioning of priorities. Trade-offs and alternatives are as important to priority setting as to budgeting.
6. We do not see any evidence, other than occasional lip service, of an overt managerial development program at division or corporate level. Such programs would seem important to: a. progress of individuals b. development of the strongest possible organization c. promotion from within	6. Design and undertake, with input from middle management, specific development programs.
7. A lack of credibility has long existed in some corporate communications. This credibility gap has been widened recently in communications re salary policy changes, severance pay and insurance policy, the establishment and discontinuance of the cost-reduction study.	7. Don't sugar coat the message. Don't assume managers are unable to see through specious arguments or explanations. The cure for this problem is obvious; we need management to communicate with us honestly and frankly so that reductions in staff, benefits, and programs can be put in perspective, particularly with respect to the anticipated results.
8. On Division matters it is evident that the flow of communications down varies from one department to another.	8. Make a greater effort to insure prompt and simultaneous downward flow of information. The distribution of the '71 Marketing Operating Plan, while it carries certain risks, is, in balance, a very positive step forward in communication.

- The meeting assumes that no perfect work site exists, and concerns expressed will provide top management and the convenor with a problem census which later can be used to direct searches for causes and solutions.
- The concern group may or may not be involved in the later problem-solving, but in either case that will be announced initially to participants.
- Convenor announces to the concern group that feedback to its members about actions to be taken will occur by some specific date.
- Convenor should insist on these norms for the meeting:

  Solutions should *not* be explored by participants in the concern group; that remains management's responsibility, for later.

  Anonymity shall be scrupulously respected, both in the concern group and in later meetings with management.

  Evaluation, criticism, or defense of contributions should be minimized.

These guidelines are not sacrosanct, of course, and other organizations have begun to experiment with less-bounded varieties of similar complements to the formal structure. Consider a "microcosm group" of twelve members selected to be representative of all work groups, hierarchical levels, and major demographic classes in an organization of 250 members.[7] The microcosm group not only assisted in developing a survey and feedback intervention, but had a charge that was time-extensive: to facilitate the improvement of communication between hierarchical levels and individual work units.

Why Such Simple OD Designs Can Succeed

The growing reliance on designs that supplement the formal authority structure implies a clear message: that existing formal relationships may be variously inflexible and unresponsive to problem situations, and in some cases those relationships constitute or contribute to the difficulties.

To suggest the breadth of the advantages possible with such simple OD designs, more specifically, seven factors that help explain why and how the open report in Exhibit 1 came to be generated. *First,* all middle managers involved had been exposed to a sensitivity-training experience in the year or two preceding their involvement in this feedback design. The OD design, indeed, was presented as an organizational extension of that initial training, as an opportunity to put into practice the values, attitudes, and behavioral skills that had been worked on in T-groups. This earlier training experience presumably contributed to the preparation of reports.

Second, in cases such as the one above, the OD feedback design amounts to taking the cork out of the communication bottle. The very act of requesting feedback thus may generate a gushing forth of repressed material. Indeed, the catharsis may be so dominant that the products of such designs, once expressed, may be more pointed than is appropriate. Once the concerns are ventilated, they should be easier to set in a more realistic perspective.

Third, there may be a tendency to give a new authority figure a chance to prove self. If he makes a point of asking for feedback and commits many hours of time to the task, employees probably assume that the request means what it says.

Fourth, the design's use of groups may help express information that individuals might feel inhibited about revealing. Often, such feedback designs make organization members aware of how many things they do share. Such reinforcement of observations is very potent stuff indeed,[8] and care is appropriate lest these social processes inhibit reporting the off-beat or deviant notion that could be significant. Many of the reports in this case indicate minority opinions, which is a healthy sign.

Fifth, anonymity may help generate openness, although that particular sword cuts several ways. In this case, anonymity for individuals was possible. But the group clearly owned its report and had to be willing to discuss it face-to-face with the division manager. This feature may have smoothed some of the edges off some reports, but the manager preferred not to deal with anonymous feedback.

Sixth, competition between groups can encourage openness, up to a point. Beyond some indeterminate point, that competition could help generate reports with a quality of "Can you top this?" This quality may be false to reality.

Seventh, action provides the major motivator of openness in such OD feedback designs. Initially, the hope of action may be enough. Beyond that, only the expectation of action is likely to be a motivator. Feedback without action will be perceived as manipulative, or worse. Indeed, if no action is anticipated in response to feedback, it hardly matters whether the feedback is open or accurate. Hence, the division manager was careful to act on the feedback reports wherever he could, to initiate studies where necessary, and to explain lack of action where he had no other choice, for the new manager was serious about reestablishing viable vertical communication linkages between himself and middle managers.

Temporary Formations for Problem-Solving
Character and Consequences of Collateral Organizations*

Dale Zand correctly describes the overall bias of the OD literature in a recent article, and he also details a useful corrective for that bias in his description of "collateral organizations." These Zand defines as parallel, continuously

*This section depends heavily on Dale E. Zand, "Collateral Organization: A New Change Strategy," *Journal of Applied Behavioral Science,* Vol. 10 (January 1974), pp. 63-99; and Dale E. Zand, Matthew B. Miles, and William O. Lytle, Jr., "Enlarging Organization Choice Through Use of a Temporary Problem-Solving System" (mimeographed).

coexisting units "which a manager can use to supplement his or her existing formal organization. Collateral organizations have norms differing from those usually in force, and are used to identify and solve apparently intractable problems, and are carefully linked to the 'regular' organization. No new people are required."[9] In effect, Zand extends and elaborates on the limited-purpose and temporary sensing groups described immediately above.

The contrast between the typical OD bias and the notion of collateral organizations may be developed briefly. Simply but accurately, much of the OD literature advises replacing of what may be called the "authority/production-center" system of organizing, like the traditional model for organizing discussed in Chapter 2. The prescribed replacement is a "knowledge/problem-centered" system, with characteristics like those attributed to the unorthodox model in Chapter 2. Managers, however, often get anxious about any such wholesale replacement, for bureaucratic systems may be useful for organizing certain kinds of work, and no doubt will be variously relied on at times in most or all organizations.

That is, subtle snares inhere in the OD thrust toward replacing traditional systems for organizing. For example, Zand explains that "poorly conceptualized OD efforts" may lead organization members to believe that it will never again be necessary to "need directive behavior, specialized assignments, and limited communication." These expectations must prove unrealistic, Zand adds, usually sooner rather than later. The costs can be severe. "Upon 'regressing' to the authority/production mode," Zand explains, "managers feel guilty and disappointed. Subordinates are frustrated and dissatisfied at relinquishing their newly found influence. Managers and subordinates frequently conclude that organizational development is a sham." Moreover, organizations whose primary mode is knowledge/problem-centered may also unrealistically resist flexibility in their reliance on one structural mode. Zand notes that "research units and educational institutions resist using the authority/production mode when it is needed, fearing that the primary, participative mode would not only be displaced but would be unrecoverable."[10]

Hence, Zand's emphasis on collateral organizations complements the usual OD bias toward displacing traditional systems. His thrust is toward designing creative, problem-solving organizations—toward facilitating their flexible use by managers, *along with* traditional organizational systems rather than as a *replacement for* them.

Two Kinds of Organizational Problems

Zand's prescriptions rest on conceptual foundations, admittedly incomplete and partial, which must be described, even if briefly. The basic ideation underlying the notion of collateral organizations distinguishes between two kinds of

Exhibit 2 Characteristics of Well-Structured and Ill-Structured Problems

Element	Well-Structured Problems	Ill-Structured Problems
Variation of output with hours of work	Known Proportional	Unknown Nonproportional
Variation of output with number of people	Known Proportional	Unknown Nonproportional
Characteristics of input and output	Countable Quality accurately measurable Errors detected quickly, precisely	Not countable Quality difficult to measure Errors difficult to detect
Information available	Relevant Accurate Complete	Uncertain Inaccurate Incomplete
Solutions	Few are feasible All are known Best one determined easily	Many are feasible Few are known Best one difficult to determine
Experts	Past solution of similar problems is a reliable indication of expertise	Many claim to be expert, but past experience is an unreliable guide to expertise
Methods of control	External standards such as output targets, hours allowed, cost goals can effectively control performance	External standards are inapplicable and misleading
Feedback about results	Occurs shortly after action Can be attributed to the action	Occurs long after the action Cannot be attributed only to the action

Source: Reproduced by special permission from *The Journal of Applied Behavioral Science.* "Collateral Organization: A New Change Strategy" by Dale E. Zand, Vol. 10, no. 1 (January 1974), p. 67.

organizational problems: well-structured and ill-structured. Exhibit 2 defines major characteristics of both kinds of problems. Of course, not all problems can be sorted confidently into one of the two categories, but the basic distinction is a valuable one.

Two Corresponding Ways of Organizing

Given these two types of problems, Zand reasonably proposes that each should be served by a different structure or way of organizing. Essentially, he characterizes these two structures, which he calls authority/production-centered and knowledge/problem-centered, respectively, in terms of the differences shown in Table 1. These two pure types will exist in various combinations in the world of organizations, of course. But the essential distinction is both useful and straightforward: "The authority/production form is concerned with mobilizing people and equipment to maximize output of a finished product. The knowledge/problem form is concerned with processing or inventing knowledge to solve problems."[11]

Zand's basic argument merely requires stating. He begins by distinguishing two types of organizations, as well as two basic types of problems that can be expected in all large organizations. Those distinctions, in effect, generate the four-cell matrix in Figure 1. Although major gaps exist in the available literature, and despite the general character of Zand's distinctions, two of the four matrix cells match a problem with an organization type, and two cells suggest mismatches. Figure 1 sketches some of the recurring outcomes that Zand expects,

Table 1 Two Broad Types of Organizations

Element	Authority/Production-Centered	Knowledge/Problem-Centered
Levels of authority	Many	Few
Division of labor	High	Low
Links to others in the organization	Few	Many
Source of influence and power	Position in the hierarchy	Ability to identify and solve the problem
Use of rules and procedures	High	Low
Primary purpose	Maximize output	Analyze or invent knowledge to solve problems

TYPE OF PROBLEM	TYPE OF ORGANIZATION: Authority/Production	TYPE OF ORGANIZATION: Knowledge/Problem
Well-Structured	I High output Rapid processing Small number of errors in output Members low in authority report low satisfaction Tends to reject unsolicited innovations	II Lower output Slower processing More errors in output More satisfying Accepts unsolicited innovations
Ill-Structured	IV Lower output Slower processing Low-quality solutions Low in creativity Orderly, but not functional	III High output Rapid processing High-quality solutions High creativity Appears disorderly but is functional

Figure 1 Some probable recurring patterns of consequences of four combinations of types of problem and types of organization. [Reproduced by special permission from *The Journal of Applied Behavioral Science.* "Collateral Organization: A New Change Strategy," by Dale E. Zand, Vol. 10, no. 1 (January 1974), p. 69.]

based on the available research. Quadrants I and III represent the well-matched cases of problems/organizations, but note that the expected consequences are not all favorable in either case.

Of course, reality is more complex than Figure 1 allows. Every organization must cope, more or less simultaneously, with both well-structured and ill-structured problems. For example, a specific firm may face both the well-structured problem of efficiently producing its existing product line, as well as the ill-structured problem of what that product line should be in 3 or 5 years.

Common thoughtways do not reflect this complexity. The typical executive thinks of developing *an* organization, and thereby virtually guarantees various dilemmas. If the one chosen organization tends toward the knowledge/problem-centered model, one class of problems may be handled well at the expense of doing less well on those problems more easily amenable to an authority/production-centered model. If, as is far more likely, the decision goes to the latter model, the organization may handle well the repetitive problems but respond poorly to unexpected problems that "fall between the cracks" of the existing authority structure, job descriptions, and so on.

OD interventions often represent counterprescriptions to just such cases of mismatch and, as long as the one-organization model is accepted, these interventions can be ineffectual or even seriously counterproductive. Consider Zand's brief picture of the multiple dissonances that can be set in motion by such OD interventions as sensitivity training or Grid laboratories, which focus on improving the manager's skill in individual and group behavior but may neglect some basic organization realities. Zand observes that when "a manager applies his new knowledge to his formal organization, he usually encourages open questioning of goals and methods, which blurs formal boundaries between jobs." Both good and bad news can result. As to the latter, Zand notes that both supervisors and subordinates may interpret such actions "as undermining authority and disrupting the formal organization, so they resist and discard his changes. The manager is in theoretical limbo, without concepts, he cannot explain to other managers what he is doing in terms they can understand."[12]

Slipping Between the Horns of Dilemmas

Basically, Zand recommends a direct way of avoiding the dilemmas implied by the one-organization assumption. To wit: consciously elaborate a multiorganization model. This model includes the formal or primary structure which persists, as well as one or more collateral structures that may come and go as old problems are resolved and new ones surface.

Generic Features of Collaterals

For Zand, collateral organizations have a family of characteristics which set them apart from the primary or formal organization structure. Of these characteristics, six are especially noteworthy.[13]

- The purpose of the collateral organization is to identify and deal with problems to which the formal or primary organization is poorly adapted.
- A collateral organization seeks to complement the formal organization creatively. It basically proposes to establish new combinations of people, with new channels of communication, to work on specific problems.
- A collateral organization does not displace the formal organization. Both are available to a manager, who chooses one or the other, depending on the problem.
- A collateral organization consists of the same people who work in the formal organization.

- The outputs of the collateral organization are inputs to the formal organization. This linkage with the formal organization is critical.
- A collateral organization seeks to emphasize norms, that is, expectations of how people will behave, that may differ from norms of the formal organization. The different norms facilitate new ideas and new approaches to obstacles, especially ideas and approaches that are less subject to the tunnel vision introduced by the specialization and vested interests associated with the formal organization.

In sum, then, the collateral organization seeks to provide a useful answer to a practical need. That need, essentially, is to permit managers to respond to urgent issues that poorly fit the existing formal systems of authority and jurisdiction and to do so without being seen as subverting the formal system.

Designing a Collateral for a Specific Context*

Now we turn to illustrate the usefulness of the collateral organization concept and to outline some social technology for introducing one. We do not intend to delve deeply into the interpersonal or social dynamics of the development process.

Fred Anderson, manager of the Maintenance and Laboratory Service Division of Ajax Corporation, a large research and development company, was concerned about the cost effectiveness of his unit. His division had been performing more work with the same budget, and although objective standards were difficult to establish, he felt improvement was possible. Since the Service Division employed 300 of the 3000 people in Ajax, it was a major expense.

The Service Division had been formed 2 years earlier by consolidating into one unit activities that had previously been performed by small groups in each of the major research and engineering divisions of Ajax. After consolidation, the foreman's job changed from supervising only craftsmen in one specialty (such as machinists or electricians) to supervising a team which could completely build and repair complex laboratory facilities. Thus, at the level of the foremen and below, the organization took on some properties of a *matrix*. Specialized craftsmen were assigned to different projects as needed, and they usually worked on several projects with groups of varying size and membership. In addition, for the first time, foremen and craftsmen were rotated between the company's two locations, 20 miles apart.

Middle managers advised Mr. Anderson that the foremen were at the crux of the division's difficulties and would be the key to any improvement effort. They

*Reproduced by special permission from *The Journal of Applied Behavioral Science*. "Collateral Organization: A New Change Strategy," by Dale E. Zand, Vol. 10, no. 1 (January 1974), pp. 76-85.

described the foremen as unwilling to stress high output, reluctant to discipline workers, resistant to cost reduction and work changes, and tending to promise work dates that frequently were not met.

Mr. Anderson consulted OD specialists. They observed that formen were affected by the behavior and attitudes of their managers, and that the problems Mr. Anderson was trying to solve were complex, ill-defined, and substantially different from the well-structured routines of daily manager-foremen relations.[14] The consultants proposed, and management accepted, a sequence of collateral organizations involving both managers and foremen (Figure 2).

Collateral Phase 1. All sixteen managers in the division met for 3 days away from the plant in order to (1) identify and solve work problems of concern to managers and foremen, and (2) learn a collateral mode of problem-solving.

To help introduce the collateral mode, the OD specialists constrained the managers to work on one element of problem-solving at a time, in a method called "staged problem solving." They also facilitated information flow, wider use of resources, and norms that encouraged questioning and creativity by placing managers in different groups with varying membership.

First, the managers developed an inventory of problems while working in three "diagonal slice" groups (no manager and immediate subordinate in the same group). Then, in a plenary meeting of all sixteen managers, the groups discussed their problem inventories and consolidated them. At first the small groups were "stiff" and concerns were stated indirectly. However, with the aid of process observations by the OD specialists, role playing, small-group exercises, and the discipline of discussing each group's product in plenary session, this stiffness disappeared.

Next, each group diagnosed causes of a subset of problems. A written summary of each diagnosis was immediately duplicated and distributed to all the managers. The managers met again in plenary session and each group explained and discussed its diagnosis. By this time the managers were deeply involved in the effort. Highly relevant problems had been identified, and causes were being discussed without disguising names or incidents. The managers were stimulated by the open exchange of views and the increasing probability that several important problems might be solved.

On the second day of the meeting, the OD team arranged for the managers to meet in three peer groups. The groups were given the following tasks: (1) assign priorities to problems, (2) nominate managers to task forces that would recommend solutions to Mr. Anderson at the meeting, and (3) nominate managers to a steering committee that would take control of the remainder of the meeting and also guide the collateral organization after returning to the plant and the hierarchical (primary) organization.

Linking to the formal organization. To assure that the collateral organization would tie into the formal one, the managers were asked to use the following criteria for nominating candidates to a task force: (1) at least one manager should have formal authority to act on the problem; (2) several should be technical and procedural experts on the problem; (3) at least one should know and represent the views of people who would be affected by a solution.

The managers elected a five-man steering committee and asked the division manager to serve as chair. Thus, they connected the collateral organization's steering committee to the highest authority in their formal organization.

The steering committee formed task forces for the high-priority problems and assigned every manager (including themselves) to a task force. The task forces rediagnosed their assigned problems and developed solutions.

Then, in plenary session, each task force presented and discussed its progress. All managers freely questioned, commented, and provided additional inputs. The task forces absorbed the new inputs and met again to refine their proposals. By this stage, involvement was intense. Groups worked late into the night to prepare their recommendations for the next day. The norms in these groups very closely followed the knowledge/problem-centered mode: A manager's position was secondary to his contribution.

During the last half-day, each task force presented its recommendations in plenary session. To clarify that the organization was shifting back to its primary mode, the OD team explicitly stated that the Division Manager, Mr. Anderson, could respond in any of the following ways: (1) He could accept the task force recommendation, designate a manager to implement it, specify a completion date, and state how a report of progress would be given to all the managers. (2) He could suggest modifications, discuss them, and approve a modified recommendation. (3) He could withhold a decision, pending additional information or alternatives, and authorize the task force to continue its work back at the plant. (4) He could withhold a decision if in his judgment the proposal was not appropriate now but might be at a later date. (5) He could reject the recommendation and not give any reasons.

There was a good deal of excitement and joking as Mr. Anderson stood at the front of the room waiting to hear each group's statement of the problem, review of causes, and recommended solutions. During the presentations, managers freely called from the floor for clarification or elaborated a point when they felt it was misunderstood. The cohesiveness of the managers was noticeably higher than before the 3-day meeting.

By this time much information that had been known only in isolated pockets of the formal hierarchy had been exchanged across the organization. Managers had demonstrated their trust in one another through the openness of their discussions during the preceding two and one-half days. With this background, solutions that were not feasible or not integrative were readily discarded

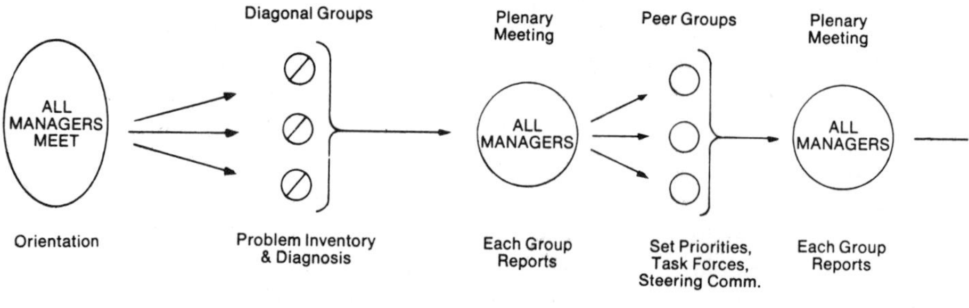

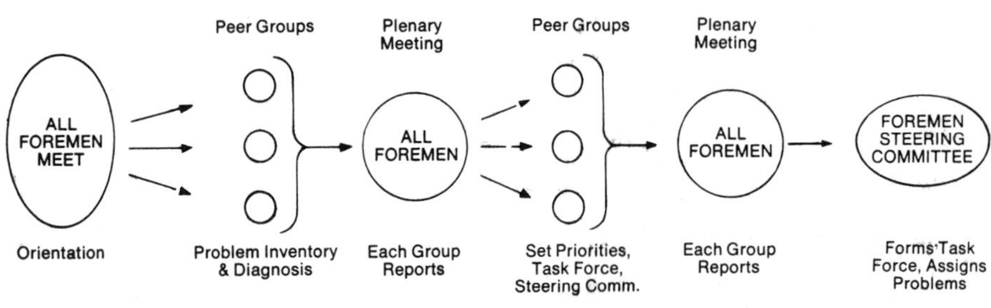

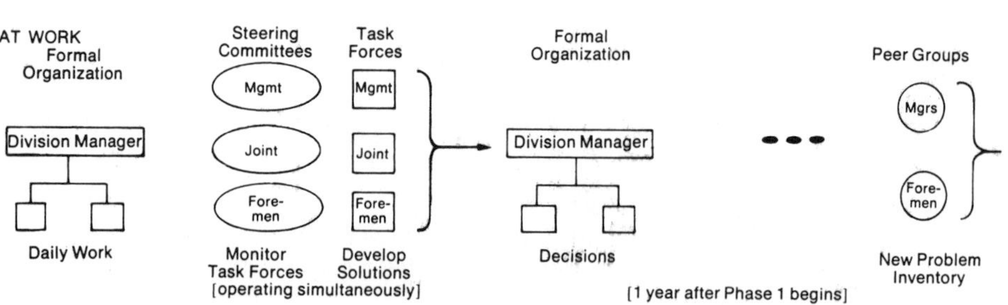

Figure 2 Multiphase collateral organization. [Reproduced by special permission New Change Strategy," by Dale E. Zand, Vol. 10, no. 1 (January 1974), pp. 81-82.]

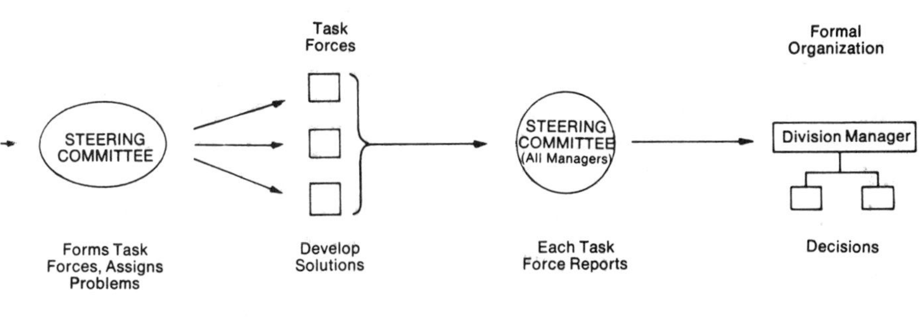

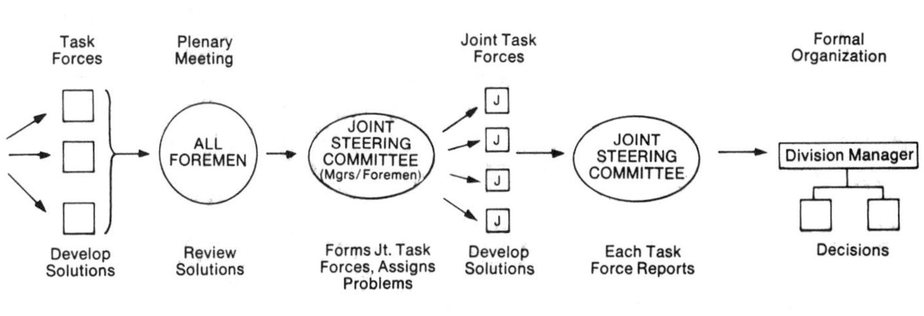

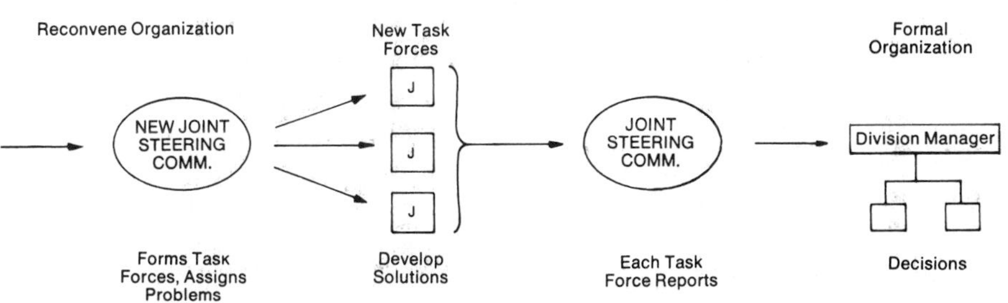

from the *Journal of Applied Behavioral Science.* "Collateral Organization: A

in the task forces. As a result, the final recommendations were appropriate and well thought out. Mr. Anderson neither rejected nor withheld a decision on any of the recommendations.

Results: Collateral Phase 1. A new information system for managers was instituted. A new strategy for recruiting engineering and scientific specialists was approved. Middle managers were delegated additional decision powers. A task force was established to redesign the division's organizational structure.

The managers also made plans to follow-up in the hierarchical organization problems they had identified but did not have time to solve during the 3-day meeting. Finally, they agreed they would join the foremen in a collateral organization if the foremen invited them. They discussed how they might work with the foremen in a collateral mode.

Collateral Phase 2. All eighteen foremen met for 3 days at the off-site location 1 week after the managers' collateral organization experience. The OD specialists had decided to separate managers from foremen to prevent tension and distorted communication between levels from interfering with learning to work in a collateral mode. The managers' collateral organization was developed first so they could decide from personal experience whether to approve a collateral organization for foremen. The procedure and activities in the foremen's meeting were similar to the manager's meeting.

Linking two collateral organizations. Anticipating the need to link the managers' collateral organization to the foremen's collateral organization for work on common problems, management had agreed to the OD specialists' recommendation that foremen be permitted to invite managers to join them the last day and a half. The foremen (contrary to management's stereotype of foremen as insensitive) did not wish to offend any manager by not inviting him and negotiated with management to have all managers join them, except for five who had to be left to run the division.

A joint steering committee of foremen and managers assigned both foremen and managers to joint task forces. Comprehensive, ill-structured issues had been identified for work. There was tension within the joint task forces as managers and foremen who knew each other by name but had never worked closely together before prepared to discuss problems that had been suppressed, distorted, or circumvented in the formal organization. Some foremen became guarded when a manager tried to dominate, but the issues and the withheld information that had been constraining the organization were nevertheless introduced via the "impersonal" written task force reports.

During the last half-day, the joint task forces presented their recommendations to Mr. Anderson (format as before), who immediately made several important decisions. Procedures for working on unsolved problems after returning to the plant were also established.

Results: Collateral Phase 2. The recommendations approved by Mr. Anderson included the following: Foremen were given wider latitude in authorizing overtime to complete a job without their supervisor's approval; they could authorize workers' time off without pay; they could purchase parts that were delaying job completion up to $200 per job without going through time-consuming formal purchasing procedures. These measures helped cut costs and sped completion of jobs.

Mr. Anderson also decided that task forces concerned with the responsibilities of foremen, the training of foremen, the merit and performance review system, providing proper engineering support, and reviewing pay differentials between foremen and workers were to continue their investigation after they returned to the plant and the hierarchical organization.

Of the thirty important problems which had been identified, nine had been assigned to task forces and three had been resolved. Completion and review dates had been established for the others, and procedures had been developed for following through on the remaining problems. An attitude survey showed that managers and foremen felt they had learned much about one another and about problem-solving. They were enthusiastic about the collateral organization.

Collateral Phase 3. After returning to the plant and the hierarchical organization, task forces of managers, foremen, and joint membership continued their work. Progress was slower than expected because of daily work pressures.

There also was testing of the authority/production mode. Some foremen task forces, impressed with their new influence potential, attempted to circumvent middle managers and moved directly to the joint steering committee or the division manager with short-term work issues. Senior foremen quickly sensed the resentment this was arousing among middle managers and redirected the foremen task forces to the issues they had been assigned. Managers of other divisions in the laboratory were skeptical about allowing foremen on task forces. They were also concerned that foremen might usurp higher management's authority. Mr. Anderson was able to reassure the other divisions that this dual mode of operation need not spread to other divisions unless they wanted it. He was also able to convince them on the basis of preliminary results that the performance of the maintenance division would improve over the long run.

Based on the measure of identifying and solving ill-structured problems, the collateral mode contributed to the organization's effectiveness. After 9 months, six of the nine original high-priority problems and five secondary problems were solved. All but three task forces had completed their assignments and were dissolved. Work was to begin on twelve less critical problems.

The collateral organization was self-operating; no OD specialists were used. One year after the first meetings, a new division manager (promoted from within the division) continued the collateral organization with the aid of the joint steering committee. Using small groups, a new inventory of problems was developed, three new task forces were formed, and progress was reviewed with the steering committee until the new problems were solved.

To obtain information about attitudes toward the collateral mode, interviews were conducted 18 months after the start of the project. Five managers and five foremen representing all levels of management, every task force, and both steering committees were interviewed. Each respondent felt strongly that the collateral mode was extremely useful and strongly supported its continuation.

Some Issues Generic to Collaterals

Zand does not intend to argue that the collateral strategy is fail-safe, of course, but rather he maintains that the approach raises the probability of success. Any help is welcome, for the problems are substantial. Three points help illustrate why success is often problemmatical on issues for which the collateral organization is appropriate.

First, the primary factor limiting the probability of success is the very nature of the "ill-defined problems." No pussy-cats need apply; these problems are all bearlike. Probabilities of success are thus low.

Second, interdepartmental conflict can be so severe as to defy the collateral strategy. Consequently, individuals may be little predisposed to put very much energy into breathing life into their units of the collateral organization, which are after all peopled largely by a conflictful "them" from the primary structure. No direct evidence exists. Analogically, however, efforts to use micro-units to work on macro-issues seem to support two generalizations. Thus, the micro-units generally seem capable of developing empathy, understanding, and appropriate skills for effective interaction, even for those in such conflict as Catholics and Protestants in Ireland, or Arabs and Jews in Israel. However, the macro-issues tend to be highly resistant to change, and it even seems the case that the caring and sharing in micro-units can exacerbate the intensity of the macro-issue conflict, as by increasing the guilt about that intractability, by generating feelings of regression from comfortable micro-unit interaction, and so on.[15]

Third, the use of collateral organizations may initially increase the number of problems going to groups for solution, which may bother some managers. The increase is likely to be temporary, however.

Fourth, collateral organizations are likely to increase the stress on middle managers, who are often substantially stressed as it is. Zand explains:[16]

> Higher managers may discover that middle managers have been distorting and editing the upward flow of information. Lower managers may discover they can influence higher management decisions more easily than they thought possible. Both higher and lower managers discover they need less

time to identify and solve complex problems. Management may be prompted to redesign the hierarchical organization and redefine the role of middle managers.

Fifth, and finally, some employees may find it difficult or impossible to switch back and forth between the collateral and the formal modes. They need a structure and relationships that do not change—stability and consistency are massively significant for them.[17] This is an especially salient issue, of course, when a manager is inflexible. Attempts to use the collateral mode may then result in major resistance. Zand reports no such problems with managers, but he does note that several nonsupervisory employees had difficulty with switching modes, finding that discomforting and confusing.

Notes

1. Robert T. Golembiewski, *Organizing Men and Power* (Chicago: Rand McNally, 1967), esp. pp. 31-117.
2. Philip J. Browne and Robert T. Golembiewski, "The Line-Staff Concept Revisited: An Empirical Study of Organizational Images," *Academy of Management Journal,* Vol. 17 (September 1974), pp. 406-417.
3. For a more detailed OD design for personnel selection based on the laboratory approach, see Donald C. King, "Selecting Personnel for a Systems 4 Organization." Paper presented at NTL Conference on New Technology in Organization Development, New York, October 8-9, 1971.
4. For some relevant theory, see Ralph H. Turner, "Role-Taking, Role Standpoint, and Reference Group Behavior," *American Journal of Sociology,* Vol. 61 (January 1956), pp. 318-321, 326. For an application, see R. Fred Ferguson, "Field Experiments: Preparation for the Changing Police Role." Mimeographed, undated.

   For an OD use of the role approach similar to the description above, see Roger Harrison, "Role Negotiation: A Tough-Minded Approach to Team Development," in W. Warner Burke and Harvey A. Hornstein (eds.), *The Social Technology of Organization Development* (Washington, D.C.: NTL Learning Resources Corporation, 1972).
5. For other similar designs, see Matthew B. Miles, P. H. Calder, H. A. Hornstein, D. N. Callahan, and R. S. Schiavo, "Data Feedback and Organizational Change in a School System." Paper presented at Annual Meeting, American Sociological Association, August 29, 1966; John L. Aiteen, "Notes on Employee Surveys as O.D. Stimulants," mimeographed (Midland, Mich., Dow Chemical Co., undated); and Richard J. Ward and Glen H. Varney, "Organizational Assessment: A Deep Sensing Approach," pp. 395-399, in Robert L. Taylor, Michael J. O'Connell, Robert A. Zawacki, and D. D. Warrick (eds.), *1976 Proceedings,* Academy of Management.

For an insightful analysis of how degenerative interaction systems can develop in large organizations, and how the laboratory approach can help moderate or reverse them, see Jerry B. Harvey and D. Richard Albertson, "Neurotic Organizations: Symptoms, Causes and Treatment," Parts I and II, *Personnel Journal,* Vol. 50 (September 1971), pp. 694-699 and (October 1971), pp. 770-777.

6. "Sensing Technique at TRW Elicits Open Response from Employees," *World of Work Report,* Vol. 2 (December 1977), p. 138; and William B. Cash, Jr., and Robert L. Minter, "Concern Meetings: A Useful OD Tool," *Training Directors Journal,* Vol. 32 (March 1978), pp. 44-45.
7. Clayton P. Alderfer, "Improving Organizational Communication Through Long-Term Intergroup Intervention," *Journal of Applied Behavioral Science,* Vol. 13 (October 1977), pp. 193-210.
8. Robert T. Golembiewski, *The Small Group* (Chicago: University of Chicago, 1962), esp. pp. 9-26 and 46-56.
9. Dale E. Zand, "Collateral Organization: A New Change Strategy," *Journal of Applied Behavioral Science,* Vol. 10 (January 1974), p. 63.
10. Ibid., p. 70.
11. Ibid., p. 68.
12. Ibid., p. 65.
13. Ibid., p. 71.
14. Dr. Zand acknowledges his gratitude to Matthew B. Miles and William O. Lytle, Jr., who were on the OD team with him. This case is based upon *Enlarging Organization Choice Through Use of a Temporary Problem-Solving System,* by D. E. Zand, M. B. Miles, and W. O. Lytle, Jr. (mimeographed, available from author).
15. Illustratively, see Leonard W. Doob and William J. Foltz, "Voices From A Belfast Workshop," *Social Change,* Vol. 5, no. 3 (1975), pp. 1-3 and 6-7.
16. Zand, "Collateral Organization," p. 87.
17. T. W. Adorno, E. Frenkel-Brunswick, J. Levinson, and R. N. Sanford, *The Authoritarian Personality* (New York: Harper, 1950); and Victor H. Vroom, "Some Personality Determinants of the Effects of Participation," *Journal of Abnormal and Social Psychology,* Vol. 59 (1959), pp. 322-327.

Chapter 4

FACILITATING COORDINATION AND OTHER CRUCIAL LINKAGES

Four Designs that Accept but Seek to Modify Effects of Extant Structures

This chapter complements the preceding one. Like that chapter, the present one accepts the existing formal structuring of work. Unlike Chapter 3 however, the focus here is *not* on interventions that provide a kind of temporary midcourse correction, while essentially preserving the quality and style of the formal structure of work. Rather, this chapter emphasizes designs that have the broader ambition of variously upgrading the quality of working life while retaining an extant structure of work.

The total sense of the contrast between these two chapters is suggested by an analogy. The concept in Chapter 3 of an organization unit or system is akin to that of the object ball in billiards; it will often change direction or speed after impact, but no change in essence occurs. The object ball remains a billiard ball. Chapter 4 moves toward inducing basic changes in fundamental processes of organization units. To be fanciful, it is as if this chapter seeks to develop different characteristics in our metaphorical object ball—characteristics of marshmallows, of spiny cactus, or whatever.

Specifically, this chapter deals with four kinds of designs that impact with substantial force on the existing organization of work—that seek to facilitate coordination in one degree or another—but which stop short of the actual restructuring of work. The major sections below deal with, in turn:

- An effort to reorient the style and relationships in a substantial number of units within a field sales division, a kind of renewal of the processes of existing units of formal organization

- An attempt to reduce interdepartmental conflict or, to put it positively, to increase the cohesiveness of a number of specialties reporting to an integrative executive
- Anticipating and seeking to moderate the kinds of slippage common between "line" and "staff" officials, a kind of preventative intervention to make both classes of officials more effective in performing certain shared responsibilities
- Management by objectives, or MBO, a common surrogate for OD, which proposes a philosophy or style for overcoming many of the fragmenting tendencies induced by traditional ways of organizing work

The first intervention has a dual goal: to induce norms and processes within a large number of similar organization units that will support viable *vertical* feedback linkages. The target is a central one, for formal organizations live or die in terms of the adequacy of what goes up, and what comes down, its formal channels of communication. In the present case, there was real and growing concern that lower-level employees were telling the variously varnished truth, and often too late to be of optimum use. Similarly, there were real problems with the policies and decisions that trickled down the structure.

The second intervention also deals with a critical kind of problem–improving *horizontal* linkages between units of an organization. The OD vehicle is called the confrontation design. Horizontal linkages have been neglected in the literature,[1] and more's the pity. To be sure, superior-subordinate or command relationships are important in determining what happens in organizations. But lateral relationships between peers, whether collaborative or antagonistic, often are critical determinants of the effectiveness and of the quality of life in complex organizations.[2] Intergroup relationships are also central, especially given the common strategy of creating unity in one social unit by differentiating it from other units in ways that complicate collaboration.

The third section below focuses on a ubiquitous and major source of interunit conflict in organizations, that between line and staff. Their incomplete integration characterizes life in many complex organizations. The design below seeks to anticipate these integrative problems, via a learning design for establishing expectancies and relationships between line and staff officials that will help cushion some of the inevitable tensions and dilemmas that are expected. The design applies preventative medicine, as it were, at a particularly sore spot in many organizations.

In the concluding section below, the focus shifts to a major managerial intervention, MBO. Its goal constitutes nothing less than providing a philosophy and style which induces self-discipline that contributes to coordination and other significant linkages between individual needs and organization demands. Experience with MBO applications will be reviewed, and its uneven record of success will be explained in terms of a general failure to respect certain values and guidelines consistent with OD.

Renewing Numerous Formal Units in a Large Organization
Changing Relationships and Style Rather than People, on a Mass Scale

Both the risk and the reward of OD efforts escalate when the target is permanent work groups. Successes, and failures, will tend to live far beyond the OD intervention. The focus below is on one such high risk/reward design and some of its consequences. The design immediately involved some 400 managers and salesmen who staffed 33 geographic marketing units. Thus the design not only dealt with permanent groups, but with substantial numbers of them. Indeed, the design may be unique in this respect.

Stability-Oriented Becomes Survival-Oriented

The 400 participants in the design had not long before experienced several major traumas. Market conditions required a cutback of some 20 percent in the national field-sales force, and the 400 were the survivors. More cuts were possible.

In addition, a new head of marketing had been appointed shortly after the cutback in personnel. He had resigned from the very marketing division he now headed. The circumstances of his resignation are relevant. He cut his blooming relationship via a strong and widely circulated letter. The marketing division was on a collision course with reality, his letter announced. He emphasized, among other factors, that officials were essentially avoiding a number of tough decisions forced by market conditions, communications were worsening, and a growing make-believe atmosphere inhibited a flexible response to a rapidly changing marketplace. Necessary action was avoided by a "paralysis of analysis" and vain hopes for a better day. He was back 3 years later, in command this time.

Moreover, a new marketing strategy would soon be put into effect, complete with a revolutionary information system that was being installed in about one-third the regions and would soon be extended to all. Previously, specific performance of individual salespersons had been difficult or impossible to assess. Hence, the prime focus was on the style of saleswork, as well as on elaborate rules seen as "mickey mouse." The necessary change had two goals:

- To introduce the new information system, which clearly individuated salespersons, had a quantitative bias, and stressed relations between managers and the sales staff

- To preserve collaboration between salespersonnel as well as between them and their managers

The derivative subtleties were numerous. Although changes in measuring individual sales performance would no doubt reduce the centrality of regional identifications and interaction, important collaborative work still had to be done in the regions. "I used to be a member of a football team," one salesman aptly described the change. "Now, I'm for many purposes a sprinter on a track team." In addition, more fluid and rapid interchanges between the field and headquarters would be increasingly necessary as the new marketing strategy took effect. Historically, the field had been a zealous and effective defender of its own autonomy. Multiple allegiances suddenly became a more important part of the game.

All in all, then, major motivations encouraged a long-run team-building effort at the regional level. The present design was the opening wedge of that effort, and thereby it is at once significant and limited.

Designing for a Regenerative System

The situation in the marketing division was a delicate one, which could easily become worse. The design had two basic goals:

- To begin *team*-development activities for the thirty-three regional sales groups, and to face problems as they were, as openly and directly as possible
- To begin to develop a new climate for the total field-sales organization, consistent with these basic thrusts of the new marketing head:

  To "tell it like it is," from all levels

  To avoid "promising rose gardens" to stimulate sales-force morale in bogus or unrealistic ways

  To develop open communication linkages—up, down, and across the marketing organization—to increase the validity and reliability of information available in the system for the hard decisions that still had to be made

In terms of the vocabulary introduced earlier, the overall goal sought to reverse a degenerative system that was worsening, and fast. The fear was patent: that the trauma of the reduction-in-force would freeze salesmen into protective behavioral patterns that would increase the chances of maladaptive responses to the changes in products and markets that were needed, and which the national sales meeting would help introduce.

The learning design was clean in its structure, if ponderous in execution. A national sales meeting was called, the first in the firm's recent history. The sequence of the learning flow, with an approximate balance of time and emphasis, can be sketched as:

Team development in regions to encourage openness, willingness to risk, etc.	→	Presentations by various senior officials about marketing-relevant prospects and plans, which were then variously responded to, critiqued, etc., by sales force

Whenever possible, the basic strategy was to induce action or decision in relation to issues as they came up. The point of it was a sense of marketing newly on the move. At times, it was possible to respond on the spot. In many other cases, action was not possible. Alternatively, then, ongoing deliberations were described, and, whenever possible, likely dates for decision or action were shared.

The public theme of the regional team-development design unrelentingly emphasized feedback, in stereo, as it were. Over 2 days, the regional units gave and received feedback about:

- Managerial tasks and styles,[3] as preferred by the men and as practiced by their regional managers
- Functional roles,[4] as they were present or absent in each of the regions
- Individual needs[5] of each regional member, as these were satisfied or frustrated in regional interaction
- Properties of each region as an organization unit[6]
- Skills in giving and receiving feedback[7]

The design of each learning unit was similar: brief cognitive inputs were used to help men organize their own experiences as members of a regional team, with the goals of seeing themselves and others more clearly and of beginning to build more effective and satisfying relations. In the case of functional roles, for example, a resource person sketched the differences between three kinds of roles and described their relevance to team functioning. The roles were: task-oriented, group maintenance, and self-oriented. Then, each participant was requested to look at himself individually and his colleagues in terms of their roles in the regional unit, noting which specific individuals tended to fill which roles. Each participant used a special form which listed numerous examples of the three basic roles. Subsequently, region members could share and discuss their role identifications, as they wished. Most wished to do so, and discussions tended to be lively and animated. Each learning unit closed similarly, also. The format for summarizing and transitioning was this, roughly:

> You have had a couple of hours to look at the various roles people play in your region. Some things you have seen no doubt please you, and some

> concern you. It is our philosophy that it is best to have both kinds of things out in the open, as much as you feel safe in doing so. We hope that sense of safety grows, not only in your region but in your dealings with your bosses and the people who work for you.
>
> Later, as you know, you will have a chance here to test that sense of safety outside your region, as you meet with various corporate officials.
>
> Remember, your management has agreed to provide the resources, should you wish to do more later than we have been able to do here with the notion of roles.
>
> Now, there's another notion in the behavioral sciences that may help in developing the kind of open and collaborative system that can help make work more meaningful and satisfying. . . .

Several details complete this rough sketch of the design. *First,* members of each of the thirty-three regions sat at separate circular tables in a large ballroom. Sometimes they would be in "general session," as when getting a cognitive input to focus their team-development activities. At other times, each region would focus on its internal processes. *Second,* six resource persons moved between the groups when they were in the latter mode, clarifying or whatever. *Third,* the resource persons had been the T-group trainers for a number of the participants, including at least all of the thirty-three regional managers. Some prior relationships of trust existed, then. These were no doubt critical contributors to the acceptance of the design. *Fourth,* each regional manager had previously met in longer and more intense team-development situations with his superior, the division manager. The regional managers were to do only what their superiors had done perhaps 12 to 18 months before. There was some reasonable concern among regional managers before the present experience, but it was of low intensity. If the concern had been high in even several managers, the design would have been modified.

Three Kinds of Design Consequences

Three varieties of data imply the substantial impact of this brief design for team development in a large population. The experience clearly "pulled the cork" for many salesmen, for the following several days of presentations were responded to with considerable directness and force. In contrast, the developing motto in the field had been: "The silent way is the safe way—you may be next!" The new marketing head was especially pleased by the extra sessions the salesmen felt were necessary to clarify a wide range of points with headquarters. The degree of involvement of the majority of the salesmen is implicit in the fact that it was their recreation and sleep time they were investing to get the answers they wanted. At the impressionistic level, then, the meeting was a clear success, both as to team development and in the sessions that followed.

Two administrations of a 24-item version of the Likert Profile provide extensive data which support these impressions. For present purposes, it is necessary to note only that the form of the Profile used here taps seven organizational dimensions.

1-2 deal with leadership

3-6 deal with motivation

7-13 deal with the character of communication

14-16 deal with interaction and influence

17-20 deal with decision-making

21 deals with goal setting

22-24 deal with the character of control

The administrations were spaced by some 4 months, with the training intervention coming midway between them. Some 329 salesmen responded, both times. The salesmen were asked to describe their own regions, as much as that was possible.

To conserve space, no data are reported here, but they clearly suggest pervasive effects of the design. Specifically, about 72 percent of the changes in mean scores were in the predicted direction. Viewed from another perspective, four of the thirty-three regions accounted for somewhat more than 33 percent of the negative scores. And two of those four regions at least approached breaking even in terms of scores toward or away from the laboratory values defined by System 4 of the Likert Profile.

A word is necessary in explaining what is meant by the term "predicted direction" of change in this case. Consultants had designed for specific effects whose desirability the salesmen themselves had overwhelmingly reflected in their Ideal responses to each item on the first administration of the Likert Profile. The Now scores on the Likert Profile items, in short, were to change in the direction of the Ideal scores. Consultants generated the design predicted to help the salesmen move in the direction they preferred.

A final batch of data suggests there is a cutting edge to such team development designs. Such designs induce rising expectations about what work should provide, and, hypothetically, those expectations in turn create one or both of two outcomes: greater demand for need satisfaction, and a sharp negative reaction if those needs are not met. In the present case, for example, salesmen were asked to describe their regions in terms of four of Halpin's[8] scales, each of which is tapped by several questionnaire items. The scales are:

Disengagement describes a group which is "going through the motions," a group that is not "in gear" as far as its task is concerned.

Hindrance refers to members' feeling that management burdens them with duties and requirements that are deemed busywork and that management does not facilitate their work.

Table 1 Some Results of a Mass Team-Development Design

	Disengagement (10 items)	Hindrance (5 items)	Esprit (9 items)	Intimacy (6 items)
Relationship of Postintervention Scores to Preintervention Scores	Higher in seven cases, two of which reached the .05 level	Higher in all five cases, two of which reached the .05 level	Higher in six cases, one of which reached the .05 level	Higher in three cases, one of which reached the .05 level
	Lower in three cases, none of which reached the .05 level		Lower in three cases, none of which reached the .05 level	Lower in three cases, none of which reached the .05 level

Note: The data summarized here are for 289 salesmen whose before and after scores were compared item by item. Mean scores for all salesmen on each item are compared.
Source: See Note 61.

Esprit refers to members' feeling that their social needs are being satisfied and also that they are enjoying a sense of task accomplishment.

Intimacy refers to members' enjoyment of friendly social relationships during work, a need satisfaction that may be independent of task accomplishment.

Unlike the Likert items, which respondents were instructed to apply to their own regions, the Halpin items tended to relate to the broader managerial system. This was especially the case for the disengagement and hindrance items, but esprit is also affected.

These summary data in Table 1 add to a very slim literature on mass team-building;[9] they imply optimism that real progress is possible in brief periods; but major loose ends must be acknowledged. That is, changes in the Likert Profile items suggest some major improvement in the climate of relationships within the regions. But the data from the Halpin disengagement and hindrance scales seem to indicate that development of more favorable relationships at the regional level does not necessarily carry over to other levels.

Four Concluding Notes

Evaluating the magnitude of the changes reviewed is a tentative business, especially for four reasons. *First,* the convention for estimating "team development" by averaging the self-reports of individual salesmen is clearly inelegant, and could bias results significantly. For example, the typical response of managers to the results above is: "No, it was a better experience for the salesmen than that." What do they mean? Their own conventions for measuring impact were more complicated than an equal weighing of responses, and those personal conventions generated more "positive" results. More or less, the managers weighed any self-report in terms of such factors as the following.

- Does the report come from a salesman who is variously influential, or from a follower?
- Does the report come from a salesman rated as excellent, or satisfactory?
- Does the report come from a salesman who has demonstrated an ability to observe and describe what is going on outside himself, or from one who strongly tends to project what is going on inside himself as a purported description of the outside world?
- Does the report come from a salesman who is known as a "tough grader," or one who sees most everything in glowing terms?
- Does the report come from a salesman who keeps his own counsel, or from one who reads the election returns first?
- Does the report come from a dependent salesman, or a chronic malcontent?

The mere aggregation of self-reports is innocent of such distinctions, and thereby can mask relations that do exist or highlight spurious relations.[10]

Second, the present data provide at least some support for the reasonable notion that not every salesman or each region had the same need for change. Thus, all five deviant regions on Likert II ranked well above the median on Likert I. This suggests that the present design was not particularly useful for those who needed change least. Alternatively, the dynamics of the learning experience might have led some high Likert scorers to downgrade their region on Likert II because of new data about the fragility of what previously seemed solid relationships, and so on.

Third, alternatively, those five deviant regions had more than their share of salesmen who responded to Likert I in socially desirable ways. The reduction in Likert II scores in such a case would be a positive learning outcome. The OD design, as it were, would have expanded the definition of what was socially desirable, or at least what was admissable in an analysis of organization interaction. Such an effect could have permitted some salesmen to feel comfortable in providing more "negative" self-reports. Evidence confirming this surmise has been published elsewhere.[11]

Fourth, despite points of commonality, the instruments used here differ widely in coverage, methodology, and approach to scaling. Perhaps the major difference between the two scales can be expressed in terms of their unity versus their heterogeneity. Space does not permit great detail, but the Halpin data generate heterogeneous factorial structures. In sharp contrast, the Likert data seem to tap one large phenomenal domain.

These considerations do not imply that Likert is superior to Halpin, but they do suggest a difference. Note, however, that a strong argument for the essential similarity of the Likert and Halpin instruments has been advanced.[12]

Improving Horizontal Relations in Large Organizations
The Confrontation Design Generates Intergroup Cohesiveness*

The thrust of this section seeks to selectively engage laboratory dynamics in learning situations that do not employ T-groups. The focus is on horizontal linkages between units at more or less the same hierarchical level whose contributions have to be integrated smoothly into common flows of work. Please note this section complements Boss' analysis in Chapter 6 of Part 1. He utilized the confrontation design on intragroup issues. The present analysis uses that design to deal with issues between groups.

The Ubiquity of We/They Relations

To begin, the target here is no rare bird: it is everywhere. Ineffective and conflictful horizontal relations, often referred to as "we/they" or "win/lose," derive from omnipresent sources, and often have significant consequences. For example, the basis for differentiation can lay in tasks, hierarchical status, race, religion, sex, or between generations; and those bases for differentiation can be historically rooted, or they may be as ephemeral as the latest dictates of fashion.[13] This section focuses on phenomena that are truly ubiquitous, then.

*This section draws heavily from Robert T. Golembiewski and Arthur Blumberg, "The Laboratory Approach to Organization Change: Confrontation Design," *Journal of the Academy of Management,* Vol. 11 (June 1968), pp. 199-210. For a more detailed technical report, see Robert T. Golembiewski and Arthur Blumberg, "Confrontation as a Training Design in Complex Organizations: Attitudinal Changes in a Diversified Population of Managers," *Journal of Applied Behavioral Science,* Vol. 3 (December 1967), pp. 525-547. See also Golembiewski and Blumberg, "Training and Relational Learning," *Training and Development Journal,* Vol. 21 (November 1967), pp. 35-42. Other similar designs are described by Robert R. Blake, Jane S. Mouton, and Richard L. Sloma, "The Union-Management Laboratory: Strategy for Resolving Intergroup Conflict," *Journal of Applied Behavioral Science,* Vol. 1 (January 1965), pp. 25-57; and Richard Beckhard, "The Confrontation Meeting," *Harvard Business Review,* Vol. 45 (March 1967), pp. 149-155. For an overview of available research, see Frank Friedlander and L. Dave Brown, "Organization Development," *Annual Review of Psychology,* Vol. 25 (1974), pp. 329-331.

Organizational Paralysis as a Common Consequence

We/they relations can be a source of conflictful growth for people in groups, but that possibility usually seems a long shot. The conflictful phenomena of we/they are typically complex, significant, and difficult to manage—a wicked combination. The difficulty can be suggested briefly by sketching some typical properties of intergroup relations when they take on a win/lose character.[14]

- The cohesiveness of the involved groups increases sharply.
- The closing of ranks tends to smother dispute or differences within groups that could have led to a reexamination and enrichment of initial positions.
- A centralization of leadership and power tends to occur, which may be functional for the crisis situation but can imply longer-run internal problems when the intergroup competition is settled.
- Selective perceptions and evaluations begin to flourish: Our group is all good; theirs is all bad.
- Negative stereotypes about Other develop.
  Motives of Other become suspect.
  Intellectual distortions about Other grow.
  Commonalities are minimized, and differences are exaggerated.
  Stereotypes trigger feelings which may be incongruent with objective realities but which nonetheless reinforce stereotypes.
- Comprehension of the position of Other is reduced.
- The capacity for mutual empathy is impaired.

Such dynamics clearly lead to degenerative interaction sequences, as described at several points above, which complicate relationships between individuals as well as groups. It is not dramatic to refer to such situations as "paralysis." The fear of doing the wrong thing tends to inhibit doing anything, especially the important things.

Seven Features of the Intergroup Confrontation

The confrontation design directly addresses such intergroup paralysis. Although confrontation designs can vary widely in specifics, seven core features particularly distinguish them from learning designs using T-groups. *First,* confrontation designs involve as participants individuals who are hierarchically and/or functionally involved in some common flow of work. The attitudinal changes reported here concern four levels of the same marketing organization and some nine of its component activities. Immediately, then, the confrontation design seeks learning that has direct on-the-job application.

Second, confrontation designs involve two or more organizational entities whose members have real and unresolved issues with one another, for example, labor and management. In this case, the focus was on the relations between various headquarters activities and supervisors of a field-sales force. Confrontations are highly structured and content-oriented, in this sense; T-groups are not.

Third, confrontation designs involve the mutual development of images as a basis for attempting to highlight unresolved issues. In this case, five basic learning aggregates were instructed to individually choose Relevant Others, that is, any organization positions or units with which more effective relations were considered necessary to do an effective job. For each of these Relevant Others, participants were instructed to develop three-dimensional images based on the following questions:

- How do we see ourselves in relation to the Relevant Other?
- How does the Relevant Other see us?
- How do we see the Relevant Other?

The 3-D Images were to be written on large sheets of newsprint. Each Learning Aggregate prepared its 3-D Image in isolation.

The 3-D Image, in effect, instructs participants to engage processes of both feedback and disclosure. But, both processes are far more limited and controlled than in a T-group, by intention. Thus both feedback and disclosure are written, and hence more deliberate, in 3-D designs. Moreover, the 3-D Image focuses on organizational groups, not individuals; items in 3-D Images are tested in advance before they are communicated, by individuals who have a common organizational stake in what gets communicated.

Several factors complicate the learning design in this case. For example, only four of the five basic learning aggregates were formal units of organization; the fifth was a categoric group composed of specialists from various headquarters' units. Moreover, even the four formal organization units were but recently established. Such factors probably reduced the potency of the design. In general, we expect the confrontation experience to be more potent as each basic learning aggregate is more than a categoric group, that is, as its members share social norms and mutually identify.[15] To the degree that a Basic Learning Aggregate posesses such qualities of real "groupiness," so should they be able to consensually validate and reinforce the learning of each group member.

Fourth, sharing 3-D Images provides the first step toward mutually working through any relational problems. In this case, consultants scheduled blocks of time during which willing Relevant Others confront one another. A consultant was present at each confrontation.

Fifth, confrontation designs assume that significant organizational problems often are caused by blockages in communication. Confrontations "free up" people to "level" in communicating and thus set the stage for authentic interaction and effective problem-solving. Some objective dilemmas, such as a critical lack of money, cannot be resolved by confrontation designs, of course. In such cases, the ideal outcomes are greater clarity in communicating about the dilemmas and greater willingness to collaborate in doing as much as conditions permit.

Sixth, confrontations are short-cycle affairs. The confrontation design about which data will be reported here, for example, took some 12 scheduled hours. In contrast, a typical stranger experience in sensitivity training lasts 2 weeks.

Seventh, confrontation designs are seen as springboards for organizational action. Since such a design is typically brief, however, real limits exist as to what can be accomplished. Participants were instructed to do only two things: to try to understand the 3-D Images communicated to them, and to seek some areas of agreement where mutually beneficial accommodations might be made. In addition, core groups were set up following the confrontations to work on specific organizational issues. These core groups were formed as a terminal training activity, some work was begun in the groups, and plans were made for future meetings.

In sum, the learning in confrontation designs does not have to be transferred or made relational. It *is* relational.

Selected Initial Effects of One Application

Some initial effects of one application of the confrontation design will be illustrated in two ways. The representative 3-D Image in Exhibit 1 reveals that participants did not trifle with the design. The figure reflects many unresolved issues, some of which were surprises and none of which had been admitted to public dialogue between the parties.

Providing more rigorous support of the efficacy of the confrontation is an involved matter. Our primary data concern attitudinal changes, derived from a questionnaire administered before and immediately after the experience.[16] Only impressionistic data about behavioral changes are available, but they reinforce the attitudinal changes that seem due to the confrontation.

Expectations about intended changes in attitudes toward specific units were not simple. The consultants distinguished:

I. Units which were deeply involved in the design, toward which the most favorable shifts in attitudes were expected.

II. Units which had little or token representation in the design, toward which only a slight drift toward more favorable attitudes due to a halo effect was anticipated.

Exhibit 1 Sample 3-D Image by Regional Sales Group I with the Promotion Department as the Relevant Other

A. *How Members of Regional Sales Group I See Themselves in Relation to Promotion Department:*

1. Circumvented
2. Manipulated
3. Receiving benefits of their efforts
4. Nonparticipating (relatively)
5. Defensive
6. Used
7. Productive
8. Instrument of their success
9. Have never taken us into their confidence in admitting that a promotion "bombed"
10. The field would like to help but must be a two-way street

B. *How Members of Regional Sales Group I Feel Promotion Department Sees Them:*

1. Insensitive to corporate needs
2. Noncommunicative upwards, as holding back ideas and suggestions
3. Productive in field-sales work
4. Naive about the promotion side of business
5. Unappreciative of promotion efforts
6. Lacking understanding about their sales objectives
7. Belligerent
8. Overly independent operators
9. Not qualified to evaluate the promotions sent to us
10. Honest in opinions

C. *How Members of Regional Sales Group I Characterize Promotion Department:*

1. Autocratic
2. Productive
3. Unappreciative of field efforts
4. Competent with "things" but not "people"
5. Industrious
6. Inflexible
7. Unrealistic
8. Naive
9. Progressive in promotion philosophy and programs
10. Overly competitive within own department
11. Plagiarists who take field ideas but do not always give credit

Source: See Note 61.

III. Units which had created substantial new business during the design, toward which the least favorable shifts in attitudes were expected. Basically, two units did not participate fully in the confrontation. For example, one produced only a two-dimensional image, its members refusing to describe how they saw themselves.

In addition, three types of criteria questions or items were distinguished *a priori.* For each of these, different predictions seemed appropriate. The three types of questions were:

A. Volitional Criteria Questions, 11 items which tapped attitudes considered relatively easy to change (for example, How much do you want to collaborate with Unit Z?) or attitudes deemed particularly sensitive to the confrontation design (for example, How much information have you received from Unit X?)

B. Objective Criteria Questions, ten items which tapped attitudes that could hardly be changed positively on the basis of the confrontation design, but which might very well drift negatively as people felt more free to be open about their attitudes toward self and others (such as, What is the level of productivity of Unit Z?)

C. Combined Criteria Questions, composed of eleven volitional and ten objective criteria questions, on which a general drift toward favorable changes in attitudes was expected

These expectations may be summarized in the 3 X 3 matrix in Table 2. Interpretively, pre- and postconfrontation administrations of the questionnaire were expected to reveal that the most favorable[17] shifts in attitudes would be reported towards the deeply involved organization units on the volitional items. On the objective items, the expectation was that attitudes toward all organization units would tend to change negatively, and most sharply for the unfinished business units.

The pattern of attitudinal changes above was not only expected, it was intended. Designing for "negative" or "unfavorable" shifts in attitudes on the objective criteria questions may seem perverse, but the learning design was a dilemma/invention model that captures much of the essence of the dynamics of

Table 2 Expected Shifts in Attitudes Due to Confrontation Design, by Type of Organization Unit and Kind of Attitude

		Types of Units		
		I. Deeply Involved	*II. Under-represented*	*III. Unfinished Business*
Types of Criteria-Questions	*A. Volitional*	Most favorable shifts in attitudes	Moderately favorable shifts in attitudes	Least favorable shifts in attitudes
	B. Objective	Least unfavorable shifts in attitudes	Moderately unfavorable shifts in attitudes	Most unfavorable shifts in attitudes
	C. Combined	Strong favorable shifts in attitudes	Slight favorable shifts in attitudes	Least favorable shifts in attitudes

Source: See Note 61.

T-groups. Let us simplify grievously. The consultants concluded that members of the host organization had entered into a mutual defense pact. In short, lack of openness served to obscure basic organization dilemmas. The confrontation design attempts to induce the public recognition of such dilemmas via greater openness and risk-taking, by explicitly dealing with the reality perceived by organization members. Hence, negative changes in attitudes on the objective criteria questions do not signal a dangerous deterioration of morale. Rather, such changes establish that dilemmas requiring attention have been acknowledged. During a confrontation, organization members are encouraged to activate the "dilemma" part of the dilemma/invention learning model, by seeing themselves and others as less productive than they were willing to admit previously. At the same time, however, the confrontation design encourages organization members to work harder on the "invention" aspects of the learning model. That is, the design is intended to favorably change the attitudes of organization members on the volitional criteria questions, toward a greater desire to cooperate in coping with organizational dilemmas.

Table 3 establishes that these complex expectations are generally supported by attitudinal changes in the host population. The ratios in Table 3 derive from changes in before and after attitudes of all participants toward each of nine target positions or units of organization, including their own. A ratio greater than 1.0 indicates that favorable changes in attitudes outnumber unfavorable changes; a ratio less than 1.0 indicates that negative or unfavorable changes in attitudes are more numerous.

Sampling the data in Table 3 reveals, for example, that deeply involved units attract the most favorable shifts in attitudes, as expected. Favorable changes in attitudes toward those units at a minimum are 14 times more likely than unfavorable changes. The other two types of units, in contrast, experience approximately a 2:1 ratio of positive to negative changes. All three types of units, within a narrow range, experience unfavorable attitudinal shifts on objective items. Roughly, unfavorable attitudinal changes outnumber favorable changes by 2-5 to 1. The negative trend was anticipated. As anticipated, also, the data do not even suggest wholesale rejection. Thus, the deeply involved units were the targets of roughly the same proportion of favorable to unfavorable changes on the objective criteria questions as the new business units. In addition, although the data are not reported here, individuals describing their own unit saw themselves just as "unfavorably" on the objective criteria questions after the confrontation as did others describing them. So, the drift toward negative changes was not an "us good guys" and "those bad guys" phenomenon.

Two capsule characterizations seem appropriate. After the confrontation, individuals seemed more willing to undertake a task that they saw as more demanding than they had thought. This describes an orientation that is conducive to effective learning and change.

Table 3 Summary Data Concerning Attitudinal Changes Toward Nine Units of Organization, Based on Pre- and Postconfrontation Administrations of Questionnaire

			Types of Organization Units or Positions		
			I. Deeply Involved	*II. Under-represented*	*III. Unfinished Business*
Types of Criteria Questions	*A. Volitional*	Ratio ± Changes	14.00 (28/2)	2.33 (28/12)	1.86 (13/7)
		Ratio ± Statistically Significant Changes	Infinity (14/0)	4.45 (9/2)	1.67 (5/3)
	B. Objective	Ratio ± Changes	.65 (13/20)	.42 (13/31)	.38 (6/16)
		Ratio ± Statistically Significant Changes	.25 (1/4)	0 (0/10)	.18 (2/11)
	C. Combined	Ratio ± Changes	1.86 (41/22)	.95 (41/43)	.83 (19/23)
		Ratio ± Statistically Significant Changes	3.75 (15/4)	.82 (9/11)	.58 (11/19)

Note: Numbers in parentheses indicate the raw number of positive/negative changes.
Source: See Note 61.

More broadly, without making too much of such data, the summary data in Table 3 suggest the antithesis of a degenerative communication process.

Some Qualifications About Initial Effects

Although data support the efficacy of one spin-off of sensitivity training, four points must be stressed by way of qualification. *First,* the data trends in Table 3 probably understate the power of the confrontation design. Briefly, the learning situation was very complex in the present case, closure often was not possible when confrontations were held, and some mutually desired confrontations were not held because of lack of time. More favorable attitudinal changes should show up in cases where there are fewer loose ends.

Second, no direct evidence about behavioral change is presented here, but various data strongly imply behavioral changes. For example, the history of the core groups was characterized by an excess of zeal, if anything. Specifically, some core groups attempted problem-solving in areas beyond their jurisdiction, against which consultants had strongly cautioned and advised. Predictably, superiors in the broader control system restrained some of the core groups.

Third, the confrontation design seems widely applicable and safe, but some potential host organizations may not be culturally prepared for it. No doubt, most culturally unprepared organizations would be aware enough to avoid soliciting such an experience. But consultants still face a real responsibility of judging the preparedness of the host organizations and its personnel to profit from what is for the most organizations a novel vehicle for exerting influence.

Should the consultant misjudge an organization's preparedness, however, the most probable damage is the loss of a useful opportunity for development. That is, the confrontation design includes a wide array of safety features. Consider the large number of points at which participants must make collaborative judgments about the degree of openness they are willing to risk. For example, the groups used in confrontation designs give each individual a range of resources which can advise against or support various statements in a 3-D Image. In short, the 3-D Image requires conscious risk taking and multiple testing for commitment. And that is intended by the design. For we can really learn only as we risk and make real commitments.

Safeguards also inhibit taking the easy ways out of avoiding a confrontation or weaseling in the preparation of images. That is, any group developing a 3-D Image will be alert to the design property that watering down their image to guarantee safety may invite ridicule as their image is compared unfavorably to images developed by others. The derivative tension is very real, and it seems to result in a kind of escalation of truthfulness in which the relative merits of openness and closedness are very consciously weighed. As it should be, then, a major share of the responsibility for the success or failure of a confrontation design rests with members of the host organization. They are, after all, the ones who basically must live with the results.

Fourth, no particular skills are required of participants in a confrontation design, but skilled consultants should be available each time images are actually shared. Such a resource person can intervene if things go badly, and can always serve to encourage behavior that respects laboratory values, as well as to model for other participants the greater openness which is the goal of the confrontation design. Far more likely, however, the particular usefulness of the consultant lies in encouraging participants to confront each other at deeper levels when he or she suspects some varnishing of the truth is taking place.

A Technical Note

Note that different effects may have resulted if a "fishbowl" or "group-observing-group" vehicle had been used in the confrontation. A fishbowl formation would have had each group observing every other group in the *act of preparing its 3-D Image.* In the present case, participants saw the product of each other's processes but had mostly to infer those underlying processes. As Robert R. Blake notes in another connection, the fishbowl highlights some critical data. He explains:

> The fishbowl permits each group to see the other group members working together. . . . This permits the second group to observe group culture, tradition, power relations, and esprit . . . , to say nothing of hearing the content discussed. The same is true when the second group gets in the fishbowl. What this means is that critical aspects of behavior, usually unrevealed . . . , are brought into view. . . . The *image production* and exchange approach . . . obscures social process.[18]

Essentially, then, the present vehicle limits, and deliberately so, the degree to which one group gets acquainted with another. However, the fishbowl is likely to be most appropriate when two groups are involved.[19] This is a major limitation.

Persistence of Initial Effects*

Did the effects persist? The standard questionnaire exploring attitudes about interdepartmental relations was administered three times to test whether the observed attitudinal changes persisted over time. Administrations I and II were 5 days apart; Administration III followed by some 7 months. All comparisons below involve Administration II versus Administration III and are based on questionnaire responses of forty-five managers at several levels in subunits of the marketing division of a large corporation.

Any marked persistence of attitudinal changes suggests the usefulness of the confrontation design as one technique in the repertoire of organizational change agents. Since no planned reinforcement of the effects of the confrontation experience was attempted by managers or consultants during the interval between Administrations II and III, any persistence of effects implies the potency of the design.

Intervening Divisional History

The target organization experienced rough times in the 7-month period between Administrations II and III, which makes particularly noteworthy any persistence of attitudinal change. Six interacting elements suggest the fuller range of forces operating on the marketing division in which the research was conducted.

First, a significant government action was taken against one major product. This was a double blow. The anticipated loss in sales would have significant effects on division performance. Moreover, the government action sharply limited promotion efforts on other products as well, and promotional skills were the division's major strength. Morale among the field-sales force was hit especially hard, and headquarters-field relations were sorely tested.

*This section draws heavily from Robert T. Golembiewski and Arthur Blumberg, "Persistence of Attitudinal Changes Induced by a Confrontation Design," *Academy of Management Journal,* Vol. 12 (September 1969), pp. 309-318.

Second, division dependence on a few old products, on which patents had lapsed or were soon to run out, was highlighted by the government action.

Third, division sales and profits fell by nearly 20 percent in the 7 months following the confrontation, with profound consequences. The division traditionally promised ambitious profits to corporate, and delivered, the reward being substantial autonomy from corporate oversight. As sales and profits tumbled, corporate interventions escalated, and headquarters-field relationships worsened in critical regards.

Fourth, crucial interdepartmental issues were raised as some budgets were cut sharply and others hardly at all, to help achieve the profit target for the current year. Such cuts were widely perceived as Band-Aids. Budget-cutting it was, however.

Fifth, corporate policies toward the division seemed to change abruptly. The overall divisional effect was to give more attention to protecting the "Big No. 1," one's department and/or one's job. The potential for interdepartmental conflict zoomed upwards, with the paradoxical effect of encouraging greater corporate oversight when what existed was already considered too much.

Sixth, several significant personnel actions reduced responsibilities and salaries of key division employees. The derivative tensions exacerbated an already delicate situation.

Minimal Expectations About Persistence

The effect of time on the attitudinal changes induced by the confrontation design cannot be strictly isolated, therefore, but some insight is possible. In this spirit, for volitional items only, one simple and conservative decision rule is proposed to judge the persistence over time of attitudinal changes induced by a confrontation design.

> *Decision Rule I:* The confrontation design can claim to have affected persisting attitudinal changes if comparisons of Administration III versus II show that statistically significant negative changes occur on the volitional items in only a minority of cases.

Decision Rule I is reasonable, perhaps even rigorous. The division's history implies massive impetus toward worsening interdepartmental relations and, as Table 4 shows, considerable potential existed for downward readjustments in attitudes. That is, comparing Administration II to Administration I, positive changes were observed on a total of 90 percent of the volitional items referring to deeply involved units or positions.[20] And, 46 percent of all changes were positive and statistically significant. The effects are less marked but still substantial for the two other classes of organization units or positions. Any major decay over time in attitudinal changes induced by the confrontation design, then, can reasonably be inferred only from major statistically significant negative changes in attitudes, Administration III versus II.

Table 4 Percentage Summary of Changes in Attitudes, Volitional Items Only, Administration II Versus I

	Three Classes of Organization Units Which Were Targets of Attitudes		
Volitional Items	*Three Deeply Involved Units* ($N_1 = 30$)	*Four Under-represented Units* ($N_2 = 40$)	*Two New Business Units* ($N_3 = 20$)
Positive Statistically Significant Changes	46.3%	45.0%	25.0%
Positive Statistically Insignificant Changes	43.7	10.0	37.5
No Changes	3.3	15.0	2.5
Negative Statistically Insignificant Changes	6.7	25.0	20.0
Negative Statistically Significant Changes	0.0	5.0	15.0
	100.0%	100.0%	100.0%

Note: The percentages above are based on ratings by 45 managers of each of nine units on 10 Volitional Items. The total data base, then, includes 4,050 ratings. Ninety tests of significance were run on the differences between the means of each of the 10 items for each of the nine positions or units. The percentages are based on these ninety tests of significance. Hence $N_1 + N_2 + N_3 = 90$.

Source: See Note 61.

For the objective items, given the massive imponderables, a standstill criterion estimates the efficacy of the confrontation design.

> *Decision Rule II:* The dilemma/invention model will be supported if Administration III of the standard questionnaire reveals no major negative trends on objective items when compared to Administration II.

Operationally, "no major negative trends" is defined as an approximate balance of positive and negative changes on objective items, comparing Administration III with Administration II. For the objective items, a substantial negative trend was observed between Administration II versus I, as Table 5 shows.

The 7 months of turbulent organizational history also permit a fortuitous test of two basic questions about the confrontation design. Do the more open and critical attitudes it induced make an organization especially vulnerable to massive environmental forces such as those described above, which will occur now and again in every organization? If so, applications of the confrontation design would be potentially dangerous. Alternatively, is there any evidence that the improvements in volitional items also induced by the confrontation design have the opposite effect of making an organization more effective in coping with such massive environmental forces?

Tests of Minimal Expectations

A test of Decision Rule I strongly implies that the confrontation design had useful effects in the 7-month period between Administrations II and III of the standard questionnaire. That is, on the volitional items, the substantial

Table 5 Percentage Summary of Changes in Attitudes, Objective Items Only, Administration II Versus I

	Three Classes of Organization Units Which Were Targets of Attitudes		
Objective Items	*Three Deeply Involved Units* ($N_1 = 44$)	*Four Under-represented Units* ($N_2 = 33$)	*Two New Business Units* ($N_3 = 22$)
Positive Statistically Significant Changes	3.0%	0.0%	9.1%
Positive Statistically Insignificant Changes	21.2	15.9	13.7
No Changes	15.2	13.6	4.5
Negative Statistically Insignificant Changes	48.5	47.8	27.2
Negative Statistically Significant Changes	12.1	22.7	45.5
	100.0%	100.0%	100.0%

Note: The percentages above are based on ratings by 45 managers of each of nine units on 11 Objective Items. The total data base, then, includes 4,455 ratings. Ninety-nine tests of significance were run on the differences between the means of each of the 10 items for each of the nine positions or units. The percentages are based on these 99 tests of significance. Hence $N_1 + N_2 + N_3 = 99$.
Source: See Note 61.

improvements in attitudes following a confrontation experience tend to persist. In this sense, the confrontation design seemed to provide a cushion against massive environmental forces; it did not amplify them. Specifically, Table 6 provides summary data establishing that Decision Rule I is met. Only one attitudinal change in ten was negative and statistically significant, overall, comparing Administration III with II. Nearly 60 percent of the additional cases also are negative, but these changes were usually small and can confidently be attributed to random variations in the data.

The powerful impact of the brief confrontation experience on Volitional attitudes also can be suggested by comparing Tables 4 and 6. For example, over three times as many positive statistically significant entries appear in the former as do negative statistically significant ones in the latter. This suggests, of course, that the improvements in attitudes about interdepartmental relations induced on volitional items by a brief confrontation design are substantially preserved despite 7 months of harrowing organization history.

The summary data in Table 7 also meet Decision Rule II, suggesting that a runaway-train effect did not occur between Administrations II and III of the standard questionnaire. More broadly, the data suggest that the confrontation design set in motion dynamics that increase an organization's ability to cope with a hostile environment. Of the attitudinal changes between the two administrations, one-third are negative and statistically significant, to be sure. But more than a third of the changes trend positively or do not change. Another third trend negatively but do not reach usually accepted levels of statistical significance. Given that massive environmental forces encouraged a major worsening of the relationships between organization units, this record does not suggest a runaway-train effect.

Other Supporting Evidence

Substantial evidence, in sum, supports the persistence over time of the attitudinal effects of a confrontation design, despite the uncertainties involved. In addition, the confrontation design has by now gained a serious niche for itself in the OD literature.[21] Early successes with the design have encouraged numerous applications. In one case, for example, a confrontation design was utilized to turnaround the operations in a plant that was losing $1,000,000 a year and was scheduled for shutdown. Within a year after the confrontation, the yearly loss had been reduced by four-fifths.[22] Notably, also, cross-cultural results imply that the design is not narrowly culture-bound.[23]

Such applications are intriguing, but much needed specificity about the confrontation design is obviously lacking. The conditions under which it works best, for example, are imprecisely unknown. Nor is it clear when the design is contraindicated.

Table 6 A Percentage Summary of Changes in Attitudes, Volitional Items Only, Administration III Versus II

	Three Classes of Organization Units Which Were Targets of Attitudes			
Volitional Items	*Three Deeply Involved Units* ($N_1 = 30$)	*Three Under-represented Units* ($N_2 = 30$)	*Two New Business Units* ($N_3 = 20$)	*Weighted Average*
Positive Statistically Significant Changes	0.0%	0.0%	0.0%	0.0%
Positive Statistically Insignificant Changes	13.3	20.0	20.0	17.5
No Changes	13.3	10.0	5.0	11.2
Negative Statistically Insignificant Changes	56.7	53.3	70.0	58.8
Negative Statistically Significant Changes	16.7	16.7	5.0	12.5
	100.0%	100.0%	100.0%	100.0%

Note: The percentages above are based on ratings by 45 managers of each of eight units on 10 Volitional Items. The total data base, then, includes 3,600 ratings. Eighty tests of significance were run on the differences between the means of each of the 10 items for each of the nine positions or units. The percentages are based on these 80 tests of significance. Hence $N_1 + N_2 + N_3 = 80$.

Source: See Note 61.

Table 7 Percentage Summary of Changes in Attitudes, Objective Items Only, Administration III Versus II

	Three Classes of Units Which Were Targets of Attitudes			
Objective Items	*Three Deeply Involved Units* (N_1= 30)	*Three Under-represented Units* (N_2= 33)	*Two New Business Units* (N_3= 22)	*Weighted Average*
Positive Statistically Significant Changes	3.0%	6.0%	9.1%	5.7%
Positive Statistically Insignificant Changes	15.2	27.3	22.7	21.7
No Changes	5.0	6.0	18.2	7.9
Negative Statistically Insignificant Changes	33.3	30.3	18.2	28.4
Negative Statistically Significant Changes	43.5	30.3	31.8	36.3
	100.0%	99.9%	100.0%	100.0%

Note: The percentages above are based on ratings by 45 managers of each of nine units on 11 Objective Items. The total data base, then, includes 4,455 ratings. Eighty-eight tests of significance were run on the differences between the means of each of the 10 items for each of the nine positions or units. The percentages are based on these 88 tests of significance. Hence $N_1 + N_2 + N_3 = 88$.

Source: See Note 61.

Caution About Diagnosing Two Kinds of Processes

Let us build on the need for greater specificity about where and when the confrontation design seems most applicable. Suggestive if not conclusive considerations imply that the previous and extended discussion of a useful design must be tethered firmly, that the design may ill suit certain conditions. As everywhere, diagnosis is critical, and one can have too much of even the very best things.

Jerry Harvey provides explicit direction for this one-more-time emphasis on the primacy of diagnosis. He urges differentiating two kinds of processes that can develop between individuals or groups: the crisis of disagreement, or "real conflict," where the dilemma is that people differ in their views of reality and/or in what to do about those views; and the crisis of agreement, where the underlying dilemma derives not from difference but from implicit and unexpressed similarity. Exhibit 2 goes into detail in describing the behavioral processes underlying a crisis of agreement, as well as the central elements that conceptually can be said to reinforce it. This description draws very substantially from Harvey,[24] and may oversimplify his significant treatment. In any case, the central notion in a crisis of agreement can be expressed in terms of "the Abilene Paradox"—the situation where several people behave in ways that they mutually dislike or reject because each of them presumes that all others prefer that behavior. To avoid being a party-poop, then, they all go along on a unanimously unpreferred course of action.[25] Oppositely, we all know what a crisis of disagreement is. Papa wants to watch the Super Bowl, for example; mama wants to see the ballet; and they each either say so, very affirmatively, or one pouts because the other monopolizes the TV set without thinking of the other's preferences or perhaps even caring about them. I have tried my hand at describing the crisis of disagreement in Exhibit 2, using Harvey's style of approach.

Most people knowingly nod their heads when introduced to the crisis of agreement, for they can recall cases that fit that type. But Harvey's distinction has profound implications for OD interventions, and far more so than for stimulating sardonic reverie.

Specifically, a crisis of disagreement—the kind more or less assumed in the literature as *the* only kind[26]—seems well-suited to learning vehicles like the confrontation design. Basically, the design provides procedures and rests on a set of norms concerning when and how to express differences—precisely what is required by the crisis of disagreement. Relatedly, the design is from an important perspective a device for reducing distance—between those at different levels of the hierarchy, or between those experiencing a "communication gap." And, confrontation designs may reveal new data, even as they typically reflect some perceptions that participants share and as they induce a shared experience that can be a powerful bonding agent for overcoming mutual difficulties. The sum and substance of it: Participants typically find that expression of the differences was not so fearsome as they believed; participants often get new data whose value they recognize; participants often feel a sense of greater closeness; and they are likely to feel a release of energy, by hypothesis, energy that was previously used to repress differences or to assuage anxiety or uncertainty. I assign a high probability to such consequences, given a crisis of disagreement, although qualifications must be specified. To illustrate:

> Several partners were considering a merger with a larger firm, and serious concerns began to develop in a once-cohesive partnerships.
>
> They requested a confrontation experience, based on direct participation of one of the partners in a prior and "successful" application. I introduced the design this way: "I estimate the chances are 9 in 10 that—when we finish several hours from now—you will be more united than you are now, more clear on where you stand, with more energy to make the important decisions about the merger." "Of course," I added, "you also may learn something during our time together, you may have a suspicion reinforced, that may drive you further apart. That could happen."
>
> Extensive discussion highlighted several such divisive issues, previously not fully appreciated, which were so great as to induce one of the partners to leave. The issues were basically economic, and constituted a "given" for some that one partner could not accept. His greater clarity about the point induced the dissolution of the partnership.

Exhibit 2 A Schematic Contrast of Two Types of Crisis

Crisis of Agreement[a]	Crisis of Disagreement
A. Underlying behavioral processes	A. Underlying behavioral processes
1. Organization members experience pain from some specific collective problem(s), with feelings about impotence or incompetence deriving from the failure to resolve or manage the problem(s) somehow.	1. Organization members may or may not experience pain from some specific collective problem(s), but such problem(s) do exist although consciousness-raising about them may be required.
2. Members share the same private concept of problem(s) facing their organization, and individually recognize the same or similar underlying explanations or causes of the problem(s), if any are acknowledged.	2. Members do not share the same private concept of problem(s) facing their organization, and individually have very different underlying explanations or causes of the problem(s), if any are acknowledged.
3. As individuals, many or all organization members have similar and compatible preferences for coping with the problem(s).	3. As individuals, many or all organization members have different and incompatible preferences for coping with the problem(s).
4. As individuals, many or all organization members see the same or similar solution as appropriate for resolving or managing the problem(s).	4. As individuals, many or all organization members see different or incompatible solutions as appropriate for resolving or managing the problem(s).
5. In public settings, organization members consistently do not communicate accurately to one another—about their preferences, beliefs, knowledge of causes and consequences of organization problems—and hence mutually create a false or misleading collective reality. The probable result is a low-energy system—careful, perhaps polite, and very conscious of roles and jurisdictions.	5. In public settings, therefore, organization members may deal with one another in two basic ways: probably in a minority of cases, to risk open conflict, hostility, etc., attendant to the expression of disagreements probably in most cases, to avoid the risk of acrimony (as by agreeing not to disagree openly on certain issues) but at the expense of suppressing real issues and conflict.

6. Given a false or misleading collective reality, on definite balance, collective decisions get made that reflect neither member preferences nor their real views of reality, with the results more than likely being counterproductive both for individual and organization goals.

7. Greater member pain is likely, and a sense of both individual and collective incompetence and impotency probably will grow.

8. The cycle is set to repeat itself, probably with greater speed and intensity as well as with a lessened probability of corrective action.

B. Central elements reinforcing the process

1. *Action anxiety:* Individuals are conscious and cogent about analysis and their own preferences, but fearful of taking or suggesting action.

The openly conflictful organizations probably will be high-energy systems, with substantial but perhaps incompatible personal commitment and involvement, great but perhaps fruitless expenditures of effort, and so on. The suppressing organization probably will be characterized by low levels of energy, commitment, and involvement.

6. The probability seems high that both adaptations—if for different reasons—will lead to a false or misleading collective reality, over time. Openly conflictful organizations may develop polarizations that inhibit or preclude members from communicating accurately with one another. Suppressing organizations may create the same effect by defining certain subjects as off-limits.

7. Greater member pain is likely in both cases, and a sense of both individual and collective incompetence probably will grow.

8. The cycle is set to repeat itself, probably with greater speed and intensity, as well as with a lessened probability of corrective analysis and action.

B. Central elements reinforcing the process

1. *Legitimacy anxiety:* Organization members are uncertain about the rules of the game for public analysis and preference-stating, which may either inhibit analysis, and/or encourage aggressive acting-out in preferences or descriptions of reality.

Exhibit 2 (Continued)

Crisis of Agreement[a]	Crisis of Disagreement
2. *Negative fantasies re action:* Very serious consequences are assumed to follow from any action consistent with what members believe should be done or know to be the case.	2. *Negative fantasies re analysis:* Very serious consequences are assumed to follow from any attempts at analysis of what members believe should be done or is the case, as in "opening a Pandora's box."
3. *Fear of separation:* The prime existential risk underlying action anxiety and negative fantasies inheres in a fantasied separation from others—as in being fired or losing friends.	3. *Fear of unsatisfactory inclusion:* The prime existential risk is being incorporated with others having unacceptably different sets of preferences of what should exist or views of what does exist.
4. *Primacy of risk over certainty:* The risk of confronting others with what individual organization members know or prefer seems too great, given the fear that others will reject the confronter. In sum, the fear of rejection is more motivating than the certainty of what one knows, even though the failure to confront probably will mean failure to problem-solve and, consequently, pain for organization members.	4. *Primacy of we vs. they:* The risk of confronting others with disagreements about what individuals know or prefer seems too great, given the fear that this will only further polarize participants. In sum, the fear of polarization is more motivating than the hope of some accommodations whose achievement would neither be taxing nor require unacceptable concessions, even though the failure to confront probably will mean failure to problem-solve and, consequently, pain for organization members.

[a]Based on Jerry B. Harvey, "Consulting During Crises of Agreement," esp. pp. 162-165, in W. Warner Burke (ed.), *Current Issues and Strategies in Organization Development* (New York: Human Science Press, 1977).

A Design Poorly Suited to a Crisis of Agreement

But what about the suitability of a confrontation design for a crisis of agreement? Not very promising, this argument maintains, and perhaps the design may even be seriously counterproductive in many cases. Consider a sketch of the contra-case. Crises of agreement need to encourage the expression of similarities, not differences; instead of being the solution, the low social distance and the overly high importance invested in maintaining relationships constitute important parts of the problem. Moreover, group confrontation in such cases at best will reinforce what everyone already knows. Hence, that design may only deepen despair that no action has been taken, may raise questions about courage and competence in not taking action even when the issues are quite clear, may imply serious issues of trust about why colleagues did not share what they all really knew, and so on. Paramountly, perhaps, crises of agreement often may be rooted in an unrealistically high estimate of the abilities of fellow group members, encouraging each member to repress private attitudes and to think: I'm the only one out of step in this high-powered group, so I better keep quiet. Once the unshared agreements become clear, group members may be seriously shaken about their own gullibility and the obvious inadequacies of others. In short, the crisis of confidence may deepen.

A brief case also implies the awkward fit of a confrontation design to a crisis of agreement. To get the bottom line, two management groups responded to a 3-D Image as part of an OD program—an Operating Committee, and the collection of managers reporting directly to them. Among other products, the two groups independently generated these outputs for discussion:

How Operating Committee Believes Subordinates See Operating Committee	How Subordinates See Operating Committee
Not communicative enough	Divergent and disunified
Floundering, indecisive	Lacking evidence of authority and decisiveness
Defensive, unreceptive	Spend too much time on non-key issues
Too involved in day-to-day operations and decisions	Poor catalyst
Overcautious	Do not communicate a sense of direction or purpose
Under tight corporate control, and disadvantaged in competing for corporate resources	"Nice guys" [i.e., not very competent]
	Too much resistance rather than encouragement

Intervenors did not diagnose a crisis of agreement; indeed, they did not then think in such terms. The 3-D design, in brief, had bubbled up from the enthusiasm of the subordinates, all of whom had been through a sensitivity-training experience. Their firm was facing a very uncertain future–falling demand and no new products–and had been hoping for the best for a year or more. The subordinates made a facile transfer of their T-group learning. "As soon as the Operating Committee learns how we see them," the prevailing optimism may be summarized, "the tough decisions will be made, fast." The Operating Committee, more or less fresh from their own independent T-group experiences, agreed to the design.

The 3-D confrontation design initially generated more heat than light, more despair than optimism. Participant reactions were diverse, but with a definite central tendency. When the two lists above (among others) were taped to a wall, the subordinates grew very angry. "I'll be damned," one of them said. "They knew exactly how we saw them, and they haven't done diddly-squat about it. I wasn't even sure how my colleagues felt until we did the 3-D! Op Com is either too dumb to have their present jobs; or they don't at all respect our unanimously negative views, which implies they think we're too narrow and immature for our jobs." At first, members of the Operating Committee tended to be sheepish and withdrawn. "We each thought that's how it would come out, but we really didn't talk about it–I guess with an unspoken hope that things would be better." Frustration and anger soon began to show. "I guess we were silently colluding to be hopeful–hoping to protect each other and our subordinates. And what do we get for it? We get dumped on."

Intervenors also came in for their share of attention, and reasonably so. "That's a great trick you [intervenors] did with marking pens and newsprint," one Operating Committee member noted with mixed sadness and anger at self as well as consultants. "I hope you can quickly yank another rabbit out of your hat–something that will save face and solve our problem."

No rabbits were pulled out of hats, of course, and things stayed wild and woolly for a long period. The eventual outcome? The required tough decisions got made, and quite expeditiously, and the rough implementation got done with general agreement and relative goodwill. But everyone did not live happily ever after. Several changes were made in Op Com membership, for example. And several times it appeared as if Op Com might try to punish their more vocal subordinates for saying discouraging words. Over a period of months, however, matters did get resolved in ways that were broadly accepted. Why? No one can really say for certain. Intervenors do believe, however, that the prior and successful T-group experiences were significant–and perhaps determinative–in these complex outcomes. And intervenors are now absolutely certain that a 3-D design does not optimally suit a crisis of agreement.

A Design Better Suited to a Crisis of Agreement

In sum, the prime goal in crises of agreement should focus on motivating action based on existing commonalities, and crises of disagreement seem to respond to sharpening differences, generating new data, and encouraging analysis. The trick in the former case is to stress the commonalities while at the same time convincing participants that the failure to recognize publicly and express those commonalities earlier is no rare disease. If mismanaged agreement constitutes the dilemma, resolution can be quick, almost instantaneous. The key involves emphasizing the agreement so that it really gets heard, without reducing self-esteem and competence. This may seen easy, but that appearance is very deceptive, and especially so where continued membership is so valued that no one will risk saying the dischordant word for fear of rejection, even though many (or even all) colleagues privately take the same position.[27] I have in mind a person who at once privately had desperate doubts about our Viet Nam policies, yet was publicly one of their major architects. He confided his doubts to his diary but not to his colleagues who, tragically, shared his private doubts but were no more able to express them. One hears—tragedy of all tragedies—that their public stonewalling was encouraged by a fear of crossing President Lyndon Johnson, whose support for the war was unqualified at first but who later privately began to have the same grave doubts as many of his major advisors. Johnson was not able to back down himself from his earlier position, and he got no help in that regard from his advisors, even though many of them yearned for a change and Johnson himself may have welcomed a face-saving opportunity to do so.[28]

The goals of the two kinds of crises seem to require different designs, then, as is suggested by two prototypic questions:

> *Crisis of Disagreement:* "Oh, so that's how things are, how we differ. . . ! How can we remedy that?"
>
> *Crisis of Agreement:* "Yes, I knew that all along. But you can't do anything about it. Lord knows we tried. It's just a painful given."

Phrased in such terms, the two kinds of crisis imply several underlying developmental sequences. To illustrate, it may be the case that crises of agreement constitute a more serious stage following failure to resolve an initial crisis of disagreement. For example, efforts to resolve the latter may have excited emotions and so on, and the resulting pain may have encouraged general public repression of the causes, which nonetheless remain to do their work. It might also be that some institutional contexts—for example public employment with a protectionist civil service system—might encourage the evolution of crises of disagreement into crises of agreement; or such contexts may directly tend to create more crises of agreement as reasonable responses to the "fact" that "you just can't do anything about that here, at least not in our work lives."

Exhibit 3 Sketch of a Design for Crisis of Agreement

A. Key diagnostic questions

1. In general, how are things going in the organization?
2. What in particular is going well?
3. What are some specific organization problems which need to be solved?
4. What actions do you think need to be taken to solve them?
5. What problem-solving actions have you and others attempted, and what were the outcomes?
6. If you have not taken action, what prevents your taking action to solve them?

B. Diagnostic guidelines

1. If answers to question 1 are consistently positive, the organization presumably experiences neither conflict of disagreement nor conflict of agreement. Only reporting back to confirm the health of the organization is necessary.
2. If answers to questions 1-4 consistently differ, the organization may be presumed to be in a conflict of disagreement. A design like the confrontation design would be appropriate.
3. A crisis of agreement may be presumed when these conditions are met by responses from many or all organization members.

   Pain and conflict get emphasized in responses to questions 1-3.

   Agreement about organization problems surfaces on question 3.

   Agreement about probable solutions also exists on question 4.

   Much rationalization about why what should be done cannot be done gets expressed in responses to questions 5 and 6.

   Evidence is presented about actions actually taken, especially in response to question 5, that are contrary to what respondents believe should be done.

C. An intervention for crisis of agreement

1. Sort the interview data into the basic themes of agreement.
2. Themes get reported back in a public session in ways that use respondents' own words as much as possible but that protect anonymity.
3. All those interviewed then write a collective summary of all of the data supporting each theme of agreement, decide on the action-implications of the themes, and plan specific actions.
4. Summarize the theory of agreement sketched in Exhibit 2, to reinforce understanding of why and how members were inhibited from sharing agreements with each other.
5. Individual organization members are coached, in private, about actions they might take in light of the agreements shared with their colleagues.

Source: Based on Jerry B. Harvey, "Consulting During Crises of Agreement," esp. pp. 169-171, in W. Warner Burke (ed.), *Current Issues and Strategies in Organization Development* (New York: Human Science Press, 1977).

Harvey suggests a design that seems suited to crises of agreement. Exhibit 3 sketches the details. Basically, he recommends privately asking organization members the six questions presented in the exhibit, with assurance that the anonymity of respondents will be respected. The exhibit should be self-explanatory, and more detailed analysis is available elsewhere for interested readers.[29]

Note here only that Harvey's design has three thrusts, specially attuned to the needs of a crisis of agreement. *First,* and paramountly, his design seeks to provide major intellectual supports for why and how colleagues were not able to share agreements with one another. This feature no doubt serves to reduce sheepishness or guilt, as if to say: It happens a lot, for understandable reasons. So don't be too hard on yourselves.

Second, the intervenor can come to play an active coaching role, *privately,* to help get individual members over the rough spots and, perhaps, to save face in some complex senses as well as to begin working through tough issues in private situations. Here, the intervenor may make good use of "worst case" analysis. A crisis of agreement rests on fears that very bad things will happen if the private positions are revealed. The intervenor can then help play a critical game: What would be the worst thing that would happen if private positions were shared? The "worst" might not be so bad. Or if the "worst" were really wicked, intervenor may help develop strategies for coping or for getting out from under.

Third, Harvey's design contrasts with a confrontation design. You can almost hear the "whoosh" of released energy following a successful confrontation design. Indeed, the major problem there is building bounded arenas for action, lest participants exuberantly seek to involve the external world, whether peacefully or kicking and screaming. Harvey's design suggests a more fragile flower, perhaps because a crisis of agreement tends to be associated with low-energy states to begin with. That is, the major issue in Harvey's design seems careful nurturance rather than boundary-building.

Building Ties Between "Line" and "Staff"
A Design for Facilitating Entry and Transfer of Learning

The focus shifts to a design with heroic ambitions, which seem to have been realized in significant part. The design seeks to win a doubleheader, as it were. Thus, it takes on the effects of an apparently inevitable tension in large organizations,[30] that tension between "line" and "staff" which complicates the problems of entry by the latter. And the design also seeks to increase the probability of transfer of learnings first gained in small, contrived groups into the large, back-home organization. Hence, the patent significance of the design sketched below.

Entry and Transfer as Central Problems

No doubt, entry and transfer are major problems. Entry is more straightforward issue, if often a difficult one. Generally, the entry of "staff" officials, like OD intervenors, into "line" activities is variously tense and circumscribed. As two seasoned observers conclude of overall line-staff relationships, in fact, "there probably is no other area of management which in practice causes more difficulty, more friction, and more loss of time and effectiveness."[31] This is a drab litany, and implies that any easing of the problems of entry is very welcome indeed. In the present case, entry was facilitated by the fact that each staff person was assigned to service a specific division and was, in that sense, "their man" as well as a headquarters' staff man. However, as is often the case, line officials saw staff as "trainers" more or less outside the flow of work, while staff believed they could be more effective if they came to be seen as persons who "work regularly and consistently in the organization with the manager."[32]

Let us summarize briefly. Entry not only involves getting into the act, as it were, but also doing that in desired ways. Staff personnel in this case were concerned with the latter kind of entry.

"Transfer" has been emphasized at several points above, and especially in Chapter 3 of Part 1. The problem is generic to all learning. That is, it is all well and good to learn how to hit the ball out of the park in batting practice, but that learning has to be transferred to game conditions. In the present case, trainers were concerned that their essentially classroom approach was too limited to produce adequate transfer of learning into the workaday organization. So, the entry and transfer issues are yin and yang.

Three Design Essentials for Enhancing Entry and Transfer

The design for simultaneously working on both entry and transfer was built around a T-group experience for managers, with the following three added elements:

- The design provided for active participation by internal trainer-consultants (T-Cs) who were not the T-group trainers.
- The systematic reliance on a single conceptual framework for viewing management and organization.
- The use of extensive data collection and feedback to heighten learning for both managers and T-C.

Internal Trainer-Consultants

The T-Cs—staff assigned to service individual managers who volunteered to participate—played important roles in the design. The design's basic goal sought to "establish an open and trustful relationship"[33] between each T-C and his manager. To that end, T-Cs observed the managers throughout their T-group experience, and sought to help the managers profit from that experience in ways that would at once facilitate transfer of learning for the managers and entry of the T-Cs in the back-home organization. Specifically, T-Cs[34]

- Collected back-home data prior to the T-group about each of their managers from subordinates and peers
- Consulted with their manager regarding experiences in the T-group, as well as about the back-home data
- Sought to develop the kind of relationship during the training that would facilitate later cooperation with the manager back at the work site

Unifying Conceptual Network

The design's intent was to interpret all managerial learning and organization applications in terms of Likert's four managerial systems,[35] which have been introduced at several points above. Such a single framework would help managers and T-Cs interpret what was occurring both at the training and the work sites, and that framework also could be used to estimate progress or regress by the manager.

Multiple Data-Collecting Instruments

Using the single conceptual framework, managers received data describing three classes of behavior:[36]

- The manager's behavior in his organizational role, data for which were provided by the manager's peers and subordinates prior to the T-group experience
- The processes of a manager's T-group, as well as of each individual member's behavior
- The processes of an organization simulation that was part of the laboratory in which the managers participated

The values of such multiple-source data are several. Thus, the data could heighten T-group learning, as well as facilitate later transfer. In addition, managers might come to appreciate the value of collecting quantifiable data about human behaviors and relationships, which was not common in the host organization. And, the nontrainer skills of the T-C also could be showcased.

Sketch of the Design

Exhibit 4 provides substantial detail about the design with double-barreled ambitions: to ease entry and to facilitate transfer. Those design details are self-explanatory.

Some Consequences of the Design

Although no systematic research has been undertaken, it appears that about 25 percent of the managers experiencing such a design did go on to make significant improvements at the work site, with the aid of the T-Cs. This implies that the design did in fact have favorable effects on both entry and transfer. As the four developers of the design conclude:[37]

> The entire project to date has yielded several results which are considered highly valuable. It is clear that a successful relationship has been built between the Trainer-Consultant and his managers. From all observations of the T-Cs, their managers seem to see them as useful resources, understand the nature of their role, and are desirous of utilizing them as adjuncts in the manager's back-home application efforts.
>
> Almost all of the managers have either initiated application activity or have voiced intentions of doing so.

For those 25 percent of the managers who have not attempted any detectable back-home OD activity, one or more of three factors seem significant.[38] *First,* some managers do not seem to have benefited from the laboratory experience, and for whatever reason have not been motivated to develop open relationships with their subordinates back-home.

Second, certain parts of the broad organization culture do not support work-site OD efforts. That is, even if a manager had a very positive experience in his T-group and was highly motivated to extend his learning, back-home barriers could inhibit change. Sometimes, the manager's boss would not support the required change effort.

Third, T-C inadequacies or errors have been significant in stifling OD change efforts. By implication, some managers may quickly lose confidence in a T-C who is not perfect. Or, perhaps some managers were looking for an excuse to avoid a change-effort that was both difficult and chancy. In any case, as close observers conclude, the "game" that the T-C must play is definitely not for novices.[39]

Exhibit 4 A Schema of a Design for a Laboratory/Consultation Model for Organization Change

A. Prelaboratory phase: preparing internal trainer-consultants

1. 2.5 days. Trainer-Consultants (T-Cs) met to prepare for working with 25 line managers. There were three major emphases:

   To contribute to the final design of the training laboratory, with especial emphasis on the timing and nature of consultations between T-Cs and their line managers.

   To brief T-Cs on the instruments whose data would be fed-back to line managers, and to examine ways of interpreting and using that data.

   To discuss and role-play the building of the consultant role.

B. Four laboratory phases

1. 2 days. Concentrated T-groups for managers focused on personal and interpersonal issues, featuring a full-day marathon. T-Cs had three primary roles: they

   Observed the behavior of their managers in interacting with others.

   Met with their managers in three private consultations.

   Collected, tabulated, and fed data back to their managers.

2. 2 days. T-Grouping was combined with exercises and theory, with emphasis on group and organizational issues. T-Cs had three more scheduled private consultations with their managers, with the goal of comparing the manager's behavior in the T-group with his performance on several structured tasks.
3. 1 day. Focus is entirely on collecting and analyzing data, T-Cs consulting with their line managers about four kinds of data: systematic perceptions of the manager's back-home behavior previously collected from organizational subordinates and peers.
4. 1 day. Self-choice of activities by participants.

C. Postlaboratory work

1. T-Cs continue their consulting with their managers back-home, with this approximate record of follow-on:

   About 25 percent of participating managers have not persisted in any change effort beyond an initial meeting with their subordinates.

   About half of the managers continued change efforts, but these were not rated as "totally effective" by the appropriate T-Cs.

   The remaining 25 percent of the managers continue to work on change efforts that have already led to "significant improvements."

Source: Based on William G. Dyer, Robert F. Maddocks, J. Weldon Moffitt, and William J. Underwood, "A Laboratory-Consultation Model for Organization Change," esp. pp. 312-316. Reprinted from W. Warner Burke and Harvey A. Hornstein (eds.), *The Social Technology of Organization Development* (Fairfax, Virg.: NTL Learning Resources Corporation, 1972). Reissued: La Jolla, Calif.: University Associates, 1976. Used with permission.

A Common Surrogate for OD
Dynamics and Hazards of Management by Objectives Applications*

Management by objectives, or MBO, appears to be the most pervasive management idea of the last decade, although its roots go back at least a quarter-century.[40] MBO has achieved escalating acceptance not only in industrial organizations, but also in medical institutions, school systems, and government agencies.[41] MBO is not restricted to the United States, and appears to be just as popular in England.[42]

The present analysis of MBO rests on two motivations, in addition to the need to acknowledge its ubiquitous presence. Thus, MBO often is presented as a kind of convenient surrogate for true Organizational Development: a handy one-design remedy for most of what ails almost all organizations. Moreover, although reams have been written about MBO, especially pro[43] but also con,[44] little empirical evidence indicates that MBO produces performance improvements.[45] Clearly, then, organizations have adopted MBO on faith or on the basis of unsubstantiated testimonials, many of them in the form of case studies.

Some Seductive Properties of MBO

How and why has so much enthusiasm been generated by so little evidence? A major part of the explanation certainly includes the seductive appeal of MBO. Not only does it promise to meet central needs in today's organizations. Moreover, MBO seems straightforward and uncomplicated; therefore, just about anyone can teach it, learn it, and implement it. It is also compatible with common sense or conventional wisdom. That is, it appears to be what good managers should be doing, but somehow have not found the time to do. As Levinson puts it:[46]

> The intent of clarifying job obligations and measuring performance against a man's own goals seems reasonable enough. The concern for having both superior and subordinate consider the same matters in reviewing the performance of the latter is eminently sensible. The effort to come to common agreement on what constitutes the subordinate's job is highly desirable.

MBO's promise and apparent straightforwardness are easy enough to illustrate, as in Figure 1. That figure constitutes a flow chart of how MBO rests on three attractive principles:

- Knowledge by superior and subordinate about what is expected at work
- Continuous and effective feedback as to results and evaluations of work

*Expressly written for this volume by Jan P. Muczyk of Cleveland State University.

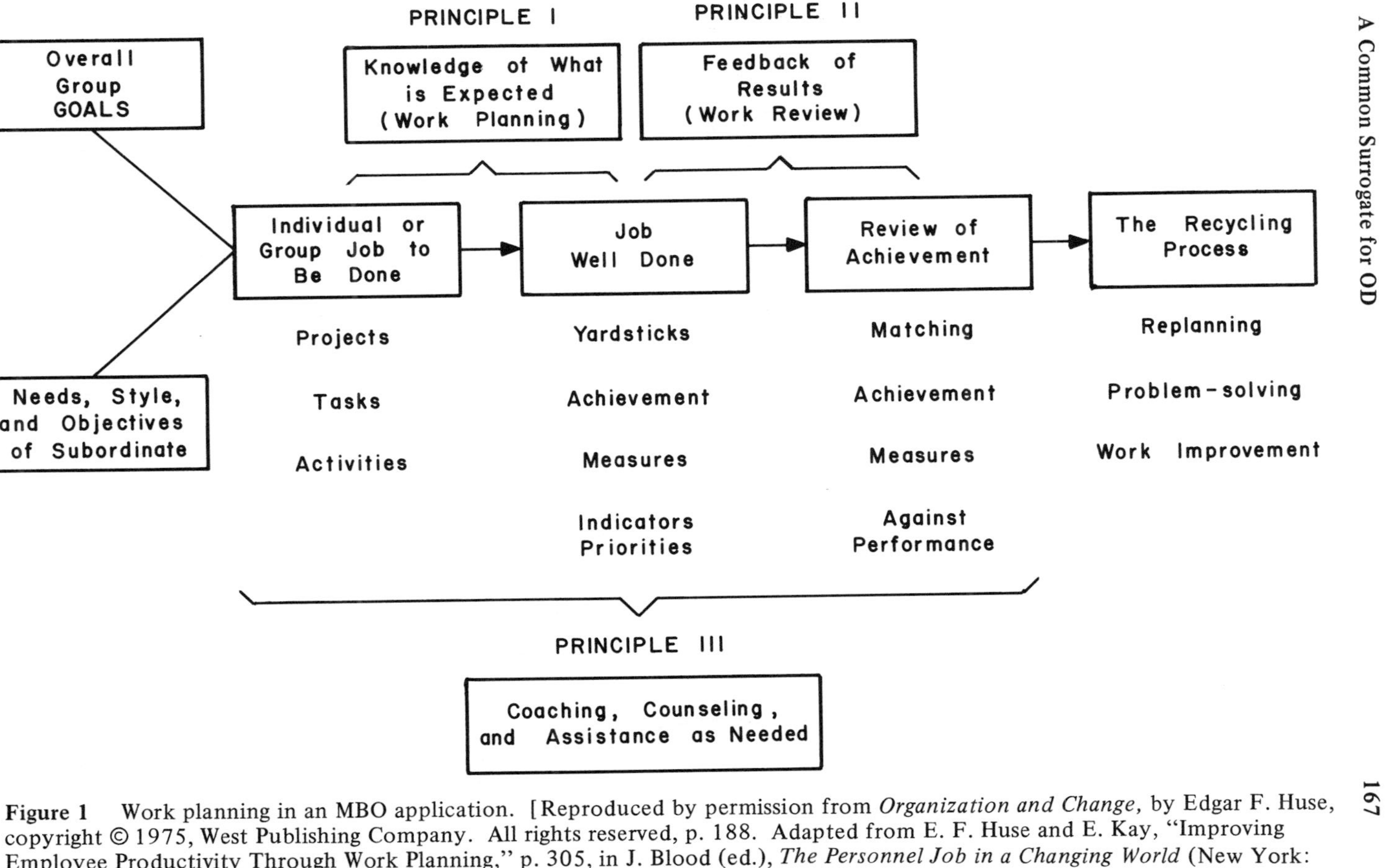

Figure 1 Work planning in an MBO application. [Reproduced by permission from *Organization and Change*, by Edgar F. Huse, copyright © 1975, West Publishing Company. All rights reserved, p. 188. Adapted from E. F. Huse and E. Kay, "Improving Employee Productivity Through Work Planning," p. 305, in J. Blood (ed.), *The Personnel Job in a Changing World* (New York: American Management Association, 1964).]

- Necessary support for both managers and their subordinates for coaching, counseling, or other useful assistance

Furthermore, MBO often is offered as a solution to just about any problem an organization faces. Consider this formidable battery of reasons why different organizations have adopted MBO:

- To improve the effectiveness and efficiency of the organization
- To provide employees the opportunity to influence their work
- To provide members opportunities to develop their potentials
- To improve the ability of the organization to cope with technological and market changes, as well as the changing nature of the work force
- To reward members in accordance with their contributions

In addition, perhaps most significantly, MBO appeals to many as a participative form of management in an era clamoring for greater organizational democracy and power equalization.

Given what MBO might do, or what it is advertised as doing, then, no wonder that few discouraging or even questioning voices are heard. Nobody wants to risk killing the goose said to lay so many golden eggs. Consultants of every ilk have little trouble convincing organizations they need MBO. Indeed, MBO has become in too many instances the snake oil for contemporary organizational medicine shows. Its popularity has no doubt been abetted by the credibility that some academics have lent it through almost unqualified support in the management literature.

Major Problems with MBO

This is one place where questions about MBO will be raised, but the exercise certainly intends no hatchet job. This discussion hopes, in fact, to separate the baby from the bath water. But, hatchet jobs are easier to bring off, and we here accept the risk of trying to draw distinctions where polemics are more prevalent. But so be it. Wish us luck.

Let us begin with two conclusions and a procedure for supporting those conclusions. *First,* the goals associated with MBO are certainly worthwhile pursuing and, coincidentally, are compatible with OD values. *Second,* however, the typical MBO application seeks to attain its aims in ways often characterizable as inadequate and counterproductive. The overall sense of this second point can be briefly established here by Morrisey's warning that managers typically fail to recognize that MBO is "a *human*, not a mechanical process," not "an administrative procedure or reporting system." Where such a concept of MBO has taken root, he warns:[47]

> it should not come as a surprise to learn that there is something less than wholehearted commitment on the part of most managers in the organization. It is conceivable, of course, that introduction of the steps in this process in an arbitrary, mechanical manner may produce a higher level of performance . . . if for no other reason than someone "up there" finally told them specifically what was expected. However, that is not where the real payoff comes from the use of this process.

Supporting these two conclusions will require the bulk of this section. The immediate procedure will be to take, one at a time, a look at a number of central steps in MBO applications, and to illustrate how OD perspectives and designs can facilitate the typical MBO application. A concluding emphasis seeks to show how disappointing OD applications can be shown to rest on inadequacies of the typical MBO process.

Joint Goal Setting

Typically, MBO applications rhapsodize about the joint effort by superior and subordinate pairs to set goals for task and self-development. To simplify some, MBO proponents maintain that joint goal-setting serves a truly imposing array of attractive goals. For example, it can:

- Encourage participative management
- Bring about greater commitment to organizational goals
- Afford the subordinate greater freedom, since MBO is ends-oriented rather than means-oriented
- Reduce uncertainty about superior's wants and expectations, thereby minimizing dysfunctional behavior
- Enchance the development of a subordinate's potential

Let us tether the enthusiasm that such attractive goals inspire in many. The evidence permits only this substantially more cautious proposition: Given appropriate supporting values and behaviors—and especially given an organization patterned after the unorthodox model in Chapter 2—MBO can serve an imposing array of attractive goals. However, these derivative qualifiers of enthusiasm about MBO, among others, are highlighted by experience:

- The appropriate supporting values and behaviors—as in high trust, openness and owning, plus low risk—seldom exist.
- Few MBO applications do much by way of inducing or reinforcing such supporting behaviors or attitudes.

- Indeed, much support for MBO comes from those who see it as a vehicle for preserving the very bureaucratic values and behaviors which heighten the need for MBO.
- Most MBO applications occur in traditional organization structures and, indeed, are basically intended to remedy the structure's defects while preserving that structure, the style of supervision it encourages, and so on.
- And, for the clincher, MBO would be easy to install and would tend to work like a charm—given appropriate supporting values and behavior, and given the unorthodox structure sketched in Chapter 8—but MBO would not be much needed under those two conditions.

Let us survey some of the experience which motivated the cautious proposition offered above, and which provides perspective on the qualifications just listed as to whether MBO will work as most maintain. Consider a central problem. Kerr questions whether joint goal-setting among unequals is possible, in the absence of substantial changes in common managerial ways. He notes:[48]

> The supposition that the superior can comfortably go from "boss-judge" to "friend-helper" and back again is central to MBO. . . . The research literature provides abundant evidence that hierarchical status differences produce some very predictable effects upon interaction patterns, subordinate defensiveness, and quantity and quality of communications, which "stack the deck" against joint goals set by unequals.

That is, one does not convert authoritarian managers into participative ones by simply instructing them to involve subordinates and to give them greater freedom of action. Superiors can, and frequently do, impose their objectives on subordinates.[49] One cannot usually expect superiors who have goals of a 10 percent increase in output, and who will be evaluated in accordance with these goals, for example, to permit their subordinates a lesser goal no matter how well-reasoned their case. Similarly, hierarchical organizations frequently dictate the means by which work is accomplished through policies, procedures, and job descriptions—inflexible methods at times dictated by technological imperatives, union contracts, and by prescribed reporting relationships and interactions. In the absence of fundamental changes in such constraints, joint goal-setting may more approximate a new but limited ratification procedure of what has been in effect decided by those who always made the decisions before MBO.

These considerations imply the shallowness of joint goal-setting in the absence of a debureaucratization of organizations which is a precondition for substantial freedom of action. As such, most MBO applications may not only be inadequate, but they may even work opposite their announced goals. Consider only two cases in point. That is, it appears in various ways that MBO reinforces the bureaucratic model,[50] that it is hierarchy-serving in the significant usual absence of appropriate participative values, behaviors, and structures. For example, the traditional organization of work has been criticized for failing to provide suitable means for dealing with horizontal and diagonal relationships where the performance of many individuals is dependent on the quality of communication, coordination, and cooperation between workers and work groups, at the same or different levels of the organization. In effect, MBO promises attractive consequences, and without the difficult changeover to the unorthodox model described in Chapter 2. Joint goal-setting in MBO, however, remains a vertical, dyadic process which is usually silent with regard to the means by which multiple horizontal and diagonal competing interests are resolved. Similarly, the announced intent of joint goal-setting is to provide the subordinate clearer direction. But, this promise is quite hollow unless the individual controls enough of a total flow of work to be meaningfully responsible for it.

Given such problems, MBO applications often will lead to this outcome: continual increases in quantifiable objectives, but no change in authority or control over a reasonably complete flow of work. How many managers will accept as a satisfactory goal the maintenance of last year's level? Even Scientific Management recognizes a limit, and does not require higher standards each year.

Construction of Action Plans

This critical analysis moves to another attractive MBO feature, the emphasis on action plans. The putative advantages emanating from this central component of MBO are formidable. They include:

- Better planning through greater awareness of the relationship between goals and plans
- Elimination of duplication of effort and resources
- Creation of better controls and an acceptance of their necessity

But, certainly not just any "action plan" will do. Planning is most meaningful when it concerns a discrete flow of work—some sequence of activities that hang together and are essentially responsive to some manager's industry and direction. But traditional structuring of work emphasizes parts more than related wholes. Moreover, simply requiring subordinates to submit plans will not automatically make them competent planners. Planning skills have to be described and developed. In their absence, action plans are likely to be implemented in a ritualistic manner and can degenerate into merely a flood of paperwork. This will especially be the case in instances where many goals are set or are revised frequently.

Periodic Reviews

Periodic reviews of progress toward goals are strongly advocated as an integral element of the MBO process. The motivation is direct and convincing. Such reviews:

- Provide more and better performance feedback
- Improve mutual understanding and coordination
- Catch problems before it is too late

Yet, periodic reviews can be used with equal facility for opposite goals. Thus, in the absence of appropriate values and behaviors by superior and subordinate, the periodic reviews may appear to be, or even come to be, coercive controls to threaten subordinates who are not meeting schedules, or to pressure the successful into attaining more and more. Periodic reviews can even delude a manager into substituting infrequent and largely superficial reviews for his continuing responsibility to supervise, encourage, develop, reward, and discipline subordinates.

Results-Oriented Performance Appraisals

Who can argue with the notion that individuals should be evaluated on the basis of results? Indeed, performance evaluation should be predicated on what the persons do, as opposed to who or what they are. Supposedly, results-oriented performance appraisals make the performance evaluation process more relevant, thereby gaining acceptance by the subordinate. Furthermore, such appraisals provide the opportunity to give or withhold rewards on grounds that are well understood and considered fair by the subordinate.

Results-oriented appraisals do not, however, resolve the quandary of measuring achievement. Setting measurable objectives, their desired levels, and assessing the degree of attainment remain extremely thorny issues, MBO or no. Sometimes these issues can be eased by structural reorganization. As Chapter 2 illustrates, alternative structures imply very different answers to this central question: How do managers insure that their subordinates are pursuing goals of comparable importance and difficulty? Other questions are uniformly difficult no matter what the structure. For example: How does one reward a subordinate who exceeds easy goals by a large margin, as compared to one who barely falls short of attaining difficult ones? Here, perhaps the only hope is to keep superior-subordinate linkages as regenerative as possible, using the terminology introduced in Chapter 1 in Part 1.

Moreover, certain goals do not readily lend themselves to expression in quantitative terms, but are nonetheless important to overall performance. Here, patently, working relationships must be based on trust and reciprocity.

Otherwise, there will be ample opportunity to fantasize about enemies even when they do not exist, and nurture aplenty in which real antagonisms and resistances can grow. The literature pertaining to reliance on statistical controls is replete with examples of undesirable organizational consequences resulting from the efforts of workers to meet statistical measures to "look good,"[51] come hell or high water. Subordinates might even view a goal as a performance ceiling: It is never to be surpassed, no matter what. In light of the fact that workers have a tendency to build slack into their work, and apparently more so as they feel distrustful and threatened,[52] such a norm can have a negative impact on performance even while MBO seems to be working.

MBO Disappointments as Failures of Process

Even unwavering advocates of MBO have conceded over the years that it has had an occasional failure, and evidence is mounting that MBO has more clear failures than successes.[53] In fact, we may be approaching an era when more time is spent taking MBO out than putting it in. Of course, many individuals will attempt to "patch up" MBO as its shortcomings become better known, for example, as by including group goal-setting and group evaluation of performance. Already so many versions of MBO exist that the rubric has lost much of its original meaning.

These disappointments with MBO have been dismissed quickly, by and large. Thus, an individual failure is typically attributed to such causes: it was poorly implemented; it did not have support of top management; it was adopted in ignorance; it degenerated into too much unnecessary paperwork; it was not tailored to the needs of the specific host organization, and so on.

This argument challenges MBO more, suggesting as it does two points. *First,* MBO qua technique encourages certain cross-currents that undercut explicit MBO objectives. *Second,* MBO applications typically give little explicit attention to developing the values and behaviors necessary to support MBO.[54] The implicit and inadequate argument seems to be, rather, that a working MBO program will generate the values and behaviors required to get an MBO application going in constructive ways. Clearly, that puts matters the wrong way around.

The usual MBO ethos seems seriously inadequate in multiple particulars. A mechanistic application of MBO is just old wine in new bottles. That is, it is Scientific Management for all levels of an organization without the benefit of systematic setting of performance standards, and it depends on a reward or punishment psychology. A ritualistic implementation of MBO, ironically, serves to reinforce bureaucracy in a hierarchical organization rather than solve the problems created by it. Formalistic MBO programs invite an extensive manual of forms which require, among other things, codification through job descriptions, recording goals and their revisions, progress reports, and written action plans. An already busy manager operating in a loosely structured and dynamic environment, coping with unforeseen day-to-day exigencies by whatever means that work, easily can become frustrated by the added red tape. This person may respond by either completing the forms in a cursory manner immediately before their due date, or by simplifying the job so that he or she is complying with the letter of the law, that is, not doing anything that is not required by the "system."

Approaching MBO via OD[55]

To put the main point in another way, the position here argues for approaching MBO via OD values, diagnosis, and learning designs. This builds on the point, already established, that the reasons for adopting MBO and its hoped-for consequences are congruent with OD values. What almost all MBO applications lack, however, is an emphasis on a learning technology sufficient to induce and maintain the behaviors and attitudes required by such values.

Moreover, OD implies a data-based analysis of needs in different technical, managerial, and human subsystems, using an array of diagnostic methods. MBO applications seem insensitive to the fact that not all organizations face identical problems. This seems awkward. If we learn only one thing from existing research, it should be that no simple formula deals with the myriad of specific organizational obstacles standing in the way of attaining OD values, MBO notwithstanding. Organizations would be better served by appreciating the enormity of the challenge and by abandoning the search for simplistic nostrums.

The arguments presented above do not constitute a plea for abandoning MBO concepts, that is, but for integrating them with higher-order theoretical perspectives. Consider the emphasis on goal setting. The relationship between conscious goals and intentions and task performance is clearly established in laboratory studies. However, goals must be accepted by the subordinate before they have a positive impact on performance.[56] Since the MBO goal-setting requirement does not necessarily engender goal acceptance, OD techniques should be employed to seek such acceptance. Such joint MBO/OD strategies are recommended for implementing other MBO components as well.

Once the major impediments to MBO in a specific organization are diagnosed, finally, suitable OD interventions must be selected, and their efficacy measured against the baseline data obtained during the needs-analysis phase. These interventions or learning designs can cover a vast range. If top management is unsure of its goals, for example, the change agent should assist with goal and policy clarification. Further, if structural problems seem central, attention must be directed to reorganizing interdepartmental and intradepartmental work flows. This may require job restructuring, redefining authority and responsibility, or redirecting communication flows. These may be required to provide relief from day-to-day exigencies that occupy much of the time of most managers and force them to be reactive rather than proactive. The catalog of possible OD interventions and designs is longer still. Thus, certain motivational problems may call for job enrichment. Alternatively, interpersonal or interdepartmental conflicts may require team-building workshops or other conflict-resolution techniques. If a sound management information system is lacking, then one must be created. Otherwise, timely performance feedback will be unavailable for any purpose. If decision-making skills need updating, then instruction in decision theory and techniques should be instituted. When leadership skills are deficient, appropriate training is in order. Equally obvious, a number of problems in any organization can only be resolved by replacing incumbents who cannot perform satisfactorily.

OD is not sure-fire protection against the unintended and undesired consequences of a mechanistic application of MBO or any other cure-all, of course, for there are also charlatans with their own quick and easy (if not inexpensive) OD formulas. Moreover, we have much to learn about organizations and ways of improving them. In spite of these limitations, OD as a growing body of theory and experience provides a greater potential for realizing MBO aims than does the simple MBO formula. A few consultants have already attempted the required integration of the MBO technique with an OD perspective.[57] Until that integration is well in hand, the MBO formula must be viewed with caution, for it will often be placebo at best, and at worst it will either aggravate or induce serious organizational maladies.

How Not to Succeed at MBO*

Many of the insights above about the useful conflation of MBO and OD were gained the hard way: they derive from an unsuccessful MBO program implemented in a large bank by the author.[58] A review of the MBO literature reveals that the problems encountered by the author have also been experienced by others frequently enough so that they cannot be dismissed as a deviant case.

The sad but learningful experience in the bank is easy enough to summarize. When it came to a final reckoning, those exposed to MBO did not perform any better than their non-MBO counterparts. This outcome seems explainable on the following grounds.

- That the implementation of the MBO program deviated from the ideal in several respects.
- OD strategies were not pursued concomitantly as vehicles by which to enhance the probability of attaining MBO aims.

*This section was written expressly for this volume by Jan Muczyk.

Violating Some Useful Guidelines

To begin, the bank's MBO application violated three guidelines that OD experience suggests are useful, if they clearly are not ultimate requirements. Orthodox OD opinion, of course, urges dealing with networks in organizations that have substantial control over their structure and policies. This usually means starting with officials at the top of an organization, and working down. Note that it is also often appropriate to start with lower-level officials who have substantial authority over a related flow of work. The MBO application in the bank met neither condition. Moreover, in effect, the MBO technology was grafted to a managerial culture and a set of traditions that were not systematically analyzed for congruence with MBO requirements. That was two strikes against a successful MBO application. Had the author actively involved top management in the implementation of the MBO program at the lower levels of the organization, it probably would have had a better chance of acceptance. As it was, a number of branch managers and their assistants perceived MBO as another fad, given that top management was not directly involved.

In addition, the normal pressures exerted by top management in behalf of the success of a program introduced on a more permanent basis were absent. The MBO participants cooperated in the study because of a genuine interest in MBO, as a favor to the researcher, or to comply with the wishes of top management which were that the researcher receive cooperation. If the latter two reasons were responsible for the participation, the subjects might have been motivated simply to go through the motions of the program rather than commit their psychic and physical energies to the success of MBO.

More significant, the bank's reward system was not integrated with the MBO program. A formal performance appraisal system independent of MBO did exist, but it was not held in high regard by branch managers and their assistants. Consequently, individuals who set higher goals and attained them had no assurance that they would receive greater rewards than persons who set lower goals or failed to attain the high goals that they set. Most managers would not miss the implied message, given that they otherwise had ample demands on their energies and allegiances.

Finally, the study lasted only 1 year. It is quite possible that a complex managerial system takes considerably more time to produce an impact.

As central as the preceding factors are, however, the author remains convinced that the MBO program suffered much more from the failure to employ appropriate OD diagnosis and designs for each phase of the MBO application. In other words, the implementation of the MBO program in the bank was overly mechanistic.

Neglect of Data-Based Diagnosis

The first blunder in the implementation process was a failure to conduct a data-based diagnosis of organizational problems. (A variety of action-research models appropriate for such a job are reviewed at many points in this volume.) The convenient assumption was made that MBO would effectively deal with whatever problems existed in the organization. Oppositely, however, some of those existing problems not only were recalcitrant, but they also fundamentally undercut the MBO approach. Diagnosis would have indicated that separate and prior action was necessary, as a stage in moving toward MBO. For example, branch managers reported to a regional manager who also was a senior branch manager in that region. However, as a practical matter, the branch managers received their direction from and reported to the various functional areas of central bank management. As a result, the joint goal-setting process between a branch manager and the regional manager was in most instances perfunctory, if not illusory, with the regional manager simply rubber-stamping the goals set unilaterally by the branch manager. Since no pressures encouraged the setting of challenging goals, most branch managers played it safe and set very modest goals. The game was a difficult one to win, however it was played. In one instance, a regional manager used the MBO program as an opportunity to try to assert command for the first time. He called in the branch managers in his region who were part of the MBO group and issued them their goals for the next 6- and 12-month periods. As one would suspect, his action caused considerable resentment.

Failure to Use OD Interventions and Perspectives

To make an obvious point, had an organizational diagnosis been performed before installing the MBO program, the usefulness of a variety of OD perspectives and interventions would have been highlighted. Patently, for example, the position of regional manager would have to be upgraded before the joint goal-setting phase could be implemented in any meaningful way. Similarly, the design for the MBO application would have sought ways to involve total work groups in planning and execution,[59] a potential for necessary change which was not utilized in the bank. To simplify, use of the group as a vehicle for change makes available its power for changing work, culture, and norms, and also may engage longer-run forces that can support the MBO application over the inevitable rough spots. Paramountly, perhaps, such work-group involvement is useful, perhaps even crucial, in defining organizational as well as individual goals in ways that increase ownership and reduce both the sense and reality of goals and tasks having been imposed from on high. If attention to work-group involvement is inadequate, Huse concludes definitively, "the effectiveness of an MBO approach may, over time, be greatly reduced."[60]

The story is a similar one in a number of other critical areas. For want of diagnosis, either the wrong interventions were chosen, or the interventions were not accorded corrected priorities, or both. To illustrate, an organizational analysis also would have revealed that branch managers spent an inordinate amount of time reacting to daily exigencies. Consequently, they did not have sufficient time to plan, develop their subordinates, evaluate them properly, develop new clients, exploit existing markets, and so on. Restructuring the branch manager's job was necessary to permit the delegation of many day-to-day responsibilities. Such a strategy would have freed the managers to engage in managerial functions while at the same time enriching the position of assistant branch manager, thus accelerating the process of developing subordinates.

The job restructuring approach by itself would probably have had a minor impact unless accompanied by a systematic management development program, with prior diagnosis again being critical. Most branch managers had no formal managerial training, and few had a college education. On the other hand, the assistant branch managers were better educated and considerably younger, they being the products of a bank's recent program to prepare for the future. In a number of instances, the branch managers were threatened by their younger, better educated "heirs apparent." Given the fact that the bank is a status-conscious organization, a great deal of groundwork was necessary as a precondition to an MBO program. Upgrading the planning and organizing and controlling skills of managers through traditional training programs were, at a minimum, part of this necessary groundwork.

Diagnosis also would have emphasized the usefulness of other OD learning designs. For example, laboratory methods and team-building approaches could have been employed for the purpose of establishing a superior-subordinate climate which would improve the probability of genuine joint goal setting. This requires substantial consensus, delicate role negotiations, productive periodic review sessions, and a better understood performance evaluation process, which in turn would lead to a more equitable distribution of rewards.

Make no mistake about it, to pound home a critical point, there is nothing in the MBO approach per se that automatically answers the tough questions. In MBO, as elsewhere, those tough questions require a climate of interpersonal trust and openness. MBO needs these as prerequisites far more than it helps nourish them as consequences. For example, determining areas in which goals are to be set is typically a difficult task for many jobs. The bank experience proved to be no exception. The branch managers participating in the MBO program listed the categories that they believed were important to the success of their branches and the bank as a whole. The respective lists were merged and the duplications eliminated. This exercise produced an exhaustive list of performance categories without priorities or relevance to the special needs of the various branch managers. The list was a veritable embarrassment of riches, but not very useful in terms of providing direction to the MBO participants. Again, the MBO subjects played it safe and set goals in categories that appeared in the financial control reports issued by corporate headquarters, and for the most part ignored long-run goals associated with self-development or the development of subordinates. In the long-run, the neglected goals were more central to the organization than the short-run goals which were set, but the managers focused on what was measured by the organization at the time. That is at once eminently reasonable and significantly limiting.

The failure of MBO at the bank convinced top management to abandon it after a 14-month trial period. By this time it was too late to start over, correctly. This sad experience is being repeated in many organizations, and will continue to be repeated as long as consultants are selling MBO as a "canned" approach. MBO must be melded with appropriate OD techniques which provide the necessary processes by which to attain MBO aims. MBO, in turn, offers the structure and performance orientation which the "softer" OD approaches lack. Hopefully, it will prove to be a happy marriage.

Notes

1. Henry A. Landsberger, "The Horizontal Dimension in Bureaucracy," *Administrative Science Quarterly,* Vol. 6 (December 1961), pp. 299-332.
2. Leonard R. Sayles, *Managerial Behavior* (New York: McGraw-Hill, 1964), esp. pp. 58-82.
3. A case study involved the selection for promotion of a manager from a list of possibles. This task had the projective quality of encouraging participants to surface and analyze their criteria for assessing a manager's style and performance, first in the case study and for later application to their own flesh-and-blood manager.
4. The traditional distinctions were made. See Robert T. Golembiewski and Arthur Blumberg (eds.), *Sensitivity Training and the Laboratory Approach* (Itasca, Ill.: F. E. Peacock, 1977), pp. 84-88.
5. Schultz's FIRO-B Model of needs was used, but participants used only verbal guidelines to rate their own needs, as opposed to the available questionnaires. See William C. Schultz, *FIRO-B* (New York: Holt, Rinehart, Winston, 1958).
6. Participants analyzed data from six items of the Likert Profile, which they had previously completed and which had been scored for them. Note that none of these data are reported here.
7. The basic design followed the guidelines for feedback in Chapter 1 of Part 1 of this revision. A few samples were analyzed by a resource person, but the basic focus was on pieces of feedback previously written by participants as part of the subdesign. These were further analyzed in the regions as

individuals felt free to share their feedback items and to analyze them in terms of the guidelines.

8. See Andrew W. Halpin and Don B. Croft, *The Organizational Climate of Schools* (Chicago: Midwest Administration Center, 1963). Four other OCDQ scales were researched but, because of space, are not considered here.

9. The results here are more optimistic than in the only other report about mass team-building. See Reuben T. Harris and Jerry L. Porras, "The Consequences of Large System Change in Practice," pp. 298-302, in Jeffrey C. Susbauer (ed.), *Proceedings '78,* Annual Meeting, Academy of Management, San Francisco, Calif., August 1978.

10. Robert T. Golembiewski, *The Small Group* (Chicago: University of Chicago, 1962), pp. 57-66. See also Ted L. Huston and George Levinger, "Interpersonal Attractions and Relationships," esp. pp. 118-120, in Mark R. Rosenzweig and Lyman W. Porter (eds.), *Annual Review of Psychology,* Vol. 29 (Palo Alto, Calif.: Annual Reviews, 1978).

11. Robert T. Golembiewski and R. Munzenrider, "Social Desirability as an Intervening Variable in OD Effects," *Journal of Applied Behavioral Science,* Vol. 11 (July 1975), pp. 317-332.

12. John W. Hall, "A Comparison of Halpin and Craft's Organizational Climates and Likert's Organizational Systems," *Administrative Science Quarterly,* Vol. 17 (December 1972), pp. 586-590. See also Robert Munzenrider, *Organization Climate.* Unpublished doctoral dissertation, University of Georgia, 1976, esp. chaps. 4 and 5.

13. For a useful discussion of the sources of we/they in groups, consult Clayton P. Alderfer, "Group and Intergroup Relations," especially, pp. 242-281, in J. Richard Hackman and J. Lloyd Suttle (eds.), *Improving Life At Work* (Santa Monica, Calif.: Goodyear Publishing, 1977).

14. Robert R. Blake, Herbert A. Shepard, and Jane S. Mouton, *Managing Intergroup Conflict in Industry* (Houston: Gulf Publishing, 1968), esp. pp. 1-49. See also John A. Seiler, "Diagnosing Interdepartmental Conflict," *Harvard Business Review,* Vol. 41 (September 1963), pp. 121-132. Useful conceptual elaboration is provided by Alan C. Filley, *Interpersonal Conflict Resolution* (Glenview, Ill.: Scott, Foresman, 1975).

15. For a detailed analysis of such group properties, see Golembiewski, *The Small Group,* pp. 9-26.

16. For details, see Robert T. Golembiewski and Arthur Blumberg, "Confrontation as a Learning Design in Complex Organizations: Attitudinal Changes in a Diversified Population of Managers," *Journal of Applied Behavioral Science,* Vol. 3 (December 1967), pp. 529-536.

17. The terms "favorable" and "unfavorable" are convenient shorthand only. On the volitional criteria questions, attitudinal changes reporting an enhanced willingness to collaborate are "favorable"; on objective items,

attitudinal changes reporting a lower degree of perceived productivity are "unfavorable." On both kinds of items, the directions of scales were varied on the questionnaire to inhibit the development of response sets. However, the data were uniformly processed so that favorable changes are scored (+) and unfavorable changes are scored (−).

18. Robert R. Blake, "The Uses of the Past," *Journal of Applied Behavioral Science,* Vol. 7 (October 1971), pp. 519-520.

19. Michael Blansfield, Robert R. Blake, and Jane S. Mouton, "The Merger Laboratory," *Training Directors Journal,* Vol. 18 (May 1964), pp. 2-10, for example, deal with a case where N = 2.

20. Recall that data were gathered about three classes of organization units or positions. "Underrepresented" units or positions had only one or no representatives at the experience, and no major changes in attitudes toward them were expected. "New business" groups were those whose performance in the confrontation design was such as to raise new issues that were not resolved. Note also that one underrepresented organization unit was dropped from Administration III. Originally, some of its members were scheduled to participate, but this did not prove possible.

21. Michael Beer, "The Technology of Organization Development," pp. 950-951, in Marvin D. Dunnette (ed.), *Handbook of Industrial and Organizational Psychology* (Chicago: Rand McNally, 1976).

22. Wayne Boss, David J. Gouws, and Takeshi Nagia, "The Cross-Cultural Effects of Organizational Development Interventions: A Conflict/Confrontation Design," *Southern Review of Public Administration,* Vol. 1 (March 1978), pp. 486-502.

23. Edgar F. Huse and C. A. Barebo, personal communication, 1976.

24. The prime reference here is Jerry B. Harvey's "Consulting During Crises of Agreement," esp. pp. 162-171, in W. Warner Burke (ed.), *Current Issues and Strategies in Organization Development* (New York: Human Science, 1977). See also Jerry B. Harvey and D. Richard Albertson, "Neurotic Organizations: Symptoms, Causes, and Treatment," Parts I and II, *Personnel Journal,* Vol. 50 (1971), pp. 694-699, 770-777; and Jerry B. Harvey, "The Abilene Paradox: The Management of Agreement," *Organizational Dynamics* (Summer 1974), pp. 63-80.

25. The effect can exist for various reasons—"conformity," "social comparison processes," "groupthink," and so on. On this central detail, consult Peter B. Smith, *Groups Within Organizations* (New York: Harper and Row, 1973), esp. pp. 14-15. The effect can operate in trivial matters, as well as in the most profound. Consult and compare Solomon Asch, "Effects of Group Pressure on the Modification and Distortion of Judgments," in Dorwin Cartwright and Alvin Zander (eds.), *Group Dynamics* (Evanston, Ill.: Row Peterson, 1960), with Irving Janis, *Groupthink* (Boston: Houghton Mifflin, 1972).

26. As in Allan C. Filley, *Interpersonal Conflict Resolution* (Homewood, Ill.: Dorsey, 1974), esp. p. 7.
27. For revealing (and terrifying) examples, consult Janis, *Groupthink.*
28. For some evidence tending to confirm this interpretation, see David Halberstam, *The Best and the Brightest* (New York: Random House, 1969), esp. pp. 632-658.
29. Harvey and Albertson, "Neurotic Organizations."
30. Robert T. Golembiewski, *Organizing Men and Power: Patterns of Behavior and Line-Staff Models* (Chicago: Rand McNally, 1967).
31. Harold D. Koontz and Cyril J. O'Donnell, *Principles of Management* (New York: McGraw-Hill, 1968), p. 291.
32. William G. Dyer, Robert F. Maddocks, J. Weldon Moffitt, and William J. Underwood, "A Laboratory-Consultation Model for Organization Change," p. 309, in W. Warner Burke and Harvey A. Hornstein (eds.), *The Social Technology of Organization Development* (Fairfax, Virg.: NTL Learning Resources Corp., 1972).
33. Ibid., p. 310.
34. Ibid.
35. Rensis Likert, *New Patterns of Management* (New York: McGraw-Hill, 1961).
36. Dyer, Maddocks, Moffitt, and Underwood, "A Laboratory-Consultation Model for Organization Change," p. 311.
37. Ibid., p. 318.
38. Ibid., p. 316.
39. Ibid., p. 317.
40. Peter Drucker, *Practice of Management* (New York: Harper, 1954), first used the term "Management by Objectives."
41. John Ivancevich, "Changes in Performance in a Management by Objectives Program," *Administrative Science Quarterly,* Vol. 19 (1974), pp. 563-574.
42. J. Wickens, "Management by Objectives: An Appraisal," *Journal of Management Studies,* Vol. 5 (1968), p. 365.
43. William D. Heier, "Implementing an Appraisal-by-Results Program," *Personnel,* Vol. 47 (November 1970), pp. 24-32.
44. Most prominently, see Stephen Kerr, "Some Modifications in MBO as an OD Strategy," *Academy of Management Proceedings,* August 13-16 (1972), pp. 39-42; and H. Levinson "Management by Whose Objectives?" *Harvard Business Review,* Vol. 48 (July 1970), pp. 125-134.
45. For an exception, see Ivancevich, "Changes in Performance in a Management by Objectives Program;" and Ivancevich and S. Klein, "A Three-Year Longitudinal Study of MBO: A Preliminary Report," *Midwest Division Academy of Mangement Proceedings,* April 24-26, 1975, pp. 316-317.

For overall perspective on the quality of research on MBO, see Mark McConkie, "Managemement by Objectives in Public Agencies." Unpublished doctoral dissertation, University of Georgia, Athens, Ga., 1977.

46. Levinson, "Management by Whose Objectives?"

47. George L. Morrisey, "Making MBO Work: The Missing Link," *Training and Development Journal,* Vol. 30 (February 1976), p. 3.

48. Kerr, "Some Modifications in MBO as an OD Strategy," p. 40. See also Mark L. McConkie, "A Clarification of the Goal Setting and Appraisal Process in MBO," *Academy of Management Review,* Vol. 4 (January (1979), pp. 29-40.

49. Levinson, "Management by Whose Objectives?"

50. Ivancevich and Klein, "A Three-Year Longitudinal Study of MBO."

51. George Strauss and Leonard R. Sayles, *Personnel* (Englewood Cliffs, N.J.: Prentice-Hall, 1967), pp. 357-365.

52. For a review of the underlying research and ideation, see Robert T. Golembiewski, *Behavior and Organization* (Chicago: Rand McNally, 1962), esp. pp. 123-148.

53. Jan Muczyk, "A Controlled Field Experiment Measuring the Impact of MBO on Performance Data," *Academy of Management Proceedings,* August 10-13, 1975, pp. 363-365; and S. Singular, "Has MBO Failed?" *MBA* (October 1975), pp. 47-50.

54. For an exception, see Richard E. Byrd and John Cowan, "MBO: A Behavioral Science Approach," *Personnel,* Vol. 51 (March 1974), pp. 42-50.

55. The integrative approach here is suggestive only. For a model of what is needed, see Glenn H. Varney, *An Organization Development Approach to Management Development* (Reading, Mass.: Addison-Wesley, 1976).

56. E. Locke, "Toward a Theory of Task Motivation and Incentives," *Organizational Behavior and Human Performance,* Vol. 3 (1968), pp. 157-189.

57. See, for example, Arthur C. Beck, Jr., with Ellis D. Hillmar, *A Practical Approach to Organization Development Through MBO* (Reading, Mass.: Addison-Wesley, 1972).

58. Muczyk, "A Controlled Field Experiment Measuring the Impact of MBO on Performance Data."

59. The importance of group phenomena in MBO is emphasized by Wendell L. French and Robert W. Holloman, "Management by Objectives: The Team Approach," *California Management Review,* Vol. 17 (Spring 1975), pp. 13-22; and Arthur C. Beck, Jr., and Ellis D. Hillmar, *Making MBO/R Work* (Reading, Mass.: Addison-Wesley, 1976).

60. Edgar F. Huse, *Organization Development and Change* (St. Paul, Minn.: West Publishing, 1975), p. 187

61. Robert T. Golembiewski, *Renewing Organizations: The Laboratory Approach to Planned Change* (Itasca, Ill.:F. E. Peacock, 1972).

Chapter 5

TOWARD SEPARATION AND "SMALLER IS BETTER"
Perspectives on Neglected Imperatives in Life

Although separation and decline are as much facts of life as integration and growth, one would never know it from reading almost all the OD literature.[1] Bolman punches the point home, with emphasis on an uncomfortable question: Have we reached the point in many cases where "growth" and "progress" are antagonistic if not opposed? Bolman isolates two questions in dealing with this macro-query. He notes:[2] "Some of those questions are technical: how can we help organizations to cope effectively and humanely with no-growth and negative growth conditions? Some are questions of our own values as professionals: to what extent are we so caught up in the 'bigger-is-better' world view that we are part of the problem rather than part of the solution?" The extent of being caught-up seems substantial. OD has prospered most where organizations are already very large, are growing very rapidly, or both.

Adapting Organizations to Human Needs
Three Basic Strategies

This chapter seeks to correct the existing imbalance in OD applications between separation and integration, and between growth and smaller-is-better. The approach has two motivators: to suggest what is lost in the imbalance, as well as to illustrate how it can have serious unanticipated consequences. The present focus is on three basic strategies for OD interventions, using Bolman's useful categories:[3]

- Empowering individuals and small systems in large organizations
- Facilitating in low-growth and negative-growth contexts
- Managing termination processes

The view here is that these strategies can be variously reinforcing or exclusive, so no unqualified generalization about them is possible except that they are useful foci for organizing the discussion to follow.

Empowering Individuals and Small Systems

One way to respond constructively to the problems of massive organizational size in general—as well as to the need to limit growth or even reduce size in order to permit more flexible responses—involves empowering individuals and small systems in large organizations. This can be done, following Bolman, in three major ways: by redistributing power, so that the have-nots gain some control at the expense of the haves; by seeking mutual empowerment of (for example) labor as well as management; or by variously decoupling larger systems.

Several general propositions may be made about these three ways of acting on the first strategy. *First,* in some or many cases, the approaches may be mutually exclusive. Thus redistributing power means in the present usage unilateral rather than mutual empowerment. *Second,* the three approaches to the empowering strategy may generate variable resistance. Thus "losers" often will resist redistributing power, but we can often expect an accepting response if all or many parties foresee mutual empowerment. *Third,* however, it often will be difficult to determine whether a specific action will lead to a redistribution of power or mutual empowerment. For example, decoupling a large system could lead to one effect or the other. *Fourth,* to fine-tune the previous point, any OD intervention often will have various mixes of effects for various classes of organization members: some members will see a redistribution of power in which they only lose; other members may see some mutual empowerment mixed with some loss of control; and some members may see everything coming up roses.

Subsequent discussion illustrates several ways of empowering individuals and small systems in larger organizations. The first two major sections below will deal with:

- The general case for separation and integration as dual imperatives in life, with a brief case study of the mischief caused by an OD design
- A specific merger of two small units, including a design for gathering appropriate data for determining the character of the merger

Facilitating in Low-Growth and Negative-Growth Contexts

More narrowly, OD interventions can also be seen as facilitative under unfavorable economic conditions. The demotion experience detailed in Chapter 4 of Part 1 of this revised edition seems to qualify, for example. Two additional illustrations here suggest the fuller range of appropriate OD interventions:

- A multifirm consortium for meeting individual needs as well as for responding to bad economic conditions–recession, inflation, cutbacks, and so on
- Using small teams to increase productivity when market conditions sour and greater efficiency is necessary

The third section below introduces the consortium notion; and a fourth section details the case of productivity increase. Note that both examples may be interpreted as a mutual empowerment of employees and management. At the very least, a redistribution of power seems implied.

Managing Termination Processes

OD interventions also can be useful in extremis, although they have seldom been so applied. The two emphases below

- Review how OD values and designs can facilitate an employee's being fired, phased-out, or just leaving an organization–"facilitate" in terms of both the individual and the employing organization
- Illustrate the debriefing, or interment, of work teams whose missions have been completed

The fifth and sixth sections below dwell on these two perspectives on managing termination processes.

A Warning About Unexpected Consequences
A Primer on Tearing Asunder What OD Hath Brought Together

The first perspective on integration and separation seeks to establish the duality's commonness in nature, as well as to illustrate some serious effects of its neglect in a large organization. As the subheading announces, this section is a warning about the unexpected consequences of a narrowly *gemeinschaft* spirit in a fundamentally *gesellschaft* world. More specifically, OD interventions can be so successful integratively that they later complicate convenient or necessary uncouplings and can inhibit attempts to empower small systems in very large ones.

Integration and Separation as Dual Imperatives

That integration and separation characterize so much of our lives is trivial to establish. There are so many examples near-at-hand that one is led to demand equal time for integration and separation. Consider these examples of complete integration → separation cycles:

- A project team quickly gears up to do a critical research task, and then is phased out.
- People marry, and then a spouse dies.
- "Children" leave home and start their own families.
- A young married couple sees divorce as the only alternative to enervating one another over a lifetime.
- Families leave one neighborhood and settle in another.
- Kids change schools, either because of graduation, relocation, busing programs, or whatever.

Ubiquitous as such examples are, far more attention is normally given to integration rites than to separation. Take only one contrast. Many young marrieds get in a whirl of ceremonious and celebrative activities, but nothing comparable exists for the newly divorced. It is almost as if the latter were a failure, and the former an unqualified good. We all know better, of course. Divorce may be the very best thing for many people; and the prognosis for the newly married is not very good, on the average. But the human spirit and our institutions often strain counter to reality.

Relatedly, the rites of separation also can be seen as more painful than those of integrating or unifying. Consider the old T-group design of having groups trade members. The task is trying for all. Even less favored members are unlikely to be put on the "trading block," few will volunteer, and even T-groups with very brief histories tend to become very protective of "their own." The ego boost of being selected seems no general match for the fear of being unselected, with the potential guilt and sense of abandonment which might be triggered in self and others.

Everyone wants to get invited to the prom, in short, whatever the expected quid pro quo. And no one wants to receive a "Dear John (or Joan)" letter, even if it clearly is for the best.

Alcan's Experience of Failure Through Success

These dual imperatives also characterize much life in organizations, of course, and the old biases also hold there. For every thousand team-building experiences, there are no doubt no more than a few OD experiences dealing with "team-killing" or "team-burial." And that bias often has costs, sometimes severe ones, because the world of organizations may as insistently demand separation one day as it exhorted integration only a short time before.

Consider Alcan.[4] At one point in its development, it was a huge but essentially simple and monolithic organization devoted to producing alumina. It was reasonable to have the goal of the firm being "one big family." Its members had many of the same socializing experiences, its technology was common and straightforward, and its objectives narrowly focused on a homogeneous product line. To be sure, like its home, Canada, Alcan was a vast mix of languages and cultures. How reasonable it seemed, then, to prescribe massive doses of in-house T-groups to provide that common experience and social adhesive that could help build crosswalks between organization members who differed in their native homes and cultures but who shared a common product and technology.

What was functional at one point in time, however, became seriously dysfunctional at another. The bonds of loyalty and affection that derived from the T-groups, in short, came to thwart what was seen as a major business need: to diversify into manufacturing and marketing from the far simpler business of producing alumina. Given the major differences in technologies, markets, and so on, it seemed reasonable to divide the "one big family" into at least two profit centers. This separation required a movement, in effect, from the traditional to the unorthodox structure discussed in the initial section of Chapter 2 above.

The required movement was inhibited by several classes of factors, however. One class of factors included objective dilemmas such as: The best and the brightest personnel reasonably would be steered to the marketing and manufacturing areas, which would become more the go-go of the organization. Alumina production would become more and more of a hardworking but drab step-sister, useful but not very glamorous. The reasonable desires of corporate officials to see the new ventures succeed no doubt would be reflected in more rapid advancement, higher salaries, and so on, all of which are powerful motivators to leave the old and join the new. However, the sense of the "one big family" reinforced by the large doses of in-house T-grouping constituted a serious obstacle to the required structural change, which would have been difficult enough. For many, feelings of guilt and abandonment severely complicated the transition toward separation. For others, the business need to separate constituted a regression from the goal of "one big, happy family," progress toward which had engaged so much energy over a number of years.

As this chapter argues, integration and separation are dual imperatives of organizational life. Neither can be neglected, each has implications for the other, and each has costs which cannot be avoided but which can be anticipated and prepared for.

Merger as an Exercise in Integration and Separation

It Takes Two to Make One-and-a-Fraction*

Applied behavioral scientists spend most of their time working on problems that pertain to a single group or organization. This section seeks to be different. Its purpose is to highlight the dynamics that develop when two organizations join forces to create one functioning unit. Empowering individuals and especially small systems often will depend on this ability to uncouple and recouple, and especially in ways that imply mutual empowerment far more than a simple redistribution of power. The case below highlights one OD design that sought mutual empowerment and which seems to have succeeded.

There is a small but growing body of literature,[5] predominantly from the business world, that is concerned with organization mergers and emphasizes financial effects. In a survey of factors that may lead to the success or failure of mergers, to cite a rare exception, John Kitching focuses on matters of management and organization, albeit not in great detail.[6] He indicates, for example, the necessity of having competent "managers of change" and of setting up clear reporting relationships in the newly formed organizational structure. Kitching's data also indicate that in 81 percent of the merger "failures" reported, reporting relationships were unclear and there was a tendency to change them often.

From the point of view of behavioral scientists, the financial and economic components of mergers are part of a total mix of problems that focus on such things as expectations about norm development, role change, leadership style, decision-making processes, and goal orientation. This section deals with these latter factors, via a case study of a merger.

Situation Inducing Merger

This case of merger had an unexpected beginning in a 2-day training session on consultation skills for twenty-three members of two geographically separate but

*This section is taken largely from Arthur Blumberg and William Wiener, "One From Two: A Behavioral Science Design for Merging Organizations," mimeographed. A number of stylistic and organizing changes have been made. Reproduced by special permission from *The Journal of Applied Behavioral Science*. "One from Two: Facilitating an Organizational Merger," by Arthur Blumberg and William Wiener, Vol. 7, no. 1, pp. 87-102. Copyrighted by NTL Institute, 1971.

contiguous units of a private voluntary community organization. The participants comprised the total professional staff of the two organizations which also included the usual array of supporting activities. These units, though both parts of a large national organization, had no formal or reporting relationships with each other. Members of the two units might meet at professional, regional, or national conferences, but for all practical purposes they were separate. Each had its own governing board, did its own fund raising, and developed its own programs.

These two organizations offered field consultation and guidance services to local constituent units within their respective geographic areas. One very important structural and functional difference did exist between the two. The larger of the units, hereafter called organization A, also provided direct program services to communities where no local constituent units were in operation, in addition to providing field consultation. In effect, then, the larger organization performed both line and staff operations, in contrast to the other, whose function was for the most part limited to staff activities.

It became evident to the consultant shortly after the training session had started that though the exercise was going well, the enhancing of consultation skills was not uppermost in the minds of the participants. Discussion revealed an underlying issue: that the national organization had recently decided, in the interests of program and resource utilization, that the two organizational units would be merged. The merger was scheduled for a year later. To complicate matters, no decision had been made about who would be the new executive of the merged organization. It could conceivably be the current executive of either organization, or neither. The unknowns thus involved job tenure, working relations, leadership, program development, and a host of other personal and organizational issues.

The matter of consultation skills had lower priority than the merger, the participants agreed. At the consultant's suggestion, they also agreed to engage with each other in activities that might lead toward the resolution of the problems complicating the creation of one productive unit from two.

It seemed abundantly clear that the first need of these two groups was to free their intergroup communications so that they would be able to talk with each other in meaningful terms about the coming merger. The practical question was: What is there about our two existing organizations that will aid our work together, and what will hinder us? In other words, the initial part of the total change effort was devoted to collecting data about the manner in which each group perceived itself and the other. Based on the results and analysis of this effort, the two organizations and the consultant would be in a position to plan further.

The consultant engaged the two groups in a three-dimensional confrontation exercise, as described above. Given the manageable size of the group, even if other instruments were at hand, this probably would have been the right decision. The exercise is simple, and has training as well as data-collection potential. Exhibit 1 details the 3-D Images produced by the two organization units.

Two major points are obvious from even a cursory scanning of Exhibit 1.

- The prospective merger would have to join two organizations which, though having similar goal orientations, were quite different in a number of very important ways.
- The differences in the organizations were known to each other. That is, the manner in which each organization described itself tended to be congruent with the way it was described by the other. In addition, the estimates that each organization made of how the other would describe them were, in general, accurate.

With an eye toward the merger, some major issues clearly would have to be handled. *First,* organization A saw itself as task or project-oriented, while organization B's description implied that, if concern were devoted to process issues, task and project accomplishment would flow naturally. Differences between these orientations can be profound.

Second, it appeared there were qualitative differences in the nature of the interpersonal and group communications that took place within each organization. Organization A's self-picture included nonleveling and avoiding confrontation. Feelings were not shared, which reasonably could lead to a fair amount of energy being expended in trying to find out just what the other person was really saying. The quality of the communications in organization B was different. The impression conveyed is that a good bit of leveling occurred, members reflected high trust, and the system was quite open. And, organization B's members clearly saw themselves as a superior unit because of these characteristics.

Third, perhaps underlying the difference between the two organizations, and contributing generically to the problems that the two groups might meet when they joined forces, were attitudes about authority. One gets the feeling that organization A's members tended to be dependently oriented. The authority orientation of organization B seemed to be more independent with, possibly, a liberal sprinkling of counterdependency.

By engaging in the confrontation exercise, then, two developments took place that would play a major role in helping the organizations plan for the joint future. Data had been collected which indicated organizational problem areas that would have to be dealt with if the merger were to take place effectively. Moreover, the data were shared publicly by the two groups in a nondefensive manner. In other words, this public sharing was the beginning, hopefully, of the development of a norm for the merged organization that would encourage and

Exhibit 1 Results of Three-Dimensional Confrontation Exercise Concerning Organizations A and B

Organization A

I. *Perception of Ourselves*

1. Project- and task-oriented
2. Three staffs with separate functions (fragmented)
   a. services to local units
   b. district services
   c. governmental services
3. Individual empire builders
4. Reluctance to recognize merit and skill of each other
5. Don't know why one does what he does and how he feels
6. Style of work is 'block'
7. Not cohesive
8. Don't level—withdrawal from confrontation
9. Some change—now provide local unit service (was district-oriented and operators of activities)
10. Fast pick-up on board decisions and tasks
11. Staff participation in policy formulation

II. *Our Perception of B*

1. Issue-oriented—take stands and let it be known
2. Crusaders
3. Aggressive toward organizational goals and objectives
4. Sensitive to needs of each other
5. Swinging staff
6. Total unit knows where they stand and look to them for direction.

III. *Our Estimation of How B Perceives Us*

1. Cautious-status quo keeper
2. Building individual empires
3. "Country boys"—not cosmopolitan
4. Part of establishment viewed as unit with no shining stars (or rabble rousers)
5. Older—set in their ways
6. Resist change

Organization B

I. *Perception of Ourselves*

1. High degree of leveling with each other
2. Enjoy catharsis
3. Gutsy group—willing to take risks
4. Not task-oriented
5. Like to develop own agenda
6. Flexible
7. Free to change
8. Diversified internal resources
9. Proud bastards—we're glad we're humble
10. Innovative
11. High trust—open—brainstormers

II. *Our Perception of A*

1. Conservative on issues/race/money/politics
2. Task-oriented
3. Not together
4. Up tight
5. Lack openness with each other/others
6. Tradition-bound
7. Unwillingness to take risks. Scared? Of what?
8. Desire to be cooperative
9. Solid—dependable—safe

III. *Our Estimation of How A Perceives Us*

1. Way out—extremists
2. Controversial
3. Bunch of individualists
4. Quick triggers
5. Vocal
6. Swinging staff
7. Going too far—too fast
8. Bunch of proud bastards
9. Threatening but possibly explosive enough to carry them to new "things"
10. Insensitive to their kinds of work problems

maintain an openness of communication about organizational and interpersonal matters.

An Enlarged Data Base for Diagnosis

From the consultant's viewpoint, the data collected from the confrontation session constituted an inadequate base for any deliberative strategies for change. The point was this: The data obtained from the confrontation design were interesting, but useful only for a limited purpose. What would be needed, if future consultant-client contact developed, would be a way of helping the two organizational groups formulate workable behavioral guidelines for their new organization to which all could commit themselves. It was also critically important that these guidelines be based on rational inquiry and deliberation as well as feelings. This latter point derives from the notion that questions about and conflicts of emotionality are crucial in opening a system and catalyzing it into action. But to base the action solely on emotional data is hardly a defensible posture in planning for change.

In addition to the practical problem of change, the consultant was curious about these two organizations from an academic viewpoint. The confrontation data indicated glaring differences between A and B. How would these differences show up in some sort of quantitative measure? From a diagnostic point of view, were there elements of each organization's character where little or no incongruence existed? What factors could conceivably account for the differences that had been observed and, in all probability, would be observed if additional data were to be collected?

In order to help answer both the operational and academic questions, permission was received to administer the Likert Profile of Organization Characteristics[7] and FIRO-B[8] to all members of each organization. Likert's Profile was chosen because it permits a measurement of the organizational characteristics as they are currently seen by the members and also solicits an ideal image of the organization. It was felt that the latter point would be of particular importance if the two organizations did agree to work and train together prior to the merger. In a sense, the measures of the ideal image of their organization could provide goals around which forces could be mobilized to create and agree upon behavioral norms that might induce goal attainment.

As noted elsewhere, Likert's instrument is based on the idea of characterizing the management system of an organization in terms of seven organizational processes. Form J-2 of the instrument was used. It contains eighteen items, each of which is rated on a 20-point scale. There are four major subdivisions of each scale. Each is described in some detail and corresponds to Likert's notion of management systems—System 1, Authoritative-Exploitative; System 2,

Benevolent-Authoritative; System 3, Consultative; and System 4, Participative Group. Respondents are asked to rate each item according to the manner in which they *Now* see their organization, and also according to the *Ideal* they prefer for their organization. The results may be reported in either tabular or profile form.

The use of FIRO-B as another means to collect potentially important data was, frankly, more of a fishing expedition than it was based on any theoretically derived hypothesis. Given the differences that had developed, FIRO-B data were desired by the consultant in response to curiosity. Could it be that the organizational differences were related to differences of the interpersonal need structures of the members? FIRO-B, essentially, taps three kinds of dimensions: inclusion, affection, and control.

The Premerger Design

Given the opportunity to collect formal data, the consultant clarified the design. It included, at the discretion of the client systems, two additional meetings: one with organization A which would be an attempt to help that group open its internal communications, and one in which both A and B would get together for a data-feedback and planning session. The consultant's services were requested for these meetings, and they were held.

The meeting with organization A was a 2½-day affair. It was not a T-group. Rather, the session focused on what might be termed "organizational garbage," and attempted to clear out the clutter of unresolved issues and confusions that appeared to have developed over a period of years. The issues dealt with seemed not to focus on matters of personality but on questions of policy clarification, more precise implications of organizational decisions that had been made, and issues of role conflict and ambiguity.

One very important decision was made during the meeting. Members of organization A whose function was to offer direct program services, in contrast to the field consultative function, decided that their best interests would not be served by being part of the merger. They opted out, which was within their prerogative. This decision meant that future planning and deliberation concerning the merger would involve only those members of the two organizations who would conceivably be part of the new consolidated organization. Some eight members of each organization were thus excluded.

It appeared to the consultant that the most valuable result of the session with the members of organization A was that people said things that had been on their minds for a long time. No one had been punished. A good bit of behavioral feedback, though not here-and-now oriented, had been given and, more importantly, received. It was apparently the first time that this group had met in order to have a look at themselves, and from the comments of the participants, the effort had been well worthwhile. They had achieved a start on the road that might enable them to communicate with organization B members on a level that both groups desired.

There was a side effect to the meeting which, though not related to its substance, was critical to the success of the merger program. Some sense emerged as to where the merger program might go. Indeed, it was at the close of this meeting that the consultant was asked specifically if he had time available to meet with both organizations in order to help them examine the data and make plans concerning the development of norms and operating procedures of the consolidated unit. The meeting was scheduled. Time conflicts permitted only a 1-day session which would be held during a 4-day meeting of the two organizations.

The design for the session was simple. Its two phases were feedback and action. As conceived by the consultant, the design would involve a brief review of the history of the problem, the presentation of the results of the data collection, and the convening of subgroup task forces around particular issues that arose from the data analysis. The job of the task forces would be to analyze the issues in depth and then propose a set of operational guidelines that would, hopefully, constitute the functional and procedural norms of the merged group.

Feedback re Characteristics of Two Organizations

The data were presented to the two organizations by use of a typical Likert Profile. Because of the length and complexity of the Profile, it is presented here in summary form, rather than item by item. No meaning is lost in this convenient substitution.

A comparison of Tables 1 and 2 reveals marked differences between the two organizations on Now scores. Organization A is clearly a System 3 or Consultative unit; the mean Now scores for B are all within System 4, Participative Group. The Ideal scores for both organizations are System 4. In sum, A's members would like their organization to be at the level at which organization B apparently was already operating. The latter point was, of course, central to the future program activities. In effect, the Ideal scores also implied the operating norms that would be necessary for the merged organization to develop and maintain, if conflict were to be minimized and productivity enhanced.

Tables 1 and 2 are also consistent with the 3-D Images developed in the confrontation exercise in which both organizations participated. That is, the systematic data obtained from the administration of Likert's Profile tends to confirm the sense of the confrontation results. It is possible that the confrontation exercise itself could be structured somewhat differently so that more focused data could be obtained, thus providing a quick measure of organizational or group characteristics.

Table 1 Profile of Organization A

Organizational Characteristics	*Mean— Now Scores*	*S.D.*	*Mean— Ideal Scores*	*S.D.*	*T*	*Level of Significance*
Leadership processes	11.53	3.9	17.16	4.6	3.83	.01
Motivational forces	11.94	3.2	17.16	4.6	3.97	.01
Communications processes	12.53	3.8	17.23	4.6	3.57	.015
Interaction-influence processes	12.27	4.3	17.99	4.7	3.96	.01
Decision-making processes	12.52	4.6	17.05	4.9	3.18	.025
Goal-setting processes	11.13	3.3	17.21	4.7	4.58	.01
Control processes	12.37	4.3	16.83	5.2	3.44	.02

Table 2 Profile of Organization B

Organizational Characteristics	*Mean— Now Scores*	*S.D.*	*Mean— Ideal Scores*	*S.D.*	*T*	*Level of Significance*
Leadership processes	17.29	3.1	17.87	2.8	1.79	N.S.
Motivational forces	15.87	3.5	16.87	3.7	2.00	N.S.
Communications processes	17.91	1.1	18.78	1.1	2.15	N.S.
Interaction-influence processes	18.18	1.3	18.99	1.0	1.77	N.S.
Decision-making processes	17.74	1.5	18.34	1.4	1.64	N.S.
Goal-setting processes	17.21	1.8	18.15	1.6	1.62	N.S.
Control processes	16.79	1.4	17.62	1.4	1.97	N.S.

The administration of FIRO-B revealed no significant differences between A and B members concerning questions of interpersonal compatibility or levels of interpersonal needs. Whatever the reasons for the differences between the two organizations, they seemed not to be related to interpersonal needs or compatibility, at least in the way these are measured by the FIRO-B instrument.

Planning Organizational Norms by Task Force

After the data were presented, task forces were formed by asking people to volunteer to work on proposals about those organizational issues in which they were most interested. Each task force would bring back to the total group its recommendations concerning operating norms that would, hopefully, induce a System-4 orientation in the merged organization. The group would react to the proposals, which would then be refined into document form. The final document described a management style preferred by members of the recently merged region. The document was addressed:

- To those suggesting candidates for the executive post
- To those making the decision on the executive post
- To those candidates for the executive post wishing to examine how the staff could work best to achieve a high level of productivity

In a sense, then, the two organizations had combined to "tell it like it is," both to those who would be making decisions about the new executive and to potential applicants for the position. The staff members involved were saying, in effect: "These are the organizational conditions under which we see ourselves working most productively. It would be to the best interests of our organization and us if our needs and desires regarding these conditions were congruent with those of the new executive." The substance of the final document is given in Exhibit 2.

Though the executives of A and B were present at the meeting at which the basics of the document were formulated, neither signed the document, reasoning that this was a staff matter. Moreover, both might be candidates for the position in question.

Exhibit 2 A Preferred Management Style for a Newly Merged Region

The C Region Staff agreed upon the way in which the staff members can work best to achieve a high level of productivity.

There is consensus by the staff on:

1. decision-making processes
2. processes which would motivate us
3. goal-setting processes
4. type of leadership for this management system

We would like to share these characteristics of our Regional Staff Team with you.

Decision-Making Processes

Our staff feels that decision making in an open participative atmosphere is a staff competency of high priority. If a member of the C Region Staff, including the Executive, is in need of data for making a decision, the process would call:

1. For him to state to the staff the locus of the decision-making, i.e., an individual staff man, the Executive, the Regional Staff, other.
2. For the issue requiring a decision to be identified.
3. For all available data to be put on the table.
4. For a thorough testing of all opinions.
5. For choices to be clearly stated.
6. For the final decision and the reasons for the decision to be shared quickly with the staff.

The C Region Staff feels it important that each staff man be supported with an agreed-upon decision-making process which he may confidently exercise while in the field. We expect a supportive

Exhibit 2 (Continued)

stance of our action by the Executive and our Staff Associates. One process would require answers to the following questions:

1. Has the problem been identified?
2. Have sufficient data been collected?
3. What are the options?
4. What is the decision?

In our relationships to all decision-making which affects this staff, an open initiative-consultative approach would be exercised by staff members. Therefore, we see our staff affecting decision-making at all levels through our interactional process with other Regional Staffs, Headquarters staffs, local staffs, or others.

Processes Which Motivate us

Running throughout our work together is our unanimous feeling that we are motivated to our highest level of productivity through participative management exercised at the optimum.

We believe that the processes of "Management by Objective" provide the best vehicle for achieving organizational objectives.

An open communication system of vertical and horizontal dimensions is essential to motivation as we demonstrate our initiative-consultative functions.

We are motivated by a continuing process of evaluation of our individual and staff work.

We believe that our motivation to be highly productive is correlated to the trust level experienced by the staff members, including the Executive.

Goal Setting

We believe it to be our management responsibility to have a process which sets goals by involving all staff affected by work related to achieving those goals.

We make use of a linkage system with other units (headquarters, local, other) to participate in establishing goals which affect us.

Likewise, the use of the consultative method in setting our own goals has consistently involved others beyond our Regional Staff.

Leadership Processes

We are in agreement that there are some essential guidelines for a leadership style for this staff team.

This team produces best with a participative leader who provides the following:

1. A generous amount of participation from fellow staff members in his style of leadership.
2. A wide-open gut-level system of vertical and horizontal communication.
3. A sharing of leadership through the group in the planning and execution of overall responsibilities.
4. An open access to the power structure of the organization (lay and staff).
5. A management of the agreed-upon processes developed by the staff.

In our interpersonal staff relations we agreed that we would work best with an Executive who supports a supervisor-supervisee role which calls for mutually agreed-upon goals for the supervisee with his supervisor to be shared with the staff.

Job segments and the standards of performance, the elements of job accountability for each staff man, should be fully tested with the entire staff, including those job segments and standards of performance expected of the Executive.

Conclusion

In conclusion, this document is a description of how the C Region Staff agrees it could work best to achieve a high level of productivity. It is not intended to describe the functions of our work but to relate how we see ourselves working effectively toward the achievement of those functions accepted by this Regional Staff as appropriate to the Movement.

You may well find this information to be useful to you in achieving your stated task.

Epilogue

The executive of organization A became the executive of the newly merged organization. Organization B's executive accepted a comparable position as director of another merged unit in a different section of the country. Informal discussion with the new executive of organization C and some of his associates indicated that they viewed the process of planning for the merger as having been very effective. In their words, they were "off and running" and felt they were quite a bit ahead of the other organizational units that had merged through one process of another. Perhaps most significantly, the staff developed through the whole process, what seems to be a more articulate sense of their own power and trust in each other.

A Model for Mergers?

The organizational situation we have described does not bear a one-to-one relationship to merger conditions that exist in the world of business and industry. For example, though there was a parent unit involved and its influence was felt, this was not a case of one organization "taking over" another. Rather, the present merger created one supraorganization from two equals. In addition, though financial matters were important, because the organizational goals were oriented toward service and not profits or enlarged share of the market, the eventual success of the merger cannot be measured in usual business terms. Finally, the units in question were rather small ones and no doubt avoided major issues involved in larger-scale mergers.

Nevertheless, the events that have been discussed bear enough similarity on a process level to the broader picture so that some tentative statements may be made concerning the human problems of mergers and the potential resolution of these problems.

First, inherent in any merger situation is the substantial potential for tension and distrust among those individuals whose positions and function will be most affected. Even if assurances about job tenure are given, the tensions will derive from questions of ambiguity about role and reporting relationships. This suggests, immediately, the necessity for an open acknowledgment of the tension-creating situation. Conditions must be created where people can talk about their concerns and have them listened to and understood.

Second, mergers mean change. It is not honest to say that "business as usual" will be the order of the day. There will be changes in procedures, operating norms, reporting relationships, and management styles, among others. The confrontation design, or some modification of it, could help to lay the groundwork for such changes to proceed in a productive fashion. As well as providing a substantive input into the situation, the confrontation design can help create the openness that will be required as the merger process develops.

Third, some operational and quantifiable means of pinpointing specific organizational differences need to be employed if those primarily involved in the merger are to be given the opportunity to examine organizational differences in a deliberate and intelligent fashion. It is not enough to acknowledge that differences exist and "we will take care of them as we go along." The utilization of Likert's Profile of Organizational Characteristics in the present case was very helpful.

Fourth, despite the small size of the units involved in this merger, the case provides real analogues relevant to merger teams dealing with far larger entities. Merger teams typically run to no more than ten or so to a side, roughly the present size. Probably the major difference between this merger and one involving larger organizations is the effect of numerous levels. The present case involved only two levels, headquarters and the two field units. Larger mergers require integration between more hierarchical levels, and perhaps also between such categoric groups as labor and management which may be involved at each level.

Fifth, perhaps the most critical point of all in the present case, and probably in all mergers, is the need to obtain the collaborative involvement of those individuals whose jobs will be most directly affected by the merger. Via this involvement around both the process and substantive issues of the merger, it may be possible for people to feel a sense of ownership of the commitment to the new organization.

Sixth, in some merger designs, it might be important to use a fishbowl or group-observing-group[9] formation. This design alternative seems most appropriate where the members of the two units are strangers to one another and where observing the process of each group by other people provide very rich data and insights. In this case, although the 3-D Images were developed by the individual groups in isolation, little was probably lost. The point-by-point correspondences of the 3-D Images, for example, suggest that the members of both groups had a detailed knowledge of one another. A group-observing-group design could help generate similar data for relative stranger groups.

Multifirm Employment in a Consortium
Spreading the Risk in Negative-Growth Contexts

Let us shift attention to a more narrow focus—how can OD contribute to ameliorating hard economic times? Consider those growing legions of people whose career development has been abruptly blocked by no-growth or by decline, perhaps temporarily, perhaps permanently. Brynildsen describes these legions, globally but with verisimilitude:[10]

> Typically they are fairly competent, probably somewhat obsolete technically, making a very reasonable income, somewhat bored, and unwilling to take many risks in order to find a job which could be more challenging and exciting. In short they are under-utilized and have had their personal and professional growth stifled.

These growing cadres are in important senses organizational products, and they can have profound effects on organizations. That is, in the flush times of the preceding decade or so, many organizations essentially became paternalistic in their efforts to grow more humane, promotions and pay increases probably came quicker than previously, and many employees no doubt developed life styles predicated on more of the same. Commonly, also, salaries escalated sharply, even though individuals had skills that were obsolescing and/or appropriate only to a specific technology. Few firms upgraded their work forces, as by earmarking for retraining some portion of spending that went for salaries.

Economic times have changed and may remain harsh for an indefinite time. Some human products of the last decade have been variously unbuckled from their organizations, but many remain—less turned-on by their work, often less productive, and perhaps even looking down the somber road of a decade or two of going nowhere. The presence of such a cadre can have profound effects on what an organization is capable of doing in the present and what dreams it has for the future.

Are there ways of facilitating adaptations to this increasingly common condition, and especially via mutual empowerment of both the employee and the employing organization? Brynildsen suggests an interesting way of dealing with slow-growth situations. He proposes a consortium of perhaps fifteen employing organizations in a given geographical area which would "pool benefits, seniority, salaries, etc."[11] These portable benefits would make shifts in career or employer somewhat easier, depending upon the inventiveness reflected in organizing any specific consortium. These more facile shifts might have important or even profound consequences for employer and employees, three of which Brynildsen emphasizes:[12]

- Fluctuating needs for personnel might be coped with collaboratively.
- Smaller organizations might be able to acquire talents or expertise which were previously unaffordable.
- Dealing with marginal performers might be easier, with positive effects on applicable standards of performance.

Much reshaping of work and attitudes clearly would be required by such a consortium. For example, the notion of loyalty to *an* organization constitutes a major obstacle to the notion. The consortium idea basically rests on a greater sense of loyalty to self, to profession, or to special skill. And many reasons exist why both individuals and firms would find comfort in a simpler notion of loyalty.

Consequently, the consortium idea may not be a wave of the future. But it does suggest a kind of systemic innovation that will increase OD's usefulness in foul weather as well as fair.

Energizing Teams as a Response to Hard Times
Increased Output Under Inflation, Recession, and Negative-Growth

As the economic harder times of the last few years have rolled on—with threats of shortages of raw materials and energy, instabilities in money markets, escalating wages, and concerns about the quality of work—managers have reason to taunt OD practitioners: "Where are you now that I really need you?"

OD practitioners and their technologies have not been pioneering responses to slow-growth or no-growth, perhaps reasonably but no less unfortunately. That is, meeting individual needs is easiest during economic boom-times. Moreover, OD is a child of prosperity of the late 1950s and early 1960s, probably a little-troubled prosperity never to be seen again; OD practitioners have some reason to be pleased with past progress; and there is still plenty to do in firms and industries which are still faring well. So taking to the storm cellars until the most ominous economic clouds scud over has its attractions.

This section seeks to meet hard economic times, head-on, by increasing productivity. In the short-run, of course, this may mean fewer jobs; it may even suggest a redistribution of power that profits only management. In the longer run, however, the key to prosperity no doubt lies in escalating productivity, which may be the only real road to mutual empowerment for labor and management.

A Proactive Design

Little OD work has taken a head-on approach to establishing its appropriateness to economic wind-and-rain as well as sun, but the "production team" approach to increasing productivity at Honeywell Aerospace illustrates what can be done. Facing the twin body-blows of industrial recession and continuing inflation, Honeywell inaugurated PTP (Production Team Program) in a department building electronic navigation systems for NASA spacecraft.[13] The results? During 1974-1975, production increased 14 percent while manpower was reduced 39 percent, without the introduction of any new technology or labor-saving machinery. These percentages imply a tangible saving of some $1.5 million.

What motivated such results? Honeywell personnel trace them to the interaction of a guiding philosophy and several operating principles. The philosophy –which is seen as accounting for "the largest part" of the results–fits comfortably with dominant OD values. Two internal observers express that philosophy as "management's belief that the road to increased productivity involves engaging employees at all levels in the process of making needed improvements. PTP was the vehicle for achieving this involvement and reducing the false separation that exists in many organizations between problem solvers and non-problem solvers."[14] This philosophy gets activated by six "operating principles," briefly described in Exhibit 3. They are

- Team identification
- Accountability
- Competition
- Feedback
- Recognition
- Regular problem-solving meetings

Overall, these operating principles are consistent with the nontraditional structuring of work described in Chapter 2 above and tap the power of group processes and norms.

Only the "team meeting" component needs further development here in terms of two points. *First,* prior to the initial meeting of each team, a leader is designated by management and participates in a 9-hour training course. The content deals with both process (leading effective meetings, listening, and problem-solving) as well as with such topics as planning and work simplification. *Second,* at the initial team meeting, members get a review of departmental history and objectives, leading to a discussion of the role the team can play in subsequent meetings. Teams can deal with both specific production issues, with relationship issues, or both. In any case, a general process is prescribed for each problem or issue:[15]

- Define the problem or issue
- Develop alternatives
- Decide on a solution
- Develop an action plan
- Implement the plan

The need for teams to implement plans gets particular attention, because the teams "do not exist merely for the purpose of listing problems and possible solutions to be tossed back into the lap of management for implementation."

Exhibit 3 "Operating Principles" in Honeywell Aerospace's Production Team Program

---

Team Identification
In forming teams, factors such as similarity of assembly skills, physical location, and existing organizational structure are considered by behavioral scientists and industrial engineers. The objective is to identify teams of people with common goals and problems. Differentiating a department into teams of eight to twelve employees rarely requires major organizational shake-ups.

Accountability
A system is developed for collecting and recording the teams' weekly level of performance, using the ratio of total actual labor hours to industrial engineering standards.

Competition
Each team's improvement on its own past productivity is measured, on the model of a moving point such as a golf handicap, using simple formulae.

Feedback
Each team's relative improvement is plotted on a large public display board, which also contains individual pictures of all team members. "These team boards," Honeywell officials report, "are useful for providing feedback on team accomplishments, as well as strengthening the identification that each individual has with the team and its goals."

Recognition
Each month, the team with the greatest improvement in productivity is recognized at a departmental meeting, getting a citation and a small gift. A picture of that team gets prominent display in the production area.

Regular Problem-Solving Meetings
Each team has regular meetings, at least bi-weekly for an hour. These "are the key ingredient for sustaining lasting improvements in productivity," Honeywell officials report, "and gradually replace feelings of powerlessness with an awareness of cost and productivity problems and a 'can do' attitude."

Source: John M. Donovan and Wingate Sikes, "The 'Production Team' Increases Productivity at Honeywell," Honeywell Aerospace Division, St. Petersburg, Fla. (no date), pp. 2-4.

The team is directed to attend to the full problem-solving cycle. "While the process may be painfully slow at times," Honeywell officials note, "it does develop a greater commitment on the part of the team to making the solution work, and it brings a broader understanding of the problems faced by management."[16]

What Really Happened?

This brief description only skims the surface, of course, and grievously simplifies the fuller understanding that would support a reasonable assessment about PTP's long-run adequacy as a specific management/employee exchange process. Specifically, PTP implies presently unanswerable questions. For example, is the situation a temporary one, built on an unrecognized fiction? Thus employees may really have gained control unilaterally at the expense of management, which may induce a backlash once that becomes clear. Or management may be the only winner, with the control that employees believe they have gained being freedom only to enrich the corporate coffers. Time probably would soon tell if either of these were the case, with direct reflections in costs and output.

Put otherwise, it seems reasonable that PTP in the long-run must rest firmly in what was called mutual empowerment in the introductory section of this chapter. The underlying exchange process between labor and management must be a healthy and balanced one. If employees come to believe that the design is unilateral only—to increase profits while people are fired for their success or that of their colleagues—enthusiasm for PTP reasonably would plummet. The judgment is not an easy one; for the survival of an organization can be morally consequential, and it may well be the case that a specific organization will have to increase productivity to stay alive even as that displaces some employees to provide continued employment for many others.

Reduction-in-Force as a More Constructive Experience
OD for Those Being "Let Go"

If the attention given to training and socializing a new employee is given a score of 100, the time and effort given to helping dismissed employees adapt to their new conditions is probably no more than 0.1 on the same scale. This imbalance implies a major potential for polluting labor-management relationships, or at least for encouraging a lawyer's paradise of legalistic safeguards of job tenure.

What factors lead to this judgment about an unsatisfactory imbalance between OD work devoted to "letting go" versus "holding on"? Clearly, those factors have both empirical and value components, subtly intermixed, and a brief catalog must suffice here. Although major progress has been made concerning physiologic dangers at work, less is known about the physiologic and psychological consequences of nonwork. The anecdotal literature suggests that termination can have profound physical and emotional effects;[17] and joblessness has been closely linked to social integration and political behavior as well as to extremism.[18] Chapter 4 of Part 1 provides striking evidence of what effects job loss can have on (for example) individual depression. But such effects may not be consistent,[19] and they are still unclearly related to basic physiologic or emotional processes.[20] Second, very little has been done in an action-research sense with available information about the effect of the social environment on the health of employees.[21] Third, letting-go implies an especially high possibility for mischief because today's reductions-in-force have less to do with "removals for cause" than they have to do with new technologies and obsolescing skills, changes in business strategies, mergers and unbucklings, phasing-out of project teams, industrial relocation, and so on. An employee can with justice often note that departure represents "no fault of mine." "Failure" often merely signals a change of direction by the employing organization.

This section provides several perspectives on why and how the relative effort given to those being "let go" should be increased. We summarize by way of introduction. To begin, the processes of letting-go have a powerful impact on many employees, both those who remain and those who do not. From both practical and moral standpoints, it is appropriate to dissipate that impact, preferably by channeling it into constructive effort. Moreover, a number of guidelines will be suggested as useful in recognizing more fully the massive potential impact of job loss. Finally, some relevant designs for such an increased emphasis will be presented, in terms of design detail and also of central thrust.

Impact of Being Let Go

Judging from what happens when a person is fired, work remains very central for many people. This generalization perhaps applies especially to professional and skilled employees, but the generalization seems to hold rather more than less for all employees. Broadly, Lehner concludes that dismissal seriously affects many survivors as well as victims. He notes:[22]

> Dismissal is usually direct, sudden, and irrevocable. The act is often performed with guilt feelings by the person responsible and experienced with anger and shock by the person dismissed. The absence of either skill or regret is too often evident. Too many managers simply regard the firing of an employee as an unpleasant duty to be accomplished as quickly as possible.

Specific and perhaps even shocking evidence also implies the impact of firing. In one case, for example, approximately twenty-five released employees were tested several days after dismissal as to their present emotional state, with particular regard to their anxiety, depression, and hostility.[23] For what it is worth, all scores for all employees were higher than the mean scores for recent admissions to a large urban mental hospital of patients identified as schizophrenics.

Whether looked at broadly or in terms of specific effects, the impact of loss of job implies the centrality of work for most people. To be sure, we all know people who were relieved to lose a job, perhaps even genuinely happy. And there seems no doubt that many people are quite willing for awhile to enjoy their new leisure and whatever unemployment compensation they receive—to catch up on being with their family, on hunting, fishing, and so on. But for many people, perhaps most people much of the time, work is too central for its loss to go unremarked in major ways. Lehner expresses this differential but significant meaning of work in revealing terms. Thus, individuals may perceive their work as representing one or more of the following:[24]

Self-confirmation, a sign that the person is a valued contributor to society

Self-assertion, in that the person is a producer and thereby leaves a mark on his or her environment, either by individual effort or by contributing to some broader effort

Self-aggression, in that the person may try to outdo others, perhaps even succeeding in that from time to time

Self-love, which then permits the person to love others

Self-fulfillment, in that the person derives pleasure and rewards from work

Self-therapy, in that work can serve as a tranquilizer, with its demands stabilizing the person's inner turmoil

Slippage Between What We Prefer and How We Act

In at least one sense, constructively managing the multiple impacts of being let go is straightforward. Managers need do only what they seem to prefer, on very definite balance. Consider Stybel's study of thirty cases of executive dismissal in both public and business organizations.[25] Typically, his informants all but universally agreed as to how people should be terminated. Thus they emphasized early warning, remedial coaching, documentation of performance, probation, and so on.

However, managers seldom do what they prefer, with ironic consequences. Thus, rather than giving early warning, those doing the firing usually avoid direct confrontation about the issues, send only subtle cues that may escape the subordinate, and eventually waffle about the reasons for a dismissal to save face all around. Those doing the dismissing also make three assumptions that often return to haunt: That all or most others understand the reason for a dismissal; that others' focus of concern in dismissals is on whether they are justified or justifiable; and that in any case people's memories are very short when it comes to firings. What are the haunting consequences of all this? Surviving organization members may or may not understand a dismissal or agree with it, but their memories are very long and focus on the way dismissals were done. These processes are often seen as ineffective—for good reason, given the incongruence between common preferences and the actual dynamics of dismissal—or even unjust. Organizational myths tend to get created and they (bigger than life and often fancifully embroidered) in turn often become constraints that control how managers go about making dismissals.

Some Guidelines for Really Caring

Given these reasons for the centrality of work, both practical and moral considerations encourage caring about doing better in the matter of dismissal. Practically, either the dismissal itself or the process of the dismissal can send strong feelings swirling through an organization, feelings which may make a bad thing for some much worse for many more. Morally, perhaps the real respect that employees are accorded while at work will for many be highlighted by these last rites. If employees are valued in some basic sense, and especially if the dismissal is no fault of their own, especial care should be taken to reflect that value in end-of-game play.

Lehner suggests some useful guidelines to serve these practical and moral needs.[26]

- Management should strive to come to perceive dismissal in the framework of the dismissed rather than approaching it merely from a narrow managerial point of view.
- Cutback victims should have the longest possible notice, the potential risk being that an employee may "lay down on the job," but the probable pay-off being that the dismissed as well as other employees will recognize the effort to achieve some degree of mutual problem-solving and collaboration even in extremis.
- As much information as possible should be provided about other employment opportunities.
- Services which facilitate job hunting should be provided.
- Opportunities should be investigated for *partial lay-offs,* especially for professional employees, such that an individual has the option of continuing to work for a day or so a week—as a "permanent part-timer,"[27] by job-sharing,[28] or on a consulting basis, perhaps even while working for more than one firm.
- Management should be more aggressive in providing opportunities for group counseling or workshops, under competent guidance, to help ease the shock of dismissal and hopefully also to transform anxiety, despair, or self-pity into renewed enthusiasm.

Some Useful Last-Rite OD Designs

There has been some, but only a little, experience and research on designs appropriate to work toward the guidelines just introduced. A design discussed in a

Exhibit 4 Major Foci of an Income Development Workshop

Purpose

To aid dismissed professionals in adding to their immediate income in ways that do not necessarily involve their specialties.

Main Topics

1. The focus is on questions to be discussed in small groups, with the goal of reducing or better coping with job-loss trauma. The questions include:

   How did you feel when you got the lay-off notice?

   How did you deal with those feelings?

   How do you feel now?

2. Learning from the experience of others who generated additional income, to help induce the conclusions: "If they did it, so can I."
3. Individuals focus on the question of what they *can do* to make additional income. Inventories of experiences, resources, and desires are developed—by the individual and with the help of other group members.
4. Possible new goals are explored in response to the question: What would I *like* to do?
5. The next focus is on surveying the possibilities for working on the results of emphases 3 and 4. This phase emphasizes individual work on action plans.
6. Individual action plans are shared with the group, and new possibilities may be suggested and explored.

Source: From George F. J. Lehner, "From Job Loss to Career Innovation," esp. pp. 221-222. Reprinted from: W. Warner Burke (ed.), *New Technologies in Organization Development: 1* (La Jolla, Calif.: University Associates, 1975). Used with permission.

previous chapter, the demotion design in the first section of Chapter 4 of Part 1, clearly provides one sample of what might be done. Exhibit 4 sketches another design, that of a workshop dealing with income enhancement. Note that the workshop might include as many as fifty to sixty participants at a time, composed of five to ten small groups, each aided by a resource person.

Several common features of these appropriate designs can be extracted. *First*, ultimately they seek to trigger a change in the dismissed person's mode of functioning.[29] For example, Lehner stresses these two shifts:[30]

Active ← passive
Reactive → proactive

Many other similar shifts might be added. Self-pity → problem-solving is but one example of a far longer list.

Second, the implied pay-offs of such designs have a kind of yin/yang quality, a blending of opposites. Illustratively, such designs seek to energize a sense of individual ownership of and responsibility for developing plans to cope, but clearly with the organization's general support and also with the help of groups of fellow copers. Similarly, such designs seek to direct attention to the inner turmoil triggered by the job loss, but basically to facilitate action-taking, rather than merely to engage in endless rounds of self-analysis and self-pity. Relatedly, the goal is to seek new solutions unique to the individual, using as one resource the most basic of human collectivities, the small group whose members share a common need or predicament.

Third, such designs are rooted in the context of OD values. This analysis need not, should not, repeat what has been laid out fully, perhaps even tediously, in Chapters 1 through 3 of Part 1. But the point requires illustrating, lest its significance go unappreciated. For example, such designs seek collaboration and support in the very maw of what is for most people a deindividuating, solitary, and fragmenting experience. It may even be said that it is especially in such situations that the truest meaning and relevance of OD values can be found.

Burying the Organizational Dead
Psychological Debriefing of Ad Hoc Teams

A final and rapidly increasing kind of separation requires brief note. The reference is to project teams, which come and go in myriad forms and numbers. When a project team is terminated, an affair clearly ends, but reassignments often follow. Typical cases include the shutdown of a research team, a task force, or a new-venture team. While considered here as a way of managing termination processes, clearly, the effective burial of project teams relates to the other two strategies introduced at the outset of this chapter—as facilitative during bad times (or even good), and is intended to empower individuals and small systems by closing the books on yesterday's business.[31]

Such organizational dead now crowd the landscape, one major product of our burgeoning adhocracy, and ample evidence testifies that we do not handle the corpses very effectively. That is, intense feelings—loyalties and counter-loyalties—often develop in such ad hoc groups, and managers typically work hard to get members to develop strong attachments early in the game, to motivate individual effort and collaboration. Seldom do the same organizations institutionalize sorrow or relief, or even proper internment, however, when the go-go has gone and the team is disbanded.

This author has participated in several efforts to "close the books" on such ad hoc teams. The designs have been brief—a half-day or so—and simple. Some informal and off-site location is chosen, such as a rented beachhouse with facilities for eating and otherwise enjoying. The design elements usually emphasize such questions:

- What did you most enjoy about the project?
- What bugged you the most?
- What is your guess about what bugged others most, especially specific individuals or groups present at the experience?

Provisional experience is that such debriefing opportunities are good fun and seem to release much data–typically to be washed away quickly by talk, food, and drink–that might later pollute other organizational relationships. Closure is often so rapid and obvious that one can almost hear the doors slamming on experiences–recalled, and then filed away or forgotten. The experience is sometimes tender; it can be maudlin, and sometimes even pointed. But, the need for a debriefing experience is often strong, and participants often develop rites and traditions that leave no doubt as to the significance of what is transpiring. Consider one set of teams that accepted authoritarian direction because of unusual circumstances. When disbanded, these teams developed the tradition of a formal dress-up dinner to which the superior is invited. After drinks but before any serious discussion, the gussied-up superior is taken to a special room–with as much force as is necessary–is de-pantsed, has his bare feet dipped in a soluble paint, and is marched across the ceiling, upside down. There his prints join those of his predecessors. The message seems plain: We accepted tight control from you because we acknowledged its necessity. But our reactions to it were very real, and often very negative. And we want you to remember that the past is now gone, and we want a very different relationship should we work together again. Then comes the debriefing.

Notes

1. For a brilliant exception that deals with personal and professional concerns, see Robert Tannenbaum, "Some Matters of Life and Death," *OD Practitioner*, Vol. 8 (February 1976), pp. 1-7. There are few such studies with an organizational flavor. For an intriguing example, see Rick Lundquist, "An Organization's Choice to Die: An Anthropological Case Study of Cultural Change," pp. 373-377, in Robert L. Taylor, Michael J. O'Connell, Robert A. Zawacki, and D. D. Warrick (eds.), *1976 Proceedings*, Academy of Management. However, careful readers of the literature can find the theme even in some of the path-finding OD work, as in Arthur H. Kuriloff's *Organizational Development for Survival* (New York: American Management Association, 1972).
2. Lee Bolman, "Organization Development and Limits to Growth: When Smaller Is Better, Can OD Help?" Paper presented at 1978 Annual Meeting, Academy of Management, San Francisco, Calif., August 9-12, p. 2.

3. Ibid., p. 3.
4. Alexander Winn, "Reflections of the T-Group Strategy and the Role of Change Agent in Organization Development." Unpublished MS, February 1971, esp. pp. 250-256.
5. See, for example, *Mergers and Acquisitions* published by Mergers and Acquistions, Inc., 1725 K St., N.W., Washington, D.C.
6. John Kitching, "Why Do Mergers Miscarry?" *Harvard Business Review*, Vol. 4 (November 1967), pp. 84-101.
7. Rensis Likert, *The Human Organization* (New York: McGraw-Hill, 1967).
8. William Schutz, *FIRO-B* (New York: Holt, Rinehart, Winston, 1955).
9. Robert R. Blake, "The Uses of the Past," *Journal of Applied Behavioral Science*, Vol. 7 (October 1971), pp. 319-320.
10. R. D. Brynildsen, "Some Thoughts on Broadening Career Development Thrusts," *OD Practitioner*, Vol. 9 (January 1977), p. 13.
11. Ibid., p. 14. Many other innovations could serve such needs, of course. E.g., some organizations are beginning to experiment with job-sharing, as when husband/wife professionals share duties at home and at work. Perhaps one of every five larger organizations permits job-sharing. See John W. Seybolt, "Career Development: The State of the Art Among the Grass Roots," *Training and Development Journal*, Vol. 33 (April 1979), p. 18. An unusual job category—"permanent part-time"—also implies many of the same advantages. Such arrangements not only serve individuals; they also can provide flexibility for organizations adjusting to economic ups-and-downs and they might even generate increases in productivity. On the latter point, see Catalyst, Inc., Position Paper, "Part-Time Social Workers in Public Welfare" (New York: Catalyst, Inc., 1977).
12. Ibid.
13. John M. Donovan and Wingate Sikes, "The 'Production Team' Increases Productivity at Honeywell," Honeywell Aerospace Division, St. Petersburg, Fla. (no date).
14. Ibid., pp. 1-2.
15. Ibid., p. 5.
16. Ibid., pp. 5-6.
17. Alfred Slote, *Termination: The Closing at Baker Plant* (Indianapolis, Ind.: Bobbs-Merrill, 1977); and Thomas D. Taber, Jeffrey T. Walsh, and Robert A. Cooke, "Developing a Community-Based Program for Reducing the Social Impact of a Plant Closing," *Journal of Applied Behavioral Science* (1979, in press), pp. 1-2.
18. Susan Gore, *The Influence of Social Support in Ameliorating and Consequences of Job Loss*. Unpublished doctoral dissertation, University of Pennsylvania, 1973; and Michael Aiken, Louis A. Ferman, and Harold L. Sheppard, *Economic Failure, Alienation, and Extremism* (Ann Arbor, Mich.: University of Michigan, 1968), esp. p. 152.

19. Stanislav V. Kasl, Susan Gore, and Sidney Cobb, "The Experience of Losing a Job: Changes in Health, Symptoms and Illness Behavior," *Psychosomatic Medicine,* Vol. 37 (March 1975), pp. 106-122.
20. Sidney Cobb, "Physiologic Changes in Men Whose Jobs Were Abolished," *Journal of Psychosomatic Research,* Vol. 18 (August 1974), pp. 245-258.
21. Slote, *Termination,* p. 14.
22. George F. J. Lehner, "From Job Loss to Career Innovation," p. 213, in W. Warner Burke, ed., *Contemporary Organization Development* (La Jolla, Calif.: University Associates, 1975). For a report of a related effort, see James H. Judson, "Training Through Plan Phase-Out," *Training and Development Journal,* Vol. 30 (August 1976), pp. 22-23.
23. The instrument was the Multiple Affect Adjective Check List introduced in Chapter 4 of Part 1.
24. Lehner, "From Job Loss," p. 216.
25. L. J. Strybel, "Managing Human Resource Termination." Unpublished doctoral disseration, Harvard University, Cambridge, Mass., 1978.
26. Lehner, "From Job Loss," p. 216.
27. Pat Bagchi, "Job-Sharing," *Peninsula Magazine,* Vol. 1 (April 1976).
28. Catalyst, Inc., "Part-Time Social Workers in Public Welfare."
29. Lehner's design stresses socio-emotional and process-oriented interventions, for example, while a "rational approach" would emphasize providing advice and information to those released about their rights and entitlements–unemployment compensation, food stamps, company benefits, and so on. For a conceptual treatment, consult Gerald Zaltman, David H. Florio, and Linda A. Sikorski, *Dynamic Educational Change* (New York: The Free Press, 1977). For a "rational" intervention, see Taber, Walsh, and Cooke, "Developing a Community-Based Program"; and Jeffrey T. Walsh and Thomas D. Taber, "Assessing the Effectiveness of Nonprofessional Counseling During a Plant Closing." Paper presented at 84th Annual Convention, American Psychological Association, Washington, D.C., September 1976. A more narrowly utilitarian point of view gets expressed by Ken Leiniveber, "Showing Them the Door," *Personnel,* Vol. 53 (July 1976), pp. 66-68.
30. Lehner, "From Job Loss," p. 223.
31. Although only anecdotal data are available, this author joins a number of observers in concluding that serious effects often follow in the wake of closing-out project teams–marital dischord, serious drinking, depression, and so on. These effects may be seen as reflecting the difficulty of "coming down" without aid or conscious design from the involving and often-frenetic activities that characterize a project team's last days which leave many unresolved issues that can herniate members, especially those with dominant or exclusive task-orientations unaccustomed to dealing with socio-emotional issues.

Chapter 6

ELIMINATING UNNECESSARY ORGANIZATION CONSTRAINTS

Reducing Some Avoidable Costs of Managing Time and Status

The Hippocratic oath contains a major exhortation, perhaps is even built upon it. "Above all, do no harm," goes that exhortation.

Organization designers have not been similarly restrained, that seems abundantly clear. The organizational version of the medical doctor's oath, that is, might very well be: "Above all, impose no unnecessary constraints." Organization designers seem to have gone overboard in this regard, but in the opposite direction of industriously creating and maintaining systems that the sociologists see as generating "surplus repression," in what is particularly revealing terminology. This is increasingly seen as awkward. Hence, the growing number of suggestions that "demotivating" features of work be removed, and that care be exercised lest controls have serious and unanticipated consequences.[1]

This chapter fits the tradition of "above all, do no harm." It illustrates the cost of overcontrol in two particulars–time and status. The message is simple, but profound: Some constraints on individual behavior are clearly required in large organizations, but it does not follow that more constraints are better, nor that complete constraint constitutes the ultimate good. Specifically, the two long descriptions below commonly imply that no great harm follows relaxing two common constraints at work:

- Allowing employees, within limits, to exert greater control over their work hours
- Eliminating one troublesome status distinction, that between salaried and hourly wage personnel

Indeed, on balance, these two relaxations of constraints seem to generate real benefits for both employees and management, in addition to producing no serious negative effects.

Greater Employee Control over Workday

Flexi-Time as One Avenue for Expressing Central OD Values*

A mature OD also will have to encompass interventions that are structural and apply throughout organizations. This section seeks to contribute to that maturity by detailing the character and some of the consequences of one broadly applicable structural intervention. The intervention is called Flexi-Time, and will be viewed from three perspectives:

- As a modest step toward providing greater freedom and self-determination at work, which are central values in OD
- As a simple intervention that can generate substantial changes in work relationships, as well as in the quality of life for both employees and supervisors, changes which have often been advertised but which seldom have been documented by research designs that seek to avoid at least the most obvious methodological difficulties
- As providing a base of experience and evidence that will encourage similar applications to other kinds of work at all organization levels

Two applications of Flexi-Time (F-T) are discussed. The first is a pilot study, and the second deals with the extension of that intervention to most of the headquarters operations of the corporation which hosted the pilot study.

Advantages and Disadvantages of the Flexi-Time Approach

The thrust of flexible work hours is simple in concept, but applications must be tailored to specific sites. Let us describe one such tailoring effort.

*This section derives from a number of sources: Robert T. Golembiewski, Rick Hilles, and Munro Kagno, "A Longitudinal Study of Flexi-Time Effects," *Journal of Applied Behavioral Science,* Vol. 10 (December 1974), pp. 503-532; Robert T. Golembiewski, Samuel Yeager, and Rick Hilles, "Factor Analysis of Some Flexi-Time Effects," *Academy of Management Journal,* Vol. 18 (September 1975), pp. 500-509; and Robert T. Golembiewski, Rick Hilles, and Samuel Yeager, "Some Attitudinal and Behavioral Consequences of a Flexi-Time Installation: One Avenue for Expressing Central OD Values," pp. 87-120, in Dennis P. Slevin and Ralph H. Kilmann (eds.), *The Management of Organization Design: Research and Methodology* (New York: American Elsevier, 1976).

Exhibit 1 Flexi-Time Model

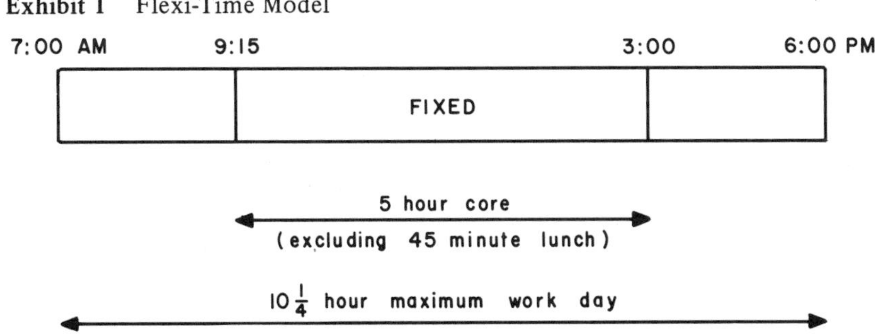

Initial Flexi-Time Model

A middling-liberal version of flexible work hours evolved from discussions between a personnel representative and research and development (R&D) officials, as Exhibit 1 implies. Illustratively, an individual may start work any time between 7:00 and 9:15 AM and stop between 3:00 and 6:00 PM. These comprise the flexible work hours, which the employee can change from day to day. An employee must be at work only during the five core hours.

Some Constraints

There are significant constraints on this variable schedule. Assume an employee works a 35-hour week. Because of wage and hour laws, weekly roll or non-exempt employees may not work more than 8 hours in any one day without being paid overtime. Therefore, a weekly roll employee may work only one 5-hour day in a week while accumulating 35 hours without getting into an overtime situation. Semimonthly roll employees—who are salaried—have greater flexibility in this regard. When an employee works a 40-hour, 5-day week, obviously, constraints assume even greater proportions for wage earners. Excluding overtime, the time of beginning work determines the end of the workday.

Four other details of this initial Flexi-Time model deserve emphasis. *First,* the flexible work hour preferences of employees are *subject to work requirements of the immediate supervisor.* On occasion, the demands of the job or the preferences of a supervisor may require that certain hours be kept. This will apply particularly when an employee's work must mesh with another individual or team. *Second,* the lunch period is not flexible. *Third,* hours worked in excess of thirty-five in a week may not be "banked" for a following week. This version of F-T thus involves a 1-week accounting period. *Fourth,* the pilot study Flexi-Time application involved the accurate recording of each person's accumulated time. Supervisors of the two experimental units in this case decided to continue use of a time clock, while the comparison unit continued to use time sheets.

Some Anticipated Advantages

Experience in other firms suggests some very real advantages of flexible working hours. The following advantages seemed most likely in the organization studied.

- The flexible work-hour system may minimize lost work hours. For example, in organizations with fixed working hours, employees frequently take time off for personal business, formally or informally. Under flexible work hours, time off for personal business is legitimate, but employees tend to take care of personal business on their own time.
- Overtime may be reduced. Some experience indicates that flexible hours allow easy adjustments to variable work loads. Therefore, overtime compensation may be reduced.
- Sick leave may be reduced. For example, individuals who oversleep can legitimately come to work, as opposed to calling in sick to avoid being recorded as late.
- Productivity may increase, qualitatively and quantitatively, although this can only be measured in this case by changes in attitudes *about* productivity in the three R&D units studied here. Some evidence indicates that employees on flexible hours are more inclined to stop work only after a task has been completed, thereby reducing start-up time on the following day and avoiding downtime at the end of the workday. Moreover, flexible work hours permit an employee to plan work hours to more closely coincide with the most productive hours.
- Flexible work hours may provide a better work climate for employees, thereby resulting in improved morale.
- Flexible work hours may reduce rush-hour traffic problems.
- Flexible hours may provide quieter periods for more concentrated work and thought.

Some Potential Disadvantages

To provide some balance, the Flexi-Time intervention implies potential problems. The most significant disadvantages follow.

- Because core hours cover only 5 hours a day, informal communication such as spontaneous meetings and phone calls might be impaired.
- Overtime might increase if a weekly employee's presence is routinely required when salaried employees are working more than 8 hours.
- The positive impact of flexible hours may be diminished by the negative effects of requiring use of a time clock or other recording devices.
- The increased flexibility enjoyed by employees may be perceived by some managers as a threat to their control.

- Once employees experience flexible hours, many may not want to return to a fixed-hour system.
- The cost of support services may increase.
- The flexible work schedule may require increased supervisory time and may divert supervisors from more important tasks.

As Expressing Central OD Values

The pilot Flexi-Time installation attempted to provide one tangible avenue for expressing central OD values. The host organization had for several years sponsored OD efforts that sought to establish greater freedom and responsible self-determination at work, involving the top seven hierarchical levels of a substantial business enterprise.[2] Flexi-Time provided one way of expressing those central values that was simple, direct, definite, and tangible. Specifically:

- Flexi-Time is less likely to violate autocratic norms among management or employees, even though some managers may resent the loss of control over employees involved in flexible hours and may seek to limit employee use of flexible hours.
- Flexi-Time effects can be felt very early and on a day-to-day basis, as in less fighting of traffic, whatever and whether long-run benefits accrue.
- Flexi-Time requires changes only on a day-by-day basis, and only from those employees who desire change from normal work hours.
- Flexi-Time does not require any major predisposition "to participate," or the learning of any skills.
- Flexi-Time typically affects an entire work force, or major segments of it.

Five Reinforcing OD Values and Understandings

Five "values and understandings" which stemmed from the broader ongoing OD effort, or were significantly augmented by it, facilitated the Flexi-Time installation. These five emphases deal with both the "why" and "how" of the Flexi-Time installation's beginning and acceptance.

First, many participants saw consultants in an aura of trust against a background of risks mutually and successfully run. The two prime consultants, to be specific, had participated with many members of the host organization in a wide range of OD activities: T-groups, team-building, confrontations between superior and subordinate, and more.

Second, at least some central participants perceived that the OD program led to real progress toward the kind of organization they valued and in which they could succeed with joy. From this perspective, Flexi-Time was another step toward significant personal and career goals.[3]

Third, the F-T program of action-research evolved in ways consistent with the thrust of the broader OD program. For example, great care was taken to design and implement Flexi-Time in a "bottom-up" fashion. This required inputs from, and involvement by, supervisors and managers. For example, a group of R&D managers were asked early in the game to develop a list of potential advantages and disadvantages of the basic idea of Flexi-Time as it applied to their specific work site. This was intended to have multiple effects: to disseminate knowledge about the intervention, encourage discussion about its anticipated effects, signal real concern about the "fit" of Flexi-Time variants to specific work sites, encourage realistic tests of variants, and develop questionnaire items intended to test actual advantages or disadvantages of specific applications.

Fourth, the promise of greater employee choice through Flexi-Time implied welcome relief for R&D, which had been under great pressure "to produce" for several years. To explain, among similar signs of belt-tightening, R&D had experienced constraints on adding people, despite a growing project workload. Hence the attractiveness of Flexi-Time, which promised greater employee freedom and satisfaction, and at little or no cost.

Fifth, the motivation for Flexi-Time was rooted in a cautious willingness on the part of R&D officials to test new approaches which might have a positive impact on "morale" and productivity, especially those approaches which had little or no direct costs. Flexi-Time met both criteria in several interacting senses, which can only be illustrated here. For example, normal work hours encouraged some downtime, as when chemical reactions would not be started until the next day because they could not be completed before the normal end of a workday, and because there was no procedure for carrying forward credit for such work.

Major Features of a Pilot Study

Three organization units at one R&D field site were chosen for study, each representing a different scientific discipline. Two units, henceforth called experimentals, had Flexi-Time installed. The third unit, the comparisons, was used as a benchmark against which to compare any changes reported by experimentals.

Both "soft" and "hard" data were gathered. Soft data involve changes in attitudes reflected on two questionnaires at three points in time. Basically, the questionnaire items sought evidence about the degree to which Flexi-Time had triggered the several anticipated advantages and disadvantages listed above. The questionnaires were administered on this approximate schedule:

Day 1	Day 15	Day 195	Day 375
Pretest	Flexi-Time installation	Short-post	Long-post

Company records also provide a variety of "hard" data, dealing with absenteeism, cost of support services, number of sick days, and time of arrival and departure.

Questionnaire data were solicited from occupants of two roles: employees and supervisors. Thus, managers at several levels responded to two questionnaire forms, one as employees of the corporation and the other as supervisors of specific sections or units. Nonmanagers responded to only one form. These forms are referred to below as:

- Employee form, responded to by both managerial and nonmanagerial personnel, whose eighteen items sought such information: "What is the impact of current work hours on your personal productivity?" (The eighteen items are described in Table 2.)
- Managerial form, responded to only by supervisors, whose twelve items sought such information: "What is the productivity of your employees?" (The twelve items are described in Table 5.)

Evidence indicates that supervisory respondents distinguished the two roles. All questionnaire items elicit responses on scales with seven equal-appearing intervals whose extreme points were anchored by such descriptions as "high" and "low." The directions of the scales were randomly reversed to reduce the probability of response set.

Data were solicited only from individuals who were permanent employees during the 375-day period of observation. The subjects performed jobs with a substantial range of abilities, training, and income. Details are not provided here, however. In sum, the numbers of employees involved are given in Table 1.

Table 1 Total Responses to Two Questionnaire Forms

	Employee Form		Managerial Form	
	Pretest and Short-Post	Long-Post	Pretest and Short-Post	Long-Post
Experimental unit A	15	12	5	5
Experimental unit B	22	20	6	6
Comparison unit	21	18	4	4
Totals	57	50	15	15

Three Major Analytical Tracks in Pilot Study

Basically, data about the effects of the Flexi-Time installation were analyzed in three distinct ways. *First,* all responses to the employee form, from both employees and supervisors, were factor analyzed, and effects of the installation were interpreted in terms of the major dimensions isolated thereby.

Second, item analysis was employed on responses to the managerial form, where factor analysis is not appropriate because of the ratio of managers to items.

Third, a variety of separate analyses were run on behavioral effects of the Flexi-Time installation. In contrast, the preceding two tracks emphasized self-reports *about* attitudes or behavior.

Respondents in Their Role as Employee: Track 1

All responses by both managers and employees to the first administration of the employee form were factor analyzed,* with each item being assigned to one and only one factor. Typically, this means an item was assigned to that one factor on which its loading was greatest, relative to the six other loadings. Every item, excluding only item 14, was assigned in this way. Item 14 was assigned to Factor III rather than IV, despite its slightly higher loading on IV, because it contributed more to the columnar loadings on Factor III. The resulting structure was relatively "clean," although the matrix is not reproduced here to conserve space. Seven factors accounting for 70 percent of the variance were isolated, using a Varimax procedure after rotation with Kaiser normalization. Specifically, the analysis establishes that the employee form elicits data across a substantial phenomenal range.

Verbal interpretations of the individual items contributing most to the separate factors permit a tentative description of the psychological space tapped by the employee form. Specific predictions about expected effects of the Flexi-Time installation on each of these dimensions also can be made.

Table 2 attempts this useful if tentative mapping-cum-predictions. The verbal descriptions fit the item loadings rather comfortably, overall. Note that the factor descriptions represent statements of ideals to be worked toward. Loadings of items 2, 8, 12, and 15 on Factors IV, V, and VII imply that the actual situation at pretest was seen as mixed by respondents. Factor V, for example, contains negative loadings on items 8 and 12, which indicates substantial conflict over scheduling with both coworkers and supervisors before Flexi-Time. Similarly, Factor VI implies difficulties with scheduling. The "expected

*For a variety of technical reasons, some associated with analyses beyond the present one, N = 50 in the factor analysis. This N corresponds to the total number of subjects who responded to all three administrations of the employee form. On the pretest, by way of comparison, N = 57.

Table 2 Factor Descriptions and Component Items as Ideals to Be Approached, Along with Expected Effects on Each Factor, at Three Points in Time, of Flexi-Time Installation

Factor	Expected Effects of Flexi-Time Installation: Short-Post vs. Pretest, Long-Post vs. Pretest	Expected Effects of Flexi-Time Installation: Long-Post vs. Short-Post
I. Participative work site with good communication	Increase, or at least maintain	Maintain, or at least do not decrease significantly
Item 01. Substantial participation in decisions re work		
Item 11. Good quality of communications re work assignments		
II. Positive impact of work hours on person and productivity	Increase	
Item 03. High satisfaction with work hours		
Item 05. Lessened traffic congestion		
Item 07. Positive impact of work hours on personnel productivity		
III. Flexibility, personal and work-related	Increase	Maintain, or at least do not decrease significantly
Item 06. Ease of attending to personal business		
Item 09. Substantial flexibility to schedule work		
Item 14. Ease of arranging meetings		
Item 17. Availability of others for "spur of the moment" meetings		

Table 2 (Continued)

Factor	Expected Effects of Flexi-Time Installation: Short-Post vs. Pretest, Long-Post vs. Pretest	Long-Post vs. Short-Post
IV. Reinforced motivation to contribute beyond standard Item 15. Substantial inclination to work more than standard workweek Item 18. Good quality of support services	Increase	Maintain, or at least do not decrease significantly
V. Unconflictful work site Item 04. Positive reaction to use of time clock Item 08. Infrequent conflict with coworkers over scheduling Item 12. Infrequent conflict with supervisors Item 16. Good quality of communication re activities in company of personal interest	Increase, or at least maintain	Maintain, or at least do not decrease significantly
VI. Work-site attractiveness and availability of human resources Item 10. Desirability of department as place to work Item 13. Common availability of others when needed	Increase, or at least maintain	Maintain, or at least do not decrease significantly
VII. Ease of scheduling work Item 02. Ease of scheduling work involving others	Increase, or at least maintain	Maintain, or at least do not decrease significantly

effects" are based on perhaps-arbitrary goals of the interventers. Illustratively, for Flexi-Time to be successful, it was considered that Factor III—"flexibility, personal and work-related"—should reflect increases over time. In contrast, increases would be attractive on Factor V—"unconflictful work site"—but maintenance of existing levels was acceptable.

Operationally, an individual's score on each factor of each administration of the employee form was calculated by adding the reported scale values of each of the items assigned to any factor. For present purposes, all scores are reported as varying in the same direction.

The reactions of both managers and nonmanagers in their role as employees to Flexi-Time were substantially positive. Two sources of data establish the point.

Responses to Open-Ended Questions. Responses to open-ended questions soliciting feelings "about current work hour policy and its effect on the way you do your job" were all but unanimously favorable. For example:

- Extremely favorable. It allows much more flexibility in setting up and running reactions—particularly those which involve more than 7 hours, but not overnight. I am much more willing to stay later to work up a reaction, knowing that I can leave early later in the week.
- Although I don't use the flexible hours because of a car pool I am in, I think they are excellent and I hope to use them in the future.

The only criticisms were directed at the time clock, which most saw as a necessary evil. Perhaps even more impressively, eight of eighteen persons from the comparison unit spontaneously recommended an early Flexi-Time application at their own work site.

Responses to Standard Questionnaire. Responses to the employee form also imply that Flexi-Time contributed significantly to improvements in the quality of the work environment. Specifically, Table 3 lends support to three broad conclusions. *First,* the table implies that the F-T impact should be reasonably clear in comparisons of attitudinal trends by experimentals versus comparisons. That is, not a single statistically significant difference exists on the seven factors, before the intervention.

Second, Table 3 reflects that Flexi-Time had a moderate intended impact on all respondents over the first 6 months of its application. Specifically, four of the seven differences on the short-post favor the experimentals, and two of the differences attain statistical significance.

Third, at T = 1 year, Table 3 reports massive changes in attitudes. That is, six of the seven differences on the long-post are in the expected direction. Moreover, four of these six differences attain the 0.05 level.

Table 3 Mean Aggregate Scores, Experimentals (N = 32) Versus All Comparisons (N = 18) on Three Administrations of Employee Form

	Pretest Scores[b]			Short-Post Test Scores			Long-Post Test Scores	
Factor	Experimentals	Comparisons	Factor	Experimentals	Comparisons	Factor	Experimentals	Comparisons
I	9.78	8.50	I	10.25	9.22	I	9.91	9.50
II	11.97	12.00	II	18.19[a]	13.06[a]	II	18.97[a]	13.50[a]
III	18.25	18.11	III	22.44[a]	16.39[a]	III	23.22[a]	17.44[a]
IV	9.19	9.33	IV	10.19	10.33	IV	9.84	10.39
V	19.63	20.56	V	20.34	20.39	V	21.06[a]	19.44[a]
VI	10.50	11.17	VI	11.06	11.28	VI	11.09	10.17
VII	5.72	5.72	VII	6.03	5.83	VII	6.34[a]	5.44[a]

[a] Indicates pairs of scores that attain or surpass 0.05 level on t-test, one tailed.
[b] The means vary in size due to the variable number of items defining the several factors.

Distinguishing the responses of managers and nonmanagers to the employee form seems to require no major qualification of the conclusion that responses of respondents in their role as employee were favorable to Flexi-Time. The data are not reproduced here.

Reactions of Managers: Track 2

The reactions to Flexi-Time of those in supervisory roles also can be reflected in two ways: via responses to open-ended questions about work-hour policy, as well as via standard questionnaire items.

Responses to Open-Ended Questions. Almost all Experimental supervisors responded positively to the Flexi-Time program. One or two noted that it did not influence their work site very much, and several criticized the use of the time clock. But the bulk of the responses were overwhelmingly positive, as these illustrations establish:

- Very enthusiastic. Makes every week different. Productivity of my subordinates has not suffered from core hours—probably has increased because of better overall morale. Commuting has become easier—less time on the road—and less hectic. Occasionally, when working from 7:15 to 3:00, I find traffic almost minimal. Will find it difficult to ever return to 8:45 to 4:30 *routine.*
- Excellent. At least in [my] area flexible work hours are the answer to a prayer. Employees willing to stay with long experiments—on the old system they would have been rushed and maybe ruined. Employee work has improved dramatically with a parallel increase in productivity.

Responses to Standard Questionnaires. Interpretations of responses of the supervisors to the questionnaire items cannot be so direct. Consultants anticipated that supervisors qua employees would enjoy the personal benefits of Flexi-Time, but might also see the program more in terms of its potential for inducing conflict, or for increasing the probability that some skill or service would be unavailable when needed. Hence, there were two expectations about supervisors' reactions to Flexi-Time:

- As employees, supervisors were expected to show an attitudinal pattern similar to that of nonmanagerial personnel on short-post and long-post tests.
- As managers, the minimum expectation was that pretest attitudes would not worsen over the first 6 months of the installation, and would probably improve on the long-post.

The evidence supports two conclusions. *First,* supervisors did seem to distinguish the two roles. *Second,* the expectations above were generally met. The number of supervisors is small, of course. Consequently, tentativeness is appropriate in interpreting the data.

Supervisors as Employees. Table 4 provides convincing evidence that responses of managers to the employee form do not differ significantly from those of nonmanagers. Specifically, managers and nonmanagers differ significantly on two factors on the pretest. One of these significant differences still exists on the long-post, and that where managers report higher scores on the factor "reinforced motivation to contribute beyond standard." This result is not surprising.

Supervisors as Managers. Supervisors also met expectations in their responses to the managerial form, which contains twelve items.

The impact of Flexi-Time over its first 6 months on the attitudes of supervisors as managers is reflected in Tables 5 and 6. The minimum expectation about Flexi-Time was that it maintain the status quo, as supervisors view various facets of their managerial responsibilities. Hence, the "desired effects" in Table 5 are usually phrased as negatives: do not lower significantly, do not increase significantly, and so on.

Table 5 implies that the minimum expectation of no deterioration on the managerial form was basically met. Definitely, also, supervisory attitudes did not improve substantially. All changes are nonsignificant.

Approximately 1 year after installation, a long-post test attempted to assess whether short-post supervisory attitudes toward Flexi-Time developed into real concerns. Overall, supervisors as managers report impressive changes on the managerial form, comparing the long-post to the short-post. This pattern contrasts sharply with the no-change condition at 6 months after installation. Specifically, as Table 6 shows, twenty of the twenty-four changes reported by Experimental supervisors are in the desired direction, with nine being statistically significant. Note especially that on the "worst" item, item 8, supervisors from one experimental unit report that problems with other supervisors re work hours have remained unchanged over the first year of the Flexi-Time application, while supervisors in the other experimental unit report somewhat but not significantly greater problems in that regard. In contrast, Table 6 shows only twelve desired changes for experimentals, with none achieving statistical significance, over Flexi-Time's first 6 months.

An In-Process Summary. The data above support two conclusions: a potent if delayed impact of Flexi-Time on the attitudes of supervisors as managers; and the program's positive reception by all respondents as employees. Close observers can account for the difference between experimentals and comparisons in

Table 4 Mean Aggregate Scores, *Experimentals Only*, Managerial (N = 11) Versus Nonmanageral Respondents (N = 21) on Three Administrations of an Employee Form

	Pretest Scores[b]			Short-Post Test Scores			Long-Post Scores	
Factor	Managerial Respondents	Nonmanagerial Respondents	Factor	Managerial Respondents	Nonmanagerial Respondents	Factor	Managerial Respondents	Nonmanagerial Respondents
I	11.55[a]	8.86[a]	I	10.91	9.91	I	10.64	9.52
II	12.36	11.76	II	17.64	18.48	II	19.55	18.67
III	17.27	18.76	III	22.27	22.52	III	23.27	23.19
IV	11.36[a]	8.05[a]	IV	10.45	10.05	IV	11.45[a]	9.00[a]
V	20.00	19.43	V	19.55	20.76	V	20.36	21.43
VI	10.00	10.76	VI	10.55	11.33	VI	11.55	10.86
VII	5.82	5.66	VII	5.82	6.14	VII	6.27	6.38

[a] Indicates pairs of scores that attain or surpass 0.05 level on t-test, one-tailed.
[b] The means vary in size due to the variable number of items defining the several factors.

Table 5 Summary of Differences on Pretest Versus Short-Test Supervisors in Experimental and Comparison Units, Managerial Form

Items on Managerial Form	Pretest Differences, Supervisors,[a] Experimentals (Es) vs. Comparisons (Cs)	Desired Effect of Flexi-Time on Experimental Supervisors	Short-Post Differences, Supervisors,[b] Experimentals (Es) vs. Comparisons (Cs)
1. Productivity of your employees	Es report lower productivity	Do not lower significantly	Es report higher productivity
2. Morale of your employees	Es report lower morale	Increase	Es report higher morale
3. Quality of support services	Es report better quality	Do not lower significantly	Es report lower quality of services
4. Degree of conflict with employees over scheduling	Es report more conflict	Do not increase significantly	Es report less conflict
5. Quality of communications about work assignments	Es report lower quality	Do not worsen significantly	Es still report lower quality of communications
6. Flexibility to undertake projects or experiments	Es report less flexibility	Do not reduce significantly	Es still report less flexibility

7. Effort required to account for employees' time	Es report less effort	Do not increase significantly	Es now report more effort required
8. Problems with other supervisors re work hours	Es report few problems	Do not increase significantly	Es report fewer problems
9. Opportunities for employees to work independently	Es report fewer opportunities	Do not reduce significantly	Es still report fewer opportunities
10. Effort required to schedule work assignments	Es report less effort	Do not increase significantly	Es still report less effort
11. Your employees' attitudes at work	Es report less positive attitudes	Improve	Es report more positive employee attitudes
12. Overall performance of your employees	Es report lower overall performance	Do not worsen significantly	Es report better overall performance

[a]Significance of differences was determined by t-test two-tailed. Any differences achieving the 0.05 level or greater is indicated by the term "significantly" in the description of effects.
[b]Significance of differences was determined by t-test, one-tailed. No differences attain the 0.05 level.

Table 6 Summary of Changes Reported by Supervisors on Managerial Form, Long-Post Versus Pretest[a]

Items on Managerial Form	Experimental Unit A, Long-Post vs. Pretest (N = 5)	Experimental Unit B, Long-Post vs. Pretest (N = 6)	Comparison Unit, Long-Post vs. Pretest (N = 4)
1	+	+	–
2	+*	+*	0
3	–	+	+
4	+	+*	–
5	+	+*	–
6	+	+*	–
7	+*	+*	+
8	–	0	+
9	+	0	+
10	+*	+	+
11	+	+	–
12	+	+*	–

[a]Note: + designates a change toward a desired effect; – designates a change opposite a desired effect; 0 designates no change; * designates a change that achieves the 0.05 level of statistical significance, or beyond, by one-tailed t-test.

terms of no systemic variable other than the presence or absence of Flexi-Time. No doubt many other nonsystemic factors do contribute to the pattern of attitudinal change. But it seems reasonable to conclude that, in this case, a structural intervention was able to trigger a variety of changes in the quality of life at the work site, as both employees and managers viewed it.

Some "Hard" Data About Flexi-Time: Track 3

The F-T impact also can be estimated in terms of a variety of measures of behavior. Some observers refer to such behavioral measures as "hard," while measures of attitudes are "soft." We do not assign a somehow different level of reality to the two kinds of data, but patent differences do exist. Thus, measures of attitudes are typically obtrusive, and that obtrusiveness can induce reactions in respondents that complicate interpretations of any data acquired. Moreover, measures of attitudes are more or less subject to conscious faking or to differential perceptual biases or skills of respondents.[4] Four kinds of "hard" data are available in this case. They include:

- Variations in time in and time out
- Changes in the amount of overtime
- Changes in rates of absenteeism
- Changes in cost of support services

Time In and Time Out. Perhaps the most obvious impact of Flexi-Time, and for some the most worrisome, is reflected in a discrete behavior: The time people enter their work site and when they leave. Some managers are concerned that wildly skewed distributions may occur, creating horrendous scheduling problems under Flexi-Time.

The experience in the present firm indicates substantial but only marginal use of the F-T arrangement. Table 7 provides data from a 10-month period, with months 6-10 covering the summer vacation months. More or less, under Flexi-Time most employees keep to the standard workday of 8:45 AM through 4:30 PM, plus or minus 30 minutes. Specifically, nearly 82 percent of the times-in during months 1-5 are recorded in the interval 8:15 to 9:15 in Table 7. In the summer months, the percentage drops, but only to about 75 percent. For times-out, a little over 60 percent are recorded as 4:00 to 5:00 PM for the winter months, with the figure falling only to 55 percent in the summer months. Hence, the F-T pattern seems to be, grossly, to work later one day and leave earlier on another. Apparently only a few people check in early and check out early. The only noteworthy additional trend is a flattening of the distributions of both arrival and departure times on Mondays and Fridays, especially in the summer months, on which days employees are somewhat more apt to report or depart somewhat earlier or later than on other days of the week.

Overtime. On the face of it, overtime decreased very sharply in the first 6 months of experience with Flexi-Time, and has stayed at the lower level for an additional 6 months. Overtime was never a very big item, but it was reduced by some three-quarters after the F-T installation.

Several factors urge against a robust conclusion on this point, however. Coincident with the F-T installation, management had decided to minimize overtime. In addition, a major user of overtime in one experimental unit was phased out just before the F-T test began. Moreover, only about 30 percent of the employees in the experimental units are weekly roll employees, and their overtime history may therefore be an unreliable indicator of F-T effects in situations where paid overtime is possible for a greater proportion of a work force. Salaried employees, those on the semimonthly roll, do not qualify for

Table 7 Percentage Distributions of Time In and Time Out (Approximately 10,000 Employee Workdays)

Times In (AM)	Months 1-5 (%)	Months 6-10 (%)	Times Out (PM)	Months 1-5 (%)	Months 6-10 (%)
6:45	0.04	0.02	3:00	1.3	2.8
7:00	0.3	0.9	3:15	7.2	11.1
7:15	1.7	2.6	3:30	5.5	6.7
7:30	6.4	7.3	3:45	3.9	4.7
7:45	3.2	5.1	4:00	5.1	6.1
8:00	4.5	7.5	4:15	6.4	7.7
8:15	12.0	15.0	4:30	15.1	14.1
8:30	21.0	23.2	4:45	20.8	17.7
8:45	25.3	18.2	5:00	12.8	9.8
9:00	16.6	11.7	5:15	8.1	6.8
9:15	6.9	6.7	5:30	5.1	4.8
9:30	1.9	1.7	5:45	3.7	3.0
9:45	0.1	0.1	6:00	2.3	3.2
10:00	0.1	0.1	6:15	1.1	0.9
			6:30	0.6	0.4
			6:45	0.4	0.05
			7:00	0.2	0.14
			7:15	0.3	0.05
			after 7:30	0.3	0.2

overtime. Finally, the general opinion is that the experimentals now are working on missions that have less potential for overtime.

Consequently, the decrease in overtime cannot be directly attributed to the F-T arrangement. But the program no doubt helped management work toward its policy of minimal overtime use.

Absenteeism. Table 8 provides summary data about absenteeism which reflect sometimes striking changes, but whose interpretation cannot be definite. Overall, that is, total paid absences dropped by over one-third in the experimental units, comparing the full year after the F-T installation with the prior 12 months. In contrast, a group of employees doing much the same kind of work at another company site a few miles distant, but without Flexi-Time, experienced an

Table 8 Absences in Two 1-Year Periods Before and After Flexi-Time Installation[a]

Time	Experimental Units (N = 43)		Comparison Group (N = 41)	
	Total Paid Absences	Absences of Single Day or Less	Total Paid Absences	Absences of Single Day or Less
Nov. 1971 to Sept. 1972	277 days	71	180 days	81
Nov. 1972 to Sept. 1973	179.5 days	80	207.5 days	98
Changes	−97.5 days	+ 9 occurrences	+27.5 days	+17 occurrences
	−35 percent	+12.7 percent	+15.2 percent	+21 percent

[a]Flexi-Time introduced October 1972.

increase in absenteeism of some 15 percent over a similar period. Note that the experimentals and comparisons started from substantially different bases, however. One cannot say how much of the initial difference was due to bad medical luck, and how much to different employee or supervisory standards about acceptable levels of absenteeism. But it seems safe to conclude that absenteeism under Flexi-Time decreased, in the face of an increase among employees of similar skills and training without Flexi-Time.

Table 8 requires three additional points of clarification. Thus, it considers all "paid absences," whether for sick leave or other reasons. Only 5 days of absence were not paid in the 2 years of observation, and they all occurred in the comparison group in the first year. So, the reduction in "paid absences" in the experimental unit did not result from a sudden increase in absences for which pay was denied.

Note that the "comparison group" in Table 8 is not the same as the "comparison unit" referred to above. For a variety of technical reasons, meaningful retrospective absence data were available for a substantial group of company employees only at another nearby site, who also had pretty much the same skills, training, and missions as did the experimentals. The data refer only to those individuals in the three involved organization units who were employed during the full period November 1971 through September 1973, that is, those employees about whose reactions to F-T management was most concerned. Turnover among both experimentals and comparisons was moderate, approximately 10 percent per year.

Finally, the expected decrease in absences of a single day or less did not occur. Short-term absences could have resulted from oversleeping before Flexi-Time, for example, and the new work hours were expected to reduce them. However, experimentals increased such absences by nearly 13 percent, as compared to the comparisons who increased by 21 percent from a somewhat higher base.

In conclusion, although there is no one way to interpret the data in Table 8, the evidence implies an F-T impact on absenteeism. Employees exposed to Flexi-Time reduced their absenteeism, in the face of a substantial increase in absenteeism among employees of comparable skills, training, and pay. The expected decrease in short-term absences did not occur among experimentals, however, although comparisons reflected an increase of some 50 percent.

Cost of Support Services. Many managerial innovations claim advantages in fact gained only by shifting costs to other parts of the system. Evidence implies that no such balloon-squeezing occurred under Flexi-Time. Thus, attitudinal data imply no serious F-T by-products, such as new drains on the time of supervisors or heightened conflict about scheduling. Moreover, it also seems that Flexi-Time has *not* resulted in increased costs of centralized support services provided to the experimental units. These costs include personnel, as well as a variety of supplies and expenses related to day-to-day activities.

The cost data can be reviewed breifly. Overall, the average number of support personnel has been reduced by approximately 15 percent, comparing the year before to the year after the F-T installation. Similarly, the cost of all support services has now been reduced by approximately 12 percent. These costs include one-time charges for new equipment and new procedures that came on-stream in the first F-T year, during which period concerted efforts were being made to improve the quality of support services.

Given the usual indeterminacies, conservatively, costs for support services at least have not increased in the short run, and substantial savings can be expected in the longer run. Note that average employment in the two experimental units has otherwise remained essentially stable since the F-T installation. Of course, not only Flexi-Time was impacting on support services. The campaign to improve equipment and procedures for support services also contributes to both savings and costs.

A Flexi-Time Application in a Large Diversified Firm

The pilot study was clearly encouraging, then, but the OD team did not recommend extending Flexi-Time to all employees. That might have worked, but it violated the OD mode. Rather, recommendations to top management urged a more permissive proposal that allowed various levels of management to adopt *some* flexible work-hour program suitable to their own needs, in consultation with corporate personnel and consistent with such broad uniformities as the number of hours per workweek. The multiple intentions should be patent:

- To extend to broader ranges of employees the possibilities for greater freedom and self-determination at work implicit in flexible work hours, as illustrated by Flexi-Time
- but to do so without reducing or negating the sense of commitment or ownership of several levels of managers
- and to do so while recognizing that various combinations of tasks and diverse collections of people can imply their own logic that will require various models of the core notion of flexible work hours.

The description below details the first 6 months of experience with this permissive F-T policy in a host firm that is larger and more diversified than any other in which reasonably rigorous research has been attempted, with the firm having an extensive product line and being involved in the full range of activities, from research and development through marketing. In addition, this report gives separate attention to the reactions of nonsupervisory as well as of supervisory personnel.[5]

How Employees Manage Their Time

Unlike the pilot study, the broader application permitted many variations on the elemental theme that employees can exercise an increased degree of control over when they begin and stop work each day. Generally, two factors determine how much control over work schedules can be exercised. *First,* the F-T policy adopted by top management defines a maximum condition which various operating units may exploit in variable degree or not at all, depending upon their choice and the demands of work. The maximum condition is exactly the same as in the pilot study just reviewed.

Second, employees have differential flexibility in controlling the length of their workday. "Nonexempt" employees, that is, those covered by the federal Walsh-Healey Act, may work as few as 5 hours in a given day under flexible work hours, but they can work no more than 8 hours unless they receive supervisory approval for overtime pay. "Exempt" employees may work as few as 5 hours in a given day, or as many as 11.

Specifically, four programs, ranging from least flexibility to most, illustrate the differential flexibility possible for various groups of employees in the large diversified firm. Normal hours of work range from 35 to 40 hours per week.

- In the mailroom, employees are paid by the hour and work a 40-hour week. Consequently, their starting time determines their quitting time, unless overtime pay is approved.
- Manufacturing office employees are in the main nonexempt and work 7¾-hour days. Consequently, they can work only an additional 15 minutes per day before running into an overtime situation. Employees can determine when they will begin work in the interval 7 to 9:15 AM, and they can bank only ¼-hour per day, barring overtime. Any accumulated time may be used to shorten one or more of the workdays in the week of the accumulation.
- Nonexempt employees in the customer service unit work a 7-hour day, and can bank up to 1 hour a day, credits which can be used to shorten other workdays. However, all employees must provide their supervisors with advance notice of their arrival and departure times so that customer coverage can continue without interruption.
- Employees in most other areas of the firm—R&D, marketing (excluding field sales), corporate personnel, and so on, work a 7-hour day. Exempt employees can bank as many as 4 hours a day, and nonexempt employees can bank 1 hour per day. All employees can variably begin and finish work on scientific days as long as they respect the core hours,

although policy provides that supervisors have the discretion to require exceptions when work requires.

Some 2150 employees came to work under some F-T program, about 40 percent of whom are covered by federal wage-and-hour laws and thus cannot take maximum advantage of the firm's flexible work-hours policy. In addition, one unit, manufacturing-production, with some 650 employees, rejected the opportunity to develop a suitable F-T program. Two other groups of employees, the field sales force and security, did not participate in flexible work hours. The former already had substantial control over their hours of work, and the latter kept rigidly fixed schedules due to the nature of their work.

Diffusing the Work-Hours Innovation

The introduction of flexible work hours in the host firm was broadly experimental and participative. The main events in diffusing the innovation include:

- The favorable results of the pilot application were broadly disseminated.
- Senior executives were advised to authorize only that subordinate managers develop with the help of corporate personnel some flexible work hours variant suitable to their specific work site.
- Twenty-three work-hour area representatives (ARs) were appointed by appropriate middle managers to help develop the several flexible work-hours programs, to evaluate the success or failure of the individual applications, and so on, with the active involvement of corporate personnel.
- Results were assessed and reported in the aggregate to top management 6 months after the local variants were implemented. In addition, each of the twenty-three ARs got data concerning their own work force for further dissemination to involved managers and employees.

Evaluating the Innovation

The focus here is on the evaluation of the first 6-months' experience with flexible work hours. Evaluation was based on three basic kinds of data:

- Attitudes of both supervisors and employees about their work and the work site, as revealed by both forced choice and open-ended questionnaire items that differ from those used in the pilot study
- Absenteeism
- Overtime

Work pressures militated against any design other than a posttest only. No control or comparison group was utilized because there were major perceived differences between the population under F-T programs and those three classes of employees not covered: security, field sales, and manufacturing-production.

Several procedural details serve to introduce the data. *First,* attitudinal data came from a sample of 183 supervisors and 274 employees in sixteen of the twenty-three work areas. The population surveyed amounted to some 21 percent of those exposed to F-T programs over the past 6 months.

Second, the seven work areas not surveyed comprise about 12 percent of the total relevant population, because their ARs choose not to participate in the voluntary survey. Pressure of other business was cited by some ARs, but the common reason for nonparticipation was the overkill attributed to the survey. Most nonparticipating ARs claimed to know well the positive attitudes toward Flexi-Time of their few ($\overline{X} = 35$) employees, and hence felt a survey was redundant and a waste of time. In contrast, the sixteen participating ARs were responsible for clusters of an average of 120 employees each with, credibly enough, less opportunity to assess reactions to the flexible work-hours programs confidently.

Third, area representatives did not follow any single pattern in polling clusters of nonsupervisors. ARs were urged to generate approximately a 10 percent sample of nonsupervisors, at a minimum, but several had areas with large differences in skills, wages-rates, and so on. They sampled more extensively. Random methods of selecting individual respondents were recommended, but job demands and availability of specific individuals required departures from randomness.

Fourth, ARs were urged to get as many responses as possible from supervisory employees, who might be especially sensitive to problems with the programs. The 183 returns from supervisors comprise approximately 30 percent of all supervisors from areas with participating ARs.

Nonsupervisors Evaluate Flexible Work Hours. The reactions of nonsupervisors run strongly positive, on balance, concerning their first 6 months of experience with the several flexible work-hours programs. The positive reaction is especially noteworthy because the approximately 1400 nonsupervisory employees in the sixteen work areas participating in this study included about 875 nonexempt employees, and are limited in their ability to use flexible work hours without getting into overtime situations. Perhaps the most convenient overall indicators of nonsupervisory opinion are responses to the question: "How would you describe your reaction if [the firm] were to return to the previous fixed hours policy?"

Reaction	N	%
Very positive	9	3
Positive	7	3
Neither positive nor negative	31	11
Negative	83	31
Very negative	141	52
No answer	3	–
	274	100

In sum, 83 percent of nonsupervisory employees reflect a strong preference for the continuation of the new work-hour programs.

Table 9 reflects a variety of reasons for this strong preference to retain flexible work hours. In general, the benefits to most employees seem considerable, as in reduced traffic congestion and ability to attend to personal business. The costs do not appear great. Thus, about 11 percent of the respondents see others as less available when needed, and the same proportion of respondents also see the availability of support services as having been adversely affected by flexible work hours. Overall, only a few employees report any negative impacts on their productivity or job performance.

Supervisors Evaluate Flexible Work Hours. The 183 surveyed supervisors provide reactions as occupants of two roles: as individual employees, and as supervisors. As employees, supervisors are about as positive about flexible work hours as nonsupervisors, in sum. Hence the data are not detailed here. Illustratively, 81 percent of the supervisors express a negative reaction to a return to fixed hours, while 9 percent favor it. The corresponding figures for nonsupervisors are 83 and 6 percent, respectively.

Supervisors in their managerial role also respond favorably to flexible work hours, but somewhat less uniformly in some issue areas. Since flexible work hours might so complicate the task of the supervisor as to wash out any advantages experienced by employees, these reactions deserve close scrutiny. Table 10 provides summary data. Thus, some supervisors report adverse consequences: 12 percent see their flexibility in scheduling as having been reduced somewhat; 17 percent see some reduced employee coverage of work situations; and 18 percent report having to spend more effort accounting for employee's time. These indications do not appear to represent acute problems, however. Moreover, they seem overbalanced by positive effects. Thus, 85 percent of the supervisors report that flexible work hours impact favorably on employee morale; 45 percent see an improvement in overall performance; and 32 percent attribute enhanced productivity to the innovation.

Table 9 Impact of Flexible Work-Hour Programs on Nonsupervisory Employees[a]

Reaction	Your Productivity		Availability of Others When Needed		Traffic Congestion to and from Work		Ability to Attend to Personal Business During Day Out of Building		Availability of Support Services		Communication with Others re Work		Your Job Performance	
	N	%	N	%	N	%	N	%	N	%	N	%	N	%
Very favorable	176	64	31	12	112	42	136	50	28	10	51	19	97	35
Favorable	80	29	90	33	90	33	87	32	93	35	73	27	93	34
About the same	13	7	120	44	63	23	44	16	117	44	135	50	83	30
Unfavorable	–	–	28	10	3	1	2	1	30	11	11	4	1	1
Very unfavorable	–	–	1	1	2	1	4	1	–	–	–	–	–	–
No answer	7	2	4	–	4	–	1	–	6	–	4	–	0	–

[a]*Stimulus*: Compared with the previous fixed hours, how would you rate the impact of flexible work hours on the following items?

Table 10 Impact of Flexible Work-Hour Programs on Supervisors[a]

Reaction	Productivity of Your Employees		Your Flexibility in Scheduling		Employee Coverage of Work Area		Amount of Your Effort Required to Account for Employee's Time		Morale of Your Employees		Overall Performance of Your Employees	
	N	%	N	%	N	%	N	%	N	%	N	%
Very favorable	12	7	14	8	11	6	9	5	50	28	24	14
Favorable	47	27	36	20	34	19	21	12	104	57	57	32
About the same	115	66	109	60	104	58	116	65	27	15	94	53
Unfavorable	—	—	23	12	30	17	32	18	—	—	—	—
Very unfavorable	—	—	—	—	1	—	1	—	—	—	—	—

[a]*Stimulus: As a supervisor,* in comparison with previous fixed work hours, how would you rate the impact of flexible work hours on the following items?

A kind of bottom-line measure perhaps especially reflects the quality of supervisory reactions to the programs. They were asked: "Under flexible work hours, to what degree do your employees abuse work-hour policies?"

Reaction	N	%
A great deal	–	–
Quite a bit	6	2
Some	17	10
A little	28	16
Very little or none	123	71

Most estimate that the degree of abuse under conventional work hours was similar, if not greater!

Trends in Absenteeism. Most observers expect that F-T programs will decrease single-day absenteeism due to oversleeping, minor and passing physical complaints, and so on. Two stratified, random samples of fifty supervisors and fifty nonsupervisors were drawn to test for absenteeism effects, comparing a 5-month period in 1974 with the same period in 1975. The samples were stratified to reflect proportions of the several job classes of involved employees, with random choices of individuals filling each job class's share of the 100 cases. Only sick days are considered here, for all of which the employees were paid. Various company rules apply but, generally, supervisors check on "sick days" only when absences surpass certain public maxima. Employees also can take a fixed number of "personal days" off with or without pay. These are not considered here.

The data on absenteeism, on balance, imply the flexible work-hour programs had the intended effect. As Table 11 shows, the expected decreases in a single-day sick absences did occur, a decrease that is particularly notable in the

Table 11 Comparison of Sick Days During Two 5-Month Periods

	Total Sick Days		Single-Day Absences	
	December 1973- April 1974	December 1974- April 1974	December 1973- April 1974	December 1974- April 1974
Exempt employees	74	67	27	26
Hourly employees	117	168	51	41
Totals	191	235	78	67

fact of a substantial increase in total sick days reported. There is no particular reason to expect flexible work hours to impact on multiple-day illness or total sick days.

Trends in Overtime. Some observers have worried that flexibility for salaried personnel would only result in burgeoning overtime costs for hourly workers. For example, a research scientist might use flexible hours to finish a long experiment and sleep late the next day. But his flexible response might require lab helpers who are paid by the hour. The scientist's flexibility, in short, might require increased overtime. Federal legislation, of course, limits to eight the number of hours that can be worked on a straight-time basis during any given day for hourly rate employees.

It seems safe to conclude that flexible work-hours programs in the host firm did *not* increase overtime. In fact, comparing the first 5 months in 1975 with the same period in 1974, overtime costs were down more than 21 percent. This trend cannot be credited to the flexible work-hours programs alone; indeed, the host firm was making a concerted effort to minimize overtime. But, flexible work hours clearly did not frustrate management efforts to reduce overtime, and they also may have encouraged employees to make more efficient use of their most productive work periods.

As Encouraging Other Applications

These results encourage the further dissemination of the flexible work-hours innovation, especially as guided by OD values. At very little start-up cost, major and favorable attitudinal shifts occur among both employees and supervisors. Available "hard" data are more difficult to interpret, but flexible work hours patently did not increase costs of absenteeism or overtime, and probably decreased them.

Summarizing the Available Literature*

Let us provide an overview as counterpoint to the detailed analysis of two specific cases just reviewed. A growing literature supports the general efficacy of Flexi-Time installations, in a wide variety of contexts—in industry, service, and commerce; in government and business; and here and abroad. Most of that literature is descriptive or broadly clinical, but some detailed studies exist.

Let us provide perspective on that burgeoning literature, a first-cut at a complex subject that has two emphases. Thus, the general characteristics of

*For a more extensive treatment, see Robert T. Golembiewski and Carl W. Proehl, Jr., "A Survey of the Empirical Literature on Flexible Workhours: Character and Consequences of a Major Innovation," *Academy of Management Review*, Vol. 3 (October 1978), pp. 837-853.

available studies will be detailed, and the behavioral consequences of Flexi-Time installations will be sketched, as far as "hard data" permit. Finer-tuned analyses specify differences in specific F-T programs, the degree of discretion they permit, specific site characteristics, the effects on employees' attitudes and opinions, and so on.[6] Here the focus will be on undifferentiated F-T programs, which essentially permit some degree of employee choice about when to start and stop work, while also requiring a 5-day week with a larger or smaller number of core hours during which all employees must be at work. The studies dealt with include only those which make a serious effort to gather a range of data about Flexi-Time effects, from records, surveys, and so on. Even this loose criterion disqualifies most publications, which tend strongly to be anecdotal and impressionistic.

General Characteristics of the Universe of Studies

Exhibit 2 presents those studies of separate installations reported in sufficient detail to be useful here, as well as the two available summaries of applications at several sites, and directs attention to several important features of the available research. Three highlights from that exhibit deserve mention. *First,* it implies that available research may be criticized on technical grounds. For example, few studies utilize control or comparison groups. Despite the very tough problems in isolating real "controls," they do help eliminate hypothetical causes for observed effects alternative to the Flexi-Time intervention. Relatedly, few studies provide longitudinal perspective. Many studies use a posttest-only design, for example, which complicates the interpretation of results and does not encourage carefree assignment of observed effects to the installation. Many studies use post-only designs without comparison groups, moreover, which precludes the application of statistical techniques to provide consistent estimates of trends in data over time. And those post-only designs typically permit only such weak conclusions: X percent of respondents after Y months of experience with Flexi-Time report that they want to retain it. Typically, studies lack even the simplest statistical treatment.

Second, the available studies obviously cluster in clerical, white-collar contexts. This obviously raises serious issues about the generalizability of the results to manufacturing or industrial contexts.

Third, the studies involve union and nonunion settings, although we cannot be precise about either the managements or unions involved. Reasonably, however, the willingness to experiment with the design implies something about both management and union style, for example, concerning the appropriate mix of freedom or coercion. Care is appropriate, then, about generalizing the findings here to management or union contexts that may be variously labeled "authoritarian," "hard-nosed," "System 1," "9, 1," and so on.

Exhibit 2 Overview of Flexi-Time Studies

Study	Setting	Union Involved?	Study Design	Comparison Group(s)?	Hard/Soft Data?	Statistical Treatment?
Canada Trust[7]	All functions in a trust company; 80 employees	Yes	Post/long-post	No	H/S	None
Dorking[8]	574 members of design-drafting department	?	Pre/post	No	H/S	None
Evans[9]	232 clericals in a British insurance company	?	Pre/post/long-post	Yes	S	None
Golembiewski, Hilles, and Kagno[10]	R&D units, approx. 60 salaried and hourly employees	No	Pre/post/long-post	Yes	H/S	t-Test for differences between means
Golembiewski and Hilles[11]	All functions in pharmaceutical firm employing about 4000	No	Post only	No	H/S	None
Hopp and Sommerstad[12]	Aerospare and micro-circuit units in a computer firm	?	Generally, post only; some pre/post comparisons	Yes	H/S	None
Lufthansa[13]	50% of the 6700 ground personnel of an airline	Yes	Generally, post only; some pre/post comparisons	No	H/S	None

Exhibit 2 (Continued)

Study	Setting	Union Involved?	Study Design	Comparison Group(s)?	Hard/Soft Data?	Statistical Treatment?
Mueller and Cole[14]	Washington, D.C., offices of a federal agency	?	Generally, post only; some pre/post comparisons	?	H/S	None
Port Authority[15]	850 nonunionized employees	No	Pre/post	No	H/S	None
Prudential[16]	950 staff members of the main office of a British insurance company	Yes	Post only	No	H/S	None
Salvatore[17]	110 employees in a Canadian federal agency	Yes	Generally, post only; some pre/post comparisons	No	H/S	None
Santa Clara[18]	Juvenile-adult probation department	Yes	Pre/post/long-post	No	S	None
Thornton[19]	50 members of personnel department in a Canadian federal agency	?	Pre/post	No	H/S	None
Walker, Fletcher, and McLeod[20]	Two British Civil Service offices, 125 employees	?	Post only	No	S	None

Weinstein[21]						
Company AB	Application clerks in a U.S. business	No	Generally, post only; some pre/post comparisons	No	H/S	None
Company CD	Variable	No		No	H/S	
Company EF	Clerical staff in a U.S. business	No		Yes	H/S	
Martin[22]	Summary of 40 applications	?	Generally, post only; some pre/post comparisons	?	H/S	None
Wilton and Harrison[23]	Summary of 21 applications, ranging from 37 to 2700 employees	In two companies	Generally, post only; some pre/post comparisons	in 17 cases	H/S	None

Survey of Behavioral Consequences

Although available studies deal with both attitudinal and behavioral consequences, this analysis will practice economy. Attitudinal consequences basically are just as positive as the data presented above in connection with the two case studies. Behavioral consequences present a more challenging target for analysis, and monopolize attention here.

Flexi-Time applications often get advocated as positively impacting on a number of significant behaviors at work. For example, most proponents argue that Flexi-Time tends to reduce absenteeism and sick leave, especially those of the 1-day variety, as well as tardiness. The rationale is transparent. An employee who sleeps late, or a parent with a suddenly sick child, or a buyer with an urge to take advantage of a sale, might under the conventional system call in sick rather than risk a hassle about a late arrival. Flexi-Time also is often thought to reduce turnover, by making for more attractive conditions at work.

In contrast, others maintain that Flexi-Time only increases costs. Thus, more employees might have to be hired; costs of supervision might increase; and overtime charges might rise, particularly as workers covered by Walsh-Healey provisions remain to provide support services for exempt employees who are "flexing" a workday longer than 8 hours.

Exhibit 3 summarizes the available data, often reporting specific magnitudes. The exhibit also uses general terms—"no appreciable effect," or "reduced"—to provide the most suitable summary of reports by researchers.

What do available data suggest? *First,* "hard" measures get little attention. Exhibit 3 has many empty cells, and several studies listed in Exhibit 2 did not even attempt to generate such data, and hence are omitted from the third exhibit.

Second, Exhibit 3 implies that the benefits of Flexi-Time applications outweigh their costs. Few cases of "negative" effects exist in the relevant literature; many cases of "positive" effects appear; and only a few researchers report that applications do not seem to have definite effects on "hard" measures.

Third, at the very least, the data imply that Flexi-Time has low behavioral costs, even if one chooses to question the generality of its positive behavioral effects. Note, however, that supervisors seem to make a number of adjustments under F-T—as in a greater willingness to rely on self-control and more common use of mechanisms for "programmed coordination."[24] These adjustments may be considered short-run costs, although most supervisors seem to make them with no great difficulty. Moreover, those adjustments would typically be preferred by most employees. Indeed, the lag time in the development of great supervisory enthusiasm about F-T—which a section above (see p. 228) suggests took over 6 months—may reflect the period of supervisory experimentation with such new attitudes and mechanisms.

Exhibit 3 Overview of Behavioral Effects of Flexi-Time Installations

Study	Sick Leave or Absenteeism	Tardiness	Turnover	Overtime	Trends in Costs
Canada Trust	Absenteeism reduced			Reduced 73.4%	
Dorking	Over a 12-month period: 1-4 hour sick leave absences decrease by approximately 70%; 5-7 hour sick leave absences decrease by 33%; and full-day sick leave absences decrease by 8%				
Golembiewski, Hilles, and Kagno	1-day absences increase but at half the rate for comparison group; long-term absences decrease by 35% in F-T units while comparison groups increase by 15%			Reduced 75%, but other programs also operating	Slight decrease in costs of support services as well as personnel
Golembiewski and Hilles	While total sick days increase by over 20%, single-day absences decrease by about 14%, comparing the year after F-T to the year before			Reduced 21%, but other programs also operating	No appreciable change in personnel costs
Hopp and Sommerstad	Sick leave declines in all but the summer months	Tardiness declines	Lower in one quarter of program; higher in two summer months of program		
Lufthansa	Reduced			Reduced	

Exhibit 3 (Continued)

Study	Sick Leave or Absenteeism	Tardiness	Turnover	Overtime	Trends in Costs
Mueller and Cole	Sick leave decreases by 7%; annual leave decreases by 10%		"Lowest turnover rate in 5 years"	39% of offices report small decrease, 23% a substantial decrease, and 15% a small increase	
Port Authority	"No appreciable effect"			"No appreciable effect"	
Prudential	Reduced			Reduced	
Salvatore		Reduced			
Thornton				Reduced	
Weinstein					
Company AB			Reduced		
Company CD			Reduced		
Company EF	No change		Reduced		
Martin	Absenteeism decreases in 65% of the organizations rated	Decreases in 89% of the organizations rated	Reduced in 16% of the organizations	Increases in 5% of the organizations and reduced in 28%	Utility expenses increase in 8%, decrease in 11% of cases Unit costs increase in 3%, decrease in 20% of cases
Wilton and Harrison	Half-day and 1-day absences decrease in 52% of the companies, increase in 4% No change in longer absences		Reduced in 14% of the cases	Reduced in 66% of the cases	

Eliminating Invidious Distinctions, Especially Unnecessary Ones
The Blue-Collar Worker Goes on Salary

Sometime in the mid-1800s, the difference between salaried and hourly workers evolved. Before then, to simplify, there existed only entrepreneurs and hands-for-hire. The latter were paid by the hour or the piece, essentially out of concern that productivity would be sustained only by such motivators of diligence. Salaried personnel had a meaningfully distinct status, and their fidelity to the job inhered in their ownership status.

Basically, the difference between salaried and hourly workers still persists, even though the ranks of the salaried are now ballooned by huge numbers of white-collar employees. While to be salaried was once a mark of some distinction, there being so few of the species, the armies of the salaried today are perhaps 40 percent larger than all hourly workers combined. But the distinction persists in most organizations, and with it some categoric judgments about the differential trustworthiness of employees, their ability to be responsible, and so on.

The question is not whether the distinction is invidious, for that it surely is. Rather, *the* question concerns whether the distinction is necessary or useful. Available evidence suggests the distinction encourages substantial mischief in organizations.[25] A long excerpt below—taken from the work of Robert D. Hulme and Richard V. Bevan—supplies important if not conclusive corroboration of that conclusion.

What? Put Everybody on Salary?

A number of companies recently have put all employees on salary, including production workers. The plans vary widely in details, but Exhibit 4 presents the basic features of a typical salary plan for production people. Its goal is to remove an invidious distinction between employees and, in effect, to test whether that difference in treatment was necessary.

Why Not Treat Adults as Adults?*

When we examined five salary plans—those of Gillette, Polaroid, Kinetic Dispersion, Avon Products, and Black & Decker—we identified solutions to the problems set out in the preceding paragraphs and to a number of other difficulties associated with blue-collar salaries. Many of the solutions are either specific

*The remainder of this section essentially reprints Robert D. Hulme and Richard V. Bevan, "The Blue-Collar Worker Goes on Salary," *Harvard Business Review* (March-April 1975).

Exhibit 4 Principal Features of a Typical Salary Plan

Purpose of the plan	It provides for plant employees to be salaried; it represents a principal element in establishing uniform employee relations polices for everyone.
Eligibility	All employees are eligible after 3 months of service.
Time recording	Employees are no longer required to punch time clocks; supervisors will record lateness, absence, and sickness for control purposes.
Basis of payment	All employees will be paid biweekly, at a salary rate determined from their hourly rate prior to the changeover.
Payment for time not worked	No deduction will be made from salary for absence for any reason, unless absences other than sickness total more than 15 days in any 12-month period.
Sick pay	For absences after 15 days in any 12-month period due to sickness, payment will be made under the sickness and accident plan.
Timekeeping and attendance standards	Although salary will not be withheld unless an employee exceeds the limitations above, attendance records will be an important factor in evaluating performance for merit increases and promotion opportunities.
Probationary employees	Employees in their first 3 months of service will not be paid for absences of any kind, except for short periods of lateness at the supervisor's discretion.
Administration	Supervisors will be responsible for maintaining attendance records; any questions or comments should be directed to them.

Source: Robert O. Hulme and Richard V. Bevan, "The Blue-Collar Worker Goes on Salary," *Harvard Business Review* (March-April 1975).

management controls and policies or specially directed communication efforts. But, whatever the details, the salary approach has meant a fundamental shift in the employee relations framework to a presumption of maturity on the part of all workers.

Polaroid Corporation in Cambridge, Massachusetts, for example, bases its "unification" program on the premise that adults should be treated as adults. To introduce the program, management launched an educational effort encouraging individuals to recognize that they are responsible for their time and must use their own judgment in determining whether an absence is necessary.

Polaroid, along with the four other companies we studied, was convinced that equal treatment of all employees would evoke a favorable response from the work force. In general, the expectations of these companies have been fulfilled, but those who believed that improved attitudes would lead *directly* to improved productivity have been disappointed. It is those who believed an improvement in attitudes is a *good objective in itself* who have come closest to seeing their hopes fulfilled. Most important, these companies did not expect the salary concept to ameliorate all their labor relations problems. If they had, the arguments of those opposing salary plans for production employees would have been strengthened.

We shall review some of the companies' experiences with their salary plan vis-à-vis the role and reaction of labor unions, the effect of absenteeism, the response of supervisors, and the effect on work-place attitudes. Exhibit 5 highlights some of the aspects of their plans. In summary, we shall offer some criteria for determining the capability of a company to switch to a salary structure for its blue-collar workers.

Role and Reaction of Labor Unions

A common denominator in the salary plans studied was the development and introduction of each by management initiative, rather than response. As we have noted, the fear that a union would seek to trade this initiative for a more traditional benefit has stopped many companies from extending salary payment systems to unionized operations. However, companies that have made this change report that union reaction has not been a problem.

Management Proposes; Labor Approves

An example is Kinetic Dispersion Corporation, a Buffalo, New York manufacturer of equipment for the paint and food industry. In 1962, when the United Auto Workers organized the company's employees, Kinetic's president had been considering placing the entire work force on a salary basis. He believed strongly in equal treatment for all employees and could find no justification for a two-tiered wage system—hourly for production workers and weekly for other employees. He was concerned about the inequity of hourly people losing income when absent for good reason, while salaried employees suffered no deduction.

When Kinetic's management introduced the idea of salaries during the company's first contract negotiations with the union, local UAW officials believed that the issue was sufficiently important to recess negotiations and consult with their international leaders in Detroit. With the full approval and active interest of UAW headquarters, the local accepted the company's proposal

Exhibit 5 Selected Aspects of Salary Plans

Company	Union Status	Date of Change-over	Objective of Changeover	Treat-ment of Time Clocks	Absence Rate for Workers Affected by Plan (%)[a]			Employee Reaction	Employer Appraisal
					Before	After	Current		
Avon Products	Nonunion	1972[b]	Eliminate distinctions in treatment of office and factory employees	Removed	4.1	4.4	4.2	Some preimplementation resistance from management; favorable postimplementation reaction, including that of supervisors	There were no specific gains, but management is satisfied that the approach is an essential part of its philosophy
Gillette	Nonunion	1955	Provide a logical alternative to improved sick leave	Retained	4.6	4.7	4.7	Generally favorable reaction, but initial minor concern about loss of status of clerical employees	Management is satisfied with the results

Black & Decker	Nonunion	1971	Improve employee relationships, with consequent benefits to operational effectiveness	Removed	1.5[c]	2.3	2.0	Introduction of plan a contribution to favorable attitudes; some supervisory concern over payment decisions	Response generated by the plan has enabled continued productivity improvements
Kinetic Dispersion	Union (UAW)	1962	Eliminate distinctions and provide security of income	Retained	—[d]	—[d]	—[d]	Plan welcomed, but misused initially	Management is reasonably satisfied, although problems were far more severe than anticipated
Polaroid	Nonunion	1966	Unify hourly and salaried employees	Retained until 1972	5.0	6.0	6.0	Benefits of plan well accepted, but no fundamental change of attitude	Management is not unhappy and considers program now controlled

[a] Basis of measurement may vary, so figures are not comparable between companies.
[b] Weekly salary plan was introduced in 1972, but 1968 changes equalized treatment in most cases.
[c] This applies for sickness only.
[d] Rates were not measured; substantial increase occurred after changeover.
Source: Robert D. Hulme and Richard V. Bevan, "The Blue-Collar Worker Goes on Salary," *Harvard Business Review* (March-April 1975).

for a salaried bargaining unit. The union did not attempt to trade off the proposal for some other demand, nor did the company use it to limit other benefits in the contract.

The wording of the provision on salaries was broad, stating that after a 60-day probationary period any employee would be paid in full for up to 3 months' absence in a year. The type of absence was not spelled out, and the contract gave the company no discretion to withhold payment, even when the supervisor thought the absence unreasonable.

The first year of the contract was expensive for Kinetic. Absences increased substantially, and many of the excuses for not coming to work were spurious. Management discussed the problem with UAW officials and warned that if the abuses continued, the salary plan would be unilaterally withdrawn. The union did not want this to happen; the salary plan dovetailed neatly with the idea of a guaranteed annual wage, which the late Walter Reuther was then advocating.

Hence the UAW agreed to amend the contract and give the company the right to withhold payment if it deemed an absence to be unreasonable. A substantial improvement in the absence rate followed—the result of a combination of union pressure and management action. Working together, union and management had preserved the concept. In fact, the salary program at Kinetic has been so successful over the years that only one grievance over nonpayment has gone to arbitration. The company's position was upheld. The positive response of the UAW to this kind of plan is consistent with research findings published in 1974 in Canada by David Peach.[26]

Different Degrees of Eliminating Distinctions

Avon Products, a larger company than Kinetic, has had an equally favorable experience of paying salaries to production workers.

Avon Goes Almost All the Way

For many years Avon has made few distinctions between clerical and production employees. Vacations, benefits, and general personnel policies have been similar for both groups. Before 1968 the major difference was a more liberal sick leave policy for office employees than for hourly production employees. In 1968 Avon amended this program and granted hourly workers the same sick leave benefits as all of the salaried employees. In addition, the company introduced a policy that allowed all employees to be paid who were absent for valid personal reasons.

With the installation of the sick leave plan, the only remaining differences were the use of the time clock, frequency of payment (weekly for production, semimonthly for office), deductions for lateness, and some aspects of salary administration. In January 1971 Avon formally introduced a "weekly salary plan," eliminating all but one of these differences: rather than receiving merit raises, production workers still receive automatic increases, a procedure suited to paced production work.

Black & Decker's Selective Application

Black & Decker Manufacturing Company of Towson, Maryland, on the other hand, has been selective in its application of its salary plan. During the past 4 years the company has extended its plan to an increasing number of plants on a systematic basis. Employees who are paid weekly salaries are permitted up to a maximum of 10 days' paid absence during a year for acceptable reasons, such as sickness or personal emergency. Supervisors have the responsibility of determining whether an absence should or should not be paid.

Although Black & Decker is enthusiastic about the concept of an all-salaried work force, it has delayed extending salaries to every employee simultaneously at all locations for two reasons:

- Company policy has been to widen the scope of the salary plan gradually, concentrating on solving problems as they arise. There has been no urgency to implement the change for uniformity's sake alone.
- The company believes that a complete understanding of the concept and the intent of the plan is paramount and that supervisory training in the "pay/no pay?" decision-making process is essential to the success of the plan.

Effects on Absenteeism

The introduction of a salary plan is almost always accompanied by an initial surge of absenteeism as employees test the new program. In some cases, the surge subsides without specific management action, but in others it is serious enough to require extensive control measures—either increased supervisory pressure or direct limits to paid time off.

Even in situations where companies have predesigned extensive controls and put them into operation immediately, the increase in absenteeism tends to occur. And although it generally drops back to a steady level after several months, it is usually higher than before. In the companies we studied, the rate of absences increased by an average of 15 percent, equivalent to less than 1 percent of payroll. In terms of cost, however, the effect on payroll is greater than this because absences not paid in the past are now paid under this approach.

Informal Guidelines

At Gillette, the idea of an all-salaried work force rose directly from a review in 1955 of sick leave benefits. At the time of review, the absence rate of 4.6 percent among production employees compared with one of 3.5 percent for salaried personnel.

Gillette anticipated an initial increase in the total rate of absenteeism to 5 percent, a figure management believed to be reasonable for a change expected to have a beneficial effect on worker attitudes. Actually, absenteeism among production workers did not increase significantly immediately after the introduction of the new plan and has since settled at 4.7 percent, only marginally above the original rate.

To assist supervisors in deciding when a worker should be paid for a personal absence or whether corrective action should be taken if someone appears to be abusing the program, Gillette established guidelines that set a 12-day annual standard for absence control. This is broken down into shorter periods, and the supervisor reviews the records to determine when an employee's absence rate is running ahead of standard.

The 12-day limit is an informal one, but understandably, the guidelines do not apply to a long absence for sickness. Payments for absences beyond the guidelines continue, provided valid reasons are forthcoming. However, excessive absences may become the basis for managerial action–for example, a warning meeting, counseling, or dismissal.

Peer Pressure

At Avon during the period 1966 to 1967 sickness absence for all nonexempt employees totaled 3.9 percent. For the hourly group the rate was 4.1 percent. After the 1968 implementation of a company-wide paid sick leave plan, the rate increased to 4.2 percent overall and 4.4 percent for the hourly group. Subsequent rates have varied from 4.0 to 4.3 percent for all nonexempt employees and 4.1 to 4.3 percent for the former hourly group.

Between the 1968 introduction of the sick leave plan and the 1971 installation of the all-salary program, the total absence rate averaged 5.6 percent. Since the conversion, the absence rate has averaged 5.3 percent. According to Avon the salary policy reduced abuses by permitting employees to request limited amounts of paid time off instead of reporting that they were "sick" for the full day. Also, the counseling and control efforts of supervisors were enhanced.

Generally, an employee who comes in late is paid, but if he or she is late a substantial number of times, this fact is recorded for evaluation purposes. Avon considers less than half a day's absence as a lateness and more than that an absence, and the supervisor makes the pay or no pay decision. A personal absence is paid if the supervisor believes it is justified.

The work unit is an added pressure that helps control absenteeism at Avon. A typical work unit consists of a group of employees on a packing line, each with a specific location and function. Although a small degree of flexibility exists, in most cases a gap in the team is readily apparent and has an immediate impact on the group's ability to sustain output. Thus, peer pressure exerts an effective control on attendance.

Response of First-Level Supervision

Reaction among supervisors to their new responsibilities in making pay or no pay decisions varied considerably in the companies under study. Many supervisors seem to resist the initial implementation of these programs, partly out of confusion and partly out of fear of added responsibility. However, over a period of time and with proper guidelines and support from management, these fears abate and supervisors take their administrative and judgmental responsibilities in stride.

Better Decision-Making

Initially, supervisors at Black & Decker were not entirely happy with some aspects of their company's salary plan. In particular, they found it difficult to make judgments about performance appraisal and equitable payment decisions. To help these supervisors, the company issued additional explanatory guidelines that emphasized plan objectives and also introduced a new merit performance review system. Supervisors now have a high degree of understanding of the plan and the philosophy behind it and are administering controls effectively.

Higher Standards

At Avon, supervisors generally have been pleased about exercising their own judgment in these pay or no pay matters. Avon believes the increased challenge and responsibility have been instrumental in enhancing the attractiveness of the supervisor's job to the point where the company is able to continue to raise its standards and recruit and retain more college graduate supervisors than before. More important, the approach is entirely consistent with its management style of treating employees as individuals and of handling employee relations matters based on the facts of the situation.

Impact on the Working Environment

The objective of the salary plans among the companies we studied has been to sustain efforts to develop a sense of unity among employees. In this regard, these plans represent a fundamental step toward implementing management's employee relations philosophy.

Good Management-Employee Relations

Black & Decker's experience is indicative. The company believes that introduction of salaries has been a contributing factor to sustaining historically good management-employee relations. Since 1966, employment at Hampstead has risen by 5 percent, while output has increased 80 percent. Technological developments deserve the credit for part of this productivity increase, but much of it is due to operational economics and improvements in working practices. Continuing, substantial operational changes have been readily implemented and accepted in part because the salary plan has supported the development of favorable attitudes.

Employees there believe that through the plan they have been given something that other workers in the local community do not have. It encourages them to identify more closely with the company and its management. A contributing factor to these positive attitudes, according to the company, is the work ethic in Hampstead's rural location. A high proportion of the work force consists of long-term skilled employees; 50 percent have been employed there for more than 10 years.

Mature Behavior

At Polaroid, the objective in placing all employees on salary is to minimize differences between the employee groups. As expected, hourly employees were happy with the program, but perceived it at first as no more than a new fringe benefit. There was no immediate indication of any significantly changed attitudes. Nevertheless, Polaroid now sees signs of the expected mature behavior among employees. This reflects the experience of other companies in which employees have begun to accept the responsibility of reporting to work in situations where formerly they might have stayed away.

Conditions for Probable Success

In the course of our study, we identified a number of criteria for determining whether the salary approach is a viable alternative. The *primary* criteria follow:

- Management-employee relations are open and cooperative.
- The labor force is reasonably stable, mature, and responsible.
- First-level supervisors have the ability and personal confidence to use their judgment within the context of the plan.

- Time-recording procedures generate adequate and accurate absence-control data and accounting information.
- Prevailing absence rates are not unusually high.
- Advance communication of the purpose and operation of the plan can be extended effectively to all employees and can involve all levels of management.
- If there is a union, relations with it are good.
- The plan provides for unobstructed exercise of maximum management discretion.

We conclude that to pay salaries to all employees could be a worthwhile objective for many organizations. The criteria just cited indicate the major conditions necessary for probable success. As an isolated action, the salary approach may create more problems than it eliminates. But, as part of a broad program of positive employee relations, it can develop a favorable, productive, and economically feasible response.

Notes

1. W. Warner Burke, "Organization Development in Transition," *Journal of Applied Behavioral Science,* Vol. 12 (1976), p. 370.
2. Stokes Carrigan, "Organization Development in a Pharmaceutical Setting," in J. Jenning Partin (ed.), *Current Perspectives in Organization Development* (Reading, Mass.: Addison-Wesley, 1973).
3. For a broad perspective, see Allan R. Cohen and Herman Gadon, *Alternative Work Schedules: Integrating Individual and Organizational Needs* (Reading, Mass.: Addison-Wesley, 1978). F-T is one of a number of innovations that can variously serve OD values. For example, F-T can help make adjustments to phases in the life cycle sketched in Chapter 4 of Part 1. See also ibid., pp. 18-32. F-T also can better meet the changes in life styles that are becoming more of a factor in major organizational issues. For example, see Amitai Etzioni, "Opting Out: The Waning of the Work Ethic," *Pscyhology Today,* Vol. 11 (July 1977), pp. 18ff.
4. Robert T. Golembiewski and Robert Munzenrider, "Social Desirability as an Intervening Variable in Interpreting OD Effects," *Journal of Applied Behavioral Science,* Vol. 11 (March 1975), pp. 317-332.
5. For some details, see Robert T. Golembiewski and Richard Hilles, "Flexi-Time in a Large Firm: The First Six Months," *Monthly Labor Review,* Vol. 100 (February 1977), pp. 56-59.
6. Consult Robert T. Golembiewski and Carl W. Proehl, Jr., "A Survey of the Empirical Literature on Flexible Workhours: Character and Consequences of a Major Innovation," *Academy of Management Review,* Vol. 3 (October

1978), pp. 837-853; and Stanley D. Nollen and Virginia H. Martin, *Alternative Work Schedules, Part 1: Flexitime* (New York: Amacom, 1978).

7. Canada Trust, Personnel Resources, "Flexible Working Hours at Canada Trust." Canada Trust, September 1974.
8. Kenneth L. C. Dorking, "Flexible Work Hours: A One Year Review." Paper presented at the 15th Annual Convention of the American Institute for Design and Drafting, Arlington, Texas, April 8, 1975.
9. Martin G. Evans, "Notes on the Impact of Flexitime in a Large Insurance Company: Reactions of Non-Supervisory Employees," *Occupational Psychology,* Vol. 47 (1973), pp. 237-240.
10. Robert T. Golembiewski, Richard J. Hilles, and Munro S. Kagno, "A Longitudinal Study of Flexi-Time Effects: Some Consequences of an OD Structural Intervention," *The Journal of Applied Behavioral Science,* Vol. 10 (1974), pp. 503-532.
11. Golembiewski and Hilles, "Flexi-Time in a Large Firm."
12. Michael A. Hopp and C. R. Sommerstad, "Reaction at Computor Firm: More Pluses Than Minuses," *Monthly Labor Review,* Vol. 100 (February 1977), pp. 69-71.
13. Lufthansa, "Flexitime in Germany and Britain," *European Industrial Relations Review* (January 1974), pp. 5-11.
14. Oscar Mueller and Muriel Cole, "Concept Wins Converts at Federal Agency," *Monthly Labor Review,* Vol. 100 (February 1977), pp. 71-74.
15. Port Authority of New York and New Jersey, Planning and Development Department, "Flexible Work Hours Experiment at the Port Authority of New York and New Jersey," December 1975.
16. Prudential Insurance Co., "Flexitime in Germany and Britain," *European Industrial Relations Review* (January 1974), pp. 5-11.
17. P. Salvatore, "Flexible Working Hours: The Experiment and Its Evaluation." Personnel Branch of the Department of Communications of the Government of Canada, January 1974.
18. Santa Clara County, California, Juvenile and Adult Probation Departments, "Flexitime Summary Report," unpublished MS, 1975.
19. L. V. Thornton, "Report on Flexible Hours Experiment in the Personnel Branch," Personnel Branch of the Department of Consumer and Corporate Affairs, Ottawa, Canada, April 1973.
20. James Walker, "Flexible Working Hours in Two British Government Offices," *Public Personnel Journal,* Vol. 4 (July-August 1975), pp. 216-222.
21. Harriet Goldberg Weinstein, *A Comparison of Three Alternative Work Schedules: Flexible Work Hours, Compact Work Hours, Compact Work, and Staggered Work Hours* (Philadelphia: The Wharton School, University of Pennsylvania, 1975).

22. Virginia Hider Martin (ed.), *Hours of Work When Workers Can Choose* (Washington, D.C.: Business and Professional Women's Foundation, 1975).
23. Marjorie Wilton and Gordon F. Harrison, "The Time of Your Life: A Report on Flexible Working Hours," Haskins and Sells and Associates, March 1975.
24. Lee A. Graf, "The Impact of Flexitime on the First-Line Supervisor's Job," pp. 185-189, in Jeffrey C. Susbauer (ed.), *Proceedings '78,* Annual Meeting, Academy of Management, San Francisco, August 12-15, 1978.
25. Rosabeth Moss Kanter, *Men and Women of the Corporation* (New York: Basic Books, 1977), esp. pp. 37-39.
26. David Peach, "Salaries for Production Workers—What Happens?" *The Business Quarterly* (Spring 1974), pp. 67-79.

Chapter 7

RECONSTITUTING THE BROAD WORK ENVIRONMENT
Four "Total System" Interventions

In one way or another, the six preceding chapters look at pieces—at organization structure, at coordination, at conflict between organization units, at temporary supplements to the permanent authority structure, and so on. This chapter seeks to bring it all together, in two distinct senses. Thus, the focus below will be on four "total system" interventions, although the units vary greatly in size. Moreover, the focus here will distinguish three orders, or waves, of change. They are, to simplify:[1]

> *First-Order Change*: OD programs typically involve interventions with some limited target subsystem of a complex organization, such as team-building by a small group of executives which lead to significant but restricted changes in attitudes, perceptions, and behavior among participants.
>
> *Second-Order Change*: OD programs typically require second-order changes, that is, changes in other subsystems which are not direct targets of specific interventions, as in the case of employees of supervisors who are targets of an OD intervention.
>
> *Third-Order Change*: OD program effects also should appear in various bottom-line effects, as in such aggregate measures of system effectiveness as productivity.

Despite the patent significance of third-order change, the literature is thinnest where it should be most robust. That is, what needs doing is relatively clear in concept,[2] but little appropriate research exists. As has been shown in several of the chapters above, first-order change due to OD interventions is well established, both in concept and research.

This chapter draws attention to third-order change, via four total system interventions. Thus, the first section focuses on changes in system performance by a local police force, following introduction of a new incentive compensation plan. Little attention is given to changes in intervening processes, behavior, or attitudes.

The second total system intervention illustrates an effort at third-order change in some performance indicators in an industrial plant, following attempts to create a new climate for interaction along with appropriate skills. In addition, this second example attempts to measure both first-order and second-order changes. This makes it a valuable addition to a slim literature.[3]

A third total system intervention also has a comprehensive focus in tracing a broad range of changes, but this time from a broad philosophic point of view. The previous application has a researcher's natural-science flavor. In contrast, this third example details the consequences of an effort to embody respect and concern for employees in an industrial setting. The consequences are reflected in measures of systemic performance, as well as in attitudes of employees towards their work and themselves.

The fourth systemic intervention is in many senses the most comprehensive, and the most general. It deals with a broad effort to improve the "quality of working life" via survey feedback. The specific foci here are dual: an attempt to specify the central content of the "quality of working life" concept; and a critique of one application of the QWL strategy and approach whose goal is long-run improvement in system performance. Only the first few leaves will be taken from this particular artichoke, given considerations of space and the solid treatments available in the literature.

Reinforcing Motivation to Do Well
An Innovative Compensation Program in Local Law Enforcement

This initial section presents a double challenge. Thus, it deals with a significant but neglected approach to change: that via deliberate structuring of compensation plans. And the locus is in government, where attention to performance is both critically needed and usually lacking.

The opportunity and challenge can be sketched briefly. Little research exists about compensation plans in OD efforts,[4] despite several central attractions of such a focus. Extrapolating from Walton, such an emphasis has several virtues when compared to interaction-centered OD designs.[5]

- People pay real attention to compensation systems.
- Employees with lesser verbal and human relations skills might find it easier to generate the behaviors and attitudes implied by the compensation system than by (for example) a team-building design.

- Employees with lesser needs for active involvement may still respond to the stimulus of an appropriate compensation system.
- It is always a good idea to reward desired behaviors and attitudes, and a compensation plan can powerfully motivate what is required to make an OD effort work.[6]

Looked at from another point of view, government agencies pose an especial opportunity and challenge for the organizational change agent. That is, government operations now account for some 22 percent of our gross national product, and governments employ nearly one-fifth of our total work force. Moreover, the leveling off of that growth curve is nowhere in sight. Thus, Spiegel concludes: "Government is *the* growth sector today."[7]

There is an added element of drama in the government focus. Thus, it is easy to foresee a collision between immovable object and irresistible force. For the demands for government services are increasing, while a resistance among taxpayers seems to be developing toward growing governmental budgets. More and more politicians scramble to get out in front of this resistance, to become its "leaders."

There seems one approach to these unreconcilable demands for more services at stabilized or marginally increasing costs. That way out: a major emphasis on productivity improvement to maintain or even reduce the level of public spending without a corresponding deterioration in public services. Slowly but surely, that conclusion is beginning to pervade the consciousness of influentials,[8] after a decade or more of feverish emphasis on increasing the level of spending rather than its quality and productivity.

This section seeks to describe one approach to productivity enhancement in public agencies, in the strategic area of law enforcement. Note that the spirit of the intervention is applicable to a broad range of public service delivery systems.

Four Strategies for Improving Productivity

Four generic strategies seem appropriate for maintaining the quality of public services in the face of growing demand and stabilizing budgets,[9] with a major emphasis on law enforcement. *First,* more intensive applications of technology can help, as in the use of computers to help store and process information useful in police work. *Second,* efforts can be made to organize more effectively a given set of police resources. Some police departments have been reorganized so as to reduce interdivisional conflict and to increase teamwork between various specialties, for example.[10] Or, existing small police jurisdictions can be enlarged to take advantage of economies of scale, even though bigger is not always better.[11] *Third,* as in Chapter 6 of Part 1 of this revision, efforts may be made to improve interpersonal and intergroup processes. Such improvements may later lead to enhanced procedures, policies, and structures, as that chapter also illustrates. *Fourth,* efforts can be made to increase the motivation of law enforcement officials by developing a set of incentives.

There seems little question but that the fourth strategy implies the greatest leverage. For openers, some four-fifths of police budgets cover people costs.[12] Moreover, evidence implies that we are very far from making cost-effective use of police personnel. Note that the costs of police services for cities of similar crime rate and size are reported to vary by a substantial 400 percent.[13] Such huge disparities in cost imply major opportunities for improving the productivity of some law enforcement agencies.

Five Difficulties in Measuring Productivity

The problems of increasing government productivity are compounded by an elemental and yet profound truism. How can you with certainty increase what can be measured only with substantial difficulty? That is, even if you succeed, you might not get to know it! Consider only five such problems of measuring productivity in providing police services.[14]

- Crime statistics are often inadequate; for example, actual crime has some variable probability of being reported.
- The effects of law enforcement activity on criminal behavior are difficult to determine,[15] so one cannot predict very confidently the results of (let us say) greater expenditures on foot patrolmen.
- It is typically insufficient to measure any single component of the criminal justice system (for example, police work) without somehow relating that component to all others (for example, the courts, jails, pardons and paroles),[16] but we cannot now specify such systemic interrelatedness either conceptually or operationally.
- Even if all components of the criminal justice system are adequately measured, profound chicken-or-egg issues bedevil necessary judgments about what causes what in which degree; for example, few reported drug busts may indicate police work that is either so effective that most pushers know better than to test it, or that is ineffective because judges are so lenient with pushers that writing up an arrest is not worth the effort, among many other possibilities.
- To measure the quantity of some police service is often easy or unrevealing, but the judgment about quality is typically crucial and difficult.
- "Local conditions" profoundly influence what constitute "good police services"; there is no simple and sovereign measure of what constitutes "good services," comparing even apparently similar jurisdictions.

One Good Try, Difficulties Notwithstanding

The City of Orange, California, sought to heighten police performance via a "performance incentive plan."[17] That is, city officials were not immobilized either by the significance of the challenge to improve productivity or by its difficulties. Details are important in understanding what they did, and why As part of regular collective bargaining in Orange, major crimes are separated into two categories.

Relatively Repressible by Police Effort	Relatively Unrepressible by Police Effort
Rape	Homicide
Robbery	Aggravated assault
Burglary	Larceny
Auto theft	

The rationale for the distinction between the two types of crime rests on the presumed degree of control police have over them. Rape, robbery, burglary, and auto theft are "repressible" because police action is seen as influencing the probability of their occurrence. Oppositely, Staudohar adds: "Homicide was thought to be essentially 'nonrepressible' because it is a crime of passion usually occurring among family members. Larceny frequently involves theft within a business firm, while assault is a crime of passion often occurring spontaneously in or just outside bars; each of these crimes is less susceptible to police control."[18]

Performance Incentive Plan (PIP)

To simplify somewhat, variations in the reported rates of the four repressible crimes were tied to cash incentives. Salary increases of 7.5 and 6.0 percent were granted effective July 1973 and July 1974, respectively. In addition other incentives could be earned according to this skeletal formula:

> Effective March 1, 1974, an additional salary increase of 1 percent would be granted if the rates of the four repressible crimes were reduced by 3 percent, as compared to an earlier base period. An additional salary increase of 2 percent would be granted if the rates fell 6 percent or more.
>
> Effective March 1, 1975, for a period of 20 months beginning July 1, 1973, specified reductions in crime rates would lead to additional incentives
>
> 8% reduction → 1% increase in salaries,
> 10% reduction → 2% increase,
> 12% reduction → 3% increase.

The agreement also made provision for population growth, as well as for such details as what would constitute "reported crimes" and how they would be verified.

Significantly, the agreement included 136 police, including even those sergeants and lieutenants who are not covered by Orange's collective bargaining contract. Their inclusion was motivated by a desire to preserve salary differentials between supervisors and other police, and also to avoid any conscious or unconscious resistance by police not covered by the collective bargaining agreement but who were direct supervisors of covered police. These supervisors could make or break the incentive plan. Top police officials, captain and above, were not covered by the incentive plan.

Appraisal of Experience with PIP

Although the glare of national publicity sometimes creates differing impressions[19] of PIP, at least five conclusions seem appropriate in reviewing the performance incentive plan.[20] *First,* repressible crimes were reduced in both phases. The initial decrease approximated 17 percent, well above that required for the maximum incentive of a 2 percent salary increase, which became effective March 1, 1974. For the 20-month period, the decrease was 12.6 percent, this figure being only slightly above that required for the maximum 3 percent increase which became effective March 1, 1975.

The most elemental results are these, then. Reported crimes decrease substantially during both periods, but less so in the second. In cold cash, the average salary increment amounts to about $20 per month per employee covered by the incentive plan.

Interpreting these elemental results cannot be straightforward, especially because the data-base in this case implies several imponderables. Thus, one observer credits Orange only with being "the first city in the country to arise from the bargaining table with a contractual incentive plan for lying [about] crime statistics."[21] More moderately, there are several senses in which the police statistics might be subject to scrutiny.

- The statistics refer only to one facet of a very complex job, on which police probably spend only 10 to 20 percent of their time.[22]
- The police are not the only agency which combats crime.
- Misclassification of crimes is possible.[23]
- The reporting of crimes by victims is highly variable.[24]

Such features, and others as well, imply problems in interpreting the Orange data. Independent studies imply that misclassification was not a problem in

Orange, however.[25] Moreover, programs like that in Orange typically encourage *greater* reporting of some crimes by citizens.[26] So it is possible, perhaps even probable, that the Orange program not only reduced the number of target crimes, but did so in the face of an enhanced tendency by citizens to report crimes due to a greater optimism that something would be done about them. Staudohar observes that, in this sense, PIP was "designed with a built-in bias *against* success."[27]

Second, police under the incentive plan seemed to talk more with both citizens and themselves, and various police and citizen programs were developed to inhibit crime, especially via advice and information concerning burglary. In addition, increased coordination seemed to develop between shifts and police specialties. The impact of PIP on such changes cannot be confidently assessed, nor can the degree to which they (and not PIP) contributed to reductions in crime.[28] Reasonably, however, PIP is one contributor to the changes in target crimes.

Third, police personnel increased from 113 to 118 during the incentive plan's early days and remained there, an increase of some 4.5 percent. It does not seem reasonable, therefore, to explain the reported decreases in repressible crimes as substantially resulting from a larger police force.

Fourth, the plan surfaced some problems of measuring performance. For example, no data about the quality of police services were gathered, and these would be useful in a more refined incentive system. Similarly, the reporting of crimes was central to the plan, and it involved police officials in a situation with some potential for conflict of interest. Staudohar emphasizes the key role of the watch commander, whose duty it is to reconcile any differences between radio-call slips regarding crimes with the reports filed at the end of each shift by the involved officers. Staudohar acknowledges "that a conflict of interest arises, because the watch commanders are covered by the incentive plan in that all personnel up through lieutenant get the same percentage pay adjustment whether in or out of the bargaining unit." The conflict of interest may be more apparent than actual, he goes on, but the possibility does urge caution in interpreting the results in Orange.[29] And, future plans probably should audit criminal data to reduce such doubts.[30]

Fifth, total reported crimes increased somewhat in Orange. The overall increase is in large part due to the burgeoning incidence of larceny and aggravated assault, both unrepressible crimes by Orange's definitions. Comparisons with other cities imply that similar or greater increases in unrepressible crimes occurred quite generally. Hence, it does not seem the case that Orange's reduced rates of repressible crimes were gained by simply shifting police effort from unrepressible crimes.

Concluding Comments

No single categoric evaluation of PIP seems appropriate, then, and other police departments no doubt will have to tailor plans to their own local conditions. Staudohar's verdict seems serviceable. Despite its limitations, he concludes that "the Orange plan is an innovative experiment which will hopefully stimulate similar schemes in other cities. Future efforts should seek to refine and improve the model."

Many open issues remain, but some reasonable components of such future attention seem reasonable enough. *First,* growing attention in OD has been given of late to compensation or incentive systems,[31] and that bodes well for the future. Little published information about the mode of developing and implementing the Orange plan has been published, and it is here that OD perspectives might be very valuable in future efforts. The analysis of useful guidelines for MBO, detailed in Chapter 3 also should prove useful in this connection. Overall, historical materials amply testify to the power of social relationships in neutralizing incentive systems, as in the ample literature on "rate setting" compared to the far slimmer one on "rate busting." The "future efforts" for which Staudohar calls will have critical behavioral components, of that there can be no doubt.

Second, one key issue in such future use will involve matching types of compensation and incentive systems to the types of tasks involved.[32] The historical record seems clear enough on the point. Many incentive systems only exacerbate interpersonal or interunit conflict—as when additional compensation for one set of actors often encourages efforts to relocate responsibility for error or shoddy work, for example, by "throwing dead cats in other people's backyards"—when no one organizationally related set of actors has formal responsibility for a complete task,[33] which is the case in the traditional way of structuring work reviewed in Chapter 2.

Two OD perspectives are relevant here. Thus, the materials in Chapter 2 on restructuring work often will be critical. Briefly, an incentive system imposed on the traditional structure of work often will create problems—complex wage rates and record keeping, further inducements to interunit conflict, and so on.[34] Such problems, in fact, contributed mightily to the general abandonment of incentive systems where traditional organizing concepts dominated, which was almost everywhere in industrial work and at many other sites as well. So, a restructuring of work often will be useful or necessary for a "clean" incentive system that not only motivates individuals but, far more significantly, facilitates an entire flow of work. One of the virtues of autonomous teams, for example, centers around the possibility of several crucial simplifications of incentive systems that reinforce effort by teams or groups responsible for a total flow of work.[35]

Third, the comments above imply a conceptual great leap forward consistent with OD values which can be facilitated by OD perspectives and designs. Typically, compensation systems are seen as an elite prerogative, with payment going directly to individual persons or jobs. In contrast, the comments above imply an emphasis on "group incentives" to all those involved in a discrete flow of work, often divided among team members by some process acceptable to them.[36] Relatedly, the comments above imply a strong role for employees[37] or their representatives[38]—as in a worker's council or some such body—in actually developing incentive systems, within broad policy guides set by management. Initial experience with such experiments has been positive. In some cases, indeed, individual employees play a major role in determining the character of their compensation package. Consider "cafeteria benefits." Up to a specified dollar maximum, employees in some firms can design their own benefits package: X dollars for this coverage, Y dollars for vacations, and so on. Such plans have two attractive features, despite their problems. Thus, they clearly imply a movement toward greater employee choice and freedom. Moreover, such programs also rest on a responsiveness to different stages of human or career development, whose importance is sketched in Chapter 4 of Part 1. Thus, employees with children might seek greater dental insurance coverage; those approaching retirement might opt for larger coverage for catastrophic illness; and so on.

Improving Organizational Performance
Complicated Data Relevant to Three Orders of Change*

The direct way to induce third-order change involves self-conscious design, measurement of the consequences of the design on some target population, verifying its derivative effects on other populations, and, finally, observing its efforts on systemic performance. That seems straightforward enough, although it has seldom been done,[39] for substantial reasons that need not be repeated here.

This section describes one exception to the usual neglect, an effort to improve organizational performance in a plant of some 3000 employees oriented

*Much of this section heavily depends on John R. Kimberly and Warren R. Nielsen, "Organizational Development and Change in Organizational Performance." Copyright 1975 by the *Administrative Science Quarterly,* Vol. 20 (June 1975), pp. 192-206. See also Larry E. Pate, Warren R. Nielsen, and Richard T. Mowday, "A Longitudinal Assessment of the Impact of Organization Development on Absenteeism, Grievance Rates and Product Quality," in Robert L. Taylor, Michael J. O'Connell, Robert A. Zawacki, and D. D. Warrick (eds.), *Proceedings* (Annual Meeting), Academy of Management, Orlando, Fla., August 14-17, 1977, pp. 353-357.

toward an assembly-line model. The motivation for the OD intervention is direct. As Kimberly and Nielsen explain:[40]

> First, the plant was a major unit in a division which had been considered very successful in the past, but which in recent years was experiencing decreases in production, quality, and profits and increases in absenteeism, turnover, and grievance rates. Second, there was a general feeling in the plant that supervisors and managers were not working together and that the first-line supervisors did not see themselves as part of the team and some effort was needed to rectify this situation.

A Sketch of the Design for Change

The OD design extended over some 15 months of Plant A's history, and there is literally nothing uncomplicated that may be said about it. Much of its essential thrust can be suggested by two emphases, one concerning the target population and the other describing a multiphase program.

Target Population and Expected Effects

The target population of the OD interventions was the nearly 200 supervisors of production at Plant A. They represent five levels of organization, as Figure 1 shows. Specific training interventions were directed only at the 200 supervisors. Derivative changes in their behavior and skills, in turn, were expected to induce changes in the 2600 hourly employees that would result in improvements in overall performance. Figure 2 charts the expected three-stage flow.

- First-order changes are induced in the 200 supervisors by training interventions.
- Second-order changes in the 2600 hourly employees are expected to result from these new supervisory behaviors and skills.
- Third-order changes also are expected to result in enhanced total system performance.

Eight-Phase Program for Change

How the changes in supervisory behavior and skills were induced can be suggested somewhat more specifically by Exhibit 1. The overall design is a familiar one, whose flow might be sketched as: diagnosis ↔ skill enhancement ↔ planning for action ↔ team-building ↔ implementing plans for action. The expected payoff of these interacting and increasingly complex steps involves broad systemic change in total performance.

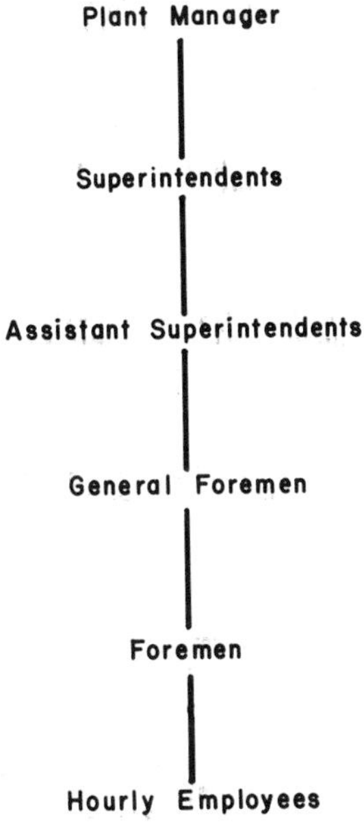

Figure 1 Levels of organization in Plant A.

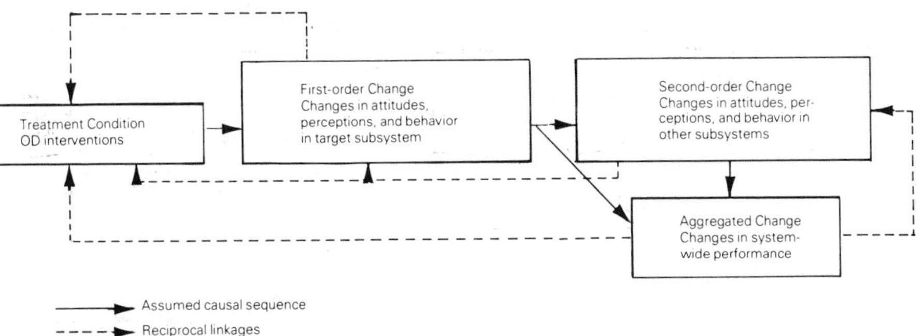

Figure 2 Major and reciprocal linkages in a systemic OD program. [*Source*: Based on John R. Kimberly and Warren R. Nielsen, "Organization Development and Change in Organizational Performance." Copyright 1975 by the *Administrative Science Quarterly*, Vol. 20 (June 1975), p. 195.]

Exhibit 1 Eight Phases in Change Program

Initial diagnosis. The diagnosis consisted of three stages. First, a series of interviews was held with a sample of 15 supervisory and managerial personnel including the plant manager and his immediate staff. Second, group meetings were held with those interviewed to examine the results and to determine problem areas and priorities. And finally, the plant manager, his immediate staff, and the external consultants met to finalize the change design.

Team skills training. Foremen, general foremen, assistant superintendents, and superintendents participated with their peers in groups of approximately 25 individuals in a series of experience-based exercises during a 2½-day workshop.

Data collection. Immediately following the team skills training, all foremen completed two questionnaires. The first concentrated on organizational health and effectiveness and the second asked them to describe the behavior of their immediate supervisor—general foremen or assistant superintendents.

Data confrontation. In this phase, various work groups were asked to review the data described above and determine problem areas, establish priorities in these areas, and develop some preliminary recommendations for change.

Action planning. Based on the data and conversation during the data confrontation, each group developed some recommendations for change and plans for the changes to be implemented. The plans included what should be changed, who should be responsible, and when the action should be completed.

Team-building. Each natural work group in the entire system, including the plant manager and his immediate staff of superintendents, then met for 2 days. The agenda consisted of identifying blocks to effectiveness for the specific group and the development of change goals and plans to accomplish the desired changes.

Intergroup building. This phase consisted of 2-day meetings between groups that were interdependent in the plant. The groups met for the purpose of establishing mutual understanding and cooperation and to enhance collaboration on shared goals or problems.

Data collection. Two questionnaires were administered a second time.

Source: From John R. Kimberly and Warren R. Nielsen, "Organization Development and Change in Organizational Performance." Copyright 1975 by the *Administrative Science Quarterly*, Vol. 20 (June 1975), pp. 192-193.

A Sketch of the Confirming Evidence

The change program lasted 2 years, from initial diagnosis to final data collection, which precludes any simple summary of what occurred and why. Moreover, because the intervention was plant-wide and no comparable plants existed in the parent corporation, no "controls" or "comparisons" are available in this case.

Hence, alternative explanations of the results below cannot be rejected out of hand, but the most credible explanation of the results attributes them to the OD intervention.

First-Order Changes

The training interventions pretty clearly induced expected changes in the target population, the 200 managers and supervisors in the plant. There are first-order changes, of course. Table 1 suggests the range and extent of such first-order changes over a 15-month period, based on questionnaire responses from a sample of the production foremen. In summary, the table reports on ten aspects of supervisory behavior, substantial increases in all of which occurred over the period of observation. All of these changes are presumptively desirable, as in the case of a perceived increase in the kind of supervisory behavior scored as "willingness to change." The large t-values in all ten cases merely establish that the observed increases almost certainly cannot be due to random causes. As Kimberly and Nielsen conclude: "After the initiation of the OD program, the first-line supervisors perceived their managers as encouraging more subordinate involvement in such activities as planning, decision making, and direction of group activities." The two researchers go on to observe that the "managers were

Table 1 Reported Changes in Ten Aspects of Supervisory Behavior

	Mean Scores		
Item	January 1970 (N = 90)	March 1971 (N = 87)	t-Value[a]
Listening	3.45	4.48	3.90
Expressing ideas to others	4.14	5.07	3.60
Influence	2.85	4.05	4.55
Decision-making	3.43	4.40	3.82
Relations with other	2.85	3.86	3.82
Task orientation	4.20	4.85	2.76
Handling of conflict	3.71	4.33	2.14
Willingness to change	4.28	5.00	3.26
Problem-solving	3.30	4.25	3.06
Self-development	3.24	4.01	2.71

[a] All values in this column designate a difference that surpasses the 0.05 level of statistical significance.

Source: From John R. Kimberly and Warren R. Nielsen, "Organization Development and Change in Organizational Performance." Copyright 1975 by the *Administrative Science Quarterly*, Vol. 20 (June 1975), p. 197.

also perceived as making greater effort to hear and understand the subordinate's position on problems and work goals as well as making use of subordinate's skills in problem solving."

Second-Order Changes

By implication, also, changes seem to have occurred in subsystems other than the target population. The point is especially clear in a summary of changes reported in nine aspects of the plant's "organization climate" found in Table 2. These before versus after variations in climate are consistent with the changes in supervisory behavior just reviewed, and they also suggest second-order changes affecting employees other than those directly exposed to the training design. Kimberly and Nielsen emphasize that "the change for all items was in the predicted direction." They conclude that major changes in organization climate occurred after the OD intervention. Specifically, they note that "the organizational participants perceived greater levels of trust and support in the target sub-system, conflicts were handled more openly, and the skills and resources of the participants were more fully utilized. In addition, they saw greater opportunities for autonomy and self-direction."[41]

Table 2 Reported Changes in Nine Aspects of Organization Climate

	Mean Scores		
Item	January 1970 (N = 90)	March 1971 (N = 87)	t-Value[a]
Trust	3.73	4.78	5.09
Support	3.76	4.36	2.37
Open communications	3.04	4.64	6.83
Understanding of objectives	4.52	5.29	3.64
Commitment to objectives	4.40	5.17	3.58
Handling of conflict	3.79	4.91	4.88
Utilization of member resources	3.80	4.78	4.14
Self-direction, autonomy	3.20	4.77	5.88
Supportive environment	3.24	4.56	5.28

[a] All values in this column designate a difference that surpasses the 0.01 level of statistical significance.

Source: From John R. Kimberly and Warren R. Nielsen, "Organization Development and Change in Organizational Performance." Copyright 1975 by the *Administrative Science Quarterly*, Vol. 20 (June 1975), p. 197.

Third-Order Changes

Kimberly and Nielsen also sought to measure critical bottom-line change in four ways. These are third-order changes, and are especially revealing of the potency of the OD intervention. The authors expected:[42]

- Significant increases in units produced
- Significant decreases in the variance in units produced
- Significant increases in the level of the quality index
- Significant decreases in the variance of the quality index
- Significant increases in the profit index

There is no way that the several tests of these expectations can be reproduced here, for they are both complex and lengthy.[43] Generally, however, the expectations are confirmed. In the one case in which an expectation is not confirmed, in addition, a credible explanation exists. To explain, four of the five expectations are met. Thus, production variance decreases, rates of quality increase, variance in quality decreases, and profits increase. However, no change occurs in rates of production. On reflection, this unexpected finding does not surprise the researchers. They explain that "the figures for the same period led to the conclusion that rates of production are likely to be largely determined externally, by corporate policy and market conditions." However, neither policy nor market conditions are really controllable by plant participants in the OD program. Hence, Kimberly and Nielsen conclude, in retrospect, rates of production should not be affected one way or the other by the OD interventions. The authors conclude: "Later discussion with the plant manager and his immediate staff suggested that this interpretation corresponded closely to their perception of reality."[44]

Concluding Observations

All in all, then, the OD intervention sketched above had the expected effects, considering all three orders of change. The two researchers are suitably cautious about their results, and yet they emphasize the credibility of those results, given what is presently known. Such a balanced view seems appropriate.

Doing Away with the Factory Blues
A Holistic Approach Showing Respect and Concern for Employees

"Factory work" triggers a flood of thought-polarities: necessary but dirty; the base for an advancing economy but better left to others, or the children of others, often immigrants, and so on. So pervasive are these polarities that they assume the status of a common wisdom, about which nothing fundamental can be done except to flee the factory personally, if at all possible, or at least to strive to free one's children from that bondage.

A Précis of the Problem

The heart of these polarities seems to be that the typical factory has not been able to solve, perhaps has not even usually addressed, a basic question: Why are factories so socially and emotionally sterile?

U.S. Eaton Corporation, spearheaded by some of its employees like Donald N. Scobel who authored the following description, decided to try to chase away some of those old, factory blues. Scobel might not be comfortable in referring to this long-run effort as a major OD change problem, for he speaks more in terms of an ethical determination to treat employees as trustworthy and productive, rather than in the language of the behavioral scientists' "time-extended interventions to induce an appropriate culture." Indeed, Scobel seems to have some good laughs at the expense of behavioral scientists, twitting them as high-priced gurus who see only bits and pieces rather than the whole person at work.

But what Scobel describes is an OD program, sharing its basic values if seldom using its terminology. In addition, the description below clearly deals with all three orders of change emphasized in this chapter. For better or worse, then, Scobel takes his place among the OD contributors to this volume. He writes about an approach that has been extended since 1968 to over 5000 employees at thirteen plant sites which may be described as medium-heavy industrial.

The "Eaton Story" Begins as a Management Exercise*

It all began 7 years ago when the manager of Eaton's Battle Creek, Michigan engine valve plant decided to build a new facility in Kearney, Nebraska. He asked his managerial staff and the Cleveland headquarters employee relations people how he might avoid the deterioration in employee/management relationships in Nebraska that had occurred over the decades in the Michigan plant.

In response to this challenge, a few managerial people representing the full spectrum of functional disciplines at Eaton isolated themselves to discuss and evaluate traditional policies and practices that affect employee relations. They

*The following material through the remainder of this section is from Donald N. Scobel, "Doing Away with the Factory Blues," *Harvard Business Review,* Vol. 53 (November-December 1975), pp. 133-142. Copyright ©1975 by the President and Fellows of Harvard College; all rights reserved.

summarized their composite critique in a report to the Battle Creek manager that took the form of a "letter" written as if by a factory employee who is explaining why he brings so little of himself to his workplace.

The Employee's Letter

Dear Sir:

What you are asking me, as I see it, is why am I not giving you my best in exchange for the reasonable wages and benefits you provide me and my family.

First, I'm not trying to blame anybody for why you don't see the "whole" me. Some of the problem is company policy, some is union thinking, some is just me. Let me tell you why, and I'll leave it to bigger minds than mine to figure out blames and remedies.

I'll begin with my first day on the job eleven years ago—my first factory job, by the way. I was just 19 then. Incidentally, my cousin started work in your office as a clerk typist on the same day. We used to drive to work together. She still works for you, too.

The first thing I was told that day by the personnel manager and my foreman was that I was on 90 days' probation. They were going to measure my ability and attendance and attitude and then make up their minds about me. Gee, that surprised me. I thought I'd been hired already—but I really wasn't. Although the foreman tried to make me feel at home, it was still sort of a shock to realize I was starting out kind of on the sidelines until I proved my worth. In fact, the only person who told me I "belonged," without any strings attached, was my union steward.

You know, that first day my foreman told me all about the shop rules of discipline as if I were going to start out stealing or coming to work drunk or getting into fights or horseplay. What made it even worse was when I later found out that no one told my cousin she was on probation. I asked her if she had seen the rules, and here it is eleven years later and she still doesn't know there are about 35 rules for those of us working in the factory.

What it boils down to is that your policies—yes, and the provisions of our union contract—simply presume the factoryman untrustworthy, while my cousin in the office is held in much higher regard. It's almost like we work for different companies. . . .

Sir, why must I punch a time clock? Do you think I'd lie about my starting and quitting times? Why must I have buzzers to tell me when I take a break, relieve myself, eat lunch, start working, go home? Do you really think I can't tell time or would otherwise rob you of valuable minutes? Why doesn't the rest room I must use provide any privacy? Why do I have to drive my car over chuck holes while you enjoy reserved paved parking? Why must I work the day before and after a holiday to get holiday pay?

The Employee's Letter (Continued)

Are you convinced I will extend the holiday into the weekend—while, by the way, my cousin is thought to have more sense than that?

I guess I'm saying that when you design your policies for the very few who need them, how do you think the rest of us feel?

Sir, do you really think I don't care or don't know what you think of me? If you are convinced of that, then you will never understand why I bring less than all of myself to my workbench.

You know, sir, in my eleven years, I've run all kinds of machinery for you, but your company has never even let me look at what the maintenance man does when he has to repair one of my machines. No one has ever really aked me how quality might be better or how my equipment or methods might be improved. In fact, your policies drum it into me good and proper that you really want me to stay in my place. And now, *you* want to know why *I* don't pour it on? Wow! Don't you realize that I may want to contribute more than you let me? I know the union may be responsible for some of this—but again, I'm trying to explain why, not whose fault it is.

You know, sir, I would like a more challenging job, but that isn't the heart of the matter, not for me at least. If there were a sense of dignity around here, I could not hold back the effort and ideas within me, even if my particular job was less than thrilling. Many of my buddies do not want a greater job challenge, but they do want their modest contributions respected. . . .

It has been said, sir, that factory people look upon *profit* as a dirty word. I don't feel that way, but you know, it's almost as if *love* is the dirty word here.

Why don't I give my best? Well, I guess I have a kind of thermostat inside me that responds to your warmth. Do you have a thermostat inside you?

Very truly yours,

Management's Response to Its Own Critique

The above letter all but spells out its own solutions. The epilogue of the report to the Michigan manager said: "To avoid industrial decay, build a plant around the presumed correctness of the letter writer." And this is what the manager of the new plant in Nebraska, and all managers of Eaton do. . . .

The First Steps

At the new Eaton plants, management puts out a written handbook in which it commits itself to a counseling rather than a rules-penalties process; to weekly departmental meetings where employee inputs are sought; to manager roundtables and an "open floor" concept; to a uniform office-factory benefit system; and to a foundation of concern, trust, and participation. The handbook states that ". . . an important concept here is that people are individuals . . . and a company must relate to uniqueness if there is to be a full measure of personal growth and contribution to organizational objectives. The emphasis is upon employee involvement in matters that affect him and sharing the responsibility for an effective operation. It's a mutual fulfillment."

What Eaton does in the formal training of supervisors under the new model is remarkably minimal. In a two-day seminar, the group of supervisors spends the first day just talking about why people work and what they want out of life. The consensus usually is that "we are all into this for pretty much the same reasons." The group invariably believes there are personal differences in motivational priorities, but does not believe these differences can be categorized for any class or group of employees, or that different categories of motivational factors are inherently more important. Although behavioral scientists have dissected this premise almost to death, it is true that most people desire a sense of community at work. Recognizing this fact helps supervisors and managers see that treating employees under the same roof with different value systems does not make much "human" sense.

During the second day of the seminar the supervisors review the basic components of the new approach and consider how that approach helps build a common value system of respect and participation. The reason training can be minimal is that the supervisor steps from the seminar into a workplace where the new commitments and ground rules are in effect immediately. Another plus is that it is not necessary to have "behavioral science superstars" to understand or apply the new approach. Supervisors of varying competencies are usually at ease with this approach only after brief exposure. Very few clamor for the old regimentation, or see it as essential to their ability to supervise. One supervisor simply said, "Nothing fancy about this. It's just being human with biblical roots." Eaton is trying to resurrect fairness through identifiable policy changes that are fundamentally fair.

Policy Changes

Space prohibits listing all aspects of this new approach. In essence, personnel policies and presumptions that are based on mistrust and lack of care are discarded and replaced, where necessary, with ones that reflect concern and mutual respect.

Illustrations of the New Approach. The following are a few examples of how this attitude is applied to actual policies and processes.

- At the new Eaton plants, the hiring process is a meaningful, two-way exchange, which replaces the structured interview and the more common "get-me-twelve-warm-bodies-by-Tuesday" factory-hiring syndrome. Applicants and their spouses are invited in small groups to an after-dinner "coffee" where the plant's products, processes, and philosophy are discussed. Both factory and office employees take the group on a plant and office tour and encourage the applicant to spend additional time in departments that seem most attractive to him. Personnel people ask the newcomer to express his job preferences within his general skill level for initial placement or for later transfer if there is no opening in the department he selects. The people conducting the tour introduce the applicant to people he may be working for and with. With this open review of the job, the job seeker ends up knowing more about the company and its people than they do about him. This process extends to a drill press operator or a file clerk the concern and dignity that industry usually extends only to its applicants for managerial posts.

- There is no probationary period. Supervisors evaluate individually any problem that might arise with a new person. Although it can happen that supervisors may have to let someone go, the policy presumes that people are eager to work and to be dependable employees, rather than the opposite.

- The plants do not use time clocks, buzzers, or similar controls. Although the company needs records of time allocations for many legal as well as good business reasons, it assumes that individuals can accurately record their own times.

The dual value system mentioned by the "letter writer" no longer exists. . . .

- All factory and office people also share the same benefit package. Levels of certain benefits vary with salary, but the system is uniform. Payment for casual absence is often a dynamic distinguisher between office and factory status. At the newer Eaton facilities, all people are paid for both casual and long-term absences and are under the same pay system for long-term absences.

- Office and factory supervisors hold departmental meetings at least once every two weeks to discuss issues that the employees themselves raise. Often the supervisor will have an employee lead the discussion.

- The plant manager chairs a periodic roundtable with representatives from all office and factory departments who are selected in whatever way the department decides. The participants prepare the agenda of concerns and the minutes, as well as post follow-up action notices on central and departmental bulletin boards.

- An "open floor" concept replaces the old "open door" policy. The "open door" implied to a factoryman, "If you want to do business with a staff person, you must come up to his front office." The new approach makes the factoryman's workplace as important an "office" as anyplace else in the facility. So that territorial barriers are specifically torn down, the personnel department and other staff people make a point of conducting business at the employee's workplace as well as at their own.

- In a variety of ways, factory, supervisory, and lower-level office people participate in managerial meetings and functions. . . .

• At some locations, factory and lower-level office people are editors of the plant's newssheets. Often the recreational, social, and community affairs activities are independently managed, including direction of the fiscal aspects, by joint committees of factory and office people. Special committees (little ad hocracies) are formed from time to time to handle contingencies.

• It is common for factory people to volunteer to be plant tour guides, to be involved with food service, plant safety, and fire protection matters, even to the extent of codirection of these activities.

I hope the above list gives the reader some idea of what Eaton is trying to do. In addition to these items, there are two important kinds of experiences that flow from this approach. For employees who want them, there are opportunities to be involved in developing the scope of their jobs or in increasing their participation in decision-making.

Job Involvement . . . . Management wanted first to restructure the work climate and then to be responsive to spontaneous employee drives for greater job involvement as these drives emerged. What followed clearly, and almost quantifiably, resulted from the new work culture.

In the new plants, almost all employees seek better and more rapid performance inspection and feedback. In some cases, some of the inspection duties have been taken over by the employees themselves and blended into their own manufacturing responsibilities and operations. Interestingly, until people achieve job proficiency, they want guidance on how to improve their performance. . . .

Almost a third of the work force diagnoses its own job methods and scopes. At one plant, a janitor persuaded his boss that he, rather than the purchasing department, could order local cleaning supplies because he would give it higher priority than they would. He was allowed to do so, while other janitors wanted no part of the telephoning and paper work. . . .

These experiences in job involvement result from a specific policy of laissez-faire. Management responds positively to involvement but does not attempt to structure it.

Participation in Decision-Making. It is integral to many aspects of the new approach that employees should participate in decisions. This extends to specific decisions that affect work and the work life. For example, if a plant is on a two-shift, 5-day operation, and business expands, the different departments will discuss different work-schedule options, such as weekend work, extended daily hours, or a third shift that could be used to handle the increase. Often management will express its thoughts and invite reactions; more often, the options are put to a vote. In either case, employee inputs are specifically invited before any decision is made. . . .

Even in layoff circumstances, decision participation is invited. Although people do not like to vote on only negative alternatives, such as a reduction of the work force versus a reduction in working hours, if the company submits its preferred course to employee consideration, it will often find the attitudinal "pulse" and more often than not receive ideas for policy redirection. During one temporary layoff, plantwide discussion brought forth more layoff volunteers than were needed! In almost all cases, when the employees participate in decisions, they cooperate to the full with the final decision. As one manager put it, "I can no longer conceive of making a decision of major impact on any segment of that work force without first inviting meaningful dialogue."

Employees React to the Changes

Although some problems have arisen under the new approach (I will discuss these below), nothing so far indicates that the basic concepts are off the mark. In fact, there are some interesting comparisons that can be drawn between the new model facilities and the older plants, indicating that the new approach increases both productivity and worker satisfaction.

Measures of Success

At the new plants, absenteeism (casual as well as sick leaves) ranges from 0.5 to 3 percent, compared with 6 to 12 percent at traditional locations. Turnover is similarly reduced. With the new approach, voluntary separations average under 4 percent annually, compared with up to 60 percent at traditional plants.

In the new plants the hourly product output (for identical blueprints of products run on similar equipment) will range from parity to 35 percent more than at the traditional plants. Of more importance to Eaton, however, is the longer range performance where trends are comparable. . . .

On the other hand, new facilities often have a worse plant safety record than the older plants. Management speculates that this decline in safety is caused partly by the new work force's unfamiliarity with industrial hazards and by the fact that carelessness creeps in when people strive so hard to increase production. In any event, the safety problem has led employees to involve themselves more in plant and departmental safety activities.

Actions Speak Louder Than Words

These measurements are interesting, but are subject to all the problems involved in accurately comparing even seemingly like facilities. . . . One can tell what is happening at the new plants and what the work force's effect is on productivity more by examining actual events than by measuring output. . . .

- A plant manager at one of the older plants visited a new model facility and wrote in his report to a vice-president, ". . . I'd sum it up by reporting that when the first shift ended you couldn't tell it was quitting time! No clocks to line up at! No rushing to cars! No tires screeching! Some people finished the last piece in their machine. Many casually took showers. Some went out to the picnic area and gossiped over a bottle of pop. Several stayed to play baseball or horseshoes in the back field. Some went to a variety of committee meetings. The point is that the exodus was so gradual it went unnoticed. Unbelievable!". . .
- One New Year's Day, almost all the employees at one plant responded to a TV news bulletin that the plant was within an unexpected flood area. Most labored around the clock so the plant could be fully operational the next day. . . .

These examples show how the new approach affects employees at work, and were perhaps best summarized by one manager when he said, "On those especially frustrating days I still know in my bones that nothing intentionally destructive is going on around here."

Problems of Implementation

Although the humanistic approach to employee relationships has not failed at any location, there have, nevertheless, been growing pains. With varying degrees of severity, most of the following problems have occurred at one or more plants.

Initially, Eaton concentrated its effort on employee relations in the factory. Although very few office people were averse to bringing dignity and fairness to the factory employees, when the factories were filled with camaraderie, the office people became envious of the "feeling." The office people did not have the sense of involvement with their workplace that management had assumed they did, and once the issue was raised it was clear why. Some plant managers did not include the office people in their roundtable discussions, and when they did conduct departmental meetings, which was infrequently, the meetings seemed pallid in comparison to factory meetings.

Management in the new plants solved these problems by stressing participation in the offices and ensuring more meaningful interaction between the office and factory employees so that all could share the same work climate. What Eaton had seen originally as a factory revitalization now involves the entire workplace. . . .

There are different problems that arise when things go almost too smoothly. At a few places, for instanct, the sense of goodwill was so pervasive that the company did not react to a few individuals who were exploiting the trust placed in them. The other employees became restless and brought pressure on these people directly as well as on management to deal with these individuals. In most cases, the peer pressure and counseling procedure has been effective, and the individuals responded positively.

Despite the implementation problems I have cited, the approach has been accepted in most new locations. Although not without its skeptics, the concept is now a familiar idea throughout the company, and many managers of traditional plants, which have varied histories of problems with factory and office employees, are searching out ways to apply the new approach at their own plants, where practices, policies, and attitudes are already firmly established.

The Backward Glance

Eaton's efforts at some older plants are still in early stages, and it is too soon to report significant successes or failures. It is already apparent, however, that remodeling is slower and more complex than building anew. It is equally evident, nevertheless, that meaningful changes can be made at traditional locations without great risk or investment. As at new locations, the company must express its commitment; the absence of commitment makes the ideas seem vague and philosophical rather than action-oriented.

Understandably, it is much more difficult to convince supervisors, employees, and their unions in the older plants that change is not threatening and can take place with fairness and dignity. This task has become easier at Eaton since the word has now spread that the new plants are such fulfilling places to work in. It is still, however, a great challenge to managers in the traditional plants to bring everyone together without fanfare into a common constructive process, to get them to believe that management means what it is saying. If management tries to impose the new approach, it runs the risk of appearing as if it were just another management attempt to impose its will upon the employees. Because of these problems, managers in some older plants are using different approaches to attain the same ends.

At one old plant, there is a joint company-union initiated effort to transform the workplace climate through a variety of participative endeavors. These include such experiences as employees themselves rearranging an entire stockroom area more efficiently or management entrusting employees in a certain department with the responsiblity of resolving their own absentee problems. At another location, the company has approached the union to recast the provisions of the labor agreement in language that assumes trust and respect between parties. The point is to see whether constructive relationships can emerge from changes in legalistic language and principles previously inscribed in stone.

More commonly, however, Eaton is trying to adapt its new plant experiences to traditional places. . . .

The union, of course, must be integrally involved in the entire change process. As management takes on a new role, so must the union and the employees. All three must involve themselves in some new processes that have them working together toward some common objectives. Working together seems to bring about change far sooner than does eons of dialogue.

From our early efforts to reduce alienation at traditional workplaces, it seems that decision participation must come into play early in the process. This comes slowly at first for people not accustomed to participating, but the encouragement to participate begins to narrow the credibility gap and most people join in after a few invitations.

Lastly, management must discard traditional policies and practices that presume or embody mistrust. Where these policies are rooted in provisions of a labor agreement such as the probationary concept or a host of other rigid systems, the company and union must work these out together. And this teamwork is not likely to occur unless the union and employees are playing a part in the entire change process.

Postscript

What Eaton is doing is not complex. When one observer suggested we were only getting the "Hawthorne effect," we glowed and said that was exactly right. All we are trying to do is "bottle" the Hawthorne effect, and share respect and concern with employees.

It is significant that about a quarter of the companies that research the Eaton approach and visit a facility adapt some form of the process for one or more of their own locations. . . .

Those companies that have tried the Eaton approach have confirmed our experiences. They report:

- This approach is fundamentally fair and makes sense even if doesn't prove to be a panacea.
- It is based on some very specific and simple actions that can be implemented by existing personnel.
- The company can rely on its own innovators, and not, as one inquirer put it, on "a behavioral guru."
- The approach does not require a large financial investment, and even a 1 percent increase in plant utilization or a 2 percent drop in absenteeism brings a substantial return on investment.

Enhancing the Quality of Working Life
A Concept Sketched and One Approach Illustrated

Perhaps the most common reflection of a greater social role by both government and especially business organizations is the growing emphasis on the quality of working life of their employees. What organizations do to their employees, in short, now gets some of that attention that has been fixated on what employees can do for their organizations. The underlying motivation is not all Christian charity. Rather, even maintenance of the existing level of employee contributions will no doubt require enhancement of what organizations offer their employees, including (perhaps especially including) nonmonetary benefits.

The approach to dealing with the quality of working life here has two themes. Thus, the concept is elaborated, and one attempt by a large organization to do something about the quality of working life will be briefly described. The point of both themes is the same: to understand; and to seek to do something with that understanding.

What Is QWL?

This introduction starts at the beginning, which is not usual for discussions of the quality of working life, or QWL. Discussions tend to quickly turn to purple prose, either of praise or condemnation. We stand with Walton, who gives major attention to the concept. He asks rhetorically:[45]

- How should QWL be conceptualized, and how can it be measured?
- What are appropriate criteria for measurement, and how do they influence each other?
- How is each QWL criterion related to productivity, if at all?
- Is an individual QWL criterion more or less applicable to all employee groups?

Walton's conclusion is firm: "These questions are central to both research on the quality of the human experience in work organizations and action programs which seek to improve that experience."

With no pretense of being exhaustive here, Walton's analysis will be relied on to sketch the breadth of the usual content of QWL concepts. Walton's useful effort is variously paraphrased and quoted directly in Exhibit 2.

Several points are patent in the convenient but obviously simplified summary in Exhibit 2. *First,* that exhibit clearly charts a long trail awinding, even for the most progressive of organizations. There should be no dearth of QWL things that need doing, for a long time to come.

Second, the elements reasonably encompassed by a QWL concept are not all consistent. Indeed, several of the elements are in more or less direct oppostion. For example, the growing sense of constitutionalism may encourage a legalistic emphasis that detracts from more personal or humanistic elements in QWL, such as the growing sense of community among an organization's members. The challenge is to blend and balance.

Exhibit 2 Some Salient Features of the Concept "Quality of Working Life"

1. *Adequate and fair compensation*, which is a subject issue that involves such complex questions as:
   - Does the income meet both the standards of the recipient as well as social standards of what is sufficient?
   - Does the pay received for one job bear some reasonable relationship to the pay received for other comparable jobs?
2. *Safe and healthy working conditions*, which refers to a broad and increasingly stringent set of conditions defining a healthy work environment
3. *Immediate opportunity to use and develop human capabilities*, which implies such job qualities, among others as:
   - Autonomy: autonomy and self-control relative to external controls
   - Multiple skills: the degree to which work uses a wide range of skills and abilities rather than repetition of the same narrow skill
   - Information and perspective: the ability to get meaningful information about the total work process and the results of their own action, so that employees can appreciate the relevance and consequences of their actions
   - Planning: the degree to which work includes planning as well as implementation of activities
4. *Future opportunity for continued growth and security*, which refers to such complex aspects of working life as:
   - Development: the extent to which one's current activities help maintain and expand one's capabilities rather than lead to obsolescence
   - Prospective application: the expectation to use expanded or new knowledge and skills in work assignments
   - Advancement opportunities: the availability of opportunities to advance in ways that are recognizable to others at work as well as to family members
   - Security: employment or income security
5. *Social integration in work organization*, which includes this broad range of work-site attributes:
   - Freedom from prejudice: acceptance of the worker for work-related traits, skills, abilities, and potential without regard to race, sex, creed, and national origin, or to life styles and physical appearance
   - Egalitarianism: the absence of stratification in work organization

Exhibit 2 (Continued)

- Mobility: the existence of upward mobility for employees
- Supportive primary groups: membership in face-to-face work groups that supply help, support, and affirmation of the uniqueness of each individual
- Community: the sense of community in work organizations that extends beyond face-to-face work groups
- Interpersonal openness: the way members of the work organization relate their ideas and feelings to one another

6. *Constitutionalism in the work organization,* which includes the following central features:

   - Privacy: the right to personal privacy
   - Free speech: the right to dissent openly from the views of superiors in the organization without fear of reprisal
   - Equity: the right to equitable treatment in all matters
   - Due process: governance by the "rule of law" rather than the rule of men in such matters as equal opportunity in all aspects of the job, privacy, and dissent, including procedures for due process and access to appeals

7. *Impact of work on total life,* which relates work-site effects—both positive and negative—to marriage, the family, and so on

8. *Social relevance of work life,* which refers to the socially beneficial or injurious effects of the employing organization and its products or services

Source: Drawn from Richard E. Walton, "Quality of Working Life: What Is It?" *Sloan Management Review,* Vol. 15 (Fall 1973), pp. 11-21. Reprinted by permission.

Third, no agreement exists about which of these QWL elements are related to productivity, or how. The questions are substantial. Much QWL improvement will be costly, for example, and productivity improvements are a major (sometimes the only) source of the required resources.

But, short-run QWL expenditures may be useful, perhaps even necessary, although no corresponding increases in productivity are expected. There are real storms a-brewing around many of today's organizations, some due to the contentious spirit of the times, but others clearly related to conditions at the work site that have not kept pace with broad social developments and aspirations. And, sometimes, the best that the captain of a ship can do is to keep it afloat, while waiting for calmer weather. The appropriate performance criterion under such conditions is not: Did the ship arrive on time? Rather, the focal question is whether the captain did what was prudently necessary, perhaps even more than was absolutely necessary, to assure that the ship would dock safely, however late.

Perspectives on QWL Enhancement Through Survey/Feedback

More or less commonly, survey/feedback designs get used as the method of choice for enhancing the quality of working life, at least as the entering wedge.[46] The few pages below cannot presume to settle the complex issues involved. Yet, useful perspective can be provided for a few strategic points, all the more usefully so since they often get neglected, or get obfuscated in technical argument.

The general posture here concerning reliance on survey/feedback may be expressed in two words: yes, but. Employee surveys provide a convenient means of learning about concerns among the organizational legions, at a specific point in time, and at a cost that is minuscule compared to the potential yields in information and employee goodwill. But, surveys do not provide a ready answer to every manager's dream. Extracting value for dollars spent requires sophistication by users in the design and interpretation of surveys. Surveys can lead to considerable mischief, if too much is expected of them, or if they are interpreted incautiously.

The present approach to making more of the "yes" and less of the "but" considers only four points, although convenient resources provide detail and perspective for those with specialized interests.[47] In turn, attention will go to the following:

- Some up-front cautions for survey users
- Notes on institutionalizing the survey/feedback process
- A sketch of *the* two significant issues in designing surveys, and hence in interpreting their results
- An outline of a useful OD mode for dealing with survey/feedback results

Some Preliminary Cautions

Let us start with a list of "don'ts" for survey users. Managers contemplating use of a survey are well-advised to respect certain cautions very early in their decision-making. Illustratively, potential users of surveys:

- Should only in extremis authorize a survey to "buy time" or to "take the heat off."
- Should authorize a survey only if they are willing to risk exposing how things really are. Unwilling managers will be better off spending the

money on a consultant who will give them what they want or, better still, not spending the money at all.

- Should not authorize a survey unless they are willing to seriously consider doing something about what the results reveal, if anything.
- Should realize that surveys only generate data, and do not necessarily provide useful information.
- Should not authorize a survey unless they appreciate that problems may be unearthed by surveys, but solutions seldom are.
- Should be careful about authorizing off-the-shelf surveys, and specifically those which imply some ideal vision of what a management system should be. Management may end up looking bad in terms of standards of success built into the survey instrument that management does not understand, accepts only in part, or which management might even reject on close analysis.
- Should authorize one-shot surveys only in rare cases. The willingness to at least consider a series of readings over time usually should be a precondition to an initial survey.

Institutionalizing the Survey/Feedback Process

A survey may be much ado about nothing, in the absence of very early and effective institutionalization of the total process to increase the probability that something will be done with the results once they become available. Some kind of "steering group" which owns the survey process seems all but inevitable to provide the nurturing, resources, and credibility that a survey/feedback process typically requires. Such institutionalization provides reinforcement and thrust for the process—all the way from early concept to action planning after results become available. Basically, two kinds of steering groups are available:

- A *core group* composed of the highest levels of line and staff officials, with responsibility for the full survey and feedback cycle, from design to action-planning and follow-up
- A *task force* composed of officials of various ranks—hopefully chosen for their reputations as straight-shooters, and containing both respected comers as well as those who have topped-out—whose major assignment will be to shepherd the survey process, make a report to top officialdom, and then variously transfer implementation activities to the permanent authority structure

Note that a steering group will be particularly useful, even necessary, when unions are involved. Plainly spoken, unions often will see surveys as threats to their ties with employees. Unions also use surveys less frequently, as far as

I know. So, their lower confidence in surveys, as well as their lesser sophistication in using their results, may inspire less than enthusiastic initial reactions. Consequently, union officials might well be represented on the task force or core group described above. In any case, their acceptance (if not active support) of a survey typically is critical.

Tastes may differ in this regard, but I strongly prefer a core group. Its members may be very busy people, and may find it inconvenient to give active dedication to the survey. And respondents may have some concern about the survey data being so available to those who may be major sources of dissatisfaction. But a core group powerfully signals that the organization means business with the survey, and the core group's members will no doubt be useful in the implementation phases of the survey process. Of course, relying on a core group brings prevailing organizational conflicts and politics directly into the survey process, right at the start. But that fact can provide a great opportunity as well as a major challenge to the survey process, for at least two reasons. Thus, working on those politics and conflicts may be very valuable, and I believe it best to do so early–up-front and personal, as it were. Moreover, if such politics and conflicts are to preclude a complete process, I would prefer that the scuttling comes early in the game. Effort would be saved, and the risk of disillusioning–perhaps even of unwisely exposing–respondents would be reduced.

A task force also can be useful in helping establish the early credibility of the survey process, in creating the important belief that survey data will not be used punitively, and so on. Task force members probably will be more available, and more likely to see the success or failure of the survey as more directly impactful on their careers than members of a core group.

Task force have their liabilities, however. Early in the survey process, members may come to see themselves as "in the middle"–between the employees and top officialdom–and may become so protective of the respondents as to become obstacles in the planning of the survey. Moreover, toward the end of the survey and feedback process, task forces may provide less muscle and experience for implementation. Indeed, implementation may be seriously complicated because a task force is deliberately set outside normal authority channels, and this elemental fact may induce dynamics that complicate transfer from the task force to the regular authority structure. Indeed, the very act of surveying may imply some inadequacy or incompetency in the normal authority structure, and survey results may make as many enemies as friends among an organization's officialdom. That is to say, regular authority figures may have multiple reasons to drop the baton proffered them by a task force.

Opinions may differ about the relative preference for task force or core group, of course, and some organizational conditions may require one or the other. My opinion on one point remains absolute, however. Without some early institutionalization, via a task force or a core group, the odds do not favor a full survey/feedback cycle.

Two Central Considerations About Surveys

Two central considerations should preoccupy surveys. To begin, they need to be rooted in a clear statement of values or goals prescribing what the organization *should be.* Absent specificity about values or goals, the survey will neither be able to ask the appropriate questions, except by chance, nor will it be obvious what the survey results really mean, or what to do about them. Surveys do not somehow sidestep the tough value issues of what should exist—the balancing of ethical considerations with the realities of specific organizational environments. Rather, rightly viewed, surveys highlight the need for such tough analysis.

Surveys must be sensitive in numerous ways to the fact that organizations become infused with value, then, and the earlier the better. Indeed, survey applications will profit from a concerted effort at *prior* clarification of values:[48] What values do and should guide this organization as we go about doing our thing? This is a critical way of evaluating your internal or external consultants, as a matter of fact. The consultant should as a matter of all but universal practice get the client—even try to force the client, if necessary—to consider what values presently distinguish the client's organization, as well as to ponder whether those values that now infuse the organization really constitute the ones that the client wants to preserve at this particular stage in the organization's development.

In sum, powerful reasons support value clarification. You have to know what an organization is and wishes to be—to be in touch with what that organization values—to make effective and consistent response to survey findings. For example, assume a survey reports general agreement that managers should be more encouraging to subordinates. So what? Judgments of value alone can help answer that: So what? The normative questions cover a broad range. Should subordinates' needs be responded to? What specific practices or policies constitute coddling of subordinates, now, in our specific organization? And so on and on. Moreover, if an organization's values are inconsistent, or if serous differences about them exist, acting on the results of a survey will be difficult or impossible. A good survey will help in testing for differences in values, but it cannot resolve them.

Let us get the other megaissue up front. Surveys also must be rooted in a comprehensive model of reality, of the world *as it is.* Surveys cannot merely "count the leaves on trees," to rely on that useful metaphor that reminds us to distinguish information from data. Surveys should focus on the significant features of life in organizations, the key processes and dynamics, meticulously selected from among those countless features that could be variously measured or counted. Absent such grounding in a model of reality, survey results can constitute nothing more than bothersome detail. A serviceable model of reality provides three kinds of information.

- Dimensions that describe the significant features of organizational life.
- Data that detail where a specific organization stands on these important dimensions.
- Given where a specific organization stands on such dimensions, a useful model of reality highlights processes and dynamics that might be affected to move the organization toward its preferred goals or values.

We cannot here resolve for the reader the many ticklish issues involved, but consider the central dilemma. In sum, the use of the results of surveys involves raising self by one's bootstraps. Action based on a survey both depends upon a comprehensive model of reality and, ideally, will contribute to the testing and elaboration of such a model. If we were to wait for that model to appear full-blown, alternatively, not only would we never survey, but the development of more useful models also would be delayed.

So we have to begin with the best we have in developing a survey instrument, while striving to make what we have better. Most surveys do not score very high in this particular. They usually seek only data that seem of immediate relevance to the user, and they seldom are developed or interpreted in terms of some explicit model of reality. This can be risky business.

Schema of an OD Implementing Mode

Getting valid and reliable data from a survey certainly constitutes a good start toward the success of a survey/feedback intervention, but even solid institutionalization might not be able to inhibit the misuse of "good data." Prudent caution in the overall design of the survey/feedback intervention is required. Managers can be tempted to use survey data unwisely, to illustrate, as in seeking to "motivate" some individuals or work units. Even worse, survey data could be used as the public excuse for taking action against managers already viewed as inadequate, but action against whom waited a propitious incident.

Solid safeguards should be built against such awkward uses of survey data. Basically, a survey effort should be based on vigorous resolve to maximize learning and improvement, as contrasted with organizational analogues of search and destroy missions. A little mutual trust and confidence can go a long way in such cases.

Or, managers can design a survey-based program of improvement in ways that reduce the temptation for doing foolish things with survey results. For example, one large soft-goods firm adopted this strategy when they inaugurated a major survey:

- Aggregate survey data were reported directly to top management, but break-out data by departments remained the sole property of individual department managers and the task force which was the steering group for the survey-feedback effort.
- Individual task-force members were assigned as liaison to specific departments of the host firm and helped them interpret departmental survey results.
- Each department manager was told only that he rated higher than, lower than, or about the same as most departments. The "other departments" were not identified specifically.
- Each department head was mandated to appoint a team, including himself, with responsibility for identifying opportunities for useful change suggested by the survey data, as well as for designing and implementing changes, if any.
- The task-force member sought to work with his departmental team to formulate a plan of action, if considered appropriate.
- A follow-up survey was scheduled 12 months after the initial survey. At that time, and for the first time, top management would see the results of the two surveys. Here, progress, or lack of it, could be analyzed, department heads would have to account for their stewardship, and so on.
- Periodic resurveys would be made to generate time-series data to monitor the "vital signs" of the system over time.

This may seem the long way around the barn, but it seeks to avoid the carnage that can result from less reasonable designs. The strategy puts learning or change first, but without forgetting that assessing the quality of stewardship is appropriate after a reasonable opportunity for constructive response by department managers to the survey data.

Sketching One QWL Effort

The OD literature has been enriched recently by variously complete reports on several comprehensive QWL programs, often joint union-management ventures.[49] The most publicized programs have been associated with the American Center for Quality of Work Life of Washington, D. C.—which has generated ten QWL projects, including efforts at the Rushton mine,[50] the Bolivar, Tenn., manufacturing site,[51] and the Tennessee Valley Authority.[52] In a few other cases (e.g., at SmithKline Corp.),[53] QWL efforts were launched and financed as in-house efforts in nonunion situations.

The joint-QWL programs have an especial relevance, for at least four reasons. Thus, unions are everywhere; the multiple-authority structures for unions and manager imply intriguing problems for intervention and analysis; and, as Huse notes correctly, "OD has had little to say about the role of unions and the part they play in OD."[54] In addition, the programs seem to have been well-funded,[55] or at least had resources available to them well beyond all but a few OD efforts.

Hence the focus here on one joint union/management QWL program—that at the Bolivar plant of what was Harman International Industries, Inc. Its basic thrust vibrates in these words:[56]

> . . . to create an American model of industrial democracy: a model that is acceptable to unions and that might stimulate future union efforts. The project is based on the view that a national movement to improve the quality of work is unlikely to succeed without union support and that union leaders are practical people who can't be expected to struggle for abstract concepts like 'humanized work' or self-management without something concrete to point to. If the project is successful, the workers and management . . . will develop programs that not only change the character of their work but that also can be adopted by unions as goals for collective bargaining.

None of the documentation is complete, but a very good idea of the QWL designs and consequences can be gained by a brief review of the Bolivar program, whose principal investigators/intervenors have left a good and growing record of their still-developing evaluation of the first 6 years of QWL activity. Bolivar investigators isolate six more-or-less distinct phases of effort. Exhibit 3 provides a variety of details about these phases, which imply grist for later analysis and also were used by the researchers for time-series analysis of data.

The review here cannot go into any detail about the six stages. Rather, four emphases will dominate: underlying goals or objectives will be specified; then three major design-elements in the Bolivar experience will be sketched; in addition, the results through late-1978 will be reviewed; and, finally, some conclusions by way of hindsight will be offered. Note that the description below involves five sets of major actors, in addition to corporate and local management, international and local union officials, and Bolivar employees:

- An Advisory Committee with variable but top-level representation from labor and management
- An Ad Hoc (later Working) Committee of plant-level union and management representatives
- Thirty-three groups at the work-level, each composed of a supervisor, union steward, and employees
- An intervention team of highly variable composition called the "project staff" or the "WIP program staff," which (among other things) collected 1973 data for a survey/feedback design and otherwise helped introduce work-site innovations

- An evaluation staff from the Institute of Social Research, University of Michigan, which in 1974 took over formal evaluation of the Bolivar efforts.

Exhibit 3 Different Phases of the Bolivar Program, with Selected Key Events

Phase I (May 1972-March 1973, base-line period)

Negotiations and decision to participate, at level of corporation and international union.

Bolivar plant votes October 1972 to participate, unanimously, following a UAW meeting for all employees to discuss the "humanization of work."

Corporate informs Bolivar management that Work Improvement Program (WIP) would start; WIP originally was planned as a "job satisfaction" and "personal development" program.

Phase II (April 1973-February 1974, study and interview phase)

Two-hour structured interviews re plant conditions with over 300 employees begin by evaluation staff, summer 1973.

Ad Hoc Committee at plant level established October 1973–composed of five management employees and five union officials–begins looking at working conditions and survey data. Becomes Working Committee in November 1973.

"Shelter Agreement" signed to protect employees from loss of pay, job security, or seniority due to WIP.

Top-level Advisory Committee established as part of shelter agreement protecting employees.

Final Technical Report completed February 1974.

Phase III (March 1974-January 1975, experimental phase to try new and alternative ways of structuring work and expanding WIP)

March 1974 begins with two major goals: to feedback the survey data; and to educate naive union, management, and employees about different methods for improving quality of working life.

Survey/feedback apparently lacks broad support.

Three experimental groups set up for sociotechnical restructuring in April 1974.

Experimental groups increase output and raise issues of employee compensation.

Corporate and work force supports Earned Idle Time (EIT) as compensation in experimental groups, while union and plant management rejects EIT.

Formal assessment of QWL project begins June 1974, by Institute for Social Research.

A few more sociotechnical experimental groups formed July 1974.

Seminars, Educational classes start.

Recession causes lay offs, end of experimental groups.

Exhibit 3 (Continued)

Phase IV (February 1975-December 1975, first year of plant-wide diffusion of results from experiments)

Recession forces lay off of 33% of hourly work force, and union/management letter invites those laid off to participate in In-Plant School.

Thirty-three core groups—each composed of foremen, job steward, and employees appointed or elected.

In-Plant School starts—blueprint reading, welding, Bible studies, black studies, etc.

WIP ratified by vote of local union in April 1975, EIT goes plant-wide.

Working Committee not proactive: reacts mostly to departmental EIT plans.

Pre-Assembly Core Group begins supervision experiment.

Phase V (January 1976-December 1976, second year plant-wide: search for new directions)

Core Groups do not function as expected.

Advisory Committee stifles Working Committee, which focuses on EIT plans.

Growth in various forms of top-level union/management collaboration, for example, in sharing profitability information.

Cost-savings-sharing plan gets proposed at top levels, but is never instituted.

WIP becomes EIT to most of work force.

Continuation of WIP and third-party educators/evaluators is discussed.

Formal assessment QWL project continues fall 1976, survey by Institute of Social Research.

Phase VI (January 1977-February 1978, third year plant-wide: continued search for new directions)

Harman leaves parent corporation and becomes Under-Secretary of Commerce.

Parent company is sold.

"Paradox of democracy" concerning EIT, and negative effects on employees' health.

Formal assessment as QWL project moves to completion: various reports and books available or in final stages.

Debate about the kind and degree of future commitment to WIP, if and how it gets built into ongoing management/union activities.

Source: Based on Barry A. Macy, "A Theoretical Basis for and an Assessment of the Bolivar Quality of Working Life Experiment: 1972-1977." Paper presented at 1978 Annual Meeting, Academy of Management, San Francisco, Calif., August 9-12, 1978. See esp. Table 2. See also Robert L. Duckles, "Work, Workers, and Democratic Change." Unpublished doctoral dissertation, The Wright Institute Graduate School, Berkeley, Calif., 1976, pp. 218-231; and the Harvard Project on Technology, Work and Character, *The Bolivar Project: Final Technical Report,* February 15, 1974, Appendix A. Mimeographed.

Underlying Goals or Objectives

At base, the Bolivar project was rooted in the congruent philosophies of Dr. Sidney Harman and Irving Bluestone—the first being the president of Bolivar's parent corporation, and the latter, vice-president of the United Automobile Workers Union whose local was the collective bargaining agent at Bolivar. With the help of Dr. Michael Maccoby, Director of the Harvard Project on Technology, Work and Character—four basic principles were enunciated in terms of which the Bolivar plant would be restructured by management, union, and work force.[57]

- *Increased security.* The first area of security involves health and safety, which we intend to improve by creating the best possible environment, with a minimum of hazards. Security against loss of job is more difficult to achieve, as the Harman Automotive Division is part of a market which is subject to fluctuations that are beyond our control. No one can promise that a worker will never be laid off. In the *overall* sense, security from loss of job depends on effectively operating the plant to assure recovering the major portion of the available business, so the plant continues in business and continues employing workers.
- *Increased equity.* By making the distribution of work, the organization of work, the rewards of work, and the rules under which we work as fair and as reasonable as they can be.
- *Increased individuation.* By recognizing that all people are not the same, but have different interests and needs, and by increasing the opportunities for people to develop in their own ways.
- *Increased democracy.* By giving each worker more opportunities to have a say in the decisions that affect his life, including his work life.

Evidence implies that an incomplete clarification of values underlay these four principles, perhaps because of the euphoria[58] that seems to have permeated the initial mutual discovery by Harman and Bluestone of shared philosophies. In any case, understanding of the basic values seemed to zig and zag. From the start, Macy emphasizes, the purpose of Bolivar "was *not* to increase productivity."[59] Indeed, he notes the belief that "had Harman called for a productivity improvement program, the UAW would not have participated. . . ."[60] However, Harman corporate announced to Bolivar officials that a "Work Improvement Program" would begin, which rings differently from the previously planned "Job Satisfaction" program. In any case, somewhat later still, a contingency plan evolved. A "shelter agreement" signed by both labor and management not only insured that workers would not lose their job as a result of any changes at Bolivar, but also specified that:[61]

> The purpose of the joint labor-management . . . program is to make work better and more satisfying for all employees, salaried and hourly, while maintaining the necessary productivity for job security.
>
> The purpose is *not* to increase productivity. If increased productivity is a by-product of the program, ways of rewarding the employees for increased productivity will become legitimate matters for inclusion in the program.

But incomplete consensus about values still existed. Somewhat later, illustratively, Harman urged a fifth major principle for Bolivar: "mutuality."

One need not dig very deep to hazard a reasonable guess as to what Harman's addendum to the four principles may have signaled. The UAW's immediate self-interest seems clear enough: raising productivity, absent an offsetting increase in demand, means fewer jobs. Reasonable enough. But what of Harman's stake? Suppose WIP increased productivity as well as generated a more decent and fulfilling work site. A request for "mutuality" for management would make sense in such a context, lest the benefits of increased productivity go only to employees.

Survey/Feedback at Bolivar

As is common in QWL efforts, for openers, Bolivar utilized survey/feedback as "a first step toward creating new cooperative processes to improve work."[62] Data were gathered via 2-hour structured interviews with 300 Bolivar employees concerning supervision, working conditions, the union, health and safety, and so on. The data were embodied in a *Final Technical Report,* dated February 15, 1974, whose direct tone may be suggested economically by this snippet from the Report:[63]

> The production floor is dirty and disorderly, . . . noisy. A shortage of storage space and the pace of production which overworks the luggers and towmotor operators results in parts and materials being pushed into every available corner. . . . Many machines are kept in poor repair. . . . The atmosphere is stuffy and irritating to some. . . . There are holes in the roof, and pools of water on the floor. In winter, there is inadequate heating. . . . Comfort and sometimes safety have been ignored in the all-out effort to maximize production and profits.

The fate of the survey/feedback intervention can be essentially summarized in terms of four themes. *First,* the survey generated a sheaf of results—suggestively, the 429-page working report of survey findings was called "the telephone book." Small wonder.

Second, the report seemed to pull no punches about the Bolivar work site, which was deficient in numerous regards related to the health, safety, and morale of employees. Workers were most concerned about the former issues, but dissatisfaction with and alienation from work got some attention.

Third, major physical improvements were made in the work site by "the end of Phase IV," Macy tells us, which he dates as December 1975. Available information does not permit certainty, but it appears that the survey data helped encourage such improvements.

Fourth, however, the feedback of the survey data seemed lame. The survey data were discussed in the Working Committee, and with some impact, it seems. The power of the design in plant-wide rounds of feedback does not seem to have been exploited, however, or perhaps even contemplated. For example, it is not clear what (if any) design the feedback was to follow–i.e., "waterfalls" or "cascades," as contrasted with a "bottom up" approach. But Macy sees one point as undeniable. When the *Final Technical Report* became available–nearly a year after the survey interviews began–its broad impact was definitely underwhelming. "The Bolivar workforce, the union, and the management did not show much interest in the results of the survey phase," Macy concludes: "only a handful of workers ever saw or wanted to see the results included in the *Final Technical Report.*"[64] One doctoral committee seems to have been impressed, however, since the data got embodied in a PhD dissertation.[65]

Sociotechnical Intervention at Bolivar

Given that the survey and feedback element did not catch fire, whence came the pizzazz at Bolivar? Not much doubt exists on the point. Early in Phase IV of the Bolivar intervention, sociotechnical experiments with existing workflows were begun. Following the model sketched in Chapter 2 above, which was introduced at Bolivar in a seminar by Einar Thorsrud who had substantial European experience with sociotechnical applications in industry,[66] experimental groups involving sixty workers were set up on the shop floor. The experiments began in April 1974 and were instituted by the Working Committee and the WIP project staff. The experiment both succeeded and failed in distinct senses.

Success came quickly and was clear as early as June 1974. Several experimental work teams demonstrated that they could absorb sociotechnical principles, as well as apply them to restructuring their own work which (to simplify) had been industrially engineered so that specific time standards for various jobs were available. Output previously averaged about 85 percent of standards, but the experimentals soon reached well beyond 100 percent. What to do with this sudden surplus? Consistent with sociotechnical principles, specific *groups of employees* were given three options:

- Going home early, but with a full-day's pay
- Getting a bonus–extra pay for exceeding applicable standards of performance
- Earning bonus hours to spend in various in-plant activities–for example, attending classes in-plant

Some experimental groups opted to take early-leaving for what became known as Earned Idle Time or EIT, and that decision implied some tough issues that in the long run saw failure ride the shoulders of success. As early as October 1974, for example, EIT was shown to have some serious negative effects on the quality of working life. And details to be reviewed below clearly indicate that EIT was a double-edged sword, not only in its direct effects on employees but also in its tendency to become WIP rather than only one element in that program.

Let us develop only the general point here. Quickly, Macy notes, the "majority of other hourly workers at Bolivar became upset because of what they regarded as an 'inequity' and voiced demands that everyone in the plant be included in the experiment."[67] WIP hung in the balance, as a consequence, but UAW official Bluestone was especially instrumental in continuing local union support. Relatedly, the number of people in the experimental program was increased, while the Working Committee decided that the experimental program could not be extended plant-wide because of the lack of industrial-engineering standards on some jobs, scheduling problems, and the like.

This set of decisions did not stick long, however, and WIP tended to become EIT, with unanticipated consequences for all. A downturn in the auto market led to a temporary plant shut-down and the layoff of a third of the work force in December 1974 and January 1975, but pressure for EIT only escalated. In April 1975, a plant-wide election endorsed WIP—by 80 to 20 percent—and specifically sanctioned the extension of EIT. Despite concerns about inequities between "production" and "non-production" employees, major power-wielders—some members of the Working Committee, top company officials, and union leaders—decided not to block the local membership's desire for EIT. They did steer the local membership a bit, however. The Working Committee, with the strong urging of the Advisory Committee, ruled out a bonus for production workers for output above standard. EIT might be used to:[68]

- Leave the plant early
- Discuss work-related matters
- Take part in education programs

In summer 1978, about 70 percent of the entire "direct" and "indirect" Bolivar work force is on EIT.[69] About 20 percent of Bolivar's employees have attended educational classes. There is "still no financial incentive in the WIP," Macy notes in late 1978.[70]

Core Groups at Bolivar

Coincident with the February 1975 decision to expand EIT, 33 "core groups" were established, at least one for each department. A core group included the immediate supervisor, the union steward, and appointed or elected employees. A major effort—over 1100 paid hours—was devoted by the project staff to weekly meetings which, Macy explains, "covered how, when, and where the WIP got started; the progress of the program; and where it was headed. . . . The Core Groups were to carry this same message to members of their departments."[71] The intended action-objectives—apparently those of the Work Committee and the project staff—were to[72]

- Expand the WIP to all production or direct labor departments, following the model of the original experimental groups
- Begin meetings and experiments in indirect labor management departments
- Start a broad educational program

At times, the core groups seemed to meet all expectations, as in the supervision experiment in the Pre-Assembly Core Group begun in October 1975.[73] Basically, on Pre-Assembly initiative, ten volunteers got a direct sense of supervision and gained experience for possible future promotion. How did this occur? Volunteers individually spent substantial time tracking and observing a supervisor; later they had controlled practice with real-time foremanship for half-days during a 3- to 5-day period; and subsequently Pre-Assembly operated without a foreman, instead rotating the job among several volunteers who would rather do it themselves.

Although the experiment was not adopted, the Pre-Assembly Core Group reflected WIP at its best. In summary form, observers see it as reflecting Bolivar's three new S's—Spirit, Structure, and Study.[74] Thus the experiment was described as reflecting a new "mutuality, respect and concern for each individual," in strong contrast to the "spirit of hostility, resistance, and conflict between management and workers that was evident when the program first started." In addition, the experiment implied the viability of new structures, especially the core group and the Working Committee—which authorized Pre-Assembly to go ahead—but also including the top-level Advisory Committee which inspired and supported WIP. And the Pre-Assembly experiment also emphasized Study. Although their efforts did not get built into everyday supervision in direct ways, three observers conclude that ". . . participants deepened their understanding not only of the technical and economic aspects but the human and social aspects of their work."[75]

The core groups never quite made it, for numerous reasons. Basically, they started late and at a difficult time—when approximately one-third of the work force was laid off during the recession of fall 1974—and soon their broad charge got diluted by local desires for plant-wide EIT. The vote ratifying such extension came in April 1975, and soon the WIP apparatus was up to its institutional neck in monitoring EIT. Thus it is estimated that the Working Committee—which was empowered to approve EIT plans for each department—was spending 55 percent of its time monitoring such plans.[76] An in-plant education program started during Phase IV—"to counterbalance the EIT program"[77]—and the experiment in supervision described above began in October 1975. But the Work Improvement Program substantially became EIT. Worse still, EIT apparently became a kind of love/hate object for many at Bolivar. Thus the October 1977 issue of the plant paper carried a letter by one employee, who apparently spoke for a broader constituency. The letter read:[78]

> Production is a great thing to have. Everyone likes to get out early, but they should be more considerate of people. I have worked on several lines since I have been in the department. All of the people on the line want to get those parts down the belt. "If you are sick you should have stayed at home, roll them parts. We want to get out of here by twelve." [Signed by Union member of Assembly Department]

Moreover, attention at Bolivar seemed to refocus on useful exchanges between corporate and the international union. Thus a Cost-Saving-Sharing Plan got detailed attention, although corporate and the international union were unable to agree on either the components that would comprise the underlying formula, the formula base from which savings would be measured, or how any savings would be shared. Consistently, also, the Advisory Committee seemed to limit the initiative of the Working Committee. Whatever the reasons, Macy is willing to describe the period beginning January 1976 as being characterized (among several other particulars) by the "non-functioning nature of Core Groups."[79]

Three Classes of Effects at Bolivar

A very attractive feature of the Bolivar documentation derives from the numerous indicators that were tracked by the evaluation team. Three classes of indicators were distinguished,[80] and trends in them provide an overall view of how Bolivar people respond to QWL. Basically, the data cover various periods, ranging from 45 to 56 months.

Impact on People. Data on ten measures of QWL impacts on Bolivar people provide a mixed picture, comparing T_1 (summer 1973) to T_2 (fall 1976). Neglecting a variety of technical and statistical considerations, some of potentially great significance,[81] the individual employee who remained at Bolivar from T_1 to T_2 experienced these eleven effects:

- Overall job satisfaction did not change significantly.
- Alienation did not change significantly.
- Depersonalization significantly improved.

- Somatic complaints *significantly increased.*
- Mental health *significantly decreased.*
- Race discrimination did not change significantly.
- Suggestions made did not change significantly.
- Self-reported absenteeism *increased significantly.*
- Organization climate did not change significantly.
- Effort did not change significantly.
- Ideas kept to self *increased significantly.*

Macy reports data from several populations—rather than just one population, as above—but his conclusion about the more complex comparisons proves serviceable in the present case as well. From "an individually relevant perspective, the quality of working life at Bolivar did not seem to change significantly. In fact, in quite a few instances, it declined."[82] In the list above, specifically, only *one* significant difference (depersonalization) was expected. Moreover, in six cases no significant changes were reported. Indeed, finally, four statistically significant changes were in a direction opposed to expectations of what would constitute an improved quality of working life.

Impact on the Union. Whatever else, QWL seemed to have left the union at T_2 where it was at T_1, in the perceptions of respondents. The data leave no doubt about the point. In sum, respondents perceived *no* significant changes in the union on *any* dimension, comparing 1973 to 1976 data. Nine union-relevant variables were measured.[83]

Impact on the Plant-as-Organization. Perceptions of the plant-as-organization changed in many specific particulars, but mostly in unintended and surprising ways. Twenty-nine variables were measured in all. In brief summary, using only matched data from individuals surveyed in both 1973 and 1976,[84] three clusters of effects can be distinguished. First consider two classes of major changes.

Statistically Significant Increases in	Statistically Significant Decreases in
Skills required to perform job	Feedback re job
Supervisory participation	Supervisory facilitation
Group participation	Supervisory closeness
Amount of influence over task decisions	Supervisory support
Adequacy of resources	Supervisory respect
Job security	Group satisfaction and integration
	Satisfaction with pay
	Equity of pay

Statistically Significant Increases in	Statistically Significant Decreases in
	Intrinsic and extrinsic rewards following good performance
	Intrinsic and extrinsic rewards following poor performance

In addition, no changes were observed on 11 other variables.

If the pattern of significant changes is contrary to intent, on balance, the data do not surprise. In fact, the organization-level results square nicely with data about individual-level changes reported above. Job changes did occur, in which individuals participated to higher degrees than before, as the statistically significant increases above reflect. At the same time, EIT led to peer pressure, supervisory disaffection, and employee dissatisfaction with relations at work, with pay, and so on.

Impact on Financial Measures. For those looking at the bottom-line only, Bolivar QWL seems to have been a good thing to do. Paradoxically, although the program failed to improve the quality of working life, it had a very attractive cost/benefit ratio.

Despite substantial statistical problems[85] with the panoply of variables used to measure financial effects,[86] "the numbers" stereophonically reflect the major impact of WIP. Generally, the Michigan evaluators estimate a major decrease T_2 versus T_1 in "counterproductive behavior and performance"–from 8.5 percent of sales in the interval May 1972 through March 1973, to 6.7 percent of sales in the interval January through December 1976.[87] Illustratively, also, productivity per employee increased from $131 to $161, in constant dollars, over the 56-month period of measurement. At the same time, quality also improved; scrap decreased 16 percent, and customer returns plummeted by approximately 50 percent.[88]

Hindsight re Bolivar

So what happend? And why? Hindsight is not always 20/20, of course, but it can be instructive. In the spirit of learning rather than second-guessing, then, five major points get inspired by the Bolivar data:

- The Bolivar program released or engaged real forces
- using a very general model for intervening
- which was not tethered by consistent values
- whose application also may have been based on limited diagnosis and prescription
- and whose reported results may reflect serious methodological issues.

Real Forces Released or Engaged. The Bolivar experience covers a substantial chunk of time during which big changes took place—major personnel layoffs occurred, as did a spurt in demand; major figures in the QWL effort moved on and off the stage; and so on. The effects reported nonetheless suggest the powerful forces that exist, waiting to be engaged, for good or ill; and the brief narrative above implies that intervenors were successful in engaging some substantial part of such forces, although not always as intended because of accidents, bad luck, and incomplete knowledge.

General Model of Intervention. For good or ill, Bolivar operated on a very general model of intervention, which also seemed to vary over time—and about which little specific information is available, with changes in program designs, as well as with the comings and goings of program staff. The latter were especially pronounced. The general character of the intervention mode stands in sharp contrast to evaluation at Bolivar, which is detailed, elegantly done—within the limitations of the Institute of Social Research coming on-board in midstream—and widely disseminated.[89]

The intervention/evaluation imbalance is noteworthy, for at least three distinct reasons. *First,* OD follows *the* basic rule of data-processing: Garbage in, garbage out. As a general rule of thumb, then, the balance of detailed and specific attention should go to intervention modes and designs. An elegant evaluation effort can only, in general, establish the quality of the intervention post hoc. An effective intervention will remain in place without any evaluation, in contrast. Something would be lost, to be sure. That is, a "good evaluation" no doubt will reinforce the effects of a potent OD intervention. And a *super* "bad evaluation" may tell us why "the patient died," which can be a very powerful learning experience.

Second, again at a general level, a comprehensive OD effort faces an incredibly difficult challenge. To put matters at their absolute simplest, such an effort must integrate subtle "process" and complex "content." That is, not only must interpersonal and intergroup processes be made regenerative—which implies the development of appropriate attitudes, behaviors, and skills—but the client system must variously come to appreciate the need to master and apply major and often still-developing substantive knowledge, while working to remain in control of the learning or change.

Providing balanced attention to "process" and "content" can pose challenges almost as formidable as developing a container for the universal solvent. What does that mean, specifically? We can illustrate here only. Thus we know tolerably well how to get individuals in groups to be process-wise—in touch with their feelings, and so on. T-groups usually can do the job; and designs like the 3-D confrontation also typically work in such ways. Process-related learning also can generate a strong sense of personal involvement and ownership: the data and the diagnosis belong to the client, to put it directly. So far, so good. But suppose a newly regenerative interaction system reveals a basic dissatisfaction with supervision? To a degree, clients can work out aspects of what improved relationships would be like.

But what of bringing to bear what we know about supervisory styles—as related to knowledge of what leads to what, but more especially to knowledge of how to achieve desirable states? Severe problems immediately become apparent. Descriptively, to illustrate, we know what factors tend to be most closely associated with employee satisfaction. In order, the following factors seem the most important in inducing high satisfaction:[90]

1. A "nurturant" supervisor
2. Adequate help, assistance, guidance
3. Few problems such as safety hazards, poor hours, or poor transportation
4. Fair promotional policies
5. Supervisor not supervising too closely
6. A technically competent supervisor
7. Autonomy in matters affecting work
8. A job with "enriching" demands

Following Strauss, this list indicates that supervisory behavior will be critical in satisfaction. "Of the eight factors," he observes, "three refer directly to supervisors (1, 5, and 6), three are often primarily their responsibility (2, 7, and 8), and even the remaining two (3 and 4) are substantially subject to the influence of supervisors."[91]

If these factors truly describe, then the obvious next question may seem to be prescriptive: How should supervisors behave or believe in order to be nurturant, provide adequate help, and so on?

Well, the next question is prescriptive, but it is far less obvious than the question above. *The* question involves not only prescribing behaviors or values, but doing so in ways that facilitate change in individuals, and in ways that also permit substantial commitment and ownership of the learning process by the learners themselves. The reader is referred to Chapter 1 of Part 1, and especially the discussion of psychological success in learning.

The overall image should be that of a tightrope, perhaps precariously swinging. Clearly, too much insistence on the "content" of such detailed knowledge may sour the "process"; and relatedly, single-minded preservation of a healthy "process" without due attention to "content" issues can leave people quivering with the desire to change but frustrated silly about not knowing how to go about doing what they know needs to be done. As the man said, integrating process and content in organizations is both crucial and difficult.

Third, a number of more detailed points raise questions about the model of intervention at Bolivar. I emphasize they are "questions" or "concerns" rather than "certainties." Three points reflect these questions, building on clues gleaned from diverse sources.

- At the outset, the concept of intervention at Bolivar emphasized three features. Thus only intervenors using a "client-centered approach" were considered.[92] Harking back to Lewin, moreover, reliance was placed on this basic force-field motion: that change is better facilitated by (for example) reducing the impact of inhibitors of the desired behavior, as opposed to increasing the direct stimulators of that behavior.[93] The implied rationale? Increases in stimulators ("driving forces") would be likely to increase old inhibitors ("restraining forces") or to induce the development of new inhibitors. Finally, group-oriented interventions were much preferred, as "when effort is targeted at the groups involved, rather than at individuals. . . ."[94]

These notions are consistent with the laboratory approach to OD, but they are quite general and also seem to have been inconsistently applied at Bolivar. Thus Macy notes that the Working Committee originally was "forced on" WIP in early stages[95] when, in sharp opposition, that demand would better have been accepted with thanks and, better still, would have long before been anticipated in an intervention mode that is group-oriented. Similarly, the early interview/feedback intervention reflects no group-based features, either in design, data-gathering, or action-planning,[96] except for reliance on the once-resisted Working Committee. Substantially later, in contrast, the intended use of the core groups clearly coincided with the three general features of intervention mode detailed above.

- The earliest intervention emphasis was on macro-structure and broad goals, for certain. The Advisory Committee and the Working Committee can certainly be considered major structural achievements, in an adversary and litigious context. These structures evolved out of negotiations which consumed much time,[97] one guesses to assure ". . . that the outcomes valued by each of the subsystems are given equal weight in conducting and judging the overall success of the change program."[98] Structurally, also, a very early decision provided that a "third party" would do the intervening and evaluating.[99] These two third-party functions were at first combined, and then later divided between a WIP project staff and a team from the University or Michigan's Institute of Social Research. The four principles—apparently going as far as could be gone without forfeiting the program[100]—provided the spirit or values for this macro-structure.

Indeed, one may almost say that explicit interventions dealt *only* with macro-structure and broad goals. Suggestively, no explicit interventions seek the kind of socioemotional preparation sketched in Chapters 1 to 3 of Part 1, with the possible (but not probable) exception of the truncated survey/feedback intervention. This fact does not derive from lack of need. The prior condition of labor/management relations can safely be described as having many features of degenerative interaction systems, of cycles of mistrust, and so on. And the intervening/evaluating third-party components added unpredictability to the already-complex set of multiple loyalties, authoritative structures, and interests.

This dominant structural bias cuts two ways. On the one hand, it does not repeat the error of much OD. Practice often has been so interaction-centered as to neglect or undervalue structural effects on behavior, even so much so in cases as to preclude taking structure into account in theory and strategy.[101] The effect has very real roots deep in the heart of often-opposed central tendencies. Thus the interaction-oriented design has roots in the T-group background, and often comes along with a metaphysical pathos that emphasizes love/acceptance/inclusion. The structure-oriented design has quite different wellsprings, which emphasize power/hierarchical distinctions/in-ness and out-ness. Often the twain are not accommodated.

Problems aside, structure-oriented designs must have a prominent place in OD. At Bolivar, very practically, the structural entry seems well-designed to ease initial concerns that the QWL program serve both union and management interests. The point is of special moment, given that the conditions favoring union/management joint ventures are very complex and rare.[102] At the same time, however, interaction-centered designs will be appropriate in inducing attitudes, values, and skills consistent with the new structures. The point does *not* escape Bolivar intervenors or evaluators. The new structures would profit from effective feedback, for example; and enhanced trust clearly was required to make the structures work. The underlying values/skills do not seem to be overabundant at Bolivar; and obvious opportunities for confrontation designs or team-building abound. But no interaction-centered designs seem to have been employed. For example, the general failure of the core groups seems to have been recognized in early 1976. In mid-1978, Macy reports that the "Working Committee had recently begun to have discussions with some core groups about their problems and possible solutions."[103]

- Beyond the basic structural innovations, the intervention style may be characterized in two basic ways. Early on, the dominant mode seems to approximate what Chapter 1 in Part 1 calls "instrumental process analysis." Witness this rare description: "The role of the project staff was to raise questions aimed at providing a full description of the nature of the work, its purpose, methods, and organization, as well as an understanding of the sources of information, materials, and supplies. . . ."[104] With apparently few exceptions—as in inviting Thorsrud to present a seminar on sociotechnical principles hopefully to stir motivation for changes in work—this facilitative and structural mode seems to have dominated.

This intervention style cannot be evaluated with certainty. By implication, however, little attention in intervention designs was given to the "interpersonal process orientation"—to skills in diagnosis and action relevant to building new cooperative relationships.[105] That would be counted a loss by those who value an interaction-oriented entry, as by being open about and owning feelings and reactions, or by those who prefer the mixed interaction/structure emphases characteristic of most team-building. But initial-entry via structure also can muster substantial support. For example, forms or patterns of work organization that, like the joint-committees at Bolivar, encourage participation and cooperation can have "very significant impact, on the nature of work, the character of work environment, and the nature of labor-management relations. . . ."[106]

How you begin has characteristics of a "judgment call"; but explicit designs for structural, interaction, and policy changes must *all* be accorded attention somewhere along the way in any comprehensive QWL effort. And this constitutes a tightrope-walking act for the client-centered intervenor. Consider how narrow the *media via* can be:

- Intervenors can bring to bear outside resources to stimulate client's knowledge and perhaps motivate, as was done at Bolivar in connection with sociotechnical principles, and that may be perceived as directing the client. In turn, this may limit ownership and active learning, while breeding dependence.
- Intervenors can play a more strictly reactive role, either deliberately and/or because of lack of substantive knowledge, thereby leaving client without needed resources, owning failure rather than success, and perhaps feeling frustrated with self and intervenor in ways that may be difficult to recognize. This will especially be the case if intervenors are otherwise decent and caring people, and hence difficult to criticize.

Only a regenerative system can over the long-run provide the feedback and disclosure necessary to fine-tune specific dynamics to avoid both situations sketched above.

In connection with the core groups, introduced well into the program's life, a more explicit and complementary intervention style is acknowledged. Thus Duckles[107] emphasizes his indebtedness to Piaget's work[108]—an "educational approach" that stresses "active learning." Duckles sees WIP as "unique" in this sense: "The study is not conducted by outside experts alone, but is an active co-learning endeavor that the project staff undertakes *with* the employees."[109] Three participants underscore the intervenor's role in these terms ". . . the 'third-party' staff on this project analyze work with people at all levels of the organization and help them to develop their ideas into specific changes. . . . [Any decisions are] reached by the *people* involved and approved by management and the union. . . ."[110]

Rightly interpreted, Piaget's "educational approach" seems well-attuned to the intervenor's tightrope-walking act described above. A brief explanation of this approach suggests the point, and also implies how easy it is for the intervenor to stray off the straight and very narrow.

To Understand Is to Invent was first published in French in 1948, and an English translation appeared in 1973. Piaget's special interest was why students (in today's vernacular) were turned off in large numbers by the physical sciences, and especially by mathematics. Basically, Piaget sees the fault in the mode of teaching rather than in the subjects or the students. Overall, he prescribes a learning-situation that:

- Stresses an interdisciplinary approach
- Places great demands on teachers to integrate a range of materials, both of process and substance, and especially to work in teams
- Provides an "active" role for the learner, especially in hands-on experimentation rather than in being a passive recipient of knowledge handed down by others, in memorizing, and so on
- Reorients the teacher into a designer of learning opportunities as opposed to a controlling and lecturing central figure
- Focuses on the concrete versus the abstract, the latter being defined as that "without relation to an actual need" of the learner[111]
- Emphasizes groupings of students in contrast to individual learners, since learning requires collaboration and exchange between people

Basically, Piaget proposes that people come to own and retain learning when it "is theirs"—via experimentation and discovery triggered by felt-needs. Not that the individual is required to rediscover all human knowledge. The individual starts by recreating or rediscovering, but only "until the time when he will be happy to be guided and taught."[112]

Piaget sees substantial similarities between intellectual and ethical development. Thus Piaget proposes that if the individual ". . . is intellectually passive," he will not know how to be free ethically. Conversely, if his ethics "consist *exclusively* in submission to adult authority, and if the *only* social exchanges that make up the life of the class are those that bind each student individually to a master holding all power, he will not know how to be intellectually active."[113]

Piaget's argument of what needs to be done—given his caveats that we then still lacked a technology for doing it, and that we were in 1948 only beginning to develop a suitable empirical base—is both radical and subtle. Basically, he proposes an orientation *for openers.* Thus he seeks ways of educational pump-priming, for providing the learner with a methodology that will serve in the future, and especially for avoiding an early turnoff by autocratic experts. On the other hand, at critical points he underscores that he is not proposing that all learning–ethical and intellectual–must be totally or even substantially rediscovered by each person or generation. For example, note that in the key passage quoted immediately above, Piaget calls for a *shift in the balance* in the processes of intellectual and ethical learning. Hence I underscore these central words of Piagets: exclusively and only. Put otherwise, Piaget seems to acknowledge that openers for learning, as important as they are, do not provide exclusive or convenient access to the total learning process. He is not unambiguous on the point. But he appears to imply that, at some point, not clearly defined, a "mutual respect" can develop between "new" learners and those "more experienced" that will permit using *and* leaping over the shoulders of the past. This "time when [the new learner] will be happy to be guided and taught" seems to have two major characteristics: the "more experienced" person will have learned to take on colearner qualities and yet retain any reasonable expertise; and the new learner will have a methodology sufficiently in place to somewhat separate the intellectual or ethical wheat from the chaff.

Compelling evidence implies that biased and variable attention was accorded to Piaget's ideology for intervening, however, which clearly seeks to maximize ownership and involvement by the learner. Four points serve to sketch the character of the compelling evidence.

First, the central figures at Bolivar clearly were very strong on the ideology of self-determination. Apparently Piaget was in this sense taken *very* seriously by intervenors. Given cases in which "grandiose fantasies" about "doing good" for humankind motivated intervenors to take forceful initiatives which might have seriously compromised employee ownership and involvement,[114] one gets the impression that intervenors often were at a polar extreme. Thus Duckles acknowledges taking "the ideology of self-determination to an extreme when I do not even make appropriate comments or raise questions that need to be raised."[115]

Second, the record does not contain much evidence at Bolivar of the several kinds of interventions emphasized throughout both parts of this volume–human-processual or technostructural approaches as they relate people, and technology through organizational processes and structures. Thorsrud's sociotechnical seminar seems the major exception, perhaps *the* exception. What did intervenors do? Basically, they sought to create space and time–as by scheduling periodic meetings of employees and managers–where participants could "*break out* of the traditional ways of relation to each other that are dictated by the system."[116] No evidence exists of the application of designs to facilitate such "breaking out"–as by inducing feedback, explicitly building skills, moving toward regenerative systems, and so on. And although he acknowledges the value of (apparently rare) confrontations to the "new tradition of frankness" at Bolivar,[117] Duckles provides no evidence of designs that explicitly facilitate and legitimate openness, perhaps out of reasonable care that retribution might follow.[118] In any case, Duckles tells us in connection with one confrontation only that it "took courage," was a "great emotional strain" on the employee, and that her derivative pain is "one of the powerful inhibitors" restraining others from similar confrontations.[119] These facts can be interpreted as evidence of the commitment of the intervenors to self-determination, or as timidity.

Third, the general hands-off style at Bolivar was reasonable, given the experience of the intervenors. As Duckles observes: "None of us had any experience in such a program in this kind of setting."[120] In this case, Piaget's prescriptions were not adhered to: he certainly implied both substantive and processual interventions by knowledgeable resource-persons who (to be sure) were not to act like autocratic experts. The intervenors at Bolivar did include experienced social scientists. But that experience was focused on describing organizational situations rather than in prescribing and achieving a specific, desired organizational situation; moreover, that social-science expertise does not seem to have much influenced interventions at Bolivar.[121]

Fourth, although the ideology basically emphasized employee self-determination, practice at Bolivar seems to have been inconsistent. Consider this contrast. The mode at Bolivar implies a less robust intervenor's role than, for example, that sketched in the first section of Chapter 6 (Summarizing the Available Literature) in connection with a Flexi-Time application. As Bolivar is described—a nonconfrontive environment with an economically and psychologically dependent work force[122]—careful efforts may have been appropriate to nourish employee ownership and involvement. But practice sometimes violated this general prescription in significant ways. Thus WIP was inaugurated when "about half" of the employees raised their hands in agreement, and no hands were raised in opposition.[123] Similarly, the extension of EIT (in the words of a friendly observer) largely skipped-over the processes of self-determination in "the desire to please as many people as possible." The consequences: EIT ". . . is seen by many, not as something that employees have accomplished for themselves, but as something that has . . . been granted to them,"[124] more or less in the traditional mode.

Lack of Tethering by Consistent Values. Although at this remove one cannot be certain about the full range of values that guided Bolivar, the issue has such transcendant significance that one must use available sources to gain as much insight as possible. In addition to being tentative, the development below will be complex, consisting of three major themes. Thus analysis will deal, in turn, with: the place of values in OD; the treatments of values by intervenors at Bolivar; and a review of the evidence implying that inconsistent values underlay Bolivar and/or that a consistent set of values was not effectively set in a place.

To begin, above all, OD implies a basic agreement about values that should characterize the work site.[125] The point must be qualified in two ways, but still remains robust. As Chapters 1 to 3 in Part 1 should make clear, those values can fade and blur; and they do contain inconsistencies and forces in opposition. But the central tendencies seem clear enough, with (as in the case of the guidelines for feedback) quite specific working rules of thumb sometimes being available. As the chapters beyond the introductory three make plain, on balance, the technology of the laboratory approach to OD can lay substantial claim to being able to energize that central set of values—certainly not in all cases, but definitely in more rather than in fewer cases.

Let us be more specific about the general learning model in OD. The meta-values of OD emphasize choice and are seen as need-fulfilling in several senses, especially in that competent individuals require effective feedback and disclosure. That is to say, all things being relatively equal, individuals strongly prefer regenerative interaction. In interaction-centered approaches, individuals get learning experiences with values, attitudes, and skills that are appropriate for generating what individuals generally prefer. Although the challenges will differ depending upon whether stranger or family experiences are employed, in both cases learning must be transferred and/or translated into organizatioal behaviors, structures, or policies. Boss' discussion in Chapter 6 of Part 1 nicely illustrates such a comprehensive OD process, beginning with interaction-centered designs that facilitate later changes in policies and structures.

If the point of entry is through policies or structure, as in job enlargement or Flexi-Time, the approach must be somewhat more complicated. Thus the concept must be introduced in ways that permit the clients to conclude that their needs can be met by the concept, a conclusion ideally arrived at without damaging the client's sense of ownership. In addition, the application of the concept also should respect OD values. The description of Flexi-Time in Chapter 6 above illustrates one approach to touching both of these bases.

So much by way of recalling the critical role of values in OD and how they interact with empirical conditions. Because of the subtlety of the issues, tracking the Bolivar concept of values presents some real challenges. Three points underlay this conclusion.

First, at its best, the Bolivar treatment of values focuses on the "four principles," which are global, hard to be against in any abstract sense, and come with little guidance for being translated into action. This is a difficult combination and troubles, for at least three reasons. Thus the principles do not provide specific operational guidance, as Bolivar intervenors sometimes reflect.[126] And they seem seriously incomplete, as Harman's recommendation of "mutuality" suggests. In addition, the principles more tolerably deal with the extreme cases than with the kinds of issues likely to be encountered in practice. Witness Duckles' reasonable development of the point that each principle must be considered along with all others in a systemic way, in discussing the specific content of the Bolivar "spirit":[127]

> Individuation cannot be taken to the extreme of a separate program for each employee, but it can act as a limit on democracy in that the majority of employees cannot decide that the wishes of any minority are of no consequence.
>
> In the same spirit, it would be inconsistent for the majority to decide that a minority of employees should be laid off, for some gain of the majority. This would violate the principle of security.

The questions remain, nonetheless. When push comes to shove, as it often will, is it individuation or democracy, on balance?

Second, at its worst, the treatment of values can get very careless at Bolivar. Given that intervenors were not political or social philosophers, the usages still surprise in several particulars. In a general sense, that is, interpretations about what Bolivar should do wandered over a huge spectrum. Should WIP contribute to increased satisfaction and personal development? Or should it be a Work Improvement Program, with a definite tilt toward increased productivity? Or should Bolivar be an "industrial democracy," interpreted in ways that would jolt everyone to the right of Jean Jacques Rousseau, at least as popularly viewed? Should workers only have "a say" about what affects their lives, or is self-determination the goal?

Consider a few examples of this normative casualness. Sometimes the treatment suggests a kind of congenial invisible hand. In one source, for example, the reader learns that the joint-membership committee "structure has developed a new cooperative mode."[128] This could be taken to imply that structure can induce appropriate behavior and values. This may be the case, but it probably begs a crucial chicken-or-egg question. In other cases, value issues get submerged in a kind of unrestrained groupism. For example, Duckles notes that Bolivar employees do not compare to some European employees who have legislative mandates to appoint workers to corporate boards of directors. "This is not ruled out in the Bolivar Project but," Duckles adds, "if it ever happens, it will be because Harman employees have decided this is something that they want."[129] Whichever of several interpretations one places on these words, care seems appropriate. In the case of the far more trivial issue of bonus pay for EIT, boundaries *were firmly set for* Bolivar employees, as the new committee structure was definitely intended to guarantee, over the broadest range. Nonetheless Duckles sometimes seems to reject *any* statement of values, other than that which evolves in situ. Consider this discussion of consensus, which governs decisions in the Working Committee: "One member of the committee who is not in accord with a proposal can hold up the final decision. This is not because of a policy that was set forth in the beginning, but because the members of the committee take each other's views seriously."[130]

Third, at other times, intervenors reflect that they intend to work toward a range of value-loaded behaviors, skills, and attitudes—which is of course what any program of change must do, whether explicitly and consistently or implicitly and at sixes and sevens—but without much specificity.[131] Thus Duckles argues that "the development of democracy" requires, among other factors:[132]

- Nonstereotypic ways of relating
- Learning management skills
- Developing commitments to groups and group processes
- Learning to deal with human differences

Duckles here implies, but does not specify, a number of values for Bolivar. Is openness, for example, nonstereotypic? And how does one go about attaining openness if it is? Clearly, value-constraints are appropriate. Certainly, for example, Duckles does not mean to imply that commitments to *any* groups or processes are desired or desirable. The essential point can be put positively by using "participation" as an illustration. Prescribing participation implies a value, to be sure, but not a specific or even revealing one. Without nit-picking, participation must be diversely specified by a range of values. For example,

- Which of the many kinds of participation—representative systems or whatever—are at issue?
- What limits constrain the range of legitimate impact of whatever direct or representative forms are chosen?
- What value-loaded skills are required or useful?
- What guidelines prescribe operational ways of approaching those skills?

The full range of prescriptive "oughts" are relevant, indeed crucial. As Argyris notes, acceptance of the high-level "should" does not necessarily imply the induction of appropriate skills.[133] Moreover, the former without the latter can be seriously counterproductive.

Let us now turn to the final of the three themes of this subsection—a review of the empirical evidence to make a best-guess about whether consistent values underlay Bolivar and/or were effectively or generally set in place there. That is, the subsection above may be picky; it may fixate on words while the real payoff inheres in what actually happens.

The change in focus does not change the basic conclusion. Whether by design or circumstance, that is, *the* essential manifestation of WIP was a structural one, which seemed too little constrained by values of the kind detailed in Chapters 1 to 3 of Part 1. Six points suggest the dimensions of the implied argument, but hardly exhaust it.

First, and paramountly, the normative system at Bolivar in important particulars does not seem capable of inducing the behaviors and attitudes appropriate for the new structures. More specifically, the new structure implies regenerative interaction, or something very much like it. It does not seem to exist, overall. Oppositely, indeed, the evidence implies that the 1978 Bolivar has major characteristics of a degnerative interaction system, with strong suggestions of a crisis of agreement, and with no explicit ameliorative designs in sight. Note that, as Macy observes, EIT's dysfunctional features were obvious very early in the game—in fact, several years before the availability of the data sketched in the section above concerning adverse EIT effects on employees.[134] In addition, foremen and supervisors (who are not on EIT) saw (see) it as causing major problems, including cheating on quantity and quality. This apparently requires additional supervisory effort and creates friction with employees consistent with the Michigan results reviewed above. Obviously, the norms and processes for getting such data into decision-making did not work well, at the very least. More likely, EIT was extended before any realistic effort had been undertaken to develop an appropriate culture for supporting and constraining EIT. Illustratively, the core groups seem reasonable vehicles for inducing appropriate norms and processes for regenerative systems *throughout Bolivar,* assuming for now that the Advisory Committee and Working Committee had developed such cultures in their microcosms, as observers often state or imply. But the core groups started with several serious handicaps: They came three years after WIP started; EIT got extended just as they were barely started; it appears that the core groups were motivated to sell EIT, as much as anything else, rather than culturally cushion its application; and we learn that core groups did not function well, whatever their intended mission. In sum, various Bolivar subunits—the experimental sociotechnical groups, or the Pre-Assembly Core Group—might have developed values that suitably adjusted work changes to the cultural norms and nervous systems of the employees. There is no evidence of such an effort for the broader population which quickly was allowed to vote on EIT, however.

Second, to refine the guess-cum-evidence above somewhat, note the failure of the 1973 survey data to evolve into an impactful survey/feedback intervention. This bobtailed intervention could have provided early and broad experience with regenerative interaction systems.

What accounts for the 1974 fizzle of the feedback of the 1973 data? The record is far from complete, but it appears that useful guidelines did not support the survey/feedback intervention in important particulars. Several sources provide positive statements of such useful guidelines.[135] At Bolivar, several counterproductive features characterized the abortive survey/feedback process, whether or not they were somehow unavoidable in the complex and uncertain atmosphere that certainly existed at Bolivar:

- There does not seem to have been broad and open participation in the design of the survey instrument, as by using "sensing groups" to suggest items, while also building credibility for the survey and involving all organization ranks at very early stages.[136]
- There seems to have been no clear schedule re the survey and its implementation.
- Approximately 9 months intervened between beginning the survey and release of *Final Technical Report,* which is far too long to sustain broad interest.[137]
- There was no clear mechanism for dealing with survey data *at all levels:* the Advisory Committee did exist at corporate/international levels, and the Working Committee at the plant level seemed very helpful in working with the survey data; but nothing like the core groups existed to disseminate findings and to action-plan throughout the system.

In short, an incomplete action-research model can be associated with the 1973 survey data, which implies loss of major opportunities to signal the appropriateness of more regenerative interaction sequences, as well as loss of opportunity for system-wide practice with the values and skills underlying them.

Relatedly, *third,* available evidence implies inadequate attention to the cultural preparedness of the host organization.[138] To be sure, the point must be variously qualified in specific cases, but the point applies far more than less. Note that at the very top levels, a serendipitous enthusiasm and extensive interaction seem to have bonded together the very top management and union officials. But even there, early normative agreement seems to have been seriously incomplete, even naive. Consider Harman's late addition of "mutuality" to the four guiding principles. More broadly, intervenors were aware that changes in jobs would have to be supported by an appropriate culture—values reflected in policies, supervisory practices, and so on. Thus Macy observes:[139]

> Joint committees place two types of strains on their union and management members. Traditional union-management relationships are built on bargaining skills, explicit agreements, and mechanisms to enforce those agreements. Cooperative union-management relationships are built on problem-solving skills, gentlemen's agreements, and trust. Both union and management members of cooperative committees must learn problem-solving skills. They must also learn to trust one another, the consultants, and the evaluators. Building trust may be the more difficult problem.

An orthodox OD effort would early address such issues—whether in stranger T-groups, in family teams, or whatever—but available documents do not detail how (or if) the broad cultural preparedness of the host was designed for. For certain, however, "spelling out the [four] principles that . . . should govern the worklife of hourly employees and managers alike" was seen as a (the?) prime way of seeing that Bolivar did not stay "locked into a hierarchical bureaucratic system."[140] And intervenors clearly intended "a new style of leadership in both management and the union," even as they recognized that the four principles "do not provide a detailed blueprint of steps to be taken and concrete goals to be achieved."[141] The requirements?[142]

> Managers needed examples of how to analyze problems cooperatively and stimulate participation in decision-making. Union leaders needed to learn how to bargain cooperatively (in such a way that both sides gain) without weakening their position in adversary collective bargaining.

Some "new structures, processes, and relationships" did develop,[143] especially at the top levels in the Advisory Committee and the Working Committee—without which Michigan's Institute of Social Research concludes "the WIP program probably could not have survived the last four years."[144] But lower-level analogues were rare, and not the results of specific designs where they did develop.

Whatever the specific approaches to such value-loaded skill-training and cultural transformation, the preponderance of evidence implies that it was not effective at Bolivar, especially at the working level. To be sure, the job was awesome, especially because of the historically adversary relationships of labor and management at Bolivar and such calamities as massive layoffs. But the conclusion remains. Indeed, one may argue that the work culture deteriorated during WIP at Bolivar. Witness that perceptions of the union change not at all, and that changes in Bolivar as an organization constitute a mixed bag, at best, containing many changes in directions opposed to those intended/implied. Better said perhaps—with noteworthy exceptions in the Advisory and Working Committees—direct learning designs for such normative-or value-shaping do not appear to have received major attention. As for the employees, they are broadly described as industrially unsocialized, let alone sophisticated about managerial causes and consequences. Substantial effort was expended in somehow training the core groups. But that came late in the Bolivar experience and the Michigan evaluators (at least) express disappointment that the core groups did not function as intended.

Fourth, all concerned seemed to have been genuinely surprised at rediscovering the "paradox of democracy" in EIT's providing attractive release time but yet polluting the quality of working life. That is, the learning involves recognition that a majority can choose unwisely in the purported service of its own interests which, in turn, implies the lack of value constraints emphasized above. That this surprises at all, of course, implies that too little initial attention was given to fundamental consideration of the value consequences of the basic institutional approach: "democracy" at best guarantees only that *desired* goals will be acted on, not that *desirable* goals will be chosen. Moreover, if anything, "democracy" does not mean a one-time vote: it implies a continuous processing of wants and needs, a review of experience, and so on, as well as cultural values and processes capable of supporting that major effort. As Duckles rightly observes: " . . . democracy is more than a preplanned format for participating in decision-making."[145]

The surprise also surprises in several other senses. Thus the Bolivar management and employees were quite unsophisticated, the latter being people of the land with little industrial experience living in an economy just moving out of dependence on agriculture, with many of their hearts probably more in the fields than in the plant. "Guided democracy" might reasonably have been more explicitly in the air. Perhaps it was, indeed. In significant senses, officialdom had implied early that it was aware of such a paradox—that is, they did not trust the prevailing values or processes. For example, both union and management officialdom at some times firmly "guided" the employees—as in forbidding a bonus; and at other times these same officials *decided not to obstruct* employee desires for EIT interpreted as early release—whether because of "industrial democracy" or pure politics, or of patient wisdom or lack of wit and will, we do not know and cannot safely speculate.

Fifth, given the adversary relations that had characterized union/management relations, one can at least raise the issue of whether or not the Bolivar experience existed at two distinct levels. Structurally, the Advisory and Working Committees may have been seen as *the* arenas for the company and management to authoritatively express their manifold interests, blocking one another when necessary via their role of consensual decision-making. Amorphously, the "four principles" could have existed as generalized wishes or hopes—increased satisfaction and personal growth or Work Improvement Program, or even industrial democracy, with no explicit concern about "What's in it for all of us." In any case, the apparent failure to raise aggressively differences in values or ideologies may have cost in at least four senses.

- Bolivar may have forfeited a reasonable approach to change. Although this does not always characterize practice, many OD designs rest on notions of reciprocity or exchange. Relevantly, the reader can consult the development of the notion in Chapters 3 and 5 of Part 1, as in the discussion of role negotiation, contracting, and so on.

In multiple contrast, Bolivar seems to have variously blurred the sharp edges of ideological or practical differences in goals, values, or needs, perhaps to get something going. For example, the four principles can hardly be opposed, in the abstract;[146] verbalisms in effect unrealisticaly downplay or put off the tough issues of trade-offs, as in the early insistence that WIP was oriented toward increases in satisfaction rather than in productivity; or suitable trade-offs could not be arranged, as in the cost saving-sharing proposal. Exceptions to this generalization clearly exist,[147] but the point still applies.

• The approach at Bolivar may have lost a useful opportunity to abort the program. Granted that Bolivar might not have been possible at all if Harman had emphasized productivity as well as satisfaction, that does not preclude choice, and it certainly does not negate early value clarification.[148] Sometimes the intervenor can best say: "Nature abhors an asymmetry. People cannot simply give without getting. Let's clarify all the values; and if we cannot figure out some realistic basis for exchange, I'd advise against going much further."

Blurring the tough issues will be especially hazardous when they can be reasonably expected to arise. When sociotechnical approaches work, as Chapter 2 above suggests, increased productivity *and* satisfaction often result. Aggressive forethought seems appropriate. Even when the early possiblity of productivity increases was dealt with up-front at Bolivar, however, it had a very tentative, bye-and-bye, and narrow focus. As Duckles notes: "*If* increased productivity is *a by-product* of the program, ways of *rewarding the employee . . . will become* legitimate matters for inclusion in the program."[149] If circumstances give us enough time to consider a range of reasonable alternatives, Duckles might have added, and if rewarding the firm as well as the union for such success also became legitimate objects of concern. Events proved less benign, it appears, in the groundswell of enthusiasm for EIT.

• The approach at Bolivar may have precluded a useful flexibility. Understandings can change, and differences in values may unexpectedly emerge. When EIT as early-leaving developed in the experimental sociotechnical groups, for example, Harman might reasonably have asked in the absence of the data that the Michigan evaluation team presented later—What's in that for us? Workers get to leave early; that can cause jealousies; and it may even encourage shoddy performance just to get done. I had in mind improving the work site, not encouraging employees to abandon it! Did such a position underlay Harman's suggested fifth principle—"mutuality"? That guess does not offend.

• The approach at Bolivar may have failed. By hypothesis, the new structure proved no real constraint against the popular appeal of EIT. The attempt to finesse via structure the specification of values and constraints, in sum, could have encouraged the build-up of forces that overwhelmed the structure. However, note that officials did rule out a bonus for work beyond standard.

Sixth—and the point almost startles—even cases of the successful induction of an appropriate culture or normative context at Bolivar seem to be dealt with vaguely, at arm's length. Thus Macy observes: "Perhaps the most impressive thing about the project is that an initial climate of experimentation, trust, and faith was produced in the organization."[150] The specific referent is the "*local* management and *local* union representatives and . . . *top* corporate and *top* union officials." The penetration seems limited, however. The thirty-three core groups, Macy reports in late 1978, have not been meeting regularly for about 2 years. Moreover, Macy provides no details about this central if limited outcome re climate; indeed, in a sense he appears to argue that no details can be provided about how the outcome was induced or came about. "One of the great unknowns in organization change research," he explains, "is how this is done."[151] Given our still-fragmentary understanding, Chapters 1 to 3 in Part 1 argue oppositely that we do know much about what happens in climate-setting and why.

Issues of Macro Diagnosis/Prescription. Only a very wise person can tell what the Bolivar data really mean, but some reasonable speculations imply that they are to a substantial degree results of inadequate diagnosis and prescription, especially in connection with work standards and associated reward/punishment systems. For example, consider only one speculative but realistic notion that can account for the characterization of WIP/EIT:

> Basically, the industrial standards were inconsistent: "loose" in some cases, "tight" in others. This could have been the objective case, but it is necessary only that substantial numbers of opinion leaders believe it to be the case.
>
> As is common, these standards would rest on "unfair" considerations: differential power in the departments–including negotiating skills or centrality in the flow of work–or on historical accidents. Those who merely worked hard and produced a lot would find their standards rising without corresponding recompense. Those who played the game effectively might keep their standards low without arousing suspicion.
>
> To make a long story short, EIT could simply have made a bad situation worse. Groups who had dogged it before EIT could easily raise their output and go home early; previously industrious groups would get screwed again.

This hypothesis has a general credibility, given other experience as well as data from Bolivar.[152] Moreover, the interpretation fits nicely with Bolivar results summarized above: for example, that good work after WIP is less likely than before to lead to reward, and that poor work is less likely to lead to punishment.

This hypothesis also could be further elaborated. Why did people at once raise their productivity, improve the quality of their work, and yet report a worsening quality of working life? Try these explanatory contributors, for openers: Job security was enhanced; wages and fringes rose over 40 percent during the WIP interval, more or less;[153] the physical work site was improved in some (many?) particulars; and there may have been *no comparable place to go,* given the early-industrial phase through which the once-pastoral Bolivar area was going and the economic ups and downs that might have raised the salience of staying put, growing concerns notwithstanding. Increased pressure at work—coercion to finish early, or whatever—could simply have increased even faster than such added inducements to stay in the system. Relatedly, the sense of broad injustice or inequity concerning EIT could have burgeoned, even as specific individuals liked the free time for themselves. Absolutely, employees are "better off"; relatively, they are "worse off." The criticality of "relative deprivation" has long been appreciated, of course, especially when the referent is "the good old days."

Consider another tack which contributes to the hypothesis above but does not depend on it. It seems at least clear that other compensations for EIT were possible and that they could have other consequences for union, management, and employees. Consider the situation if a new basic union contract—as does that of the United Mine Workers—tied management contributions to pensions or insurance *to the amount of physical output* rather than to persons working or hours worked. Conceivably, given suitable job security for employees already on-board, that would change the force-field for the union. As it was—since concern about protecting the number of jobs remained very important for the union, and since continuation of WIP also was important to union power figures like Bluestone—EIT as-early-leaving seemed unavoidable.

The general point did not escape those at Bolivar, of course, but it seems a matter of too little and/or too late. Thus an In-Plant School was started, but that was nearly a year after the EIT boomlet began and just about the time that EIT went plant-wide. Even more significant, perhaps, a cost-savings-sharing plan was proposed in Phase V, but failed to attract sufficient top-level support. That plan explicitly raised *the* issue—What's in it for all?—and could have channeled EIT effects in different directions.

Linking QWL to the Host. The Bolivar experience is not conclusive on an issue facing all QWL efforts: how to link the QWL apparatus to the normal structures for decision-making. Broadly, two major possibilities exist,[154] which might be used alone or in combination:

- Utilize the usual decision-makers in the new QWL roles.
- Utilize individuals not normally in command who develop QWL recommendations for the usual decision-makers.

At Bolivar, the Advisory Committee was clearly the "same people in new roles." The Working Committee included traditional power figures and their representatives in new roles; the core groups included normal power figures as well as employees chosen (by management?) or elected, apparently by employees.

The chapters above provide several examples of variations for this crucial change-role. These examples include both ad hoc and limited efforts, as well as such comprehensive efforts as those encompassed by variants of Zand's "collateral organization."

The two basic alternatives have mixed advantages/disadvantages. Power wielders in the new change-role can provide substantial leverage, but it may be difficult for them to develop new behaviors appropriate for the QWL effort.[155] If the power figures were really good at that work, epigrammatically, QWL would not be necessary. At least, major efforts to induce and reinforce behavioral change is indicated. Alternatively, staffing the new QWL roles with individuals not holding power roles might permit greater selectivity and might reduce the training burden. But these individuals may lack clout; they may compromise the QWL effort by a derivative superabundance of caution about being Judas-goats; and their very existence may generate conflict by threatening the normal decision-makers.[156]

In addition, Bolivar philosophy about linkage seems to have zigged and zagged. Note that the Working Committee proved extremely valuable in the translation of ideas for change into practice, in the view of the Michigan evaluators. This does not surprise, for OD programs require such linkages. What does surprise is Macy's intriguing aside that the Working Committee was "initially forced on the Bolivar WIP by the National Committee on Productivity," which made a grant supporting some of the program.[157]

Methodological Issues. Finally, the Bolivar results may be an artefact of various features still beyond the normal state of the art. For example, Chapter 8 below raises a number of confoundments and constraints on OD applications, including uncommonly made distinctions between alternative concepts of change that would require different, even opposite, interpretations of the Bolivar results. The reader may wish to play that game at the appropriate time. For now, consider only one possibility. The "bad" data from Bolivar may not mean that things there got worse. Indeed, things may have improved, but just not as rapidly as the expectations of employees burgeoned about what constituted a tolerably just and fair organization! An apparent OD "limited success," that is to say, may have been successful in a not-so-obvious but more profound sense.

Costs and Benefits of Interventions in Large Organizations
Some Generalizations

This and the preceding six chapters have described and analyzed a broad range of OD interventions in large organizations. Those chapters support at least ten generalizations, which are briefly detailed here.

Generalization 1

OD efforts stress the "organic" versus the "mechanistic" nature of organizations.[158] As opposed to traditional organization theory, that is, the emphasis is on assembling the competencies necessary to do the job, on team development, and on problem-solving. Similarly, as opposed to traditional organization theory with its emphasis on functional specialization, OD applications stress organizing around flows of work, projects, or matrix overlays.[159]

This orientation is at once boon and bane. Taken reasonably far, the orientation highlights the emerging character of institutions, encourages flexibility and adaptation, and also mobilizes major motivational forces that can be blunted by mechanistic approaches. This is the thrust of many interaction-centered OD efforts, such as the program discussed in Chapter 1 which sought to induce a specific style of interpersonal and intergroup relations in a large organization.

Taken too far, however, the organic orientation fixates attention on the quicksilver of interaction, while neglecting broader institutional features such as policies, structures, compensation systems, and so on. Epigrammatically, the need is to tie together OD values and perspectives with such systemic interventions as Flexi-Time (Chapter 6), MBO (Chapter 4), or compensation systems (Chapter 7). Preceding chapters establish that such an integration is possible, if still uncommon.

Generalization 2

Relatedly, the OD literature stresses the ideal of a change program simultaneously affecting behavior, structure, and policy and procedure.[160] The ideal of simultaneous or comprehensive change is closely approached in only a few cases, however.

Short of simultaneity, the literature also implies some guidelines for the order of sequencing components of total OD efforts. Tushman's analysis seems apt.[161] He considers only "behavioral" and "structural" interventions, and isolates two orders of precedence:

- Structural, then behavioral, change
- Behavioral, then structural, change

Tushman makes three main points. First, the second strategy tends to dominate in most OD applications. Second, whatever strategy leads an OD program, "a dual approach is . . . more effective . . . than either taken alone. . . ." Third, in organizations with a relatively certain technology, the structural-behavioral strategy seems the more appropriate.

In addition, changes in structure or policy and procedure may be especially useful as first-stage interventions in organizations which are not yet "culturally prepared" for interaction-centered interventions, or where the integrity of the chain of command is highly valued. Many military or paramilitary organizations may have such a character, for example.

Generalization 3

Both simultaneity and comprehensiveness of OD efforts pose significant difficulties for many reasons, one of them being the different philosophic orientations underlying interaction-centered and structure-centered approaches. Consider the issue of psychological ownership. That constitutes no obvious problem for interaction-centered designs, whose practice and theory are steeped in voluntarism, immediate experience, and so on. In contrast, structure-centered approaches tend to be rooted "out there"—in the organization behavior literature, in theoretical linkages of covariants expressed in technical language, and so on—rather than "in here" as is much more the case with interaction-centered designs. The appearance of studies with a strong OD orientation taking a structural approach thus is a highly welcome sign of progress, but nonetheless implies the need for safeguarding the sense of ownership.

Generalization 4

Where to start an OD intervention? The conventional wisdom prescribes "the top," or as close as possible thereto, for obvious reasons. But the evidence reviewed above, as well as independent research,[162] suggests that advice may be too restrictive. This list of loci inspired by Beckhard and Harris seems to do nicely:[163]

- The top management of a system
- The top of a subsystem which is "autonomous enough"
- Groups or organizations known to be ready for change because they anticipate pain or discomfort in its absence
- Groups or organizations presently experiencing pain or discomfort
- New teams or systems without a history and no clear models for operating
- Staff units that can serve as models, or which will aid in the implementation of later interventions
- Temporary project systems, the reasons for and duration of whose existence and tenure are problem-defined

Generalization 5

Points of organizational tension or uncertainty are strategic ones for applications of the laboratory approach in organizations. The fragmentation may set department versus department, line versus staff, headquarters versus the field, or labor versus management.

Generalization 6

These strategic targets for change or choice impose correspondingly great demands on the adequacy of the theory underlying OD applications designed to remedy matters, but these demands often exceed our practical and theoretical grasp. Four particulars will drive the point home. *First,* OD still lacks a relatively comprehensive theory to guide its applications.[164] Numerous bits and pieces of useful theory were reviewed above, of course, and they permit some optimism that we are on the correct track. Moreover, retrospective case analysis implies that the basic OD approach is viable. To be specific, Dunn and Swierczek tested hypotheses relevant to change, using a substantial number of studies of a broad range of approaches to change as the data base. They conclude that three conditions stand out as characteristic of successful efforts of change:[165]

- Collaborative modes of intervention
- Participative change-agent orientations
- Strategies emphasizing high levels of participation

No surprises here for OD fans.

Second, this theoretical deficit inheres in the inadequate volume of "rigorous research" dealing with applications of the laboratory approach to organization change. Thus, Edgar Schein and Warren Bennis noted in 1965 that:

> Discouraging, but not unexpectedly, the research effort seems weakest in those situations where the risks are highest and the tasks are most complex. We are referring to the uses of laboratory training in inducing change in organizations. In some organizational change programs, a great deal of attention is being paid to research, but not enough research is yet being done.[166]

There have been real improvements over the decade-plus since 1965 in this puny state of the literature. But the generalization still applies, and in uncomfortable degree, at this later date. For example, three observers conclude a broad 1977 review of the literature in this way: "Although there is an abundance of literature on OD, there is very little research on its effects that can withstand the rigorous testing most social scientists would expect." These observers add:

"Furthermore, there is research available on only six [types] of interventions of the wide variety reported in the literature."[167]

Third, existing OD research has important methodological and design limitations, although overall judgments often will differ depending upon which view one takes of the proverbial glass of water—as half-full or as half-empty. Thus, Porras and Berg conclude in their survey of a small population of studies that "the overall quality of OD research methodology was spotty."[168] But they still emphasize that 50 percent of the studies in their survey utilized relatively strong research designs, and they emphasize that their panel of studies does not permit support of what they call that "common myth about OD research, i.e., that very little OD research has been done that deserves the designation of 'scientific.' "[169] Oppositely, Peggy Morrison notes in her study of twenty-six pieces of OD research that "only three met all [twelve] criteria" that Campbell and Stanley have proposed for judging the validity of a design's results. She concludes: "The present underdeveloped state of the art of OD evaluation demonstrates that practitioners must (1) determine appropriate measures for assessing; (2) develop more adequate instruments for measuing change related to OD; and (3) consistently utilize more rigorous designs for their studies."[170]

Despite such differences in how one evaluates what exists, however, some points seem beyond dispute. Thus, more OD studies with longitudinal designs would be most welcome, for numerous methodological reasons. Thus only about a quarter of the studies in a recent survey of the literature, a select population to begin with, have time frames of more than 12 months.[171] Clearly, that complicates judgments about the persistence of any changes. Moreover, despite their strong representation in the small Porras and Berg population of studies, few experimental or quasiexperimental designs existed in a batch of nearly 600 OD sources.[172] In addition, the all-but-universal lack of controls or comparison groups complicates the explanation of observed effects in terms of the OD intervention.

Fourth, most OD research has a strong focus on limited outcomes such as the before and after change in an individual's ability to emphathize with others. Commonly, input or process variables receive less attention, as do the second-order and third-order changes described in the opening pages of this chapter. Exceptions to these generalizations exist, both early and late. But the generalization still holds.

Straightforward summary is possible concerning this fourth problem with the laboratory approach to organization change. With rare exceptions, OD approaches to organization change have not been validated in the broader sense of tracing their influence on such desirable states as high productivity and high satisfaction, or of tracking the processes involved.[173] Powerful reasons explain this less than robust condition, of course, but its effects are nonetheless real. Primary among them is the possibility that the emphasis on self-reports of attitudes and perceptions will simply induce respondents to react in terms of what they correctly perceive as the desired outcomes of interventions. "Given the strong value system underlying the use of OD in organizations," three acute observers note, "the use of such measures poses serious threats to the internal validity of the research."[174]

Generalization 7

Evidence suggests that OD designs can have similar effects over a range of relevant conditions, but there is also every reason to believe that major increases in our theoretical and applied knowledge are both possible and desirable. Convenient targets for such greater specificity include:

- Designs that are age-specific or relate to the stage of a person's development[175]
- Designs that are size specific and relate to the number of participants
- Designs that are culture sensitive or personality sensitive, as in their interaction versus structural bias to suit different hosts or clients
- Designs that relate to differences in the host organization, such as stage of development, maturity of product line, and so on

Growth in such specificity will signal the emergence of an increasingly comprehensive OD theory as the next chapter indicates.

Moreover, and a related issue, knowledge about the relative power of different designs under the same or similar conditions has a patently high value. To team-build or to intervene at a sociotechnical level? Or both? These constitute the central analytical/applied targets at issue here.

Growth in both kinds of specificity will signal the evolution of an increasingly sophisticated OD; and there clearly remains a long way to go on both kinds of issues. The value of the goal and our limited progress toward it get ready illustration in the work of Pasmore and King. In comparable (but not identical) units of the same organization, these researchers contrasted the effects on attitudes and productivity of three OD designs:

- *Survey/feedback*, which followed a "bottom up"[176] flow of feedback—with feedback meetings initially being held by several groups of employees, who developed action plans to be considered by management—in contrast to a "waterfall' or "cascade" of meetings down the organization.
- *Sociotechnical*, which Passmore and King describe as including "autonomous work groups, integrated support functions, challenging job assignments, job mobility, facilitative leadership, managerial decision

information for operators, and continuous learning and evolution."[177] This reflects the usual wisdom. Note, however, that the employees in this case were neither handpicked nor was their work site specially built for the sociotechnical organization of work. The presence of these two conditions is said to facilitate sociotechnical applications, so Pasmore and King had a tougher case.

- *Job redesign* by task force committees of union, management, and employees from each area of the plant, responding in part to survey results. Job rotation began, employees were able to learn and perform a range of tasks, and some of the most repetitive tasks were eliminated. But these changes stopped, of apparent necessity, far short of the substantial control of the work possible under the sociotechnical mode.

Avoiding details, Pasmore and King observed major similarities and differences over the 2½-year duration of their action research, varying their treatments according to a definite schedule.[178] Basically, attitudinal changes resulting from all interventions were basically similar,[179] although some edge went to combined sociotechnical and survey/feedback interventions.[180] However, only the sociotechnical intervention resulted in major savings in costs and improvements in productivity. "Major" in this case proved substantial indeed.[181] Based on past experience in the firm, approximately 1.1 million units were expected during start-up, whereas action production was 1.45 million units. Moreover, start-up costs were nearly 8 percent lower than estimated. In addition, industrial engineering standards indicated a crew of 126 to 129 employees would be required, but only 104 were used. This implied a cost-saving of at least $164,000, by conservative estimate.

As attention-getting as these comparisons are, however, they do not exhaust what needs to be known. For example, it is not clear whether the specific character of the experimental site was determinative, and thus whether other sites might yield different comparisons. The list of such issues could be extended greatly. But the general point should be clear. Pasmore and King have brought us a useful distance; and they also imply how much farther we must go.

Generalization 8

Despite the findings sketched above, danger as well as value may inhere in sociotechnical interventions, and especially in structural interventions that place little or no emphasis on the processes of application. Patently, that is, structure constitutes a powerful determinant of behavior, as Chapters 2, 3, and 6 above particularly imply. However, structural interventions may encourage autocratic impositions, mechanistic approaches to human systems, or approaches that are concept-oriented rather than being application-oriented. This often seems to be the case with job enrichment, for example. With care, however, OD values and orientation can guide structural interventions in significant ways.

Generalization 9

A number of designs reviewed in the seven chapters on interventions in large organizations seem to work even as they imply potential dilemmas.[182] The reference is perhaps most pointedly to Chapter 5, but the concern applies to other chapters as well. For example, debriefing designs for those being let go by an organization raise such issues:

- They may be mere Band-Aids that cover major underlying problems.
- They may be manipulative in the sense of being only "cooling-out" experiences.
- They may provide temporary catharsis only.
- They may generate value or ethical issues for intervenors who are concerned that the meager and limited benefits do not justify the costs and risks to participants.

For some, indeed, OD is to be feared as a formidable arsenal of designs that only make the demands of the "organization imperative" more effective and less escapable.[183] In this view, the demands of "organization" are everything, and people are to bend (or be bent) to that imperative, preferably with little overt fuss, but kicking if necessary.

This author does not subscribe to the alarmist view. But one point is inescapable. As with any technology, the more sophisticated OD designs and theory become, the more dangerous they can be in guileless or malevolent hands. The other side of that coin is that OD's potential for good also increases under the same conditions. Eternal ethical vigilance, then, is the inescapable concomitant of growth in human knowledge.

Generalization 10

Several broad conclusions seem implicit in OD applications in large organizations. They are usefully listed here, in conclusion, relying on Friedlander and Brown's summary.[184]

- OD is not a short-term process.
- The support and active involvement of top management is useful and probably necessary, especially to encourage the commitment of those at lower levels of organization.

- The support of top managment is not enough, because every OD effort of any scale requires major support from multiple levels of the hierarchy.
- Unambiguous interpretation of the results of OD efforts is difficult even under the best of circumstances.

Notes

1. John R. Kimberly and Warren R. Nielsen, "Organization Development and Change in Organizational Performance," *Administrative Science Quarterly,* Vol. 20 (June 1975), pp. 194-195.
2. Richard Beckhard, "Strategies for Large System Change," *Sloan Management Review,* Vol. 16 (Winter 1975), pp. 43-56. For a critical overview of what is called "multifaceted OD," see Frank Friedlander and L. Dave Brown, "Organization Development," *Annual Review of Psychology,* Vol. 25 (1974), pp. 332-333. See also Frank Friedlander's *Purpose and Values in OD* (Madison, Wisc.: Organization Development Divison, American Society for Training and Development, 1976), esp. pp. 12-15.
3. Prominent among the few other examples of such early comprehensive studies are Robert R. Blake, Jane S. Mouton, Louis B. Barnes, and Larry E. Greiner, "Breakthrough in Organization Development," *Harvard Business Review,* Vol. 42 (November 1964), pp. 133-135; and Alfred J. Marrow, David G. Bowers, and Stanley Seashore, *Management By Participation* (New York: Harper and Row, 1967). For recent examples, consult Carl A. Bramlette, Donald O. Jewell, and Michael H. Mescon, "Designing for Organizational Effectiveness: A Better Way," *Atlanta Economic Review,* Vol. 27 (September 1977), pp. 35-41; and Bramlette, Jewell, and Mescon, "Designing for Organizational Effectiveness; How It Works," *Atlanta Economic Review,* Vol. 27 (November 1977), pp. 10-15.
4. Michael Beer, "The Technology of Organization Development," p. 977, in Marvin D. Dunnette (ed.), *Handbook of Industrial and Organization Psychology* (Chicago: Rand McNally, 1976); and Thomas H. Patten, Jr., and Karren L. Fraser, "Using the Organizational Reward System as an OD Lever," *Journal of Applied Behavioral Science,* Vol. 11 (December 1975), p. 457.
5. Richard E. Walton, "Contrasting Designs for Participative Systems," *Personnel Administration,* Vol. 30 (December 1967), pp. 35-47.
6. The rub, of course is that employees must perceive accurately what the compensation plan signals as the appropriate behaviors/attitudes in OD contexts. On this critical point, see Steven Kerr, "On the Folly of Rewarding A, While Hoping for B," *Academy of Management Journal,* Vol. 18 (December 1975), pp. 769-783.

7. Arthur H. Spiegel III, "How Outsiders Overhauled a Public Agency," *Harvard Business Review*, Vol. 53 (January 1975), p. 116.
8. This consciousness was reflected, for example, in the Symposium on Productivity in Government, *Public Administration Review*, Vol. 32 (November 1972). Abundant signs–both conceptual and mensural–indicate that this growing attention to productivity still has a very long way to go. The point is convincingly made by Raymond D. Horton, "Productivity and Productivity Bargaining in Government: A Critical Analysis," *Public Administration Review*, Vol. 36 (July 1976), pp. 407-414.
9. Paul D. Staudohar, "An Experiment in Increasing Productivity of Police Service Employees," *Public Administration Review*, Vol. 35 (September 1975), p. 518.
10. John P. Kenney, *Police Administration* (Springfield, Ill.: Charles C Thomas, 1972); and Kenney, "Team Policing Organization: A Theoretical Model," *Police*, Vol. 16 (August 1972).
11. Vincent Ostrom, *The Intellectual Crisis of American Public Administration* (University, Ala.: University of Alabama, 1973), esp. pp. 117-122.
12. Staudohar, "An Experiment in Increasing Productivity of Police Service Employees," p. 518.
13. National Commission on Productivity, *The Challenge of Productivity Diversity* (Washington, D.C.: General Service Administration, 1973), p. 23.
14. These come basically from Staudohar, "An Experiment in Increasing Productivity of Police Service Employees," p. 519.
15. National Commission on Productivity, *Second Annual Report*, March 1973 (Washington, D.C.: U.S. Government Printing Office, 1973), p. 48.
16. Robert C. Lind and John P. Lipsky, "The Measurement of Police Output," *Law and Contemporary Problems*, Vol. 36 (Autumn 1971), p. 569.
17. National Commission on Productivity, *First Annual Report*, March 1972 (Washington, D.C.: U.S. Government Printing Office, 1972), p. 9, names the process "productivity bargaining."
18. Staudohar, "An Experiment in Increasing Productivity of Police Service Employees."
19. See *Business Week*, January 4, 1974, p. 37; *Newsweek*, Vol. 83, April 1, 1974, p. 69; *Time*, Vol. 104, September 16, 1974, p. 86; and *Wall Street Journal*, October 2, 1973, p. 1.
20. Staudohar, "An Experiment in Increasing Productivity in Police Service Employees," pp. 520-521.
21. Dorothy Guyot, "What Productivity? What Bargain?" *Public Administration Review*, Vol. 30 (May 1976), p. 340.

22. J. Albert Reiss, *The Police and the Public* (New Haven, Conn.: Yale University, 1971).
23. Guyot, "What Productivity? What Bargain?" p. 341.
24. U.S. Department of Justice, Law Enforcement Assistance Administration, *Criminal Victimization Surveys in the Nation's Five Largest Cities* (Washington, D.C.: U.S. Government Printing Office, 1975).
25. Paul D. Staudohar, "Reply to Professor Guyot," *Public Administration Review,* Vol. 30 (May 1976), p. 344.
26. Guyot, "What Productivity? What Bargain?" p. 341.
27. Staudohar, "Reply to Professor Guyot, " p. 344.
28. Ibid.
29. Staudohar, "An Experiment in Increasing Productivity of Police Service Employees," pp. 521-522.
30. Ibid., p. 522.
31. Walton, "Contrasting Designs for Participative Systems."
32. Earl Vinson, W. Anthony Kullisch, and Richard W. Beatty, "Incentive Systems and Task Types as OD Intervention Targets," pp. 363-367, in Robert L. Taylor, Michael J. O'Connell, Robert A. Zawacki, and D. D. Warrick (eds.), *Proceedings* (Annual Meeting), Academy of Management, Orlando, Fla., August 14-17, 1977.
33. Robert T. Golembiewski, "A Behavioral Approach to Wage Administration: Work Flow and Structural Design," *Academy of Management Journal,* Vol. 6 (December 1963), pp. 367-377.
34. For the classic exposition of the general point, see Erick L. Trist and H. Murray, "Some Social and Psychological Consequenses of the Longwall Method of Goal-Getting," *Human Relations,* Vol. 4 (February 1951), pp. 3-38.
35. Robert T. Golembiewski, *Men, Management, and Morality* (New York: McGraw-Hill, 1965), esp. pp. 231-258.
36. Ibid., pp. 233-236.
37. Edward E. Lawler, "Workers Can Set Their Own Wages–Responsibility," *Psychology Today* (February 1977), pp. 109-112.
38. "Organizational, Wage System Changes Boost Productivity at Volkswagen's Auto Repair Shops in Stockholm," *World of Work Report,* Vol. 3 (January 1978), p. 4.
39. Friedlander and Brown, "Organization Development," pp. 313-320.
40. Kimberly and R. Nielsen, "Organization Development and Change in Organizational Performance," p. 192.
41. Ibid., p. 190.
42. Ibid., p. 195.

43. Ibid., pp. 197-203.

44. Ibid., pp. 203-204.

45. Richard E. Walton, "Quality of Working Life: What Is it?" *Sloan Management Review,* Vol. 15 (Fall 1973), p. 11.

46. See, for example, John A. Drexler, Jr., and Edward E. Lawler III, "A Union-Management Cooperative Project to Improve the Quality of Work Life," *Journal of Applied Behavioral Science,* Vol. 13 (October 1977), pp. 373-387; and Nelson Frye, George Seifert, and Joseph P. Yaney, "Organizational Change Through Feedback and Research (OD) Efforts," *Group and Organization Studies,* Vol. 2 (September 1977), esp. pp. 296-305.

47. David G. Bowers and Jerome L. Franklin, *Data-Based Organizational Change* (La Jolla, Calif.: University Associates, 1977); David A. Nadler, *Feedback and Organization Development* (Reading, Mass.: Addison-Wesley, 1977); and Robert T. Golembiewski and Richard Hilles, *Toward the Responsive Organization: The Theory and Practice of Survey/Feedback* (Salt Lake City, Utah: Brighton, 1979).

48. For guidance about such an effort, consult Howard Kirchenbaum, *Advanced Value Clarification* (La Jolla, Calif.: University Associates, 1977).

49. For a review of a number of QWL programs, see Edgar Weinberg, "Labor-Management Cooperation: A Report on Recent Initiatives," *Monthly Labor Review,* Vol. 99 (April 1976), pp. 13-22.

50. P. S. Goodman, *Assessing Organizational Change: The Rushton Quality of Work Experiment* (New York: Wiley-Interscience, in press).

51. Barry Macy, Edward E. Lawler III, and G. Ledford, *The Bolivar Quality of Work Experiment* (New York: Wiley Interscience, in press); and Barry A. Macy, "A Theoretical Basis for and an Assessment of the Bolivar Quality of Working Life Experiment: 1972-1977." Paper presented at 1978 Annual Meeting, Academy of Management, San Francisco, Calif., August 9-11, 1978.

52. Tennessee Valley Authority, *The Quality of Work Program and the TVA Experiment, September, 1974-December, 1975* (Chattanooga, Tenn.: Tennessee Valley Authority, 1976).

53. The detailed history of the SmithKline experience has not been written, although a number of interpretive overviews and a covey of research reports are available. For the overviews consult: *SmithKline Quality of Life Survey* (Philadelphia,Penn.: Human Resources Network, October 29, 1976), 8 pp.; and Golembiewski and Hilles, *Toward the Responsive Organization,* esp. chaps. 1-4. For some of the research reports, see Robert T. Golembiewski, Rick Hilles, and Munro Kagno, "A Longitudinal Study of Flexi-Time Effects," *Journal of Applied Behavioral Science,*

Vol. 10 (December 1974), pp. 503-532; Robert T. Golembiewski, Keith Billingsley, and Samuel Yeager, "Measuring Change and Persistence in Human Affairs," *Journal of Applied Behavioral Science,* Vol. 12 (June 1976), pp. 133-157; and Robert T. Golembiewski and Samuel Yeager, "Fine-Tuning Survey/Feedback Interventions: Differentiating Respondents in Terms of Performance Appraisals," pp. 348-352, in Robert L. Taylor, Michael J. O'Connell, Robert A. Zawacki, and D. D. Warrick (eds.), *Proceedings* (Annual Meeting) Academy of Management, Kissimmee, Fla., August 14-17, 1977.

54. Edgar F. Huse, *Organization Development and Change* (St. Paul, Minn.: West, 1975), p. 65.
55. Michael Maccoby, "Statement," U.S. Senate, Select Committee on Small Business, *Hearings,* December 2-4, 1975 (Washington, D.C.: Government Printing Office, 1976), p. 193.
56. Michael Maccoby, "Changing Work," *Working Papers,* Vol. 2 (Summer 1975), p. 44. Cited in Macy, "A Theoretical Basis for . . . Assessment," p. 2.
57. These principles come from "*Questions and Answers About the Work Improvement Program: Joint Effort of Harman International Industries and the UAW,*" Bolivar, Tenn., October 1974. See also Neil Q. Herrick and Michael Maccoby, "Humanizing Work," esp. pp. 64-66, in Louis E. Davis and A. B. Cherns (eds.), *The Quality of Working Life* (New York: The Free Press, 1975).
58. See Macy, "A Theoretical Basis for . . . Assessment," esp. pp. 19-20.
59. Ibid., p. 20. My emphasis.
60. Ibid.
61. Robert Duckles, "Humanizing Work: The Bolivar Project," *Survey of Business,* Vol. 12, no. 5 (1977), p. 25.
62. Maccoby, "Statement," p. 193.
63. Michael Maccoby, Harold Sheppard, Neil Q. Herrick, and others, *Final Technical Report: The Bolivar Project,* pp. 11-12. Submitted to the National Commission on Productivity, February 15, 1974.
64. Macy, "A Theoretical Basis for . . . Assessment," p. 27.
65. Patricia Colling (ed.), *Dissertation Abstracts International* (Ann Arbor, Mich.: University Microfilm International, 1976), pp. 1894-1895B.
66. See his *Model for Socio-Technical Systems* (Oslo, Norway: Work Research Institutes, 1976).
67. Macy, "A Theoretical Basis for . . . Assessment," p. 28.
68. Ibid., p. 33.
69. For a popularization of the sunny side of EIT, see "How Workers Can Get Eight-Hour Pay for Five," *Business Week,* May 19, 1975, p. 5.
70. Macy, "A Theoretical Basis for . . . Assessment," p. 33.

71. Ibid., pp. 31-32.
72. Ibid., p. 31.
73. Margaret M. Duckles, Robert Duckles, and Michael Maccoby, "The Process of Change at Bolivar," *Journal of Applied Behavioral Science,* Vol. 13 (June 1977), pp. 393-398.
74. Ibid., p. 398.
75. Ibid.
76. Macy, "A Theoretical Basis for . . . Assessment," p. 34
77. Ibid., p. 33.
78. Ibid., p. 35.
79. Ibid., Table 2.
80. Barry A. Macy and Philip H. Mirvis, "A Methodology for Assessment of Quality of Work Life and Organizational Effectiveness in Behavioral-Economic Terms," *Administrative Science Quarterly,* Vol. 21 (June 1976), pp. 212-226, provide details concerning each of the attitudinal, behavioral, and financial indicators.
81. For a splendid overview of such measurement issues, see Donald T. Campbell, "Keeping the Data Honest in the Experimenting Society," pp. 37-76, in Howard W. Melton and David J. H. Watson (eds.), *Interdisciplinary Dimensions of Accounting for Social Goals and Social Organizations* (Columbus, Ohio: Grid Inc., 1977).
82. Macy, "A Theoretical Basis for . . . Assessment," p. 47.
83. Ibid., Table 5.
84. Ibid., Table 4.
85. Ibid., pp. 53-55.
86. Macy and Mirvis, "A Methodology for Assessment."
87. Macy, "A Theoretical Basis for . . . Assessment," p. 58.
88. Ibid., p. 57.
89. For example, see Macy and Mirvis, "A Methodology for Assessment," and Edward E. Lawler III, "Adaptive Experiments: An Approach to Organizational Behavior Research," *Academy of Management Review,* Vol. 2 (October 1977), pp. 576-585.
90. George Strauss, "Managerial Practices," p. 299, in Richard Hackman and L. Lloyd Suttle (eds.), *Improving Life at Work* (Santa Monica, Calif.: Goodyear, 1977).
91. Ibid., p. 299.
92. John A. Drexler, Jr., and Edward E. Lawler III, "A Union-Management Cooperative Project to Improve the Quality of Work Life," *Journal of Applied Behavioral Science,* Vol. 13 (July 1977), p. 382.
93. Ibid., pp. 385-386.

94. Edward E. Lawler and John A. Drexler, Jr., "Dynamics of Establishing Cooperative Quality-of-Worklife Projects," *Monthly Labor Review*, Vol. 101 (March 1978), p. 23.

95. Macy, "A Theoretical Basis for . . . Assessment," p. 25n.

96. For detail on group-oriented features that can be built into all stages of survey/feedback design, consult David A. Nadler, *Feedback and Organization Development* (Reading, Mass.: Addison-Wesley, 1977), pp. 55-81 and 144-165; and Golembiewski and Hilles, *Toward the Responsive Organization*, esp. chaps. 1-6.

97. See Drexler and Lawler, "A Union-Management Cooperative," pp. 375-385; and Lawler and Drexler, "Dynamics of Establishing Cooperative Projects," pp. 23-26.

98. Thomas A. Kochan and Lee Dyer, "A Model for Organizational Change in the Context of Labor-Management Relations," *Journal of Applied Behavioral Science*, Vol. 12 (January 1976), p. 63.

99. Duckles, "Humanizing Work," p. 24.

100. Macy, "A Theoretical Basis for . . . Assessment," p. 20

101. Kochan and Dyer, "Model for Organizational Change," pp. 63-64, stress this critical lacuna in OD.

102. Ibid., esp. pp. 65-72; Kochan and Dyer develop a comprehensive set of hypotheses about the conditions favoring/discouraging joint ventures by management and unions.

103. Macy, "A Theoretical Basis for . . . Assessment," p. 66n.

104. Duckles, Duckles, and Maccoby, "Process of Change at Bolivar," p. 392.

105. As Macy and Peterson observe about another QWL program: "Little skill building and training in group process issues was provided. . . . However, the joint information gathering and feedback activities . . . are expected to have facilitated greater information and experience sharing among the members than is often the case." Barry A. Macy and Mark F. Peterson, "Evaluating Attitudinal Change in a Longitudinal Quality of Work Life Intervention," p. 32, of a mimeod MS which will be Chapter 20 in Stanley Seashore, Edward E. Lawler III, Philip H. Mirvis, and Cortlandt Cammann, *Observing and Measuring Organizational Change: A Guide to Field Practice* (New York: Wiley-Interscience, in press).

106. P. S. Goodman and Edward E. Lawler III, "New Forms of Work Organization in the United States," p. 1. Monograph prepared for International Labor Organization, March 1977.

107. Duckles, "Humanizing Work," p. 26.

108. Jean Piaget, *To Understand Is to Invent: The Future of Education* (New York: Grossman, 1973).

109. Duckles, "Humanizing Work," p. 26.

110. Duckles, Duckles, and Maccoby, "Process of Change at Bolivar," p. 390.
111. Piaget, "To Understand Is to Invent," pp. 98-99.
112. Ibid., p. 99.
113. Ibid., p. 107. My emphases.
114. Robert L. Duckles, *Work, Workers, and Democratic Change.* Unpublished Ph.D. dissertation, The Wright Institute Graduate School, Berkeley, Calif., 1976, p. 32.
115. Ibid.
116. Ibid., p. 115.
117. Ibid., p. 138.
118. Ibid., pp. 137-140.
119. Ibid., p. 138.
120. Ibid., p. 27.
121. Duckles distinguishes six types of employees from their survey responses, for example, which typology he uses to describe events at Bolivar. But it does not appear that this categorization of employees directly influenced any planned interventions. See ibid., pp. 208-217.
122. Ibid., p. 138.
123. Ibid., p. 11.
124. Ibid., p. 148.
125. Marvin R. Weisbord, "How Do You Know It Works, If You Don't Know What It Is?" *OD Practitioner,* Vol. 9 (October 1977), pp. 1-8, nicely and kaleidoscopically makes the point. See also Chapters 1-3 in Part 1.
126. Duckles, Duckles, and Maccoby, "Process of Change at Bolivar," p. 389.
127. Duckles, "Humanizing Work," p. 26.
128. Duckles, Duckles, and Maccoby, "Process of Change at Bolivar," p. 391.
129. Ibid., p. 23.
130. Ibid., p. 26.
131. Maccoby, "Statement," p. 193.
132. Duckles, "Work, Workers, and Democratic Change."
133. Chris Argyris and Donald Schön, *Organizational Learning: A Theory of Action Perspective* (Reading, Mass.: Addison-Wesley, 1978).
134. Macy, "A Theoretical Basis for . . . Assessment," p. 47, makes the point in referring to the evaluation of the three original sociotechnical experimental groups, using a structured interview administered by Harold Sheppard.
135. Consult Nadler, *Feedback and Organization Development,* pp. 144-165; and Golembiewski and Hilles, *Toward the Responsive Organization,* esp. pp. 105-177.

136. Re sensing groups, see Golembiewski and Hilles, *Toward the Responsive Organization*, pp. 49-50.

137. In the SmithKline Corp. QWL effort, in contrast, a tight schedule was proposed, widely advertised, and adhered to: sensing groups begin in last week of August; survey distributed in mid-October; results by individual items to *all* organization members by Thanksgiving; and detailed analyses available for top-level review in January-February, with periodic reporting re any actions taken or deferred.

138. Macy and Peterson, "Evaluating Attitudinal Change," p. 32.

139. Macy, "A Theoretical Basis for . . . Assessment," p. 14.

140. Maccoby, "Statement," pp. 192-201.

141. Duckles, Duckles, and Maccoby, "Process of Change at Bolivar," p. 389.

142. Michael Maccoby, *The Quality of Working Life: Lessons from Bolivar* (Washington, D.C.: The Institute for Policy Studies, 1976), p. 6.

143. J. Herman and Barry A. Macy, "Labor-Management Relationships in Collaborative Quality of Working Life Projects." Paper presented at the Quality of Work Life Assessment Conference, University of Michigan, Institute for Social Research, Ann Arbor, Mich., July 14-15, 1977.

144. Macy, "A Theoretical Basis for . . . Assessment," p. 26.

145. Duckles, "Humanizing Work," p. 23.

146. See the insightful criticism of participation "introduced from the top down as symbolic solutions to ideological contradictions," as a reflection of someone's feelings of guilt, and so on, in George Strauss and Eliezer Rosenstein, "Workers Participation: A Critical View," *Industrial Relations*, Vol. 9 (1970), esp. pp. 198-201.

147. Consider that in the Pre-Assembly Core Group experiment with supervision, an interesting trade-off was arranged. Volunteers and the company would split the time-costs 50/50. That is, half of the experimental time of volunteers came from the company releasing them from production, and the other half came from each individual employee's EIT earnings. See Duckles, Duckles, and Maccoby, "Process of Change at Bolivar," p. 394.

148. For one approach to value clarification, see Kirschenbaum, *Advanced Value Clarification.*

149. Duckles, "Humanizing Work," p. 25. My emphases.

150. Macy, "A Theoretical Basis for . . . Assessment, " p. 60.

151. Ibid.

152. Duckles, "Work, Workers and Democratic Change," esp. pp. 80, 98, 105-106, and 126. By one estimate, some standards may be as much as one-third "looser" than others at Bolivar.

153. Macy, "A Theoretical Basis for . . . Assessment," p. 62n.
154. For a broad discussion of the differences, consult Golembiewski and Hilles, "Toward the Responsive Organization, pp. 31-35 and 49-51.
155. As is suggested by Kochan and Dyer, "Model for Organizational Change," esp. pp. 60-62.
156. Strauss, "Managerial Practices," esp. pp. 357-358.
157. Macy, "A Theoretical Basis for . . . Assessment," p. 25n.
158. Herbert A. Shepard, "Changing Interpersonal and Intergroup Relationships in Organizations," in James G. March (ed.), *Handbook of Organizations* (Chicago, Ill.: Rand McNally, 1965), pp. 1115-1143.
159. Golembiewski, *Men, Management, and Morality*.
160. Richard Beckhard, "An Organization Improvement Program in a Decentralized Organization," *Journal of Applied Behavioral Science,* Vol. 2 (January 1966), pp. 3-26.
161. Michael Tushman, *Organizational Change* (Ithaca, N.Y.: New York State School of Industrial and Labor Relations, 1974), esp. p. 73.
162. William N. Dunn and Frederic W. Swierczek, "Planned Organizational Change: Toward Grounded Theory," *Journal of Applied Behavioral Science,* Vol. 13 (April 1977), esp. pp. 147-148.
163. Richard Beckhard and Stanley M. Harris, *Organizational Transitions* (Reading, Mass.: Addison-Wesley, 1977), pp. 42-43.
164. Michael Beer, "On Gaining Influence and Power for OD," *Journal of Applied Behavioral Science,* Vol. 12 (January 1976), pp. 48-51.
165. Dunn and Swierczek, "Planned Organizational Change," p. 135.
166. Edgar Schein and Warren G. Bennis (eds.), *Personal and Organizational Change through Group Methods* (New York: Wiley, 1965), p. 323.
167. Newton Margulies, Penny L. Wright, and Richard W. Scholl, "Organization Development Techniques: Their Impact on Change," *Group and Organization Studies,* Vol. 2 (December 1977), p. 428.
168. Jerry I. Porras and Per Olaf Berg, "Evaluation Methodology in Organization Development: An Analysis and Critique," *Journal of Applied Behavioral Science,* Vol. 14 (April 1978), p. 151.
169. Ibid., p. 157.
170. Peggy Morrison, "Evaluation in OD: A Review and an Assessment," *Group and Organization Studies,* Vol. 3 (March 1978), esp. p. 42.
171. Larry E. Pate, Warren R. Nielsen, and Paul C. Bacon, "Advances in Research on Organization Development: Toward A Beginning," *Group and Organization Studies,* Vol. 2 (December 1977), pp. 449-460.
172. Larry E. Pate, "A Reference List for Change Agents," in J. William Pfeiffer and John E. Jones (eds.), *The 1976 Annual Handbook for Group Facilitators* (La Jolla, Calif.: University Associates, 1976).

173. For exceptions see Louis B. Barnes and Larry E. Greiner, "Breakthrough in Organization Development," *Harvard Business Review,* Vol. 42 (December 1964), pp. 139-164; and Chris Argyris, *Interpersonal Competence and Organizational Effectiveness* (Homewood, Ill.: Dorsey, 1962).

174. Larry E. Pate, Warren R. Nielsen, and Richard T. Mowday, "A Longitudinal Assessment of the Impact of Organization Development on Absenteeism, Grievance Rates and Product Quality," in Taylor, O'Connell, Zawacki, and Warrick (eds.), *Proceedings* (1977), p. 353.

175. Consult Stanislav V. Kasl, "Work and Mental Health," esp. p. 98, in W.J. Heisler and John W. Houck (eds.), *A Matter of Dignity* (South Bend, Ind.: University of Notre Dame Press, 1977).

176. P. Tolchinsky and William A. Pasmore, "Survey Feedback: A Bottom Up Approach." Unpublished MS, Purdue University, Lafayette, Ind., 1976.

177. William A. Pasmore and Donald C. King, "Understanding Organizational Change: A Comparative Study of Multifaceted Interventions," *Journal of Applied Behavioral Science,* Vol. 14 (December 1978), p. 459.

178. Ibid., p. 460.

179. William A. Pasmore, *Understanding Organizational Change.* Unpublished doctoral thesis, Purdue University, Lafayette, Ind., 1976.

180. Pasmore and King, "Understanding Organizational Change," p. 466.

181. Ibid., pp. 464-465.

182. A range of related issues is raised by Richard E. Walton and Donald P. Warwick, "The Ethics of Organization Development," *Journal of Applied Behavioral Science,* Vol. 9 (November 1973), pp. 681-699.

183. David K. Hart and William G. Scott, "The Organizational Imperative," *Administration and Society,* Vol. 7 (November 1975), pp. 259-285.

184. Friedlander and Brown, "Organization Development," p. 333.

Section 2

ISSUES RE INTERVENING AND INTERVENTIONS

Chapter 8

A SAMPLER OF CONSTRAINTS ON ORGANIZATION DEVELOPMENT APPLICATIONS

Confoundments and Complications of What Needs Doing

Organization Development is as much of a paradox as all of life. In both, we often have to act long before we have a good scientific grasp of the relevant reality. In both, also, it is tempting to make a virtue of this necessity.

This chapter acknowledges the first similarity. OD applications are substantially ahead of our ability to comprehend what is happening and why in relatively precise conceptual terms,[1] just as is much of life.

This chapter seeks to avoid making a virtue of necessity, however, specifically by emphasizing how our lack of knowledge implies several prominent constraints on OD applications. Act we must, in many cases, that is. But we should never delude ourselves about how much of what we do is by guess and by golly, and how much is firmly rooted in theory as well as experience.

There are many ways of demonstrating how knowledge lacunae constitute constraints on OD applications, and the sampler here focuses on only five questions that illustrate those constraints. The question-form is appropriate, because we presently know more good questions than adequate answers.

First, how much can we reasonably expect of OD efforts, and why? Such questions come easily, but working answers are Everyhuman's choice. I can only add personal perspective here, even if it is the perspective of someone who has sweated and worried over the issues for a long enough time to be in touch with the more obvious problems.

Second, what major constraints on OD applications, if any, inhere in differences between host organizations? Some groundwork has been laid. Previous discussion should have established that available models of the change-process in organizations represent roughly the same developmental state as the daguerrotype represents in photography. What is needed, in contrast, is the analogue of a high-resolution motion picture, with instant replay capabilities! The second section below illustrates existing progress toward this critical capability.

Third, which of several alternative OD designs are most impactful under specific conditions? To T-group or to team-build, and under which conditions? These issues demand vigorous attention. The third section below highlights the multiple value of comparative analysis of OD interventions, and also reviews the results of one major effort at comparative analysis.

Fourth, what constraints should be applied to feedback and disclosure? The focus is on the reconceptualization of "openness" as a property of a communication system, rather than a personal quality.

Fifth, is our basic concept of "change" adequate? This late chapter may seem a curious time at which to raise the point, but the plain fact is that without a clear and valid concept of change it will be impossible to determine which OD designs have what effects. And right now, common concepts of change seem too simple. Far worse, they may be quite misleading. What appears to be a successful OD intervention may be a dud, or even seriously counterproductive. Obviously, then, one cannot overstate the importance of a valid concept of change.

How Long Does It Last? How Much Gets Done?
Entropy Has All the Trump Cards

We start with that megaquestion: How much should we expect of OD? But we start with that question only to shunt it aside as a snare and a delusion or, at best, a debator's question. The practically relevant choice—about any OD program or intervention or, indeed, about all of life—is at once more elemental and tougher. That choice:

- Should decisions about an OD program be made to seek to make it last as long as possible?
- Should decisions about an OD program be made to seek to get as much done as possible?

Sometimes these questions are not opposed alternatives, but most often they are.

The view here is that the second choice is all but required in OD because of the way the world is. To explain, the natural order of things and institutions seems to be *entropic*: that is, people and their institutions trend toward death and decay, they inexorably run down. Consequently, the questions cannot be: Will OD overcome entropy? Entropy, as the subheading of this section puts it, has all the trump cards. Hence the need to do as much as possible before the inevitable occurs, because to do nothing merely accelerates the entropic coming and makes the waiting more unpleasant.

OD cannot avoid the ultimate tragedy of life, for individuals or organizations. But it can help enrich the quality of that life, while it lasts and before the inevitable comes, making life more heroic and less punic, and perhaps even significantly extending the productive spans of both individuals and organizations.

Some Common Forces in Balance

That entropy has much the better of it can be suggested by sketching some common forces in balance in organizations embarking on OD programs. Epigrammatically, the constructive human forces always have to contest with what the late Alexander Winn called "the irrational and destructive impulses of man."[2] The factors predisposed to OD efforts come and go, flourishing under somewhat special circumstances, including the following.

- The OD effort is in critical senses the product of the integration of the interests of a staff insider and the needs of a line official who has responsibility for a substantial organization unit and some autonomy in its management.
- The responsible line official has a "conversion experience," some precipitating episode that highlights the inadequacies or awkward consequences of the manager's style which he or she is motivated to avoid.
- Typically, the build-up of a variety of organization pressures precedes an OD effort. These pressures signal that traditional ways of coping or doing business will become increasingly awkward, and the wise manager takes heed early enough to have a fighting chance.
- Sufficient resources–in time, money, and goodwill–are available.
- The "good experiences" of other organizations with comparable characteristics often supply major motivation for an OD effort in the newly shaken organization.
- The host organization's own accumulating "good experiences" help sustain and expand early OD beachheads.

These predisposing features, which wax and wane, must sufficiently overbalance a set of counterforces to an OD program. The major forces in opposition include the following.

- Recognizing the need for a change is difficult because of the political inadvisability in some organizations of owning up to any "defect" for fear that it will be used against the unit in bargaining situations or that it will contribute to an "unfavorable climate of opinion" that may work against the unit.

- All OD programs test and usually challenge existing power relationships, and the more so as the OD interventions are potent, and most people will tend to resist disturbing a balance of power which favors them.[3]
- OD interventions themselves may induce stress and pain, and hence may contribute to their own dilution or demise.[4]
- Personal ambitions can provide a highly volatile component in OD programs, those of the persons "pushing" the OD program, as well as those who have a vested interest in the status quo. The success of an OD program can create new problems of organizational power, in fact, as well as solve operating problems.
- Given a history of authoritarian management, requests to be open and trusting are likely to be viewed with varying degrees of suspicion.[5]
- The responsible line officials, conversion experience and all, often become conflicted about how much openness they want, from whom, and about what, and especially so after receiving some disliked or unwanted openness. This conflict can reinforce incredulity or suspicion in other organization members.
- The responsible line official can opt to satisfice as conditions improve due to early OD interventions, and this individual's support may wane as the OD effort succeeds.
- Resources can become scarce, very suddenly, or they can be reallocated.
- Some organization members can utilize an OD program's products, such as increased openness, to identify members for later punishment. Or, the myth may develop that this occurs.

These constitute hardy opposing forces, patently. Some derive from objective dilemmas, others from convenience or ignorance, and some from the elemental fact that humans have great potentiality for mischief or even evil as well as good. Many of these counterforces grow at least in proportion to the success of the OD effort. Practically, then, the lifeline of even a successful OD program may look like this:

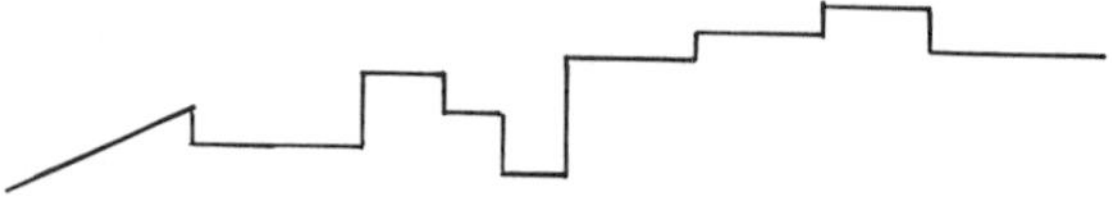

A more ebullient lifeline has such an onward and upward slope:

The latter is not in the cards, realistically. Indeed, paradoxically, aspiring to the latter lifeline for OD programs may encourage simplicism in diagnosis and prescription, manipulation of the accepting, intolerance of those unwilling to be converted, and an ambition for too much, too soon. Our developing but still primitive knowledge might not be able to support the weight of all that zealotry. Pascal captured much of the paradoxical sense of the point in his Pensee 358: "Man is neither angel nor brute, and the unfortunate thing is that he who would act the angel acts the brute."

Guidelines for Optimists

Given such forces in balance, then, no wonder that OD programs typically face severe constraints, sooner or later. Hence the inappropriateness of Stephenson's pointed question. "If, as OD practitioners suggest, current organizational behavior is costly," he asks, "why does it persist?"[6] One's first impulse is to answer: For the same reasons that war, famine, and pestilence persist: our lack of wit, moral conviction, and technology to eliminate them. More moderate positions soon come to the fore, however, such as: Given the formidable character of typical counterforces, the flourishing of OD provides substantial testimony about the lofty aspirations of the human spirit and the grave needs of today's organizations.

Blaise Pascal once said of man that he is so much less than God, yet so much more than a reed. Much the same may be said of OD. Compared with the ultimate, it is nothing much, but compared to what commonly exists in organizations, it is everything.

For optimists, then, two guidelines for OD seem appropriate. One principle urges remembering that the key issue is how much you get done, not how long you take to do it. A second principle urges a somewhat adventuresome humility about what can reasonably get done, given what is known and what seem reasonable extensions of what is known. The trick is thrusting toward greater knowledge while keeping both feet planted in the evolving and accumulating experience and literature relevant to OD. Tricky, that.

Pessimists will have an easier time of it. Like Seidenberg,[7] they can merely wait as organizations suffocate in their accumulating offal, or perhaps even rejoice as that prediction comes closer to being fulfilled.

What Do We Know About Differences in Host Organizations?
Some Elemental Distinctions to Be Encompassed by a Satisfactory Typology

Respecting our own advice, this section seeks to forward OD by standing solidly on what we know or can be substantially certain of.

This section begins with a neglected truism: that host organizations differ in significant ways, which OD designs would do well to take into account. This amounts to a kind of primitive belief that defies uncomplicated proof and encourages easy acceptance. The present approach is to provide five perspectives on the truism introducing this section:

- That organizations may be distinguished at least in terms of their stages of development, as well as in terms of their basic mission and role
- That organizations are not mere technical structures, that they become institutions infused with value and hence take on more or less distinguishable "characters" or "styles"
- That differences of note seem to exist between "government" and "business," at least as a useful first approximation
- That organization "cultures" vary widely, both in government and business, and these differences must be accommodated by effective OD designs
- That organizations do and/or should have different degress of "coupledness"

Organizational Growth Stages and Missions

Host organizations for OD applications will differ in at least two major senses. These differences may affect both the need for OD programs and the probability of their success, and derive from stages of organizational growth[8] and from organization missions.[9] The position here is like that of the "contingency theorists," who urge seeking many *theories* of organization rather than *a theory.*[10] That is to say, the need for an OD effort tends to increase for organizations at specific stages of growth and for organizations having certain kinds of missions. OD efforts can succeed when the predisposing variables are not favorable, however, as several cases in point establish.[11]

Four Growth Stages

One set of organization theories must deal with where organizations are in their stages of development. As a starter, organizations beyond some minimal size may be conceived of as passing through at least four major stages of growth, which are more or less sequential but which can occur in various combinations:[12]

- Growth at some single site, as by expansion of a plant, or restaurant, or whatever
- Growth by adding field units, as when replicas of the original single site are developed at new geographical locations

- Growth by adding functions or activities, as when an organization begins to add internal resources that were previously supplied by outside sources because the organization was previously too small to economically justify them
- Growth by diversification, as when organizations add product lines, goods, or services

Two points about these stages are critical. Even very large organizations can exist without exhausting early strategies for growth. Du Pont during World War I was already a monster corporation, for example, but it was still at the stage of growing by adding field units. Also, even apparently minor extensions of an organization's mission can have profound organizational consequences. Consider that a convenient way to enjoy the relative simplicity of early stages of growth is to have a homogeneous product line, such as producing a raw material. When that mission includes (for example) fabricating as well as producing the raw material, however, quantum increases in complexity occur as new functions are added and as complexity burgeons.[13]

Growth Stages and Need for OD. The several growth stages imply different needs for OD interventions. That is clear even at this point. Consider only the quantum increases in problems of communication characteristic of the stages for growth. Given expansion at a central site, problems of communication do increase. But experience suggests that even very large organizations at a single site can be monitored by very few individuals who do not miss much that goes on.[14] Communication and organizational problems rapidly increase when field units are added.[15] As new functions are added–the third strategy for growth–such internal problems increase additively. As new products or services are added, the potential for conflict, misunderstanding, and confusion probably increases exponentially.

Several factors underlie this sharp increase in potential for trouble, and the increasing relevance of OD, under the fourth stage of growth. Just a few will be listed. Obviously, the integrative burden increases sharply as a larger number of functions have to be brought to bear at appropriate times on an increasingly large number of programs or products or services. Then, too, many of the functional specialists have more or less different training, backgrounds, interests, professional values, vocabularies, and even distinct ways of thinking and problem-solving.

Four Kinds of Organizational Missions

The ingenuity of the human constitutes the only limit on distinguishing organizations in terms of the character of their basic missions, so bare illustration must suffice here. Perrow's approach is both simple and useful, distinguishing organizations in terms of their basic search processes and of the variety of problems or stimuli to which they must respond. Figure 1 generates four basic kinds of organizational missions, based on a rough twofold differentiation of each basic dimension. Examples of the four basic kinds of missions come to mind easily. A pin factory clearly would have a routine mission, just as the design of the C-5A transport would be a nonroutine mission.[16] And the fabrication of aluminum stock for a variety of uses implies an engineering mission. These examples have a thing-bias, of course, but similar distinctions can be made between people-changing organizations.[17]

Organizational Missions and Need for OD. Organizations stand in need of OD interventions more or less in direct relationship to the degree that they approach a nonroutine mission. As the approach occurs, problems in communication begin to increase under the organization structure consistent with the bureaucratic

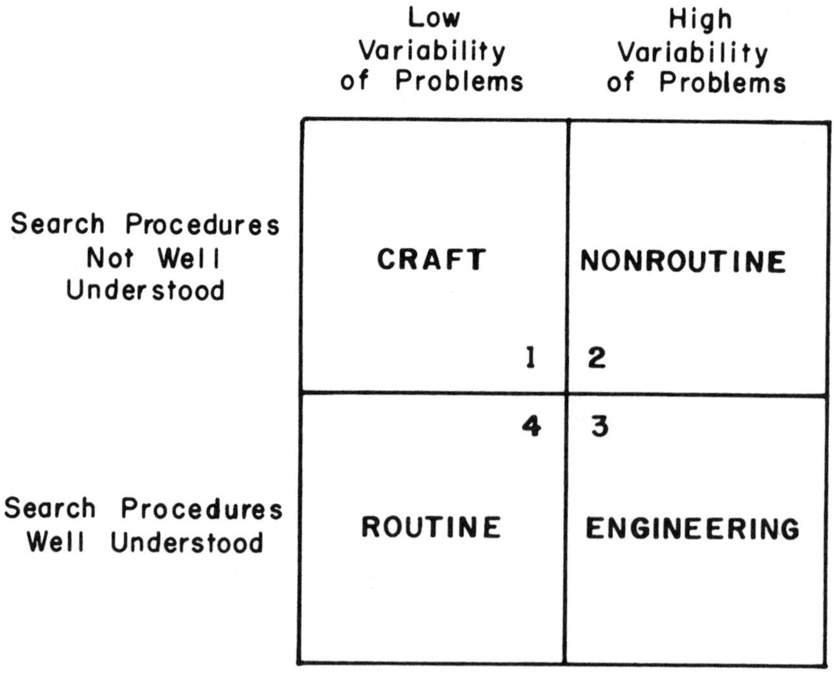

	Low Variability of Problems	High Variability of Problems
Search Procedures Not Well Understood	CRAFT 1	NONROUTINE 2
Search Procedures Well Understood	4 ROUTINE	3 ENGINEERING

Figure 1 Some examples of four kinds of organizational missions. (*Source*: Adapted from *Organizational Analysis* by Charles Perrow. Copyright 1970 by Wadsworth Publishing Company Inc. Reprinted by permission of the publisher, Brooks/Cole Publishing Company, Monterey, Calif.)

model, and increasingly troublesome outcomes tend to proliferate. Perrow captures the essence of the challenges to both communication and orthodox structural arrangements in this description of nonroutine missions:

> supervisors of production work closely with the technical people in the administration of production since the latter cannot call the shots for the former on the basis of routine information sent upstairs. Indeed, job descriptions may be such that it is difficult to distinguish the supervisory level from the technical level. Both groups are free to define situations as best they can. Therefore, both have considerable power with respect to such matters as resources and organizational strategies.[18]

Nonroutine missions for organizations have increased spectacularly since World War II, although routine missions still abound. Perrow notes: "Most firms fit into the quite routine cell."[19] But, even firms clearly classifiable as having a routine mission, on balance, contain some or many subunits that have nonroutine missions. Moreover, most organizational environments are dynamic, at least at certain stages. Thus, operations in any new power plant probably have major nonroutine aspects, even though the mission can become routine after a few years.[20] Finally, many or most organizations are being variously shaken today by major external forces. As Argyris explains:

> Two major changes that are presently occurring in our society are (1) a break with traditional authority and (2) the growth of democratic ideology and accelerated rate of change. To the extent these observations are validated, mechanistic organizations will be in difficulty because they may no longer attract the youth that they will need to manage their organizations.[21]

This argument must be extended to OD in organizations with routine missions. Some have vigorously doubted OD's usefulness in organizations with routine missions; others have just as stoutly maintained that such organizations are precisely those that are most likely to be need-depriving, and hence provide the primary targets for OD interventions.[22]

This writer has friends in both camps, and in this case he finds it possible to agree with all his friends. For example, organizations with routine missions are more likely to induce and sustain autocratic styles of supervision, and hence OD designs facilitating upward feedback may be particularly useful in such organizations. For similar reasons, OD interventions intended to change the broad style and structure of a routine mission organization—let us say, to Likert System IV—should be looked at carefully. For it may be the case that the organization's basic markets and technology tend to encourage a more centralized and autocratic management style. Such an intervention might be seriously counterproductive. That is, if a System IV style got broadly accepted, it might only inhibit doing what needed to be done, which implies failure by way of success.

Thus, guilt or anger over regressing might be felt in an organization accepting System IV ideals when some members did what needed doing in a directive and nonparticipative way. Designs like those presented in Chapters 3 and 4 would be safer in routine mission organizations, specifically.

Toward Understanding Organizational Character

As is well known but inadequately appreciated, organizations are not merely legal or technical structures. They become "infused with value," they take on a character that is a normative mosaic of what that organization represents and of the values for which it stands.[23] Thus, we highlight central aspects of the character of organizations when we say they are a "good place to work," a "tight ship," or a "hell hole"; or we complain that some organization "can't make up its mind what business it is in."

Four "Ideologies" or "Orientations"

Roger Harrison describes one parsimonious way of thinking about an organization's character by distinguishing four "ideologies" or "orientations" that give organizations their distinctive flavors.[24] Brief descriptions reflect his basic distinctions.

> *Power Orientation.* The dominant motive here is to dominate the environment and to emasculate the opposition, whether that opposition be competing organizations, peers, or subordinates. The coin of the realm is power or influence, with the basic comparison being strength versus weakness, and the basic outcomes being "wins" and "losses." Superficially, the power orientation may be reflected in a paternalistic facade, or an exploitative one.
>
> *Role Orientation.* The dominant goals here are rationality and orderliness, with a corresponding preoccupation with legality, legitimacy, and responsibility. The focal questions are: Who has the authority to perform which acts? Such an orientation, on the negative side, can lead to errors of omission, jurisdictional conflicts, and a history of too little, too late.
>
> *Task Orientation.* The basic question here is: What needs to be done? Goal achievement is the prime value, and if role definitions are somehow awkward, so much the worse for them. Authority derives from getting the job done, rather than from power or position. Organizations with such a dominant orientation can be trying and demanding for their members, and they are prone to errors of commission and overexuberance.
>
> *Person Orientation.* The basic motive here is to serve the needs of its members. Members can be narcissistic, or helpful and caring. The work is so organized as to meet individual needs, even when this creates role unclarities or blunts task-centeredness.

Harrison notes that very few pure types exist. But most organizations can be described in terms of some distribution of the four ideologies, often with a dominant ideology as well as a clear back-up ideology.

Each of the ideologies, Harrison explains, has both attractions and disadvantages, as viewed from the perspective of the person and the organization. Exhibit 1 illustrates the point, focusing on three major personal and three organization concerns.

Harrison's approach to an organization's character or ideological orientation has multiple uses. For example, it suggests one common source of conflict. Assume that an individual prefers role orientation, and also finds self in an organization whose dominant character sanctions a task orientation. The potential for conflict is patently high.

Organizational Orientations and OD Interventions of Choice

More or less obviously, also, any prescription for an OD effort should be sensitive to these complex mixes of personal preferences and organizational styles, which can be measured by an available questionnaire. Thus, for example, a person with a high power orientation, and no intention of modifying it, might be discomforted by a 3-D confrontation with subordinates. Similarly, many of the designs above would be appropriate only in limited ways for an organization with a dominant power orientation, *and* with an unflinching resolve to preserve it. Uses of OD designs in such cases might be seen as Band-Aids or as mere "cooling-out," as just another (if subtle) set of techniques in the arsenal of the autocrat who prefers to cover the mailed fist with a velvet glove. Further, if the dominant back-up ideology of most or all relevant organization members were the person orientation, designs like family T-groups might be the design of choice for inducing the transition. If the dominant back-up ideology of most or all of those relevant organization members were the role orientation, in contrast, designs like the role negotiation intervention might be more appropriate.

But such speculations need to be recognized for what they are. That is, the plain truth remains that we are only a little way down the track of knowing which OD designs are optimally appropriate for which mix of personal preferences and extant organizational styles. One can imagine two significant classes of outcomes of many OD efforts:

- The design or intervention that succeeds for the wrong or an inadequate reason
- The design or intervention that fails because it is awkwardly matched with an organization's style or an individual's preferences

Neither type of outcome is desirable, and the first, despite being superficially attractive, also implies the lesser potential for learning. Consequently, it is

Exhibit 1 How Four Orientations Meet Local Concerns of People and Organizations

A. Three concerns of people:

	Security against economic, political, and psychological deprivation	Opportunities for voluntary commitment to worthwhile goals	Opportunities to pursue one's own growth and development independent of organization goals
Power orientation	Low: At the pleasure of the autocrat	Low: Unless one is in a sufficiently high position to determine organization goals	Low: Unless one is in a sufficiently high position to determine organization goals
Role orientation	High: Secured by law, custom, and procedure	Low: Even if, at times, one is in a high position	Low: Organization goals are relatively rigid and activities are closely prescribed
Task orientation	Moderate: Psychological deprivation can occur when an individual's contributions are redundant	High: A major basis of the individual's relationship to the organization	Low: Individuals should not be in the organization if they do not subscribe to some of its goals
Person orientation	High: The individual's welfare is the major concern	High: But only if the individuals are capable of generating their own goals	High: Organization goals are determined by individual needs

B. Three organizational concerns:

	Effective response to dangerous, threatening environments	Dealing rapidly and effectively with environmental complexity and change	Internal integration and coordination of effort—if necessary, at the expense of individual needs
Power orientation	High: The organization tends to be perceptually ready for a fight	Moderate to low: Depends on size, pyramidal communication channels are easily overloaded	High: Effective control emanates from the top

Exhibit 1 (Continued)

	Effective response to dangerous, threatening environments	Dealing rapidly and effectively with environmental complexity and change	Internal integration and coordination of effort—if necessary, at the expense of individual needs
Role orientation	Moderate to low: The organization is slow to mobilize to meet increases in threat	Low: Slow to change programmed procedures, communication channels are easily overloaded	High: Features a carefully planned rational system of work
Task orientation	Moderate to high: The organization may be slow to make decisions but produces highly competent responses	High: Flexible assignment of resources and short communication channels facilitate adaptation	Moderate: Integrated by common goal; but flexible, shifting structure may make coordination difficult
Person orientation	Low: The organization is slow to become aware of threat and slow to mobilize effort against it	High: But response is erratic; assignment of resources to problems depends greatly on individual needs and interests	Low: A common goal difficult to achieve and activities may shift with individual interests

From Roger Harrison, "Understanding Your Organization's Character," *Harvard Business Review,* Vol. 50 (May-June 1972).

necessary to resolve firmly to reduce the number of both outcomes. This will require acknowledging the elemental facts that organizations have different characters and that their members have different preferences about what orientations should be dominant.

Is Government that Different?

OD gets applied more often and more extensively in industry than in government. That truism reflects the special obstacles to OD which exist in government organizations, and two sections below provide perspective on these special obstacles. In sum, the two sections focus first on the available research literature and then on the intervenor's role. This provides double-header perspective, as it were, that helps explain the special problems facing public-sector OD.

Theoretical and Practical Comparisons Derived from the Literature*

The review here of the literature focuses on eleven propositions comparing government and manufacturing organizations, following the conceptual work of the late James Thompson.[25] The propositions derived from a search of the literature and relevant theory, leavened by the author's own experience. Table 1 summarizes the differences. The catalog is not meant to be exhaustive, but hopefully its elements are testable. If they do nothing other than foster debate, however, they have achieved their purpose.

Proposition 1. The major technology of industry is "long-linked" while that of government is "mediating." Industry and government often vary with respect to technology, and these variations generate differences at the managerial and institutional levels.[26] Thompson would describe industrial manufacturing technology as "long-linked," which "involves serial interdependence in the sense that act Z can be performed after successful completion of act Y which in turn rests on act X, etc."[27] Production of specific products requires specific machines and tools, work-flow arrangements, and selection of operators. Repetition helps eliminate imperfections. With a constant rate of production, resource input can be standardized so none is underemployed.

In contrast, government more often involves a "mediating technology," which links clients who are or wish to be interdependent. This requires operating in standardized ways, with multiple clients distributed in time and space. Bureaucratic categorization and impersonal application of rules are applied to assure that segments of the organization act compatibly.[28]

Noteworthy differences also characterize lower levels of organization. In government, work patterns are somewhat varied compared to the repetitive work which may be machine-paced in industry.[29] Productivity among individual employees also can vary much more in government than in industry, where the pace and output are more standardized. However, lower level employees in industry often seem to develop more unfavorable attitudes. Quality and waste are more likely to become problems, as in absenteeism, turnover, slowdowns, and grievances. Where work is more varied, these problems are less visible. For this reason, a manufacturing organization is more likely than government to seek to alleviate the problems induced by repetitive operations via OD, as by job enlargement or quality of working life interventions.

*This section comes from Peggy Morrison, "A Comparison of Organization Development in Government and Manufacturing Organizations," pp. 6-22. Paper completed in partial fulfillment of qualifying procedures for Ph.D. Candidacy, University of Cincinnati, December 1975.

Table 1 Organizational Differences in Government and Manufacturing Organizations

Variable	Government	Industry
Type of technology	Mediating	Long-linked
Use of new technology	Less	More
Goals	Subject to change more often	Subject to change less often
Definition of system boundaries	Vague	Clearer
Openness of system boundaries	Greater	Less
Influence of political environment	Greater	Less
Interests and values represented	Highly diverse	Much less diverse
Influence of interests and values represented	Greater	Less
Competing identifications, affiliations, and loyalties in command linkages	Highly diverse and complex	Much less diverse and complex
Number of authoritative decision-makers	Multiple sets	One or a few sets
Strength of linkages in organizational hierarchy	Weaker	Stronger
Definition of the *top* of the organization	Vague	Clearer
Concern for maintaining status quo	Higher	Lower
Job security	Greater	Less
Concern for worker productivity	Less	More
Rewards for innovation	Less	More
Concern for employee satisfaction	Lower	Higher
Adaptive structures	Underdeveloped	Better developed
Habit of procedures and caution	Stronger	Weaker
Legal habit	Stronger	Weaker
Means of expanding domain	Horizontal–increasing populations served	Vertical–increasing services rendered via control of organization's own contingencies
Changes in top leadership	More frequent and far reaching	Less frequent and less dramatic

Table 1 (Continued)

Variable	Government	Industry
Stimulus to which responsive	Political process	Market place
Source of input from the environment affecting organizational existence	Legislature or law-making body	Profit
Ability to measure outcomes	Less	More
Level of competition with similar organizations	Low	Higher
Concern for management and nonmanagement relations	Very little	More
Level of training and expertise of managers	Lower	Higher
Management's knowledge of OD	Less	More
Discretionary funds available to managers	Very little	Much more
Application of OD	Seldom and on a small scale	More often and on a broader scale

Proposition 2. Industry tends to expand its domain vertically, while government expands its domain horizontally. "Organizational domain" refers to the organization's technology, the population served, and the services rendered.[30] Manufacturers try to expand their domains through vertical integration, especially regarding activities crucial to their existence. For example, a steel manufacturer wishing to have more control of its contingencies may expand both "backward" and "forward," as it were, backward into its production sequence by running its own iron ore mines and refineries, and forward by undertaking the manufacture and sale of specific steel products. On the other hand, government organizations often seek to expand their domains horizontally by increasing the populations served.[31] On a local level, this may involve a city government annexing part of the county so that its boundaries and domain are expanded. On a state level, this would include a state claiming takeover of services heretofore left to local government.

Important ideas about governance both induce and reinforce such differences. While market forces may encourage a Rockefeller to develop an empire, for which the rewards can be regal, many political institutions inhibit similar empire-building by public officials. J. Edgar Hoover can amass considerable and long-lived power, but separation of powers and checks and balances severely restrict Napoleonic instincts. For example, Atlanta legislators have resisted efforts by administrative agencies to become more responsive to client needs—as by funding an internal ombudsman—because the legislators believe that client representation is their business.

Given the difference in how they expand their domains, both government and manufacturing provide opportunity and need for OD. When a manufacturing organization expands its domain by opening new plants and/or taking on new technologies, however, OD is more often employed in the process. For example, when Proctor and Gamble opens a new plant, external and internal OD agents are involved from the very beginning.[32] When government expands its domain, the emphasis is on legal efforts to encompass the increased population served.

Proposition 3. Organizational goals of a government more drastically and frequently change than the goals of an industrial organization. Thompson defines organizational goals as the "future domains intended by those in the dominant coalition."[33] The "dominant coalition" may mean organizational members or nonmembers. In the case of government, organizational goals are much more subject to drastic and frequent changes because of the various sources of possible dominant coalitions: the Congress, executive branch, judicial branch, voting or client publics, or government employees themselves. An industrial organization is subject to some of these forces, of course. But its dominant coalition is less likely to change as often or as dramatically as in government.

According to Thompson, "When power is widely dispersed, compromise issues can be ratified but cannot be decided by the dominant coalition in toto."[34] In government, power is much more widely dispersed than in a manufacturing organization. Therefore, dominant coalitions will probably struggle and compromise their desires more than they might in industry. Because of the frequent confusion in government organizations, consequently, a public manager may at once initiate an OD program and feel that it represents an exercise in futility. A major obstacle to OD in government is that the frequently changing goals give employees the impression OD cannot help, because *nothing* can help. Employees feel powerless in influencing these goals, much less in setting them.

Proposition 4. Government is open to a much wider range of influences than is an industrial organization. Katz and Kahn follow an open-system approach to organizations. The functional interdependence of roles ties people together and the norms for roles apply regarding what constitutes doing a good job,[35] in all organizations. However, how government handles its business is much more influenced by the values held by government employees and by pressure groups than in industry. What Katz and Kahn refer to as system openness, or susceptibility to external influences, is much greater in government than manufacturing organizations.

Relatedly, "boundaries" of a public system often defy circumscribing. Katz and Kahn define "boundaries" as the demarcation line or regions for the definition of appropriate system activity, for admission of members into the system, and for other imports into the system."[36] Since such boundaries are more difficult to define in government than in industry, "the organization" is more difficult to characterize and differentiate in the public sector.

This difficulty in defining organizational boundaries affects the use of OD by government. Primarily, a large and shifting set of actors and interests may have veto power over OD efforts in public agencies. The controlling actors and/or interests tend to be fewer and more stable in industry. For example, many of government's important decisions are made visible by the mass media, which can sometimes mobilize diverse constituencies whose restiveness may help veto OD efforts, as was the case with Project ACORD in the U.S. Department of State.

The political environment has a greater impact on the internal workings of government than of manufacturing organizations. Timothy Costello has discussed differences in private- and public-sector management in his article on the planned change undertaken in New York City during John Lindsay's administration.[37] He maintains that the periodic changes in top leadership are more drastic and far-reaching in government than in industry, with severity of change being buffered somewhat by such stabilizing features as a city manager or established high-level civil servants. This deprives public OD efforts of powerful figures who maintain any changes and reinforce new learnings. This often seems critical in OD success.[38]

The reverse side of this coin? The persisting interests in government tend to be stabilizing forces with a vested interest in what exists. Hence, stopping or changing any public program once it is started is often difficult because of the vested interests that develop around it, despite lack of use or even need.[39] These vested interests impede organizational change in government more than in industry, although such interests also exist in industry and are likewise obstacles to OD there.

Leadership in government has to be more responsive to a greater range of environmental pressures regarding which social problems should be tackled and in what order. Often these environmental pressures overrule the government employees having information and expertise relevant to the problems. Who gets what, that is to say, may be more salient than administrative effectiveness or efficiency. Technical knowledge regarding how the organization can most effectively and efficiently reach its goals may be ignored, consequently, in public sector OD. Who gets what is *the* game.

Proposition 5. Profit can serve as a useful measure of organizational effectiveness in manufacturing organizations, whereas a similar quantitative measure often does not exist for government. For a manufacturing organization, profitability is one central measure of organizational effectiveness.[40] Profit influences an organization's ability to import energy (people, facilities, materials). For government, the decision about funds for energic input is made by the legislature, in form and often in fact, and legislatures often respond to highly particularistic interests and constituencies. Continuing a specific service is likely to be more focal than overall levels or mixes of appropriations. Relatedly, industry can store up profits for future needs, which can encourage conservation and cost consciousness. In contrast, if a government department underspends its budget one year, chances are the legislature will decrease its budget the next year. This may provide a powerful disincentive to effective public management of resources.

The relative difficulty in measuring outcomes of government as opposed to industry may in turn have an effect on management practices. With more measurable outcomes, the industrial manager can more acutely feel the need for organizational change, and also may be able to pinpoint more specifically what needs to be changed. In government organizations, far less effort is made to measure outcomes and the need for organizational change may not be as obvious to the manager. That is, no itch, no scratch.

Proposition 6. The management hierarchy in government is fragmented by complex and shifting linkages of elected, appointed, and career personnel; such linkages are stronger and better defined in manufacturing organizations. Since OD programs as a general rule should begin at the top, fragmentation raises problems for government. The major problem involves choosing which "top" to consider. Beginning with elected or appointed politicians who change frequently generates resistance from civil service personnel. Beginning in the upper ranks of the civil service maximizes the chances that the OD program will have ongoing support, but may bring resistance from budget officers or political appointees. There seems no way out. Indeed, the problem may inhere in deeply cherished ideas about political governance. In the federal government, for example, one observer notes: "Congress has a definite interest in cultivating a certain level of distrust within and between government agencies so as to encourage flow of information to legislators. No OD program in a business organization will face such an array of hurdles. . . ."[41]

Golembiewski considers the multiple set of authoritative decision makers in government one of the major factors complicating OD in government.[42] He cites the death of an OD program because of a lack of integration between the two relevant subcommittees–one substantive, one appropriations–and the agency. The failure was also attributed to tradition, jealousy, and separation of powers.[43]

Proposition 7. Career personnel in government civil service can have a more negative impact on change efforts directed at programs in which they have a high degree of ownership than personnel in manufacturing organizations. Management can exert more influence over getting industrial employees to participate in change than public executives may be able to muster against civil service personnel. This is a more-or-less proposition, of course, but a significant one. Especially given their protected status, employees can wage successful war against the termination of a public program. Consider Nixon's effort to dismantle the Office of Economic Opportunity. Employees of OEO programs around the country obtained a restraining order to prohibit him. At the same time, Community Action Agencies in local communities were suddenly trying to convince their communities how important they were, trying to muster previously lacking community support to back them in their battle.[44] Employees of a business organization can believe deeply in programs, of course. But their status is less guaranteed, and they typically will have less access to friendly legislators who control the firm's life-blood. Hence, their managers can be less cautious about change in many cases. Labor unions, of course, can provide support for both government and business employees.

Such obstacles to change within government constitute obstacles to OD. Anything that implies the possibility of change for either government or manufacturing organizations is likely to be perceived as threatening, but government employees have more potential means of blocking or at least minimizing the change.

Proposition 8. Industry is output-oriented, whereas government is throughput-oriented. Katz and Kahn in their typology of organizations classify manufacturing organizations as productive or economic organizations "concerned with the creation of wealth, the manufacture of goods, and the providing of services for the general public or for specific segments of it."[45] They consider government as managerial or political because its activities are concerned with the adjudication, coordination, and control of resources, people, and subsystems.

The differences can be profound and multiply apparent. For example, industry places much more emphasis on worker productivity than does government. Industry also more often provides rewards for productivity and innovation. Therefore, there is less impetus for either productivity or innovation in government, and thus less impetus for OD.

Rosenbloom notes that the largest employer group in the U.S., government, has shown the least concern for worker productivity.[46] Whereas industrial productivity has steadily increased, government is in the throes of a real crisis. Rosenbloom is not surprised. Government is more fragmented, often less informed about relevant technological opportunities, and provides little or no reward for greater productivity; the output is inelastic and the work force difficult to reduce. Moreover, few or no competitors threaten to take over their domain if a government or its agency fails to increase productivity. Rosenbloom thinks we need to increase productivity in the future, especially as this relates to state and local government services. Costs will rise drastically unless substitutes for labor-intensive services are developed.

Proposition 9. Job security is greater in government than in industry. Labor unions in industry and civil service in government are alike in that they both protect the job security of their members and make arbitrary hiring and firing difficult. There seems a major difference, however. Industrial workers often are laid off because of declining demand for their products and increasing costs of production, but this occurs less frequently in government, or at least with much greater difficulty. Public lay-offs have occurred recently, as in New York and Detroit, but they are more rare and seem to occur far later than would be the case in industry.

Industry is more sensitive to the market place, and government is more responsive to the political processes of compromise and accommodation among the multitude of groups which may affect government decisions.[47] When budgets are cut or monies frozen for one department, particularly in the federal government as Nixon did for almost 2 years, work comes to a standstill but manpower reductions may not occur. When funding for federal housing programs and other programs under the U.S. Department of Housing and Urban Development was frozen for almost 2 years, HUD employees in federal, regional, and area offices showed up but did little work.[48] Shifting those personnel to other areas in the federal bureaucracy would have been difficult, and there was always the day-to-day hope that monies would be unfrozen and activities could resume. Such a waste of human resources and financial resources is far less likely in industry or commerce, although firms in "managed industries" can at least for a time reach profit targets even with profligate use of resources. As in new cars and autos, however, foreign competition may sooner or later raise hob with such noncompetitive conveniences.

No available data certify the greater job security of public employees, but that is clearly part of the common wisdom and is reflected in angry tones when (as in New York City) substantial numbers of civil servants were furloughed or released due to financial problems. Government organizations may also attract people more interested in "security" than in other aspects of the job, and these employees may tend to remain longer. This entrenching of personnel with major control over their own longevity with the organization may be one of the major obstacles to OD in public agencies.

Proposition 10. Public administrators are less knowledgeable and understanding of the use of OD than managers in manufacturing organizations. Top management support and use of OD obviously will depend on knowledge and understanding of OD. For complex reasons, public administrators tend to be more caboose than engine when it comes to the discovery and diffusion of managerial innovations. Consider the still-recent expansion of graduate programs in public administration, which are puny indeed compared to counterpart programs in industry and commerce. In the public sector, that is to say, administrators are less likely to have acquired any formal management or administrative training. Many employees were political appointees, in fact, who got covered later by "wall-to-wall" extensions of civil service systems. City managers constitute the most notable exception to this generalization.[49]

Proposition 11. Economic pressures toward innovation, and a willingness to pay for innovations, are related reasons for the noticeably greater amount of OD done in industry than in government. If there is a high correlation between innovation in an organization and the amount of discretion allowed, as seems probable, public work may suffer significantly. That is to say, the amount of discretion industrial managers can exercise in stimulating innovation seems generally greater than government managers have at comparable levels of responsibility.

Consider only a single point. At the time of a major study of consulting services to the federal government, the maximum daily rate for consultants to HEW and DOL was $138 and for OEO was $100, although the individual's stature could play a large role in the rate of pay. Nonetheless, most OD consultants could then easily get $250 to $400 per day for consulting in industry. The difference does impact on the enthusiasm OD consultants have for working with the federal bureaucracy, as well as with other levels of government.[50]

Intervention Guidelines Distilled from Experience*

A useful sense of how OD in the public sector faces special challenges can be suggested by three guidelines I developed from my own experience at the politics/administration interface, those top levels of public agencies where political appointees interact with career employees, sometimes to "make policy," sometimes to monitor programs. The three guidelines come from a longer list of nineteen developed for another purpose, and seek to provide both direction and counsel for public-sector intervenors, to provide insight, and to improve effectiveness within the context of typical OD values and goals. OD values and goals emphasize openness, trust, and win-win interaction, which many observers see as variously in conflict with political realities. What follows constitutes an effort

*Derived from Robert T. Golembiewski, "Intervening at Top Levels in Public Agencies: Managing the Tension Between OD Principles and Political Power." Paper presented at "OD–1978." San Francisco, Calif., April 5, 1978, 100 pp.

to accommodate those values and common realities, while avoiding both purism and opportunism.

Guideline 1. The OD consultant's basic concern should be with "the system," as contrasted with specific units or individuals. The objective dilemma should be obvious. Intervenors will work with and for individuals or groups, and yet essential guidance comes from accommodating a sense of the possible to some concept of the ideal at a systemic level that transcends individuals and groups. The same overall sense of "out-ness" leavened by a degree of "in-ness" characterizes private-sector consultation, of course. But, the pushes and pulls to me seem different or at least greater in the public sector, in general, perhaps due to the institutional features sketched above.

Two derivative needs require underscoring. Paramountly, this guideline requires that the intervenor variously help groups and individuals develop a sensitivity to systemic needs, which is to say that they often will be encouraged to take perspectives and positions contrary to their own immediate individual or group interests and traditions, for which they receive mostly (or only) psychic gratification. Operationally, moreover, the OD intervenor at the interface needs a well-developed system of values, a philosophy for action which he or she can make substantially clear to others and which can be applied to many sets of operating conditions. Also important, but in a secondary role, the OD intervenor will be expected to have a model of how some major desired effects can be attained in organizations. Clients at the interface typically do not demand perfection in knowledge or control of reality, but they usually do demand consistency in articulating and working toward some relatively clear goals in relatively effective ways.

Much the same needs bedevil OD intervenors in the private sector, of course, but operating at a systemic level in the public sector presents two classes of greater challenges: one emotional, the other associated with the pervasive multileveledness of OD consultation at the interface. The first challenge requires developing *hope* that things can be different, and the second requires *competence* involving skills and theory about how to make a difference at so many levels, often simultaneously, when so many forces make it so hard to make a lasting difference.

Prevailing Emotional Tone. The modal emotional tone concerning their "system" among those at the interface, in my experience, when they really let their hair down, ranges from despair that it is unredemptively bigger than all of us, at the worst, to the resigned but acerbic humor reflected in the public bureaucrat's pencil—erasers on both ends. Depending upon one's position at the interface, views of causality may differ. Politicals, both appointed and elective, tend to sputter and fume about the unresponsive and resistant bureaucracy; and career officials tend to despair about if not disparage passing political fads and personalities.

The general emotional tone takes manifold forms, of course, some aggressively hostile but most definitely trending toward withdrawal or resignation. Perhaps the most poignant form of the latter adaptation I recall involved a grandmotherly (and hierarchically senior) envoy from an agency who–in part tactically, but with basic sincerity–urged an OD team:

> Please go home. You can't help us; nobody can help us. We're all stuck in this, and there's no way out. I sacrificed everything for the agency in my best years–my personal life and all. But it just rolls on and gets worse. Please go home to your families. You may be able to help them. Save your energies for where it may do some good.
>
> Please leave us alone. Don't make the mistake we made. It doesn't pay.

She simply could not envision getting geared up for another disappointment.

Pervasive Multileveledness. Exacerbating these deficiencies in emotional tone at the interface, and no doubt also contributing mightily to that tone, is a pervasive "multileveledness." Life gets complicated fast, in short, what with everything at the interface being so subtly related to everything else.

Let us get somewhat more specific about what it means to say that the key words in a systemic perspective at the public interface are multilevel, as well as about what is meant by implying that the OD intervenor should discipline self to act in this way. The demands in the public sector are sometimes similar to those in the private sector, again, but the former locus will likely pose unique or at least more intense problems.

Two specifics must suffice here. *First,* most intervenors specialize in either interpersonal *or* rational-technical models. This bias need not be troublesome at many levels of organization; indeed, it often will simplify the consulting contract. The politics/administration interface seldom permits that kinds of specialization, however, and failure to be sensitive to multilevel issues can be serious.

At the politics/administration interface, *second,* OD interventions must be multilevel in another ubiquitous and significant sense. Taking the systemic view typically means that the OD intervenor finds self working betwixt and between the *professionals* and the *politicals.* I italicize because by "professionals" I do not simply mean engineers, chemists, behavioral scientists, and the like; nor by "politicals" do I refer only to elected officials. Rather, I seek to focus on two generalized roles:

- The professional role emphasizes specialized knowledge, empirical science, and rationality.
- The political role focuses on negotiation, bargaining, elections, votes, and compromise.

Complex projects require both roles, often played by the same persons. Thus, an engineer might play a political role, and an elected official also might play a professional role. One of the major confounding characteristics of the public interface, in fact, is that the same individual often has to wear both hats, in lightning-like sequence or even simultaneously.

The role specialization of politicals and professionals at the politics/administration interface is reinforced by many practices and traditions in this country, a specialization which exacerbates the tension between the two orientations which will appear in all organizations. Indeed, the interface may be defined as that uneven seam between politicals and professionals. Popularly elected legislators seldom have administrative roles, for example, except in some commission forms of government, and constitutional and institutional provisions generally separate legislative and executive and administrative branches, each with different constituencies. This specialization exacerbates the "built-in aversion between the professional and politics,"[51] an aversion that derives from the basic way each tends to test for truth-value: One seeks truth in stable technology, as it were, and the other in volatile constituency-building. The twain may never meet. In the ideal case, however, the interface will be characterized by a mutual humility: professionals will recognize that technology cannot make value choices, that only humans can and often only by utilizing processes that may be broadly characterized as "political"; politicals will recognize that no amount of negotiation or exchange can change some realities or quasirealities; and both will seek to define with appropriate precision in diverse issue-areas what is "political" from what is intractable to its processes.

Of course, politicals also exist in the private sector, but in nothing like the profusion nor with the multiplicity of independent power-bases characteristic of the public sector. And, private-sector analogues of political institutions, such as the board of directors, tend to be weak replicas of popularly elected legislatures, despite contemporary efforts to politicize those institutions, as by stockholder protests and so on.

Costs and Benefits of Systemic Bias. Taking the systemic view of the interface, then, is no easy piece. It places the intervenor directly at a major tension point, where attitudes of despair or at least resignation often will dominate. And the intervenor's theory and philosophy also must be substantially complete and compelling as to both substance and salesmanship. And even where the intervenor can come through in these senses, as if they were not challenge enough, clients often will charge that a consultant is "playing god" by insisting on a systemic perspective, and some clients with parochial loyalties and identifications may seek to "clip the consultant's wings." This restraint is likely to be all the more insistent to the degree that the OD intervenor acts impactfully.

By far the greatest difficulties with taking a "systemic view" inhere in determining just what that is. Intemperately interpreted, such a view could provide a rationale for whatever an intervenor prefers, for whatever "my guts tell me." That is not the prescription here. Along with liberal dollops of realistic humility and a passion for testing, in contrast, the organizationally relevant literatures provide major perspective for seeing the forest as well as the trees. For example, the huge literature on behavioral and attitudinal consequences of alternative structural arrangements can provide invaluable guidance, even though that literature is far from complete. Similarly, an intervenor in a team-building experience would do well to keep in mind the substantial knowledge we have about phases of group development. Moreover, on a case-by-case basis, I believe that one can usually distinguish the more systemic from the less systemic perspective. This book contains several such examples, most proximately the illustration provided by the second point immediately following.

The virtues of the first guideline are numerous, nonetheless. *First,* it avoids tiresome issues of "who is the client?" When only individuals or small groups are involved, clarity about "who is the client" patently is useful and even invaluable. At the politics/administration interface, however, the client is typically Janus-like with multiple and competing interests. Preoccupation with trying to define "client," then, may be paid for in terms of cultivating local loyalties and loss of systemic impact. The consultant should busy self with helping to seek and solve problems rather than with defining sponsorship, while being as clear as possible about whatever multiple clients are being served by any single intervention.

Second, patently, an identification with the system versus the parts reinforces the intervenor's interstitial role, and also should signal that the intervenor intends to rise above "office politics." The preachment here does not prescribe some kind of above-it-all-ness. Oppositely, it prescribes playing "systemic politics," better and more credibly.

> A chief executive had decided on a major appointment, he informed an OD consultant. The proposed appointee was saleable for various reasons, but (it soon became clear) had the basic attraction of being no threat to the chief executive. In fact, the CEO was bypassing an individual with better credentials for the job, but who also posed a greater threat to the CEO.
>
> The appointment might be good "ward politics," the consultant agreed, but its systemic implications were serious. To illustrate, the CEO over time had importuned several subordinates to develop "strong back-ups," for all the usual public reasons but also to make it easier for the CEO to reassign and terminate employees. CEO encouraged others to "put it on the line," but when he had his chance he—like they—was motivated to take the easy way out. Few would be fooled, the OD consultant guessed.
>
> The CEO reconsidered his choice, and discussion soon shifted to the topic of highlighting how the CEO had "bitten the bullet to set an example for

one and all." This would be "good medicine for the system." Besides, the CEO concluded, the odds were better than even that the new appointee soon would "dig his own grave with his mouth."

When informed that the OD consultant thought it wise to spend some time with the new appointee, the CEO first balked but finally agreed, in terms I found realistic although lacking in charity. "If you can help him, that will help me, if I play it with any finesse. And if you mess him up, or can't help, that also will help me."

This prescription for a systemic orientation may seem to increase the consultant's vulnerability, and it apparently clashes with the reasonable advice that the change agent needs *a* client, first and foremost. But recall I write here only of the politics/administration interface. Tactics well designed to secure and safeguard *a* client, in short, often are counterproductive for maintaining a systemic role. I have become quite fatalist in this regard, and assign a very high probability to one of three outcomes in cases of interstitial consultancy:

- Either the consultant comes into a situation in which a "balance of power" initially recognizes the value of some external playing an interstitial role
- or the consultant quite quickly can encourage such a balance of power
- or the consultant is very unlikely to ever become effective in trading back and forth across the politics/administration interface.

The need to legitimate the interstitial role quickly at the politics/administration interface rests on numerous considerations, two of which have a distinct prominence in my experience. Unless that occurs quickly, the consultant likely will either come to be, or come to be seen as, identified too closely with one of the subsystems to be a credible interstitial player. Moreover, appropriate balances of power at the interface typically are temporary, which also seems generally true of lateral or horizontal linkages between separate units of organization at more or less the same level. So, the premium definitely is on getting something done quickly. This implies a certain disciplined boldness.

Celerity also is appropriate in the third case above. "Getting out quick" when a supporting balance of power does not exist, or when it cannot be quickly induced, often will enhance a consultant's credibility as well as leverage when the situation changes, as it almost certainly shall. "This just is not a propitious moment," the OD intervenor announces, in effect. "There will be other, better times."

The argument for planned interstitiality can be made even more sharply. It is often dangerous to seek to attach self—or to be content with having attached self—to a limited set of actors near the politics/administration interface. For political officials are vulnerable, or at least short-lived, and changes there typically result in several rounds of changes in immediate subordinates, among both patronage and career employees. Since OD programs often will have long lead-times, establishing a tie with a system versus a specific regime is not only difficult but may be necessary.

> The demise of Project ACORD in the U.S. Department of State can be traced quite directly to its basic attachment to the office of the deputy undersecretary for administration with much less support (and even opposition) at two superordinate levels. When the undersecretary left, numerous other departures followed, and Project ACORD soon folded.

Third, an intervenor's focus on "the system" can be a damn good thing for, far more often than not, few others at the interface will be equipped or motivated to understand and evaluate systemic issues. The specialization prevalent at the interface inhibits such a view, for example. Thus, "politicals" may be very active in developing the kind of agreements we call "policy," and they later may get involved in episodic "case work" for individual constituents, but beyond that, more than likely, their attention will be spotty. The usual preoccupation among politicals, even among those in executive or managerial roles, is to get reelected or reappointed, not to manage some system. Their focus likely will be segmented and superficial, that is, centered around those interests which can be welded into a *sufficient constituency.* For them, the OD intervenor can be useful in reminding them about what they are so likely to forget.

Professionals also may need systemic help, if for different reasons. Thus, they often specialize in a function, in contrast to the specialization of politicals in stages of the policy-making and implementation cycle. That functional specialization may constitute a trained incapacity, and its effects are perhaps most clearly seen in the budget process. Each functional specialty tends to fight for its own programs, which are particularistic but intensely advocated. Politicals may exacerbate these ubiquitous tendencies, moreover, as in playing favorites to guarantee access or to provide open lines of communication. Powerful members of Congress, for example, may use such an approach for dual purposes: to help control the presidency or political appointees; and to facilitate agency response to interests important to legislators.

The intervenor also typically has experience in many more organizations than the client, whether political or professional. And intervenor's reading and study should be broader still. Such experience and knowledge, which by design is unfettered by day-to-day operating problems, often permits the consultant to sensitize clients to what may be "around the corner," to anticipate and prepare for it, or perhaps to encourage them to venture beyond their probable vested interest in what exists today.

Guideline 2. Public-sector interventions often will require some features that are unique, or at least differ in noteworthy degree from much private-sector practice.

The associated argumentation is complex and problematic, but three perspectives can provide some brief sense of the meaning here.

First, many public agencies reflect conditions or stages that do not permit unqualified acceptance of the usually appropriate counsel that OD interventions should build strength and build on strength. Roughly, some systems cannot lose for winning, and others cannot win for losing. At the risk of being merely precious, the latter cases do not permit building strength and building on strength. Rather, the orientation may be to inspire some hope, even by risking dependence of the client on the consultant, while building on acknowledged and pervasive weakness, if not perversity.

How to distinguish such conditions or stages, specifically? Many approaches might be taken. Elsewhere, I try to differentiate "regenerative" from "degenerative" systems; at another point, a "crisis of disagreement" is distinguished from a "crisis of agreement." Consider systems that are "degenerative" or experiencing a "crisis of agreement." For bare illustrative purposes here only, the same input of data via the same OD design could have such profoundly different effects in the two systems:

- "Oh, so that's what's wrong. How can we remedy that?"
- "Yes, I know that's what's wrong. There's just no way to change that around here. It'll always be that way, or at least so long that I'll never live to see it change."

The image is that of a hill. Depending upon which side of the hill on which you find yourself (A or B), going the same distance in the same direction will either get you closer to the peak (A′) or still further away from it (B′).

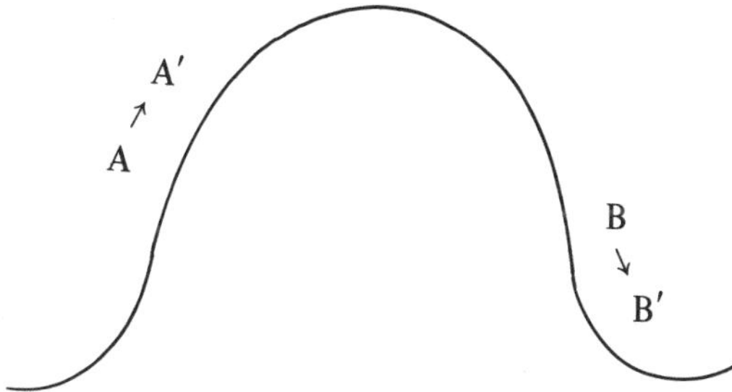

I am convinced about three points: the distinction is critical; clues about the condition usually are available; and public agencies are far more likely than private-sector organizations to have advanced degenerative symptoms or characteristics of a crisis of agreement. I cannot strictly prove my contentions, of course.

Second, by implication, OD interventions appropriate to one organizational condition or stage might be inappropriate at another, perhaps even seriously counterproductive. Let me briefly illustrate what I mean. I have found that group designs are less useful in what I consider degenerative systems. I tend to deal far more with single individuals, personally and as a go-between, with parties mutually aware of my role, and especially so when some new issue is being worked. "Privatized" designs, such as third-party interventions and role negotiation exercises, also can prove very useful. Patently, this approach reduces the risk for principals, and permits face-saving should things not work out. Typically, when things do work out, success does not want for parents. After a successful iteration or so, actors at the interface typically take up-front positions.

> In one case, political officials were cautious about confronting a CEO with their view that he required a strong back-up. They did not want to offend the man, nor to reduce his clout by too-obvious demands that he acquiesce. The politicos did feel the need for greater confidence that a capable replacement was in the wings, but they wished to proceed with no public notice. The CEO wanted to appear neither obdurate nor a patsy for a possible take-over by training his own replacement. I was invited in by one side, but soon was accepted by the other.
>
> I traded back and forth, carrying information, but also contributing to strategy and tactics. I also strived to build as much openness as possible into a situation that had very narrow parameters, as by helping those involved articulate and share the political implications of the transaction, as well as their emotional reactions to it.
>
> Once that issue got worked through with minimum dislocation, the political officials sought similar action by other key executives. "We'll use the [CEO] model," I was told, "so we won't need you." And that pleased me.

Let me provide another perspective on the decreased usefulness at the interface of such "public" interventions as group confrontations between hierarchical levels or various "mirroring" exercises. Their results in public agencies might only confirm a basic fact that everyone already knew: that the system is pervasively degenerative, which means essentially that openness, owning, and trust are so low, and risk is so high, that candidness about the system permits only the conclusion that conditions will not be changed by anyone, even given herculean effort and uncommon good fortune. Things are so bad that publicly acknowledging the point only makes matters worse, deepens despair.

Third, a key issue–perhaps *the* issue–then becomes how the *hope* of remedial change can be nurtured in the face of massive squelchers of that hope. Somehow, that hope might get kindled by itself, or a determined political in high office may come along–as seems to be the case with Governor Hunt of North Carolina–who seems seriously bent on renewing the state administrative system, and who can successfully avoid the charges of empire-building. Short of those happy happenstances, the analysis below has two emphases. A first emphasis considers some things an OD intervenor consciously can try in a degenerative system that might be ill advised in a regenerative one. The second emphasis seeks to generalize implications for the OD intervenor's role.

Some Personal Experience. What kinds of things have often worked for me? Without prescribing them for any other OD intervenor, let met sketch a brief catalog of semiparticulars.

I have found that more personal risk-taking by the intervenor seems appropriate in degenerative systems. Instead of being personally upfront—to develop the point by contrast—the usual prescription for the OD intervenor as facilitator sagely encourages getting clients to own attitudes and behavior, to express themselves openly, and so on. To which many public-sector clients will respond: "That's easy enough for you to say, but very much harder for us to do." And so it is. One way to generate some hope that regenerative features can be built into an organization is for the OD intervenor to be the "point-man," relying on infantry jargon. If the point-man lives, as it were, that implies some safety for others and all can advance.

The concept of OD intervenor as point-man cuts several ways, of course. Thus, it may result in building dependence, and it clearly builds on the "weakness" of suspicion, mistrust, and so on. But, having a point-man is often part of the culture of degenerative systems, and beginning from where the system is typically constitutes good advice and sound practice. Moreover, the risks for the OD intervenor are in the general case far less substantial than for system members, and some pump priming may be helpful symbolically, while any associated modeling may be useful to all concerned.

I have found that my point-man posture most often is directed at some power figure, say a CEO or an executive, with a reputation for staunchness if not insensitive autocracy. If we can make it, as it were, subordinates may feel a glimmer of hope. Whether we make it or not, however, the signals can be very revealing to others.

> A powerful staff executive and I got into an animated discussion about leadership styles in the very early stages of a mutual consideration of the usefulness of team-building for him and his immediate subordinates.
>
> In the heat of those early moments, he jerked a marking pencil from my hand, and sallied forth to cover several pages of newsprint, lecturing me and his subordinates.
>
> I grew restive after 15 minutes or so, and consciously debated a deliberately-facilitative but avoiding comment like: "Now, Ernst, it might be helpful at this point for us to review people's reactions to the last few minutes to see if they're getting what they expected from this meeting."

> Rather, given my guess that his subordinates would not take that bait, I noted: "It's clear to me that either you have not understood what I tried to say earlier, or that I did a very bad job of it. And your knowledge of the research literature on leadership styles seems very weak to me. Give me the marker, Ernst, and I'll start again if the misunderstanding is general."
>
> The room grew very quiet. Ernst returned to his seat and, very revealingly, said: "I deserved having my chain yanked. That was good for me–I was beyond my depth. But"–he added with no smile at all–"only one time this week."
>
> Ernst has saved everybody much time, and some possible grief. There would be no team-building, we all seem to recognize at once, especially since Ernst would be retiring in less than two years. One week between feedback efforts is a long, long time.

Where "the system" is alleged to be the inhibitor, an OD intervenor should test aggressively. In some cases, the essential cause may lie in some unapproachable, unalterable, and unavoidable source. There the intervenor may resort to "worst case" analysis. The focus here is on the basic question: "What would be the worst possible outcome if you (or your agency) did X?" Sometimes "the worst" turns out on inspection to be pretty mild stuff, or various ways of blunting the effects of "the worst" might be brought to life. It might even be possible to work toward changing "the system."

But cases clearly exist in which the worst consequence of evasion is very wicked, while "playing the game" is costly for participants. Here the intervenor faces a dilemma. Should he or she be content with Band-Aid interventions, as in "cooling-out" designs for disaffected participants? Or should he or she push for preventive interventions that reduce or eliminate the source of disaffection? There are no general answers, and sometimes it ends up being a little bit of both. Appropriate design elements can help guarantee that it is not all alleviation and no prevention.

In one case, I agreed to an ameliorative effort by CEO, whose basic style involved a preference for laissez-faire but a quick reliance on potent authoritarianism when things did not go well in his eyes. I suspected he periodically built up concern and even hostility in his subordinates, although his timing in scheduling "ventilation" sessions was pretty good. He would then drive the resulting "era of good feelings" into the ground, I feared, with no change in his behavior. I shared my concerns with him. "Now that's the kind of openness I want," he said. "If you can only get my colleagues to do half as well."

> I agreed to serve as the intervenor, but in the opening session noted my concern that the CEO was a "cast-iron sponge," who would obligingly pass through all feedback and respond to little or none of it. I explained the design thus would have two components: a confrontation phase between CEO and the group of his subordinates; and a contracting period, when

> CEO and they would bargain about what one party wanted the other to STOP, START, or CONTINUE. I advertised my major interest in seeing that any contracts would be met.
>
> The CEO smiled benevolently. "Just what we need," he said, "agreements arrived at in public which we can all share in—both in formulating and enforcing." He joined in enthusiastically, agreeing later to "start" a major policy in return for an agreement by his subordinates to "stop" something they were doing. There were promises of greater things to come.
>
> The experience was a smash success. About a week later, the CEO gave a party for me and several others he saw as central. At the party, I learned at table that the CEO had changed his mind about the major policy he had agreed to "start." The change would be communicated to others at "some later date."
>
> The CEO asked each guest to speak briefly and, of course, I opened my remarks by saying: "I resign." CEO had made the agreement in public session and, if a change was unavoidable—which I doubted—then that arena was the one in which the change should be considered. And if his employees were as incensed as I about the surprise change, I concluded ominously, there would be trouble.
>
> "Bob G. raises a point we neglected," said the CEO, unruffled. "Day-to-day pressure encourages one to neglect the fine points, you know. We shall reconsider. Good gurus are hard to find, you know."
>
> A week or so later, I learned that the new policy, almost rescinded privately, was reinstated the same way.

Of one thing I am certain in cases of "the system" as inhibitor. I think little of the OD intervenor in effect saying: "Look how easy it is for me to thumb my nose at the system. Why don't you try it? It's fun." The consultant might only precipitate clients into harmful situations, whose effect the consultant might experience in only attenuated degree, or escape altogether.

Some Implications for the OD Role. These samples of personal behavior can support some useful generalizations. Better put, perhaps, those behavioral samples should be viewed *only* within a context which distinguishes three intervenor roles:

- Generating the *need for change*
- *Implementing* a program of change after system members perceive the need for change
- *Modeling* aspects of the kinds of behavior appropriate to some needed change perceived by system members

The illustrations above of behaviors that have worked for me in seriously degenerative systems should not be read as efforts to generate a need for change;

that is, they do not relate to the first role-component. In my view, except in extreme situations, the client system must come to perceive that need. In certain exceptional cases, the intervenor must in conscience adopt such a role. But intervenors should do so with full recognition that this will probably disqualify them from either implementing or modeling roles, when and if some system comes to recognize that need for change. And intervenor's enthusiasm about a need for change may pose serious risks for system members. They may find it awkward or even dangerous to buy into an intervenor's concept of the need for change. The issue will be especially real in autocratic organizations with a history of harsh treatment of deviants.

The illustrations above of behaviors that have worked for me in advanced degenerative systems, oppositely, argue only that OD intervenors should do more modeling of behaviors appropriate to some change perceived by a client. Very often, the OD's role is perceived to be that of an implementer who only enters a system, helps highlight the need for change, and may provide appropriate skill-training. The illustrations above go beyond this implementer concept of the OD intervenor's role.

Guideline 3. The public sector "production function" is very complex, especially in two senses: The weighting of its numerous components may be highly volatile over time, and its more stable and heavily weighted components have little or nothing to do with effectiveness or efficiency, as conventionally understood. The sense of this guideline may seem unnerving for the OD intervenor, suggesting as it does the unavailability of a reliable compass by which to steer, as it were. In the private sector, for example, increased satisfaction of organization members at no added financial cost often will constitute a specific and discrete goal for an OD effort.

Establishing that this guideline is not a nonguideline will take some doing, with a modest first step being a general definition of the "production function." Despite dispute about the details of measurement, most would agree that such a function should provide for some input-output comparison, which includes quantitative and qualitative aspects of productivity, as well as some sense of the satisfaction of organization members or long-run morale.

Patently, a production function could play a critical role in organizational choice, so its characterization above in the public sector assumes negative significance. Much has been written about the virtues for managerial control in the private sector of a marketplace and of "profit" or "loss." The reliance on profit is most meaningful at or toward the top of most organizations, however, that overwhelming majority organized in a centralized mode relating functionally specialized departments. And typical profit calculations take into account only a narrow range of considerations—economic ones, and usually only short-range economic ones at that. Until recently, that is, profit calculations usually were made without considering the costs borne by the environment (as in pollution, hit-and-run mining or timber-cutting, and so on) or those costs borne by organization members (as in boredom, alienation, poor quality of working life, and so on). So, the adequacy of usual calculations of "profit" can be overstated easily, but the concept does provide some sense of a desirable and collective goal, it permits some measurement of performance, and it does encourage some degree of self-control.

Let me hedge in several senses, without changing the essential position here. The point is not so much that a production function is impossible in the public sector, as some have argued. More essentially, the position here has two central features: that many of the components of that function are highly variable over time, variable as to both number and weighting; and that the stable components of that function often relate only or mostly to very broad considerations as to what is seen to be necessary or appropriate to preserve or enhance the ultimate systemic parameters, the perceived legitimacy of the regime. The basic focus of the public-sector production function is thus on keeping the polity sufficiently together, to put it in crude terms, rather than on producing specific goods and services. The underlying criterion of "effectiveness" is a very broad one, and considerations of "efficiency" are subservient in fundamental senses. Consider the role of "spoils patronage." History shows it to have been wildly inefficient in particulars, but major claims can be made for its fundamental effectiveness at certain stages in the development of viable and relatively popular regimes in Great Britain and the United States, as through the nurturing of political parties which in turn are significant in our representative political system.

The public-sector production function patently leaves much room for maneuvering and the imagination, for "effectiveness" is defined basically in cosmic terms and "efficiency" calculations pale in comparison. This provides little or no guidance to decision-making, for elite or citizen. The task of statesmanship is to create a rolling readjustment, as it were: to preserve the essential and substantial consensus underlying any nonauthoritarian regime, moving toward systemic effectiveness *and* efficient use of material and human factors of production. That few regimes do well over any length of time in this rolling readjustment seems patent, as is evidenced by the fact that authoritarian regimes are the norm to which few lasting exceptions exist. Two temptations seem universal. Thus, regimes can so narrowly define those who determine systemic effectiveness that regimes either tumble, as in the case of most aristocracies, or they come to apply massive repression in seeking to keep the have-nots in check. Alternatively, regimes can profligately and suddenly expand expectations about who gets how much of what. Then prevailing supply and demand relationships usually get seriously out of phase, ballooning inflation sets in, and so on. In the latter case, of course, repression is often taken as the only apparent alternative to systemic disintegration.

Another hedge. There will be periods—of brief and sporadic reform movements, for example, or popular wars or causes—when the public-sector production function takes on substantial clarity and stability as to what "effectiveness" means. But even then that definition is narrow, will likely have no relation to efficiency as normally viewed, and it typically will be "politics as usual" before very long.

Variability of Organization "Cultures"

Finally and briefly, OD applications are conditioned by the subtle qualities of host organizations—their beliefs, and values, and specific ways of doing things. For want of a better term, these diverse subtle qualities are referred to as organization "cultures."

OD applications have to be suited to these cultures or, at least in extreme cases, a design may fail or create unnecessary problems. Given the goals of enhanced feedback and disclosure, to illustrate, not all possible approaches will be optimum for a specific organization culture. Indeed, some designs may be poison. Thus a very stiff and correct organization culture may respond well to a design like role negotiation, while a family T-group might seem a grossly improper invasion of historic ways of doing business.

There is no generic way to guarantee such "fit" between individual cultures and specific OD designs. But some rules of thumb are helpful, among the more important of which are the following:

- The initial primacy in OD is on diagnosis not on design, a bias which should help indicate an organization's culture and permit educated guesses as to appropriate design.
- OD seeks to induce specific processes that approach quite definite goals, but one should begin from where a system is and then move toward more satisfactory intermediate conditions. OD should not seek to leap to some "ultimate desirability" such as the "end of bureaucracy," whatever that means.
- OD emphasizes participant choice and, if the change agent respects that emphasis and cultivates it, the host can provide signals re any violation of culture, with the rationale being that the person wearing the shoes is more likely to know if they pinch than the bootmaker or salesperson.
- OD programs and designs should provide a number of explicit go/no-go points of choice, which allow and encourage hosts to express themselves as to degree of fit between their culture and an OD design. This helps build a sense of ownership at the same time.
- OD programs are no doubt best structured if they include both internal and external change agents, with the former being especially sensitive to

existing cultural pathways and the latter being somewhat less likely to become a captive of them.

The Degree of System "Coupledness"

In an elemental sense, as recent discussion in the literature has usefully highlighted in the case of "coupledness,"[52] a system is not a system. Empirically, that is, systems will differ in "where they are," in their development condition. Prescriptively, in addition, systems will differ in "where they should be," because of some technological features or because of some higher-order goals or values. Thus the markets or technology of the cardboard carton industry all but require a "tightly coupled" or "highly bounded" system. Oppositely, superordinate values, which in higher education are expressed in terms of "academic freedom" or of the conditions thought to facilitate inquiry, can prescribe a "loosely coupled" system.

These elemental distinctions imply two significant points. Directly, in empirical and/or prescriptive senses, a system may fall anywhere along this continuum: underbounded → overbounded. Table 2 illustrates some of the differences between systems at the two end-points of this continuum. Moreover, as Table 2 implies, OD interventions appropriate for a system at one end-point may be seriously counterproductive for a system at the other end-point.

Four Perspectives on Coupledness

Four major points summarize the present state of reliable knowledge relevant to differences in coupledness, whether actual or ideal. *First,* the issue of

Table 2 A Few Characteristics of Underbounded and Overbounded Systems

System Characteristics	Underbounded	Overbounded
1. Authority relations	Unclear and overlapping authority	Well-defined hierarchy and authority
2. Role definition	Uncertain definitions of roles and jobs	Strict and constraining definitions of roles and jobs
3. Management of human energy	Resources are dispersed, physically and emotionally, and difficult to harness	Resources are blocked and difficult to release

Source: Selected from Clayton P. Alderfer and David N. Berg, "Organization Development: The Profession and the Practitioner," p. 104, in Philip H. Mirvis and David N. Berg (eds.), *Failures in Organization Development and Change* (New York: Wiley, 1977).

appropriate boundness is a dynamic one and implies the long-run need to fine-tune organizations as they experience changes in markets, technologies, and so on. Consider one small transit agency, which coped well enough (was appropriately bounded, if the reader will) under the guiding notion that its management was a collection of independent professionals and specialists who reacted to problem-situations, either by direct solution or by passing problems on to appropriate specialists.[53] The results were positive, overall. Indeed, the agency is described as an innovative and high-energy system. As the agency grew rapidly in size, however, this basic reactivity became increasingly troublesome: the system grew more and more underbounded. Growing energies got invested in unproductive work: for example, determining who was responsible for failure to respond to some problem. Moreover, the reactive mode led to many surprises, many unanticipated problems, and their accelerating accumulation stressed relationships and herniated the agency's problem-solving. Hence a sense of powerlessness tended to grow, yeastlike. Individuals with heightening frequency did not know who was responsible for what; they did not have all the available information; they could not convince others to change their priorities; and so on. In a few words, the system became obviously underbounded.

Second, there seems no doubt that much OD practice deals with the consequences of overbounded responses to underbounding. For example, the situation described above might inspire determined applications of the traditional theory of organization, what in Chapter 2 of this book was called a Figure 1 structure. The very probable effect? A dysfunctional overboundedness probably would result from the traditional structuring of work for two reasons—that structure implies overkill for the diagnosed problems in the transit agency; and that structure may ill-suit a growing and innovative organization, which the transit agency is described as being.

Third, some experience suggests a useful approach to tethering interventions in an underbounded system so as to provide useful structure which does not skid into an overboundedness. For example, Cammann and Berg cite the usefulness of a three-stage design:[54]

- Diagnosing an organization's key organizing processes and activities in order to show how they are related to existing organizational conditions
- Creating opportunities for organization members to learn new attitudes and skills, with the goal of managing or changing those processes or acitivites that are inducing the undesired/undesirable conditions
- Replacing the structural arrangements that evolved in response to the "old" organizing principles and concepts, in a continuing fashion, with structural arrangements more in tune with the "new" processes and activities

Stage 2 would utilize various conventional OD designs—for listening, collaborative, or win-win relationships, and so on—respecting the processes and values detailed in the first three chapters of Part 1. Step 3 seeks to avoid a precipitous rush into overboundedness—as often happens via a determined imposition of the orthodox bureaucratic structure discussed in Chapter 2 above. Specifically, the products of Step 2—full exploration of the consequences of alternative structures and experimentation with evolving arrangements—would serve as regulators in Step 3.

Stages 1 and 3 will be highly specific to the host organization, of course, but Cammann and Berg[55] do offer four "basic underlying principles" which consultants tried to respect in their own behavior and also sought to build into the host organization:

- *Commitment to valid and systematic information*—both positive and negative data concerning thoughts, feelings, as well as events—and to its use in decision-making
- *Commitment to mutual influence,* as by involving all relevant individuals and groups in decision-making, as contrasted with various power-oriented alternatives
- *Commitment to learning,* as in experimenting with new behaviors and exploring the consequences of alternative courses of action
- *Commitment to strong yet permeable organizational structures and boundaries,* so as to give necessary direction to energy while facilitating the flow of information and also permitting responsiveness to changing conditions

Fourth, fine-tuning boundedness encounters special difficulties with the commitment to mutual influence. Or to put it otherwise, participants are likely to read less *mutual empowerment* into change-situations than they see *redistribution of power.* The latter case implies losers as well as winners, and in the long-run the real or imagined losers might have second thoughts about legitimating the diminution of their own power, even if they did not resist from the outset. In many OD efforts, for example, the organizational elite will agree to share power because things are going poorly. Thus performance may be suffering, or turnover may be growing, or the elite may be dissatisfied with the animosity created by their actions. So the elite may permit, even encourage, efforts such as confrontation designs or role negotiation, which imply a redefinition and redistribution of legitimate power. As matters improve, however, the elite may be less amenable to power-sharing, and may variously press toward the *status quo ante.* The nonelite may well see this as regression and may even experience a backlash. This situation amounts to one step forward and two backward, with heightened potential for mischief.

Some such picture tends to characterize the growing but generally checkered OD experience with such underbounded systems as those in medical education and delivery.[56] They are under great pressure to attain a greater boundedness, but major actors in relevant systems seldom get convinced of the opportunities for mutual empowerment in OD efforts, which in fact usually get framed in terms of a redistribution of power about which elites tend to develop abreactive second thoughts. Consider a view of a health-care system as composed of consumers, providers, and managers,[57] who share many characteristics. As Lammert notes of them: "All share common goals and perceptions of the social good. They want to work together to provide maximum quality of care, but may be limited by their cognition of organizational problems, outmoded structures, and limited group and interpersonal skills."[58] Both goals and deficiencies can motivate attraction to OD designs and generate movement at early stages. But the major actors differ markedly in their access to traditional sources of power: for example, both consumers and administrators lack the status accorded to doctors, as well as their access to regulatory and licensing boards, further augmented by professional and political clout. And these asymmetries tend to dominate in the long run, especially as extensions of OD beachheads are made in a power-sharing mode which often will imply power-losing to the elite. Lammert concludes: "OD interventions do not reach far enough to redress [these asymmetries of power]. Thus, while short-term improvements in team relationships can be made, the power realities of the larger systems may wipe out any long-term gains."[59]

Guides for Moving Toward Appropriate Coupledness

Must OD intervenors rest content with subsystem progress, at best, and systemic checkmate in such cases of moving toward a more appropriate boundedness? Four points suggest the broader range of ways in which OD intervenors can be proactive.

Carefully Evaluate the Bureaucratic Model. First and foremost, because of the tendency to overlook the point, intervenors should very carefully evaluate the appropriateness of the bureaucratic model, whose application represents the conventional knee-jerk reaction to underboundedness. That application in many cases may be far too much of a thing good enough under other conditions. Not only may the application be more than systemic efficiency and effectiveness require, but the structure might induce massive resistance because it conflicts with useful norms and traditions, such as those related to the freedom and self-determination of professionals at work.

Neither practitioners nor theorists have been careful enough in this regard, but awareness has been growing of late. Consider the issue of the significant relationship between local school superintendents and principals. South notes that it "is a mistake to view the principal as a middle manager," as the industrial model encourages. That error has costs, especially because major communications do not flow from superintendents → principals → department heads → teachers. Much of the central content of educational policy gets determined by the "curriculum route," which variously bypasses and interlaces the often puny chain of command.[60] Hence March concludes that attempts to control schools through hierarchical directives often will be ineffective, if not seriously counterproductive. He explains: "Activities in schools are not easily or precisely controlled through hierarchical directives or managerial incentives. Rather, educational management is controlled by diffusion of ideas and the development of social and professional norms."[61]

Consider Settling for Half a Loaf, or Less. Very often, despite the potential for copping-out, OD intervenors usefully can consider narrow-gauge efforts to move loosely coupled systems in the direction of more proactive use of valid and reliable data. Perhaps paramountly, such focused interventions can highlight the possibilities for mutual empowerment in delimited areas of relatively unqualified mutual interest, and thus avoid the backlash common in broader interventions that threaten a basic redistribution of power.

Consider the use of a survey/feedback design in medical settings.[62] The objective interests of patients in such a design seem relatively direct. They are the ones acted on, and their reactions to treatment can have profound personal implications that no doubt also impact on their medical progress. If not necesarily for themselves, patients might be motivated to provide feedback that could result in better treatment for patients to come. Many patients also probably would value the chance to influence the system. What of the other common interests? The medical staff presumably would be interested in effective patient care, although the possibility that individual doctors might be evaluated poorly could restrain their enthusiasm for feedback. In one case, moreover, Navy health-care managers had a strong vested interest in knowing about patient satisfaction, as a prelude to effective action. Unflattering research results provided the basic goad for the managers, and perhaps also for some medical staff. Five Navy facilities in one study scored lowest in patient satisfaction of eleven ambulatory health-care installations;[63] and another study showed that over half of the patients in clinics were so dissatisfied with the Navy's free services that they preferred private care even though that required that they personally pay 20 percent of the cost.[64]

These overlapping interests received reinforcement from the Navy high command—which was no doubt concerned for budgetary reasons, if nothing else—and a pilot program was instituted which worked toward mutual empowerment of patients, medical staff, and management. Details are conveniently available elsewhere,[65] but seven guidelines for the design and implementation of a patient survey/feedback information system imply how it can be oriented toward mutual empowerment.[66]

- *Goals and motive should be clearly specified.* Such a system could be oriented toward ascertaining patient satisfaction so as to permit diagnosis and remedial action. Alternatively, such a system could imply a kind of search-and-destroy mission, whose practical effect is either to purge the system of staff who cause discontent, or to isolate targets for public relations campaigns that deny the discontent. The former approach implies the possibility of mutual empowerment; but the latter suggests a more complicated picture of power redistribution that could alienate patients and/or medical staff.
- *Medical staff should be involved in the design of the questionnaire and of the procedures for dealing with the data,* for obvious reasons.
- *Staff review of data should be frequent, at first.* The emphases in early review should be on comprehensive coverage of all data, criticism and debugging of the survey and all procedures, and ameliorative action-planning which determinedly seeks to avoid evaluation of individual staff.
- *Subsequent reviews can be less frequent and focus on problem areas only and associated action-planning.*
- *Some procedures for reporting data to patients should be developed,* especially if the survey/feedback process is to be continuous.

Be Explicit Early About Tigers in the Streets. Whatever the scope of the OD intervention in loosely coupled systems, early and insistent attention must be directed at power phenomena, including those associated with the intervenor. This attention would have at least three foci, which can be expressed simply here in terms of three questions. What is the distribution of authority and influence in the host unit? What are the major conflicting interests that inhere in this network of authority and influence? Which individuals or groups share common interests, whether consciously and explicitly or in unrecognized ways?[67]

Beyond such elemental diagnostic foci, this author has found useful some early and bold stage-setting. The focus is on the central problem or trauma. Is it really painful, or simply a minor discomfort? Is the motivation for an OD effort some vague sense of "getting us all together," or does it relate to enough of everyone's fat being in the same fire? Responses to such questions must be vigorously tested and probed because, lacking a basic motivation to get it on, there are many things that can happen to an OD effort, and most of them are bad. For change programs can set tigers loose in the streets, and you either ride the tigers or risk becoming their lunch. The motivation to run such risks can reasonably inhere only in a shared and painful problem whose resolution is valued enough to risk established ways and means. OD programs, to be sure, can generate substantial amounts of warmth, closeness, and shared experiences. But these commonalities tend to decay rapidly, unless reinforced by a mutually uncomfortable problem which motivates individuals to risk their individual power in the hope of gaining individual and collective control over the problem.

Let us be less fanciful and simplify by not considering puny OD efforts. A potent OD intervention can have three basic types of effects related to power, which can be briefly introduced to show how tricky the management of power phenomena can be.[68] *First,* OD efforts can lead to mutual empowerment, as in more effective control of a common problem. This may sound attractive, and it is, but you typically have to give in order to get. Thus a marriage may be mutually empowering, but it also implies limits on the power of the individual partners. So something is gained, but something is also lost. Those wishing to have their cake and to eat it as well, clearly, should steer clear of OD efforts even if the best outcomes can be guaranteed, which is seldom the case.

Second, potent OD efforts can lead to a simple redistribution of power. Put otherwise, both elites and nonelites often will interpret OD designs in such a way, which posture the intervenor must aggressively probe for and highlight. For redistribution may be acceptable to the losers but, more probably, they will resist. I advise clients that—in the absence of a willingness to seek mutual empowerment, and lacking an unusual willingness to give up power—an OD design is probably not appropriate. Many clients, especially elites, do not hear such a message, start an OD effort, and then abort it because they recognize a growing and an unacceptable threat to their power.

Third, an OD effort can lead to some form of separation or decoupling. This can solve some problems in the long run, as in a divorce. But it requires facing difficult issues of power in the short run, as in decisions about distributing children and property during a divorce. Again, those resistant to changes in power should avoid OD designs.

Be Clear About the Alternative in Extremis. A final note for OD intervenors focusses on the clarity of the stakes and the awareness of major actors about those stakes. What are the likely consequences if a power-wielder opts to endure the persistence of a problem-situation because of a concern about risking that status? In most cases, those consequences will be minor, even though the problem remains unresolved. But (in ways and at times we do not really understand) the have-nots sometimes can become mobilized by their growing frustration, either via legal channels or by overt action. Lammert alludes to that bottom-line issue in connection with health-care institutions. She observes (or does she warn?): "If change to achieve greater power and resources for the 'have-nots' is the goal, the patterns of control in the health sector will have to change, so that health institutions are controlled by those who work in them and are served by them. The consumers of health care who are aware of their powerlessness will have to learn how to gain power and resources."[69] At this point, the OD intervenor may give way to a Saul Alinsky.

What Do We Know About the Impact of Alternative OD Designs?
Comparative Studies

A third major constraint on OD applications is both straightforward and significant. We can at present only grossly estimate the impact of alternative learning designs, and we are unable to specify the conditions under which various OD designs are appropriate. This is patently a serious limitation, whose criticality will be established from two perspectives. The first sketches why it would be super to be able to match learning designs to conditions, and the second perspective details the thrust and limitations of the only comprehensive study that deals with comparative effects of alternative OD interventions.

The Great Need Established

Directly, the sophisticated applied science matches, to quite small tolerances, the remedy to the malady, the implement to the task. The countergoals are overkill and underkill. Do no evil, certainly, but do enough so that it does real good, while not doing so much as to be wasteful or dangerous.[70]

Two epigrams come to mind. It is unseemly to hunt quail with 16-inch cannons, and just as inappropriate to perservere in demolishing a concrete driveway with a fly-swatter. These illustrate overkill and underkill, respectively. The point only counsels cost effectiveness. One can have too much of a good thing in OD, as well as too little.

These few words should establish how useful it would be to possess knowledge of the comparative effects of alternative OD designs. Given an awareness of what needs doing via diagnosis, the optimal design or intervention could then be chosen. Fly-swatter designs could be matched to problems that are flies, 20-gauge shotguns would be accurately prescribed for quail, and so on.

The Slim Supply Illustrated

The problems of comparative research are so complex that little progress has been made. That is to say, two classes of questions have to be answered.

- Given a common site for application, which of several possible OD designs is preferable?
- Given any single OD design, does it have more or less the same consequences when applied in different contexts, as in two or more different social "cultures"?

Some little research has been done on the second question, as in testing for the similarly of T-group effects in Japan, Turkey, and the United Kingdom.[71] In a similar way, Boss[72] and his associated are testing for the effects of confrontation designs in nine different countries.

Available comparative work suggests that the same OD design has some of the same and some different consequences as its site of application changes. And available research implies that alternative OD designs sometimes have similar consequences.

That this available comparative research is only a little way down a long road will be established by the remainder of this section, which reviews the one available and truly comparative study. This is an analysis of six alternative OD interventions in a large number of organizations.[73] As unique as this massive and far-sighted study is, however, discussion in this and especially in the concluding section of this chapter will demonstrate that the study's findings are limited by very serious technical imponderables.

Briefing a Comparative Study

Now for a few design details, as well as results of the comparison of six alternative OD interventions in twenty-three organizations involving some 14,000 respondents. Exhibit 2 briefly describes the interventions to be compared. Prior chapters contain numerous examples of similar designs. Without going into great detail, Bowers' data show major differences between the six alternatives. Only a bare summary is attempted here,[74] but details are conveniently available elsewhere.[75]

Survey feedback: Four of five organizations show overall improvement; one shows overall decline.

Interpersonal process consultation: Three of four organizations show overall improvement; one declines.

Task process consultation: Four of five organizations show marginal overall declines; one shows marked improvement.

Laboratory training: All five organizations show overall decline.

Data handback: One of two organizations shows overall improvement, and one reflects a decline.

No treatment: Both organizations show an overall decline.

Exhibit 2 Five Alternative OD Designs

Survey Feedback. Each supervisor and manager receives data from the questionnaire responses of his or her own immediate subordinates and suggestions concerning their interpretation and use. A resource person usually counseled privately with the supervisor-recipient about the contents of the package and then arranged a time when the supervisor could meet with subordinates to discuss the findings and their implications. Feedback procedures varied from site to site.

Interpersonal Process Consultation. The emphasis is on client groups developing a capacity for forming and implementing their own change program. The goal is to surface attitudes, feelings, individual needs, reasons for conflict, informal processes, and so on, to build solid processes to support a program of change.

Task Process Consultation. This intervention typically begins by analyzing a client unit's work-task situation privately, after extensive interviews. Consultant meets privately with the supervisor at frequent intervals to establish rapport and to gain commitment to objectives and desired future courses of action. Consultant sets the stage for client group discussions by introducing select bits of data or by having another person do so.

Laboratory Training. This intervention is an interpersonal relations laboratory. A "family group" design was followed almost exclusively, with the laboratory lasting from 3 days to 2 weeks. Experiential exercises were interspersed with unstructured discussion time.

Data Handback. This is a comparison condition. Data are tabulated and returned to supervisors, but no problem-solving based on the data was attempted.

No Treatment. No data were returned to supervisors, and no developmental activities were attempted. Summary results went only to top managers.

Source: From David G. Bowers, "OD Techniques and Their Results in 23 Organizations: The Michigan ICL Study," *Journal of Applied Behavioral Science,* Vol. 9 (January 1973), pp. 23-26.

Some Qualifications About Results

If such findings could be accepted with minor qualifications only, they would provide powerful guidance. But, as both author[76] and his critics acknowledge,[77] careful qualifications about what the data mean are appropriate. Four of these qualifications will be emphasized here.

First, as Bowers himself urges, the results may be significantly influenced by the trend lines in the several organizations. Where organizations are heading, as it were, may be an important factor in determining which kinds of OD interventions are likely to be most appropriate. Specifically, laboratory training may have poorly suited the conditions in which the organizations in Bowers' population found themselves. Bowers concludes: ". . . it may be that laboratory-like, experiential learning is successful in organizations whose climate is, or is becoming, positive . . . , but unsuccessful in organizations whose superstructure is, or is becoming, more autocratic and punitive."[78] This hypothesis is attractive, especially because it could explain some part of the major differences between Bowers' findings and those of other studies,[79] including a major one by Bowers himself.[80] And some independent research also implies a similar potency of survey/feedback designs under tough conditions. Thus Solomon concludes: "These findings suggest that the survey feedback intervention tended to have its greatest impact in those situations in which it appeared to be the most needed"—that is, when subordinates were dissatisfied with their subordinates, when activities were unplanned and disorganized, and so forth.[81] Attractive, this combination. But the plain fact remains that the available literature can support no robust interpretations.

Second, differences in the mixes of member preferences and organizational styles, following Harrison's approach sketched above, may be relevant in determining which kinds of interventions are optimal. Bowers presents no relevant data on that point, but differences in such mixes clearly could influence his results in major ways. For example, persons with a strong preference for a role orientation in organizations with traditions of a role orientation would seem difficult targets for interaction-oriented interventions, which might generate major cross-pressures for participants. Intervenors in such cases should seriously consider role negotiation designs like that sketched in Chapter 5 of Part 1.

Third, interventions of the "same type" might differ profoundly. For example, evidence suggests that some designs for laboratory training or T-grouping can be built into impactful programs of organization change, even in cases where the organization is experiencing difficult and punishing times. Illustratively, see Chapter 2 above. So a T-group ≠ a T-group.

Fourth, Bowers' study utilized only one measure of change. It is not known to what degree other measures would have produced similar patterns of change, but some pessimism seems appropriate.[82] Whether or not different measures do generate different patterns of change, we still do not know which is *the* best measure.

What Constraints Limit Feedback and Disclosure?
More Openness Being Better Does Not Mean that Most Is Best

This section is just like its four companions in this chapter, in two central regards. The focus here is on what ways OD should be constrained by what we know and what we do not know. Moreover, this section implies that the specific constraints will determine which of several possible OD designs will be more appropriate, and perhaps which will be contraindicated.

Another Perspective on More/Most and Better/Best

Specifically, in the case of feedback and disclosure, this section proposes that "more of each" will not necessarily prove to be "better and better." "More" often will mean "better," in sum, but "most" could be "worse." Early chapters in the companion book make the point in several ways—by proposing guidelines for feedback, for example, as well as by focusing on four interacting variables in regenerative/degenerative systems rather than by harping on simple and sovereign recipes. Here as there, the goal is to contribute to a heightened sensitivity that will facilitate the application of designs appropriate to different situations. Where openness can be broad, both practically and safely, interaction-centered designs like confrontations may be prescribed with confidence. Where openness must be limited, other kinds of designs will be more appropriate. Thus OD values might be approached via designs like Flexi-Time; or individuals might be guaranteed anonymity, as by a survey/feedback design or by playing audio tapes for top management from concerned organization members, using a device that disguises voices but preserves the meaning of the words with which they express their concerns.

In introductory sum, this section provides yet another perspective on how and why OD cannot be free and easy—as some propose, with enthusiasm—and somehow so ad hoc that all can share equally in the spontaneous diagnosis, discovery, and prescription.[83] These are desirable goals and enhance ownership. But some would see them as a reason to keep rediscovering the wheel. Rather, OD must be tough-minded and disciplined by the best available theory and experience. Thus this section provides specifics about a general proposition: how human thought often overextends reasonable positions, making grotesqueries out of even some very fine things. That has been the typical fate of "openness," as Ken K. Smith convincingly argues below in trying to save its central core from being extended in self-defeating ways. Smith focuses on both interpersonal and organizational contexts, and his position has two major thrusts. Attaining suitably bounded openness in organizations must overcome difficult and subtle issues, no doubt of that. Also Smith's essay all but cries out for the need to do something to appropriately fine-tune that openness if we are to control our organizations. Left to themselves, that is, the politically based dynamics to which he draws attention contain the encoding of their own mutual destruction, or at least of enslavement.

Note that Smith's argument deliberately simplifies to highlight important extreme conditions. That is, he distinguishes only three kinds of organization members—uppers, middles, and lowers. In reality, greater specification would be required for fine-grained description. Thus upwardly mobile middles would be likely to behave in different ways than nonmobiles, those middles nearing retirement might differ from midcareer persons, and so on. In what amounts to a developmental concept-in-extremis, Smith extrapolates from very real features of all organizations to show that they can develop into tragic controllables.

A Political Perspective on "Openness"*

In the 1960s, organizational change and personal growth alike became caught in the social fad of advocating that people should "let it all hang out." "Be open and honest" was the easily spoken but rarely implemented rhetoric of both unsophisticated social change-agents and many of the bourgeois "radicals" whose temporary flirtation with the "counter culture" eventually matured into dedicated attempts to make it within established social structures. With the benefit of historical retrospective, we can readily see that "openness in interpersonal relations" did not become the wave of the future. I ask, with a little ironic distance, what happend to the promise of "openness"?

I'd like to start by making three preliminary comments:

1. *Openness is a characteristic of the boundary relations between two parties.* When we say someone is "closed" or someone is "open" we refer to the nature of the boundedness of their interaction patterns.
2. When we use the term "openness" we are really *referring to a property of the communication system.* In particular, how much do I let you know about what's going on inside my "private self" (and vice versa) while we're engaging in the interaction of our "public selves."[84]
3. "Openness" also refers to the *political dynamics operative in relationships.* "Openness" may be used as a way of describing the level of personal vulnerability at which an individual operates in relationships. The catch-phrase "X is an open person" can often be restated as "X seems very able to expose vulnerabilities in interactions with others." In this sense, "openness" is a comment on levels of individual vulnerability and hence on the relative power dynamics operative in relationships. And a good way to increase one's power with respect to another is to get the other to "be open" while the self remains "closed" or even feigns reciprocity.

Optimal Boundedness. I'm taking as my first focus the boundary theme, for I consider the degree of openness or closedness as *primarily* a function of boundary relationships. All of us have encountered, in various shapes and forms, the individual who is so "tight," "reactive," and "closed" that the only appropriate metaphor for describing him is "emotionally constipated." We've also had to

*Ken K. Smith, 1978. Reprinted here with special permission. An earlier version was presented at the 1978 Annual Meeting, Academy of Management, San Francisco, Calif., August 9-11.

deal with the character who absorbs immense amounts of our time and energy, who seems unable to keep anything to self, comments on everything, and appears to be suffering from emotional and verbal diarrhea. None of us would encourage the latter individual to become more open. Heaven forbid!

For such reasons, I'd argue that openness as an unlimited goal is basically inappropriate. What we're really talking about is a desirable level of both openness and closedness—optimal boundary conditions, if you will—with the extremes being overbounded or underbounded.[85] The real concern for those of us who theorize about relationships shall center on the appropriate level of boundary permeability in particular contexts, as well as on the key social processes which regulate those boundary conditions.

I thus want to switch my focus from thinking about "openness" to "optimal boundedness."

An immediate question we must address when the topic is couched in these terms is, "optimal" from whose point of view? Since we're concerned here specifically with interpersonal relationships, clearly there are the two key parties. Hence the degree of boundedness must be readjusted so that it's optimal for that *particular relationship.* This may mean, of course, that it is not necessarily optimal for either individual because the compromises necessary to make an optimally bounded relationship may require significant readjustments by both principals. This forces that we are dealing with boundaries relevant to the individuals *and* the relationship, and that both of these must be understood when dealing with the degree of openness that exists in the interpersonal situation.

Consider the example where B is relatively more closed with A than A is with B. This may be because B is a "closed person." Or it may be that the relationship is more threatening for B than for A, which causes B to experience the interpersonal situation with A to be underbounded. Hence, the degree of relationship boundedness, while being optimal for A, proves to be inappropriate for B. To cope with this, B may become more closed (more overbounded) in order to deal with the fact that he experiences the A-B relationship to be underbounded from his own perspective. Hence, the overbounded condition of individual B may well be a reasonable reaction to the character of the A-B relationship. I refer to this concept as "overbounded reactivity to underboundedness."[86] The degree of boundedness at one level of any system may be a consequence of the boundary relations at another level. If I'm sufficiently "open" to my environment and that environment is threatening, then it's only natural for me to build a wall behind which I can feel protected from threat, thereby becoming appropriately more closed.

Boundary conditions do not remain static. In the same ways as human systems are in dynamic flow, so my relationships likewise will be in flux—in some situations overbounded, in others underbounded—constantly seeking, through experience, a condition of optimal boundedness but rarely finding it, and then only for a time. No sooner created, the "optimal" changes. For this reason, it's important to acknowledge from the outset that the interpersonal boundary conditions will experience their seasonality—a time to be overbounded, a time to be underbounded—just as there is a time to fight and a time to take flight, a time to love and a time to hate.[87] In addition, not only are there times for particular boundary conditions to prevail in the different seasons of a human-systems cycle, there are also different ways to "be" over-, under-, or optimally bounded. These likewise vary depending on the forces which flow from the context in which the relevant relationships is embedded.

As an aside, I'd like to point out that when B says "A is not sufficiently open," this really means that "the A-B relationship is inappropriately bounded for my needs." But the speaker often doesn't understand it this way, failing to recognize that it's the context (i.e., the relationship) that needs changing. B may therefore mistakenly often try to change the person A, thereby transferring the focus from a mutual reworking of the relationship to placing the blame at A's feet with the imperative for A to change in order for B to feel OK. This process carries the same flavor as ethnocentrism, and the statements about "A's openness" are couched in attributive terms. The attributive nature of this concept of openness is driven home when we consider how often we think of our own behavior in this way. We may say, "*I'm* being open and honest with you." But we're very unlikely to say "I'm being closed and deceitful with you." We're likely to phrase the latter as: "I don't trust you, so why should I lay myself open to you to let me be manipulated or hurt."

Although I think "openness" in relationships is an inappropriate way of symbolizing the "desirable" boundary conditions of interpersonal interactions, there is a much more complex issue than this with which we must struggle. And that is, *all interpersonal relationships are embedded within organizational contexts,* within a culture at large, and within particular sets of meaning-structure for understanding experience. The forces which emerge from these contexts are powerful determiners of interpersonal relations in organizations. I'd like to explore the implications of this statement relying on the extension of very real forces in organizations that often are variously muted in practice. I extrapolate, even exaggerate, to point out the often unrecognized impact of organizational forces on interpersonal exchanges.

Contextual Forces. The *first* and most obvious aspect of the organizational context is that the two principals in an interpersonal encounter cannot be thought of as just two individuals. Individuals A and B may be husband and wife, or boss and subordinate, or teacher and student, and so on. Hence their interactions are constrained not only by the set of rituals and traditions they've built up with each other in previous encounters, but also by all the norms and mores that the culture at large imposes for the facilitating or blocking of particular types of interactions for the role relationship in which the individuals are encased.

Second, any particular encounter may be a living-out of some global organizational forces where the individuals are mere puppets of the prevailing social dynamic—a subordinate being passive or belligerently unresponsive to a boss's attempt to "motivate him," or a wife being adamant she'll no longer keep the house as a dutiful servant. Such responses may express an alienated condition of life that flows, like night follows day, in the wake of years of domination and oppression.

Third, an individual may represent larger groups of relevant others whose memberships are central in that person's self-identity and are carried into an interpersonal situation. For example, a young white male manager and an old black female union member, when relating, often are dealing simultaneously with age, sex, race, hierarchy, and reference groups—each of which may constrain the interpersonal encounter.

To illustrate the potency of these contextual forces, I will explore in more detail the impact of the psychological prisons that emerge between classes of actors in organizations who have differential power.

Political Forces. In any organization, we can distinguish three sets of actors: those who have the power to determine "what is" ("creative" power), those who operate primarily out of the power to resist or destroy ("blocking" power), and those who mediate between the polarities defined by the "creators" and the "blockers" ("mediating" power). Take, for example, a typical business organization, which can be viewed as a composite of three types of actors. I distinguish the *lowers* and the *uppers*—the workers whose labor is required for the will of the powerful, and the owners and corporate bosses. Sandwiched between are the mediators (middle management), who attempt to implement the wishes of the uppers by inducing the lowers into doing things which they would not normally have much inclination to do (such as stand for hours on a hot, smelly, noisy assembly line in order to provide for the basic needs of themselves and their families).

The uppers, middles, and lowers can be viewed as imprisoned by a mind-set which their relative position in the social structure encourages. This mind-set emerges from their having the power to create, the power to mediate, or the power to block.

Uppers' Bondage. The major psychological prison for uppers is their *incapacity to comprehend the consequences of their behavior.* This imprisonment flows from three organizational features with which all uppers must struggle: their primary task, the nature of their authority relations with middles and lowers, and the ways and means available to them as uppers to gather information.

In systems theory terminology, uppers must manage both critical external and internal boundaries[88] of the system in order to assure that the goals of the organization are achieved and that the internal structures are adequate for the total system's survival. That is, uppers seek to assure that the goals of the organization are achieved and that the internal structures are adequate for the total system's survival in the environment in which it is embedded. Uppers are prone to monopolize this external/internal management function and as such are dealing with extraordinarily complex issues. Hence, when once their system has been designed, uppers tend to pass on to a middle group (a group of subordinates) the task of implementing any decision which uppers make.

This structural split between decision-making and implementation leads to decisions being taken independent of their implementability–and decisions are poorer as a result. The most critical consequence of this split affects the information flow in the organization. Let's imagine that uppers make a poor decision and then delegate its implementation to subordinates who are dependent on the uppers for their rewards in the system. The implementors (middles) are unlikely to argue that the decision is poor for fear that the uppers will just find someone else to do the implementation task, or else accuse them of not being able to do their job. Should the implementation prove to be less than satisfactory, the middles are tempted to release information that only gives hints that things didn't work out. This hesitancy derives from the fear that the uppers often will not acknowledge that their decisions are at fault, but will place blame on the middles for being incompetent. To avoid this possible accusation, middles tend primarily to pass up the line attributions about the resistance of the workers, or lowers, with a constant filtering-out of information that might disconfirm the uppers' or middles' skills.

Unaware uppers may make a decision and get only 50 percent of the relevant information, and they'll be prone to consider this as 90 percent and make their next decision accordingly. If, following each decision, the uppers only get back 50 percent of the information relevant to the impact of their decision, and if uppers act as though they have most of the relevant information, it only requires three or four decision interactions before the uppers are operating on very little information. Unknowingly, they're being protected from the consequences of their behavior. This phenomenon of becoming insulated also may be found in any group engaged in some significant conflict where ethnocentrism ("we/they" feelings) has become activated.[89] Under ethnocentric circumstances, each group is prone to take whatever reality it is able to perceive from its vantage point and affirm that this is *the* reality. Of course, certain dimensions of the perceived reality will always appear ambiguous, but as Schutz[90] indicates, each "in"-group will be prone to cope with this by taking events and objects which are incoherent, inconsistent, and only partially clear (as is always the case in conflict circumstances), transforming them into a form where the "in"-group is able to see them as coherent, consistent, and clear. This crystallization, or removal of ambiguity, is important for the functioning of "within" group life and also has profound consequences for what transpires "between" groups.

Uppers suffer most from the problems this dynamic generates, although all groups engage in this process under conflict conditions, simply because their position and power have taught them to view themselves as creators and definers of the social situation. The uppers, merely by being in the position to determine what they want others to do, have already started the process of objectifying the world.[91] Hence, when confronted with ambiguous or nonconforming cues from the environment, they are most prone to resort to their regular devices of assuming that by mere acts of definition—a declaration of their wills—they can have things as they wish.

If we add the combined impact of these two insulating forces operating on uppers—the parceling out of negative information following decision-making, and the tendency to "objectify" (and then believe their objectification) of all organizational experiences—there is good theoretical support for the empirical observation of how "out of touch with reality" uppers often seem to be from the perspective of both middles and lowers.

In summary, information about the consequences of their behavior is rarely conveyed back to uppers in unfiltered, undiluted, and undistorted form, for lowers and middles tend to refrain from passing on the things they don't want the powerful to know about. Even if accurate information is given to them, the uppers have no way of really knowing if what they're being told is accurate. Uppers may attempt to gather information from multiple sources, detect discrepancies, and use the resultant convergence as the basis for their construction of reality.[92] But even then it is difficult for the powerful to determine accurately whether that opinion is anything more than a common misperception or a well-orchestrated plot by the disenchanted to convey a "false reality." In short, uppers often become so insulated from the world they create that there's no way for them to know whether what they think is going on reflects the reality that's being experienced by others in the system.

Lowers' Bondage. The major psychological prison for *lowers* is that they often *become imprisoned by the devices they design to protect themselves from the threatening actions or perceived threats of those above.* They often develop strong norms which stipulate that even potential threats must be resisted.

Individual behavior will be shaped by these protective norms and, if they threaten group unity, individuals may be sacrificed for the "common good." Deviations from this fundamental principle are interpreted as acts of disloyalty and may inspire appropriate wrath, excommunication, or constraining sanctions; often reaffirmation of group loyalty is required. Witness the harsh experience of "whistle-blowers" in most organizations.

These protective devices can serve mixed purposes. They help to keep a group united around themes critical to the totality of the members. They assist in generating the power to act in a unified manner. The protections also facilitate fraternity, heavy commitment to the group, and a high investment in the welfare of other lowers. Note also that these protective devices can generate negative forces. Dissent may be suppressed as a result of the potential sanctions threatened if cohesion is reduced. The protective devices also ensure that the individual makes himself subservient to the collective will of the group and serve to define individualism as a problem with which the total group must deal.

One consequence of the lowers feeling threatened is that their group comes to define its essence in terms of the very cohesion and unity that is required to deal with the threat. In order to feed this sense of unity, members can paradoxically come to want a continued external threat. This creates a double-bind: if the uppers cease to present a threat, that situation may be experienced by lowers as threatening, for it lessens the sense of vulnerability of the lower group, because the *lack* of overt attack challenges the very basis of unity on which their group life is often predicated. Either way, lowers often respond to uppers with suspicion. The bind reads as follows: "If they're getting at us, we've got to watch out. If they're not getting at us, we've also got to watch out because they can get at us in the long run by reducing our unity now by lessening the threat we feel." It is this process that ensures a lower group's "paranoia" which generates intense feelings of sensitivity and suspiciousness when relating to superiors.[93]

This level of suspiciousness can permeate all information that is passed to lowers, for it will be constantly dissected to see "what they're doing to us now." In addition, for a lower, hearing nothing from those above never means that nothing is happening. It often means "all hell is about to break loose" and "we'd better get ourselves together to deal with this." Lack of information may also serve to reinforce the "paranoia" of powerlessness in lowers.[94]

Another major consequence of the structural location of the lowers is that since they tend to dislike the conditions of powerlessness in which they exist, the only way they can conceive of being free is to resist by destroying the circumstances that make them feel this way. While this is natural, the problem with being in a resistive mode is that there's a tendency to "dig in one's heels" in response to another's initiatives and to become locked into primarily reactive postures. This limits one's range of options and reinforces a feeling of stagnation.

Middles' Bondage. The major psychological prison for *middles is that their very existence depends on their capacity to preserve functional relations with both uppers and lowers.* Generally, middles must earn their keep when upper and lower groups are caught in polarized tensions. Their primary task is to mediate those tensions, to provide some unifying forces to keep the system from fragmenting.

The precariousness of middles in this linking is that they must remain sensitive to two sets of interests, often pulling in opposite directions. If they cease to manage that integrative function, the extremes will become increasingly polarized and more difficult to mediate between. If middles bend to accommodate the interests of one group, they make tenuous their relationship with the other, unless they quickly counter with an equal thrust to preserve the delicate equilibrium. Failure to retain this equilibrium makes the middles ever-vulnerable to the accusation they're being "bought off" or "seduced" by the upper group or, alternatively, that they "dropped out" or "abandoned their post" to join the lowers.

There's a paradox as long as the middles remain in the mediating position. While middles must work to diminish the intense polarization of the system, they must never succeed in this task or they'll do themselves out of a role. The mediating function must preserve some tension in the system in order for the mediation role to be needed. Although middles must make sure that the problems they're set up to solve never get completely dealt with, they must make some progress in depolarizing the system in order to keep "dancing in the in-between location." The trap for the middles then is *they're dependent for their existence on the very conditions they're trying to change.*

If you ask managers in any organization about their major problem, they'll likely say "communication." Yet if you observe their behavior, you'll note that they spend a great deal of this time actually restricting communication. How could this be? The answer is that for a middle person his power, and thereby the capacity to survive in the system, is dependent on the ability to become the central link in the communication structure. They want better communication, but they also want it to pass through them. Suggest to any middle person the development of a communication channel that bypasses him, and he'll become very threatened—even if that new channel is in the interests of the system. The reason? With the polarization of uppers and lowers, they both tend to use information-withholding (uppers as a dependency-inducing routine, lowers as a protective device). And one major way middles can acquire power in the service of their role as mediators is to become the major information-sharers while the lowers and uppers act to restrict information flow. This in-betweenness often encourages distortion in the service of depolarizing the system—optimism when lowers and uppers are pessimistic, withholding data from some parties but not others, and so on. The middles will be very vulnerable if they're ever caught publicly or intentionally doing this. Their game of distortion in the service of depolarizing the system is carried out in as hidden a manner as possible.

In addition, as mediators the middles get to learn the secrets of each side, and this gives them power. If both polarities learn of the secrets, then the middles' specialness disappears. When the middles alone know both sets of secrets, they can effectively engage in a game where they give each side the impression that they will keep confidences, simultaneously giving each side the false impression that they, as middles, will be more loyal to it than the other. When these kinds of processes become central to middles' survival, it's no wonder that they work to restrict communication that doesn't pass through them. Yet they must advertise an ideological commitment to greater communication in order to keep the uppers and lowers willing to tell them what they need to know to preserve their middle power base.

Although their public goal is to unify the system, the worst that can happen to middles caught in these binds is to have the two poles actually get together with the middle acting as mediator. Invariably, the mediators will look undignified as they appear to vacillate from one set of appearances and loyalties to another to avoid being caught in their game.

Common forms of rhetoric used to describe a system's life and vitality may exacerbate matters. Usages like "unity" seem especially predominant. Yet these terms mean different things to the three types of actors. To the lowers, "unity" often represents protection from attack. To the uppers, "unity" may mean "getting the whole act together" in the service of superordinate goals. For the middles, the unity of the whole system is critical, because only that way will their tensions be lessened.

"Openness" Reconsidered. Let us return now to the original purpose of this paper. The discussion above implies much about what consitutes a reasonably bounded openness in organizations. In short, inhibitors of openness in organizations are profound, and the prognosis of our organizational society is dismal indeed unless we find ways to reasonably curb those inhibitors. And the same time, these inhibitors are so pervasive and powerful that only a consciously bounded openness can be safe in the long run.

Consider only three perspective on the global point. *First,* if interpersonal relations in organizations have to be lived-out essentially in the context of the invisible psychological prisons sketched above, two individuals caught in different sets of structural bondage probably cannot be "open" with each other without it being transformed into a living-out of the organizational forces which envelop them. That kind of openness would be either very tentative, very fraudulent, or very dangerous.

Second, reasonably bounded openness is not likely unless some meaningful ways are found to manage power differences so that all parties feel a comparable and lasting vulnerability to one another. An openness based on a heightened and lasting vulnerability of one party, while the other party is only temporarily open and can soon retire behind superior status, is unstable and potentially dangerous. The analysis above of uppers, middles, and lowers implies power-bases resting on totally different foundations–creative, resistive, or mediative–

and provides little support or encouragement for any but a shallow and temporary openness.

Third, the analysis above implies that—as individuals get forced into one of the three types sketched above—great care is appropriate whoever unilaterally suggests that people ought to be more open in their interpersonal relations in organizational settings.

Is it the middles? If so, uppers and lowers who really understand what is going on could well regard the suggestion as mere rhetoric.

Is it the uppers? If so—given the closedness of their ranks and their access to immense resources that middles and lowers can hardly comprehend, let alone get their hands on—others could view the uppers' desire for more openness as merely a new camouflage for an old game, devious manipulation. The name of that game might well be: "I want you to tell me exactly what you think even if it costs you your job."[95]

Is it the lowers? If so—given their blocking and reactive stance and common distrust of superiors, activated by the paranoia of powerlessness—uppers and middles would reasonably respond by treating the request as a joke, as some mischief, or mere stupidity.

To date, inadequate conceptual work has been done to enable these enormous inhibitors to interpersonal openness to be appropriately tackled. From my point of view, the concept of "openness" as an overall "way of being" in interpersonal relationships overlooks too many critical organizational realities. Instead, I argue that the concept of "optimal boundedness" presents an opportunity to reconceptualize the central ideology of openness in a more appropriate way because it ceases to focus on characteristics of the individuals and instead sees the boundary nature of the interpersonal exchange as an expression of major organizational forces. Such a reconceptualization, in my opinion, offers a way of thinking about the "openness" phenomenon in dynamic terms and with a holism that includes the constant interplay of multiple levels of analysis and multiple forms of reality.

What Do We Know About Measuring Change? Conceptual Roadblock to Determining Which OD Designs Have What Effects

Finally, consider the most serious qualification of results such as those of Bowers—that qualification deriving from basic conceptual problems with "change." Lack of clarity about "change," that is to say, constitutes a very serious roadblock to determining which OD designs have what effects under specified circumstances.

This section deals with a possibility of great significance that has been but little exploited in OD. By extending the boundaries of the known, to sketch this possibility, applied research can contribute to the further development of scientific knowledge while it promises conscious amelioration of the human condition. But, applied research contributes in both senses only to the degree that we know whether a particular intervention has "succeeded" or "failed." That knowledge requires not only measuring the "quantity" of change, but more especially demands confidence in the "quality" of the concept of change that underlies the measurement. Since confidence in our concept of change is not yet appropriate, much of the potential for both research and ameliorative social action is unrealized.

This section deals with an obvious but neglected truism about applied research: that an inadequate concept of change implies diminished or misguided applied research, perhaps even tragic applied research. Hence, this paper urges distinguishing three kinds of change, suggested by experience and also supported with evidence generated by exotic statistical and computational techniques. An immediate pay-off is more certain interpretation of existing research findings, whose meaning is intimately related to the concept of change underlying them.

To these ends, the discussion below has two emphases. Initially, conceptual clarification of change will show that at least three kinds seem distinguishable. Data from a study of a successful Flexi-Time intervention were used to test these conceptual classifications. Detailed statistical analysis, not presented here, supports the broad position that a unitary concept of change is inappropriate, and may be seriously misleading.

Character of the Conceptual Problem*

This discussion treads on uncertain turf as it seeks to provide both perspective and data on significant conceptual territory. The focus is on what is measured in experimental designs, and especially in those designs placing heavy reliance on self-reports. More specifically, this section deals with a central question: Change on what?[96] In short, you cannot know which OD interventions "work," or when, unless you have a clear and useful notion of what change is.

The focus here has serious implications for the OD practitioner, who cannot avoid these questions: Change on what? Change for what? The point sometimes gets short-shrift in technically oriented treatments or as a result of a self-interest,

*A later version of this section appears as Robert T. Golembiewski, Keith Billingsley, and Samuel Yeager, "Measuring Change and Persistence in Human Affairs: Type of Change Generated by OD Designs," *Journal of Applied Behavioral Science,* Vol. 12 (May 1976), pp. 133-157.

as Ross reminds us forcefully.[97] However, it is widely recognized that OD interventions are value-loaded.[98] As such, OD interventions are far less involved with raising the level of indicators of some relatively stable system than they seek to change basic concepts of the quality of organizational life that should and can exist.

Some Elemental Distinctions Between Types of Change

The point of entry to dealing with the central, indeed crucial, complexities of change will be conceptual. To begin, three types of change will be distinguished. In summary introduction, they are:

> Alpha change, which involves a variation in the level of some existential state, given a constantly calibrated measuring instrument related to a constant conceptual domain
>
> Beta change, which involves a variation in the level of some existential state, complicated by the fact that some intervals of the measurement continuum associated with a constant conceptual domain have been recalibrated
>
> Gamma change, which involves a redefinition or reconceptualization of some domain, a major change in the perspective or frame of reference within which phenomena are perceived and classified, in what is taken to be relevant in some slice of reality

Alpha Change

Most OD designs seem to recognize only alpha changes measured by self-reports, using pretest and posttest designs with or without comparison groups. Symbolically, such designs may be described as $O_1 \ X \ O_2$, where O = observation and X = experimental intervention. That is, the usual design selects some frame of reference or criteria, with "change" being estimated by fluctuations in the levels of self-reports triggered by that referent. Alpha changes, then, are conceived as occurring along *relatively stable dimensions of reality* defined in terms of discrete and constant intervals. Note that alpha changes can be nonrandom, as established by some test of statistical significance, or they can be random only. And, alpha changes might be very large or very small, or anywhere in between. The only requirement is that alpha change occur *within* a relatively fixed system or state, defined in terms of stable dimensions of reality as estimated by a measurement continuum whose intervals are relatively constant.

A parent taking a baby to the shoe store is interested in alpha change—growth in baby's feet between this visit and the preceding one. The measurement of change occurs within a relatively fixed system of stable dimensions of reality (that is, our conventional concepts of "length" and "width") as defined by indicators whose intervals are more or less constant (that is, the calibrated marks on the measuring rod against which baby's foot is compared).

Beta Change

Beta changes involve the recalibration of the intervals used to measure some stable dimension of psychological space, as in preintervention versus postintervention responses. This contrasts with alpha changes, which are measured along more or less invariant intervals tapping a stable dimension of reality.

Simply, given beta change, a parent could not know how much a child's feet had grown between visits to the shoe store. It would not be meaningful to compare this visit with the last one because the intervals on the measuring rod had somehow changed.

A beta change on a rod for measuring feet is not very likely, of course, although such rods do expand and contract some. Social measuring rods can "expand" and "contract" significantly, however, even as their conceptual definition remains the same. That is, beta changes imply potentially variable responses to shifting indicators of a stable dimension of reality. Note that the reference here is to a phenomenon beyond test-retest reliability. For change in the measuring intervals is often *an intended effect of an OD intervention,* as contrasted with some defect of the measuring instrument.

Oversimply, perhaps, instruments soliciting self-reports are more rubber yardsticks than they are socioemotional equivalents of the "standard foot" in the Bureau of Standards. That is, self-reports are rooted in cultural definitions or in an individual's knowledge and experiences, which provide meaning for such stimuli of self-reports as an instruction to rate "degree of participation in decision making." OD efforts typically impact on such cultural definitions, and they also can significantly modify or enlarge an individual's knowledge or experiences. In this sense, applying the same instrument before and after a successful OD intervention, while assuming that the intervals along which self-reports are made remain constant, may be rather like applying a given survey instrument to several different cultures, as conventionally understood. Any resulting data must be compared only very carefully, if at all.[99]

It may seem fussy to some to distinguish beta change from alpha, because both deal only with changes in condition within a relatively stable state. But, beta change does point up a significant and generic problem in interpreting behavioral research, as an extended illustration will establish. Consider the two sets of descriptions of an organization unit in Figure 2 before (Now I) and after (Now II) an OD intervention.* In a first case, assume that only alpha change

*The terminology relates to the Rensis Likert's (1967) Profile of Organization Characteristics. The Profile seeks two kinds of self-reports: Now responses which solicit data about how respondents actually see their organization unit, and Ideal responses which seek information about how respondents feel their organization should be. The focus throughout this section is on purported descriptions of existential states only, that is, on Now responses.

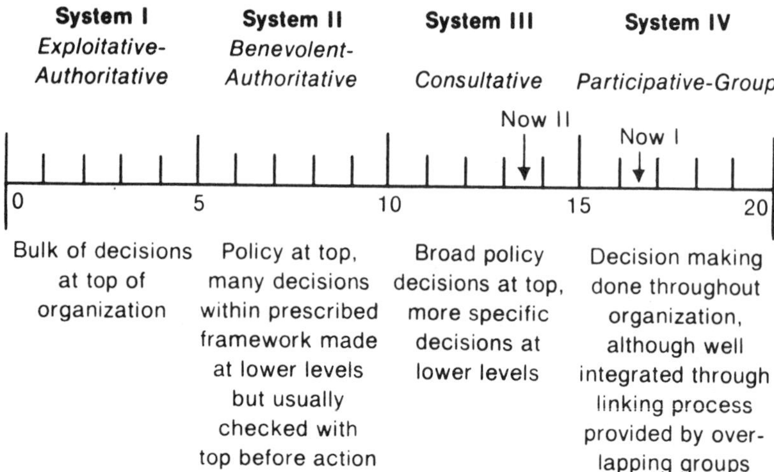

ITEM 33. *At what level in organization are decisions formally made?*

Figure 2 Pre- and posttest means on a representative item from Likert's Profile of Organizational Characteristics.

has occurred. Even here Figure 2 does not support a single or simple conclusion. The Now II score is consistent with an OD "failure" in one sense, as well as with a "success" in another. These alternative explanations provide that:

- The intervention was a failure because Now II is lower than Now I, and OD interventions should induce changes toward System IV; or
- the intervention was successful because the respondents at Now II have a more realistic view of how things really are, a firmer descriptive base for subsequent ameliorative action.

Matters get more complicated if the possibility of beta change is acknowledged. Consider employees whose pattern of responses following an OD intervention was like that in Figure 2.[100] Things in their organization units were not worse than before the intervention, respondents reported in interviews supplementing their questionnaire responses. Oppositely, in fact, respondents reported that things had substantially improved. The OD experience encouraged respondents to recalibrate Likert's intervals after the intervention in at least two ways, by hypothesis. Thus, respondents made different estimates of reality, given a clearer perception of what exists. In addition, respondents changed their intervals for measuring value-loaded terms in the Likert instrument such as "throughout the organization," "well-integrated," and "overlapping."

Interpretively, the OD experience had "lengthened" the psychological space between some intervals of the Likert instrument, while preserving the essential conceptual content of Likert's "managerial systems." The OD program had, in effect, shown respondents how much "integration" there was and could be, by hypothesis, and they recalibrated the System III and IV portions of Likert's scale. One respondent added: "I don't need to be educated about what a '3' score is! I've seen that often enough." Likert's intervals were in part rubber yardsticks, subject to expansion and contraction as personal and cultural standards were impacted by the OD intervention. Consequently, even though respondents verbally report "more participation" at Now II, their postintervention scores are lower than for Now I. The content of the System III and IV intervals had stretched "faster" or "further" than actual participation had increased, as it were. For the technical development of a similar notion, see McGee's[101] emphasis on "elastic distances" in multidimensional scaling.

Presumably, if the OD intervention had involved a month in an equivalent of Auschwitz, respondents would have recalibrated the System I portion of the Likert Profile.

There are numerous other issues associated with the "interval problem" highlighted by beta change. For example, the "response instability" that has sometimes been taken to signal a "non-attitude" in political research could in fact reflect a beta change.[102] The difference is critical. Nonattitudes can be treated cavalierly as opinional ephemera; a beta change, in contrast, may signal an important change in the intervals a rater uses to differentiate a given psychological domain. Other significant issues[103] also seem relatable to beta effects.

Gamma Change

Gamma change is conceived as a quantum shift in ways of conceptualizing salient dimensions of reality. This massively differentiates it from beta change, which refers only to variation in the intervals measuring a relatively stable dimension of reality.

This third kind of change involves the basic *redefinition of the relevant psychological space* as a consequence of an OD intervention. In sum, gamma change is "big bang" change. It refers to a change from one state to another, as contrasted with a change of degree or condition within a given state.

If gamma changes occur as the result of an OD program, clearly, interpretations of results are chancy in the extreme, and research takes on an Alice in Wonderland quality. For example, issues of instrument validity become enormously complicated when phrased in these terms: Valid for measuring which kind of change?

Bowers' study of 14,000 respondents in twenty-three organizations,[104] reviewed in the section immediately above, helps illustrate the potential relevance of gamma change. Among other tendencies, Bowers reports that survey feedback interventions were associated with "statistically significant improvement on a majority of measures" based on The Survey of Organizations Questionnaire (TSOQ). Laboratory training interventions were "associated with declines" on similar measures.[105]

In the absence of knowledge about the distribution of types of change, however, it is not possible to conclude whether Bowers' results demonstrate the greater potency of survey feedback. Alternatively, survey feedback may have triggered alpha changes, which TSOQ picked up. In contrast, laboratory training could have induced beta changes or gamma changes in the pretest versus posttest design that Bowers utilized in most cases.[106] This explanation is consistent with the different "depths of intervention" associated with survey feedback and laboratory training, respectively. Relatedly, Bowers' instrument is such that it seems more sensitive to alpha changes, as all such instruments must be. Moreover, and this need not be the case, TSOQ apparently was based on factorial studies of other organizational populations[107] than the twenty-three in the study under discussion. It is not known to what degree factorial solutions of the data from the twenty-three organizations are congruent with the base-line solutions. Nor is it known what degree of congruence exists between factorial solutions of pretest versus posttest responses to TSOQ, which could provide a clue about the incidence of beta changes or gamma changes.

Along with other points of concern,[108] then, interpretation of Bowers' results remain problemmatic because of the lack of knowledge as to the kinds of change involved. In the case of both survey research and laboratory training interventions, that knowledge is profoundly significant in interpreting Bowers' results.

In summary, two critical points apply. Gamma changes are the prime intended consquences of OD interventions. This seems the sense of typical descriptions of OD as seeking to induce a new "social order" or "culture," which implies not only recalibration of intervals but also new content for concepts describing the quality of organization life. Moreover, gamma changes are also likely to be masked by common measuring instruments whose application usually assumes only alpha change.

In sum, gamma changes may be thought of as reflecting fundamental changes in conceptualizations and expectations, a basic redefintion of the content of the referents tapped by most available measures of organization and individual processes. Consequently, gamma changes severely complicate the interpretation of the results of OD efforts.

Support for Distinguishing Gamma Change

A range of experience and evidence implies the usefulness of conceptually distinguishing the three concepts of change. That experience and evidence are briefly illustrated here, with emphasis on similar notions developed in a counseling context.

A Cousinly Concept and Other Analogues

Perspective on the usefulness of distinguishing kinds of change derives from a recent distillation of experiences about counseling. Thus, Watzlawick, Weakland, and Fisch[109] distinguish first-order change from second-order change. They explain that the former "occurs within a given system which itself remains unchanged," while the latter "changes the system itself." A nightmare illustrates their distinction, which seems to overlap substantially with the present distinction between alpha changes and the gamma variety, and which example can also be extended to beta change. They explain: "a person having a nightmare can do many things *in* his dream–run, hide, fight, scream, jump off a cliff, etc.–but no change from any one of these behaviors to another would ever terminate the nightmare." These many changes within the system are first-order changes. The authors continue: "The one way *out of* a dream involves a change from dreaming to waking . . . a change to an altogether different state." This illustrates second-order change, which seems much like gamma change. The authors could have easily defined a third type, an analogue of beta change. Via dream analysis, a person might learn that recurring dreams are more revealing than scary. Having thus expanded the nonscary or less scary intervals of a personal rating scale, in short, an individual might stay in the dream state, yet change his reaction to it. This is the sense of beta change.

Our three authors feel their distinction between two orders of change is significant, perhaps even momentous. For example, they note that failure to distinguish the two types of change can cause the "most perplexing, paradoxical consequences," as in "some of the tragicomic controversies between experimental psychologists and psychiatrists." Many of these controversies could be avoided by active recognition that when experimental psychologists "talk about change, they usually mean first-order change . . . while psychiatrists, though not often aware of this, are predominantly concerned with second-order change."[110] The difference is great. The former deals with the change of condition; the latter deals with change of state, or perhaps, with change of change.

If in a primitive analogical way only, the three types of change introduced above can be related to a stepwise model of change in OD interventions. The illustrative case is clearest for alpha change and gamma change, as the sketch in Figure 3 suggests. That is, the large vector A → B below is associated with a major change in condition but not change in state. This vector may reflect either alpha or beta change; it is clearly not gamma change. In contrast, the small vector C → D represents a minor change in condition but induces a major change in state. In the latter case, that is, a small change induces a gamma change. A very large change also might be necessary to induce a gamma effect,

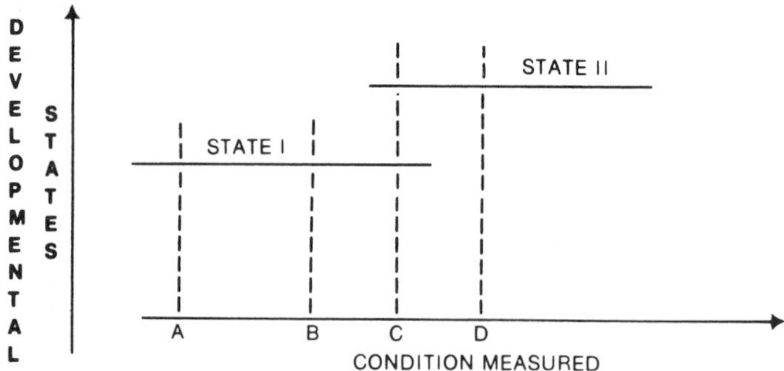

Figure 3 An illustration of alpha change in condition and gamma change in state.

depending upon the condition of the system within which the intervention is applied.

This basic concept does not violate our sense of physical properties. Thus, we all know about the difference between changes in the condition (temperature) of H_2O, and changes in its state (liquid, solid, and gas). Consider also complex homeostatis systems. They may experience a bewildering variety of changes in their conditions in highly variable order, and yet preserve their essential steady state.[111] On the other hand, common wisdom acknowledges that systems can sometimes be at such a developmental point that even minor changes in condition can induce a profound change in state. Hence the usages: the straw that broke the camel's back; the critical incident that induced a psychotic reaction; or the push we needed to get over the hump. Failure to distinguish the two kinds of change implies inadequate description and, possibly, dangerous prescriptions for action.

Much common wisdom in OD and the laboratory approach also suggests the value of distinguishing changes in condition with a state from changes in state. Thus, considerable time and effort may be expended in team development before"anything happens," and then quickly a team will "take off" and "go into orbit." The "condition measured" may be the degree of interpersonal trust, for example, substantial increases in which may be necessary before a team-to-be is willing to move to a different existential state. The change in state can then occur swiftly, even mercurially. Similar notions inhere in common concepts of developmental phases in laboratory education, as in Hampden-Turner's cyclical model of individual change,[112] in all phases of models such as that of Bennis and Shepard,[113] or in Lewin's venerable notion of unfreezing → choice or change → refreezing.[114] To illustrate, the last model clearly implies several different states, and it is important to distinguish which exists at any point. Specific behaviors or interventions appropriate in the unfrozen state of consciousness or development might be impactless or even seriously counterproductive in the frozen state.

The graphics above assume too much, of course. Specifically, analysis would be simple if we really could define and distinguish State I from State II, as in Figure 3. Usually, we have only vectors with more or less known magnitudes. However, such vectors might reflect any of the three kinds of change. That leaves too much to the imagination.

Other Research Suggesting Gamma Change

Today, we simply do not know how to distinguish the three types of change in any reasonably rigorous and consistent way. But, at least two kinds of evidence imply that the conceptual distinctions above cannot be dismissed easily. First, several independent efforts to test the adequacy of the kinds of changes sketched above have yielded positive although not exactly similar results.[115]

Second, the conceptual distinction above has been supported by some complex statistical treatments not reported here. Despite some issues with interpreting those analyses, they at least imply forcefully that a heterogeneous concept of change is necessary, with properties somewhat like those assigned to the three variants considered here.[116]

The long and short of it? The fuller possibilities of OD as applied behavioral change will depend on a satisfactory concept of change, perhaps including the present set, perhaps not. The evidence seems quite compelling that a simple concept will not permit judgments as to which OD intervention is most appropriate under which conditions.

Notes

1. The gap is stressed, for example, by Clayton P. Alderfer, "Organization Development," *Annual Review of Psychology*, Vol. 28 (1977), pp. 197-223.
2. Alexander Winn, "The Laboratory Approach to Organization Development." Paper read at Annual Conference, British Psychological Association, Oxford, Engl., September 1968, p. 3.
3. The effect is ubiquitous, and observers have generally maintained that the "total pie" of influence will be increased by OD interventions, so the "losers" will be outweighed by the "winners." For an experimental demonstration of the more complex realities, consult James F. Gavin and S. Morton McPhail, "Intervention and Evaluation: A Proactive Team Approach to OD," *Journal of Applied Behavioral Science*, Vol. 14 (April 1978), esp. pp. 188-189.
4. Ibid., esp. p. 175.
5. Sherman Kingsbury, "Tell Me Exactly What You Think, Even If It Costs You Your Job." Paper presented at Annual Meeting, Academy of Management, San Francisco, Calif., August 1978.

6. T. E. Stephenson, *Journal of Management Studies,* Vol. 12 (October 1975), p. 17.
7. Roderick Seidenberg, *Post-Historic Man* (Boston: Beacon, 1957).
8. Gordon L. Lippitt, *Organizational Renewal* (New York: Appleton-Century-Crofts, 1969), esp. pp. 29-39, presents an alternative model for organizational growth more detailed than the model used here.
9. Charles Perrow, *Organizational Analysis: A Sociological View* (Belmont, Calif.: Wadsworth, 1970), p. 19.
10. For one development of the position, see John A. Langdale, "Toward a Contingency Theory for Designing Work Organizations," *Journal of Applied Behavioral Science,* Vol. 12 (June 1976), pp. 199-214.
11. Proponents of the position that OD is appropriate in "nonroutine" organizations often label themselves "contingency theorists." For the intellectual tap-roots of that tradition, see: Tom Burns and George M. Stalker, *Management of Innovation* (London: Tavistock, 1961); Paul R. Lawrence and Jay W. Lorsch, *Organization and Environment* (Homewood, Ill.: Richard D. Irwin, 1969); and Jay W. Lorsch and John J. Morse, *Organizations and Their Members: A Contingency Approach* (New York: Harper and Row, 1974). However, favorable OD applications have been reported in situations that contingency theorists typically would see as more suitable to traditional, bureaucratic approaches. Alfred D. Marrow, David G. Bowers, and Stanley Seashore (eds.), *Management by Participation* (New York: Harper and Row, 1967), report one such successful application. See also Robert R. Blake, Jane S. Mouton, Richard L. Sloma, and Barbara Peek Loftin, "A Second Breakthrough in Organization Development," *California Management Review,* Vol. 11, no. 2 (1968), pp. 73-78.
12. Based on Alfred D. Chandler, Jr., *Strategy and Structure* (Cambridge, Mass.: MIT Press, 1962), p. 42. See also Richard Beckhard and Reuben T. Harris, *Organizational Transitions: Managing Complex Change* (Reading, Mass.: Addison-Wesley, 1977); and John Child and A. Kieser, "The Development of Organizations Over Time," Working Paper no. 51 (Birmingham, England: University of Aston Management Centre, 1976). Broad perspective derives from Larry E. Greiner, "Organization Evolution and Revolution," in Kennette Benedict and Jerry Johnson (eds.), *Seminars on Organizations,* Vol. 3 (Palo Alto, Calif.: Stanford University, 1977).
13. Chandler, *Strategy and Structure,* pp. 52-113, for example, provides detailed evidence of the structural innovations required in E. I. du Pont de Nemours & Co. See also Ernest Dale, *The Great Organizers* (New York: McGraw-Hill, 1960).
14. Henry Ford's huge River Rouge plant illustrates the point. Ford essentially ran a barony for many years, with heavy reliance on a small and loyal intelligence service.
15. Robert T. Golembiewski, *Organizing Men and Power* (Chicago: Rand McNally, 1967), esp. pp. 31-116.

16. For a classic distinction of routine versus nonroutine missions, consult the comparisons of firms in the cardboard carton versus plastic industries in Lawrence and Lorsch, *Organization and Environment.*
17. Perrow, *Organizational Analysis,* pp. 78-79.
18. Ibid., p. 81.
19. Ibid.
20. Floyd Mann, "Toward an Understanding of the Leadership Role in Formal Organizations," in Robert F. M. Dubin (ed.), *Leadership and Productivity* (San Francisco: Chandler, 1965), pp. 68-102.
21. Chris Argyris, *Intervention Theory and Method* (Reading, Mass.: Addison-Wesley, 1970), p. 87.
22. Very often, the debate is formulated in terms of "contingency theory," whose basic argument is that it "all depends" on the character of the work-flow and especially the technology when it comes to choosing an appropriate structure for organizing work. The leading early work is Lawrence and Lorsch, *Organization and Environment.* For some later developmental work on the theme, consult Lorsch and Morse, *Organizations and Their Members.*
23. Philip Selznick is the most prominent observer who insists on this point, as in his *Leadership in Administration* (New York: Harper and Row, 1957), esp. pp. 4-28.
24. Roger Harrison, "Understanding Your Organization's Character," *Harvard Business Review,* Vol. 50 (May 1972), pp. 121-123.
25. James D. Thompson, *Organizations in Action* (New York: McGraw-Hill, 1967). This analysis argues that OD applications in government face special problems. For an even less optimistic view, consult Leonard Goodstein, *Consulting with Human Service Systems* (Reading, Mass.: Addison-Wesley, 1978). Public-sector experience, however, implies a set of guidelines for OD applications that respect these special problems, and may even derive momentum from them. Illustratively, see Robert T. Golembiewski, "Intervening at the Top," in W. Warner Burke (ed.), *The Cutting Edge: Current Theory and Practice in Organization Development* (La Jolla, Calif.: University Associates, 1978).
26. Ibid., p. 12.
27. Ibid., p. 15.
28. Ibid., p. 16.
29. Rensis Likert, *New Patterns of Management* (New York: McGraw-Hill, 1961), p. 25.
30. Thompson, *Organizations in Action,* p. 128.
31. Ibid.
32. Personal conversations with Clenard Henderson, Affirmative Action Manager, Research and Development Division, and Stanley Hinckleh, Engineering Division, Proctor and Gamble.

33. Thompson, *Organizations in Action*, p. 128.
34. Ibid., p. 141.
35. Daniel Katz and Robert Kahn, *The Social Psychology of Organizations* (New York: Wiley, 1966), p. 38.
36. Ibid., p. 60.
37. Timothy W. Costello, "Change in Municipal Government: A View from the Inside," *Journal of Applied Behavioral Science*, Vol. 7 (April 1971), pp. 131-145.
38. Larry Kirkhart and Orion T. White, Jr., "The Future of OD," *Public Administration Review*, Vol. 34 (March 1974), pp. 135-140.
39. Costello, "Change in Municipal Government."
40. Katz and Kahn, *The Social Psychology of Organizations*, pp. 159-160.
41. Robert T. Golembiewski and Jack Rabin (eds.), *Public Budgeting and Finance* (Itasca, Ill.: F. E. Peacock, 1975), p. 365.
42. Ibid., 194-196.
43. Ibid.
44. The author's own experience as consultant to and evaluator of Community Action Agencies.
45. Katz and Kahn, *The Social Psychology of Organizations*, p. 112.
46. Richard S. Rosenbloom, "The Real Productivity Crisis Is in Government," *Harvard Business Review*, Vol. XI (September 1973), pp. 156-164.
47. Katz and Kahn, *The Social Psychology of Organizations*, p. 137.
48. This generalization derives from the writer's own experience as human resource consultant to communities seeking HUD funds.
49. National Training and Development Service, *First Tango in Boston: A Seminar on Organizational Change and Development* (Washington, D.C.: NTDS, 1973).
50. William G. Jarrett, "Marketing Consultant Services to Government," *Training and Development Journal*, Vol. 27 (July 1973), pp. 8 and 12.
51. Frederick C. Mosher, *Democracy and the Public Service* (New York: Oxford University Press, 1968), p. 108.
52. See Karl E. Weick, "Educational Systems as Loosely Coupled Systems," *Administrative Science Quarterly*, Vol. 21 (March 1976), pp. 1-19.
53. Cordlandt Cammann and David Berg, "Intervention in an Underbounded System," pp. 3-10. Paper delivered at 1978 Annual Meeting, Academy of Management, San Francisco, Calif., August 9-12.
54. Ibid., pp. 2, 15-18.
55. Ibid., pp. 19-21.

56. Generally, consult Marvin R. Weisbord and Leonard D. Goodstein (eds.), "Towards Healthier Medical Systems: Can We Learn from Experience?" *Journal of Applied Behavioral Science,* Vol. 14 (July 1978).
57. Marilyn H. Lammert, "Power, Authority and Status in Health Systems: A Marxian-Based Conflict Analysis," *Journal of Applied Behavioral Science,* Vol. 14 (July 1978), pp. 324-325.
58. Ibid.
59. Ibid., p. 325.
60. Oron South, "Managing Comprehensive Change in State Government: An Example of Macro-Organization Development," College of Education, Florida State University, Tallahassee, 1978.
61. James G. March, "American Public School Administration," *School Review,* Vol. 86, no. 2 (1978), p. 238.
62. Reuben T. Harris, "Improving Patient Satisfaction Through Action Research," *Journal of Applied Behavioral Science,* Vol. 14 (July 1978), pp. 382-399.
63. Reuben T. Harris, *A Multidimensional Approach to the Study of Health Care Organization.* Working Paper no. 791-75, Alfred P. Sloan School of Management, Cambridge, Mass., June 1975.
64. Reuben T. Harris and D. Whipple, "The Perceived Quality of Health Care and the Use of Military Health Facilities," *U.S. Navy Medicine,* Vol. 66 (1975), pp. 3-8.
65. Harris, "Improving Patient Satisfaction."
66. Ibid., pp. 395-398.
67. See Lammert, "Power, Authority and Status," pp. 324-325.
68. This analysis uses the categories developed by Lee Bolman, "Organization Development and the Limits of Growth: When Smaller Is Better, Can OD Help?" Paper presented at 1978 Annual Meeting, Academy of Management, San Francisco, Calif., August 9-12.
69. Lammert, "Power, Authority and Status," p. 332.
70. For a start in this much needed direction, see David G. Bowers, Jerome L. Franklin, and Patricia A. Pecorella, "Matching Problems, Precursors, and Interventions in OD: A Systemic Approach," *Journal of Applied Behavioral Science,* Vol. 11 (December 1975), pp. 391-410; and Don Hellriegel and John W. Slocum, Jr., "Towards A Comparative Typology for Assessing Organizational Change Models," pp. 363-367, in Robert L. Taylor, Michael J. O'Connell, Robert A. Zawacki, and D. D. Warrick (eds.), *1976 Proceedings,* Academy of Management. The required developments, be it noted, will depend in critical senses on the resolution of some devilish issues related to alternative research designs. For current reports on the state of the art, see Sam E. White and Terence R. Mitchell, "Organization Development: A

Review of Research Content and Research Design," *Academy of Management Review,* Vol. 1 (April 1976), pp. 57-73; and Larry E. Pate, Warren R. Nielsen, and Paula C. Bacon, "Advances in Research on Organization Development: Toward a Beginning," pp. 389-394, in Taylor, O'Connell, Zawacki, and Warrick, *1976 Proceedings.*

71. Cary L. Cooper, Ned Levine, and Koichiro Kobayashi, "Developing One's Potential: From West to East," *Group and Organization Studies,* Vol. 1 (March 1976), pp. 43-55.
72. R. Wayne Boss, David J. Gouws, and Takeshi Nagia, "The Cross-Cultural Effects of Organization Development Interventions: A Conflict-Confrontation Design," *Southern Review of Public Administration,* Vol. 2 (March 1978), pp. 486-502.
73. David G. Bowers, "OD Techniques and Their Results in 23 Organizations: The Michigan ICL Study," *Journal of Applied Behavioral Science,* Vol. 9 (September 1973), pp. 21-43. For narrower comparative studies, see Iain Mangham and Cary L. Cooper, "The Impact of T-Groups on Managerial Behavior," *Journal of Management Studies,* Vol. 6 (February 1969), esp. p. 62; and William A. Pasmore and Donald C. King, "Understanding Organizational Change," *Journal of Applied Behavioral Science,* Vol. 14 (December 1978), pp. 455-468.
74. David G. Bowers, "Back to Bower on OD Techniques," *Journal of Applied Behavioral Science,* Vol. 9 (September 1973), pp. 671-672.
75. Bowers, "OD Techniques and Their Results," esp. pp. 31-41.
76. Bowers, "Back to Bowers," pp. 671-672.
77. William R. Torbert, "Some Questions on Bowers' Study of Different OD Techniques," *Journal of Applied Behavioral Science,* Vol. 9 (September 1973), pp. 668-671; and William A. Pasmore, "The Michigan ICL Study Revisited: An Alternative Explanation of Results," *Journal of Applied Behavioral Science,* Vol. 12 (June 1976), pp. 245-251.
78. Bowers, "OD Techniques and Their Results in 23 Organizations," p. 40.
79. Sheldon Davis, "An Organic Problem-Solving Method of Organizational Change," *Journal of Applied Behavioral Science,* Vol. 3 (January 1967), pp. 3-21; and Robert T. Golembiewski and Stokes B. Carrigan, "Planned Change Through Laboratory Methods," *Training and Development Journal,* Vol. 27 (March 1973), pp. 18-27.
80. Marrow, Bowers, and Seashore, *Management by Participation.*
81. Robert J. Solomon, "An Examination of the Relationship Between a Survey Feedback OD Technique and the Work Environment," *Personnel Psychology,* Vol. 29 (1976), p. 591.
82. Robert T. Golembiewski and Robert Munzenrider, "Team-Building on a Mass Scale: Three Approaches to Measuring Effects." Unpublished MS, 1973. See also Robert Munzenrider, "Organization Climates." Unpublished doctoral disseration, University of Georgia, Athens, 1976.

83. As Marvin Weisbord seems to suggest in his "The Wizard of OD," *OD Practitioner,* Vol. 10 (Summer 1978), pp. 1-7.
84. Erving Goffman, *The Presentation of Self in Everyday Life* (Garden City: N.Y.: Doubleday, 1959).
85. Clayton P. Alderfer and David N. Berg, "Organization Development: The Profession and Practitioner," pp. 89-110, in Philip H. Mirvis and David N. Berg (eds.), *Failures in Organization Development and Change* (New York: Wiley, 1977).
86. I wish to acknowledge that this concept was developed in collaboration with Kumea Shorter and Bruce Katcher while working on a project together in a community setting.
87. Jack C. Glidewell, *Choice Points* (Cambridge, Mass.: MIT Press, 1970).
88. Eric J. Miller and A. Ken Rice, *Systems of Organization* (London: Tavistock, 1967).
89. Ronald A. Levine and Donald T. Campbell, *Ethnocentrism* (New York: Wiley, 1972).
90. Alfred Schutz, *On Phenomenology and Social Relations* (Chicago: University of Chicago Press, 1970).
91. Paulo Freire, *Pedagogy of the Oppressed* (Harmondsworth, Middlesex, Engl.: Penguin, 1972).
92. Peter L. Berger and Thomas Luckman, *The Social Construction of Reality* (Garden City, N.Y.: Doubleday, 1966).
93. Ken K. Smith, "An Intergroup Perspective on Individual Behavior," pp. 359-372, in J. Richard Hackman, Edward E. Lawler III, and Lyman W. Porter (eds.), *Perspectives on Behavior in Organizations* (New York: McGraw-Hill, 1977).
94. When typing this manuscript, my secretary and friend pointed out that using workers to illustrate the "paranoid" bondage of lowers was judgmental. She argued that the suspicion and distrust of workers was neither irrational nor excessive in view of the history of employers hiring hit-men, Mafia, scabs, and so forth, to undermine the legitimate interests of the workers. I feel that her statement is a legitimate perspective that should be expressed.
95. From the title of a paper by Sherman Kingsbury presented at the Annual Meeting, Academy of Management, San Francisco, Calif., August 1978.
96. Carl Bereiter, "Some Persisting Dilemmas in the Measurement of Change," p. 11, in Chester W. Harris (ed.), *Problems in Measuring Change* (Madison, Wisc.: University of Wisconsin, 1963).
97. Robert Ross, "OD for Whom?" *Journal of Applied Behavioral Science,* Vol. 7 (September 1971), pp. 580-585.
98. Robert Tannenbaum and Sheldon Davis, "Values, Man, and Organization," in Warren H. Schmidt (ed.), *Organizational Frontiers and Human Values*

(Belmont, Calif.: Wadsworth, 1970); and Robert T. Golembiewski, *Renewing Organizations* (Itasca, Ill.: F. E. Peacock, 1972), esp. pp. 59-110.

99. Robert T. Ward, "Culture and the Comparative Study of Politics, or the Constipated Dialectic," *American Political Science Review*, Vol. 68 (March 1974), esp. p. 199.

100. Golembiewski and Carrigan, "Planned Change Through Laboratory Methods."

101. Victor E. McGee, "The Multidimensional Analysis of 'Elastic' Distances," *British Journal of Mathematical and Statistical Psychology*, Vol. 19 (November 1966), pp. 181-196.

102. Philip E. Converse, "Attitudes and Non-Attitudes," pp. 168-189, in Edward R. Tufte (ed.), *The Quantitative Analysis of Social Problems* (Reading, Mass.: Addison-Wesley, 1970); and Robert T. Golembiewski, "The Non-Attitude Hypothesis and Types of Change," *Georgia Political Science Association Journal*, Vol. 6 (Fall 1978), pp. 103-111.

103. Susan Pepper and Lubomir S. Prytulak, "Sometimes Frequently Means Seldom: Context Effects in the Interpretation of Quantitative Expressions," *Journal of Research in Personality*, Vol. 8 (June 1974), pp. 95-101.

104. Bowers, "OD Techniques and Their Results in 23 Organizations: The Michigan ICL Study."

105. Ibid., p. 21.

106. Ibid., p. 22.

107. James Taylor and David G. Bowers, *Survey of Organizations* (Ann Arbor, Mich.: CRUSK, Institute for Social Research, University of Michigan, 1967).

108. Torbert, "Some Questions on Bowers' Study of Different OD Techniques"; and Pasmore, "The Michigan ICL Study Revisited."

109. Paul Watzlawick, John H. Weakland, and Richard Fisch, *Change: Principles of Problem Formation and Problem Resolution* (New York: W. W. Norton, 1974), esp. pp. 10-11.

110. Ibid., pp. 27-28.

111. W. Ross Ashby, *Design for a Brain* (New York: Wiley, 1954); and W. Ross Ashby, *An Introduction to Cybernetics* (London: Chapmen and Hall, 1956).

112. Charles W. Hampden-Turner, "An Existential 'Learning Theory' and the Integration of T-Group Research," *Journal of Applied Behavioral Science*, Vol. 2 (October 1966), pp. 367-386.

113. Warren G. Bennis and Herbert Shepard, "A Theory of Group Development," *Human Relations*, Vol. 9 (November 1956), pp. 415-437.

114. Dale Zand and Richard E. Sorensen, "Problems in the Measurement of Organizational Effectiveness," *Administrative Science Quarterly*, Vol. 20 (December 1975), pp. 532-545.

115. Consult Robert W. Zmud and Achilles A. Armenakis, "Understanding the Measurement of Change," mimeographed, 1978; and W. Alan Randolph and Rosemary Goad Edwards, "Assessment of Alpha, Beta, and Gamma Changes in a University-Setting OD Intervention." Paper presented at Annual Meeting, Academy of Management, San Francisco, August 1978.

116. Robert T. Golembiewski, Keith Billingsley, and Samuel Yeager, "Measuring Change and Persistence in Human Affairs: Types of Change Generated by OD Designs," *Journal of Applied Behavioral Science*, Vol. 11 (May 1976), esp. pp. 143-155. For a critique, see Michael K. Lindell and John A. Drexler, Jr., "Issues in Using Survey Methods for Measuring Organizational Change," *Academy of Management Review*, Vol. 14 (January 1979), pp. 13-19.

Chapter 9

PERSPECTIVES ON FACILITATORS OF ORGANIZATION DEVELOPMENT APPLICATIONS

How What Needs Doing Gets Done

This concluding chapter provides five perspectives on a critical resource in OD interventions: the intervenor, facilitator, change agent, the mildly deprecated guru, or whatever term is applied to that role. Generally, that resource follows a definite strategy. That is, rather than intervening directly to make things happen, the intervenor typically allows things to happen by recommending and monitoring appropriate designs that encourage or at least permit learning: a choice or a change. Occasionally, however, an intervenor will intrude self rather dramatically. Perceiving when such an intervention is necessary, knowing what specific intervention is useful, and having the presence of mind and courage to intervene: these are the essentials of the art.

It would be a mistake to assume that much more can be done here than to sketch some useful perspectives on the intervenor. To a substantial degree, intervening is an art form, and each intervenor has a personalized and idiosyncratic style. But, some things may be said with confidence.

This chapter seeks to illustrate both the generalizable and the personalized. Specifically, the first two sections below deal with the generalizable, by:

- Presenting a schema of the interventionist's world, its basic features, and some common pitfalls associated with those features
- Developing a typology of intervenors, to sketch some general classes of how intervenors go about their work

Three final sections take a personalized approach to a more elusive subject matter. That is, the focus there is on how OD intervenors:

- Conceptualize about their own style, seeking insight into some broadly personal life experiences that my relate to how they do what they do in an intervenor's role
- Reflect on some errors in how and what intervenors did
- Seek to provide some counterweight to the common view that the best OD intervention is the intervenor's "warm body" by stressing the OD intervenor's roles as theorist/scientist

A Schema of the Interventionist's World
Some Overall Features and Special Traps

Chris Argyris has given telling attention to describing the interventionist's world, and we rely on his work to paint with a broad brush some features of the role that are quite general and probably universal. Specifically, Argyris[1] distinguishes four classes of generalizations relevant to intervening, which are briefly introduced below.

Primary Tasks of Interventionist

Despite some deviations when more directive behavior is appropriate, the intervenor seeks to play a facilitative role in aiding the client or client system in coming to a better understanding of its self and its environment. Conveniently if somewhat simplistically, then, the intervenor seeks to:

- Help the client system generate valid information
- Help client use information for making more informed and responsible free choices
- Help client generate information and make free choices in ways that enhance the internal commitment of the client
- Help client to:
  Select goals with minimal defensiveness
  Define approaches to achieve goals
  Relate choices of goals and approaches to central needs
  Build challenging but attainable levels of aspiration into choices

Patently, the overall goal is to generate the valid information in ways that are ego-enhancing or at least ego-maintaining for the client, as well as in ways that reduce client resistance to or dependence on the consultant. That is a difficult combination, but well worth the effort.

Qualities Needed by Interventionist

This basic reliance on the resources of the client or client-system may be misleading, and it clearly will be if it encourages neglect of what the intervenor brings to the situation. Perhaps four intervenor qualities loom largest, and they can be detailed here briefly again relying on Argyris:

- Confidence in one's own philosophy of intervention and its derivative strategies
- Ability to perceive reality accurately, especially under stress
- Ability to perceive and accept client's attacks and mistrust, and willingness to encourage client's expression of them
- Capacity to use stressful situations as learning opportunities for self and client

In these senses, the intervenor serves as an anchor for the client or client system. "I know this approach usually works," the intervenor should ideally project, "if we hang in there long enough and can build escalating confidence in one another. Essentially, this means concentrating on the problem, not letting things like mistrust build between us, relying on our ability to perceive what is going on, and being willing to deal with whatever comes up."

Conditions Faced by Interventionist

These qualities of the intervenor as an anchor for basic processes, as an early modeler of them, are typically tested in rough seas. That is, the interventionist faces a set of conditions that encourage confusion or compromise about what is going on and why. Specifically, Argyris isolates four conditions that especially test interventionists' confidence in methodology and in self:

- A high degree of discrepancy and ambiguity:
  Between their views and those of client about causes of problems
  Between their views and those of the client about the design of effective systems
  Between consultant's own ideals and behavior
- Marginal membership in the client system, which is at once a source of a consultant's value and a problem

- Mistrust by clients, as reflected in their misperception of consultant's motives or misunderstanding of his communication
- Minimal feedback from client about effectiveness

Possible Awkward Adaptations by Interventionist

Such difficult conditions may encourage a wide variety of maladaptive responses by the interventionist, which must be guarded against. In brief summary, Argyris identifies four such maladaptive responses as most probable:

- Increases in defensive behavior, and a decrease in the use of appropriate coping behaviors
- Unrealistically high needs for inclusion in the client system or, alternatively, a decision to engage with the client system on a limited technical or specific basis only
- Unrealistic level of expectation, a compulsion for immediate and major "impact" or "success"
- High needs for confirmation or disconfirmation by client

Such responses clearly make the intervenor's needs dominant, and they can get in the way of the goal of helping the client apply resources to the problem situation. Illustratively, if the interventionist has high needs for confirmation or disconfirmation by the client, that leaves him less able to serve as an anchor for the processes to which the client is increasingly to commit self. Of course, the interventionist who believes she needs no confirmation or disconfirmation from client, or neglects or misinterprets them when they are given, is in equally difficult shape.

Some Roles that Intervenors Play
Distinguishing Classes of Similar Ways of Coping

The interventionist's world is particularly treacherous because his or her behavior will vary with the several roles that can, and often should, be played. The role demands on the interventionist are not only severe, in short, but they can be at serious cross-purposes. A brief taxonomy helps make the point.

There probably never will be a single, satisfactory way of classifying what an OD intervenor does, so this section is as quixotic as it is necessary. Unpretentiously, the approach here distinguishes five broad intervenor roles, including:

- Facilitative
- Gatekeeping

- Diagnostic
- Architectural
- Mobilizing

Roughly, the roles are listed in order of increasing obtrusiveness, as the brief descriptions below clearly imply. Table 1 also lists some *modes* of expressing those several roles, as well as some specific activities associated in practice with those roles. Numerous other ways to slice this pie have been conceived, of course. I am particularly attracted for purposes more complex than the present ones by Ottaway's focus on how change agents relate to types of change, as contrasted with the focus on roles in Table 1. Ottaway distinguishes:[2]

- Change generators, or those who raise consciousness about the need for change
- Change implementors
- Change adopters, who practice a change and normalize it

Ottaway goes on to variously subclassify these three basic types and to illustrate their complementarities and differences.

Two preliminary notes deserve emphasis concerning the panoply of roles that intervenors play. Basically, the issue has not received the attention it deserves. The value of greater attention is patently reflected in available research, some dealing with change agents in the broadest sense[3] and other research dealing more narrowly with T-group trainers.[4] Moreover, most discussions of the OD role stress its emphasis on the client's knowledge and experience and downplay the expertise of the consultant. This emphasis derives essentially from sensitivity training and process consultation, which focus on client ownership and involvement to the apparent exclusion of other goals. OD activities often require broadening these traditional role boundaries, albeit at some cost. As Huse observes:[5]

> Particularly at the more systemwide levels of intervention, it may be quite appropriate for the consultant to use his expert power to make substantive suggestions. At deeper levels of intervention, however, the use of the client's knowledge and experience become more important, with a corresponding decrease in reliance on the consultant's knowledge and expertise.

Huse also cautions that continued collaboration with the client is required, even as the change agent acts as "expert." Observers pretty much agree that the OD intervenor's roles have enlarged in the directions Huse recommends, although there are costs as well as benefits in so doing.[6]

Table 1 Some OD Intervenor Roles, with Related Modes for Expression and with Associated Activities

Typical Roles of OD Intervenor	Modes of Expressing Role	Associated Activities
1. Facilitative	Relationship improvement	Third-party consultation; role negotiation
	Process enhancement	Team-building; family T-group
2. Gatekeeping	Espousing attractive values	Writing Chapters 1-3 in Part 1
	Modeling behaviors and values in action	Giving effective feedback; acting congruently with OD values in ambiguous or threatening situations
3. Diagnostic	Designing enhancers of feedback and disclosure	3-D Images; suggesting that a management team videotape and critique its interaction
	Action research	Survey research with feedback
	Elaborating theory	As in Chapter 2's comparison of alternative structures for organizing work and their consequences
	Rational analysis	Analysis of systems and procedures; cost-benefit analysis; operations research
4. Architectural	People changing	Behavior modification; contracting
	People exchanging	Participating in a reduction-in-force or a demotion
	Structure changing	Job enrichment; MBO; role negotiation
	Policy changing	Flexi-Time; quality of working life projects; eliminating the hourly/salary distinction
	Technology changing	Disseminating basic innovations, social (as in MBO) and technical (as in computer technology)
5. Mobilizing	Inside pressure	Vertical feedback designs; team-building
	Outside pressure	Union organizing; consumer suits; organizing rent

Facilitative Role

This constitutes the primal OD role and is a quite direct transfer into the work site of the basic preoccupations of trainers in a T-group or in sensitivity training. The intervenor helps individuals and groups cope with the webs of processes and relationships within which they find themselves enmeshed, sometimes comfortably but often not. The premium is on use of client resources for diagnosis and solution, with the goal of maximum ownership via client's self-acceptance of his or her own experience. The intervenor helps to clarify that experience and the choices available to the client.

Gatekeeping Role

This second intervenor role gets somewhat more obtrusive and coercive. Tersely, no behavior or attitude may be off-limits in an OD intervention, but that behavior or attitude is not to be dealt with in just any old way. That is the central message of the first three chapters of this revision: OD is value-loaded, whether we like it or not. Nothing like a consensus about values exists among OD intervenors. A number of basic agreements do exist, as Chapters 1 to 3 in Part 1 of this revision seek to establish.

As a kind of moral conscience of an OD effort, the intervenor seeks to control norms and values, to admit or exclude specific ways in which data or relationships are to be dealt with. Effectively, the intervenor serves as professional gatekeeper, admitting this sheep and excluding that goat, as it were. Hopefully, there will be ample help from others. But sometimes the intervenor must stand lonely vigil, perhaps while under attack. How well the intervenor does at such times in modeling the attitudes and behaviors espoused in principle often will go a long way toward influencing the success or failure of OD interventions.

Intervenors gatekeep in what they espouse and practice, that is, with the latter being far more impactful than the former. Indeed, central episodes in OD interventions often in effect test whether OD intervenors really mean for self what they prescribe for others. In my experience, as the concluding section of this chapter reveals, these central episodes often involve the appropriate degree of "distance" between intervenor and organization members. If the intervenor cozies up to the superior, as by watering down negative feedback, the intervenor can come to be seen as serving those in power. On the other hand, if the intervenor identifies too exclusively with the subordinates, hierarchical superiors may reject the values the intervenor professes.

Gatekeeping requires very delicate skills indeed. Often subordinates are cautious and wait to see what happens to the intervenors when they model with their superior the values and behaviors that the intervenors advise—nay, often prescribe—that they increasingly use with their superior.

Diagnostic Role

Still more obtrusive is the diagnostic role, generally. Although the several components differ substantially, the consultant's qualities more likely will be up-front in this role because of skills, training, knowledge, or experience. Typically, that is to say, one cannot play the diagnostic role *and* the facilitative role without significant (even if sometimes subtle) shifts in the mode and character of behavior. Noteworthy dilemmas inhere in this fact. For example, how to be diagnostic in the present sense while enhancing or at least maintaining the sense of client ownership, both of which are easier to do in the facilitative role?

The four examples of diagnostic role variants in Table 1, for example, are roughly arrayed in order of how much intervenors and their skills and attributes stand front-and-center. Patently, client inputs are far more central in most feedback designs developed by the intervenor than they are in the varieties of diagnostic role called elaborating theory or rational analysis. Similarly, organization members are the experts in giving feedback to one another, even if they do so within the structure suggested by the intervenor. In elaborating theory or in rational analysis, in contrast, the intervenor is far more likely to be on his or her own turf, with implicit or explicit claims about dominant expertise and with implications for client involvement and ownership.

Architectural Role

Consider a curious duality. There has always been an architectural component in all OD interventionist activities, but the full realization of the scope and significance of this role has come slowly.[7] Indeed, common OD emphases discourage a realistic appreciation of this role, and thus perhaps discourage experimentation with it.

This duality is easy enough to understand. That is, even when the T-group was *the* only learning vehicle in the laboratory approach, enormous effort went into designing the details of learning experiences to heighten specific effects, which reflects an early architectural role. Indeed, the concern about architecture often became monumental in those early days, with massive energies going into thought and debate about design details, perhaps all the more so because trainers were still somewhat uncertain about the basic T-group technology. At the same time, however, the laboratory approach has always emphasized client involvement and ownership. This no doubt encourages a reticence about exploring the fuller dimensions of the architectural role. The belated OD emphasis on job enrichment or MBO, for example, is in part no doubt explained by the restraints on client involvement and ownership implicit in those minitechnology packages.

More recently, a substantial middle ground exists where interventionists may exercise an architectural role while respecting client involvement and ownership.

The discussion of Flexi-Time in Chapter 6, for example, illustrates one such effort at balance. But that balancing effort does not come easy, make no mistake. The overall history of MBO, for example, testifies to the fact that the architectural role can easily get out of hand, encouraging a mechanical and unilateral orientation that can undercut in practice what is in principle an attractive managerial approach.

Understandable or not, middle ground or no, one conclusion stands out concerning the architectural role. Stated in Bowers' terms, OD intervenors cannot long remain content with a "catalytic" definition of their role. Bowers notes that definition, expressed in the simplest terms, inclines ". . . toward the opinion that the client unit—person or work group—contains all of the capacity necessary to cope with its own problems, provided that it is aware of both these things (capacity and problems). The consultant . . . therefore [helps] create an interpersonal situation in which awareness can occur. His role in other words is limited to freeing up or speeding up a 'natural' capacity for constructive change."[8] This catalytic role can be useful, but it has a restricted application. This will be the case for noninteraction-oriented designs such as structural change, job redesign, and so on; and it will also be the case where theoretical understanding is required to comprehend "the problem" and to prescribe "remedies." In such cases, Bowers notes that a catalytic role often will be counterproductive.[9] The intervenor should focus on helping the client in defining the problem, putting the client in touch with the required literature or experience, and helping the client to design suitable learning vehicles.

Mobilizing Role

Pehaps least acknowledged is the OD interventionist's mobilizing role, and for substantial reasons. Let us approach the point in two ways.

First, the mobilization role has not been so subtle as to escape note. Thus, it has been recognized quite widely that OD interventions like team-building have consequences for the distribution of power in organizations and, hence, that these interventions can be profoundly political.[10] These inherently mobilizing characteristics of some OD interventions, however, do not (and should not) preclude their use. Rather, in recommending such interventions, an interventionist should advise clients about what may happen. More broadly, a few interventionists have argued for an even more overt mobilizing role, as in representing the underrepresented or in advocacy of causes from outside as well as inside a managerial system.

Second, however, there has been a tentativeness about squarely facing the fuller implications of what is generally appreciated and sometimes even advocated, in more or less extreme forms:[11] that OD interventionists usually do, and should, play a mobilizing role. The reasons for this important paradox can only be sampled here. For example, most internal OD consultants are "staff" in the traditional concept—formally advisory, outside the chain of command, and so on. No wonder, then, about *their* reticence to emphasize a mobilizing role. For that emphasis in many cases would only complicate a delicate relationship. "Staff" officials seek, ideally, to be proactive without being seen as a competitor for the authority of the "line." That is difficult to bring off, especially over a long period of time, and it is not made easier by emphasis on the mobilizing potency of the OD interventionist.

Blending Roles and Their Obtrusiveness

As in all of life, an OD interventionist cannot long avoid role difficulties except by forfeiting opportunities. To illustrate, the mobilizing role implies clear potential problems, whether in a T-group or in an organizational consultation.[12] But eschewing that role implies no long-run solution. For failure to mobilize might only limit the effectiveness of the OD interventionist, as well as narrow the areas in which he or she can be facilitative. On the other hand, too much emphasis on the mobilization role might have awkward side effects. These could include a diminished sense of ownership and involvement by clients. Worse still, excessive mobilization might encourage some unwary clients into learning situations for which they are not ready, or with which they cannot cope, or whose ratio of risk to benefit is too great. Consider the case of an interventionist who concludes that a boss "needs confronting," and zealously mobilizes subordinates to do the job. If the boss is punitive or even vicious, this might be dangerous for subordinates. That danger may not be impressive enough to deter the interventionist, who normally is more insulated from hierarchical wrath than are immediate subordinates.

And so it goes. Consequently, OD interventionists must acknowledge the general necessity for a delicate balancing of roles, even when in a specific case they opt to play it safe. The implied fine-tuning is extremely delicate and complex, and requires that interventionists be in touch with personal motives and interests, as well as be aware of the probable consequences of the designs they recommend. In addition, interventionists should be able to disclose those motives, interests, and consequences to their clients, as well as to other involved parties.

Role Differentiation and Value Issues

This diversity of intervenor roles at once requires value or ethical judgments, while it also derives both direction and confusion from the several basic sets of values underlying the OD technology and theory. So, the intervenor has only two choices: to seek synergistic integration of perspectives that are often at basic odds, or to dilute the comprehensiveness and impact of his interventions.

This complex point can be brought into focus by considering briefly the relevance of three broad systems of belief—rationalism, pragmatism, and existentialism—all of which, Chapter 2 in Part 1 emphasizes, underlay the development of OD. Friedlander highlights some critical issues when he poses these derivative value judgments for the OD intervenor:[13]

- Should intervenor foster the client's self-acceptance, by helping the client clarify his experiences and the choices available to him?
- Should intervenor suggest or design new experiences for the client so as to help him improve (for example) his problem-solving?
- Should intervenor emphasize the development and sharing of more valid models or reality?

These types of question reflect existential, pragmatic, and rationalist emphases, in order.

That the OD intervenor often cannot, and should not, restrict self to one philosophic orientation and thus to one class of these several questions, in effect, induces role differentiation and potential conflict, even as gains in comprehensiveness thus become available. "This dilemma," Friedlander observes, "presents three distinct roles for OD professionals—'the accepter or experience,' 'the change agent,' or 'the conceptual teacher-learner.' The focus is [either] on subjective awareness, [on] designing for and development of others, or objective knowledge." And therein lay critical issues for blending and choice which can enrich an intervention or hamstring it.

The Choice Domain of the Intervenor
Three Useful but Simplified Clusters of Tendencies

Another way of marking off the range of choices available to the intervenor involves sketching a choice domain, whose anchoring clusters of tendencies are sketched in Exhibit 1. Some readers might prefer to think of the three clusters of tendencies as the vertexes of a triangle, which could be labeled OD Choice Domain. Whatever one's mental picture, variants of the three alternative orientations have been prominent in the OD literature. To be sure, the three descriptions simplify, perhaps even oversimplify, and no intervenor may accept any one of them in entirety or in the bald statements of Exhibit 1. Nonetheless, the three orientations at least suggest alternative ways to go. Two of the orientations derive from the work of Stanley Herman,[14] although the presentation here clearly compresses his ideas and thus may distort them some, but hopefully not seriously so.

Exhibit 1 Three Approaches to OD Interventions

Conventional Human Relations Approach[a]	Individually Oriented Approach[a]	Technology-Oriented Approach
1. Dominant attention goes to group phenomena. The dual foci are on group-building, and then on using that normative system as support ("group helping") for efforts at choice or change by group members.	1. Dominant attention goes to the individual—to the recognition and mobilization of a person's strength and power.	1. Dominant attention goes to the structure and policies defining the job and work-site relationships, which assumes or reflects the massive impact of technology on consciousness.
2. Situational impacts on relationships and interaction get prime attention, along with causal linkages between situations and behavioral variations. These foci stress *where* and *why*, as it were.	2. *What* the individual does, and *how*, get dominant attention.	2. *What* structure and policies require of individuals and (only rarely) of groups, and *how* individuals and groups respond to those requirements, get dominant attention.
3. Analysis emphasizes "problem behavior," as well as inducing an interpersonal climate and methods suitable for managing or eliminating that behavior. The primary approach to change, then, is through the individual and his "problem behavior." Thus change occurs: When trust levels in a group are high enough so that individuals can respond nondefensively to	3. The "problem behavior" typically will be intensified or dramatized until a change in the relationship occurs. The primary approach to change, then, is through reactions of the actor and others to the "problem behavior." Thus change can occur in such ways: Others may change their reaction to the "problem behavior" as they more fully come to	3. The "problem behavior" inheres in the poor congruence of technological demands and basic or common individual needs. Since individual needs are paramount and/or cannot be violated in the long run without serious negative effects, preventive or ameliorative efforts focus on the technology. The primary approach to change or amelioration, then, is through the

feedback directed at themselves, consensually validate individual pieces of feedback, and make a choice to change or not to change in the context of group resources for analysis, for generating alternative behaviors, reinforcing efforts at experimentation, and so on.	understand the actor's intent and total behaviors. The actor may change his feeling about self as he more fully experiences and acknowledges what he is, including the "problem behavior." This may change the feelings of others toward him. The actor may change her response to others as she more clearly understands what they expect of her. Both actor and/or others accept the "problem behavior" as something that exists, an acceptance which also involves reduced tension about the behavior by self and others. Such acceptance may facilitate later substantive change. Combinations of the above.	technology seen as inducing the "problem behavior." Hence, a specific technology: Might be modified to decrease the incongruence with individual needs. Might remain unmodified, but personnel selection would isolate individuals with appropriate or less antagonistic needs, as allegedly occurs in the use of morons for highly repetitive work. Might remain unmodified, but personnel policies would be developed that recognize the deprivation of individual needs required by the technology, as in the "alone pay" supplement granted in some steel plants because individual employees have to work in confined and isolated places.
4. Aggressiveness and conflict tend to be seen as "negative forces," which should be brought to light and then resolved or reduced as soon as possible.	4. Aggressiveness and conflict are "vitalizing forces," necessary for creativity as well as for progress in relationships.	4. Aggressiveness and conflict tend to be seen as symptoms of a poor fit of individual needs and technological requirements, and hence as better reduced or eliminated.

Exhibit 1 (Continued)

Conventional Human Relations Approach[a]	Individually Oriented Approach[a]	Technology-Oriented Approach
5. Feedback from others plays a central role, but external pressure may risk mere conformity.	5. Feedback from self is seen as most central, which may deprive the individual of other resources but does maximize autonomy as well as ownership of feedback and change to which it might lead.	5. Feedback from employees about their reactions to work-site structure and policies gets priority, as mediated by academic literatures such as "organization behavior."
6. Interdependence constitutes the goal of goals.	6. The enhancement of individual autonomy and competence are the primary goals, which combine to increase the capacity of individuals to choose various modes of relating to others—competitive, collaborative, or whatever.	6. The prime goal emphasizes increased congruence of individual needs and work requirements, which may imply a basically collaborative or interdependent mode between management, union, and employees, but which also may have authoritarian features.
7. Openness about ideas and feelings is valued as a personal style.	7. Being "up-front" is valued as a personal style, which may mean being up-front even about being closed, devious, and so on.	7. The basic focus is on design alternatives and their outcomes, with little or no attention to personal style or processes.
8. Learning from new concepts, as well as experiments with new behaviors, gets priority.	8. Priority goes to increasing awareness of present behavior and its completion in ways that reduce or extinguish tension in the actor.	8. Priority goes to eliminating blockages to individual need satisfaction at the work site.

9. The consultant role is defined in terms of the observation of process and is expressed overtly as relatively inactive, neutral, and facilitative.	9. The consultant role is activist and clearly directive.	9. The consultant is activist and clearly directive, at least in interpreting the research as to useful technological variants.
10. The organizational focus is on changing cultures to make it easier for the individual to be open, trusting, and so on.	10. The focus is on increasing the competence of individuals so that they can better do whatever they want, whatever the culture of their organizations.	10. The focus is on changing job and work-site requirements so that individuals might better meet their needs and expend less energy in protecting self against a need-depriving work site.

[a]Based on Stanley M. Herman, "The Shadow of Organization Development," pp. 136-151, in W. Warner Burke (ed.), *Current Issues and Strategies in Organization Development* (New York: Human Science Press, 1977). See also Stanley M. Herman and Michael Korenich, *Authentic Management: A Gestalt Orientation to Organizations and Their Development* (Reading, Mass.: Addison-Wesley, 1977), pp. 23-37.

This analysis will be content with four uses of Exhibit 1. *First,* note that the three orientations may be compared or contrasted in suggestive terms. To illustrate, relying on Herman's work for two of the clusters of tendencies:

Conventional Human Relations Approach	Individually Oriented Approach	Technology-Oriented Approach
Group interest	Self-interest	Enlightened self-interest by system controllers; co-operation by the controlled
Belongingness	Autonomy and separateness	Compact or contract
Trust of, and openness toward, others	Caution and reserve	Trust in presently sufficient and growing mutuality between technological and individual needs
Collaboration and participation	Competition and aggressiveness	Willingness to apply, and respond to, industrial or organizational humanism
Affection and responsiveness	Dislike and resistance	Acceptance of role and motives of system controllers

Those brief identifiers more or less obviously cover much of the gamut of how people can relate to life. Some of those orientations are mutually exclusive. Even though others are more or less compatible, then, one cannot have all that Exhibit 1 contains, at least not at the same time.

Second, one can describe many of the designs above as inclining toward one or another of the three clusters of tendencies in Exhibit 1. Conveniently, let us refer to conventional human relations as CHR, individually oriented as IO, and technology oriented as TO. Most of the interaction-centered designs, for example, clearly tend toward the CHR approach, albeit in various degrees. Similarly, features of the IO approach may be read into aspects of the role negotiation designs, the demotion experience, the separation or the income-augmentation designs, or even Flexi-Time. This is the case even though, at some point or another, the IO approach can so much emphasize the D in OD that the O gets no attention. Moreover, the TO approach gets reflected in the treatments above of job enlargment, MBO, as well as in the discussion of structural variants. Note that the discussion also emphasizes that TO failures can be traced, suggestively at least, to their neglect of features of the CHR approach, such features as group norms.

Third, how then to determine where a specific intervenor or intervention comes down? For me, that choice always rests in values and ethical choices. That is, I can accept none of the three clusters of tendencies, as is, and yet any one of them might be useful. The central issue always is: Which tendency for what purposes?

The issues are seldom simple, but let us make life easy. What of the IO approach, which encourages one to such dicta as: Every person for themselves. I cannot accept that proposition in the abstract, on ethical grounds, but neither can I reject it. For my strong inclination is to reject the proposition in most cases, even as I know that certain situations dictate or at least strongly encourage just such a posture. Only the most insightful diagnosis I can muster will permit me to guess whether I can have my "druthers," or whether fixating on those "druthers" without prudent regard for the environment would be foolhardy for clients or myself. Sometimes, the mobilization of individual strength can be where it's at, because of that individual's central role in history or because he or she is a Puritan in Babylon who must be strengthened all the better to resist "the system" and perhaps to reform it. Similarly, I cannot in the abstract answer the question: to group, or not to group? The more appropriate and more complex question is: to group for what? Useful power clearly inheres in group relations. Indeed, they provide the locus within which we come to define significant aspects of ourselves. But there are groups and groups—all with more or less the same dynamics and ability to influence individual behavior of members, but with possibly extreme differences in their norms. Consider the striking contrast between the "Manson gang" and that group of twelve deep at the center of Christianity.

Fourth, Exhibit 1 may also frame a cruel irony. Single-minded devotion to any one of the clusters above may set in motion the dynamics of its own disaster. Pushed to the neglect of powerful social and institutional forces, the emphasis on "every person for themselves" could be a self-defeating cruelty. With little or no emphasis on that proposition, oppositely, we might encourage legions of yes-people and of aimless wanderers who can define self only in terms of their temporary context, and hence are soulless. The Golden Mean seeks to avoid this danger. On the other hand, pushing an idea or a concept to its limits can yield *the* breakthroughs—for good or ill, be it noted.

No easy way out exists, in sum. "You pays your money, and takes your choice." Hopefully, one prudently safeguards against the extremes of whatever choice is made. This and the section to follow look at two aspects of taking care. Those aspects involve:

- A self-portrait of how one intervenor makes those choices, with some attention to why and to the consequences of the making

- A second self-portrait of how easy it is to make inappropriate choices, with an implicit urging to actively reflect on experience as the only alternative to doing nothing or doing something poorly

A Cameo of One Intervenor
Illustrating a Specific Individual's Ways of Coping*

Push will come to shove, sooner or later, and an intervenor must come to locate self, given the snares and delusions in the intervenor's world, the multiple roles to be played, and the clusters of tendencies the intervenor has available as a choice domain, both practically as well as conceptually. The intervenor cannot play it all ways, simultaneously.

What are some of the significant ways in which push comes to shove in my case? There is a ghost in this consulting machine, in Arthur Koestler's terms,[16] but it is not easy to lay hands on it. One risks simplification and perceptual distortions, and one may inspire charges of self-aggrandizement or even seem to supply evidence of narcissism. But so be it.

Much of the difficulty in describing the spirit that infuses my consulting activities inheres in my multiple roles. Thus, most of my consulting is undertaken because of its research promise, and this implies some major cross-pressures. Moreover, perhaps half of my consulting involves executives with broad integrative responsibilities. The rest of my consulting work has a narrower training-and-development focus, reflecting my commitment to the laboratory approach to organization change, and to the evolving values and learning technologies usually referred to as Organization Development.

While glossing over some of the complications implied above, I try here to provide three personal perspectives on the elusive ghost which provides spirit and direction to my consulting activities. In turn, this narrative emphasizes:

- Some of the qualities I believe I bring to a consulting relationship
- Some of the elements I believe I search for on entry
- Some of my consulting style, behavior, or approaches, as perceived by persons with whom I have, both successfully and less satisfactorily, worked in consulting relationships as employee, collaborator, antagonist, or even curious combinations of all these and more

These perspectives view the consulting act through very small keyholes, as it were, but they focus on some central emphases in my view of myself as

*A version of this section appears in Robert T. Golembiewski, "Some Perspectives on One Consulting Style," in Dharni P. Sinha (ed.), *Consultants and Consulting Styles,* published in 1978 by Vision Books Private Ltd., 36-C Connaught Place, New Delhi 11001, India.

consultant. The first two perspectives constitute the major organizing themes. Brief descriptive excerpts from clients will be used here and there to provide illustrations or to support the narrative. Clients were asked to describe my consulting style, as a check on my descriptions of myself. No structuring cues were given to these clients, and I have selected descriptive material from their responses.

Things this Intervenor Brings with Him[17]

Any limited list of the qualities brought to any relationship must be inadequate, but it can be revealing. Hopefully, what follows contains more of the latter than the former. More or less in the order of importance, I emphasize eight qualities:

- Life-training as a participant-observer
- A bias toward the moral priority of institutions
- A conviction that any institution can be more effective and efficient, and that some are irremediably corrupt
- A bounded view of the perfectability of humankind and of our institutions, which implies that programs of change will always be strictly bounded and limited, and which assumes that interventions are not justified because they extend the time frame in which those limits are approached
- An elitism, with pluralist or even populist tendencies
- A "determined centrism"
- An interest and training in a trio of organizational perspectives: interaction; technology; and policies, procedures, structures
- An emphasis on both separation and integration

Life-Training as Participant-Observer

I was born a more or less interstitial person, and I consider the associated experiences to have been valuable in making my way in organizations without being captured by them. The overall sense of it is being "in" an organization enough to understand and appreciate and even intimately share in its culture, but no so much "of" an organization as to be a blind defender of its culture and traditions. Perhaps even more important is the sense of comfort in this interstitiality—no, make that joy and a sense of freedom in this interstitiality.[18]

The interstitiality has complex roots, no doubt. Perhaps most basic are the experiences, painful and pleasant, of a son of first-generation immigrants moving in an essentially foreign culture. The basic actors were a very real "we" and "they." The "we" referred to a Polish community around which more or less precise geographic boundaries could be drawn. "They" were always the people who ran the town and most of its businesses, and had the better jobs. "They" were English, German, and Irish, in descending order of status, and, if not necessarily enemies, "they" definitely were forces to overcome. Typically, "they" got the better of it in matters both great and small. I recall being eight or nine before realizing that the park in "their" section of town was *my* park too. To provide further detail:[19]

> We were curiously schizoid. We were proud in traditions, usually skillful in business and technology, valuing hard work, and quite well-off materially. . . . At the same time, we were somewhat embarrassed (or worse) by our second-class status in the broader community. . . .
>
> A constant motivation was inherent in such realities. From one perspective, the challenge was to prove equality or superiority. From another perspective, the goad came from a kind of self-hate generated by second-class status. The feelings generated were powerful and often conflicting—respect of those ethnic compatriots who struggled for social, economic, and political equality; sadness and some derision for those traumatized into apathy; resentment that we should have to pass special tests because of where our parents were born and the language they (and we) spoke; and real concern that we might fail to meet our expectations and those of others.

But a number of powerful factors permitted me to choose how much I would move within the Polish immigrant subculture, and how much within the dominant and surrounding but unwelcoming broader culture. Speed and strength helped in athletics, and classroom performance opened still other doors that were mostly closed to my ethnic brothers and sisters. And no doubt the engines of extending my competence—of my ambition, if you will—also were working. Whatever the causal factors, the consequences were clear. I had a deep and satisfying experience of community in my immigrant group, and I also was given (and took) an opportunity to deal intimately with less limited worlds.

Relatedly, I derive great pleasure from observing myself and others in responding to various situations and cultures, or at least from seeking to do so. Having early and consistently been in multiple cultures, I am perhaps less likely to see any one as somehow sacred and thus nonobservable and immutable. From a different perspective, I like to believe that it is really possible to appreciate diverse cultural contents, and often to learn from them. Most important, membership in multiple cultures is a major guarantor, perhaps the only major guarantor, of individual and collective freedom. Unless, of course, someone invents the perfect single culture.

More concretely, there was and is a strong element of pleasure in this multiple citizenship, especially when there are strong pressures to respond to a single culture. I recall our college team's preparation for a major football game, when stirring music blared at the practice site all week long, when signs exhorting us to overcome the athletic enemy were everywhere. Everyone's locker featured a picture of one opponent, along with colorful descriptions of what us good guys intended to do with, or to, various parts of the anatomy of those bad guys. I joined in this spirit-building and tension arousal, but within limits. For example, I had pasted a delicate poem by Emily Dickinson into my helmet. Often, but secretly, I compared its quiet stimulation with the boisterousness surrounding me and my teammates. The poem was my explicit connection with an outside culture, as it were, a symbol that I was a more diverse being than the football culture encouraged, even coerced, me to be. I would not allow myself to be captured by that one culture, despite its substantial satisfactions and rewards.

In any case, I understood quite early the varied pressures that multiple cultures could exert on me. I made a conscious and early decision between two major alternatives: to allow myself to identify with one culture, thus forfeiting the others; or to expose myself to cross-pressures, and thereby to draw from several traditions. More or less consistently, and especially when the chips are down, I choose the latter alternative.

This history has a clear application to my consulting, I believe. To oversimplify, some consultants seek to build strong confidential relationships with a client; others seek to relate clients and self through problem situations. I am in the latter class 75 percent of the time, more or less, often by choice but hopefully also because the situation requires it. One client writes of my bias to relate to clients through problems:

> [Bob] has a preference for seeing an individual interacting with others, with [him] as the observer. He appears to prefer this to simply meeting alone with a client. [He] pays particular attention to what is being communicated by the participants which he often will contrast to the words that have been exchanged.

This bias can be a painful bore, even an inexplicable one, to a client who is just blowing off steam, expressing a concern to someone with no obvious ax to grind, lonely enough to seek or yearn for human contact, or frightened that things may be slipping from his or her managerial grasp. That is, fine-tuning is often necessary. But, my central tendency remains.

Simplifying again, if consultants prefer either to be accepted or call the shots as they see them even if that jeopardizes their acceptance or liking by others, I am clearly in the second class most of the time. My specific crucible of experience has left me with strong tendencies to develop and maintain what might be called an independent frame of reference. I see this bias as critical in consulting relationships, if only because the consultant should be the most free to note that the organizational king is naked. For diverse reasons, organization members are often constrained from making such observations, even when many or all of them privately recognize the nakedness.[20] I see little reason, in general, for my doing what my clients can do as well, or better. Hence, I like to believe I specialize in the pointed observation that others probably could make, but do not feel free enough to make. This kind of specialization, of being of use to others in ways difficult for them to be of use to themselves, requires that "independent frame of reference" referred to earlier. The derivative risk is that I can be seen as too clinical, or too distant, or both—a kind of overhead observer of colonies of workers—now chortling over interesting specimens, then prattling about this feature which the workers are too busy or embarrassed to note out loud and in public.

My experience is checkered with cases in which I have been free enough, or foolish enough, to utter the discordant word. I recall my undergraduate participation in an experiment on the autokinetic phenomenon, when fellow members of an experimental group were developing norms about how far a point of light moved between successive exposures. I was obdurate. The light never moved, I knew, despite strong pressures to conform, and despite the fact that it seemed to move. I had placed a pencil upright on the table in front of me and used its point as my independent frame of reference against which to judge the movement of the light source. The social reality of fellow group members was to me no match for the external reality-check, a fact I tried vigorously but unsuccessfully to impress on them.

What the hell, many or most people might shrug, so what if the light moved or not? Somehow, that question struck me as very important. *And it still is.* I like to think that interest reflects my reading of history that each generation has known for dead-certain what soon came to be seen as the damndest, most preposterous things. Maybe somebody questioning may make others appropriately less certain in some cases.

My consulting generally involves similar reality-checking. Of course, the phenomena are more complex than a spot of light, and I seldom have such a direct measure of objective reality as that pencil. But the essentials are similar. The search for analogues of firmly planted pencils to serve as reference points still continues. So also continues the multiple conviction that what may be called intersubjective agreements are at once necessary for life, but that they also can be straightjackets for thought and action, and that in any case they should be tested as far as possible as early as possible.

Deep Commitment to Moral Priority of Organizations and Institutions

This commitment derives from the reality that organizations are ubiquitous. This may seem a simplistic point, and it would be, except that so many popular reactions to our institutions and bureaucracies neglect the point. The neglect is as manifest in the theory of Marxism as in the practice of dropping out.

According a moral priority to institutions does not reflect a denigration of individuals. Rather, it implies both a high value on individual worth, as well as a conviction that individuality can be realistically pursued by a large and growing number of people only in institutional contexts. For a few, life may perhaps be individualistic in the classic sense. For most humans, however, whether life will bring greater freedom or enslavement will be resolved in institutional contexts.

A major derivative implication requires direct statement. I am deeply suspicious of this reaction to any institution or organization: "Anything would be better." This is a powerful tether on my consultative grasp, not to mention my reach.

No doubt my commitment to the moral priority of organizations or institutions has complex and subtle roots. Whatever else, my experiences with authority figures have been overwhelmingly benign or positive. For example, very early in life I was encouraged to assume more and more of the duties of the head of my parental home, on the death of my father and given the preoccupation of my much older siblings with their own families. I stress the word "encouraged," to sharply contrast the situation with one in which a young person is cruelly thrust into the role of breadwinner. More or less oppositely, I simply was encouraged to assume as much of the adult male role as I could cope with, no doubt in large part to make my mother and sister more comfortable. My mother and I often wondered if I would now be much different had my father, a towering and determined patriarch, lived beyond my ninth birthday. My relationships with that authority figure probably would have been dramatic, at least, and he might well have influenced me in ways that would predispose me to see most authority figures differently than I do.

Authority and influence came early and easily in most other life particulars as well, and I sense no subtle unfinished business concerning those tricky issues associated with the early seeking of authority and influence that could complicate consulting relationships. For example, I seldom recall slipping into competition for authority or power with a client, which I distinguish from a difference of opinion or a disagreement about factual or technical matters or about how authority was exercised in a particular case. I engage in the latter rather freely, but I seek to convey the sense and reality of respecting authority or power figures if they will only respect their colleagues and also me. Hence, I am especially pleased to hear from one executive, himself very sensitive to issues of power, that:

> [Bob] has no interest in helping a client manipulate those around him. . . . His interest appears to be in genuinely helping people to work together so that they can achieve certain goals with forthrightness and personal satisfaction for all those concerned.

No doubt, I react very strongly to authority figures I perceive as misusing or corrupting their power. I believe I react strongly because they "let me down," and so violate my central expectations and hopes about the general constructiveness of authority relationships, and my conviction as to their universal significance. One client senses that an alternative explanation may capture some of the truth. After reading the preceding paragraphs, he noted:

> Somehow, this bothers me. [You] seem to say that you have no trouble with authority figures as long as they don't act in a way which forces you to see that they are authority figures. I know it is not quite that way, but those are the overtones.

Competition with a client over authority, whether overt or covert, might be more common for a consultant with a more traumatic or turbulent or even eventful early history over such issues. This central point is a difficult one to communicate, but the essence of it is that I am often seen as confronting authority but (I like to believe) for the purpose of generally reinforcing it. My intention is to model what I consider useful values for both superiors and subordinates in organizations. One client, whom I have helped subordinates confront over a substantial range of the executive ladder, described the process the way I like to see it evolve:

> [His concern] to facilitate improved communications further tends to stimulate group members to themselves reflect on possible communication barriers. In this role he serves as a catalyst whereby group members themselves develop analytical skills.

Expectations About Ineffectiveness, Fundamental Corruption

The observations above are not simply fat-and-happy or Pollyanna-ish. Consider one operating belief that grievously qualifies the priority that I believe should be accorded to institutions or organizations. That is, all organizations are ineffectual in variable degree, and some become unredemptively corrupt. So, most organizations have to be preserved *and* saved from themselves, and some deserve only quick burials.

The challenge motivates. Baldly, ineffective organizations—those with various degrees of what John Gardner called "dry rot"—must be reoriented and renewed. Corrupt organizations need to be rebelled against: undermined whenever convenient and toppled wherever possible.

There is no room for indolent smugness in these simple comments. The ineffectiveness of all organizations must be continually confronted and combated. And identifying organizations that merit rebellion is no easy matter, but it must be done. My early tendency was to withdraw from membership in organizations I perceived as corrupt, but I see this as a major inadequacy, if a convenient one. That is, withdrawal has been relatively uncomplicated for me, on balance, both professionally and personally. But moving on is variably reasonable, as job opportunities are scarce or plentiful, as wife and children prefer or demand to remain settled, as a person ages, as one gains experience and status that can make rebellion more impactful, and so on. I hope to do better in this critical arena.

The basic strategy for me up to now has been to seek to intervene in organizations before they somehow cross that crucial line between needing renewal and requiring rebellion. Derivatively, the inevitability of institutional ineffectiveness and perhaps corruption requires that the highest priority be assigned to the care and feeding of organizational semideviants. These are resource persons who are not so alienated from an institution as to be ineffective, but who are variously insulated from true believership so that they can meaningfully work toward a vision of the possible that includes the existing, but yearns far beyond it. The central philosophical posture is a substantial tolerance of differences, because today's curiosity may provide the innovative direction for tomorrow. The central sadness is that there are sharp practical limitations on the tolerance that is permitted in organizations or societies, given economic necessities and resources, external threats, or internal dissension.

One experience illustrates how this point can be put into practice. Some years ago, a religious denomination asked me to conduct a study of a major problem. A growing number of their local parishes were splitting over the issue of racial integration, with the consequence that some pastors and parts of some congregations were being forced out of churches. My recommendation: a central fund for displaced pastors, whose normal salary and perquisites would continue as long as they stayed in the locality in which the racial issue occurred. There the pastor could serve any parishioners with common racial views, and would also be a continuing symbol of the moral commitment of the central church to racial integration. In addition, central authorities could at least buy some time on the issue of preserving local parish autonomy, which was very important for the denomination in a theological as well as a political sense.

Bounded Enthusiasm re Human Perfectability

This view—that possible improvement constitutes the essential human challenge, but that it must be incremental at best—may be classified as fatalism or realism, but it remains an operating belief nonetheless. One of the associates of President Kennedy illustrated that philosophy in a poignant way, while the tragic events of the assasination still swirled about him. How did it feel to have the visions of Camelot so rudely smashed, so early? "Any Irish kid growing up on the South Side of Boston," came the striking reply, "knows that the world will kick you in the teeth in the end. The point is not how long it takes before the inevitable happens. The key concern is how much you get done before it happens."

The illustration applies to all human experience, I believe. At one level, death is this world's ultimate kick in the teeth, even if there are no others. At other levels, the illustration also applies to all cases of learning or change which, even if successful, also know their own kick in the teeth. Thus, learning and change may for a time be described as an accelerating curve, but soon the appropriate symbol is a plateau for rest and consolidation, which may serve as a foundation for further learning at a later time. The basic trick is to keep this learning curve from retrogressing over the long run.

Directly, then, this fourth operating belief implies a general stepwise learning curve, and my bias is to press for early location on that curve of both individuals and (more tentatively) of systems of individuals. Sometimes individuals and organizations are in a kind of "parking orbit"; and sometimes they move toward higher or lower levels of competence and insight, or seem ready to do so, as described by Hampden-Turner.[21]

Much of my consulting energy is devoted to ascertaining where potential long-run clients are on such a learning curve, and to do so early in the game. Hence, clients are likely to describe me similarly, however they evaluate my effectiveness. To illustrate: "[He seeks] to gain the confidence and respect of participants very early in the game, . . . to approach situations in a very objective manner coupled with the ability to perceive areas of tension or unwillingness to communicate." This client describes this bias toward early testing as an "effective technique," an "ability." In several cases in which he was involved, it worked that way. In other cases, the bias may be seen by others as premature or unstrategic.

In some situations, one can expect a strong motivation for accelerated change or learning, as at the start-up of a management team—a take-off point, or a fall-flat point. And that is where I prefer to be, where there is no practical alternative to attempting a learning spurt, short of probable failure. I acknowledge, hopefully without condescension, that very real challenges inhere in managing the rest and consolidation that often follow a learning spurt. But I am clear that such a challenge is not attractive to me as a consultant.

Great potential for both mischief and usefulness is found in this fourth basic bias, and the two may be tough to distinguish. Consider my bias toward the primacy of an institution in combination with the notion of the bounded perfectability of humankind and of our institutions. Clearly, an insensitive emphasis on institutional priority can be extended into support for corrupt organizations, or into palliatives that merely delay and perhaps even exacerbate needed change.

This is especially the case given the belief, for which much evidence exists, that neither individuals nor systems of them can be successfully forced into learning situations.

A Basic Elitism, with Pluralist and Populist Tendencies

This operating belief amalgamates two tendencies in tension. *First,* it implies that small minorities tend to account for a disproportionate share of the good or mischief in the world. For example, the highest versus lowest productivity clerks may differ by a factor of 10 or even 20. And Hank Aaron in his career will hit perhaps thirty times as many home runs as the average major league baseball player. Similarly, dominant influence in social systems usually is exercised by a small proportion of its membership. In such senses, the world seems fundamentally elitist, along a huge range of criteria, perhaps along all of them.

Second, however, many characteristics are required for effective performance in all social systems, and few "great men" rank high on more than a few of these characteristics. Thus, some individuals rank high on interpersonal warmth, and others on decisiveness, but relatively few people will rank high on both these criteria. In this sense, the world is at least ineluctably pluralist. The generalization holds even for small groups,[22] and it is patently applicable in complex organizations, especially under conditions of technological or product change.

Moreover, some critical, and at times, crucial, functions can be provided only by the broadest range of participants in a social system. When all is said and done, for example, that constitutes the essential rationale for representative democracy. All systems must provide effective feedback about whether the shoe pinches, about whether policies and services engender sufficient support to provide some kind of reasonable base for a peacefully evolving system. Those "wearing the shoes," patently, best provide that information. In this elemental sense, complex social systems are (or should be) open to populist inputs, for two major reasons. Thus, broad ranges of participants in any social system are likely to be aroused only episodically. So these systems should be ever open to participant inputs, because they seldom come but are often critical when they do. Moreover, or perhaps consequently, I hold as a basic goal the active involvement of increasing ranges of participants in increasingly broad areas of the governance of systems.

Determined Centrism

As the comments above suggest, I typically find myself behaving like a "determined centrist." That is, some consultants seek to exploit the full logical and practical aspects of a particular approach, but I seek to amalgamate and integrate a widening array of approaches. The first category includes a "PPBS man," an "interaction-oriented resource person," or a "quantitative type." My prejudice is to seek doggedly the central commonalities or compatibilities of numerous such approaches, as far as I can. Hence the designation "determined centrist." The consequences are numerous and of moment: life is more unpredictable for the client; I may be stamped as a shallow generalist; and trying to explain to my mother what her son does as a consultant is certainly difficult. But bias there is, and determinedly so.

An example illustrates another aspect of this centrism, if perhaps at too great length. For a manager with an autocratic bias, for example, I will often suggest interventions or learning designs with a pluralist or populist thrust. The typical confrontation design, for example, has the effect of exposing such a manager to reinforced or even novel messages from a broad range of peers, superiors, and subordinates. The focus is on what can be learned with and from the many. A manager might overreact, of course, as by a flood of recognition that he needs more acceptance than he learns he has, which makes him gun-shy about risking the new era of better feelings often triggered by the confrontation. In such cases, I can clearly see myself operating from such elitist premises: that, in some cases, the buck does stop at the manager's desk, and that, in some cases, the act of decision is and must be a solitary one that cuts across the grain of general opinion or even consensus in a manager's unit. The focus here is how the elite can do what seems to need doing, hopefully while anticipating and reducing negative reactions to it by the many, or at least while being open to reports of failure or disaffection. Determined centrism, epigrammatically, is an exercise in balance rather than in true believership.

Encompassing the Triad

After much emphasis in these volumes and elsewhere, I hesitate to again insist that effective consultation must in the long run include emphasis on a "managerial triad." But I do not hesitate for long. That triad includes:

- Interpersonal and intergroup interaction
- Organization policies, procedures, and structure
- Technology and its impact on jobs, structures, and so on

I risk overkill here for two reasons. I lust toward such comprehensiveness, even though it is typically out of reach. More elusively, I risk repetition as a counterweight to those powerful forces in organizations that inhibit integration. Thus, many observers trace the common integrative failure to basic philosophical and life-style differences between specialists who may be distinguished (to use restrained language) as "rationalists" and "humanists," or (to use more colorful language) who may be characterized as "pusher-shovers" and "toucher-feelers." Oversimply, perhaps, each camp seeks to protect itself against contamination by the other. Without question, each camp thereby limits itself in a basic way.

Bias About Integration and Separation

It is an oversimplification, but a useful one, to observe that integration has been the dominant goal of consultants basically adhering to the laboratory approach. No doubt the strong positive identifications induced in T-groups, the major learning vehicle of the laboratory approach, have provided powerful support for this tendency. And no doubt many experience far too much loneliness and alienation. For such reasons, some clients come to regard adherents of the laboratory approach as Vestal Virgins of a kind, as specialists for bringing together that which is at odds, due to misunderstandings, conflicts, and so on. As such, the integrative specialist is kept "out of the action," to be called on only when things go sour enough. The implied role is remedial or palliative, in short, as opposed to preventative. The focus is on remedying the negative consequences of immutable policies, procedures, relationships, or structures, to say the same thing in another way, rather than on helping set up policies, procedures, relationships, or structures than can reduce the probability of those consequences.

I see major problems with this kind of specialization in integration, despite its clear usefulness in many cases. It can make the consultant a mere safety valve, a dispenser of Band-Aids after the fact. Such a role is fraught with professional and ethical problems. At another level, separation is as ultimate a reality as integration, and dealing constructively with both is necessary, as Chapter 5 argues.

Things this Intervenor Searches for on Entry

Many cues compete for the attention of anyone entering any system for coordinated human activity, but I believe my attention focuses on two related sets of processes:

- "Cultural preparedness" of a host organization for self-analytic and self-corrective activities
- The motivational systems of key members of a host organization, where "key" often but not always refers to high status

"Cultural Preparedness"

I exert considerable energy assessing the extent to which members of a host organization are prepared to engage in self-analysis oriented toward self-correction. Consistent with my bias toward getting an early reading of where on a learning curve members of a host organization seem to be, I am likely to be very active and even aggressive in making that assessment.

No available measuring instrument permits a judgment about whether a specific host organization is culturally prepared for the laboratory approach to OD, but such judgments always must be made. Fortunately, nature seems to be quite benign in this case. OD designs seem applicable over a broad range of conditions in organizations with a diversity of missions, histories, and futures.

The broad applicability of OD designs in the generality of cases is comforting, but relying on "generally" will not do. Basically, prior diagnosis is necessary before all OD applications, and it may be vital in some cases. Relatedly, conditions do exist under which failure of some designs is more likely, and it is important for many purposes to know about those conditions.

Moreover, specific designs may be more or less appropriate under various conditions. In addition, the conservation of energy encourages some sense of the limitations which could reduce the probability of failure in specific cases. At least initially, change efforts could be concentrated in organizations where the probability of success is high.

Four Aspects. In the sense of making even a little needed headway, then, four aspects of cultural preparedness will be introduced and illustrated. Overall, the underlying model is a curvilinear one. To explain, each aspect of cultural preparedness can be such that an OD effort is not indicated. Up to some unspecified point, increases in all four aspects of cultural preparedness will raise the probability of both the need and the success of an OD application. Beyond these unspecified points, the need for an OD effort continues to rise, but the probability of success begins to decrease.

First, the laboratory approach to OD seems most applicable under conditions of substantial tension in a system, as a result of an organization's inefficiency, inability to adapt or change, or whatever. At very low levels of tension, as in a highly successful organization, the motivation for an OD effort may be low, even if insightful souls correctly perceive the dark clouds behind the silver lining. Where tension in the system is "extremely high," and the quotation marks are appropriate in the absence of specific meaning, an OD effort may be sorely needed, but its probability of success will be low because the tension or threat is immobilizing. For example, it is in general better to begin an OD program after major reductions in personnel have been made, rather than while that sword is hanging over people's heads.

Second, the quality of interunit relations in an organization seems an important aspect of cultural preparedness. Given "good" interunit relations–low degrees of conflict or disruptive competition and high degrees of collaborative efficiency–an OD effort is not needed very much, except as an "audit." Up to a substantial point, deterioration in the quality of interunit relations at once increases the need for an OD effort as well as the motivation to make it succeed. Beyond some unknown but very real point, the quality of life can deteriorate so much as to make OD efforts far more chancy, if not impossible.

Third, the legitimacy of focusing on interpersonal and intergroup relations constitutes an important aspect of an organization's cultural preparedness for an OD application based on the laboratory approach. Where this legitimacy is already high, the need for and impact of OD designs will be less great. Up to a significant point, decreases in the legitimacy of dealing with human relationships heighten the need for the laboratory approach and increase the probability of its effectiveness. However, the legitimacy may be so low in the cases of enough organization members as to contraindicate an OD effort. Such low legitimacy might be expressed as extreme resistance to "probing at my psyche" or abhorrence at "violations of my privacy."

Fourth, the resistance of key officials is a final contributor to cultural preparedness of a host organization. Again, despite the inability to be specific about what the words mean, "too much" resistance can be the death of OD programs. This is not only so in the trivial case that key officials can control resources, although that is a point of moment. Most people attach considerable legitimacy to an authority figure, even when that means giving that figure apparent support even when he or she does not see the obvious writing on the organization walls. At the other extreme, there may seem no such thing as "too much" support from key officials. But too enthusiastic support by key officials may be interpreted by other organization members as an effort to coopt or manipulate them.

Two Examples. I am not altogether clear as to how I make specific judgments about existing cultural preparedness, and even less so about latent preparedness. But I do make judgments at those two levels, and I tend to rely on a variety of interventions that help make those judgments early in the game. Generally speaking, these interventions are intended to be perceived as confronting the superior, even though they are sometimes perceived as fighting interventions. In either case, I attempt to model a style of relationships and, far more importantly, to give people some idea of what they might expect to happen if they began to follow that model. Two examples may help. Both involve corporation presidents, each of whom gave clear messages for me and for people in the system. Exhibits 2 and 3 provide details about two illustrative minihistories of differences in cultural preparedness. My intervention was deliberate in the first case, and unpremeditated, and perhaps naive, in the second. Characteristically, the cases came early in my involvement with new subsystems.

The two minicase studies reflect organizations with substantially different cultural preparedness. I leave to the reader the development of the specific senses in which this summary conclusion applies to the four elements of cultural preparedness sketched above. I add only the note that, for many purposes, the existence of such preparedness can be defined by the conditions under which there are no mistakes, but simply unanticipated learning opportunities. Exhibit 3 sketches such an unanticipated opportunity that went unexplored, an outcome I disliked personally and which I believed would not help the corporation, but an outcome which I judged as clearly within the legitimate prerogative of the president to determine.

Motivation of Key Officials

With as much intensity and openness as I can muster, I am much concerned in early consulting contracts with "client intent." Or, to say the same thing in other words, I am concerned to develop designs and interventions that do not

Exhibit 2 A Minicase of "Cultural Preparedness"

The president of Corporation X had been asked to give a keynote address to one of his large management groups which, more or less autonomously, had expended substantial time and resources in an OD program. I was to sit in on dry runs of his speech to assure maximum congruence between the president's comments and the design of the weeklong meeting to follow, which had an OD thrust.

An initial dry run revealed a speech more appropriate to a stockholder's meeting than the management audience. The president's emphasis was on a noteworthy increase in earnings per share (EPS) from $2.50 to $2.65. The management group was recoiling from a major cut in personnel, however, which was widely perceived as necessary but as having been too long delayed by hopeful optimism.

My reaction was strong, in a public meeting of perhaps ten observers, a reaction not at all assuaged by their early reactions which pleasantly focused on details of delivery, and so on. After perhaps 10 minutes, I noted, more or less verbatim: "Mr. President, a large proportion of your audience will be calculating how much of that $2.65 in EPS is accounted for by the salaries of their excolleagues who will not be at the meeting. I believe the tone of your proposed speech should be radically changed."

A few desultory (and, I felt, embarrassed) comments followed from other observers, but the president did not respond immediately.

After perhaps a minute, he said: "I'd like to discuss the reaction of our consultant, the big meanie. I ordered the EPS emphasis. Should I change it?"

The modeling was tried, its thrust was essentially accepted by the president, and other observers generally took the president at his word and advised change. Although his reaction was tinged with double-edged humor about the "big meanie," the president could have referred to a corpulent meanie, or even a fat one! His overall message was clear enough, in any case, especially when major changes in the speech were made, and when the "big meanie" remained active in the firm.

---

encourage more intensive self-analysis and renewal than seem realistic—concerned for superior, subordinate, and consultant.

Figure 1 conveys some sense of this concern about client intent, or more specifically, with the intent of key organizational figures who have diverse objectives relative to a specific consulting contact. The exhibit can be interpreted in terms of three particulars. *First,* it implies that major and early attention must be given to clarifying the client's orientation to any specific consulting episode. Cell I is more benign than Cell II in this regard, since the client only intends a limited impact on some specific system. But the general rule is the same in both cases: Induce, cajole, help, ultimately even try to coerce clients to isolate and face their needs and aspirations as they relate to a specific consulting episode. The injunction is dead serious even if it seems pious and

Exhibit 3 A Minicase of "Cultural Unpreparedness"

The atmosphere at headquarters of Corporation Z was bullish, if hectic, and perhaps the dominant theme was that success had its mixed blessings. For example, the president bittersweetly discussed with me and others the familial problems associated with his children (now nearing their majority) being large stockholders of shares he had earlier left in trust for them.

As part of my work, I visited a newly acquired firm, whose members included the founding entrepreneurs and many employees proud of their historic autonomy and substantial achievements.

In a private meeting with the head of the acquired firm, the mixed fruits of success was one theme. I briefly recounted the corporate president's illustration of the familial paradoxes of corporate prosperity, among many other examples and much other talk.

A 2- or 3-day meeting followed, one focus of which was a planned OD program for creating more open and trusting relationships within the corporation. I outlined an action plan, and led what I took to be an almost unanimously enthusiastic discussion. The firm's head was present, but not enthusiastic.

Shortly after the meeting, the president placed a conference call to me, with his executive vice-president also on the line. The president recounted a conversation with the firm's head in which my recounting of the discussion about familial problems was central, and reflected the latter's strong opinion about my breach of confidence. "If that is what is meant by openness," to paraphrase the thrust of the comments by the head of the firm, "we don't need any more. Lord knows what other confidences the consultant would break."

I admitted the illustration, stressed its very minor role, and emphasized that I did not consider the illustration's content as confidential in the least. Supportively, the executive vice-president reminded the corporate president that the latter had on several occasions himself used the illustration in public settings, in addition to the time I heard the president's story.

I advised confronting the firm's head about what I saw as a complex issue, preferably in the presence of the corporate president. The president did not consider the cost, effort, or risk worthwhile, given the delicacy of the early postacquisition days. What was the next best alternative? "Wall me off from the man," I said, for I did not want to burden my consulting inputs with speculations as to the firm head's intent in raising the issue.

I got my second-best choice, and expressed irony at this perhaps small matter in the context of developing an open and trusting system toward which we were contemplating major effort. The essential meaning of the conversation was clear to me. There would be no modeling of confronting behaviors in this case, whatever the severity of the breach of confidence.

Substantial and sudden changes in market conditions killed the early thoughts about an OD program, and in effect precluded a test of whether an increase in the incidence of confronting behaviors could be achieved.

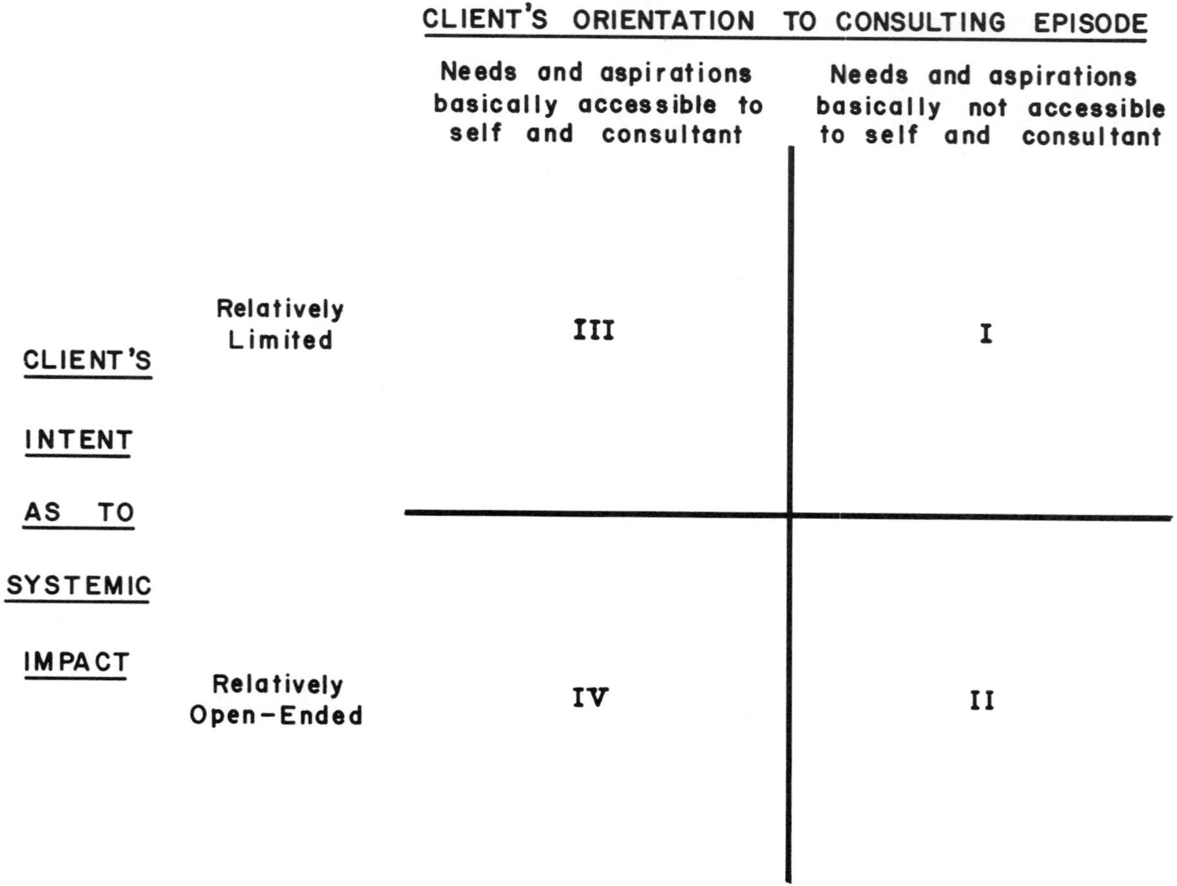

		CLIENT'S ORIENTATION TO CONSULTING EPISODE	
		Needs and aspirations basically accessible to self and consultant	Needs and aspirations basically not accessible to self and consultant
CLIENT'S INTENT AS TO SYSTEMIC IMPACT	Relatively Limited	III	I
	Relatively Open-Ended	IV	II

Figure 1 A typology of client's intent as to impact and orientation of a specific consulting episode.

simplistic. Consider six somewhat overdrawn but common sets of needs and aspirations that might not be immediately accessible to client or consultant, but which might be critical in such a design as team-building.

- "I am really concerned about my managerial potency, about my confidence and ability in making decisions. Team-building seems like a good way to share the burdens, to lighten my load of responsibility, and perhaps to avoid total criticism or blame if things go wrong."
- "Joe Wright did some team-building, and he tells me it was great. I admire Joe more than my father."
- "Many other managers in my organization are into team-building, and a guy has to adapt to organization fads however curious they may be."
- "I am an unreconstructed autocrat, but a clever and devious one. My young guys want team-development; I'll give it to them. I'd promise them anything to get them to produce more."
- "I have a new team, and I want us to get to know one another quickly, and to get some vital work done more expeditiously. My supervisory style is mildly autocratic, and I intend it to remain that way. But you can't work fluidly with people you barely know. So I'm for team development, up to a point."
- "I'd like for the rest of my team to learn what an incompetent rat Joe Brown is. He's slippery enough to play one person off against another. I want to nail him in a group situation, where his incompetence and duplicity are there for everyone to see."

Second, such diverse client needs and aspirations require surfacing not only for their own sake, but especially because they influence the choice of a suitable learning design. Some of these needs and aspirations may indeed indicate that there is no design in which I can participate with good conscience. That is, even if specific consulting episodes get sorted into Cells III and IV, this hardly justifies a consulting intervention. Rather, complex issues involving moral choices and learning designs become relevant. Consider Cell III. Assume a manager has very limited aims, as in the next to last description above: to get people in a new group to know one another better, and more quickly, to get on with some pressing job. A number of low-risk designs are responsive to that circumstance. I do not demean them, but neither am I much interested in them except as they might serve as a developmental test for a manager in the process of moving into Cell IV, whose goal is the creation at work of increasingly comprehensive systems oriented toward maximizing the simultaneous satisfaction of personal needs and organization demands.

More acute problems inhere in such cases as the last descriptive excerpt above. There may be a rare exception that I presently cannot envision, but I would not recommend or participate in team-building with the major or exclusive aim of developing group consensus about a person seen by a manager as a kind of pariah. However, I might recommend third-party consultation in that case. To the extent that team development is conceived in terms of an increasingly broad range of goals or aims, the moral judgments would become more difficult.

Third, far more critical in Figure 1 are judgments related to the scope of intended systemic impact, for that scope influences the choice of appropriate designs or interventions. For good (but hardly unassailable) theoretical and practical reasons, consultants typically seek broad systemic impact. Typically, also, consultants may be preoccupied with extending the boundaries of their science and art, which may incline them towards designs of wondrous and powerful if sometimes indiscriminate or problemmatic impact. And clients may be clear as to their needs and aspirations in a specific case, but fuzzy or unaware of differences in cost/benefit ratios between alternative designs.

There is much potential for mischief in being unclear about whether a consulting contract was in Cell III or IV. For example, one case involved a small public agency experiencing some run-of-the-mill adjustments, which had not yet influenced performance in major ways but with which the supervisor still wanted to deal. To provide some detail:

> these adjustments centered around: a new head, a young and attractive female who was somewhat unsure of her new role; a previously all-male group, on the older and somewhat stodgy side, and a little threatened by several recent personnel changes; and several new employees who were definitely mod squad aspirants if not aficionados, both male and female subtypes.
>
> The overkill prescription for this new group was three weekends of family T-grouping. The result: the revelation of nonwork material that would have tested even a far more stable group that was certain of its relations. The longrun outcome: strong feelings of guilt due to cross-pressures involving peak work demands and the humanitarian impulse to provide emotional support at work to several colleagues. The work demands tended to win out, but at substantial cost of feelings of guilt for most members and abandonment for others.

A Concluding Note

And so I have tinkered somewhat with my consulting works, revealing a lever here and indicating a balance wheel there. Though somewhat disassembled, I trust that a sense of the spirit of those parts is reflected in these observations about me as consultant, both as I see myself and as others see me.

Confessions of an Organizational Change Agent
What Sober Experience Has Taught*

Attention now turns to another way that an intervenor can take care: to reflect actively on experience, and especially to reflect on errors or unexpected outcomes.

At least in the literature, such reflection has not been very popular. That literature includes many cases of successes, documented voluminously, and numerous prescriptive treatments about the intervenor's role could be catalogued. Despite this extensive literature, however, explicit discussion of actual errors does not represent much of a thrust in OD writing. Some go as far as to suggest that the client has only self to blame.[23] Examples of errors do exist, however. These include: failure to understand why a client relationship deteriorated;[24] change overload and discrepant values; and changing only a subsystem, in which the top person was not involved.[25] Beckhard also produced a list of twelve reasons for OD failures.[26] And the first booklength treatment on the subject has but recently appeared.[27]

This section seeks to go beyond the literature in a personal way, via an account of ten errors which I believe I have made. These errors have occurred in relationship to my role as change agent working as a process consultant. For each error there is an illustrative case study in which I was directly involved. Some of the case studies could be used to illustrate more than one error but I avoided this in order to provide more examples. The ten errors relate to:

- Bottom-up change
- Creating change overload
- Raising expectations about delivery point
- Inappropriate attachment
- Trapped in one part
- Changing only a subsystem
- Inappropriate use of behavioral versus structural interventions
- Losing professional detachment
- Assuming a change is needed
- Not seeking help for self

*Reprinted from: W. J. Reddin, "Confessions of an Organizational Change Agent," in J. William Pfeiffer and John E. Jones (eds.), *Group and Organizational Studies: The International Journal for Group Facilitators,* Vol. 2, no. 1 (March 1977), pp. 33-41. LaJolla, Calif.: University Associates. Used with permission. Minor editorial changes have been made.

...nts tell me of their plans for a bottom-up change attempt I ...them of the military dictum that the penalty for mutiny is death.

> In 1959 I was a consultant to a company team planning a change program for a 20,000-employee firm. The budget was enormous. We planned a series of ten month-long residential seminars, for thirty managers each. The entire top management was to attend, except the nine man top team. The first week of the seminar was a T-group, the second was social issues at which prominent journalists and activists spoke, the third was planning and organizing, the fourth was objectives. The postseminar reaction forms were the highest I have experienced. After running three of the ten seminars, the top team canceled the allocated budget and the program was abandoned. What had happened was that successive waves of managers with a radically changed idea on how the company should be run were causing a tremendous disturbance, and we had made no preparation to enable the top team to deal with it.

I am frequently pressured by clients to make this error again but, recently at least, have not done so. The individual who makes the representation to me usually explains that the top figure is too busy, doesn't need it, could simply read the book, or if only I could speak to that person for a couple of hours. I have my armament of counterarguments and sometimes, shamelessly, even suggest that the top figure should attend an unfreeze seminar for symbolic reasons. Beckhard touches on a related problem which top team commitment and participation can avoid: "a continued discrepancy between top management statements of values and styles and their actual managerial work behavior."[28] Bennis also provides an example of this error.[29]

Creating Change Overload

It is often an easy matter to create more change than a system can conveniently cope with, thus creating change overload.

> I once held a four day team-building meeting with the top team of a food processor employing about one thousand people. The company had experienced no real change for the previous decade. The discussion came to center on the organization chart, and it was agreed to reorganize the top one hundred positions in the company. This was easier said than done. The two most powerful men on the top team were highly rigid, and in implementing, the change grew more and more authoritarian. What was designed as a healthy program of evolutionary change descended into a program to write more detailed job descriptions.

The potential for creating change overload can be high, but it is difficult to predict its occurrence. The most rigid systems are ones most likely to experience it because they are the ones least equipped to handle change. The change agent who has a continuous interface with the client should be able to identify the possibility of change overload and help with adjustment to it. If, however, his relationship is "drop in again when you are in town and let's have another team meeting in a year or so," this potential problem is difficult to monitor. I tend to avoid change overload now by requiring a continuous association and avoiding single interventions. Bennis refers to a similar error.[30]

Raising Expectations Above Delivery Point

Perhaps the easiest error to commit in organization development is raising expectations above delivery point.

> The top man of a government department decided to introduce MBO by participative means. At my suggestion, we had a meeting to discuss it. At this point, several errors had been committed. MBO, certainly in the traditional format, is not suitable for most government departments, as power is so diffuse. The top man's autocratic decision was hardly the way to introduce a participative approach and the meeting would raise expectations above delivery point. There was great excitement at the meeting about the new management style. Everyone thought things would change completely and immediately. However, over the next few months budgets were done the old way, and some key decisions were imposed autocratically. A program that might have been a success if introduced slowly, got a bad name in its opening months because of the raised expectations.

The best way to avoid this error is, from the start, to think and talk in terms of 3 to 4 years. Beckhard refers to "short time framework" as a condition for failure.[31] Another way to avoid the error is to describe every OD intervention as an "experiment," but I have never done this as it can tend to lower the responsibility of everyone involved and allows failure to be explained away too easily in terms of "we agreed it was just an experiment."

Inappropriate Attachment

Many change agents would share the view that the nature of the attachment to the client is the key element in influence attempts.

> The chairman of a 10,000-employee subsidiary of a British industrial giant invited me to dinner with his board at their country house training center. It was an epic meal and the vintage port flowed. The conversation was

witty, and I had to lean on my limited classical education to keep up with the literary allusions. In preparation for an MBO conference, I had in fact recently reread Thucydides' *History of the Peloponnesian War,* and this gave me some good lines. My first error was accepting the first invitation, and then my next was visiting in similar circumstances yet again. It was a superb, if unconscious, seduction job by the client. My relationship to this client became intellectual, witty companion. My attempts to change it were met with incredulity.

Versions of the error are failure to obtain multiple entry, attaching self too low down in the organization, interfacing with an individual not a group, slavish dependency by the client, "We really need you," or client counterdependency, "You have served your purpose." At times I have been attached as servant, master, captive behavioral scientist, visiting professor, tame seal, and resident magician. Sometimes I have to remind clients that I have not walked on water recently. Sometimes I have to remind myself.

Obtaining the appropriate attachment can be one of the most difficult things to accomplish. It can be facilitated by having a few "ground rules" which the client accepts at the start. These might range all the way from not eating with the client, a rule Tavistock once used, to never talking to any one individual alone. The attachment issue is particularly difficult for the internal change agent, and the ideal structural device is a 3-year guaranteed terminal assignment with all remuneration issues settled in advance. Beckhard refers to "overdependence on outside help" as a condition for OD failure.[32] This is one face of the multifaceted problem of attachment.

Trapped in One Part

One element of good change strategy is multiple entry, but it is all too easy to become trapped in or by one part of the organization.

A brewery used my services to improve its marketing orientation. The change program was highly successful: over 3 years the profits moved from $500,000 to $1,000,000, and the sole competitor's profit fell from $500,000 to $70,000. During this same period the position at the top of the marketing team increased in power greatly, moving from what was essentially public relations officer to sales manager and then to vice-president of marketing. All this was very well, but was not seen that way by production who had seen its considerable power and prestige erode. The OD emphasis should have then, or earlier, shifted to such interfaces within the firm and I made several unsuccessful attempts to achieve this. In the mind of production, I was the wicked consultant who had hurt them. In the mind of marketing, I was their man to use in the fight against production. All this might not be too bad, but 12 years later very low trust still exists between the two subsystems to a degree that I even now discuss with the marketing vice-president whether he ought to move on.

The possible solution to this problem is in obtaining and maintaining multiple entry and in anticipating the consequences that might arise from current change efforts. A good signal of where one might be needed is who the client most talks about disparagingly.

Changing Only a Subsystem

Changing only a subsystem was a common error of mine, especially when working with large systems.

In the early 1960s a 1000-employee division of a 3000-employee power commission engaged in a successful attempt to increase participation. Indications of this were that line crew foremen, not head office engineers, selected line tools, and meter readers wrote their own rule books and established their work norms. A major conflict boundary developed between this division and other divisions and the central systems unit. Fundamental disagreement arose over how many signatures there should be on expense accounts, what is an appropriate discretionary amount for truck drivers to spend on repairs on the road and, the biggest fight, where should computerized individual performance data be fed: to the individual, his superior, or to a staff unit? The issue is unresolved today, and in this tightly integrated technology two quite different climates exist where, presumably, any one type of climate might be better.

While the example refers to subsystems aligned vertically, the error applies equally well to systems aligned horizontally. The error then involves treatment of one level but not another. Beckhard states a particular case of this general error as "a large gap between the change effort at the top of the organization and efforts at the middle of the organization."[33]

As every system is somehow related to every other system, and since the one predictable thing about OD is its unpredictable consequences, this error is likely to be made continuously. The best way to avoid it is to establish specific measurable objectives at the start and obtain agreement to them not only from the system assumed to be directly involved but adjacent systems such as head office, owners, or politicians. If these adjacent systems, say essentially, "good, why don't you get on with it," this is at least one indication of subsystem autonomy to make the changes without impairing other relationships.

Inappropriate Use of Behavioral Versus Structural Interventions

The bread and butter of the psychologist is the random error of the sociologist. Those of us concerned with change in behavior in organizations can easily be biased too strongly to either side. Is the personality clash a function of poor role clarity or of low human relations skills? Either of these may at times explain most of the variance. But what if one chose the wrong factor in a particular case?

> I was once asked to plan a change program for a Montreal production subsidiary of a U.S.A. firm which had fired four of the subsidiary's general managers in 6 years for failure to show a profit. The trust level was low and most managers had moved to a very low level of risk-taking. After I had started to unfreeze, team-build, develop candour, etc., an independent study by the parent company uncovered major errors in the transfer-price system within the subsidiary and from the subsidiary to the parent company. When changes in these prices were introduced, profits started to appear, and the current general manager stayed 8 years. The company needed a cost accountant, but initially got a change agent.
>
> A similar error was narrowly avoided when the president of a fish packing firm turned down my idea to start team-building sessions with his trawler fleet captains. The problem was that the competing Russian fleet all cooperated with each other while his own trawler fleet captains did not, leading to much lower productivity. He pointed out to me that under Canadian Maritime Law the trawler fleet captains and crew were not employees but merchant coadventurers. Each was an independent businessman. Not only the legal system but the existing community structure and a long local history all supported this view. To imagine that much could be done by a seminar demonstrating that cooperation optimizes the system but not necessarily optimizes each individual in it was farcical. It would be rather like rearranging deckchairs on the Titanic. The clincher was when he told me about the first, and last, Christmas Eve party that the executive committee had arranged with the captains. It had to be on Christmas Eve because that was the single day of the year when all trawlers were in port. The trawler captains used the occasion to announce their first strike. Their spokesman apologized for the timing, but explained it was the first time they had been together.

Beckhard refers to precisely this error as "no connection between behavioral-science oriented change efforts and management-services/operations-research-oriented change efforts."[34] To avoid this error one must develop a wider range of conceptual tools oneself or somehow bring such tools to bear. Psychologically oriented change agents could do well to read more systems theory, sociology, and even MBO.

Losing Professional Detachment

A surgeon once told me that during operations it was not uncommon for him to tell dirty jokes to the nurses. He explained that such behavior served to maintain a psychological detachment from the patient, since psychological involvement might have affected the surgery.

> After working with one U.S.A. client intensively for 2 years, it became apparent to me that the client was talking change and had built a staff to implement it but that no change was taking place. For various reasons I was emotionally involved with this client and wanted the program to be a success. My style became abrupt and argumentative. Instead of trying to analyze resistance with the client, I was berating it for not changing. At the time I put my change in style down to my innate flexibility; after all, very few of us remain who are equally adept at Theory "X" and "Y," even when appropriate. Now I see it simply as emotional involvement leading to a lowering of effectiveness.

As a boy of 17, I was roaming Eastern Canada in the winter looking for work which was hard to find. I heard of a free 2-day residential course conducted by the St. John Ambulance Brigade, meals provided. I decided that it was my public duty to learn first aid. Never will I forget one instructor's comment that went something like this:

> Suppose you are the first on the scene of a two car collision. People and their legs are lying about and there is lots of screaming and blood. If you want to be helpful, first say to yourself: it is their problem, not mine.

His intent was to shock us, and of course he did. He was saying do not get too emotionally involved with the system you are trying to help. The implications of this aspect of the role relationship are many and contentious. Has the client really got the right not to get well? Is hoping the client will get well a poor professional posture? Is joining the client the ultimate defeat?

These days I pay more attention to my own feelings and watch for danger signals. For me, at least, they include postmeeting depression, not understanding what is going on, making remarks that are a little too smooth or crude, liking the client, wanting the client to like me, wanting an intervention to lead to a terrific success, attempting to impress the client, or obtaining much satisfaction from client praise.

Assuming a Change Is Needed

It is easy to get trapped by the belief that new is better than old or that a new label changes something.

Sometimes we attempt change when the system clearly does not need it. We never know when to give up. Two young Scouts whose younger brother had fallen into a shallow pond rush home to mother with tears in their eyes. "We're trying to give him artificial respiration," one of them sobbed. "But he keeps getting up and walking away."

Not Seeking Help for Self

The longstanding problem of those in the helping professions is not to seek help themselves. It is hardly necessary to supply an example; the prior examples attest to it. The best way I know to avoid this error is to admit first one's failures to oneself and take a fair share of the blame and then to identify others in a similar line of work who also know you as a person, and arrange for regular telephone chats concerning current clients. This is what I have done. I have not found it useful to seek such assistance from clients, or from external staff also working with the client, or those who work closely with me. They are as emotionally involved as I am and just as prone to distort, albeit in a different direction. Another more structured device has been proposed by Bennis,[35] who commented on the Clinical Pathology Conference where medical students and doctors find out why the patient really died. He believes it is a good teaching practice but, "No equivalent teaching device exists in the behavioral sciences, unfortunately, mainly because we are in a relatively early stage of developing a practice." In a footnote he continues, "There are other reasons as well, for example, the understandable desire for secrecy regarding failure or mixed successes and the difficulty of ascertaining precise causes in these complex social-change ventures."

This is clearly a highly personal account. I am not at all tempted to develop a paradigm of errors that change agents might make. This is simply my conceptualizing of part of my experience. I am sure that embedded in what I identify as errors are many of my assumptions about the human, the role of change agent, and the change process.

Intervenors as Theorists/Scientists
Whether or Not We Know It or Like It

The end-for-now of this two-book revision of *Renewing Organizations* lies just beyond the next few pages, and it is now or never for making sure a major intention has not been buried in detail. The straight-vanilla? This is a critical time for Organization Development, I argue. The possibilities of practice/application contribute much to OD's momentum; but we now know with growing precision what we need to know and still lack; and so a self-conscious emphasis on theory/science is necessary to boost OD from its present orbit into a more satisfactory and comprehensive one, while preserving the action ↔ research exchange.

How goes the effort? The issue is still in doubt, as three points establish. It seems to me that what needs doing is clear beyond a reasonable doubt; but whether that will get done—in sufficient degree, promptly enough—remains to be seen.

Theory/Science Deserves Priority Today

In the rightly ordered world, I maintain, this should be a period for consolidating advances, trimming excesses, and solidifying our knowledge base for another great leap forward. That is, theory/science should be accorded a definite priority today, so that emphasis can later shift more confidently to practice/application. Recall, in retrospect, that the last 20 years or so of OD applications rest on two lines of "pure research"—on what is often known as "group dynamics" dealing with small social units, and on survey methods dealing with large units. These are the two "stems" that French and Bell see as conflating into OD—the "laboratory stem" and the "survey stem."[36]

That two-component foundation of theory/science proved sturdy enough to support two decades of work, but the early emphasis on practice/application made some convenient assumptions that we now know to be incorrect, not only in our guts but also in conflicting results of research and experience. Thus:

An individual ≠ an individual

A group ≠ a group

An organization ≠ an organization

Specifically, an OD design suitable for one group, we now know from much practice/application, can be counterproductive for another, even though that design "often works." But we "know" this only dimly and vaguely. That is, *the* basic task has become clearer but still remains undone: to distinguish types or classes of individuals/groups/organizations, to which various OD designs can be applied so as to decrease the number of surprises and to increase the probability that intended things will in fact occur. Directly, an emphasis on theory/science must provide a firmer platform for a new round of practice/application.

Put otherwise, a fair summary of the mass of research and experience just reviewed goes this way: Things sure do get complicated, what with everything being related to everything else. This puts OD in a much more difficult place than a decade age, or even 5 years ago. Indeed, I have elsewhere argued that OD is "stuck": we are now well beyond the innocence that in 1964 proclaimed an immanent "end of bureaucracy"; but we are just now beginning to see the incredible dimensions of what needs knowing to efficiently match particular OD designs to specific existential conditions. What we know about what we need to know, that is, well serves as today's theme.

This in-betweenness or stuckness of OD—some have called it OD's "adolescence"[37]—creates all kinds of problems for intervenors. The overall feeling-tone is one of things coming unglued, with a definite tendency to doubt that some coming together will result. As one observer notes: "The overall state of the art has become more confused, troubled, and humbled by overzealous selling of professional change-agent services during the late 1960s, as well as hurt by the economic forces impinging on organizations in the mid-1970s.[38]

Consider a specific manifestation of in-betweenness or stuckness: the basic existential dilemma associated with the fact that some OD interventions—team-building, Flexi-Time, or whatever—have clearly "worked." Consider also how any emphasis on theory/science provides the only way out. Thus it is comfortable to many that OD is seen as "a new way," with adherents swelling the ranks. However, the designs "work" only more often than not, at best, so it is easy to find deviant cases. In the absence of growing knowledge about appropriate conditions for a specific design, these deviant cases will be taken to reflect the imprecision and puniness of the designs, and rightly so. This can generate broad pessimism. After the first blushes of success, then, the emphasis on theory/science represents *the* way of specifying conditions favoring applications of specific designs and, hence, of reducing the number of surprises if not trauma. Worse still, the conversion to OD has been too facile for many: they focus on the technique or the design; and they neglect the spirit, the values, the diagnosis, the building of support groups, and so on. In a word, such converts can be positive menaces, and their parade needs to be rained on.[39] Again, only an emphasis on theory/science can do that job in a constructive way.

In sum, being in-between causes discomfort that can be eased only by disciplined and massive effort—effort to add knowledge in often-exotic ways, and effort to up-grade the skills and knowledge of individuals who were perhaps able to cope comfortably at earlier stages of development but who find themselves increasingly distant from what is going on at the leading edges of research/experience. OD, as this two-book revision has taken pains to establish, rests on a foundation of values whose neglect can be mischievous, even tragic. And careful diagnosis alone, disciplined by an enlarging body of theory-science, will raise the probability of choosing the design appropriate for the conditions.

How Goes It for Theory/Science?

Substantial if casual evidence implies that this in-betweenness is being responded to in counterproductive ways, in general, for a variety of reasons that cover the gamut from realistic concerns to bare protectionism. Peggy Morrison well expresses the general point in the case of the evaluation of the results of OD interventions, about which she tells us intervenors "feel uncomfortable." She is a friendly critic, but an impactful one. She notes that some critics propose that many OD intervenors conveniently "avoid potential pain by not evaluating their own efforts." Morrison also adds to the catalog of reasons for the mixed attention to evaluation—while balancing that catalog—by observing that:[40]

> The fact that OD is so difficult to evaluate, given the adequacy of the tools available for that evaluation, leads many of us to avow that it is not possible to evaluate OD, or that verbal feedback from client groups . . . is enough evaluation. There is also the chance that our inadequate tools are not even measuring the real change that does occur and will not demonstrate the full—and to us obvious—value of OD.

The present point will profit from specificity about four themes—only selective choices from a very long list of applicable themes—which have sometimes appeared in the literature but derive essentially from the shop talk at meetings of the OD Network or the OD Division of the Academy of Management. *First,* rather than being seen as a challenge, the rigors of theory/science tend to encourage an abreaction, a neglect of the very effort necessary to get beyond the in-betweenness. I have in mind the bothered participant at a 1978 conference who, in response to an erudite and tough survey of what we know in OD, and what we don't,[41] noted in exasperation: "This is so pessimistic. You're making galloping variables out of my most cherished constants." That person spoke for many others, in fact, for most of a jam-packed audience.

The abreaction to theory/science issues takes many forms, of various severity. In large part, the consequence reflects different cultures or styles methodologists are critical and pessimistic by training; intervenors tend to be more optimistic, or in cases even blindly committed to a technology or technique; and those few intervenors who cherish research reputations must seek to respect pushes and pulls without extending them into polarizations. The abreaction also inheres in positions that in one degree seem reasonable but in other degrees boggle the mind. Witness the observation that one's best intervention is one's "warm body." That is patent at a superficial level, for interventions only get made by warm bodies. But some implications of the notion astound and befuddle. That "warm body" needs a "well-ordered head" when it comes to intellectually distinguishing (for example) crises of agreement and disagreement, and practically developing designs appropriate to specific situations. Emphasis on the "warm body" is at best a comfortable pointlessness, and at worst a wicked snare and delusion that detracts attention from theory/science concerns.

Second, a common approach to the theory/science challenge involves the proliferation of designs, techniques, and approaches—as one "fails," generate another, ad infinitum.[42] This "solution," of course, exacerbates the problem by avoiding *the* question: What specific designs apply under which specific conditions for which specific purposes? At an extreme, indeed, the proliferation can destroy the sense of a central core—as it were, herniating the sense of commonality and identity that provides thrust to OD.

Third, although I'm hopeful that they do not really mean it except in limited senses, some have virtually argued: "OD est moi." Thus Weisbord notes: ". . . I came up with an odd conclusion that perhaps OD is not singular at all, and that which OD I happen to be practicing at the moment is pretty much a function of the way I define myself—my own self image, so to speak, rather than my grasp of the 'state of the art.' "[43] In some senses, of course, Weisbord is correct. For most purposes, however, his position helps not at all, and it might even sanction a goofy kind of narcissism when a comprehensive empirical theory is needed.

Fourth, a final example of abreacting from theory/science involves a myopia, a lack of historical perspective. In one charming variant, for example, *the* central act in OD becomes the establishment of a network of colleagues with a strong bias toward practitioners.[44] Others would argue that there were earlier important networks of colleagues which, in the bargain, rested on more useful mixes of theory/science and practice/application. In addition, some observers would add that any and all networks must be cast as cabooses to the real engine in OD: the preceding three or four decades of research with group dynamics, organization behavior, and survey research, without which networks of intervenors would not have developed.

Making a Specific Case for Theory/Science

No simple and satisfactory way exists for showing how OD intervenors are perforce involved in theory/science, and especially so today—whether they like it or not, and whether or not they can or will do anything about it. But some useful illustration is possible of the point that the immediate development of OD will depend on theory/science progress. No one can now predict how the future will work itself out, but the broad directions of progress seem clear enough. Specifically, OD's basic ideational support needs upgrading. Need-satisfaction models have buoyed early OD but, as is, they are clearly inadequate. No intervenors, except by accident, can surpass the quality of their underlying models. Enhancing the quality of models underlying OD will derive only from the resolution of theory/science issues.

Need-Satisfaction Models

Without doubt, OD rests developmentally rooted in the sev
models—Maslow's pyramid of needs, Argyris' dimensions o
and Herzberg's motivators. And this implies some good ne
is bad.

Need-satisfaction models all have substantial attractions. They provide a useful first hand-hold on reality; they have the virtue of apparent simplicity and face-validity; and it has been possible to produce conditions—as in T-groups or in enlarged jobs—providing evidence that need-satisfaction is important for many individuals under many conditions. As pump-primers, then, need-satisfaction models have many attractions, which no doubt explain their extraordinary resiliency to both conceptual and empirical attack. Salancik and Pfeffer incisively phrase one version of the point:[45]

> The need-satisfaction model not only provides a rationale for organizational improvement efforts, but also provides psychological comfort to those advocating the changes. Rather than being accused of manipulating workers' attitudes, of engaging in deception . . . , or some other equally unacceptable motive, organization development practitioners can think of their work as helping individuals to satisfy their needs by improving poorly designed environments for well-designed people.

The bad news? In general, both conceptually and empirically, need-satisfaction models have been subject to major criticism,[46] despite their usefulness as first-generation efforts. Experience and research demonstrate that individuals are not necessarily attracted to need-satisfying conditions, as in job enlargement efforts.[47] What then? One could argue that individuals are not aware of how their needs could be satisfied. Or defects in implementation could be emphasized, as in earlier discussion above. However approached, the bottom line is the same. Clearly, at a minimum, the need-satisfaction models require the specification of conditions under which they will more or less apply. "Much of the time" satisfied first-generation standards, but this is another day and time. Only theory/science advances can provide this greater specificity.

Expectancy or Path-Goal Models

Observers like Vroom[48] elaborated on the need-satisfaction approach[49] and clearly remedied its simplicity. Roughly, choices in path-goal models get made because individuals evaluate second-level outcomes associated with the choices, which outcomes are differentiated in terms of how much an individual prefers them (their "valence") as well as the individual's estimate of their probable occurrence (their "instrumentality") in association with specific first-order outcomes. In addition, the individual also has an "expectancy" that a certain behavior will lead to the first-order outcome. Schematically, in the case of job enlargement:

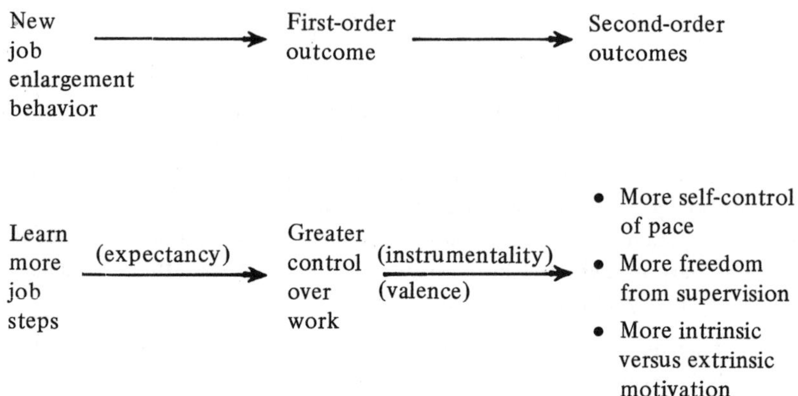

Path-goal models provide alternative explanations of (for example) "surprises" with job enlargement. Thus a job enlargement application might fail because, although an individual assigns a high valence to associated outcomes, they are also seen as improbable outcomes. Alternatively, these outcomes might appear to be probable, but not preferable. In addition, the individual may have a low expectancy that a specific behavior will lead to first-order outcomes. For example, an employee might distrust management in a job enlargement situation, fearing that the learning of new job steps would only result in a sophisticated speed-up and, consequently, in reduced control over more work for the same pay.

So far, so good, but path-goal models have been little explored and have some obvious deficiencies in the bargain. They might even increase complexity more than predictive/descriptive power. Basically, as in need-satisfaction models, the focus is still on individual predispositions and on (more rather than less) rational decision-making by individuals. Even friendly observers have highlighted the static character of common path-goal models,[50] as well as their isolation from complex stimulus situations such as work sites—with histories, technical demands, interpersonal and group dynamics, and so on.[51] Again, progress in theory/science will be required to suitably elaborate path-goal models, or to reject them.

Supraindividual Models

By implication, supraindividual models seem required to transcend the limitations of the two types of models just sketched. Two such models will be introduced here to suggest the range of what can be done by way of improving models for OD, and how it can be done.

Social Information Processing Models. Salancik and Pfeffer have taken a useful step toward urging supraindividual models on OD via a "social information processing approach." Close observers will discern numerous similar approaches in the history of organization study—as in the "political economy" approach of early commentators like Selznick, Drucker, and others. But Salancik and Pfeffer rightly remind us that many students have short memories with regard to lessons from the past. They contrast their approach with need-satisfaction models, problems with which derive from the failure "to take into account the social context in which work occurs and how this context affects attitudes and actions," as well as from neglect of "the important fact that persons spend much more time with the consequences of their actions and decisions than they spend contemplating future behaviors and beliefs." Salancik and Pfeffer conclude: "The combination of these two factors—the social context of work and the presence of consequences from previous actions—can be combined in a social information processing approach to develop new insights into people's attitudes at work."[52] At its base, the social information processing approach assumes that individuals can adapt to their social context, as well as to the consequences of their past behavior in that context. Salancik and Pfeffer consequently prescribe "that one can learn most about individual behavior by studying the informational and social environment within which that behavior occurs and to which it adapts." In the OD lexicon, this prescription urges the detailed diagnosis of the site of a potential OD intervention. And this prescription also requires comprehensive and presently unavailable theory/science.

Clearly, social information processing extends far beyond the kind of convenient specificity that need-satisfaction models do provide, and therein may lay its greatest usefulness. Consider job enlargement again, an intervention often prescribed by advocates of need-satisfaction models because of its potential for meeting human needs. Advocates of enlarged jobs from the start have warned that employees may experience early difficulty in learning appropriate behaviors, of course, which difficulty may even seem like "resistance to change" directed at an intervention explicitly rooted in heightened need-satisfaction. This is awkward, both practically and conceptually. But most job enlargement advocates explain that the difficulty is temporary, if it can be intense. And both advocate and critic are now coming to recognize that the impact of job enlargement rests on the quality of its implementation as well as on its theoretical need-satisfying properties. Social information processing adds very substantially, if not explicitly, to such explanations of job enlargement failures. Consider the impact of career stages. Illustratively, Katz proposes the need to distinguish at least three degrees of tenure as they interact with job enlargement. Thus enriched tasks "may not directly influence the overall satisfaction of employees with considerable job tenure. . . ." Moreover, "employees with a year or two on the job seem particularly receptive to the various task characteristics," apparently because they know enough to begin "getting stale" at the job. In sharp contrast, those newly assigned to jobs "may not only be unresponsive to autonomy, but may also become dissatisfied [with enlarged jobs,] especially if they are also new to the organization."[53]

The social information processing approach at once can encompass need-satisfaction models while transcending them. Consider only three variations on this theme, keeping in mind the critical qualification that the social information processing approach provides only an *orientation* rather than a *network of relations.* Only theory/science progress will make that orientation yield specific concepts and regularities. *First,* the social information processing approach can be seen as providing data about congenial/uncongenial situations for acting on the satisfaction of individuals needs. This preserves the convenience and face validity of need-satisfaction models as a first-approximation of reality, while encouraging the greater specification of conditions necessary to increase predictive power.

Second, the approach provides a congenial arena for dealing with some chicken-or-egg issues. For example, job enlargement effects may be due to causes other than meeting individual needs more closely. As some available evidence suggests, for example, positive job enlargement effects can derive less from the intervention per se than from *expectations* about those outcomes,[54] as well as from *focusing employee attention* on dimensions of performance considered significant by management but previously undervalued by employees.[55] Clearly, depending upon how things actually occur in nature, social information process can be either *additive* to the explanatory power of human-needs models or *alternative* to the theoretical underpinning of much OD work.

Third, social information processing may provide a useful contrast to need-satisfaction models. The point holds in two senses: empirically, in that the approach can be a replacement or a partial corrective for need-satisfaction models; and normatively, in that social information processing views workers differently than do need-satisfaction models. Salancik and Pfeffer put the complex point succinctly:[56]

> . . . the social information perspective holds that workers possess the ability to construct their own satisfaction by selectively perceiving and interpreting their social environment and their own past actions. Need-satisfaction models . . . excuse individuals from coping with the realities of their situations, and lodge the responsibility for workers' happiness either in the workers' need, over which they have little control, or in the task environment, over which, again, workers typically exercise little control.

Exhibit 4 Two Ideal Types of Organizational Control

Type A	Type Z
Short-term employment	Long-term employment
Individual decision-making	Collective decision-making
Individual responsibility	Individual responsibility
Frequent evaluation and promotion	Infrequent evaluation and promotion
Explicit, formalized evaluation	Implicit, informal evaluation
Specialized career paths	Nonspecialized career paths
Segmented concern for people	Wholistic concern for people

Source: From William G. Ouchi and Jerry B. Johnson, "Types of Organizational Control and Their Relationship to Emotional Well Being," *Administrative Science Quarterly,* Vol. 23 (June 1978), p. 294.

Organizational Control Models. A variety of macro-perspectives could provide content for the social informational processing approach, given major progress in theory/science that would provide presently unavailable specificity. The two ideal structural models in Chapter 2 of this book, for example, can serve such a purpose. Similarly, Ouchi and Johnson distinguish two idealized systems of organizational control, as in Exhibit 4. Basically, the approach there implies one significant difference from OD work rooted in human-needs satisfaction. As Ouchi and Johnson observe: ". . . our formulation offers an explicitly structural, macro-organizational view, founded in the literature of sociology, while the classic view is taken from an explicitly interpersonal point of view, founded in the literature of social psychology."[57] The Type A model is consistent with the traditional approach to organizing work discussed in Chapter 2 of this book. Type Z represents an idealization of common Japanese practice.

While compatible with much OD work, the focus on control systems encourages a broader range of attention in organization diagnosis than would be inspired by many need-satisfaction models. For example, the stability of employment and patterns of movement between jobs would get much attention in this sociological approach. And such differences in diagnosis might lead to very different prescriptions by change agents. Ouchi and Johnson note that OD intervenors with an interaction bias might advise workshops to improve interpersonal skills; or they might recommend survey/feedback designs to highlight problem areas in large systems. Ouchi and Johnson would recommend other interventions, alternatively or additionally suggesting ". . . that the client find ways to use part-time workers and work-smoothing devices in order to stabilize the basic workforce; that the client put professional and managerial employees through a forced job-rotation program, thus reducing specialization and increasing company-wide knowledge among employees; that the client make explicit use of symbols such as key promotions and public meetings for the purpose of expressing the new values which are to be emphasized; and so on."[58]

A Concluding Summary

In a few words, then, priority must be given to theory/science for several related reasons. But perhaps the dominant opinion leans in an opposite direction. Hopefully, this book will provide some bulk to correct that imbalance.

Notes

1. Chris Argyris, *Intervention Theory and Method* (Reading, Mass.: Addison-Wesley, 1970), pp. 128-176.
2. Richard N. Ottaway, "A Proposed Taxonomy of Change Agents," University of Manchester, 1977, esp. pp. 8-10. Mimeographed.
3. Noel M. Tichy, "Agents of Planned Social Change: Congruence of Values, Cognitions, and Actions," *Administrative Science Quarterly,* Vol. 19 (June 1974), pp. 164-182.
4. Morton A. Lieberman, Irvin D. Yalom, and Matthew B. Miles, *Encounter Groups: First Facts* (New York: Basic Books, 1973), esp. pp. 242-264.
5. Edgar F. Huse, *Organization Development and Change* (St. Paul, Minn.: West, 1975), p. 303.
6. W. Warner Burke, "Organization Development in Transition," *Journal of Applied Behavioral Science,* Vol. 12 (January 1976), esp. pp. 28-31; and Chip R. Bell, "The Trainer as Machiavelli," *Training and Development Journal,* Vol. 30 (April 1976), pp. 38-42.
7. For evidence of the value of the architectural role, see William G. Dyer, Robert F. Maddocks, J. Weldom Moffitt, and William J. Underwood, "A Laboratory-Consultation Model for Organization Change," pp. 307-320, in W. Warner Burke and Harvey A. Hornstein (eds.), *The Social Technology of Organization Development* (Fairfax, Virg., NTL Learning Resources Corp., Inc., 1972).
8. David G. Bowers, "Organizational Development," *Organizational Dynamics,* Vol. 4 (Spring 1976), p. 55.
9. Ibid., p. 56.
10. The recognition emerges forcefully, for example, in Samuel A. Culbert and Jerome Reisel, "Organization Development: An Applied Philosophy for Managers of Public Enterprise," *Public Administration Review,* Vol. 32 (March 1971), esp. pp. 160-162.

11. For a prescription of a strong advocacy role in OD interventions, see Robert Ross, "OD for Whom?" *Journal of Applied Behavioral Science,* Vol. 7 (September 1971), pp. 580-585.
12. These consequences have been established most clearly in the case of T-group trainers whose style includes a major emphasis on mobilizing, on making happen versus allowing them to happen. See Lieberman, Yalom, and Miles, *Encounter Groups,* esp. pp. 226-267.
13. Reproduced by special permission from *The Journal of Applied Behavioral Science.* Frank Friedlander, "OD Reaches Adolescence: An Exploration of Its Underlying Values," Vol. 12, no. 1 (1976), pp. 14 and 21. Copyrighted by NTL Institute, 1976.
14. Stanley M. Herman, "The Shadow of Organization Development," pp. 133-159, in W. Warner Burke (ed.), *Current Issues and Strategies in Organization Development* (New York: Human Science, 1977); and Herman and Michael Korenich, *Authentic Management: A Gestalt Orientation to Organizations and Their Development* (Reading, Mass.: Addison-Wesley, 1977).
15. Herman, "The Shadow of Organization Development," p. 135.
16. Arthur Koestler, *The Ghost in the Machine* (New York: Macmillan, 1967).
17. There are a number of other sources which provide perspective of a similar kind. See, especially, Argyris, *Intervention Theory and Method;* and Paula and Richard Franklin, *Tomorrow's Track: Experiment with Learning to Change* (Columbia, Md.: New Community Press, 1976), esp. pp. 109-116.
18. A developing line of research has begun exploring one aspect of this interstitiality–phenomena related to "marginality"–which bears on the intervenor's roles and effectiveness. See Philip J. Browne, Chester C. Cotton, and Robert T. Golembiewski, "Marginality and the OD Practitioner," *Journal of Applied Behavioral Science,* Vol. 13 (October 1977), pp. 493-506.
19. Brett Hawkins and Robert Lorinskas (eds.), *The Ethnic Factor in American Politics* (Columbus, Ohio: Merrill, 1970).
20. Irving Janis, *Victims of Groupthink* (Boston: Houghton-Mifflin, 1972).
21. Charles M. Hampden-Turner, "An Existential 'Learning Theory' and the Integration of T-Group Research," *Journal of Applied Behavioral Science,* Vol. 2 (October 1966), pp. 367-386.
22. Jane J. Mansbridge, "Time, Emotion, and Inequality: Three Problems of Participatory Groups," *Journal of Applied Behavioral Science,* Vol. 9 (March 1973), esp. pp. 361-367.
23. S. Tilles, "Understanding the Consultant's Role," *Harvard Business Review,* Vol. 39 (1961), pp. 87-99; and R. H. Woody and J. D. Woody, "Behavioral Science Consultation," *Personnel Journal,* Vol. 50 (1971), pp. 382-391.
24. "Outside Consultants to Industry: Strengths, Problems, and Pitfalls," *Personnel Psychology,* Vol. 17 (1964), esp. pp. 114-119.

25. Warren Bennis, *Changing Organizations* (New York: McGraw-Hill, 1966), pp. 152-165.

26. Richard Beckhard, *Organization Development: Strategies and Models* (Reading, Mass.: Addison-Wesley, 1969), pp. 93-96.

27. Philip H. Mirvis and David N. Berg (eds.), *Failures in Organization Development and Change: Cases and Essays for Learning* (New York: Wiley, 1977).

28. Beckhard, *Organization Development,* p. 93.

29. Bennis, *Changing Organizations,* pp. 157-160.

30. Ibid., pp. 153-155.

31. Beckhard, *Organization Development,* p. 94.

32. Ibid.

33. Ibid., p. 95.

34. Ibid., p. 94.

35. Bennis, *Changing Organizations,* p. 152.

36. Wendell L. French and Cecil H. Bell, Jr., *Organization Development* (Englewood Cliffs, N.J.: Prentice-Hall, 1973), pp. 21-29.

37. Frank Friedlander, "OD Reaches Adolescence," *Journal of Applied Behavioral Science,* Vol. 12 (January 1976), pp. 7-21.

38. Noel M. Tichy, "Current and Future Trends for Change Agentry," *Group and Organization Studies,* Vol. 3 (December 1978), p. 467.

39. Perhaps Jerry Harvey has been foremost among those urging caution rather than exuberance in what OD is and what intervenors do. See especially his "Eight Myths OD Consultants Believe In . . . and Die By," *OD Practitioner,* Vol. 7 (February 1975), pp. 1-5.

40. Peggy Morrison, "Response," *Group and Organization Studies,* Vol. 3 (December 1978), p. 399.

41. Craig Lundberg, "The Current State of Theory in Organization Development." Paper presented at the 1978 Annual Meeting, Academy of Management, San Francisco, Calif., August 10, 1978.

42. One friendly critic, for example, throws up his literary hands at the smorgasbord offered at the Fall 1978 meeting of the OD Network, which included panels, symposia, or speeches on this overwhelming collection of exotica, among others: "Neuro-linguistic programming, Weir Labs (offered often under NTL aegis as a 'deep growth' experience), dealing with death: symbolic/real, whole-person wellness, mental imaging: visual theory, the inner world of dance and OD, androgyny, metaphysics and the consultant: considering alternate realities, the white-male maze, . . . confronting the need to hold-on . . . [and] socio-technical planning for new organization settings." See Larry Porter, "The Current State of OD Practice." Paper presented at 1978 Annual Meeting, Academy of Management, August 13,

1978. Also published as "OD Practice: Some Extrapolations, Metaphors, and Inferential Leaps," *OD Practitioner,* Vol. 10 (October 1978), p. 2.

43. Marvin R. Weisbord, "The Wizard of OD," *OD Practitioner,* Vol. 10 (Summer 1978), p. 2.
44. Ibid., p. 3.
45. Gerald T. Salancik and Jeffrey Pfeffer, "A Social Information Processing Approach to Job Attitudes and Task Design," *Administrative Science Quarterly,* Vol. 23 (June 1978), p. 241.
46. Gerald R. Salancik and Jeffrey Pfeffer, "An Examination of Need-Satisfaction Models of Job Attitudes," *Administrative Science Quarterly,* Vol. 22 (September 1977), pp. 427-456.
47. Linda L. Frank and J. Richard Hackman, "A Failure of Job Enlargement," *Journal of Applied Behavioral Science,* Vol. 11 (October 1975), pp. 412-436.
48. Victor H. Vroom, *Work and Motivation* (New York: Wiley, 1964).
49. Jay R. Galbraith, *Organization Design* (Reading, Mass.: Addison-Wesley, 1966), esp. pp. 267-274.
50. As Galbraith does, in explaining his development of a "dynamic path-goal model," which also incorporates some features of need-satisfying models. Ibid., pp. 274-289.
51. Salancik and Pfeffer, "A Social Information Processing Approach," p. 224.
52. Ibid.
53. Ralph Katz, "Job Longevity as a Situational Factor in Job Satisfaction," *Administrative Science Quarterly,* Vol. 23 (June 1978), p. 220.
54. Albert S. King, "Expectation Effects in Organizational Change," *Administrative Science Quarterly,* Vol. 19 (June 1974), pp. 221-230.
55. See the conclusion of Salancik and Pfeffer, "A Social Information Processing Approach," p. 243.
56. Ibid., p. 249.
57. William G. Ouchi and Jerry B. Johnson, "Types of Organizational Control and Their Relationship to Emotional Well Being," *Administrative Science Quarterly,* Vol. 23 (June 1978), p. 311.
58. Ibid., pp. 311-312.

Author Index

Subject Index